Consumer Reports®

BUYING GUIDE

ALL NEW FOR 2004

THE EDITORS OF
CONSUMER REPORTS MAGAZINE

Consumers Union • Yonkers, New York

TABLE OF CONTENTS

Desktop computers
page 139

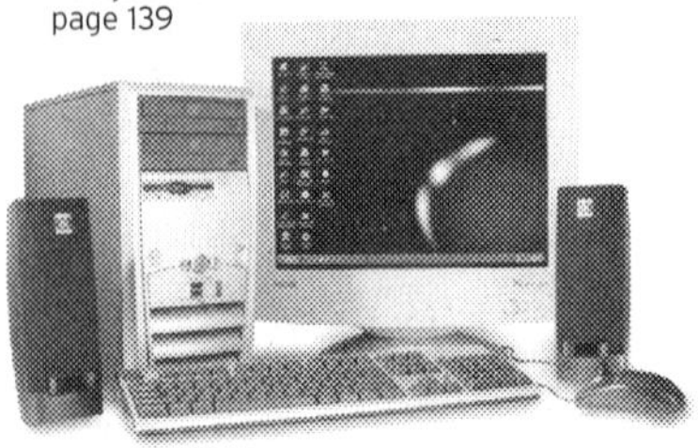

Autos
page 159

Washing machines
page 106

Digital cameras
page 45

REFERENCE SECTION

CONSUMER REPORTS BUYING GUIDE 2004

Consumer Reports (ISSN 0010-7174) is published 13 times a year by Consumers Union of U.S., Inc., 101 Truman Avenue, Yonkers, N.Y. 10703-1057. Second-class postage paid at Yonkers, N.Y., and at additional mailing offices. Canadian postage paid at Mississauga, Ontario, Canada. Canadian publications registration no. 2665247-98. Title Consumer Reports registered in U.S. Patent Office. CU is a member of the Consumers International. Mailing lists: CU rents or exchanges its customer postal list so it can be provided to other publications, companies, and nonprofit organizations. If you wish your name deleted from lists and rentals, send your address label with a request for deletion to Consumer Reports, P.O. Box 2127, Harlan, IA 51593-0316. Postmaster: Send address changes to P.O. Box 2109, Harlan, IA 51593-0298. Back issues: Single copies of 12 preceding issues, $7.95 each; Buying Guide, $10 each. Write Back Issues, Consumer Reports, Customer Relations, 101 Truman Ave., Yonkers, N.Y. 10703. Consumer Reports Buying Guide 2004 (ISBN 0-89043-979-6)

Buying Guidance at Your Fingertips

The Consumer Reports Buying Guide helps you find value and quality in today's marketplace. Start with "Secrets of Shopping Smart" on page 7 to find general tips and strategies for shopping in stores, through catalogs, and online. Next, on page 13, read our timely rundown of "10 Sneaky Shopping Traps" you might encounter—and see how to avoid them. The chapter "Fix It or Pitch It" on page 17 gives you detailed timelines and advice on when to repair and when to replace big-ticket household products, such as refrigerators, computers, TVs, and camcorders. "Finding Reliable Brands," on page 25, gives you CONSUMER REPORTS' unique brand-repair histories for TVs, computers, ranges, lawn mowers, and other household products.

Products for your home

- **Home entertainment**
- **Kitchen & laundry**
- **Home & yard**
- **Home office**

In these sections, beginning on page 35, you'll find key trends and what's new, followed by concise, informative articles that cover major purchases all around the house. When you go into the store, you'll know what to ask and what to look for.

Autos

Look here for tips on getting the best value in a new or used car. Read what's new about the 2004 models, along with Ratings and reviews of more than 200 cars, minivans, pickups, and SUVs. You'll find Reliability forecasts available only from CONSUMER REPORTS. And you can check out the best and worst used cars based on which have been the most (or least) reliable. Plus: reliability histories for 216 models.

Brand-name Ratings & reference

In the Reference Section beginning on page 233 you'll find Ratings of 967 models in 31 product categories, from blenders and camcorders to vacuum cleaners and washing machines.

Also in this section, you'll find:

- Brand Locator, a list of manufacturers' telephone numbers and Web addresses.
- An index of the last test report as published in issues of CONSUMER REPORTS magazine.
- A list of autos and other products recalled during the past year, plus information on how to find out more about product recalls.

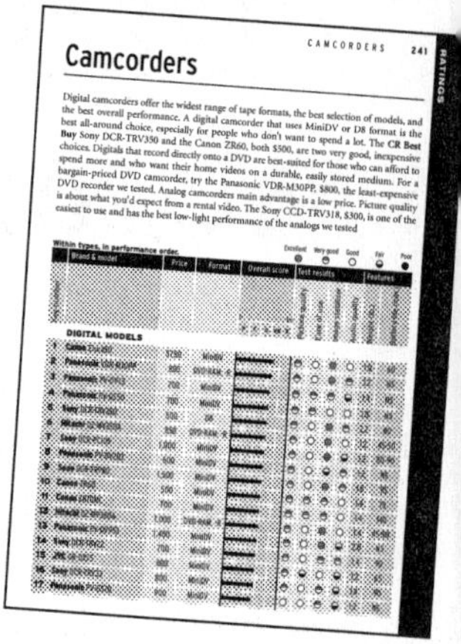

CAMCORDERS 241

RATINGS

Camcorders

Digital camcorders offer the widest range of tape formats, the best selection of models, and the best overall performance. A digital camcorder that uses MiniDV or D8 format is the best all-around choice, especially for people who don't want to spend a lot. The **CR Best Buy** Sony DCR-TRV350 and the Canon ZR60, both $500, are two very good, inexpensive choices. Digitals that record directly onto a DVD are best-suited for those who can afford to spend more and who want their home videos on a durable, easily stored medium. For a bargain-priced DVD camcorder, try the Panasonic VDR-M30PP, $800, the least-expensive DVD recorder we tested. Analog camcorders main advantage is a low price. Picture quality is about what you'd expect from a rental video. The Sony CCD-TRV318, $300, is one of the easiest to use and has the best low-light performance of the analogs we tested

Within types, in performance order.

Excellent Very good Good Fair Poor

Brand & model | Price | Format | Overall score | Test results | Features

DIGITAL MODELS

About the Consumer Reports family of products

Founded as a magazine in 1936, CONSUMER REPORTS now brings you its unbiased, trusted information in many formats. Its products and publications include CONSUMER REPORTS magazine; buying guides and magazines from Consumer Reports Special Publications; a newsletter, Consumer Reports On Health; and Consumer Reports TV, a nationally syndicated consumer news service.

ConsumerReports.org offers site subscribers a searchable version of our test findings and advice, now with wireless PDA accessibility. Auto prices and custom reports are available through the Consumer Reports New Car Price Service and Consumer Reports Used Car Price Service. You can find prices, subscription rates, and more information on all of these products and services at *www.ConsumerReports.org.* Go to "Our Publications" on the home page, then click on "More Products."

CONSUMER REPORTS specializes in head-to-head, brand-name comparisons of autos and household products. It also provides informed, impartial advice on a broad range of topics from health and nutrition to personal finance and travel.

CONSUMER REPORTS buys all the products it tests and accepts no free samples. We accept no advertising from outside entities nor do we let any company use our information or Ratings for commercial purposes.

CONSUMER REPORTS is published by Consumers Union, an independent, nonprofit testing and information organization—the largest such organization anywhere in the world.

Since 1936, Consumers Union's mission has been to test products, inform the public, and protect consumers. Our income is derived solely from the sale of our publications and services, and from nonrestrictive, noncommercial contributions, grants, and fees.

Secrets of Shopping Smart

How-to's, tips, and shortcuts that can help you find what you want fast and at a good price.

Whatever your shopping style—diligent researcher, casual browser, or determined time-saver—the current shopping scene holds new and expanding options. You can surf Web sites, leaf through catalogs, and visit every variety of store, from specialized boutiques to giant warehouse clubs. As the Web increasingly influences retailing, chances are you'll use a combination of shopping strategies. Even if you want the immediacy of buying in a store, you may want to check models, prices, and availability online. Internet companies are now publishing catalogs as selling tools.

While shopping alternatives have grown, the basic rules for smart shopping remain the same: Do your homework and determine the best value for your needs. A good place to start is with the Consumer Reports Buying Guide. The chapter that follows gives you strategies for shopping smart—in the store, online, and by catalog. Next, in "10 Sneaky Shopping Traps," we round up egregious merchandising stratagems and tell you how to deal with them. As you plan your purchases, consult this guide for more than 900 product Ratings plus brand repair histories for many product categories.

Each month, CONSUMER REPORTS magazine can also help with new product reviews and comparisons, test results, and Ratings. Our Web site, Consumer Reports.org, gives site subscribers access to the latest Ratings and archives of CONSUMER REPORTS, plus online-only content such as e-Ratings of shopping Web sites.

Store strategies

Traditional retailers are still the principal shopping choice of most consumers. Bricks-and-mortar stores allow what online or catalog shopping can't—an in-person judgment of overall appearance and important sensory qualities. Researching your purchase before you set off for the store can pay off in valuable product knowledge, time saved, and—maybe—a lower price.

Specialty stores, special service. Need help selecting a product in a category you're not familiar with? Just want a real person to help you? Smaller stores, such as audio boutiques and Main Street shops, can provide a knowledgeable staff and personal service, including special ordering. These perks may be offset by higher prices. Determine a fair price before you go, using this guide, the Web, or a retailer's catalog. Then decide how much the extra service is worth to you. Be aware that for some products, such as computers, you can get more customization by buying online. A 2002 CONSUMER REPORTS survey found that people purchasing computers over the Internet or through a catalog were generally more satisfied than people who bought them at a bricks-and-mortar retailer.

E-RATINGS

See Consumer Reports.org *(www.ConsumerReports.org)* for exclusive e-Ratings of shopping Web sites based on their credibility, usability, and content.

Bottom-line basics. Is finding the type of product you want at a good price more important than the latest technology and a large selection? Mass merchandisers such as Wal-Mart, Kmart, and Target cover many categories, with a selection of moderately priced brands from well-known manufacturers, along with their own store-brands. (Wal-Mart and Kmart together account for a huge share of total sales in many categories of appliances and electronic items.) In a recent CONSUMER REPORTS survey, Sears, Target, and Wal-Mart all received high scores for product selection.

Though return policies at most mass merchandisers are usually liberal, returns may entail time and hassle.

Big stores, big selection. Specialty chains such as Circuit City and Best Buy account for three-quarters of home-electronics sales. Home Depot and Lowe's control one-fourth of the home-improvement product market. CompUSA inhabits strip malls across the country. Sears has a network of stores and a Web site with lots of product choices for major appliances and other home products.

These chains may also feature special services, such as viewing/listening rooms for home-theater demonstrations. And although sales-staff expertise may vary, you can generally get questions answered.

Join the club. If you're willing to be flexible on brand and model, check a warehouse club: Costco, BJ's Wholesale Club, or Sam's Club (Wal-Mart's warehouse sibling). Since these stores emphasize value, not service or selection, expect long lines and little sales help. Prices are consistently low, though not necessarily the lowest. In a CONSUMER REPORTS survey, Costco was ranked among the highest clubs for quality in several categories of merchandise: electronics; books, music, and videos; hardware and tools; and small appliances.

Clubs charge an annual membership fee (generally $35 to $45). If you don't shop there frequently, that fee can undo much of your savings. But a big saving on a single purchase can pay for your membership. Most clubs will issue a limited-time shopping pass, letting you browse without joining.

Catalog strategies

Catalogs offer selection and convenience, often from established companies with proven track records and top-notch customer service. And of course they offer 24/7 access. Most catalog merchants are also online.

The catalog-Web connection can give you the best of both venues. You can browse the catalog (leafing through pages can be quicker than waiting for screens to redraw) and then order online using a catalog's "quick search" feature, or simply call the 800 number while looking at the screen.

Online catalogs typically feature more merchandise than expensive-to-mail paper catalogs. Web sites frequently feature lines not available in the paper catalog, online-only sales and bargains, even product-selection tips. Habitués of online catalog venues can snap up specials and closeouts before items go out of stock.

Ordering from a catalog over the phone or the Web is usually quick, but popular items can still be on back-order, even if they seemed to be in stock when you placed the order. If you don't receive your purchase within the promised time, check back. And before you order, check shipping fees: They can vary widely and add significantly to the cost of the order. See "Smart ordering," on page 10, for precautions that apply to both catalog and Web buying.

Web strategies

You can hunt down just about anything on the Web, from potato chips to vacation homes, but you'll find that some items are more e-commerce-compatible than others. Books, music, videos, DVDs, and computer software are big online successes because they're standardized products, and no bricks-and-mortar store is able to stock every title. Branded electronics items also lend themselves to online shopping because it's handy to select them by manufacturer and specific features. Shipping is another important factor: Small, lightweight purchases—books as opposed to, say, refrigerators—are top online sellers.

OFF THE LIST

To remove your name from most mailing, telemarketing, and e-mail lists, go to the Web site of the Direct Marketing Association at *www.dmaconsumers.org* and then click on "Consumer Assistance." Register your phone number with the National Do Not Call Registry at *www.donotcall.gov.* You can also call toll-free, 888-382-1222 (TTY 866-290-4236), from the number you wish to register.

Perhaps even more than for buying, the Web is immensely useful for researching a purchase. Information that would previously have taken many hours and many phone calls (if it could be found at all) is now available via a simple click of your mouse. Thus armed, you can make better decisions about where to buy, what to buy, and what to pay.

BUYING THROUGH AUCTIONS

Internet auction sites deal in anything people want to sell. Though sellers provide descriptions (and, often, digital images), details may be fuzzy. Except for sites operated by retailers or businesses, most auction sites do not verify the condition of an item—or whether it really exists. Thus the largest Internet auction site, eBay, suggests you get a written statement from the seller detailing condition and value, return policy, warranty information, promised delivery date, plus an address and telephone number. Ebay has increased the amount of buyer protection available for customers who use PayPal, an online payment service. Ebay also offers links to third-party companies that provide authentication and grading services.

If you purchase something at an auction site, use a credit card (not a debit card) or work out terms with an online escrow service, such as Escrow.com, which processes transactions. (Fees are based on the amount of the transaction, method of payment, and, sometimes, shipping costs.)

At pick-your-own-price sites, you name a price for, say, airline tickets, hotels, or a mortgage, and merchants come to you. Priceline originated this type of "reverse auction." The catch: You must provide a credit-card number up front. If Priceline finds the item at your price, your credit card is charged immediately, usually with no cancellation option. Nor can you request a specific brand. For airline tickets, you are only allowed to make one bid within a seven-day period for the same itinerary; for hotel rooms, within a three-day period. Simply changing your bid amount is considered a duplicate bid and will be rejected automatically.

Smart ordering

Whether catalogers or e-tailers, retailers should provide complete information about their business and policies. Here's what to look for:

Complete contact information, including a real-world location. Look for a toll-free number, e-mail and postal addresses, not a P.O. box, and 24-hour customer service. (See Brand Locator for Web addresses and phone numbers of major brands.)

Clear shipping, handling, and return policies. Review options and prices be-

REGULATIONS

Consumer protection online and off

Whenever you shop at home—online, on the phone, or by mail—you have the same safety net against theft of your credit-card number as when you shop in person. If you report misuse right away, you're liable for only $50, even on international transactions. Some Web merchants will even reimburse that $50. (Check individual Web-site policies.)

If a merchant misrepresents a product, Web shoppers and catalog patrons are entitled to the same protection and recourse. Unfortunately, if the merchant—Web or otherwise—is not in your state or within 100 miles of your home, some federal protections will not apply. For example, you may not be able to withhold credit-card payment if you have a dispute over the quality of a product. However, many credit-card issuers will try to mediate, or will at least credit your account until the dispute is settled. Barring that, you'll have to file a complaint with your state attorney general's office or local consumer-protection bureau.

Note that these protections don't apply to purchases made with a debit card.

SEARCHING

Online shopping tools

SEARCH ENGINES, PORTALS, AND DIRECTORIES

Here are some places you can start your online shopping trips.

AltaVista *(www.altavista.com)* has more than 350 million Web pages indexed.

AOL Search *(www.aol.com/search)*, available to non-AOL members too, provides returns from several other search engines and services. AOL is also a portal, a multifaceted site that combines search capabilities with other services such as shopping, weather, news, chat rooms, and much more.

AskJeeves *(www.askjeeves.com)* is a human-powered search service that returns answers (from a database of 7 million answers) to questions asked in plain English. Also offers access to other search engines.

Excite *(www.excite.com)* has more than 250 million Web pages indexed. Also a portal.

Froogle *(www.froogle.google.com)* Finds products for sale across the Web. Search for a specific item or browse through 15 shopping categories.

Go *(www.go.com)*, affiliated with Disney, uses the Google search service.

Google *(www.google.com)* The largest search engine on the Web with more than 3 billion indexed pages. Ranks pages according to the number of links that point to each page's site.

Google catalogs *(www.catalogs.google.com)* lets you search and browse mail-order catalogs online.

HotBot *(www.hotbot.com)* offers advanced searching and Web filtering features.

Open Directory *(www.dmoz.org)* uses a volunteer army of more than 57,000 "editors" to compile more than 400,000 categories and 3.8 million sites.

Yahoo! *(www.yahoo.com)*, with links to between 1.5 and 1.8 million sites, is the leading referral Web site–18 percent of all traffic to e-commerce sites originates there. Also a portal.

METASEARCH SITES

These query other search engines:

The BigHub *(www.thebighub.com)*
Dogpile *(www.dogpile.com)*
Ixquick *(www.ixquick.com)*
Mamma *(www.mamma.com)*
MetaCrawler *(www.metacrawler.com)*

SHOP BOTS

These sites compare prices, but beware of possible commercial ties to recommended merchants.

www.amazon.com offers price comparisons within the "all products" category of its search box. Goods sold directly by Amazon are listed before those sold by others.

www.consumerworld.org has its own price-comparison search as well as links to other shop bots.

www.dealtime.com searches for the best price in 18 categories, and provides helpful shopping guides.

www.mysimon.com lists 21 product categories, and allows sorting by price.

www.shopper.com is part of CNET, a Web site focusing on computers, consumer electronics, and software. You can rank results by price, and also find shipping charges, availability, and merchant phone numbers.

www.shopping.com, part of the DealTime search engine, will compare prices and features in 14 categories.

www.streetprices.com is particularly good for consumer electronics and computers.

fore you place an order. Shipping is extra with most catalog orders; some e-tailers offer free shipping when your total reaches a specified amount. When ordering from a catalog, remember sales tax, charged if the catalog company operates a store in your state.

A 100 percent satisfaction guarantee. Look for a merchant that allows returns for any reason, with no restocking fee. (Custom items and special orders may be excluded.) A good merchant will tell you as you order when items will arrive—or if they'll be delayed.

Security and privacy. At a Web site, look for the Trust-e symbol or a Better Business Bureau Online seal, both indicating that the merchant's business practices have passed an audit. As soon as you start the buying process, the site should show a symbol like a key or a lock, or a Web address with an "s" (for secure) after the "http." The best sites also cover the $50 maximum that credit-card companies charge if a card is used without your authorization.

When ordering from a catalog, look for a clearly stated list-sharing policy, with an easy way to opt out. If you don't see such a statement, ask for details—or assume that the company rents its customer lists to other merchants.

10 Sneaky Shopping Traps

With these ploys up their sleeves, sellers can easily relieve you of your money. Here's what to watch out for.

You may have earned a Ph.D. or scored over 1500 on your SAT's. But none of that matters when it comes to outsmarting today's sharp marketers. Armed with surveys, studies, an understanding of psychology, and fine print that would make Superman squint, they have developed myriad methods to help you part willingly—even eagerly—with your dollars. Only days or months later, when you study the contract closely or receive the outrageous bill, do you realize that you've been had big-time.

To help you help yourself from falling into the snares, we've rounded up the most egregious merchandising strategems and provided you with countermoves.

1 Freebies and cheapies with strings attached.

Remember when computers sold for practically nothing? What buyers later learned to their dismay was that the deal required them to sign up for three years of service with America Online at $20 a month, for a total of $720. More recently, phone companies have offered customers a cell phone for $19.95 (a $150 value). In exchange, you are given the right to pay $39.95 a month plus roaming charges and are tied to a two-year contract.

Your move: Calculate how much more you'd have to spend for the service to see whether you're really saving money over your current plan.

2 Gift certificates and similar purchases that disappear.

It's not just cottage cheese that comes with an expiration date these days. Those gift cards and certificates you buy from retailers and banks that allow the holder to purchase goods up to their face value are not valid forever. Most lose their value over time and many expire completely after one year. The end result: The merchant gets to keep the dough without providing the goods.

Your move: Make sure that you fully understand the terms of gift cards and certificates and other stored-value vehicles such as phone cards. And be sure to warn anybody you give them to that the cards should be used pronto.

3 Insurance to protect your purchase.

More and more retailers are selling extended warranties (aka product-protection plans or service contracts) on everything from cooktops to cars. Retailers think they're nifty because they often make more money on the warranty than they do on the item it covers. However, whatever they are called and wherever they are sold, extended warranties are expensive and usually unnecessary insurance. When you buy one, you're betting the product will break while under warranty and that the warranty will cost less than the repair. That's pretty unlikely. A CONSUMER REPORTS survey of product owners' experiences found that few of the products broke during the warranty period and that, typically, repairs cost about the same as the warranty.

If you buy with a credit card you may automatically double the factory warranty anyway; check with the card's issuer for details or limitations.

Your move: In most cases, forgo the extended warranty unless you are buying an expensive and delicate product. Example: a laptop computer. Fixing the display can cost $500, and the warranty typically runs $100 a year. Since the high profit margins allow some wiggle room, you may be able to bargain down the price. And in most states, manufacturers sell insurance that covers accidental damage like a display that's ruined by a spilled cup of coffee.

4 Insurance to pay off what you owe.

What if you keeled over, lost your job, or became disabled and couldn't pay off your mortgage, your credit card, or the loan on your new refrigerator? Merchants and credit-card issuers have the answer: credit-life insurance and its variants for disability and unemployment. Sounds good, but according to the Consumer Federation of America, the premiums are overpriced by about 75 percent, leaving Americans about $2 billion poorer each year. And payouts are small, indicating that people rarely collect.

Your move: Just say "no." Instead, make sure you have enough life and disability insurance. Not only are such general-purpose policies much less expensive than credit life, they also cover all your bills should something go wrong. If you lose your job, the best backups are government-provided unemployment insurance and savings.

5 Charges that hit you in the rear.

You like to think that once you've made a down payment and paid your monthly bills, you're all done. Not so fast. If you're about to turn in a leased car, for example, you can get slammed with exit charges as well. First, there's the disposition fee (the cost of prepping your car for the auction block) and charges for excess wear and tear, for which the dealer can levy astounding amounts. To soothe you, the dealer may offer to waive the charges if you simply sign up for a new car lease. Guess what? The dealer rolls the charges over into your new lease.

Your move: The disposition fee is itemized in your contract; so be prepared with a check. There is no reason, however, to take the dealer's word that repairing any excess wear and tear need cost what he or she estimates. To give yourself leverage, get an estimate from an independent garage. If it's lower, you know what to do: Get the car fixed there. Finally, shop for your new lease every bit as carefully as you did for your previous one to see whether the dealer's new offer is the best you can do.

6 Loss leaders that leave you a loser.

It's a time-worn ploy, but it always works. A toy store, for example, places a sought-after staple on sale—say, disposable diapers. You rush in to take advantage, but, by the time you reach the cash register, you've given in to the pleading of your children and purchased $200 worth of toys. What the store may have lost discounting the diapers it more than made up for on your toy splurge. The same effect occurs at warehouse stores. You enter the store intending merely to purchase cases of cheap toilet paper and tissues but wind up with $100 worth of sirloin, a leather jacket, and a flat-screen TV.

Your move: First, make a list and stick to it. Second, when shopping, don't let children—or others with urgent needs to possess new goodies—accompany you. Finally, set a spending limit and don't exceed it.

7 Zero-percent financing that costs more than zero.

To get you in the door, car dealers and merchants often offer zero-percent financing or chunky rebates. But there are catches that can cost you more than you thought. For starters, many of the car-financing deals out there are only for specific models that the manufacturer is eager to push. And rarely are dealers willing to haggle on the price when they're giving you cheap financing. Finally, you can only qualify if you have perfect credit. Merchants such as Home Depot will also award you zero-percent financing as long as you charge the amount to the store's own credit card. That's fine, but if you fail to pay on time two months in a row, your 0 percent rate rises to 20 percent or more.

Your move: With a car, figure out whether you would pay less taking 0 percent and paying full price or haggling on the price of the car and getting a car loan from your own bank. And, when it comes to 0 percent offers from retailers, make sure that you keep up the payments to avoid high interest charges.

8 Items sold separately that you can't do without.

The special price is enticing. But at the checkout counter you learn that the monitor for your sale-priced computer isn't included, the discounted handheld wireless computer requires a modem, and that the sheet set doesn't come with pillowcases. So you cough up the money for the extra but necessary items, possibly paying more than you would have for the whole package at another store.

Your move: Make sure that any package deal includes all the equipment you'll need. If you're buying a complicated item, like a computer, write out a checklist of all the features you want and then question the salesperson to make sure that the price he or she is quoting includes everything you want.

9 Charges that keep coming.

Innocently, you order from a catalog merchant over the telephone. After you complete your purchase, the sales representative on the other end offers you a three-month free subscription to any of a dozen magazines from Goldfish Fancier to Pollyanna Monthly. In a burst of enthusiasm, you say yes. In no time at all, the three months have elapsed and a charge for a full year's subscription is on your credit card. And, by the time you figure out who or where to call to stop it, you've received 12 issues.

Your move: As in all cases, don't buy impulsively. Stick to your list. And be very cautious with a merchant who already has your credit-card number. Any grunt you emit could be mistaken or purposefully misread by a sales representative as an agreement to sign up for an Internet service provider, a magazine subscription, a stolen-credit-card protection plan, and the like.

10 Bells and whistles you'll never ring or blow.

When the appliance salesclerk showed you the special dryer rack for sneakers—only $50 extra!—you thought it was nifty and you bought it along with the dryer. But, three years later, after you trip over it for the one-hundredth time in your laundry room, you realize you never use it. And so it goes with many products. Those fancy features are simply unnecessary and costly. You don't need a 12-speed blender, for example; a model with three to five speeds is fine. Automatic ice and water dispensers that add to the cost of refrigerators aren't right for every household, and they often break; what's more, replacing their filters can cost $30 to $40 a month.

Your move: To see which features make sense, you have to do your homework before purchasing. Check out the recommendations and key features sections in this Buying Guide to find out which extras will make a difference in performance and convenience and hence are worth the added expense.

Fix It or Pitch It?

When to repair and when to replace your major household items.

If a broken CD player or printer is more than two years old, replace it. But if a lawn tractor, wall oven, or projection TV goes on the fritz, it may be worth fixing even after six or seven years. Those are some of the recommendations from CONSUMER REPORTS exclusive Repair or Replace Timelines, which you'll find on pages 20 to 24 of this book.

The timelines provide year-by-year advice on when to hold—and when to fold—for 20 major household items, from computers and mowers to gas ranges and vacuum cleaners.

We drew on the experiences of 38,000 subscribers who took part in an Annual Questionnaire on broken products. Our guidelines encompass typical repair and replacement costs and the extent to which new technology makes replacing these products worthwhile.

We focused on midpriced appliances, personal-computing products, electronics, and lawn-care equipment people buy most. If you own an expensive product—say, a $4,000 pro-style range or premium tractor—even a costly repair might make more sense than replacing the item with a new model.

Of course, you can reduce your odds of facing a repair or replace decision (or at least put it off for a few years) by buying brands that have proved to be more reliable over time. Our Brand Repair Histories, starting on page 25, can help you on that score.

When it pays to replace

Replacing a broken product may be worthwhile if a current model is technologically more advanced—or when a repair is more than half the cost of replacement. Readers in our survey repaired 12 percent fewer comparable broken products than did readers surveyed in 1997. These are some of the reasons:

More bang for fewer bucks. Some 34 percent of readers who decided against repairs cited falling prices for new products as the reason, while 22 percent were driven by a desire for new features. Electronics products like TVs and computers are good examples of getting more for less.

Added efficiency. Most new fridges and washers, for example, use far less energy than older models. The most frugal also cost the most, but the long-term energy savings may make replacing a broken older model worthwhile.

High repair costs. Our surveys have shown that people usually toss broken electric shavers, toasters, and other small appliances because replacing them costs less than having them repaired. Higher-ticket items can also be expensive to repair. Intricate product designs and high labor costs explain some of that expense.

What's more, electronic problems are less obvious than mechanical ones. Ron Sawyer, executive director of the Professional Service Association, a repair-industry trade group, says diagnostic fees typically run from $30 to $60; in some cases, those fees will be deducted from the cost of repair if you decide to go ahead with it.

Shrinking parts supply. Swifter turnover for many products, particularly electronics, can mean that parts for some are scarce, even for new models. We've received reader complaints about a lack of parts for 2-year-old camcorders and 8-month-old computers.

Subpar service. Twenty-five percent of subscribers who had a product repaired reported they were at least somewhat dissatisfied with the outcome. Along with the scarcity of parts, readers' gripes included high repair fees, a long wait, and shoddy workmanship. Repair experiences tended to be worse for electronic equipment, notably camcorders, computers, and CD players. In roughly one out of three cases, the products didn't work properly after repair.

If you decide to repair

Big-ticket items like lawn tractors and projection TVs are usually worth repairing even after a long period of time because new ones are expensive. A few simple steps can ease the repair process.

Be sure it's really broken. Most owners' manuals have a troubleshooting section. Some manufacturer Web sites also provide detailed repair instructions. Several other sites to consider:

- ***www.pcappliancerepair.com.*** Provides solutions to common problems and free help with diagnosing trickier ones.
- ***www.repairclinic.com.*** Primarily a source for appliance parts, available overnight if needed. Site covers nearly 90 brands and includes troubleshooting hints, as well as a "RepairGuru" you can e-mail.
- ***www.livemanuals.com.*** This site includes simulations of how appliances and electronics equipment work, along with manufacturer addresses, phone numbers, and Web links.

Call the company. This can be frustrating: 24 percent of readers who said they tried had difficulty getting through, and almost half found the assistance wanting. But nearly 10 percent got an offer to fix or replace an out-of-warranty item for free.

Consider factory or authorized service.

REPLACE IT

Focus on digital cameras

When a digital camera conks out, should you repair or replace? We don't have sufficient survey data yet to create a timeline, but here's the advice of Consumers Union's engineers: If your camera is a one- or two-megapixel model, replace it. If it is three megapixels or higher, was made by one of the major manufacturers (Canon, Kodak, Nikon, Olympus, or Sony), and you have owned it for less than five years, have it fixed—unless the repairs would cost half as much as a new one. For other manufacturers, a broken three-megapixel or higher camera should be replaced after two years.

NIX OR FIX

Which products hold up?

This chart shows the percentage of 5-year-old products that have ever been repaired or had a serious problem, according to our Annual Questionnaire on the subject. Gas ranges had more breakdowns than electric models, for example, while self-propelled mowers failed more often than push mowers.

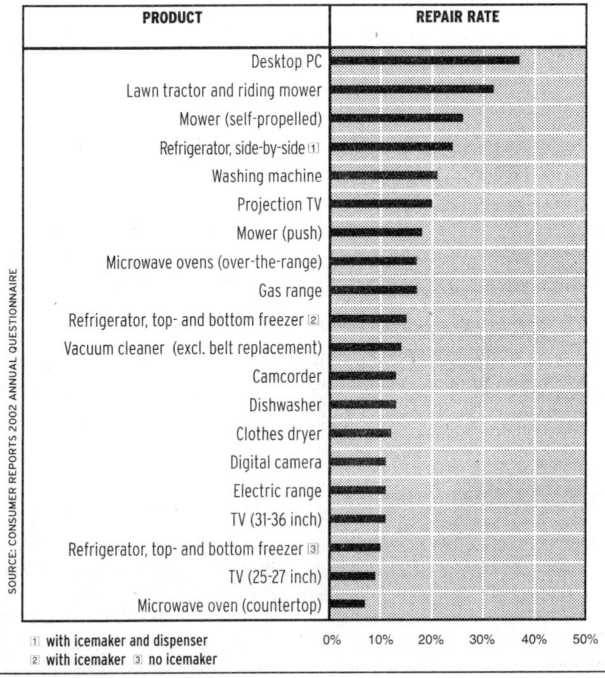

Manufacturers usually train technicians on the latest equipment. They can also hold authorized repairers to certain standards.

Check credentials. Independent repairers can be a viable choice, especially for products that are out of warranty. Ask if the repairer belongs to a trade association like the Professional Service Association. While membership doesn't guarantee integrity, it may mean repairers have had special training.

Don't take problems lying down. If you feel victimized by a repairer, you can file a complaint with your local consumer-affairs department, the Better Business Bureau *(www.bbb.org)*, or your state's attorney general's office. Also consider taking the repairer to small-claims court. Save all receipts and records. And ask to keep any parts that are replaced.

Behind the guide

Data in this guide are based largely on our 2000 Annual Questionnaire and include readers' experiences with products that broke out of warranty and were professionally repaired. **Repair problems** indicates the frequency with which readers had difficulties. Among the key problems: inconvenience; repairs that took more than two weeks; excessive cost; hard-to-find parts; and bad repairs. **Repair cost** is based on the typical range readers said they paid for repairs. **Replacement cost** denotes the typical price range for new products, as determined by our market and engineering experts. The **repair or replace timelines** show when repair or replacement makes sense in our judgment, based on the product's age, typical repair and replacement costs, and the extent to which improvements make new models superior. A white bar denotes a repair is worthwhile; a shaded bar signals a judgment call; a black bar means we advise against repair. **Special repair problems** identify difficulties that occurred more often than usual.

Lawn and garden products

☐ Repair ▒ Consider repair ■ Replace

PRODUCT	REPAIR PROBLEMS	REPAIR COST	REPLACEMENT COST	REPAIR OR REPLACE TIMELINES						
				2YR.	3YR.	4YR.	5YR.	6YR.	7YR.	8YR.
Lawn tractors and riding mowers	50%	$100-300	$800-2,500	Repair	Repair	Repair	Repair	Repair	Repair	Repair
Walk-behind gas mowers	53	50-100	200-450 (self-propelled)	Repair	Repair	Consider repair	Consider repair	Consider repair	Consider repair	Replace
			125-350 (push)	Repair	Consider repair	Consider repair	Consider repair	Replace	Replace	Replace

What to consider

LAWN TRACTORS AND RIDING MOWERS

Product outlook Trends include higher horsepower and wider cutting deck, tighter turning, better ergonomics, and automatic blade braking when moving in reverse. Stricter emissions rules that continue through 2007 have spawned cleaner-burning engines.

Special repair problems Readers reported parts were hard to get and repairs took too long.

Preventive maintenance Clean beneath the deck after each use. Change engine oil and sharpen blade each season. Clean or replace air filter and spark plug, and add a preservative to the fuel at end of mowing season. Remove and trickle-charge battery during the off season.

WALK-BEHIND GAS MOWERS

Product outlook Most now mulch, bag, and side-discharge clippings. Other mower trends include cleaner-burning engines, easier starting, and more horsepower. Many walk-behind mowers also offer high rear wheels, though some have hampered the mower's maneuverability in our tests.

Comments You may want to repair models that cost $500 or more beyond seven years, considering the price of replacement of these units.

Special repair problems Readers report that repairs took too long and weren't done correctly.

Preventive maintenance Same as for lawn tractors and riding mowers.

Personal-computing products

☐ Repair ▩ Consider repair ■ Replace

PRODUCT	REPAIR PROBLEMS	REPAIR COST	REPLACEMENT COST	REPAIR OR REPLACE TIMELINES						
				2 YR.	3 YR.	4 YR.	5 YR.	6 YR.	7 YR.	8 YR.
Desktop PCs	56%	$100-300	$1,000-2,000	Repair	Repair	Consider repair	Replace	Replace	Replace	Replace
Laptop or notebook PCs	62	100-400	1,400-2,000	Repair	Repair	Consider repair	Replace	Replace	Replace	Replace
Printers	50	50-125	100-300 (inkjet)	Consider repair	Replace	Replace	Replace	Replace	Replace	Replace

What to consider

DESKTOP PCS

Product outlook Trends include processors with a much faster clock speed; more memory; a faster modem; a larger hard drive (typically 20 to 80 GB); USB ports for high-speed connections; faster CD-ROMs, a DVD-ROM, CD-R/W, or DVD-R drive—or a combination drive for all three. Some PC models feature FireWire ports for even faster connections.

Comments Better technology often makes replacing even 2- or 3-year-old PCs more sensible than repairing them.

Special repair problems Readers reported that repairers were hard to find and repairs weren't done correctly.

Preventive maintenance Turn off the computer and the monitor before cleaning screen. Vacuum the keyboard with a soft brush. Remove and wash the mouse or track ball. Use a surge protector on your power line. If you connect to the Internet, make sure you have updated anti-virus software.

LAPTOP OR NOTEBOOK PCS

Product outlook Same as for desktop PCs, but hard drive is typically 10-30 GB.

Special repair problems Readers reported parts were hard to get and repairers hard to find. Repairs took too long and weren't done correctly.

Preventive maintenance Same as for desktop PCs.

PRINTERS

Product outlook Prices have dropped and the quality of inkjet text now approaches a laser printer's. Other trends: Some models can print photos directly from memory cards.

Comments Better technology and lower prices are disincentives for all but the simplest repairs.

Special repair problems Readers reported that repairers were hard to find.

Preventive maintenance Keep free of dirt and dust. Clean contacts with a cotton swab and alcohol.

Electronics

☐ Repair ▒ Consider repair ■ Replace

PRODUCT	REPAIR PROBLEMS	REPAIR COST	REPLACEMENT COST (TYPICAL RANGE)	REPAIR OR REPLACE TIMELINES 2 YR.	3 YR.	4 YR.	5 YR.	6 YR.	7 YR.	8 YR.
Camcorders	67%	$100-200*	$250-450-analog	Repair	Consider repair	Consider repair	Replace	Replace	Replace	Replace
			300-700-digital	Repair	Repair	Consider repair	Consider repair	Replace	Replace	Replace
CD players	59	50-100	100-250	Consider repair	Replace	Replace	Replace	Replace	Replace	Replace
Projection TVs	54	180-400	1,000-5,000 (rear projection)	Repair	Repair	Repair	Repair	Repair	Consider repair	Consider repair
25-27-in. TVs	43	85-150	200-300 (25-in.);	Consider repair	Consider repair	Replace	Replace	Replace	Replace	Replace
			250-600 (27-in.)	Repair	Consider repair	Consider repair	Replace	Replace	Replace	Replace
31-36-in. TVs	51	115-250	400-1,100 (32-in.);	Repair	Repair	Repair	Consider repair	Consider repair	Replace	Replace
			600-1,400 (36-in.)	Repair	Repair	Repair	Repair	Consider repair	Consider repair	Replace

* Applies to analog camcorders only

What to consider

CAMCORDERS

Product outlook Digital models are displacing analogs. Advantages include better picture quality for most and the ability to connect to a computer for storing/editing images. Regular 8mm is practically extinct and S-VHS-C is following suit. The VHS-C analog format is likely to last a while longer.

Comments Consider replacing a broken analog model with a digital if it's more than two years old.

Special repair problems Readers reported that repairs took too long, cost too much, and weren't done correctly. They also reported that repairers were hard to find.

Preventive maintenance Store in case to protect against dust and moisture. Clean lens with a soft cloth or special tissue. When loading, press door gently to avoid bending cassette carriage.

CD PLAYERS

Product outlook Reasonably priced multichanger and jukebox models hold up to 400 CDs. We found most new models can play CD-R and CD-RW discs.

Special repair problems Readers reported that repairs took too long and weren't done correctly.

Preventive maintenance Keep out of direct sunlight, away from heat, and where it's free of jolts to prevent skipping. Keep CDs clean and scratch-free.

PROJECTION TVS

Product outlook Some high-end models offer rectangular, movielike screens and built-in tuners that receive high-definition programming.

Special repair problems Readers reported parts were hard to get and repairers hard to find. Also repairs took too long and cost too much.

Preventive maintenance Screens scratch easily; take care when cleaning. Align the three CRTs for best picture; bumping can cause misalignment.

25-27-INCH TVS

Product outlook Some 25-inch sets have features such as a flat screen and an S-video input. Twenty-seven inch sets add more features. Entry-level HD-ready models are available starting at $750.

Preventive maintenance Keep out of direct sunlight and away from heat. Remove dust from screen and vents.

30-36-INCH TVS

Product outlook Same as 27-inch TVs. Some offer HD and other features, but cost more than $1,700.

Special repair problems Readers reported parts were hard to get and repairs took too long.

Preventive maintenance Same as for 25-27-inch TVs. Place on a sturdy stand or cart.

Appliances

☐ Repair ▒ Consider repair ■ Replace

PRODUCT	REPAIR PROBLEMS	REPAIR COST	REPLACEMENT COST	REPAIR OR REPLACE TIMELINES						
				2YR.	3YR.	4YR.	5YR.	6YR.	7YR.	8YR.
Clothes dryers	26%	$70-140	$300-500	Repair	Repair	Repair	Consider repair	Consider repair	Consider repair	Replace
Dishwashers	34	75-150	300-550	Repair	Repair	Repair	Consider repair	Consider repair	Consider repair	Replace
Electric ranges	45	85-200	400-900	Repair	Repair	Consider repair	Consider repair	Consider repair	Replace	Replace
Gas ranges	45	100-190	450-900	Repair	Repair	Repair	Consider repair	Consider repair	Consider repair	Replace
Microwave ovens	41	50-150	100-150 (countertop)	Replace	Replace	Replace	Replace	Replace	Replace	Replace
			350-450 (over-range)	Repair	Repair	Consider repair	Consider repair	Consider repair	Consider repair	Replace
Side-by-side refrigerators	37	100-200	800-1,400	Repair	Repair	Repair	Repair	Consider repair	Consider repair	Replace
Top-freezer refrigerators	32	80-185	500-800	Repair	Repair	Repair	Consider repair	Consider repair	Consider repair	Replace
Vacuum cleaners	36	30-80	80-300 (upright)	Repair	Repair	Consider repair	Consider repair	Consider repair	Replace	Replace
			200-400 (canister)	Repair	Repair	Repair	Repair	Consider repair	Consider repair	Replace
Wall ovens	57	85-250	800-1,200 (single-unit)	Repair	Repair	Repair	Repair	Consider repair	Consider repair	Consider repair
Washing machines	29	75-150	300-600	Repair	Repair	Repair	Consider repair	Consider repair	Consider repair	Replace

What to consider

CLOTHES DRYERS

Product outlook Many now have energy-saving moisture sensors and larger capacities.

Preventive maintenance Clean lint filter after each use to keep exhaust duct from clogging–a fire hazard.

DISHWASHERS

Product outlook More have dirt sensors and adjustable racks. More are also quieter, roomier, and use less water.

Preventive maintenance Keep silverware away from spray arms.

ELECTRIC RANGES

Product outlook Smoothtops are displacing coil-tops, though they aren't necessarily better or more reliable. More models have electronic controls so you can fine-tune settings. High-end models may have a gas cooktop.

Special repair problems Readers reported parts were hard to get and repairs cost too much..

Preventive maintenance Place heavy pots and pans carefully on smoothtops to avoid breakage.

GAS RANGES

Product outlook Trends include burners with 13,000 to 15,000 Btus per hour, heavy-duty grates, broad color choices, sealed burners, and glass cooktops.

Special repair problems Readers reported parts were hard to get and repairs cost too much.

Preventive maintenance Periodically clean burner ports with a needle, and be sure not to poke the igniter.

MICROWAVE OVENS

Product outlook Trends include more power and interactive displays, and sensors that adjust cooking time automatically.

Special repair problems Readers reported parts were hard to get.
Preventive maintenance Avoid turning on when empty and avoid putting metal inside.

SIDE-BY-SIDE REFRIGERATORS

Product outlook New machines must consume 30 percent less power than the least efficient models made before July 2001. New models are also quieter. Ice and water dispensers are a growing trend.
Preventive maintenance Remove dust from coils. Inspect around door seal for leaks, and keep gasket and its mating surface free of debris.

TOP-FREEZER REFRIGERATORS

Product outlook New machines must consume 30 percent less power than the least efficient models made before July 2001. New models are also quieter. Other trends include more temperature-controlled bins.
Preventive maintenance Same as for side-by-side models.

VACUUM CLEANERS

Product outlook More upright models are self-propelled, but these are heavier and harder to carry. More are bagless, but these can be messy to empty and may require frequent filter replacement. HEPA filters minimize dust emissions, but so do many others.
Preventive maintenance Change the bag or clean the filter as needed. Clean rotating-brush supports. Avoid vacuuming up string and hard objects and running over cord, which can fray and cause a shock hazard. Also inspect the cord periodically and replace it if its cover is damaged.

WALL OVENS

Product outlook More have a convection feature for faster roasting.
Special repair problems Readers reported parts were hard to get; repairers were hard to find and repairs took too long and cost too much.
Preventive maintenance Check door seals for damage.

WASHING MACHINES

Product outlook All washers manufactured after Jan. 1, 2004, must use about 25 percent less energy than previously mandated. (Standards again get stricter in 2007.) The EnergyGuide sticker on those washers reflects the new standard; models already in stores may carry the old sticker.
Comments Because front-loaders are more expensive and more fuel-efficient than top-loaders, the repair window is usually at least a year longer than for top-loaders.
Preventive maintenance Remove grit from the screen where the hose attaches to the hot-water supply.

Finding Reliable Brands

Our brand repair histories can help

Products today are pretty reliable, but some brands have been more reliable than others. Every year we survey readers on repairs and on problems they encounter with household products. From their responses, we derive the percentage of a brand's products that have been repaired or had a serious problem. The graphs that follow give brand repair rates for 25 product categories. Over the 30-plus years we've surveyed brand reliability, our findings have been consistent, though they are not infallible predictors.

A brand's repair history includes data on many models, some of which may have been more or less reliable than others. And surveys of a brand's past models can't anticipate design or manufacturing changes in its new models. Still, you can improve your chances of getting a trouble-free product by getting a brand that has been reliable in the past.

Product categories include appliances such as washers and ranges, electronic products such as TV sets and computers, and lawn mowers and tractors. Note that repair histories for different products are not directly comparable.

Because the quality of technical support may be the deciding factor when you're shopping for a desktop computer, we include a recent assessment of the PC manufacturers' technical support as well.

QUICK GUIDE

Camcorders

Camcorders are used an average of only 12 hours per year, which may influence their repair rate. We found that people use digitals for more hours than analogs, however. Among digital camcorders, JVC Mini DV and Canon Mini DV were the most repair-prone brands; for analog cameras there were small differences among leading brands. Differences of 4 or more points are meaningful.

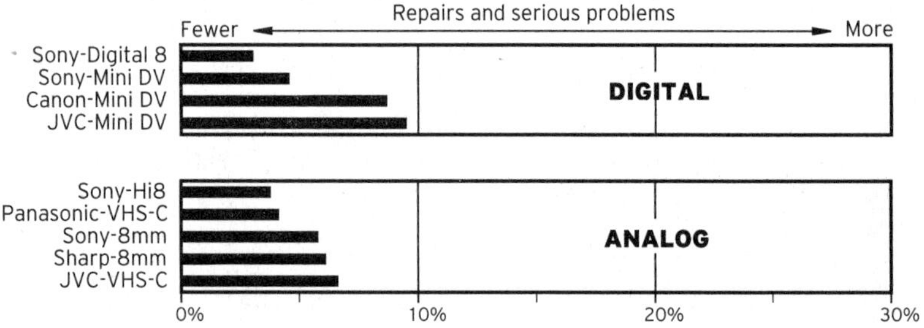

Based on more than 24,000 responses on camcorders purchased new in 1999 through the first quarter of 2002. Data have been standardized to eliminate differences among brands due to age and usage.

Computers (Desktop models)

Computers are the most repair-prone products that we ask about. In a survey of CONSUMER REPORTS readers, 4 percent bought a computer that was completely inoperable within the first month; another 10 percent had problems that month but could still use the computers. The chart shows the percentage of computers that ever had a repair to original hardware components. Micron was the most repair-prone brand. Differences of 5 or more points are meaningful.

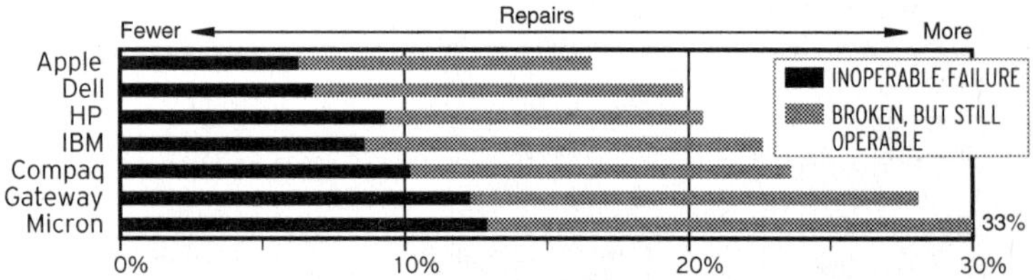

Based on more than 39,000 responses on desktop computers bought new between January 1998 and April 2002. Data have been standardized to eliminate differences attributable to a computer's age and usage.

HOW THE HELP RATES

Computer tech support

Overall, just over 40 percent of the people who used a computer manufacturer's technical support were highly satisfied with the service, based on recent experiences (since January 2002) of subscribers to ConsumerReports.org. That's lower than most other service industries CONSUMER REPORTS tracks. One in three said they couldn't get their problem solved.

Better ⊜ ⊖ ○ ◒ ● Worse

MANUFACTURER	READER SCORE (0–100)	SOLVED PROBLEM	SUPPORT STAFF	WAITING ON PHONE	WEB SUPPORT
Apple	76	⊜	⊜	⊜	⊜
Dell	64	⊖	○	○	○
Gateway	61	○	○	⊖	⊖
Sony	54	○	○	○	-
HP	53	○	○	○	○
Compaq	51	○	○	◒	○

Based on responses from more than 7,400 subscribers to ConsumerReports.org surveyed in February 2003. If everyone were completely satisfied, the reader score would be 100; 80, if respondents were, on average, very satisfied; 60, if fairly well satisfied. Differences of 4 or more points are meaningful. **Solved problem** indicates how many respondents said the manufacturer solved the problem. **Support staff** gauges how many said phone representatives seemed knowledgeable. **Waiting on phone** indicates whether respondents waited on hold too long or had other problems. **Web support** tracks problems with that type of contact. A dash means insufficient data.

Digital cameras

While our brand histories have been quite consistent over the years, this is a relatively new product with changing technology. Repair rates showed small differences among leading brands. Differences of 4 or more points are meaningful.

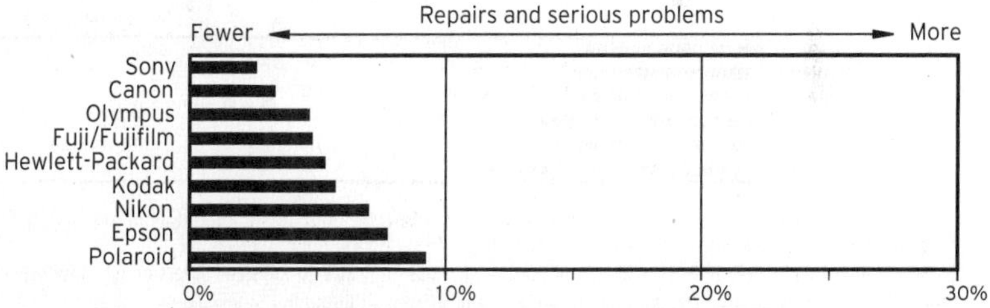

Based on more than 52,000 responses to our 2002 Annual Questionnaire on digital cameras bought new between 1999 and the first quarter of 2002. Data have been standardized to eliminate differences linked to age.

Dishwashers

Asko was the most repair-prone brand, followed by Frigidaire and Bosch. Differences of 3 or more points are meaningful.

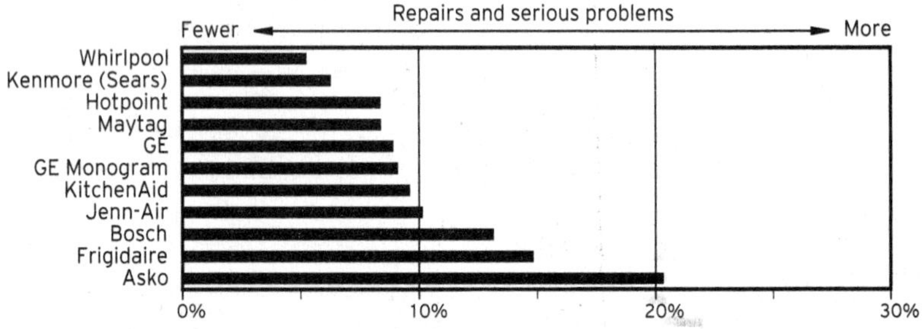

Based on more than 96,000 responses to our 2002 Annual Questionnaire on dishwashers bought new between 1997 and 2002. Data have been standardized to eliminate differences linked to age and usage.

Dryers

Gas and electric dryers have been equally reliable, with small differences among leading brands. Differences of 3 or more points are meaningful.

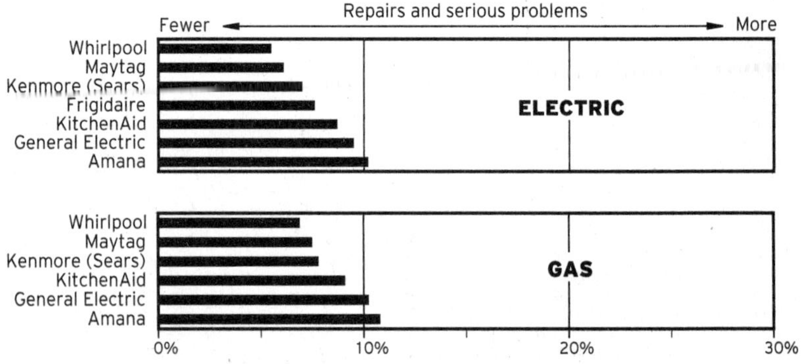

Based on almost 83,000 reader responses to our 2002 Annual Questionnaire on full-sized dryers bought new between 1997 and 2002. Data have been standardized to eliminate any differences linked to age and usage.

Lawn mowers (Push and self-propelled)

Among push models, Lawn-Boy was the most repair-prone brand; Snapper was among the more repair-prone brands of the self-propelled mowers. Differences of 5 or more points are meaningful.

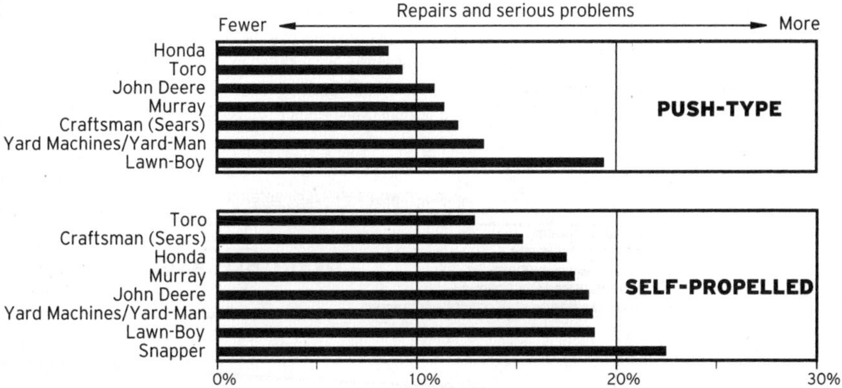

Based on 43,832 responses to our 2002 Annual Questionnaire on self-propelled and push mowers bought new between 1998 and 2002. Data have been standardized to eliminate differences linked to age and usage.

Lawn tractors and riding mowers

Cub Cadet was among the more repair-prone brands of lawn tractors. Among riding mowers, Murray (whose repair rate may in part reflect a 2002 fuel-tank recall) and Snapper were among the more repair-prone brands. Differences of 6 or more points are meaningful.

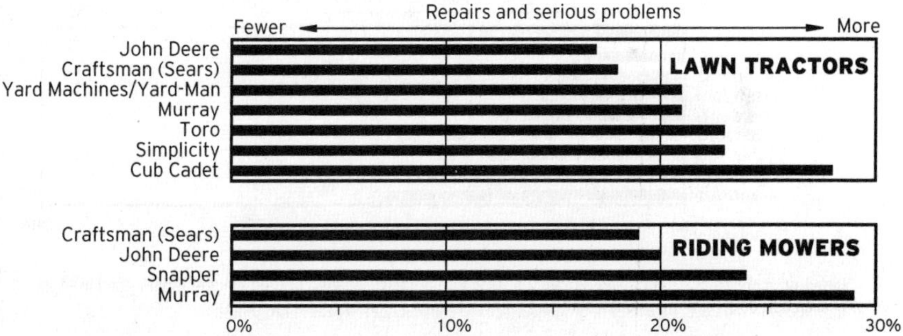

Based on more than 16,000 responses to our 2002 Annual Questionnaire on lawn tractors and riding mowers bought new between 1998 and 2002. Data have been standardized to eliminate differences linked to age and usage.

Microwave ovens

Major brands of nonconvection countertop microwave ovens generally have been quite reliable: They had repair rates of 6 percent or less, with no meaningful differences. Countertop models with convection had slightly higher repair rates. Both Sharp and GE, the brands for which we have sufficient data, had 9 percent repair rates.

Over-the-range models tend to have similar repair rates for convection and nonconvection models. Among the brands listed below, Sharp was the most repair-prone. Kenmore and Whirlpool are not included in the chart; certain models from these brands were recalled in 2002, resulting in extraordinarily high repair rates: 52 percent for Kenmore and 38 percent for Whirlpool—much higher than the repair rates for those brands from our last Annual Questionnaire. Differences of 4 or more points are meaningful.

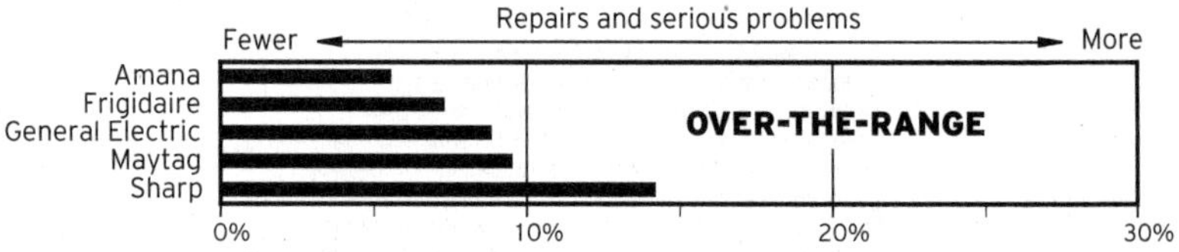

Based on more than 22,600 responses to our 2002 Annual Questionnaire on microwave ovens purchased new between 1998 and 2002. Data have been standardized to eliminate differences among brands due to age and usage.

Ranges (Electric models)

In general, electric ranges have required fewer repairs than gas models. Smoothtop models have been about as reliable as conventional coil-burner models. Jenn-Air, Amana, KitchenAid, and Maytag have been among the more repair-prone brands. Differences of 4 or more points are meaningful.

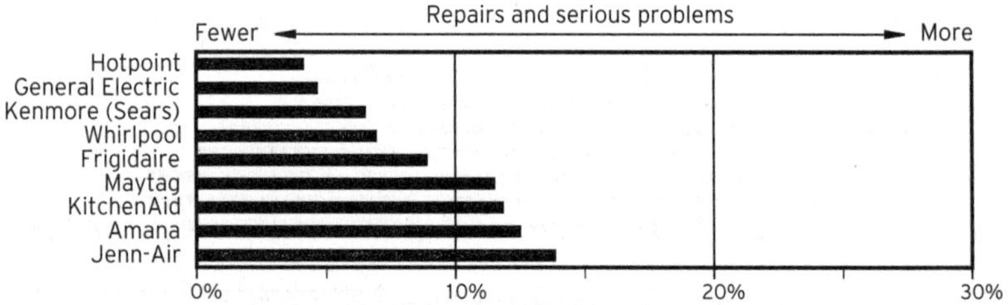

Based on more than 50,000 responses to our 2002 Annual Questionnaire covering electric ranges purchased new between 1997 and 2002. Data have been standardized to eliminate differences linked to age.

Ranges (Gas models)

Gas ranges have generally required more repairs than electric ranges. Amana was the most repair-prone brand followed by Jenn-Air, Maytag, KitchenAid, and Magic Chef. Differences of 4 or more points are meaningful.

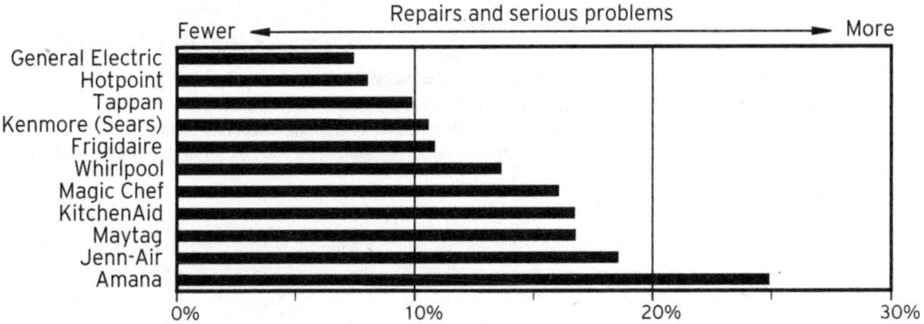

Based on more than 27,000 responses to our 2002 Annual Questionnaire covering gas ranges purchased between 1997 and 2002. Data have been standardized to eliminate differences linked to age.

Refrigerators

Regardless of configuration, the presence of an icemaker increases the chances of needing a repair. All side-by-side models included an outside ice and water dispenser, features that considerably increase the chances of needing a repair. Of models so equipped Maytag has been the least reliable. Sub-Zero is the only built-in refrigerator brand. Differences of 4 or more points are meaningful.

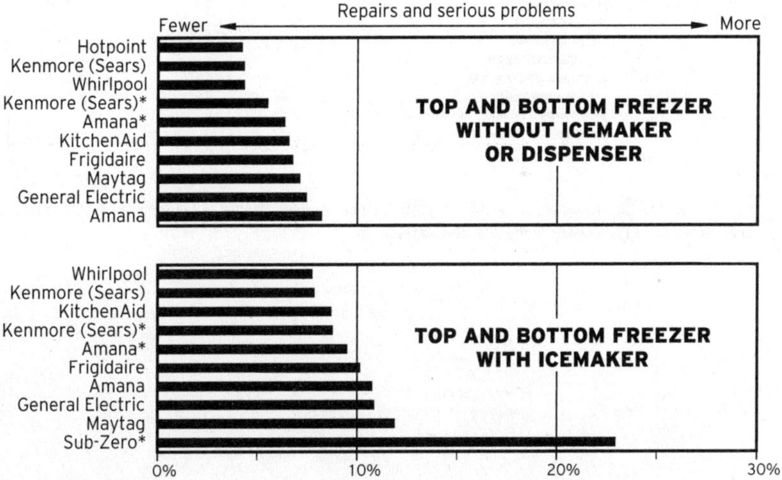

* Bottom-freezer

Refrigerators (continued)

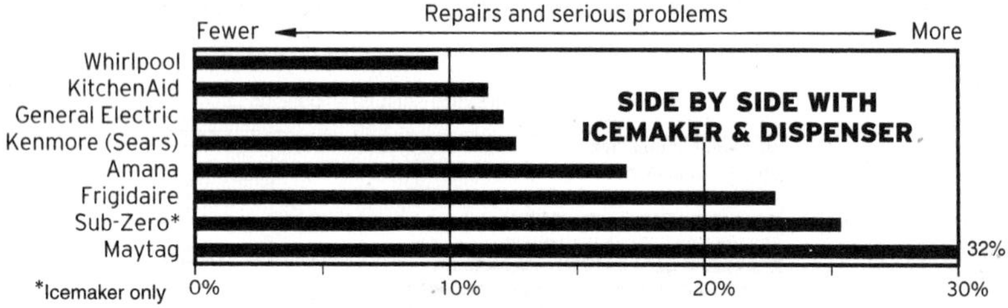

Based on more than 75,000 responses to our 2002 Annual Questionnaire on full-sized refrigerators purchased new between 1998 and 2002. Data have been standardized to eliminate differences linked to age.

TV sets (25- to 27-inch)

These models tend to be a bit older than sets in the 31- to 36-inch range. GE and RCA have been among the more troublesome brands. Differences of 3 or more points are meaningful.

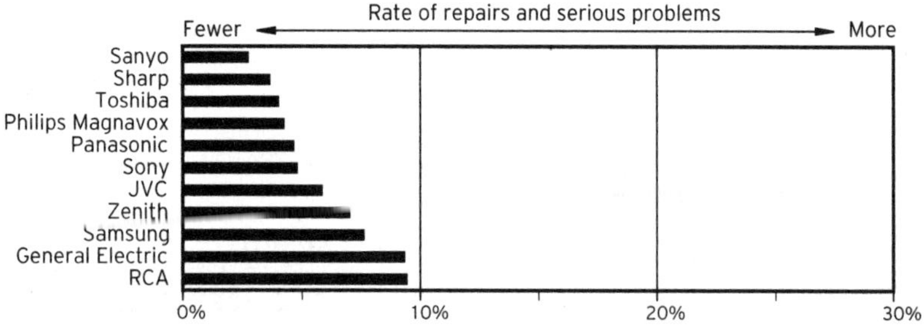

Based on nearly 75,000 responses to our 2002 Annual Questionnaire on sets purchased new from 1997 to 2002. Data have been standardized to eliminate differences attributable to age.

TV sets (31- and 32-inch, 35- and 36-inch)

Most models in our survey were fairly new and were used more often than smaller-sized TVs. RCA has been significantly more troublesome than other brands. Differences of 3 or more points are meaningful.

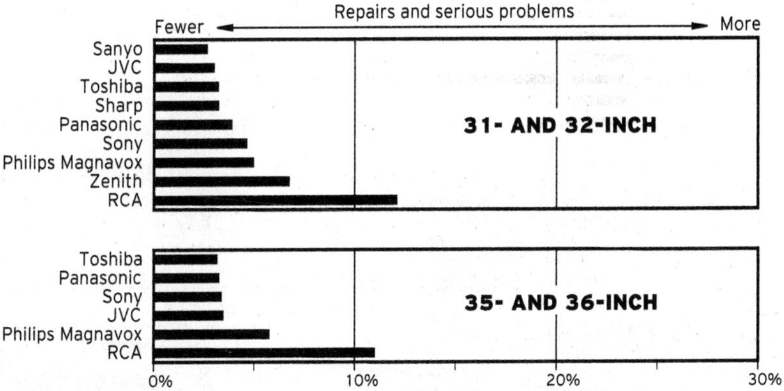

Based on nearly 41,000 responses to our 2002 Annual Questionnaire on sets purchased new from 1998 to 2002. Data have been standardized to eliminate differences attributable to age.

TV sets (projection)

Data include both HD-capable and standard sets, which showed no difference in reliability. Differences of 3 or more points are meaningful.

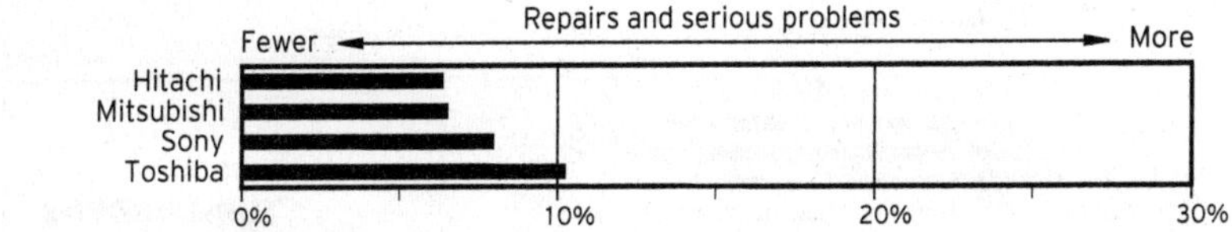

Based on 7,000 responses to our 2002 Annual Questionnaire on projection sets purchased new between 1997 and 2002. Data have been standardized to eliminate differences resulting from age and usage.

Vacuum cleaners

Eureka canisters and Fantom uprights were among the more repair-prone brands. The results shown here don't include broken belts–a frequent though usually inexpensive problem that was more common for uprights and for Eureka among canister brands. Differences of 5 or more points are meaningful.

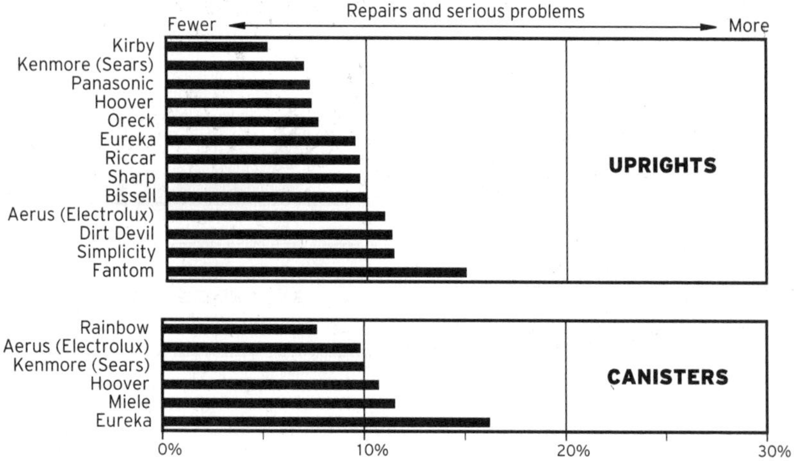

Based on more than 107,000 responses to our 2002 Annual Questionnaire on vacuum cleaners purchased new between 1998 and 2002. Data have been standardized to eliminate any differences linked to age and usage.

Washing machines

Maytag front-loaders were more repair-prone than all other brands of washers. Differences of 4 or more points are meaningful.

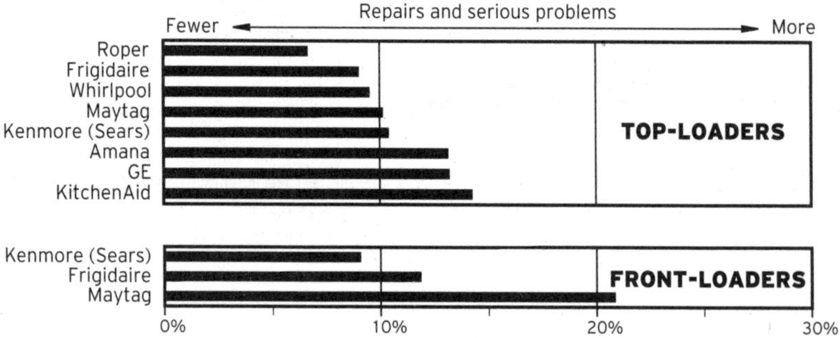

Based on more than 83,000 reader responses to our 2002 Annual Questionnaire about washers bought new between 1998 and 2002. Data have been standardized to eliminate differences linked to age and usage.

HOME ENTERTAINMENT

What's New in Home Entertainment

In recent years, digital entertainment products such as DVD players, digital video recorders (DVRs), and satellite-TV receivers have transformed the marketplace. Camcorders, cameras, receivers, cable boxes, and many TV sets have moved from analog to digital and, in the process, have made leaps in what they promise and often can deliver.

CONSUMER REPORTS tests show that digital capability often results in giant steps in performance. Audio CD players consistently reproduce sound better than turntables did. The typical digital camcorder provides much clearer video than the best of the older, analog cousins. Receivers supporting digital audio can provide more realism when you're watching movies at home than those using earlier, analog-audio standards. High-definition TV shows off not just the football game but the sweat glistening on the players' arms.

But despite digital's superiority over the analog ways of cassette tape, videotape, and traditional NTSC-standard TV, analog products will still be sold for some time to come. And if industry infighting and consumer confusion are any indication, it will be years before we see the last of the analog breed. Here's what you can see in today's home-entertainment products:

Digital movies, analog TVs. DVDs, with their capacity for extra features such as director-commentary chapters, are already replacing videotapes as the preferred home-movie choice among consumers. Meanwhile, DVD players have quickly become almost a commodity, with excellent performance the norm and prices well below $100 for an increasing number of models.

Despite the record pace of DVD adoption, however, analog TVs and VCRs are still by far the most-sold home-entertainment products, and the best of them are fine performers despite their "nondigitized" nature. VCRs are still a mainstay, though digital recorders—sold under TiVo, Replay, and other names—can record with greater speed and finesse.

The popularity of recordable DVDs has grown more slowly than predicted because of high cost, technical difficulties, and wrangles over copy-protection concerns. But DVD recorders priced as low as $500 are winning new fans in the quest for more-permanent storage of home movies. And TiVo, Replay, and similar DVRs still require you to transfer material to videotape for long-term storage.

The digital revolution in audio keeps rolling. It turns out that the introduction of CD players in 1982 was just part one of the digital revolution in consumer audio—the playback part. Part two: the current boom in digital recording options. Audio component CD player/recorders, which let you "burn" your own CDs for a dollar or two each, have been dropping in price; you can now buy one for a few hundred dollars. (The same process can also be done, often more easily, using computers.) Newer MP3 players offer huge capacity, 5 to 80 gigabytes, in very small packages. Digital-music options make music "liquid": You can pour out what you want to hear, in the order you want, in the format you choose—at home, in the car, or while jetting to Bermuda.

Improvements in digital audio technology, such as DVD-Audio and Super Audio CD (SACD), take full advantage of surround-sound speaker systems developed for movies. Such capability has worked its way into an increasing number of DVD players.

Surround sound marches on. One of the biggest attractions of DVD is its digital surround sound, most commonly represented by the Dolby Digital format. To take full advantage, you need up to six speakers (potentially more) and a Dolby Digital receiver to manage them—in addition to your TV and DVD player.

You can buy those components completely à la carte, as a receiver plus a separate matched set of six speakers, or as a "home theater in a box," which combines six speakers plus a receiver (possibly with a built-in DVD player as well). See "Setting Up a Home Theater" on the following page for more information.

Products get smaller...yet again. Manufacturers continue to shrink hard drives, batteries, and other parts of audio and video components. MP3 players can be as small as an ink pen. Portable CD and DVD players can be as thin as an inch. Many capable speakers for home theater are as small as those intended for computer use. "Executive sound systems" have shrunk minisystems into microsystems that fit readily on a desk or into flat systems that hang on a wall.

More options but fewer providers. Even as consumers' ability to control how they view and listen to content continues to expand, corporate mergers are further shrinking the number of companies that control the flow of content. Content providers now own media organizations and vice versa, with Internet service in the mix as well. General Electric owns NBC; Viacom owns CBS, MTV, VH1, Paramount Pictures, Showtime, and Blockbuster; Walt Disney owns ABC; Sony owns Columbia and TriStar; Time Warner includes AOL, HBO, Warner Brothers, New Line Cinema, Time Warner Cable, and Turner Broadcasting; and Vivendi Universal Net owns MP3.com and Rollingstone.com, among others. One result of these conglomerations is that, more than ever, what's available is affected by forces other than viewer preference.

Copyrights and wrongs. At the same time, copyright issues are limiting control of content—and possibly increasing prices. The creators and publishers of content such as movies and music have legitimate claims to legal protection of what belongs to them. But copyright concerns have led to the use of hardware that blocks you from copying a DVD title you've purchased onto a VHS tape for your personal use. (Expect similar roadblocks when DVD recorders go mainstream.)

Some recent releases of music CDs include copy protection that may distort the sound if you try to play the disc in your computer's CD-ROM drive—or even freeze up the PC altogether. And blank CDs for recording music include a surcharge to cover royalties the music industry believes would otherwise be denied to musicians.

Less privacy. Every company with which you contract for your home entertainment seems to have gone full-throttle into data mining. Rent a videotape or DVD from Blockbuster or order pay-per-view on cable, and the transaction is recorded in some way. Ditto when you buy a CD off the Web, choose a channel on your cable or satellite setup, or fill out a warranty card.

You might expect the original company to use that information to offer related products and services to you. But it's another thing to be bombarded with phone calls, letters, e-mail, and other offers from companies you've never heard of, simply because they have purchased data about you.

More complex choices all around. One more effect of the so-called digital revolution is that it's even harder to be an informed consumer. Products are more complicated, requiring you to study to make a smart choice.

More products involve a service provider, not just for Web access and cell phones but now some video equipment. Not only must you choose among competing services, but once you've chosen and bought the hardware, you're committed to that provider. Switching can involve paying hundreds of dollars more to buy new, provider-specific gear, as with satellite-TV equipment or DVRs.

More and more, electronics components need to connect with one another, requiring compatible video and audio connections for best results. And competing formats mean that early adopters cannot be sure that the format they choose will be the one that prevails, as manufacturers conjure up newer media formats, music-encoding schemes, and connection specifications.

All this, of course, means a greater challenge for consumers shopping for home-entertainment products. It's where CONSUMER REPORTS can help.

SETTING UP A HOME THEATER

Adding surround sound to a TV can transform the viewing and listening experience even more than buying a bigger set. Most TV sound can be improved by adding external speakers; a pair of self-powered speakers is a simple, easy way to do that. But for a real home-theater experience, you need a big TV, a video source (hi-fi stereo VCR or DVD player), a surround-decoding receiver/amplifier, and five speakers plus a subwoofer. Following is an overview of the whole system.

HOW SURROUND SOUND WORKS

Surround sound adds more channels to familiar two-channel stereophonic sound for stronger movie-theater realism, allowing additional speakers to carry the multichannel sound found on movies.

What you'll hear depends on three things: the format used for the source (a TV show or DVD, for instance), the software decoder (on the receiver or DVD player) used to decipher the format, and the number of speakers you have. If your gear lacks the latest, most sophisticated decoder, it can still handle a TV broadcast or DVD, but it will do so with fewer audio channels and less dramatic effect. Conversely, state-of-the-art hardware can play older material only because new decoders are generally backward-compatible with early formats. Again, you'll hear fewer channels.

The following is a rundown on the major formats:

Dolby Surround, an early version of surround sound, is an analog encoding scheme used mostly for VHS movies and TV shows. It combines four channels into stereo soundtracks. With no decoder—say, on a TV—you'll hear stereo.

With a **Dolby Pro Logic** decoder, you'll hear four channels: left, right, center (unlike Dolby Surround), and one limited-range surround channel. A newer version, **Pro Logic II,** has the same left, right, and center channels, but also has two discrete, full-range surround channels for a total of five channels. Most new receivers have Pro Logic II; older models may have only Pro Logic. You'll need four or five speakers for optimal sound.

The next step up is **Dolby Digital,** a digital encoding scheme that's also called Dolby Digital 5.1. Like Pro Logic II, it has full-range left and right channels in front and rear plus a center channel; it adds a subwoofer channel for deep bass (called ".1" because it's limited to low-frequency effects). Dolby Digital is used on digital media, such as DVDs, digital cable, digital broadcast TV, and satellite transmissions. It can also decode material that uses Dolby Surround. Virtually all new receivers and some DVD players have Dolby Digital decoders. You'll need five full-range speakers and a subwoofer for optimal sound.

DTS (Digital Theater Systems) is a rival to Dolby Digital, also with six channels. It's offered on most new receivers and on some DVD players. It calls for the same speaker setup as Dolby Digital.

Dolby Digital EX and **DTS-ES** are "extended surround" formats that add either a center-rear surround channel or an extra pair of rear-surround speakers that go behind the listener. With Dolby Digital EX, the two flavors are referred to, respectively, as Dolby Digital 6.1 (with three surround speakers) and 7.1 (with four surround speakers). Both formats are still relatively new and not widely used on either equipment or programming. At this stage, they are mostly for video enthusiasts. With them, you'll need seven or eight speakers to achieve the full effect.

THX is a certification that indicates a multichannel audio product has passed certain performance and ergonomic tests and can process sound to simulate movie-theater acoustics.

CONNECTING THE COMPONENTS

The way you connect your video and audio equipment can affect the quality of the sound and images you receive. Here's what you need to know about each.

Video connections. Even the best TV set won't live up to its potential without a high-quality video source and a high-quality connection. As described below, TV sets can have four different types of inputs, each of which accepts a specific kind of signal. Most sets 27 inches and larger have an RF antenna/cable, composite-video, and S-video input; a component-video input is found mostly on higher-end models.

Antenna/cable input, sometimes called a VHF/UHF input. This is the most common connection. It's the easiest connection to use because it's the only one that carries both sound and picture on one cable—in this case, the familiar coaxial cable. (The other video inputs carry only the picture, requiring the use of a separate pair of audio inputs to carry the sound.) The antenna/cable input is used with video sources such as antennas, cable boxes, and VCRs.

Composite-video input. This offers a step up in quality. It uses a single standard RCA-style jack—a round jack (frequently yellow) with a single pin—to pass video signals. Two separate RCA jacks are used to pass the stereo audio signals. Most video sources—including cable boxes and VCRs, as well as DVD players—have a composite video connection.

S-video input. A round jack with four pins, it accepts even better-quality signals. This input separates the signal into two—color and luminance (black and white)—which improves the image quality. This can be used to connect your TV to DVD players, satellite receivers, and digital-cable boxes, as well as digital, S-VHS, or Hi8 camcorders.

Component-video input. A three-cable connection found on some higher-end TVs, this carries potentially the best-quality signals. It separates the video signal into three signals, two color and one luminance. This input is used primarily with DVD players. On HD-ready sets, this input is specially designed to handle signals from HDTV tuners and progressive-scan DVD players.

Some TVs come with more than one S-video, composite-video, or component-video input, letting you connect several devices. On many TVs, a composite-video or S-video input is on the front of the set for easy access.

Audio connections. The picture is obviously only half the story. You will also need to hook up your sound equipment. To obtain the audio from a device such as a VCR, DVD player, cable or satellite receiver, or camcorder, you generally connect one or a pair of **audio inputs** to your receiver, which routes sound to the speakers. Stereo analog audio inputs are labeled L and R for left and right. Newer multichannel receivers will also have **coaxial** or **optical digital-audio inputs** for providing surround sound; some have both. These are used for connecting a DVD player and some digital-cable and satellite receivers. Be sure that the receiver's input matches the output of any device you want to connect—in other words, to use an optical output on the DVD player, you will need to have an optical input on the receiver. After-market converter boxes are also available.

To output the sound, every multichannel receiver will have at least six speaker terminals so it can accommodate a surround-sound system with six speakers. You don't have to use all six terminals—you can use only two for a stereo setup, for instance. Most receivers also have a **subwoofer pre-amp out,** an output that carries unamplified low-frequency signals to an active (powered) subwoofer.

Some receivers come with **5.1 inputs,** six connectors that accept multichannel analog audio signals that another device—such as a DVD player that has a built-in Dolby Digital or DTS decoder, or that plays DVD-Audio or SACD discs—has already decoded through a process that splits a signal into six or more audio channels. The inputs are typically marked Front L and R, Rear (or Surround) L and R, Center, and Subwoofer (which also may be labeled LFE, for low-frequency effects).

User manuals should be able to take you through much of the setup process. Hang on to them. Give yourself easy access to the back of the receiver and other components. You will need good lighting to read the labeling on the back panels, so have a flashlight ready. Connect audio devices first, using the cables that came with each component.

To connect speakers, you typically strip off enough insulation from the ends of the wires to connect them, without shorting, to adjacent wires. Observe proper polarity; a speaker, like a battery, has "+" and "–" terminals. (The insulation of one wire in each pair should have a distinguishing feature, such as color or striping.) Reversing polarity will cause a loss of bass or other frequencies.

You can plug almost all of your components into a two-prong AC power strip—preferably one with surge suppression. The exceptions are the three high-powered devices—the TV, receiver, and powered subwoofer. Plug those into the wall or into a three-prong AC power strip. Or you can plug all of your components into a power control center, which handles the entire system and can include surge suppression.

ARRANGING THE EQUIPMENT

Make sure your room has enough distance between you and the TV for comfortable viewing. The ideal for viewing a conventional, 30- to 40-inch set is 8 to 12 feet, which gives your eyes enough distance to knit the scan lines into a unified picture. But a high-definition TV screen has no visible scan lines, so you can sit closer. For analog sets larger than 40 inches—flat-panel or projection sets—figure on sitting more than 10 feet away. Another way of looking at it: The bigger the room, the bigger the TV can be.

Receivers generate more heat than other audio and video components, so they need to go on the top of the stack or on their own shelf, with at least a couple of inches of head space and a path for the heat to escape. If a receiver's surface becomes hot to the touch, try one of the following: turn down the volume; provide more cooling, perhaps with a small fan; use speakers with a higher impedance; or play only one set of speakers at a time.

MATCHING SPEAKERS & RECEIVER

Speakers and the receiver must match in two ways: power and impedance.

Power. Generally, the more power (measured in watts) that a receiver delivers, the louder you can play music, with less distortion. Each doubling of loudness uses about 10 times as much power. Most models these days provide plenty of power—at least 60 watts per channel.

Here's a quick guide to power requirements for various room sizes: 80 to 100 watts per channel for a large living room (15x25 feet or more with an 8-foot ceiling); 40 to 80 for an average living room (12x20 feet); 20 to 40 for a bedroom (12x14 feet). A "live" (echoey) room will need less power than a "dead" (muffled-sounding) room.

Impedance. Materials that conduct electrical current also resist the current's travel to varying degrees. This resistance, or impedance, is measured in ohms. Standard speaker impedance is 8 ohms, which all receivers can handle. Many speakers have an impedance as low as 4 ohms, according to CONSUMER REPORTS tests. All else being equal, 4-ohm speakers demand more current than 8-ohm speakers. The use of the former generally doesn't pose a problem at normal listening levels but may eventually cause a receiver to overheat or trip its internal overload switch when music is played very loud. Before buying 4-ohm speakers to regularly play loud music, check the manual or back panel of your receiver to confirm that it's compatible.

Some speakers overemphasize various frequencies when placed against the wall or tucked in a bookshelf. Manufacturers' recommendations can help you decide on the optimal placement in your particular room.

The best position for the main front speakers is roughly an equilateral triangle whose points are the left speaker, the right speaker, and you, the listener. Try to place them at about the same height as your ears as you sit. The center speaker should be atop or below the TV and aligned with, or only slightly behind, the main speakers. The left and right surround speakers can be placed alongside the seating, facing each other or the back wall. The subwoofer can go anywhere convenient—under a table, behind the sofa. Watch out for corners, though. They accentuate the bass, often making it unacceptably boomy.

THE FINE-TUNING

You can optimize the system by properly setting audio levels and taking advantage of some of your components' features.

DVD audio settings. A DVD player can output each disc's audio signal in a number of ways. The raw "bitstream" signal is undecoded; use this setting if your receiver decodes Dolby Digital and DTS audio. If you have only a digital-ready (or DVD-ready) receiver and your DVD player has a built-in Dolby Digital or DTS decoder, use the "analog 6-channel output" setting, which outputs decoded audio to the receiver. And if you have only a stereo receiver or TV (or just stereo speakers), set the DVD player for "analog 2-channel;" this downmixes the multiple channels into two.

Subwoofer adjustments. Most powered subwoofers have two controls: cutoff frequency and volume level. The former is the frequency above which the subwoofer won't reproduce sound. If your main speakers are regular, full-range types (not satellites), set the subwoofer to the lowest setting, typically 80 hertz. If they're satellites with no woofers, see the manual regarding of set up the satellite and subwoofer combination. Adjust the subwoofer's volume so its contribution is noticeable but subtle.

Receiver settings. With your receiver's user manual as a guide, adjust the receiver speaker by speaker, according to each speaker's size, distance from the listener, and sound level relative to the other speakers. With most audio systems, you should be able to sit where you will be listening and make the proper adjustments by using the receiver's remote control.

CAMCORDERS

Fine picture quality and easy editing have improved the functionality of these moviemakers. That's especially true for digital models, which are replacing analog.

Those grainy, jumpy home movies of yesteryear are long gone—replaced by home movies shot on digital or analog camcorders. You can edit and embellish the footage with music using your computer, then play it back on your VCR; you can even turn it into video shorts to e-mail.

Digital camcorders generally offer very good to excellent picture quality, along with very good sound capability, compactness, and ease of handling. Making copies of a digital recording won't result in a loss of picture or sound quality.

Analog camcorders generally have good picture and sound quality and are less expensive. Some analog units are about as compact and easy to handle as digital models, while others are a bit bigger and bulkier.

WHAT'S AVAILABLE

Sony dominates the camcorder market, with multiple models in a number of formats. Other top brands include Canon,

JVC, Panasonic, Samsung, and Sharp.

Most digital models come in the MiniDV format. New formats such as the disc-based DVD-RAM and DVD-R and tape-based MicroMV have also appeared. Some digital models weigh as little as one pound.

MiniDV. Don't let their small size deceive you. Although some models can be slipped into a large pocket, MiniDV camcorders can record very high-quality images. They use a unique tape cassette, and the typical recording time is 60 minutes at standard play (SP) speed. Expect to pay $6 for a 60-minute tape. You'll need to use the camcorder for playback—it converts its recording to an analog signal, so it can be played directly into a TV or VCR. If the TV or VCR has an S-video input jack, you can use it to get the best possible picture.

Price range: $400 to more than $2,000.

Digital 8. Also known as D8, this format gives you digital quality on Hi8 or 8mm cassettes, which cost $6.50 and $3.50 respectively. The Digital 8 format records with a faster tape speed, so a "120-minute" cassette lasts only 60 minutes at SP. Most models can also play your old analog Hi8 or 8mm tapes.

Price range: $400 to $800.

Disc-based. Capitalizing on the explosive growth and capabilities of DVD movie discs, these formats offer benefits tape can't provide: long-term durability, a compact medium, and random access to scenes as with a DVD. The 3¼-inch discs record standard MPEG-2 video, the same format used in commercial DVD videos. The amount of recording time varies according to the quality level you select: from 20 minutes per side at the highest-quality setting for DVD-RAM up to about 60 minutes per side at the lowest setting. DVD-RAM discs are not compatible with DVD players, but the discs can be reused. DVD-R is supposed to be compatible with most DVD players and computer DVD drives, but the discs are write-once. We paid about $25 at a local retailer for a blank DVD-RW.

Most analog camcorders come in one of three formats: VHS-C, Super VHS-C, and Hi8. They usually weigh around 2 pounds. Picture quality is generally good, though a notch below that of digital.

VHS-C. This format uses an adapter to play in any VHS VCR. Cassettes most commonly hold 30 minutes on SP and cost $3.50.

Price range: $250 to $500.

Super VHS-C. This high-band variation of VHS-C uses special S-VHS-C tapes. (A slightly different format, S-VHS/ET-C, can use standard VHS-C tapes.) One S-VHS-C tape yields 40 minutes at SP and costs $6.50. JVC is the only brand that offers models in this format.

Price range: $250 to $500.

Hi8. This premium variant of 8mm (an analog format that is virtually extinct) promises a sharper picture. For full benefits, you need to use Hi8 tape and watch on a TV set that has an S-video input. A 120-minute cassette tape costs about $6.50.

Price range: $200 to $400.

SHOP SMART

A camcorder's built-in microphone may pick up mechanical hum from the camcorder itself. An external microphone can deliver better sound quality. However, you probably don't need one unless you're recording music as background.

KEY FEATURES

A flip-out **liquid-crystal-display (LCD) viewer** is becoming commonplace on all but the lowest-priced camcorders. You'll find it useful for reviewing footage you've shot and easier to use than the eyepiece viewfinder for certain shooting poses. Some LCD viewers are hard to use in sunlight, a drawback on models that have only a viewer and no eyepiece.

Screens vary from 2½ to 4 inches measured diagonally, with a larger screen offered as a step-up feature on higher-priced models. Because an LCD viewer uses batteries faster than an eyepiece viewfinder does, you don't have as much recording time with it.

An **image stabilizer** automatically reduces most of the shakes that occur from holding the camcorder as you record a scene. Most stabilizers are electronic; a few are optical. Either type can be effective, though mounting the camcorder on a tripod is the surest way to get steady images. If you're not using a tripod, you can try holding the camcorder with both hands and propping both elbows against your chest.

Full auto switch essentially lets you point and shoot. The camcorder automatically adjusts the color balance, shutter speed, focus, and aperture (also called the "iris" or f-stop with camcorders).

Autofocus adjusts for maximum sharpness; **manual focus override** may be needed for problem situations, such as low light. (With some newer camcorders, you may have to tap buttons repeatedly to get the focus just right.) With many camcorders, you can also control exposure, shutter speed, and white balance.

The **zoom** is typically a finger control—press one way to zoom in, the other way to widen the view. The rate at which the zoom changes will depend on how hard you press the switch. Typical optical zoom ratios range from 10:1 to 26:1. The zoom relies on optical lenses, just like a film camera (hence the term "optical zoom"). Many camcorders offer a digital zoom to extend the range to 400:1 or more, but at a lower picture quality.

Regardless of format, analog or digital, every camcorder displays **tape speeds** the same way a VCR does. Every model, for example, includes an SP (standard play) speed. Digitals have a slower, LP (long play) speed, which adds 50 percent to the recording time. A few 8mm and Hi8 models have an LP speed that doubles the recording time. All VHS-C and S-VHS-C camcorders have an even slower EP (extended play) speed that triples the recording time. With analog camcorders, slower speeds worsen picture quality. Slow speed doesn't reduce picture quality on digital camcorders. Using slow speed, however, means sacrificing some seldom-used editing options and may restrict playback on other camcorders.

Quick review lets you view the last few seconds of a scene without having to press a lot of buttons. For special lighting situations, preset **auto-exposure settings** can be helpful. A "snow & sand" setting, for example, adjusts shutter speed or aperture to accommodate high reflectivity.

A **light** provides some illumination for close shots when the image would otherwise be too dark. **Backlight compensation** increases the exposure slightly when your subject is lit from behind and silhouetted. An **infrared-sensitive recording mode** (also known as night vision, zero lux, or MagicVu) allows shooting in very dim or dark situations, using infrared emitters. You can use it for nighttime shots, although colors won't register accurately in this mode.

Audio/video inputs let you record material from another camcorder or from a VCR, useful for copying part of another video onto your own. (A digital camcorder must have such an input jack if you want to record analog material digitally.) Unlike a built-in microphone, an external microphone that is plugged into a microphone jack won't pick up noises from the camcorder itself, and it typically improves audio performance.

A camcorder with **digital still** capability lets you take snapshots, which can be downloaded to your computer. The photo quality, though, is generally inferior to that of a still camera.

Features that may aid editing include a **built-in title generator,** a **time-and-date stamp,** and a **time code,** which is a frame reference of exactly where you are on a tape—the hour, minute, second, and frame. A **remote control** helps when you're using the camcorder as a playback device or when you're using a tripod. **Programmed recording** (a self-timer) starts the camcorder recording at a preset time.

HOW TO CHOOSE

Performance differences. Digital camcorders got high marks in our picture-quality tests. Top-performing models yielded pictures that were sharp and free of streaks and other visual "noise" and had accurate color. Audio quality wasn't quite as impressive, at least using the built-in microphone. Still, digitals recorded pleasing sound devoid of audio flutter, a wavering in pitch that can make sounds seem thin and watery.

Typically, the best analog models we tested were good—on a par with the lowest-scoring digitals. The lowest-scoring analog models delivered soft images that contained noticeable video noise and jitter, and they reproduced colors less accurately than any digital model. And while sound for 8mm and Hi8 analog camcorders was practically free of audio flutter, all the VHS-C analog camcorders suffered from some degree of that audio-signal problem.

Recommendations. If you don't want to spend a lot, an analog camcorder is a good value—many are now priced at $300 or less. Analog models may also appeal if you have little interest in video editing. If you want to upgrade, however, choose a digital model. Prices are as low as $400 and are continuing to fall.

Try before you buy. Make sure a camcorder fits comfortably in your hand and has controls that are easy to reach.

Related CR Report: November 2003
Ratings: page 241
Reliability: page 26

CAMERAS, DIGITAL

Digital photography lets you be more involved in the creation of the print than film photography. That's a plus or a minus, depending upon your point of view.

Digital cameras, which employ reusable memory cards instead of film, give you far more creative control than film cameras. With a digital, you can transfer shots to your computer, then crop, adjust color and contrast, and add textures and other special effects.

Final results can be made into cards or T-shirts, or sent via e-mail, all using the software that usually comes with the camera. You can make prints on a color inkjet printer, drop off the memory card at one of a growing number of photofinishers, or upload the file to a photo-sharing Web site for storage, viewing, or reprinting.

Digital cameras share many features with digital camcorders, such as an electronic image sensor, LCD viewer, and zoom functions. They also share some features with film cameras, such as focus and flash options. Some camcorders can be used to take still pictures, but a typical camcorder's resolution is no match for a good still camera's.

WHAT'S AVAILABLE

The leading brands are Canon, Kodak, Olympus, and Sony; other brands come from consumer-electronics, computer-imaging, and traditional camera and film companies.

Digital cameras are categorized by how many pixels, or picture elements, the image sensor contains. One megapixel = 1 million picture elements. The more pixels, the more detail the image will contain. More detail gives you more options for producing finished prints. A 1-megapixel model makes sharp 5x7-inch prints and very good 8x10s; 2- and 3-megapixel models can make excellent 8x10s and pleasing 11x14s. There are also 4- to 7-megapixel models for the amateur photo market; these are well suited for making larger prints or for maintaining sharpness if you want to use only a portion of the original image. Professional digital cameras use as many as 11 megapixels.

SHOP SMART
Once you've found the camera you like, go online to check for the best price. Unless you hit a great sale at a brick-and-mortar store, you're likely to find the best camera prices at Internet retailers.

Price range: $50 to $100 for 1-megapixel models (increasingly obsolete); $80 to $300 for 2 megapixels; $200 to $450 for 3 megapixels; $350 to $1,000 or more for 4 megapixels and up.

KEY FEATURES

Most digital cameras are highly automated, with features such as **automatic exposure control** (which manages the shutter speed, aperture, or both, according to available light) and autofocus.

Instead of film, digital cameras typically record their shots onto **flash-memory cards.** CompactFlash and SecureDigital (SD) are the most widely used. Once quite expensive, such cards have tumbled in price—a 128-megabyte card can now cost less than $60. Some cameras store shots on a MemoryStick or on a SmartMedia or xD-picture card. Others use 3¼-inch CD-R or CD-RW discs.

To save images, you transfer them to a computer, typically by connecting the camera to the computer's USB or FireWire port or inserting the memory card into a special reader. Some printers can take memory cards and make prints without putting the images on a computer first. **Image-handling software,** such as Adobe Element, MGI PhotoSuite, Microsoft Picture It, and Ulead PhotoImpact, lets you size, touch up, and crop digital images using your computer. Most digital cameras work with both Windows and Macintosh machines.

The **file format** commonly used for photos is the highly compressed JPEG format. (This is also used for photos on the Internet.) Some cameras can save photos in uncompressed TIFF format, but this setting yields enormous files. Other high-end cameras have a RAW file format, which yields the image data with no processing from the camera.

Digital cameras typically have both an **optical viewfinder** and a small color **LCD (liquid crystal display) viewer.** LCD viewers are very accurate in framing the actual image that you get—better than most of the optical viewfinders. You can also view shots you've already taken on the LCD viewer. But LCD viewers gobble up battery power and can be hard to see in bright sunlight. Many digital cameras provide a **video output,** so you can view your pictures on a TV set.

Certain cameras let you record an **audio clip** with a picture. But these clips devour storage space. Some let you record limited video, but the frame rate is slow and the resolution poor.

A **zoom lens** provides flexibility in framing shots and closes the distance between you and your subject—ideal if you want to quickly switch to a close shot. A 3x zoom is comparable to a 35mm to 105mm lens on a 35mm film camera; a 2x zoom approximates a 35mm to 70mm lens. **Optical zooms** are superior to **digital zooms,** which magnify the center of the frame without actually increasing picture detail, resulting in a somewhat coarser view.

Sensors in digital cameras are typically about as light-sensitive as ISO 100 film, though some let you increase that setting. (At ISO 100, you'll likely need to use a flash indoors and in low outdoor light.)

A camera's **flash range** tells you how far from the camera the flash will provide proper exposure: If the subject is out of range, you'll know to close the distance. But digital cameras can tolerate some underexposure before the image suffers noticeably.

Red-eye reduction shines a light toward your subject just before the main flash. (A camera whose flash unit is farther from the lens reduces the risk of red eye. Computer editing of the image may also correct red eye.) With **automatic flash mode,** the camera fires the flash whenever the light entering the camera registers as insufficient.

HOW TO CHOOSE

Performance differences. In our most recent tests, image colors looked fine. Digital cameras dealt much better with fluorescent lighting than regular film-processing labs have done. (Fluorescent lighting can give film photos a greenish cast.) Tests show that a higher pixel count alone doesn't necessarily produce better picture quality.

The image-handling software provided with a digital camera is generally easy to use. The results are usually pleasing—or readily altered if you're not satisfied. The software does have its limits, though. It can't fix an out-of-focus image, for example.

Recommendations. A 3-megapixel model is likely to offer you the best overall value: good quality at a relatively moderate price. A 3-megapixel camera provides some breathing room—files large enough for enlargements, yet not so gargantuan that you'll have difficulty saving, storing, or e-mailing them. Look for a camera with a 3x optical zoom lens and good image-handling software.

A 1-megapixel camera is fine for small snapshots or photos you e-mail to friends and family, but it's not the best choice if you want to make 8x10 enlargements.

The current high-end consumer cameras—those in the 4- to 6-megapixel range—are for people with a large budget who need a camera verging on professional-grade.

When looking at cameras, be sure you compare the so-called native pixel count. Some cameras employ software that lets them share pixels, which raises the apparent pixel count.

Try before you buy. Quite a few digital cameras offer a shallow grip or no grip at all. Some LCD viewers are awkwardly situated and could easily be soiled with nose or thumbprints. If you wear glasses, you might look for a camera viewfinder with a diopter adjustment, which may let you see the image without your glasses while using the camera.

Related CR Report: November 2003
Ratings: page 246
Reliability: page 27

CAMERAS, FILM

A point-and-shoot camera doesn't require elaborate setup before the shot. Single-lens reflex models offer maximum versatility and also can be easy to use.

A film camera remains a good choice if you want point-and-shoot simplicity and good quality for a relatively low price. The same goes for anyone who wants color prints without a lot of fuss and isn't especially concerned about ordering reprints or editing photos.

If you want more control over your pictures after you've taken them—for instance, you want to edit, publish, or e-mail them—consider a digital camera. Digitals are winning a lot of converts with their increasing capability and ease of use—without an increase in price. (See "Digital cameras" on page 45.) But you needn't go digital to get some of a digital camera's benefits: When you drop off a roll of film for processing, you can order digital storage along with your prints. Other "digitizing" options include scanning negatives or prints using a computer and scanner.

WHAT'S AVAILABLE

Major camera companies include Canon, Fuji, Kodak, Minolta, Nikon, Olympus, and Pentax. Most make point-and-shoot cameras in both 35mm and APS (advanced photo system) formats. Many of those companies also make single-lens reflex (SLR) models.

No matter what the format, cameras these days are highly automated. Practically all point-and-shoot models and some SLR models have built-in flashes. Low-priced film cameras are fixed-focus, like an old-fashioned box camera. Features that raise the price include autofocus, automatic exposure control, automatic film winding, and a zoom lens.

Compact 35mm cameras. Small, light, and inexpensive, these cameras are capable of producing exceptional photos. They're adequate for travel scenes and group shots. More expensive models include a zoom lens and many automated features. Some can shoot in panoramic mode, producing a 3½x10-inch or 4x11½-inch photo. The lens doesn't actually cover a wider angle in this mode. Instead, the panoramic shape is achieved by cropping off the top and bottom of the image.

Price range: $5 to $12 for single-use cameras; $20 and up for fixed-focus models; $50 and up for automatic, nonzoom cameras; and $70 and up for a model with a zoom.

APS cameras. APS (Advanced Photo System) models use a film cartridge that you simply drop into the camera. A magnetic coating on the film can store such information as processing instructions and the date of the snapshot. Since APS film is smaller than 35mm film, these cameras also tend to be smaller and lighter. The format allows great flexibility—you can switch from regular to wide (semi-panoramic) to panoramic in midroll. One-hour processing for this format is less widely available, however, and film and processing generally cost more.

Price range for APS models: same as for compact 35mm cameras.

35mm SLRs. Bulkier than point-and-shoot models, SLR (single lens reflex) cameras with interchangeable lenses let you see what the camera sees. Unlike a point-and-shoot, an SLR lets you compose a shot precisely, without the uncertainty of capturing content not shown in the viewfinder. Such exactitude gives you a great deal of artistic control, and the generally high-quality optics deliver the best image quality. SLRs are typically sold without a lens or are bundled with a zoom lens.

Price range: $150 and up for the camera body, $100 and up for a moderate-range zoom lens.

KEY FEATURES

A **zoom lens,** magnifying your subject two or three times or so, is available on many point-and-shoot models. The 35mm zoom lenses range from about 28 mm (fairly wide angle) to about 160 mm (a moderate telephoto). APS zoom ranges are comparable. Pricing is typically determined by the complexity of the lens design. You'll pay more for a "faster" lens, such as a 100-mm zoom that opens to f/3.5, which lets in more light than does a 100-mm lens with an f/4.5 maximum aperture.

Most cameras automate exposure partially or fully. **Aperture** governs how wide the camera should open the lens when you take a picture. Using identical-speed film and the same shutter speed, the wider the aperture a lens can manage, the better your odds of taking good pictures indoors without a flash (and the more the lens will likely cost). Shutter speed governs how long the aperture stays open during a shot. Fast **shutter speed** (1/1000 to 1/8000 of a second or so) lets you shoot fast-moving subjects.

Auto exposure regulates the shutter speed and aperture to get a properly exposed photo, whether in bright light or low light. An **exposure-compensation** feature prevents underexposure when the background is bright, or overexposure when the background is unusually dark compared with the subject. SLRs can often set the speed or aperture automatically, after you have manually set the corresponding setting as needed for a particular shot. For example, if you set the aperture, it sets the shutter speed; if you set the speed, it sets the aperture. These and more advanced compact models may offer several preset exposure modes that suit various situations.

Autofocus frees you from having to focus the camera to ensure crisp pictures; low-end cameras typically cover preset ranges, permitting quick shots but dispensing with the more precise focusing of higher-priced models. **Multi-area auto focus** reduces the risk of unintentionally focusing on the background in a scene. **Focus lock** lets you freeze the focus onto who or what appears in the center of the viewfinder, helpful for when you'd like to focus on a subject and then shift the camera's aim. Compact film cameras typically use an infrared beam to focus. **In-the-viewfinder signals** in many models let you know when the subject is too close to be in focus or when it's out of flash range.

Motorized film handling automatically advances the film and rewinds it at the end of the roll. With a 35mm camera, you drop the film in, pull out the leader, and close the camera; with APS, you merely drop the film in. **Mid-roll change,** a feature found in some APS cameras, lets you reload partially exposed rolls of film—useful if you often switch between high- and low-speed film.

Flashes cover various distances, from 4 or 5 feet to 10 feet or more. The smartest ones work with the zoom lens to broaden or narrow the beam. **Flash on demand** lets you fill in harsh shadows in bright, sunlit portraits. "Red eye" occurs when a flash reflects off a subject's retinas; **red-eye reduction** typically uses a light before the main flash to constrict the subject's pupils. (Flashes that are farther from the lens reduce red eye to begin with.)

Some cameras are **weatherproof,** handy for the beach or boating. Certain models also offer options such as a **wireless remote shutter release** or the ability to imprint photos with the date.

HOW TO CHOOSE

Performance differences. Whether they use 35mm or the newer APS film, conventional film cameras have attained a fairly high level of quality. Our tests of autofocus zoom-lens cameras have shown that the lens quality on these models is high. As a result, nearly all can produce very pleasing snapshots—sharp, properly focused, with little distortion or other drawbacks.

But, of course, the cameras don't perform identically. While SLR cameras show you exactly what will appear on film, viewfinders of even the best point-and-shoot cameras show only about 90 percent of the area that actually appears on film. With some, you see only about two-thirds of what's on film, so the prints may contain unwanted, distracting detail around the edges.

Also, don't expect too much from the built-in flash that's standard on point-and-shoot cameras. External-flash units, such as the detachable ones available for some compacts and most SLRs, provide more light for your subject than the built-in flashes.

Recommendations. Spending more gets you more features and often better optics. Nevertheless, you can expect a fairly high level of quality from 35mm point-and-shoot models, even from a very low-priced camera. Our tests over the years have shown that nearly all cameras in this class can produce very good, sometimes excellent snapshots.

Despite their smaller negative size, APS cameras often produce prints as clear as those of 35mm cameras, particularly if they aren't enlarged too much. These models also offer the versatility of switching from normal to wide-angle to panoramic shots from one frame to the next within a roll. For the very best in versatility and image quality, however, 35mm SLR models remain the best, if bulkier, choice.

Try before you buy. Be sure that you can see the viewfinder's image clearly—some cameras have a diopter adjustment to help. And make sure that the camera is easy to grip.

Related CR Report: November 2001

CD PLAYERS

The familiar console compact disc player is rapidly being replaced by more capable devices.

Delivering superb performance at an affordable price, the CD is the music medium of the moment. But regular console CD players are losing ground to digital video disk players, which can play both CDs and DVDs, and to dual-function devices that can both record and play CDs.

Niche CD players are thriving. Jukebox models can hold hundreds of discs. Portable players are now incorporating MP3 capabilities.

WHAT'S AVAILABLE

Sony dominates the CD-player category, making nearly one out of three CD players sold. Other big sellers are RCA and Technics.

Console models. Single-disc models have virtually disappeared. Multiple-disc changers, typically holding five or six discs, can play hours of music nonstop. A magazine changer holds discs in a slide-in cartridge the size of a small, thick book; cartridges double as disc storage boxes. Magazine changers aren't as easy to load and unload as carousel-type changers, which have taken over the market. Carousel changers usually let you change discs not currently in use without interrupting the music.

Price range: $100 to $250.

Megachangers. Also known as CD jukeboxes, these typically store 100 to 400 discs. Marketed as a way to manage and store an entire music collection, most let you segment a collection by music genre, composer, artist, and so forth. They flash album titles as you hunt through the discs. Inputting all the necessary data can be a tedious task (made easier on models that connect to a computer keyboard), but it's worth the effort because you can then set a jukebox to shuffle and play random selections all night or play discs only from a chosen genre. To fit all those CDs, megachangers can be quite large. In fact, some may not fit the typical stereo rack. And some are inconvenient to load, or noisy and slow in selecting CDs.

Price range: $200 to $450.

Portable players. Small, sporty, and designed for a single disc, these have simple controls. A growing number of models also play CDs you record yourself, using both the CD-R and CD-RW formats (see CD player/recorders for more on these formats) and digital file formats such as MP3 and WMA. Early portables often skipped or had poor-quality headphones. Today's players skip less, and many have good headphones that will convey decent sound. Some still have mediocre headphones, however, and you'll enjoy better listening if you replace them.

Battery life is improving, but it varies considerably from model to model. In our latest tests, battery life was typically 16 to 30 hours, but went as long as 40 hours. Some have an AC adapter, and some have a built-in battery charger. Most portables can connect to other audio gear and in that case can often play music as well as any console unit. Using a car kit, you can attach a portable player to your car's speakers.

Price range: $30 to $160.

KEY FEATURES

Console models come with more features than portables. Their **controls** should be easy to see in dim light. A **calendar display** shows a block of numbers indicating the tracks on the active disc and highlights the current track. As play continues, previous track numbers disappear, so you can quickly see how many selections are left. A **numeric keypad** on the remote takes you to a particular track more quickly than pressing Up or Down buttons.

A **remote control** is convenient and now nearly standard. The best have buttons that are grouped by function or are color-coded; they should be visible in dim light. Most CD remotes operate the player only.

Some changers and jukeboxes have a handy **single-play drawer** or slot so you can play a single disc without disturbing any already loaded. **Cataloging** capability offers various ways to keep track of the many CDs stored inside a jukebox, such as categorizing by genre.

Memory features that make track selection easy include **delete track,** which lets you skip specified tracks but otherwise play a disc from start to finish, and **favorite track** program memory, which lets you mark your preferences. **Music sampling** (or track scan) plays a few seconds of each selection. Most models can be programmed to play tracks in sequence, to shuffle play (look for "nonrepeat shuffle"), or to repeat a track. A **volume-limiter**

switch on portable players lets you hear softer passages without having other sounds at ear-splitting levels.

People who do a lot of taping will appreciate **auto edit** (also called "time fit for recording"). You enter the cassette's recording time, and the player lays out the disc's tracks, usually in sequence, to fill both sides of your tape. With **comprehensive time display,** you check time elapsed and time remaining for the current track and for the entire disc. **Running-time total** lets you total the time of tracks to be recorded to fit the maximum on a tape. **Music-peak finder** scans for the loudest passage in a track you're going to record, allowing you to adjust the tape deck's recording level correctly and quickly. **Fade out/fade in** performs the audio equivalent of a movie fade for less abrupt starts and endings. **Auto spacing** inserts a few seconds of silence between tracks.

With a **synchronizing jack,** you can connect a cable to a tape deck of the same brand so you can run both machines simultaneously. Those recording digitally to a MiniDisc recorder or a digital tape deck need a **digital output jack** in order to attach a fiber-optic or coaxial cable.

Portable CD player features focus on sound-quality enhancement and power management. Most portables have a **bass-boost control** to compensate for the thin bass of poorer headphones. Some have a **digital signal processor** (DSP), which electronically simulates the ambience of a concert hall or other venue. Skip-free performance depends on a good **buffer**—a memory feature that scans the disc, continuously storing upcoming music (typically from 10 to 45 seconds, sometimes more) so the player won't cause audio dropouts.

Most portables have a **liquid crystal display** (LCD) that shows which track is playing, and a **battery-level indicator** that warns of low batteries. (The best indicators show a shrinking scale to reflect power remaining.) An **AC adapter** runs the player on house current and enables some models to charge rechargeable cells. Rechargeable batteries may cost extra.

Colorful "sports" models tend to be pricier than the rest of the portable pack and differ in a few other respects. Their lid is secured with a **latch** and sealed with a **rubber gasket,** and they have **rubberized plugs** covering jacks for an AC adapter and headphones. The latch keeps the lid closed so successfully that some sports models are a bit hard to open. The gasket and plugs help resist sand, dirt, and moisture, though you'll need to wipe off a dusty or wet player before you open it. Keep in mind that these players are **water-resistant,** not waterproof—the difference between a splash and total immersion.

A **car kit,** standard with some portables, consists of an adapter that powers the unit through a car's cigarette lighter and a cassette adapter that pipes the player's sound through the car's tape player and speakers. (You can buy aftermarket kits at electronics or auto-supply stores.) Some adapters added noise to the sound or otherwise compromised performance in our tests. A line-out jack is a better choice than the headphone jack for connecting a portable to a component receiver or other gear.

HOW TO CHOOSE

Performance differences. Many CD players can produce excellent sound, with accurate tonal balance and no coloration or distortion. However, not all CD players are equally convenient to use. Better console models have an uncluttered front-panel display with clearly labeled main buttons grouped together by function. They also include features that make it easy to produce tapes from CDs.

For portable players, a good buffer is key for smooth, skip-free performance. Some models skipped with just a mild jouncing, others only when jolted hard. Battery life in recent tests varied from 5 to 40 hours of continuous play.

Headphones that come with portable players differ in comfort and performance. In our tests, they ranged from decent to mediocre. Comfort is very subjective, of course. Sometimes you can improve sound by buying replacement headphones. A decent set costs about $10 to $30.

Recommendations. If you're looking to play CDs in a home-theater setup, consider getting a DVD player instead of a CD player. Some are nearly as cheap as CD players these days. The price of CD player/recorders has also dropped enough to make them a reasonable alternative, with the premium for the recording functionality perhaps $100.

If you want to play only CDs, a multidisc changer will save you from having to swap discs in and out. Shoppers for portable players should weigh battery life heavily if they're frequent listeners. They should also pay particular attention to antiskip performance if they listen on the go.

Related CR Report: September 2002

CD PLAYER/ RECORDERS

They make it easy to copy the music you want onto compact discs, with no loss of quality.

Audio CD player/recorders let you make your own recordings and play back prerecorded material. They cost more than CD players without recording capability, but prices are dropping. They sell as standalone units and as components of some minisystems.

There's another way to make your own music CDs: Record them using a computer. CD drives that "burn" CDs are now standard on many computers and can be as adept as component CD player/recorders, often performing the task faster.

Both CD player/recorders and computer CD burners let you copy entire discs or dub selected tracks to create your own CD compilations. There's no quality lost in high-speed CD-to-CD dubbing. Recording speeds usually are real-time or 4x, which records four times faster. (Computer CD burners can be as fast as 16x.)

With either approach, you can record to CD-Rs (discs that can be recorded on only once) or to CD-RWs (rewritable discs that can be erased and rerecorded). The CD-R format plays on almost any CD player, whereas CD-RWs generally play only on newer disc players that are configured to accept them. Be aware that some older DVD players will have problems reading CD-R and CD-RW discs.

WHAT'S AVAILABLE

Audio CD player/recorders are sold by audio-component companies such as Denon, Harman-Kardon, JVC, Philips, Pioneer, and Sony.

Dual-tray models. One tray is for play/record, another for play.

Price range: $250 to $600.

Changer models. These hold four or five discs and let you change a disc while another is playing.

Price range: $350 to $600.

KEY FEATURES

With CD recorders, you program your

selections from up to three discs installed in the changer; the steps will be familiar to anyone who has programmed a CD changer. Most recorders give you a running total of the accumulated time of the tracks as you are programming them. The computer approach to burning CDs makes compiling "mix" discs easier than it used to be. Once a blank CD is inserted into a computer CD drive, the accompanying software displays a track list from the source disc and lets you "drag" the desired tracks into the lower panel. As you insert successive CDs, you can see the **playlist** for your CD-to-be and even change the order of the tracks, combine two or more tracks or files into one, or split a track or file into two or more.

TECH TIP
Blank discs for use in computers can't be used in CD players/recorders. Look for the words "for digital audio recorders" on the package. Discs for music cost more than ones for computers.

With both the CD player/recorder and the computer option, you must program selections from each disc in succession. **Defining tracks** on the CD onto which you're recording is accomplished with varying degrees of flexibility. How many track numbers a given player/recorder can add per disc, for example, differs from one model to another. Additionally, assigning track numbers when you're recording from cassettes may be automatic or manual. (Such track numbers are inserted automatically when recording from CDs.)

Text labeling, available on some models, lets you type in short text passages, such as artist and song names. This is a much easier procedure with a computer keyboard than with a console's remote control.

The number of **delete-track modes** grants you flexibility, whether you need to delete one track or the entire disc. One-track, Multitrack, and All-disc are three common modes. An audio CD player/recorder typically has three playback modes: **Program,** which plays tracks in a specific order; **Repeat;** and **Random Play** (or Shuffle), which plays tracks randomly.

Connection types can affect which external sources you're able to use to make a CD. A **digital input jack** may be optical or coaxial. An **analog input jack** lets you record your tapes and LPs. A **microphone input** offers a low-cost way for home musicians to make digital recordings of their performances. A **record-level control** helps you control loudness while recording digitally from analog sources—a problem you don't face when recording from digital sources.

HOW TO CHOOSE

Performance differences. Either method of burning a CD—using an audio CD player/recorder or a computer—makes a recording that's audibly (even electronically) indistinguishable from the original CD.

Audio CD player/recorders excel in versatility; you can record from CDs, LPs, cassettes, radio, and even TV (anything, in fact, that you can connect to a sound system's receiver). This method is the clear standout for recording LPs, since connecting a turntable to a computer requires additional equipment.

The computer method has advantages. Because it affords a connection to the Internet, the computer option lets you burn downloaded MP3-encoded files onto CDs. A computer offers more set-up choices when you're assembling a CD from several prerecorded discs. And, when you're recording from analog sources, the computer's CD-burning software often includes sound processing that will reduce the snap and crackle of a vinyl LP or the hiss of a cassette tape.

Recommendations. The relatively low cost of burning high-quality CDs makes CD recording a good alternative to making cassette tapes. If you're buying a CD player/recorder, first consider a changer model; its multidisc magazine or carousel will make it easy to record compilation CDs or to play uninterrupted music.

The computer-based CD-recording option allows you to record music from both CDs and the Internet. If you don't already have a CD-burning drive in your computer, you can buy one and the necessary software for about $100 to $150. If you're buying a new computer, you'll find that a CD-RW drive is standard equipment on many models. Based on our test experience, we would expect any CD-burner drive to perform competently.

DIGITAL VIDEO RECORDERS

DVRs outperform VCRs in many ways, but you'll still need a VCR to archive recordings.

Digital video recorders combine the easy navigation of a digital video disc (DVD) player with the recording capability of a video cassette recorder and the convenience of a program guide. These set-top receivers have a hard drive much like the one in a computer, generally with space for 20 to 60 hours of programming, although some can hold up to 320 hours. You can get a stand-alone DVR or one that's integrated into a satellite-TV receiver, digital TV decoder, or DVD player/recorder.

Depending on which provider and plan you choose, you may pay for the service as well as the equipment—either a one-time activation charge or a monthly fee on top of your current cable or satellite-TV bill. Newer devices with built-in DVRs offer basic functions for no fee.

Because they can record and play at the same time, DVRs allow you to pause (and rewind or fast-forward) the current show you're watching, picking up where you left off. Should you pause a one-hour show for 10 or 15 minutes at the beginning, you can resume watching it, skip past all the commercials, and catch up to the actual "live" broadcast by the end of the show. Dual-tuner models can record two programs at once, even as you're watching a third recorded program.

A DVR does not replace your usual programming source. You must still get broadcasts via cable, satellite service, or antenna. Program guides are downloaded via your phone line, generally late at night to avoid tying up the line. These guides are customized according to which broadcast channels are available in your area and to which cable or satellite service you subscribe.

WHAT'S AVAILABLE

There are only two service providers for stand-alone DVRs: TiVo and ReplayTV. Hardware prices depend mostly on how many hours of programming you can store; service charges vary. The DVRs intended for use with one provider will not work with the other. You can buy TiVo equipment directly from TiVo or AT&T Broadband, or from Hughes or Sony under their brand names.

Price range: $250 to $500.

TiVo service requires a paid subscription of $13 per month or $299 for the life of the DVR (transferable if you sell it). You can also get a DirecTV satellite receiver that incorporates TiVo capability (TiVo service charges still apply).

ReplayTV offers some models bundled with lifetime service included in the equipment price. With other models, service is separate; you can pay a one-time activation fee of $299 or a monthly charge of $13. In either case, you must buy equipment directly from the company.

Price range: $300 to $1,400.

KEY FEATURES

Most DVRs resemble VCRs in size and shape but don't have a slot for a tape or disc. (The internal hard drive is not removable.) They connect to your television like a cable or satellite receiver, using composite, S-video, or RF antenna outputs to match the input of your set.

A recorder's **hard-drive capacity** varies in actual usage. Like digital cameras, DVRs record at different **compression settings** and thus at different quality levels. For the best image quality, you have to record programming at the DVR's lowest level of compression. To get the maximum capacity advertised, you have to use the highest level of compression, which gives the lowest quality. For example, a model that advertises a 30-hour maximum capacity will fit only about 9 hours at its best-quality setting.

The **program guide** is an interactive list of the programs that can be recorded by the DVR for the next 7 to 10 days. You can use it to select the show currently being broadcast to watch or record—or you can search it by title, artist, or show type for programs you want to record automatically in the future.

Custom channels, available with some models, are individualized groupings of programs that interest you. The feature allows you to set up your own "channel" of your favorites, such as crime dramas or appearances by William Shatner, whether on "Star Trek," a talk show, or any other programming. A DVR can also record a specified show every time it runs.

A **remote control** is standard. Common features include instant replay, fast-forward, rewind, and **pause** of either recorded or live programs.

HOW TO CHOOSE

Performance differences. At the highest-quality settings, the picture quality of DVRs in recent Consumer Reports tests fell below that of most DVD players and was on a par with that of high-quality S-VHS VCRs. At the lowest-quality setting, picture quality matched run-of-the-mill VHS VCRs standard play (SP) at the best recording speed. Audio quality is a notch below CD quality.

Ultimately, the DVR's picture quality, like the VCR's, depends on the quality of the signal coming in via your cable or satellite provider. A noisy or mediocre signal will produce mediocre digital recordings.

Recommendations. TiVo and ReplayTV represent an intriguing interactive technology, but the market is still developing. Avid TV watchers are prime candidates for these devices, as are those who'd like to sort programming according to their individual viewing preferences. DVRs are also a good bet for those people who hate sitting through commercials.

If satellite dishes are an option, consider a dish receiver that includes a DVR. Keep in mind that you may have to pay a separate fee for the DVR service. Satellite DVRs work only with satellite programming and won't record from cable or an antenna.

Today's DVR can't replace a VCR, which you'll need if you want to make a permanent copy of what you record. Consider a DVR as a companion product, not a replacement, for your VCR.

Related CR Report: December 2003

DVD PLAYERS

These devices play high-quality videos as well as CDs. You can get a basic model for less than $100.

As the fastest-growing consumer-electronics product in history—more than 17 million units were sold in 2002 alone—digital video disc players offer picture and sound quality that clearly surpasses what you get with a VCR. DVDs are CD-sized discs that can contain a complete two-hour-plus movie with a six-channel (5.1) Dolby Digital or DTS soundtrack, plus extra material such as multiple languages, interviews, additional camera angles for chosen scenes, behind-the-scenes documentaries, and even entire replays of the movie with commentary by the director or some of the actors.

DVD players also play standard audio CDs. Prices on multidisc models are low enough for a DVD player to serve as a practical stand-in for a CD player. There is a catch if you record your own CDs: Some models may still have problems reading the CD-R and CD-RW discs that you record yourself.

The DVD player is still a product in transition. New capabilities include being able to play DVD-Audio or SACD, two competing high-resolution audio formats designed to offer two- to six-channel sound. Meanwhile, DVD recorder prices are soon expected to drop, to a starting point of about $500. And, despite a DVD's superior sound and picture quality, VCRs remain the least expensive alternative for recording your favorite TV programs.

WHAT'S AVAILABLE

Apex, Panasonic, Sony, and Toshiba are among the biggest-selling brands. DVD players are evolving as manufacturers seek to differentiate their products and come up with a winning combination of features. You can choose from a console or portable model. Many consoles offer built-in karaoke features and MP3 and Windows Media playback.

Standard single-disc consoles. Console models can be connected directly to your TV for viewing movies or routed through your receiver to play movies and audio CDs on your home-entertainment system. Even low-end models usually include all the video-output jacks you might want.

Price range: less than $100 to more than $800.

Standard multidisc consoles. Like CD changers, these players accommodate two or more discs, often five or seven. DVD jukeboxes that hold 400 or so discs are also available.

Price range: $150 to $1,000.

Progressive-scan single and multidisc players. These provide HD-ready TVs with a slightly sharper image by letting the set redraw 480 consecutive lines of the image 60 times per second. (By comparison, a conventional TV typically redraws every other line at that rate.) You can use a progressive-scan DVD player with a conventional TV, but you'll see the added benefit only with a set that supports the player's progressive-scan mode (480p), such as a high-definition or HD-ready set.

TECH TIP

Built-in DVD players for your car , which let kids (or anybody) watch movies from the backseat, are being offered as $1,200-plus options with new minivans, SUVs, and some cars. Similar fold-down roof players can be installed by an electronics dealer, but usually for $1,500 and up. Both offer an OK picture and very good sound.

Price range: $150 to $1,000.

Portable players. These generally come with a small wide-screen-format LCD screen and batteries that claim to provide three hours or more of playback. Some low-priced models don't come with a screen; they're intended for users who plan to connect the device to a TV. You pay extra for the portability either way.

Price range: $200 to $1,000.

KEY FEATURES

DVD-based movies often come in various formats. **Aspect-ratio control** lets you choose between the 4:3 viewing format of conventional TVs (4 inches wide for every 3 inches high) and the 16:9 ratio of newer, wide-screen sets.

A DVD player gives you all sorts of control over the picture—control you may never have known you needed. **Picture zoom** lets you zoom in on a specific frame. **Reverse frame-by-frame** gives you backward incremental movement in addition to the **forward frame-by-frame** and **slow motion** that most players provide.

Black-level adjustment brings out the detail in dark parts of the screen image. If you've ever wanted to see certain action scenes from different angles, **multi-angle capability** gives you that opportunity. Note that this feature and some others work only with certain discs. Digital video discs, unlike VHS tapes, are sectioned for easy navigation. **Chapter preview** lets you scan the opening seconds of each section or chapter until you find what you want. **Go-to by time** lets you enter how many hours and minutes into the disc you'd like to skip to. Marker functions allow easy indexing of specific sections.

TECH TIP
If you're connecting a DVD player to an older TV with only an antenna input, you'll need a radio frequency (RF) modulator ($20 to $30).

A **composite-video connection** to the TV can produce a very good picture, but with some loss of detail, and some color artifacts such as adjacent colors bleeding into each other. Using the **S-video output** can improve picture quality. It keeps the black-and-white and the color portions of the signal separated, producing more picture detail and fewer color defects than standard composite video.

Component video, the best connection you can currently get on a DVD player (but possibly lacking on the lowest-end models), improves on S-video by splitting the color signal, resulting in a wider range of color. If you use a DVD player attached with an S-video or component connection, don't be surprised if you have to adjust the TV-picture setup when you switch to a picture coming from a VCR or a cable box that uses a radio-frequency (RF, also called antenna/cable) connection or a composite connection.

One selling point of DVDs is the ability to enjoy movies with **multichannel surround sound.** To reap the full benefits of the audio encoded into DVD titles, you'll need a Dolby Digital receiver and six speakers, including a subwoofer. **Dolby Digital decoding built-in** refers to circuitry that lets a DVD player decode the six-channel audio encoded into DVD discs; without the built-in circuitry, you'd need to have the decoder built into the receiver or use a separate decoder box to take advantage of six-channel audio. (A Dolby Digital receiver will decode an older format, Dolby Pro Logic, as well.) Some players also may support **Digital Theater System (DTS) decoding** for titles using the six-channel encoding format. When you're watching DVD-based movies, **dynamic audio-range control** helps keep explosions and other noisy sound effects from seeming too loud.

DVD players also provide features such as **multilingual support,** which lets you choose dialog or subtitles in different languages for a given movie. Parental control lets parents "lock out" films by their rating code.

HOW TO CHOOSE

Performance differences. In CONSUMER REPORTS tests, most DVD players delivered excellent picture quality, all but eliminating the noise, jitters, and other aberrations typical of pictures from a VCR. They also offered CD-quality sound and, depending on the program material, multichannel capability. Some models may be more convenient to use than others. Remote controls vary considerably, so it's worth checking them out before making a purchase.

Recommendations. A DVD player offers better picture quality for movies than a VCR. Provided you have the receiver and speakers to back it up, the sound is also superior to that of a VCR. You'll need a VCR, DVD recorder, or digital video recorder (DVR) to record, however.

Even a low-end DVD player will provide excellent video and audio. A single-disc model is the least expensive option, and should do the job if you mostly watch movies. A multidisc console makes more sense if you also plan to play music CDs.

If your audio/video setup includes a receiver with built-in Dolby Digital and DTS decoding, you don't need to pay a premium to get these decoders on your DVD player. Even a low-end player will let you enjoy six-channel surround sound, assuming you have the required audio system.

If you plan to buy an HD-ready TV, it may be worthwhile getting a progressive-scan DVD player. It will work with your conventional TV now and let take advantage of the superior video quality when you get the HD-ready set.

Related CR Report: December 2003

HOME THEATER IN A BOX

No time to mix and match speakers and receiver? All-in-one systems that you hook up to your TV and VCR or DVD can minimize the hassle.

Good speakers and the other components of a home theater cost less than ever. But selecting all those components can be time consuming, and connecting them is a challenge even for audiophiles. You can save some hassle by buying an all-in-one product that combines a receiver with a six-speaker set; unless your needs are very demanding, you'll compromise little on quality.

A "home theater in a box" combines all you need for the guts of a home theater: a receiver that can decode digital-audio soundtracks and a set of six compact, matched speakers—two front, one center, two surround, and a subwoofer. You also get all the cables and wiring you need, usually labeled and color-coded for easy setup. Generally the presumption is that you already own a TV and a VCR or DVD player, although some systems come with a separate DVD player or have one built into the receiver.

WHAT'S AVAILABLE

Kenwood, Pioneer, Sony, and Yamaha account for more than half of sales, with Sony on its own commanding almost a third of the market. The cheapest models usually don't include a DVD player.

Price range: Expect to pay about $300 for a basic system and $500 to $750 for one that's capable of decoding digital signals and has a powered subwoofer. Systems aimed at audiophiles can cost $2,000 or more.

KEY FEATURES

The receivers in home-theater-in-a-box systems tend to be on the simple side. They usually include both Dolby Digital and DTS decoders. Controls should be easy to use. Look for a front panel with displays and controls grouped by function and labeled clearly. **Onscreen display** lets you control the receiver via a TV screen.

Switched AC outlets let you plug in other components and turn on the whole system with one button. The receivers offer about 20 or more presets you can use for AM and FM stations. Some receivers also offer a **sleep timer,** which turns them on or off at a preset time. **Remote controls** are most useful when they have clear labels and different-shaped and color-coded buttons grouped by function. A universal remote can control a number of devices.

SHOP SMART
If you're on a tight budget, here's a shoestring approach to home theater: Buy basic components, such as a low-priced receiver, an inexpensive DVD player, and the best speakers you can afford.

A **component-video output** on the receiver that can connect to a relatively high-end TV allows for the best picture quality; however, not many receivers have such an output. Instead, most have the next-best output, **S-video,** which is better than a composite-video or RF (antenna) connection.

Look also for an **S-video input,** which lets you connect an external DVD player, digital camcorder, or certain cable or satellite boxes. Any player you might want to connect will need the same digital-audio connections, either optical or coaxial, as those of the included receiver. And if you want to make occasional connections at the front—perhaps for a camcorder or an MP3 player—you'll need **front-panel inputs.**

Home-theater-in-a-box receivers that do not decode digital audio may have 5.1 inputs; these accept input from the decoder in a DVD player or other components with multichannel audio signals.

DSP (for digital signal processor) modes use digital circuitry to duplicate the sound measurements of, say, a concert hall. Each mode represents a different listening environment. A **bass-boost** switch amplifies the deepest sounds. You are less likely to find stand-alone receiver controls such as a graphic equalizer.

A **subwoofer** may be powered or unpowered. Either type will do the job, but a powered subwoofer requires fewer wires, provides more control over bass, and lets a powered receiver drive the other speakers.

An integrated DVD player, available with some models, typically has fewer features than does a stand-alone DVD player. Features to expect are **track programmability** (more useful for playing CDs than DVDs), **track repeat,** and **disc repeat.** If you want more features, a stand-alone DVD player may be the wiser choice.

HOW TO CHOOSE

Performance differences. Performance doesn't always depend on price, we found in recent tests of these boxed sets. The receivers generally have a very good FM tuner and adequate power, and do a fine job switching signals. Overall, however, the boxed systems don't perform as well as component systems, and their features are a notch below those of component receivers, particularly in how easy their remote controls and onscreen menus are to use.

Recommendations. Home theaters in a box offer convenience and decent sound, better than you'd get from a typical minisystem with home-theater capability. The trade-off for that convenience is that you'll generally have to settle for less than the best in receiver and speaker technology.

Related CR Report: November 2003
Ratings: page 275

MP3 PLAYERS

These devices let you play music you've either downloaded from the Web or "ripped" from your own CD collection.

Portable MP3 players store digital music in their internal memories, on removable storage media, or a combination of both. You don't buy prerecorded discs or tapes, but instead create your own digital files using software often supplied with a player. You can convert music from your favorite audio CDs to digital files on your computer—a process known as ripping—or download music from the Internet. In either case, you can listen to the files on your computer or transfer them to a portable MP3 player so you have music to go.

The term MP3 has become shorthand for digital audio of every stripe, but it's actually just one of the formats used to encode music. The abbreviation stands for Moving Pictures Expert Group 1 Audio Layer 3, a file format that compresses music to one-tenth to one-twelfth the space it would take in uncompressed form. Other encoding schemes include Windows Media Audio (WMA), Advanced Audio Codec (AAC), and Adaptive Transform Acoustic Coding (ATRAC), a proprietary format used by Sony products. Most MP3 players can handle formats in addition to MP3; the software that comes with them can convert noncompatible files into formats they can handle.

Despite copyright-infringement lawsuits by the music and movie industries, free music-sharing Web sites carry on. These sites let users download music files for transfer to MP3 players or for burning onto CDs. The music industry has responded with subscription-based services that let you stream or download music and play it on your computer. In the spring of 2003, Apple launched a service called iTunes with a per-song charge rather than a monthly subscription fee. Mac users can buy and download music that can be burned onto a CD or transferred to an iPod.

WHAT'S AVAILABLE

Major brands include Apple, Archos, Creative Labs, Panasonic, RCA, Samsung, and Sony. Other, smaller brands are on the market as well. MP3 playback has been incorporated into other handheld portable products, including CD players, MiniDisc players, cell phones, and personal digital assistants (PDAs).

Standard-capacity players. These are solid-state devices with no moving parts, which eliminates skipping, even on a bumpy road. Sizes vary, ranging from as small as a thick matchbook to the size of a deck of cards. Weight usually ranges from about 1.5 to 4 ounces. Most of the players have 64 or 128 megabytes (MB) of internal memory, which can hold an hour or two, respectively, of music ripped at a CD-quality setting. You can fit more music into memory if you compress it into smaller files, but that may result in lower audio quality.

Most standard-capacity players also have expansion slots to add more memory via card slots or "backpack" modules on the player. Common expansion memory formats include Compact Flash, MultiMediaCard, Secure Digital, and SmartMedia. Sony players may use a MagicGate MemoryStick, a copyright-protected version of Sony's existing MemoryStick media. The capacity of various types of cards ranges from about 8 MB to 512 MB and continues to increase. Memory costs have gradually dropped.

Price range: about $100 to $300 for the player; $25 to $45 for a 64-MB memory card.

High-capacity players. Also called jukeboxes, these devices have a hard drive that can hold hundreds of hours of music. The smallest are about the size of a deck of cards; others are comparable in size to a portable CD player. Weight ranges from about half a pound to 1 pound. Capacity runs from 5 gigabytes (GB) to as much as 60 GB. A 60-GB version can store more than 900 hours of music. Some 80 GB models are starting to appear as well.

TECH TIP
Figure on roughly one minute of music per megabyte to save MP3 files at the CD-quality level.

Price range: $250 and up.

KEY FEATURES

MP3 players usually come with **software** to interface with a computer. Most use a Universal Serial Bus (USB); some use the faster FireWire connection. Most support Windows, and many also support Mac platforms. The computer-to-player interface consists of a software driver that lets the computer and player communicate, along with a software application for transferring files to the player's memory. Many players are bundled with a more fully featured music-management software application, such as MusicMatch or RealOne, that helps you keep track of your MP3 files, manage playlists, and record songs from audio CDs. **Volume, track play-pause,** and **forward/reverse controls** are standard.

Audio playback formats refer to the file formats that a player is compatible with; in many cases, the music-management software bundled with a player can convert additional formats. On most models, the firmware—the built-in operating instructions—can be upgraded so the player does not become obsolete. Upgrades can add or enhance features, fix bugs, and add support for other audio formats and operating systems.

A **liquid crystal display (LCD)** screen lets you view the song title, track number, amount of memory remaining, battery life indicator, and other functions. Some new players have a color LCD screen.

Most players have some type of **equalizer,** which lets you adjust the sound in various ways. A **custom setting** via separate bass and treble controls or **adjustable equalizers** gives you the most control over the sound. Most players let you set a play mode so you can repeat one or all music tracks, or play in a random order, also referred to as "shuffle" mode. An **A-B repeat feature** allows you to set bookmarks and repeat a section of the music track.

Some players display a **list of tracks** from which you can easily make a selection. Others show only one track at a time, requiring you to advance through individual tracks to find the desired one. You can access the player's function controls via a wired or infrared **remote control** on some models.

Some players can store files other than digital-audio files, including text, image, or video files. An FM radio tuner and a built-in microphone for voice recording can be useful extras.

HOW TO CHOOSE

Performance differences. In recent Consumer Reports tests, the processing necessary to turn music into an MP3 file led to very slight degradation of the audio signal on most models, evidenced by noise or a muffling in some frequency ranges. However, if you're experiencing poor sound quality, it's more likely to be caused by mediocre or poor headphones bundled with the player. Because these can be replaced, you can easily and cheaply remedy the problem.

If you don't like the music-management software application bundled with the player, you can go online to download applications such as MusicMatch or RealOne, among others. (Check to see if there are software plug-ins designed to make such programs work most effectively with your player.)

With any portable device, batteries are a consideration. Our tests found that the players will run continuously from 5 to 35 hours before their batteries give out—a wide range. Many players use AA or AAA batteries and can accept either standard alkaline or rechargeable batteries. A rechargeable could save you money in the long run, so consider buying one (and a charger) if the player doesn't come so equipped.

Other players use a rechargeable nonstandard "block-" or "gumstick-" shaped nickel metal-hydride (NiMH) or lithium-ion (Li-ion) removable battery, which is both more expensive and harder to find. Beware of players that use a nonremovable rechargeable battery: When the battery can no longer hold a charge, the player has to be sent back to the manufacturer to be professionally serviced, which can be costly if the product is no longer under warranty.

Getting started can be tricky with some devices. When we connected some tested models to a computer, the PC often didn't recognize the player, and we had to resort to trial and error. Upgrading firmware also proved time-consuming. MP3 players use several methods for upgrading; one method, which executes the upgrade file on the PC while the player is still attached, can cause permanent damage to the player if there's even a slight interruption during execution.

Recommendations. As with computers, memory size counts. For people who like to have music in a small package, we recommend a standard-capacity MP3 player with the ability to accept external memory cards. If capacity is crucial, a larger, high-capacity model with 20 GB or more of storage would be a better choice. It will provide enough space to archive and organize a sizable library of music. However, it will likely be more complicated to use than a standard-capacity player because of the extra steps required and because of hard-drive delays while navigating through the menus or directories (folders) of songs.

If you want to minimize the odds that your player will fall behind the technology curve, look for one with upgradable firmware that can add to or enhance the features as well as accommodate newer encoding schemes or variations of MP3 compression. The more additional formats a model can play—such as WMA or ATRAC—the greater flexibility you'll have in downloading and transferring music files now and in the future.

Before you buy, make sure the player is compatible with your Windows or Mac computer (including the version of the operating system your computer uses) and that your computer has the USB or FireWire connection the player requires. Also, look for controls that are easy to read and that can be worked with one hand.

Related CR Report: May 2002

RECEIVERS

For a home-theater surround-sound system, look for a receiver that can decode Dolby Digital and DTS soundtracks.

The receiver is the brain of an audio/video system. It provides AM and FM tuners, amplifiers, surround sound, and switching capabilities. It's also the heart—most of the players in a home-entertainment system connect to it, including audio components such as speakers, a CD player, cassette deck, and turntable, as well as video sources such as a TV, DVD player, VCR, and cable and satellite boxes. Even as receivers take on a bigger role in home entertainment, they're losing some audio-related features that were common years back, such as tape monitors and phono inputs. Manufacturers say they must eliminate these less used features to make room for others.

WHAT'S AVAILABLE

Sony is by far the biggest-selling brand. Other top-selling brands include Denon, JVC, Kenwood, Onkyo, Panasonic, Pioneer, RCA, and Yamaha. Most models now are digital, designed for the six-channel surround-sound formats encoded in most DVDs and some TV fare. Here are the types you'll see, from least to most expensive:

Stereo. Basic receivers accept the analog stereo signals from a tape deck, CD player, or turntable. They provide two channels that power a pair of stereo speakers. For a simple music setup, add a cassette deck or a CD player. For rudimentary home theater, add a TV and VCR. Power typically runs 50 to 100 watts per channel.

Price range: $125 to $250.

Dolby Pro Logic. Dolby Pro Logic and Pro Logic II are the fading analog home-theater surround-sound standard. Receivers that support it can take three front channels and one surround channel from your TV or hi-fi VCR and output them to four or five speakers—three in front, and one or two in back. Most receivers supporting the Dolby Pro Logic standard are "digital-ready," which means they have the capability to send six channels of predecoded sound to the speakers. "Ready" means you must use a DVD player with a built-in digital decoder. (You won't be able to decode other digital audio sources such as satellite TV.) Power for Dolby Pro Logic models is typically 60 to 100 watts per channel.

Price range: $150 to $250.

Dolby Digital. Now representing the prevailing digital surround-sound standard, a Dolby Digital 5.1 receiver has a built-in decoder for six-channel audio capability—front left and right, front center, two rear with discrete wide-band signals, and a powered subwoofer for bass effects (that's where the ".1" comes in). Dolby Digital is the sound format for most DVDs, high-definition TV (HDTV), digital cable TV, and some satellite-TV broadcast systems. Newer versions of Dolby Digital, 6.1 and 7.1, add one or two rear channels for a total of seven-channel and eight-channel sound, respectively. To take advantage of true surround-sound capability, you'll need speakers that do a good job of reproducing full-spectrum sound. Receivers with digital decoding capability can also accept a signal that has been digitized, or sampled, at a given rate per second and converted to digital form. Dolby Digital is backward-compatible and supports earlier versions of Dolby such as Pro Logic and Pro Logic II. Power for Dolby Digital receivers is typically 80 to 120 watts per channel.

Price range: $200 to $500 or more.

DTS. A rival to Dolby Digital 5.1, Digital Theater Systems also offers six channels. It's a less common form of digital surround sound that is used in some movie tracks. Both DTS and Dolby Digital are often found on the same receivers. Power for DTS models is typically 80 to 120 watts per channel.

Price range: $200 to $500 or more.

THX-certified. The high-end receivers that meet this quality standard include full support for Dolby Pro Logic, Dolby Digital, and DTS. THX Select is the standard for components designed for small and average-sized rooms; THX Ultra is for larger rooms. Power for THX models is typically 80 to 120 watts per channel.

Price range: $500 to $2,500 and up.

KEY FEATURES

Controls should be easy to use. Look for a front panel with displays and controls clearly labeled and grouped by function. **Onscreen display** lets you control the receiver via a TV screen, a squint-free alternative to using the receiver's tiny LED or LCD display. **Switched AC outlets** (expect one or two) let you plug in other components and turn the whole system on and off with one button.

Remote controls are most useful when they have clear labels and buttons that light up for use in dim rooms. It's best if the buttons have different shapes and are color-coded and grouped by function—a goal that is seldom achieved in receiver remotes. A **learning remote** can receive programming data for other devices via their remote's infrared signal; on some remotes, the necessary codes on other manufacturers' devices are built in.

Input/output jacks matter more on a receiver than on perhaps any other component of your home theater. Clear labeling, color-coding, and logical groupings of the many jacks on the rear panel can help avert glitches during setup such as reversed speaker polarities and mixed-up inputs and outputs. Input jacks on the front panel make for easy connections to camcorders, video games, MP3 players, digital cameras, MiniDisc players, and PDAs.

A stereo receiver will give you a few audio inputs but no video jacks. Digital-ready receivers with Dolby Pro Logic will have several types of video inputs, including composite and S-video and sometimes component-video. **S-video** and **component video jacks** let you route signals from DVD players and other high-quality video sources through the receiver to the TV. Digital-ready receivers also have **audio 5.1 inputs** that accept input from a DVD player with its own built-in Dolby Digital decoder, an outboard decoder, or other components with multichannel analog signals. Dolby Digital and DTS receivers have the most complete array of audio and video inputs, often with several of a given type to accommodate multiple components.

TECH TIP
Home-theater equipment can help you make the best of an imperfect listening space. Receivers, for instance, have equalizers that can help make up for deficiencies in a room's shape.

Tone controls adjust bass and treble. A **graphic equalizer** breaks the sound spectrum into three or more sections, giving you slightly more control over the full audio spectrum. Instead of tone controls, some receivers come with tone styles such as Jazz, Classical, or Rock, each accentuating a different frequency pattern; often you can craft your own styles. But tone controls work best for correcting room acoustics and satisfying listening preferences, not enhancing a musical genre.

DSP (digital signal processor) modes use a computer chip to duplicate the sound characteristics of a concert hall and other listening environments. A **bass-boost** switch amplifies the deepest sounds, and **midnight mode** reduces loud sounds and amplifies quiet ones in music or soundtracks.

Sometimes called "one touch," a **settings memory** lets you store settings for each source to minimize differences in volume, tone, and other settings when switching between sources. A similar feature, **loudness memory,** is limited to volume settings alone.

Tape monitor lets you either listen to one source as you record a second on a tape deck or listen to the recording as it's being made. **Automatic radio tuning** includes such features as **seek** (automatic searching for the next in-range station) and 20 to 40 **presets** to call up your favorite stations.

To catch stations too weak for the seek mode, most receivers also have a **manual stepping knob** or buttons, best in one-channel increments. But most models creep in half- or quarter-steps, meaning unnecessary button tapping to find the frequency you want. **Direct tuning** of frequencies lets you tune a radio station by entering its frequency on a keypad.

HOW TO CHOOSE

Performance differences. The most recent CONSUMER REPORTS tests of receivers show that you needn't spend more than $200 to $300 to get a fine performer (unless you want a THX model; those begin at $500). Most models are very good at amplifying and tuning in FM stations, but only good for AM stations. Ease of use is often somewhat disappointing.

Recommendations. Don't buy more receiver than you need. The size of the room you're using, how loudly you play music, and the impedance of the speakers you'll use all determine how much power is appropriate. Generally, 50 watts or more per channel should be fine for a typical system in a typical 12x20 foot room. Then it becomes a question of features and usability. Virtually all new receivers support Dolby Digital 5.1 and DTS, and we strongly recommend you buy a model that supports those formats. A few receivers may support newer versions of Dolby (6.1, 7.1) that have seven or eight channels; they'd be good choices if you want the latest surround-sound capabilities.

Make sure a model you're considering has all the connection types you need, preferably in a clear, logical grouping. Explore the layout of the front panel and remote control to see how easy they'll be to use.

To compare receivers at the store, have the salesperson feed the same CD or DVD soundtrack to each one, adjust each receiver's volume to be equally loud, then select between each receiver's speaker output using the same set of speakers. Compare two receivers at a time. Stop the CD and listen for background hiss.

Related CR Report: November 2003
Ratings: page 309

SATELLITE TV

Before you opt for satellite TV, make sure a dish can be mounted on your property with a clear view of the satellite. Then choose the service provider and the hardware.

Frustration with cable companies has fueled

the growth of satellite-TV broadcast systems. Some 20 million homes now sport a saucer-shaped dish antenna.

Satellite TV offers something most cable subscribers don't get—a choice of provider. DirecTV and EchoStar's Dish Network operate nationwide. Once renowned for offering hundreds of channels but no local stations, both DirecTV and Dish Network now provide local service in many cities and outlying areas. That's the result of a 1999 federal law allowing satellite companies to offer so-called local-into-local service. In January 2002, the FCC ruled that if a satellite company offered one local channel, it had to carry all local channels in the markets where local service was offered.

People in an "unserved" household—in rural areas where an acceptable signal cannot be received via a rooftop antenna—can pick up local stations (regional affiliates of major networks) from a satellite provider. According to the FCC, you should be able to confirm your status through your satellite provider. For much of the country, however, cable remains the only way to receive all local programming, including community and school channels.

WHAT'S AVAILABLE

DirecTV and EchoStar's Dish Network have comparable programming fare, with packages offering up to several hundred channels. Movie and sports programming is strong, and foreign-language programming is available. In addition to television, both providers carry 30 to 40 commercial-free music services in many genres.

Typically, the dish and receiver are sold together and will only work with the signal of the chosen provider. Hughes, RCA, and Sony are among the companies that offer DirecTV equipment; JVC and EchoStar offer Dish Network equipment. You can also buy the hardware directly from the service provider.

Satellite dishes typically measure 18 or 24 inches. The larger dishes offer increased programming options, such as more channels, pay-per-view movies, HDTV reception, and international programming. Sometimes a second 18-inch dish may be required to receive some of those services.

Receivers accept the signal from the dish, decode it, and send it to your TV. To be able to watch different programs on different TVs at once, you'll need one receiver for each TV. To facilitate this, you need a dish with multiple low-noise block converters (LNBs). Alternatively, the receiver's RF-output jack or an inexpensive splitter may be used to send the same channel to multiple TVs.

For pay-per-view ordering and other provider contact, satellite-TV receivers must be connected to a telephone line. Typically, you use your existing line. Limited high-definition (HD) programming is available from both providers.

Price range for programming: $25 to $35 per month for basic packages with 50 or 100 channels (local-channel service adds about $5 per month); $30 to $45 for midrange packages with 100 to 150 channels; $75 to $85 a month for high-end packages with several hundred channels. Pay-per-view movies cost about $5; special sports packages are available separately.

Price range for a dish-receiver package: $100 to more than $800 for a receiver with more features. Extra receivers cost about $100 each and add about $5 apiece to the monthly bill. Some equipment may be free or offered at reduced prices as part of a special promotion.

KEY FEATURES

On the receiver, the number and type of **audio** and **video output jacks** make a difference in the quality of your picture and in the equipment you can connect. The lowest-quality connection is **radio-frequency (RF)**—the typical antenna-type connector. Better is a **composite-video output;** better still are **S-video outputs,** provided your TV is appropriately equipped, which can take advantage of the higher visual resolution of the digital video source.

An **on-screen signal-strength meter** lets you monitor how well the satellite signal is coming in. Satellite receivers with **Dolby Digital audio** capability may have optical or coaxial output for a direct digital connection to a Dolby Digital audio receiver.

Some remote controls accompanying the receiver are infrared, like TV or VCR remotes, requiring a direct line of sight to the receiver. Others use a radio-frequency signal, which can pass through walls, allowing the receiver to be placed in an unobtrusive, central location and controlled from anywhere in the house.

Remotes typically include a **program-description button,** which activates an on-screen **program-description banner.** The program guide helps you sort through the hundreds of channels.

A **program guide with picture** lets you continue to watch one program while you scan the onscreen channel guide for another. Some receivers have a **keyword search:** You can enter the full or partial name of a program or performer and search automatically through the listings.

HOW TO CHOOSE

Performance differences. The differences between the two satellite providers are subtle. Our testers saw some small defects when they viewed pictures from both satellite providers. You may notice minor visual impairments, mostly in fast-moving scenes (the most bandwidth-hungry screen content), which may be caused by expanded channel offerings at the expense of bandwidth.

Recommendations. Find out what the program offerings are in your area, including whether digital cable is available (or when it will be) and if local channels are available via satellite. It can be a major inconvenience if they're not available in your market. Choose the service, then the hardware. You need a clear view of the southern horizon and a place to mount the dish. Satellite dealers and installers will come out to assess your location. Be aware that, if you decide to switch providers, you'll need to pay for everything all over again.

Related CR Report: March 2003

SPEAKERS

Speakers can make or break your audio or video setup. Try to listen to them in a store before buying. And if you can splurge on only part of your system, splurge here.

The best array of audio or video components will let you down if matched with poor-quality speakers. Good speakers don't have to cost a bundle, though it is easy to spend a lot. For a home-theater system, you can start with two or three speakers and add others as need and budget allows. Size is no indication of quality.

WHAT'S AVAILABLE

Among the hundreds of speaker brands available, the major names include Boston Acoustics, Bose, Cambridge Soundworks, Infinity, JBL, Pioneer, Polk, RCA, and Sony. Speakers are sold through mass merchandisers, audio/video stores, and "boutique" retailers. You can also buy them online, but may pay up to $100 for shipping.

Speakers are sold as pairs for traditional stereo setups, and singly or in sets of three to six for equipping a home theater. To keep a balanced system, buy left and right speakers in pairs, rather than individually. The center-channel speaker should be matched to the front (or main) speakers. For the best sound, the rear speakers should also have a sound similar to the front speakers. The front speakers supply the stereo effect and carry most of the sound to the listener's ears. The center (or center-channel) speaker chiefly delivers dialog and is usually placed on top of or beneath the TV in a home-theater setup. Rear speakers, sometimes called surround or satellite speakers, deliver ambient effects such as crowd noise. A subwoofer carries the lowest tones.

Price range: under $300 to over $1,000.

Bookshelf speakers. These are among the smallest, but, at 12 to 18 inches tall, many are still too large to fit on a typical bookshelf. A pair of these can serve as the sole speakers in a stereo system or as the front or rear duo in a home-theater setup. One can serve as the center-channel unit, provided it's magnetically shielded so it won't interfere with the TV. Small speakers like these have made strides in their ability to handle deep bass without buzzing or distortion. Any bass-handling limitations would be less of a concern in a multispeaker system that uses a subwoofer for the deep bass.

Price range: $200 to more than $600.

Floor-standing speakers. Typically about 3 to 4 feet tall, these can also serve as the sole speakers in a stereo system or as the front pair in a home-theater system. Their big cabinets have the potential to do more justice to deep bass than smaller speakers, but we believe many listeners would be satisfied with smaller speakers that scored well for bass handling in our tests. Even if floor models do a bit better, their size and cost may steer buyers toward smaller, cheaper bookshelf models.

Price range: $300 to more than $1,000.

Center-channel speaker. In a multichannel setup, the center-channel speaker sits on or below the TV. Because it primarily handles dialog, its range doesn't have to be as full as that of the front pair, but its sound should be similar so all three blend well. Dedicated center-channel speakers are short and wide (6 inches high by 20 inches wide, for instance) so they perch neatly atop a TV.

Price range: $100 to over $500.

Rear-surround speakers. Rear speakers in a multichannel setup carry mostly background sound such as crowd noise. Newer multichannel formats such as Dolby Digital, DTS, DVD-Audio, and SACD make fuller use of these speakers than did earlier formats. You'll get the best blend if the rear pair sounds similar to the front pair. Rear speakers tend to be small and light (often 5 to 10 inches high and 3 to 6 pounds) so they can be wall mounted or placed on a shelf.

Price range: $100 to over $400.

Three-piece sets. Designed to be used as a stand-alone system or integrated with other speakers, these sets combine two bookshelf or satellite speakers for midrange and higher tones with either a center-channel speaker or a subwoofer for bass.

Price range: $300 to $800.

Six-piece sets. These systems have four satellites (used for both the front and rear pairs), one center-channel speaker, and a subwoofer. Six-piece sets save you the trouble of matching the distinctive sounds of six speakers. That can be a daunting task at home, and even more of a challenge amidst the din of a store that doesn't have a decent listening room.

Price range: $400 to more than $1,000.

Other shapes and sizes. A "powertower" is a tower speaker, usually priced above $1,000, with a side-firing, powered subwoofer in its base. Flat-panel speakers save space and cost $500 and up per pair.

KEY FEATURES

Lovers of loud sound should pay attention to a speaker's measured **impedance,** which affects how well the speaker and receiver get along. **Power range** refers to the advertised watts per channel. The **wattage** within a matched pair, front or rear, should be identical. Additionally, a speaker's power range should exceed the watts per channel supplied by your receiver or amplifier. Speakers sold to be near a TV set typically have magnetic shielding so they won't distort the picture with their core magnets.

HOW TO CHOOSE

Performance differences. What distinguishes the best from the rest is the accuracy with which speakers reproduce the original signals fed to them. Most models we've tested have been capable of reasonable accuracy. You can adjust the receiver's tone controls to compensate for a speaker's shortcomings. Making those adjust-

SOUND DECISION

Decide how much audio you want now, and expand as needed

If you want more than the basic sound from a TV's speakers, you have several options: You can move up to a stereo setup; gradually upgrade to surround sound by adding speakers and a new receiver as needed; or go straight to a full surround system.

STEREO SETUP

Requires: Any receiver and two speakers.
What it offers: The setup that used to play conventional music CDs and tapes can also provide a major sound upgrade for anything you watch on TV, whether broadcast content or VHS or DVD movies.

BASIC SURROUND SETUP

Requires: Receiver that supports Dolby Pro Logic or Pro Logic II and up to five speakers.
What it offers: You can add a few speakers to a stereo setup to get surround sound. Most VHS movies and TV programs have Pro Logic formatting, so this setup gives you the full effect.

TYPICAL SURROUND SETUP

Requires: Digital receiver that supports Dolby Digital 5.1 or DTS surround-sound format, five speakers, and a subwoofer.
What it offers: Better than basic surround setup with improved bass handling and more surround effect. Most DVD movies and some digital TV programs are 5.1.

ULTIMATE SURROUND SETUP

Requires: Digital receiver that supports Dolby Digital EX or DTS-ES extended surround-sound formats, six or seven speakers, and a subwoofer.
What it offers: A slight improvement over typical setup, with an extra rear surround channel or two. Some newer DVD movies are designed for a 6.1 or 7.1 setup.

ments is usually a minor, one-time inconvenience.

No speaker is perfect. Every speaker we've tested alters music to some degree, overemphasizing some sounds and underemphasizing others. Some speakers "roll off" entirely at extremes of bass and treble, meaning they can't reproduce some low or high sounds at all. Some speakers buzz, distort, or otherwise complain when playing low notes at window-rattling volume.

Recommendations. Look for the size and configuration that fit your listening space. Models of equal accuracy will sound different, so try to audition before you buy, using a familiar piece of music. Especially demanding: music with wide dynamics and frequencies—such as classical symphonies—and the other end of the scale, simple music, such as a solo piano performance.

Listen to the music soft and loud, for clarity and lack of harshness in the high range and a lack of boominess in the low. Start in the best position, in an equilateral triangle with the speakers, and move off-center until you find the angle at which the high frequencies become muffled. The farther you can go, the better the speakers. Sharpen your listening skills by first comparing each store's top performer with its low-priced entry-level model.

Related CR Report: November 2003
Ratings: page 316

TV SETS

Conventional TVs, high-definition TVs, flat screens, projection sets—you have more (and better) viewing choices than before, at ever-lower prices.

Conventional direct-view TVs—the picture-tube models you've been watching for years—are still what most buyers choose, and many offer outstanding performance at low prices. But of course there are other options. Want a big picture? Projection TVs have a screen measuring up to 73 inches or so, diagonally. If you'd love a screen that's only a few inches thick, you can get an LCD or plasma TV. All those TV types come in digital versions that can display high-definition (HD) signals, which offer sharper, more detailed picture quality than with an analog set. You can opt for the familiar squarish screen or a wide-screen model that simulates the movie-theater experience, better suiting much HD programming.

WHAT'S AVAILABLE

Among the brands selling TVs are JVC, Panasonic, Philips, RCA, Samsung, Sanyo, Sharp, Sony, Toshiba, and Zenith.

Conventional analog sets. Direct-view TV sets typically have a screen ranging in size from 13 inches up to 36 inches. Analog sets are usually squarish, with an aspect ratio of 4:3, meaning they're four units high for every three units wide. A 27-inch screen, once thought large, is now the norm, and these sets are among the best values among TVs. Models with 27-inch or larger screen frequently offer many features, including picture-in-picture (PIP), S-video input, simulated surround-sound effects, a universal remote control, and a comb filter. A 32-inch screen, the entry level for big-screen TV, adds two-tuner PIP and more input jacks. The largest direct-view sets have a 36-inch screen (with an occasional 40-inch set) and usually the most features and inputs.

Price: 13-inch sets start at $75 or so; 27-inch sets start at about $250; 32-inch sets start at about $400; 36-inch sets start at $600.

Projection TVs. Measuring 42 to 73

inches diagonally, rear-projection sets are the most affordable jumbo-screen TVs on the market. You can get either a 4:3 screen or a widescreen model with a 16:9 aspect ratio. Most rear-projection sets use three CRTs that have to aligned periodically to converge their image. Picture quality is usually good and sometimes very good, but doesn't equal that of a conventional picture-tube set. Viewing angle can be a drawback: The image appears dimmer as your position angles away from the center of the screen. Projection sets have plenty of features, such as two-tuner PIP and custom settings. HD-capable digital sets are becoming the norm as analog models are being phased out. Note that readers have reported that parts can be hard to get and repairers hard to find.

TECH TIP

Even the best TV won't live up to its potential unless you use a connection that maximizes the quality of the signal.

Price: analog sets start at about $1,000, HD-capable sets at about $1,500.

LCD flat panels. With a screen measuring about 10 to 40 inches diagonally, LCD TVs are only a few inches thick. They come in both 4:3 and 16:9 screen shapes and in conventional and HD models. These sets use the same technology as flat-panel computer monitors. A bright, smooth image is created by a white backlight and thousands of pixels that open and close like shutters. Slow pixel response may make fast-moving images appear fuzzy.

Price: starts at about $600.

Plasma flat panels. Also renowned for their thin profile, plasma displays tend to be bigger than LCD models, ranging from about 32 to 63 inches, measured diagonally. Most are widescreen models; both conventional and HD versions are available. With plasma technology, an image is created by a huge array of tiny fluorescent lights. Plasma displays may not include a TV tuner or speakers. Sets are often wall-mounted.

Price: starts at about $3,000.

HD-capable sets. HDTV sets can provide the best at-home viewing experience currently available. When you're watching specially formatted HD programming, the picture has more resolution and more detail than a conventional TV can display. You can get HD programming via an antenna, HD cable box, or HD satellite receiver. Even with standard (non-HD) signals from a good cable connection, a satellite signal, or a DVD player, the picture quality is often better than a conventional set's.

Two types of TV sets can display HD images. By far the more common of the two types, HD-ready sets, also known as HD monitors, can display standard-definition programs (most TV broadcasts) on their own. To display HD programs, they require a box to decode the signals—such as a digital cable box or satellite receiver specifically designed for HD programming. To get HD signals from a rooftop antenna, you'll need a separate digital-TV receiver, which costs several hundred dollars. You don't have to pay to receive the signals, however, as you do with cable and satellite. (To receive HD via antenna, you must be fairly close to a transmitter, with an unobstructed view.)

Integrated HD sets, also called HDTVs, have a built-in digital tuner that lets them display HD with only a roof antenna and no additional equipment. You may be able to receive the major networks' HD offerings, but not the premium channels available on satellite and cable. Although a digital tuner is built in, HDTV sets require an HD-capable cable box or satellite receiver to get HD via cable or satellite. Integrated sets typically cost more than HD-ready sets. Many HD sets are widescreen models because the 16:9 shape is better suited for displaying movies and other HD programming.

Price range: Depends on size and technology. The least expensive, a 27-inch direct-view set, starts at about $700. A high-end plasma TV can cost $10,000 or more.

KEY FEATURES

The **flat screen,** a departure from the decades-old curved TV tube, reduces off-angle reflections and glare, but doesn't necessarily improve picture quality. A **comb filter,** found on most sets, minimizes minor color flaws at edges within the image and increases picture clarity. An **auto-color control** can be set to automatically adjust color balance to make flesh tones look natural. **Adjustable color temperature** lets you shade the picture toward the blue range ("cooler," better for images with outdoor light) or the red ("warmer," preferred for movie-theater-like realism).

Picture-in-picture (PIP) shows two channels at once, one on a small picture inserted in the full-screen image.

Stereo sound is virtually universal on sets 27 inches or larger, but you'll generally discern little stereo separation from a set's built-in speakers. For a better stereo effect, route the signals to a sound system. A few larger TV sets have an **audio amplifier** that can power regular (unpowered) speakers connected to the set's audio output jacks, eliminating the need for a receiver. **Ambience sound** is often termed "surround sound" or the like, but this is not true surround, like that from a multispeaker Dolby Digital or Pro Logic home-theater system; rather, it's accomplished through special audio processing. Some people find the wider "soundstage" pleasing; others find it distracting. **Automatic volume control** compensates for the jarring volume jumps that often accompany commercials or changes in channel.

Virtually all TV sets come with a **remote control** to change channels and adjust sound volume and picture. A **universal remote** will control all or most of your video (and some audio) devices once you program it by entering codes. (Aftermarket universal remotes typically cost $10 to $40.) **Active-channel scan** automatically detects and memorizes active channels, eliminating the need to scan manually.

Last-channel recall lets you jump to the previously viewed channel. With channel labeling, you enter channels' names (ESPN, CNN, AMC) so you'll know where you are as you change channels. Some models offer an **Extended Data Services (XDS) decoder,** which displays channel and programming information on the show you're watching (if the station transmits that information). **Guide Plus,** which several manufacturers offer, displays program listings; the set receives program information when it's off but still in "standby."

Some features are important to specific users: **Separate audio program (SAP)** lets you receive a second soundtrack, typically in another language. **Multilingual menus** are also common. **Parental controls** include the V-chip, which blocks specific shows based on their content rating; for access, you must enter a code. A TV with **channel block-out** will block specific channels and may also prevent use of the audio/video inputs to which video games are connected.

Cable/antenna, or **radio frequency (RF)** inputs are the most basic; the next step up is **composite video. S-video input** lets you take advantage of the superior picture quality from a satellite-dish system, a DVD player, or a digital camcorder.

Component-video input offers even better quality, useful with equipment that comes with component outputs, such as some DVD players, high-definition satellite receivers, and cable boxes. For a camcorder or video game, **front-mounted A/V jacks** are helpful. Audio output jacks, essential for a home-theater setup, let you direct a stereo TV's audio signal to a receiver or self-powered speakers. A **headphone jack** lets you watch (and listen) without disturbing others.

Sets that are **1080i/720p capable** can display digital signals in those two high-definition specifications. **VGA/SVGA input** allows the TV to accept signals from a computer.

Some features are most often found on HD sets and projection TVs. **Motion compensation** can improve the smoothness of movies played on standard (not progressive-scan) DVD players. This feature is sometimes referred to as 3:2 pulldown compensation or by brand-specific names such as CineMotion. On 16:9 sets, **stretch and zoom modes** will expand or compress an image to better fill the screen shape. This helps to reduce the dark bands that can appear above, below, or on the sides of the image if you watch content formatted for one screen shape on a TV that has the other shape. (The picture may be distorted or cut off a bit in the process of stretching and zooming.) Those bars make the picture slightly smaller and use the cathode-ray tubes (CRT) phosphors unevenly, which can leave residual images on the screen over time. This "burn-in" is also a risk with any images left on the screen for long periods.

On CRT-based projection sets, **auto convergence** provides a one-touch adjustment to automatically align the three CRTs for a sharp, accurate image. It's much more convenient than manual convergence, which can require many time-consuming mechanical adjustments.

HOW TO CHOOSE

Performance differences. Most TV sets we've tested do at least a good job, many very good. HD sets generally have the best picture quality, even with conventional programming. Some of the biggest differences show up in sound quality. On most sets, the audio quality is sufficient for the usual TV fare, but for watching movies you can improve the audio by running the TV sound through a receiver to external speakers.

Recommendations. Before you start shopping, decide whether you want to stick with a direct-view set or go with a big-screen projection set or a flat panel, and whether you want a conventional analog TV or one that can handle HD signals. For the most part, CONSUMER REPORTS thinks HD-ready sets make more sense for most buyers than integrated HDTVs.

Size is another key consideration. For a fine picture plus many useful features, a 27-inch model may be the best deal. But if you have the space, you may prefer a 32-inch or 36-inch set, which are becoming more affordable. A big-screen TV is best viewed in a larger room that allows adequate viewing distance from the screen. Flat-panel LCDs and plasma sets are still fairly expensive; prices are likely to drop, as they have on other electronic gear, as these technologies mature and more sets are manufactured.

Also take into consideration how your TV will fit in with the other components of your home theater. If you plan to output sound to external speakers, you'll want audio outputs. DVD players, digital camcorders, and other devices require S-video inputs; for DVD players, a component-video input is better. Check with your cable-service provider regarding availability of digital cable service. Even if you watch mostly conventional programming now, buying an HD-capable set will give you superior picture quality now and the option of watching HD programming down the road. But you'll pay a premium for this type of TV.

Related CR Report: December 2002

Reliability: page 32, 33

VCRS

Video cassette recorders don't match the picture and sound quality of DVD players, but they're still the most inexpensive way to play, record, and archive videos.

Today's VCRs are more of a bargain than ever. Hi-fi models, which cost about $150 to $300 when we tested them in November 1998, now have list prices as low as $80—and may sell for as little as $50.

WHAT'S AVAILABLE

Panasonic, RCA, Emerson, JVC, and Sony are among the biggest-selling brands. Most VCRs are standard VHS models; S-VHS, or super VHS, models can record in higher resolution.

Monophonic models, starting at about $50, record sound adequately for playback through a small TV speaker. Hi-fi VCRs cost a little more but offer sound of near CD quality. They're much better for larger TVs with stereo sound or for connecting to a receiver that supports the basic surround-sound formats (Dolby ProLogic or ProLogic II) used on some VHS tapes. Dual-deck models, which hold two cassettes at once, let you copy tapes easily. There are also a few digital VCRs that can record digital satellite-TV content.

Price range: $80 to $250 (hi-fi); $200 and up (S-VHS); $200 to $350 (dual-deck); $750 and up (digital).

KEY FEATURES

Hi-fi models record **high-fidelity sound,** a desirable feature for a home-theater setup. **S-VHS** records more information onto a special tape for better picture detail. A newer variation, **S-VHS ET,** uses standard VHS tape.

Cable/satellite-box control, also referred to as C3 (for "cable-channel changer"), lets the VCR change the channel when you tape a program. **VCR Plus,** now quite common, lets you set the VCR to tape a program simply by punching in a code number from your local TV listings. **Memory backup** saves programming information if the VCR temporarily loses power; depending on the model, you may have a few minutes or less before the program settings are gone.

There are various "skip" features on VCRs. **Automatic commercial advance** lets the VCR bypass all commercials during playback by fast-forwarding past such cues as fade-to-black and changes in sound level. **Movie advance** lets you fly over previews at the beginning of a rented tape. **One-button skip** lets you fast-forward 30 to 60 seconds with each button press. There are also different kinds of searches: A **go-to search** skips to a section according to the time on the counter, while a **zero search** finds the place on the tape where the counter was set to zero. An **index search** forwards the tape to a specific index point set by the machine each time you begin a recording.

Editing features include s**huttle** and **jog controls,** which let you scan large segments or move forward or backward one frame at a time to find the exact spot you want. **Audio dub,** a higher-end feature, lets you add music or narration to existing recordings. A **flying erase head** lets you insert segments without noticeable video glitches.

Plug and play eases setup; you connect the VCR to the cable system or an antenna, then plug it in. The VCR reads signals from broadcasters to automatically program the channels and the clock. The latter feature is also known as **auto clock set.** Some VCRs can automatically switch from SP to EP speed, a feature called **auto speed-switching** that extends recording time and helps ensure that you don't miss a climactic scene because you ran out of tape.

A **universal remote** lets you control other devices along with your VCR. If the kids misplace it, a **remote locator** will page the remote, causing it to beep from its hiding place. **Child lock** disables the VCR's controls to keep programming from being changed.

HOW TO CHOOSE

Performance differences. Because DVD players have redefined excellence in picture quality for inexpensive video gear, none of the VCRs that we tested produced what we now consider an excellent picture. Still, most models have performed very well—and the best picture you can get from a VCR is almost as good as what you'd get from a typical DVD player.

Recommendations. For basic recording of movies and TV shows, VCRs offer great value. Even inexpensive models now offer hi-fi sound and some level of VCR Plus programming. If you have an S-VHS-C, a Hi8, or a digital camcorder, you'll want a VCR that supports S-VHS to view the improved video quality. If you're hooking a VCR into a home-theater system that includes a DVD player, note that built-in encryption contained in many DVD discs typically won't let you copy DVD movies onto videotape. Such copying is a copyright violation in most cases.

Many VCRs have four or more recording heads, but that doesn't necessarily translate into better performance than you get with a dual-head model. For the best assurance of quality before you buy, try to get a side-by-side demonstration of the models you're considering.

Related CR Report: December 2002

VCR/DVD COMBOS

These save space and reduce the need for connections. For many buyers, the compromise is worth it.

At a time when many consumers want both a video cassette recorder and a DVD player, these combo units may appeal. Their main advantage is that they fit in about the same space as a VCR, can involve less wiring than two separate devices, and can be operated with just one remote. VCR/DVD combos can play either form of media; a few models let you record DVDS onto videotapes. The combos may simplify cabling; if you're not fussy about picture or sound quality, you can connect one to your TV through a single cable. Such convenience and simplicity exact a price: a combo can cost as much as or more than a stand-alone VCR and DVD player together.

WHAT'S AVAILABLE

The top manufacturers of VCR/DVD combos are also major players among makers of stand-alone units; they include Panasonic, Samsung, and Toshiba. As with stand-alone units, combos are rapidly evolving as manufacturers seek to differentiate their products and come up with a winning combination of features. The chief classes relate to their DVD-playback capability:

Standard DVD models. These perform with typically excellent DVD quality when connected to any TV made within the past few years. VHS picture quality is comparable to that of a stand-alone VCR.

Price range: $120 to $300.

Progressive-scan DVD models. This newer generation of combos, when connected to a regular TV, delivers the same high-quality picture as a standard player. But, when paired with a high-definition TV, a progressive-scan player delivers a cleaner image—the next best thing to true HD. VHS picture quality is the same as for models with standard DVD.

Price range: $150 to $350.

KEY FEATURES

What you'll find in a combo VCR/DVD player is mostly a subset of what you get with stand-alone VCRs and DVD players, plus a few features that play off the integration of the two functions.

The DVD-player side of these units lets you take advantage of **multichannel surround sound** by routing the movie's digitally encoded soundtrack to a receiver through the **coaxial** or **optical digital-audio output.** (The receiver must have built-in decoding capability—Dolby Digital, DTS, or better—that lets it decode the multichannel audio encoded into DVD discs.) Should you want to connect the DVD's digital-audio output to a receiver, make sure its output (coaxial or optical) matches the receiver's input.

One capability affecting both primary functions of the combos is that aside from their digital-audio features they also let you take advantage of **Dolby Pro Logic** analog multichannel surround sound. This may be encoded onto DVDs, VHS tapes, and even some TV programming. Again, you'll need a receiver with Dolby Pro Logic decoding; you connect it to the combo unit's stereo audio outputs.

If you don't have the full multispeaker setup, **virtual surround sound** mimics the effects of a full surround-sound system. It sounds pleasing to some people but artificial to others. **Dynamic audio-range** control helps keep a movie's explosions and other noisy sound effects from seeming too loud.

Besides playing standard DVDs, combos (as with stand-alone DVD players) can often play discs of numerous other formats. These include **CD-Recordable (CD-R)** and **CD-Rewritable (CD-RW),** along with—depending on the model—discs in the recordable **DVD+R, DVD-R, DVD+RW,** and **DVD-RW formats.** Many models can play **MP3** music files burned onto a CD, and all can play commercial audio CDs. With some new combos, a **memory-card slot** lets you insert removable media on which you've stored MP3 music files or photos shot with a digital camera.

Some models can record a non-copy-protected DVD onto videotape. But since most movies on DVD are copy-protected, you probably won't be able to use this feature often.

The VCR side of the combo player usually offers **index search,** which fast-forwards or rewinds the tape to a specific index point set by the machine at the start of a recorded segment. Some models can automatically switch tapes from SP to EP speed, a feature called **auto speed-switching,** to extend recording time and help ensure that you don't miss a climactic scene because you ran out of tape. Also helpful on some is the ability to play S-VHS tapes at VHS quality.

What's typically missing is any form of VCR Plus, which eases the process of programming **time-shift recording** (taping a program for later viewing) by letting you enter numerical codes from TV listings instead of the program's date, time, duration, and channel.

For connecting to the TV set, VCR/DVD combos offer **radio-frequency (RF) output** for either DVD or VHS signals, a major advantage if you have an old TV with only that form of input. (The downside is mediocre image quality.) A **composite-video** connection can produce a very good picture, but there will be some loss of detail and some color artifacts, such as adjacent colors bleeding into each other. **S-video output,** on some models, can improve DVD picture quality. It keeps the black-and-white and the color portions of the signal separated, producing more picture detail and fewer color defects than standard composite video. **Component video,** the best connection these combos offer (for DVD output), improves on S-video by splitting the color signal, resulting in a wider range of color. Component video also supports a progressive-scan signal for those DVD players that provide it.

Among other features, a **screen saver** is a moving image that kicks in after a set duration of inactivity to prevent still images from burning into your TV screen. It won't, however, prevent long-term burn-in of the dark bands displayed while you're watching letterbox-format programming. With a **lighted remote,** buttons are illuminated so you can see them more easily in a darkened room.

HOW TO CHOOSE

Performance differences. Picture quality from a VCR/DVD combo is comparable to what you'd get from stand-alone devices—excellent for DVD and so-so for VHS, depending on tape speed. Owing to the number of features, both the VCR and DVD functions of combo players make them slightly more complicated to use than stand-alone units.

Recommendations. If convenience and saving space are paramount, choose from among the models that require the fewest compromises. And if space is especially cramped, consider a newer combination product that marries a TV, VCR, and DVD player to offer portability and capabilities similar to those of a TV/VCR combo. Also worth weighing into your decision: If one combo function breaks, you'll be without both until the player comes back from the repair shop.

Related CR Report: December 2003

KITCHEN & LAUNDRY

What's New in Kitchen & Laundry Products

Today's appliances are smarter, more capable, and more energy-efficient than yesterday's. New technologies and tightened government energy standards have sparked the change. A bonus is that today's appliances, large and small, are likely to be more stylish than the appliances you currently own. Here's a rundown on some of the current trends:

Added intelligence. Everything from dishwashers to mixers has been embellished with electronic sensors, controls, and monitors. "Smart" products are supposed to minimize the guesswork of knowing when the clothes are dry, the food is cooked, the dishes are washed, or the toast is browned. This technology can use water and energy more efficiently, as with a washer that automatically fills to the water level the load requires, or a refrigerator that defrosts only as necessary rather than at set intervals.

But such advances are only the first wave. Ready to debut: microwave ovens that scan bar codes on packaged-food labels and automatically set the precise cooking time and power level; Internet-connected refrigerators that scan labels and automatically reorder provisions when you're running low; and self-diagnosing appliances that can convey information to a repair center by computer, allowing a technician to make a preliminary diagnosis before a service call. Whether these products will truly fill a consumer need—or merely serve a manufacturer's need to spark sales—remains to be seen.

Faster cooking. Consumers seem to want food cooked ever faster, or at least manufacturers say they do. Titans such as General Electric, Maytag, and Whirlpool have introduced appliances that claim to reduce cooking times by as much as 60 percent over conventional means by combining various methods—microwave, convection, and halogen or quartz light bulbs. Such hybrid devices may offer another advantage: no preheating. The perceived desire for speed has even fueled a resurgence in a category from another era—pressure cookers—in safer and more consumer-friendly designs.

Improved efficiency. As of January 1, 2004, the U.S. Department of Energy is mandating that new washing machines be about 35 percent more efficient than previously required. Based on recent CONSUMER REPORTS tests, many top-loading models now on the market won't pass muster, so expect innovative designs in the future. Perhaps in anticipation of DOE regulations, manufacturers have introduced more front-loading machines, inherently more frugal because they tumble clothes through water instead of submerging them, as a top-loader does. Front-loaders consume about two-thirds less water than most top-loaders, though newly designed top-loaders are narrowing the gap. Refrigerators, which typically devour more electricity than any other kitchen appliance, are now required to be less gluttonous. In general, side-by-side units are less space- and energy-efficient than either top- or bottom-freezer models. Over the long run, a pricier model with a low annual energy cost may be less expensive than a cheaper model that uses more electricity.

Easier cleaning. More products are designed with flat, seamless surfaces, fewer buttons, and touchpad controls, making them easier to clean. Smoothtop electric ranges continue to rise in popularity. And manufacturers are offering a new stainless-steel look-alike finish known as VCM that hides the smudges and fingerprints that seem to multiply on stainless steel.

Gas ranges are cleaning up their act, too, as companies such as GE unveil gas smoothtops: Burners and grates sit atop a solid-glass surface, eliminating pesky nooks, crannies, and dripbowls—although you do have to use a special cleansing cream. Nearly all refrigerators now feature movable glass shelves bound by a lip to retain spills.

Sleeker styling. Just about every major appliance maker now offers stylish kitchen appliances with curved doors, sleek-looking hardware and controls, and a flashy logo or nameplate. Such equipment can cost twice as much as mainstream products, but extra features help justify the price tag.

Some dishwashers relocate controls from the front panel to the top lip of the door, where they're out of sight. With a front panel that matches kitchen cabinets, this design can help the dishwasher blend in with its surroundings.

Color choices are proliferating as well. Stainless steel debuted in "professional" and "semi-pro" high-end models. And brushed aluminum finishes are now widely available in mass-marketed products, along with the traditional white and black. Biscuit, bisque, or linen are replacing almond. If you prefer a splashier color for your appliance—such as cobalt blue or hunter green—look to premium brands such as Jenn-Air, KitchenAid, or Viking.

Family-friendly features. Manufacturers are using child lockouts to keep curious fingers out of potentially hazardous places. Some microwave ovens let you punch in a code to prevent accidental activation. A lockout button disables the knobs on a gas range or keeps the dishwasher from shutting down midcycle if little Emma starts poking at the keypad. Such niceties are still relatively new and not yet found on many products.

More power. Sales of powerful commercial-style, stainless-steel ranges—with four or more high-output burners rated at maximum outputs of 15,000 British thermal units per hour, or Btu/hr.—continue to rise. More typical upscale stoves come with an assortment of burners with maximum outputs from 5,000 to 14,000 Btu/hr. Microwaves continue to get more powerful, too, with 1,300 watts the benchmark, up from around 800 a few years ago.

More shopping options. Frigidaire, GE, Maytag, Sears, and Whirlpool sell almost three-fourths of all major appliances. In some categories, Sears alone sells more than several of its biggest competitors combined, and the company is trying to strengthen its position by selling white goods online. But the competitive landscape is changing. Deep-discount warehouse membership clubs such as Costco

THE APPLIANCE NAME GAME

Who makes what?

Despite all the nameplates, only a handful of companies actually make refrigerators, ranges, washers, dryers, and dishwashers. The companies typically sell products under their own brand and also produce specific models for other manufacturers. For example, we know from our laboratory inspections that GE's front-loading washer comes off Frigidaire's assembly line. Sears's Kenmore brand, the biggest name in appliances, isn't made by Sears at all. Kenmore products are made entirely by other companies. Here's a rundown of the key players and the familiar names they sell, listed alphabetically:

Frigidaire. The company, owned by Sweden's Electrolux, also makes Gibson, Kelvinator, and Tappan appliances. The Frigidaire line is typically higher priced, especially in the tony Frigidaire Gallery and Gallery Professional series. Tappan is a significant force in gas ranges. Kelvinator and Gibson are harder to find; products sold under those names are generally less expensive, with fewer features.

General Electric. One of the two biggest U.S. appliance makers (along with Whirlpool), GE is particularly strong in the cooking categories. The GE name is considered a midrange brand; GE Profile is geared toward people who want to spend more. GE Monogram, focusing on high style and a commercial look with both freestanding and built-in products, competes with boutique names like Thermador (owned by Bosch) and Viking and is distributed separately. Hotpoint is GE's value brand.

Kenmore. The nation's biggest source of major appliances, Sears has its store-brand Kenmore models made to order by companies such as Whirlpool, long a manufacturer of many Kenmore laundry machines. Kenmore washing machines and dryers are also made by Frigidaire. Kenmore Elite is Sears's high-end brand of kitchen and laundry products.

Maytag. The company that made its name in washers and dryers cultivates a premium image, with many of its products bearing the flagship name. Maytag Neptune is a line of premium laundry machines. Performa is the company's value-priced line. Jenn-Air, best known for modular cooktops and ranges, is Maytag's upscale kitchen brand. Admiral and Magic Chef are budget brands. Maytag purchased Amana in 2001 and will continue to market appliances under the Amana brand name. (Amana was the fifth-largest appliance maker, known mostly for its refrigerators.)

Whirlpool. Also strongly positioned in the laundry room, the nation's other major appliance maker sells products under its corporate name in a wide variety of prices. Whirlpool Gold products are a notch up from the mainstream Whirlpool line; KitchenAid is the company's upscale brand; Roper is the bargain brand.

European and boutique brands. Small in market share but often leaders in design and styling, brands such as Asko, Bosch, and Miele were among the first to showcase water-efficient engineering and clean-looking controls for dishwashers and washing machines. Viking is the leading manufacturer of pro-style kitchen appliances and outdoor grills. Sub-Zero is gaining market share with products sold under its own name and the Wolf brand. KitchenAid sells pro-style appliances under the KitchenAid Architect moniker. Other makers of pro-style ranges include DCS, Dacor, and Dynasty.

have expanded their selection of refrigerators, ranges, and the like. Home Depot and Lowe's, the nation's biggest home-center chains, have publicly announced they want to dethrone Sears as the leading appliance marketer.

While the Internet has become a popular way to purchase books and get travel deals, it's not much of a factor in the appliance category. Still, e-commerce experts predict online appliance sales could reach $2 billion by 2004—accounting for about 6 percent of sales.

Brand battles in small appliances. Coffeemakers, toasters, and blenders rule the kitchen countertop, with consumers purchasing more of them every year than any other countertop appliance. Three brands account for nearly three-quarters of small-appliance sales: Black & Decker, Hamilton Beach/Proctor-Silex, and Sunbeam/Oster.

Major mass retailers, where most of the products are sold, are trying to grab an even larger share of the business by gaining exclusive rights to established national brands. Hamilton Beach/Proctor-Silex, for example, makes products under the GE name (via a licensing agreement) for sale at Wal-Mart. Philips markets a line under its own name through Target. Black & Decker has partnered with chains such as Kmart. Sears sells small appliances under its Kenmore name.

COFFEEMAKERS

Most models make a good cup of coffee. Higher-priced models usually have more convenience features and fancier styling.

The popularity of Starbucks and other specialty coffee shops seems to be driving demand for a new generation of coffeemakers that seeks to replicate the coffeehouse experience at home. Customized brewing, water filtration, and thermal carafes are a few of the features manufacturers are hoping will encourage consumers to trade up. Truth is, virtually any model can make a good cup as long as you use decent coffee.

WHAT'S AVAILABLE

While manual-drip systems, coffee presses, and percolators are available, consumers buy more automatic-drip coffeemakers than any other small kitchen appliance: 17 million per year. Mr. Coffee and Black & Decker are the two largest brands, along with well-known names such as Braun, Krups, Melitta, Proctor Silex, Cuisinart, and Delonghi.

Coffeemakers come in sizes from single-cup models to machines capable of brewing up to 12 cups at a time. Ten- and 12-cup machines account for more than 80 percent of the market, although manufacturers are trying to expand sales by pushing fully featured 4-cup models.

At the low end are bare-bones coffeemakers with a single switch to start the brewing process and a plain metal hotplate; pricier models can have programmable start and stop times, a water filter, frothing capability, and a thermal carafe. Most consumers opt for the more basic models. Black and white remain the standard colors, but some brands have added other hues.

Price range: $15 to more than $90.

KEY FEATURES

A **removable filter** basket is the easiest for loading and for removing the used filter; baskets that sit inside a pullout drawer can be messy. **Paper filters**—usually "cupcake" or cone-shaped—absorb oil and keep sediment from creeping through. Models with a **permanent mesh filter** need to be cleaned after each use, but can save you money over time. Neither type of filter detracted from coffee flavor in our tests. The simplest type of water **reservoir** is one with a big flip-top lid and lines that mark the number of cups in large, clearly visible numbers. Some reservoirs are removable—so you can fill up at the sink—and dishwasher safe. **Transparent fill tubes** with **cup markings** let you check the water level while pouring.

A **thermal carafe** helps retain flavor and aroma longer than a glass pot on a hotplate. Other niceties: a **small-batch setting** to adjust brew time when you make fewer than 5 cups; **temperature** and **brew-strength controls;** and a **drip-stop feature** that lets you pour a cup before the whole pot's done. A **programmable timer** lets you add ground coffee and water the night before, so you can wake up to a freshly brewed pot. A **clock-timer** automatically turns off the hotplate at a specified or programmed time after brewing. New models frequently have a more **compact footprint** and **flat electronic-touchpad controls.** Some high-end models feature a **built-in bean grinder.** A **built-in water filter** may cut chlorine and, sometimes, mineral buildup (but a filter can harbor bacteria if you don't regularly change it).

HOW TO CHOOSE

Performance differences. In CONSUMER REPORTS tests, just about any drip coffeemaker made good-tasting coffee. The differences among machines mostly pertain to convenience. Some models have hard-to-clean nooks and crannies or unclear markings; some easily show stains.

Some programmable models were much tougher to set than others. Brewing time for a full pot took from 9 to 11 minutes; models designated as "restaurant" type—which keep a full reservoir of hot water at the ready—brewed 8 cups in less than 4 minutes.

Recommendations. If all you want is a good cup of java, there are plenty of coffeemakers from which to choose, starting at around $15. A few dollars more buys a machine that's easier to fill and a carafe that's easier to pour from. At higher prices, you get luxuries such as programmability, sculptural style, and extras such as a drip-stop feature or a grinder.

Related CR Report: December 2002
Ratings: page 252

COOKWARE

Nonstick pots and pans are easy to clean. Uncoated cookware is often more durable. Your best bet might be some of each.

Is boiling water the extent of your kitchen prowess or do you routinely take on much more challenging tasks? Could you work in the kitchen of a five-star restaurant or are you a culinary klutz? How you answer those questions is a good gauge of the price range for the cookware you need.

A basic set of seven to 10 pieces, typically one or two pots, a skillet, a stockpot, and lids, can be had for $50. At the other end of the spectrum, you can get a set of stylish and sturdy commercial-style cookware for as much as $600. And there are lots of choices in between.

WHAT'S AVAILABLE

Farberware, Mirro/Wearever, Revere, and T-Fal are the most widely sold brands. Commercial-style brands include All-Clad and Calphalon. TV's celebrity chef

Emeril Lagasse is mixing it up in the cookware market with Emerilware (made by All-Clad). Other more recent entrants in the cookware field include the appliance maker KitchenAid and the knife maker Henckels.

Choices abound. You can find aluminum, stainless steel, copper, cast iron, tempered glass, or porcelain on carbon steel; nonstick, porcelain-coated, or uncoated; lightweight or heavy-duty commercial-style; handles of metal, plastic, or wood.

Commercial-style cookware is typically made of aluminum or stainless steel. Cooking enthusiasts will appreciate the fact that these sturdy pots and pans are built to conduct heat evenly up the sides and that their riveted metal handles can be put to hard use. A stovetop grill pan often has raised ridges that sear meat and vegetables. Basic sets of cookware can be supplemented with individual pieces from open stock.

Price range: $50 or less for a low-end set; $50 to $100 for midlevel; $200 and up for high-end or commercial-style.

KEY FEATURES

The most versatile materials for pots and pans are the most common ones: aluminum and stainless steel. **Aluminum,** when it's sufficiently heavy-gauge, heats quickly and evenly. On the other hand, **thin-gauge aluminum**, besides heating unevenly, is prone to denting and warping. **Anodized aluminum** is an excellent conductor of heat and is relatively lightweight; it's durable, but easily stained and not dishwasher-safe. **Enamel-coated aluminum,** typically found in low-end lines, can chip easily.

Stainless steel can go in the dishwasher, but it conducts and retains heat poorly. It's usually layered over aluminum. Some stainless-steel pots have a bottom with a copper or aluminum core.

Copper heats and cools quickly, ideal when temperature control is important. It's good for, say, making caramel sauce. Provided that it's kept polished, copper looks great hanging on a kitchen wall or from the ceiling. Because copper reacts with acidic foods such as tomatoes, it's usually lined with stainless steel or tin, which may blister and wear out over time. Solid-copper cookware, thin-gauge or heavy-gauge, is expensive.

You might want some **cast-iron** or **tempered-glass** pieces. Cast iron is slow to heat and cool, but it handles high temperatures well, and it's great for stews or Cajun-style blackening. Tempered glass breaks easily and cooks unevenly on the stove, but it can go directly from the freezer to the stove, oven, broiler, or microwave—and then on to the table.

Most Americans opt for **nonstick** pots and pans to reduce the need for elbow grease when cleaning up. Introduced on cookware more than 30 years ago, the first nonstick coatings were thin and easily scratched. Nonsticks have greatly improved, but still shouldn't be used with metal utensils or very high heat. To improve durability, some manufacturers use a thicker nonstick coating or create a gritty or textured surface before applying the nonstick finish. Many nonstick pots and pans aren't meant for the dishwasher, but they're easy to wash by hand.

There are some advantages to **uncoated** cookware. It's dishwasher-safe, it can handle metal utensils, and it's good for browning. Uncoated cookware is also better when you want food to stick a little—say, when you want particles of meat left behind in a pan after sautéing so you can make a flavorful pan sauce. **Porcelain coatings** are easy to maintain and they're tough (although they can be chipped).

Handles are typically made from tubular stainless steel, cast stainless steel, heat-resistant plastic, or wood. **Solid metal handles** are unwieldy but sturdy. Solid or **hollow metal handles** can get hot but can go from stovetop to broiler without damage. (Check the label first; some can warp or discolor when used that way.) **Lightweight plastic handles** won't get as hot as metal ones, but can't go in ovens above 350° F—and they occasionally break. While **wooden handles** stay cool, they can't go in the oven or dishwasher. And they may deteriorate over time. Handles are either welded, screwed, or riveted onto cookware. **Riveted handles** are the strongest. Some sets have removable handles that are used with different pieces, but we've found that the handles may fit with some pieces better than others.

Cookware with a specific shape simplifies certain cooking tasks. A skillet with **flared sides** aids sautéing or flipping omelets. **Straight sides** are better for frying. **Flat bottoms** work well on an electric range, especially a smoothtop.

HOW TO CHOOSE

Performance differences. Most people now opt for nonstick pots and pans, which requires little or no oil and clean easily. But uncoated cookware is better for browning and can stand up to metal utensils. While commercial-style sets are sturdy, they're also relatively heavy and their metal handles get hot. "Hand weigh" pieces as you shop, and imagine how they will feel when full. You might be happier using lightweight pots and pans with comfortable plastic handles that stay better insulated from the heat. Cast iron and copper are great for making certain dishes, but they may not be practical as basic cookware.

Recommendations. Choose a set with pots and pans that best match your cooking style. Over time, you can supplement your set by buying from open stock. Some people prefer individual pieces in different styles—a nonstick frying pan, say, and an uncoated stockpot.

Related CR Report: December 2002
Ratings: page 257

DISHWASHERS

Models selling for as little as $350 or so can excel at washing dishes. But they may not measure up to pricier models in quietness, water and energy usage, or features.

Spend $300 to $400 and you can get a dishwasher that's a little noisy but still does a good job cleaning dirty dishes without prerinsing. To get the best of everything—cleaning prowess plus quieter operation, more convenience features, efficiency with water and energy, even designer styling—you'll have to spend $600 or more.

A dirt sensor, once a premium feature, has made its way down to lower-priced models. That's not necessarily a plus. Sensors are designed to adjust water level to the amount of soil on dishes, but we've found them to be of marginal use in our tests. And they're not as energy efficient as the federal government's EnergyGuide stickers and Energy Star designations suggest: Those labels are based on water and energy usage with completely clean loads, not the soiled dishes you'll be washing in normal use.

WHAT'S AVAILABLE

Frigidaire (soon to be renamed Electrolux), GE, Maytag, and Whirlpool make most dishwashers and sell them under their own names, the names of associated brands, and sometimes the Sears Kenmore label. Whirlpool makes high-end KitchenAid, low-end Roper, and most Kenmore models. Maytag makes the high-end Jenn-Air, mid-priced Amana, and low-priced Admiral dishwashers. GE offers a wide range of choices under the GE label and also makes the value-priced Hotpoint. Asko, Bosch, and Miele are high-end European brands; Viking dishwashers are made by Asko.

Most models fit into a 24-inch-wide space under a kitchen countertop and are attached to a hot-water pipe, drain, and an electrical line. Compact models fit into narrower spaces. If you've got the room, it's now possible to get a wider, 30-inch dishwasher. Portable models in a finished cabinet can be rolled over to the sink and connected to the faucet. A "dishwasher in a drawer" design from Fisher & Paykel, a New Zealand–based company, has two stacked drawers that can be used simultaneously or individually, depending upon the number of dishes you need to wash.

Price range: $250 to $1,300 (domestic brands); $500 to $1,800 (foreign-made brands).

KEY FEATURES

Most models offer a choice of at least three **wash cycles**—Light, Normal, and Heavy—which should be enough for typical dish-washing jobs. **Rinse/Hold** lets you rinse dirty dishes before using the dishwasher on a full cycle. Other cycles offered on many models include **Pot Scrubber, Soak/Scrub,** and **China/Crystal,** none of which we consider crucial. Dishwashers often spray water from multiple places, or "levels," in the machine. Most models typically offer a choice of **drying** with or without heat.

Some dishwashers use two **filters** to keep wash water free of food that can be redistributed on clean dishes. A coarse outer filter captures large bits and a fine inner filter removes smaller particles. Most such models are self-cleaning: A spray arm cleans residue from the coarse filter during the rinse cycle, and a food-disposal **grinder** cuts up large food particles. Some of the more expensive dishwashers have a filter that you must pull out and clean manually; these are usually quieter than those with grinders. If noise is a concern, see if better **soundproofing**—often in the form of hard, rubbery insulation surrounded by a thick fiberglass blanket—is available as a step-up feature.

Sensors determine how dirty the dishes are, or how large the load is, and provide the appropriate amount of water. But in our tests with very dirty dishes, models with dirt sensors didn't clean noticeably better than those without. Sensors that determined load size did reduce water used on small loads, however, particularly when the dishes weren't very dirty. (Among the dishwashers in the most recent tests, only some under the Sears Kenmore brand had this feature.)

A **sanitizing wash** or **rinse option** that raises the water temperature above the typical 140° F doesn't necessarily mean improved cleaning. Remember, the moment you touch a dish while taking it out of the dishwasher, it's no longer sanitized.

Most dishwashers have **electronic touchpad controls**. On more expensive ones, the controls may be fully or partially hidden, or integrated, in the top edge of the door. The least expensive models have mechanical controls, usually operated by a dial and push buttons. Touchpads are the easiest to clean. **Dials** indicate progress through a cycle. Some electronic models digitally display time left in the wash cycle. Others merely show a "clean" signal. A **delayed-start** control lets you run the dishwasher at night, when utility rates may be lower. Some models offer **child-safety features,** such as locks for the door and controls.

Most dishwashers hold cups and glasses on top, plates on the bottom, and silverware in a basket. **Racks** can sometimes be adjusted to better fit your dishes. On some models, the top rack can be adjusted enough to let you put 10-inch dinner plates on both top and bottom racks simultaneously. Our most recent tests included a Maytag model with three racks instead of the usual two: The shelf-like third rack below the others can hold large, shallow items such as platters.

Other features that enhance flexibility include **adjustable** and **removable tines,** which flatten areas to accept bigger dishes, pots, and pans; **slots for silverware** that prevent "nesting"; **removable racks,** which enable loading and unloading outside the dishwasher; **stemware holders,** which steady wine glasses; **clips** to keep light plastic cups from overturning; and **fold-down shelves,** which stack cups in a double-tiered arrangement. Stainless-steel **tubs** may last virtually forever, whereas plastic ones can discolor. But plastic tubs usually have a warranty of 20 years, much longer than most people keep a dishwasher. In our tests, stainless-steel-lined models had a slightly shorter drying time but didn't wash any better.

If you want a front panel that matches your cabinets, you can buy a kit compatible with many dishwashers. Some higher-priced models are designed to be customized; they come without a front panel so you can choose your own, usually at a cost of several hundred dollars.

HOW TO CHOOSE

Performance differences. Most dishwashers tested by Consumer Reports do an excellent or very good job, with little or no spotting or redepositing of food. Manufacturers typically make a few different wash systems, with different "levels" and filters. According to our tests, the main differences among dishwashers are in water and energy use and in noise level. The quietest models are so unobtrusive you might hear them only if you're really listening. Cycle times vary from about 1½ hours to 2½ hours. Several machines that did an excellent job at washing dishes have cycle times of less than 2 hours.

While a dishwasher uses some electricity to run its motor and its drying heater or fan, about 80 percent of the energy is used to heat water, both in the home's water heater and in the machine itself. Long-term water efficiency differences can noticeably affect the cost of the machine over its life cycle. Dishwashers in recent tests used between 5 and 12 gallons in a normal cycle. The annual cost of operation might range from about $28 to $52 with a gas water heater, $48 to $85 with an electric water heater.

Dishwashers with dirt sensors aren't as efficient as you might think. If you run very dirty loads—especially without prerinsing—these dishwashers will use much more hot water, and require more energy to heat that water, than the labels indicate. To reduce energy costs with any dishwasher, don't prerinse, wait until you have a full load, and choose the lightest cycle that experience tells you will get your dishes clean.

Recommendations. The best-performing dishwashers aren't always the most expensive. You can get fine performance at a low price if you don't insist on the quietest operation and the most flexible loading. High-priced models, including foreign brands, offer styling and soundproofing that appeal to some buyers. Foreign brands are also often more energy efficient.

Compare prices of delivery and installation. Installation can run $100 to $200 or more; removing your old dishwasher may cost an extra $25 to $50.

Related CR Report: May 2003

Ratings: page 261

Reliability: page 28

DRYERS

On the whole, clothes dryers do a good job. The more sophisticated models do it with greater finesse.

Dryers are relatively simple. Their major differences are how they heat the air (gas or electricity) and how they're programmed to shut off once the load is dry (thermostat or moisture sensor). Gas models typically cost about $50 more than electric ones, but they're cheaper to operate.

Consumer Reports has found that dryers with a moisture sensor tend to recognize when laundry is dry more quickly than machines that use a traditional thermostat. Because they don't subject clothing to unnecessary heat, moisture-sensor models are easier on fabrics. And since they shut themselves off sooner, they use less energy. Sensors are now offered on many dryers, including some relatively low-cost ones. In our most recent tests, some $350 models had sensors.

WHAT'S AVAILABLE

The top four brands—GE, Maytag, Kenmore (Sears), and Whirlpool—account for just over 80 percent of dryer sales. Other brands include Amana (owned by Maytag), Frigidaire (owned by Electrolux), Hotpoint (made by GE), and KitchenAid and Roper (both made by Whirlpool). You may also run across smaller brands such as Crosley, Gibson, and White-Westinghouse, all of which are made by the larger brands. Asko, Bosch, and Miele are European brands. Fisher-Paykel is imported from New Zealand, LG from Korea, and Haier from China.

Full-sized models. These models generally measure between 27 and 29 inches in width—the critical dimension for fitting into cabinetry and closets. Front-mounted controls on some models let you stack the dryer atop a front-loading washer. Full-sized models vary in drum capacity from about 5 to 7½ cubic feet. Most dryers have ample capacity for typical wash loads. A larger drum can more easily handle bulky items such as queen-sized comforters.

Price range: electric, $200 to $800; gas, $250 to $850. Buying a more expensive model may get you more capacity and a few extra conveniences.

Space-saving models. Compacts, exclusively electric, are typically 24 inches wide, with a drum capacity roughly half that of full-sized models—about 3½ cubic feet. Aside from their smaller capacity, they perform much like full-sized machines. They can be stacked atop a companion washer, but shorter people may find it difficult to reach the dryer controls or the inside of the drum. Some dryers operate on 120 volts, others on 240 volts.

Price range: $380 to about $1,400.

Another space-saving option is a laundry center, which combines a washer and dryer in a single unit. Laundry centers come with either gas or electric dryers. There are full-sized (27 inches wide) or compact (24 inches wide) models available. The dryer component of a laundry center typically has a somewhat smaller capacity than a full-sized dryer. Models with electric dryers require a dedicated 240-volt power source.

Price range: $700 to $1,900.

KEY FEATURES

Full-sized dryers often have two or three **auto-dry cycles,** which shut them off when clothes reach the desired dryness. Each cycle might have a **More Dry** setting to dry clothes completely, and a **Less Dry** setting to leave clothes damp and ready for ironing. Setting the dryer in between those two extremes is a good idea. Manufacturers have refined the way dryers shut themselves off. As clothes tumble past a **moisture sensor,** electrical contacts in the drum sample their conductivity for surface dampness and relay signals to electronic controls. Dryers with a **thermostat** measure moisture indirectly by taking the temperature of exhaust air from the drum (the temperature rises as moisture evaporates). Moisture-sensor models are more accurate, sparing your laundry unnecessary drying and sparing you needlessly high energy bills.

SHOP SMART
Stainless-steel drums don't improve performance in dryers, as they can in washers.

Most dryers have a separate **temperature control** that lets you choose a lower heat for delicate fabrics, among other things. An **extended tumble** setting, sometimes called Press Care or Finish Guard, helps to prevent wrinkling when you don't remove clothes immediately. Some models continue to tumble without heat; others cycle on and off. An **express-dry cycle** is meant for drying small loads at high heat in less than a half hour. Large loads will take longer. **Touchpad electronic controls** found in higher-end models tend to be more versatile and convenient than mechanical dials and buttons—once you figure them out, that is. Some models let you save favorite settings. High-end dryers have a video display with a progression of menus that let you program specific settings for recall at any time.

A **top-mounted lint filter** may be somewhat easier to clean than one that resides inside the drum. Some models have a **warning light** that reminds you to clean the lint filter. It's important to clean the lint filter regularly to minimize any fire hazard. It's also advisable to use metal ducting (either rigid or flexible) instead of plastic or flexible foil, which can create a fire hazard by trapping lint.

Most full-sized models have a **drum light,** making it easy for you to spot stray items that may be clinging to the top of the drum or hiding in the back. Some models let you raise or lower the volume of an **end-of-cycle signal** or shut it off. A **rack** included with many machines attaches inside the drum and is intended to hold sneakers or other bulky items. Models with a **drop-down door** in front may fit better against a side wall, but a **side-opening door** may make it easier to access the inside of the drum.

HOW TO CHOOSE

Performance differences. We've found that nearly all machines dry ordinary laundry loads well. Models with a moisture sensor don't overdry clothes as much as models using a thermostat, saving energy as well as sparing fabric wear and tear. If you plan on putting the dryer near the kitchen or a bedroom, pay attention to the noise level. Some models are loud enough to drown out normal conversation. Virtually all dryers can accommodate the load from a typical washer, so capacity isn't an issue unless you want to dry bulky items such as comforters.

Recommendations. It's worthwhile to spend the $30 to $50 extra for a moisture-sensor model. More efficient drying will eventually pay for the extra cost. Purchase a gas dryer if you can. Although priced about $50 more than an electric model, a gas dryer usually costs about 25 cents less per load to operate, making up the price difference in a year or two of typical use. The extra hardware of a gas dryer, however, often makes it more expensive to repair.

Related CR Report: August 2003
Ratings: page 267
Reliability: page 28

FREEZERS

Chest freezers cost the least to buy and run, but self-defrost uprights are the winners for convenience.

If you buy box loads of burgers at a warehouse club or like to keep a few weeks' worth of dinner fixings on hand, the 4- to 6-cubic-foot freezer compartment in most refrigerators may seem positively Lilliputian. A separate freezer might be a good investment.

WHAT'S AVAILABLE

Most freezers sold in the U.S. are from one of two companies: Frigidaire, which makes models sold under the Frigidaire, GE, and Kenmore labels; and W.C. Wood, which makes models sold under its own name as well as Amana, Magic Chef, Maytag, and Whirlpool. There are two types of freezer: chests, which are essentially horizontal boxes, with a door that opens upward, and need to be defrosted manually; and uprights, which resemble a single-door refrigerator and come in self-defrost and manual-defrost versions.

Chests. These freezers vary most in capacity, ranging from 4 to 25 cubic feet. Aside from a hanging basket or two, chests are wide open, letting you put in even large, bulky items. Nearly all the claimed cubic-foot space is usable. The design makes chests more energy efficient and cheaper to operate than uprights. Cooling coils are built into the walls, so no fan is required to circulate the cold air. Because the door opens from the top, virtually no cold air escapes when you put in or take out food. But a chest's open design does make it hard to organize the contents. Finding something can require bending and, often, moving around piles of frozen goods. If you're short, you may find it difficult to extricate an item buried at the bottom (assuming you can remember it's stashed there). A chest also takes up more floor space than an upright. A 15-cubic-foot model is about 4 feet wide by 2½ feet deep; a comparable upright is just as deep but only 2 to 2½ feet wide.

Defrosting a chest can be a hassle, especially if it's fully loaded or has a thick coating of ice. Since all chests are manual-defrost, you have to unload the food, keep it frozen somewhere until the ice encrusting the walls has melted, remove the water that accumulates at the drain, then put back the food.

Price range: $140 to $550.

Self-defrost uprights. These models (sometimes called frost-free) have from 11 to 25 cubic feet of space. Like a refrigerator, they have shelves in the main compartment and on the door; some have pullout bins. This arrangement lets you organize and access contents, but reduces usable space by about 20 percent. Interior shelves can be removed or adjusted to fit large items. When you open the door of an upright, cold air spills out from the bottom while warm, humid air sneaks in at the top. That makes the freezer work harder and use more energy to stay cold, and temperatures may fluctuate a bit. These models compensate by using a fan to circulate cold air from the cooling coils, which are located in the back wall.

Self-defrosting involves heaters that turn on periodically to remove excess ice buildup, eliminating a tedious, messy chore but using extra energy: A self-defrost model costs about $20 a year more to run than a similar-sized chest. For many people, the convenience may be worth the extra cost. Self-defrosting models are a bit noisier than other types, an issue only if they're located near a living area rather than in the basement or garage. While freezers of old weren't recommended for use in areas that got very hot or cold, current self-defrost models should work fine within a wide ambient temperature range—typically 32° F to 110° F.

TECH TIP
Use a freezer thermometer, under $10 at hardware and houseware outlets, to see whether your freezer is maintaining the optimum temperature of 0 degrees F.

Price range: $350 to $750.

Manual-defrost uprights. These freezers have a capacity of 5 to 25 cubic feet, of which some 15 percent isn't usable. They cost less to buy and run than self-defrost models but aren't as economical as chests. Unlike their self-defrost counterparts, they don't have a fan to circulate cold air, which can result in uneven temperatures. Defrosting is quite a chore with some. The metal shelves in the main space are filled with coolant, so if you're not careful scraping off the ice you can damage the shelves. What's more, ice tends to cling to the shelves, so defrosting can take up to 24 hours. Other models have a "flash" defrost system that heats the cooling coils to quickly melt any frost. There's no need to scrape, but, as with any freezer, you must empty the contents before defrosting. Because a manual-defrost upright's shelves contain coolant, they can't be adjusted or removed to hold large items.

Price range: $160 to $600.

KEY FEATURES

While freezers are simpler than some other major appliances, there are several features worth looking for. **Interior lighting** makes it easier to find things, especially if you place the freezer in a dimly lit area. A **power-on light,** indicating that the freezer has power, is helpful. A **temperature alarm** lets you know when the freezer is too warm inside, such as after a prolonged power outage. (If you lose power, don't open the freezer door; food should remain frozen for about 24 to 48 hours.) A **quick-freeze** feature brings the freezer to its coldest setting faster by making it run continuously instead of cycling on and off; that's handy when you're adding a lot of food. The **flash-defrost** feature on some manual-defrost upright freezers can make defrosting easier and faster.

HOW TO CHOOSE

Performance differences. We've found that most freezers of a type are similar in terms of performance, efficiency, and convenience. The usable capacity of chest freezers is generally the same as the labeled capacity; the capacity of some manual-defrost and self-defrost uprights is somewhat less than what's claimed. Operating a new 15-cubic-foot freezer costs $30 to $55 a year at typical electric rates, depending on the type. That's in the same ballpark as a new refrigerator's annual energy cost.

Recommendations. A chest freezer gives you the most space and the best performance for the lowest purchase price and operating cost. But you'll have to defrost it periodically, a real chore. For freedom from defrosting and ease of access, go with a self-defrost upright. It will cost a little more to buy and operate than a chest, but the convenience may be worth it. We don't see a compelling reason to buy a manual-defrost upright when comparable self-defrosting models perform better and cost about the same. Manual models, however, do offer more usable space for the money than self-defrost models.

Related CR Report: September 2002

MICROWAVE OVENS

You'll see larger capacity, more power, sensors that detect doneness, and stylish designs. You can get a countertop model for under $100.

Microwave ovens, which built their reputation on speed, are also showing some smarts. Many automatically shut off when a sensor determines that the food is cooked or sufficiently heated. The sensor is also used to automate an array of cooking chores, with buttons labeled for frozen entrées, baked potatoes, popcorn, and other common items. Design touches include softer edges for less boxy styling, hidden controls for a sleeker look, stainless steel, and, for a few, a translucent finish.

WHAT'S AVAILABLE

Sharp leads the countertop microwave-oven market with almost 25 percent of sales, followed by Emerson, GE, Kenmore, Panasonic, and Samsung. GE sells the most over-the-range models.

Microwaves come in a variety of sizes, from compact to large. Most sit on the countertop, but a growing number sold—about 25 percent—mount over the range. Manufacturers are working to boost capacity without taking up more space by moving controls to the door and using recessed turntables and smaller electronic components. Be warned: To gauge capacity, manufacturers tend to tally every cubic inch, including corner spaces, where food on the turntable can't rotate. In fact, the diameter of the turntable is a more realistic measurement, and we base our calculation of usable capacity on that dimension.

Microwave ovens vary in the power of the magnetron, which generates the microwaves. Midsized and large ovens are rated at 900 to 1,350 watts, compact ovens at 600 to 800 watts. A higher wattage may heat food more quickly, but differences of 100 watts are probably inconsequential. Some microwave ovens have a convection feature—a fan and, often, a heating element—that lets you roast and bake, something you don't really do in a regular microwave.

Price range: $80 to $300 (countertop models); $300 to $765 (over-the-range); $330 to $700 (convection countertop or over-the-range).

SHOP SMART

If you like to see food as it cooks, get an oven with a black-screened window, which usually provides a clearer view than a white-screened one.

KEY FEATURES

A **turntable** rotates the food so it will heat more uniformly, but the center of the dish still tends to be cooler than the rest. Most turntables are removable for cleaning. With some models, you can turn off the rotation when, for instance, you're using a dish that's too large to rotate. The results won't be as good, however.

You'll find similarities in controls from

model to model. A **numeric keypad** is used to set cooking times and power levels. Most ovens have **shortcut keys** for particular foods, and for reheating or defrosting; some start immediately when you hit the shortcut key, others make you enter the food quantity or weight. Some models have an **automatic popcorn feature** that takes just one press of a button.

Pressing a **1-minute** or **30-second key** runs the oven at full power or extends the current cooking time. Microwave ovens typically have a number of **power levels.** We've found six to be more than adequate.

A **moisture sensor** gauges the steam that food emits when heated and uses that information to determine when the food is cooked. The small premium you pay for a sensor (about $10 to $30) is worth it. A few ovens have a **crisper pan** for making bacon or crisping pizza, since microwave cooking leaves food hot but not browned or crispy.

Over-the-range ovens vent themselves and the range, with a **fan** that usually turns on when heat is sensed from the range below. The exhaust can go outside or into the kitchen; if you want the oven to vent inside, you'll need a **charcoal filter** (sometimes included). An over-the-range microwave generally doesn't handle ventilation as well as a hood-and-blower ventilation system because it doesn't extend over the front burner.

HOW TO CHOOSE

Performance differences. Most microwave ovens are easy to use and competent at their main tasks of heating and defrosting. Nearly all the ones we've tested heated a baking dish full of cold mashed potatoes to a fairly uniform temperature. We found a few ovens that left large icy chunks while defrosting ground beef, however. Be skeptical about special technologies claimed to improve cooking evenness.

Recommendations. A large or midsized countertop model is a good choice. Compact models, though less expensive, typically have lower power ratings and don't heat as fast. Your kitchen layout may dictate an over-the-range microwave, but these models cost about twice as much as large countertop models, are heavy, and may take two people—or sometimes even an electrician—to install.

Related CR Report: January 2003
Reliability: page 30

MIXING APPLIANCES

Choosing the right machine for the way you prepare foods is the trick. You may find you need more than one.

Which food-prep appliance best suits your style and the foods you prepare? Blenders usually excel at mixing icy drinks. Stick-shaped immersion blenders are handy mostly for stirring powdered drinks or puréeing vegetables in a saucepan. Food processors are versatile machines that can chop, slice, shred, and purée many different foods. Mini-choppers are good for small jobs such as mincing garlic and chopping nuts. Hand mixers can handle light chores such as whipping cream or mixing cake batter. And powerful stand mixers are ideal for cooks who make bread and cookies from scratch.

WHAT'S AVAILABLE

Blenders. Rugged construction and increased power are driving blender sales.

Ice-crushing ability is one of the key attributes that shoppers look for in a blender, according to manufacturers. But appearance matters as well, since a blender is one of the appliances consumers are more likely to leave on the countertop than store in a cupboard. As a result, you'll see more colors and metallic finishes. Hamilton Beach and Oster account for more than 40 percent of countertop-blender sales. Other brands include Black & Decker, Braun, Cuisinart, GE, KitchenAid, Krups, Proctor-Silex, Sharp, Sunbeam, Vita-Mix, and Waring, a product pioneer.

Price range: $10 to $400.

Immersion blenders—stick-shaped handhelds with a swirling blade at the bottom—are on a power trip, with models juiced up to 200 watts or more. With these devices, power seems to make more of a difference than with countertop blenders. An immersion blender in the 100-watt range didn't even have the energy to mince onions in our tests. Immersion blenders are popular for stirring soups and puréeing and chopping vegetables. Increasingly, they're being paired with accessories such as beaters, whisks, and attachments to clean baby bottles. Braun controls the handheld segment of the market.

Price range: $30 to $100.

Food processors. Several brands have introduced multifunction models designed to do the job of two or more machines. Cuisinart's Smart Power Duet comes with an interchangeable food-processor container and a glass blender jar and blade. Either attachment fits on the motorized base. Another design trend is a mini-bowl insert that fits inside the main container for preparing smaller quantities. Newer designs tend to be sleek, with rounded corners. Dominant brands are Black & Decker, Cuisinart, and Hamilton Beach.

Price range: $30 to $300.

Mini-choppers. These are sold like little food processors. Black & Decker is the foremost name here.

Price range: $10 to $20.

Stand and hand mixers. As with blenders, the big push in mixers is for more power, which is useful for handling heavy dough. You'll find everything from heavy-duty models offering the most power and the largest mixing bowls to light-service machines that are essentially detachable hand mixers resting on a stand. Models vary in power from about 200 to 700 watts. Sales of light-duty, convenient hand mixers have held their own in recent years.

KitchenAid owns about half the stand-mixer market; Hamilton Beach and Sunbeam are the next best-selling brands.

Price range: $40 to $250.

Black & Decker, Hamilton Beach, and Sunbeam are the dominant brands among hand mixers.

Price range: $10 to $75.

KEY FEATURES

With blenders: Three to 16 **speeds** are the norm; power ratings range from about 300 to 500 or so watts. Manufacturers claim that higher wattage translates into better performance, but in our recent tests, lower-wattage models often outperformed beefier ones, turning out icy drinks faster and leaving them smoother in consistency. Three well-differentiated speeds are adequate; a dozen or more that are hard to distinguish from one another are overkill.

Containers are made of glass, plastic, or stainless steel, and have a capacity of about 5 to 8 cups. A glass container is heavier and more stable. In tests, the blenders with glass jugs tended to perform better because they didn't shake. Glass is also easier to keep clean. Plastic may scratch and is likely to absorb the smell of whatever is inside. Stainless-steel looks good, but prevents you from seeing how the blending is going.

A wide mouth makes loading food and washing easier; big and easy-to-read markings help you measure more accurately. A **pulse setting** lets you fine-tune blending time. **Touchpad controls** are easy to wipe clean. A **blade** that's permanently attached to the container (typical of the Warings) is harder to clean than a removable blade.

SHOP SMART
Dial controls are easier to clean than push buttons, but push buttons allow you to change from one speed to another with a single touch.

With food processors: All have a clear plastic **mixing bowl** and lid, an S-shaped metal **chopping blade** (and sometimes a duller version for kneading dough), and a **plastic food pusher** to safely prod food through the feed tube. Some models have a wider tube so you don't have to cut up vegetables—such as potatoes—to fit the opening. One speed is the norm, plus a **pulse setting** to control processing precisely. Bowl capacity ranges from around 3 cups to 14 cups (dry), with most models holding 6 to 11 cups. A **shredding/slicing disk** is standard on full-sized processors. Some come with a **juicer** attachment. **Touchpad controls** are becoming more commonplace, too.

Mini-choppers look like little food processors, with a capacity of 2 to 3 cups, but they're for small jobs only, like chopping small quantities of nuts or half an onion.

With mixers: Stand mixers generally come with one **bowl,** a **beater** or two, and a **dough hook.** Some mixers offer options such as **splash guards** to prevent flour from spewing out of the bowl, plus **attachments** to make pasta, grind meat, and stuff sausage. Stand mixers generally have 5 to 16 speeds; we think three well-differentiated settings is enough. You should be able to lock a mixer's power head in the Up position so it won't crash into the bowl when the beaters are weighed down with dough. Conversely, it should lock in the Down position to keep the beaters from kicking back when tackling stiff dough.

Just about any hand mixer is good for nontaxing jobs such as beating egg whites, mashing potatoes, or whipping cream. The **slow-start** feature on some mixers prevents ingredients from spattering when you start up, but you can achieve the same result by manually stepping through three or so speeds. An indentation on the underside of the motor housing allows the mixer to sit on the edge of a bowl without taking the beaters out of the batter.

HOW TO CHOOSE

Performance differences. With blenders, power, performance, and price don't always go hand in hand. In our recent tests, some modestly powered, inexpensive blenders turned out smooth-as-silk mixtures, while some bigger and fancier blenders left food pulpy or lumpy.

Most food processors we've tested can shred cheese, purée baby food, and slice tough, fibrous produce such as ginger and celery without missing a beat. Kneading dough takes power, and large models handled the job with aplomb. Smaller machines force you to split the dough into batches, and, even after we did so, some labored while performing the task.

Heavy-duty stand mixers can tackle tough tasks such as kneading large quantities of dense dough. In tests, light-duty, less powerful models strained and overheated under a heavy load.

Recommendations. Choose the right machine for your cooking tasks. Blenders excel at puréeing soup, crushing ice, and making fruit smoothies. A food processor is better at grating cheddar cheese and chopping meat, vegetables, and nuts. A processor can also slice and shred. Neither machine, however, can match a mixer's prowess at mashing potatoes or whipping cream to a light, velvety consistency. For those kinds of tasks, you can buy a perfectly adequate hand mixer for as little as $10.

Most blenders we tested are competent at various tasks; most have the oomph to crush ice. Most are convenient to use. Choose a blender by noting the specific strengths of the models we tested. A mid-sized food processor is probably the best choice for basic tasks. Bigger models are geared toward cooking enthusiasts who want to create picture-perfect salads and knead large quantities of pasta dough. Mini-choppers save space but aren't too versatile.

Not everyone needs a stand mixer. But if you're a dedicated baker, a stand mixer is useful and convenient. Some weigh more than 20 pounds or so, however; keep that in mind if you're planning to store your mixer in a cabinet and haul it out as needed.

Spending more for any of these appliances will typically get you touchpad controls, extra speeds and power, and perhaps designer styling or colors to match your kitchen's décor. You'll pay more for a blender with a stainless-steel or other metallic jar than you will for one with a plastic or glass container. You'll also pay more for a stand mixer with lots of power and extra-sturdy construction.

Related CR Report: July 2003
Ratings: page 239

RANGES, COOKTOPS AND WALL OVENS

Choices can be confusing, but you don't have to spend top dollar for impressive performance with high-end touches.

If you're in the market for cooking appliances, it pays to decide whether you want a freestanding range (with a built-in oven) or a separate cooktop and wall oven. A cooktop/wall oven combo may offer you more flexibility with your kitchen design, although ranges can be less expensive than components. You may also need to make a decision regarding gas, electricity, or both; gas of course, is only possible if you have access to a gas hookup.

Electric ranges include the traditional coil-element type and the newer smoothtop models, in which a sheet of ceramic glass covers the heating elements. Both types of cooktop elements offer quick heating and the ability to maintain low heat levels.

Gas ranges use burners. Burners—even the high-power variety—tend to heat more slowly than the fastest electric coil elements because the heavy cast-iron grates sometimes slow the process by absorbing heat. On the other hand, an advantage to burners is being able to see how high or low you are adjusting the flame. Many high-end gas stoves are "professional-style" models with beefy knobs, heavy cast-iron grates, stainless-steel construction, and four or more high-powered burners. These high-heat behemoths can cost thousands, and typically require a special range hood and blower system. They may also need special shielding and a reinforced floor.

You'll find more and more shared characteristics between electric and gas ranges. For example, some gas models have electric warming zones, and "gas-on-glass" versions blend the visual response of a flame with a smoothtop's easier cleaning by placing the burners over a smooth ceramic surface. What's more, a growing number of high-end gas ranges pair gas cooktop burners with an electric oven. Fortunately, you don't have to spend top dollar for top cooking performance.

WHAT'S AVAILABLE

GE and Whirlpool are the leading makers of ranges, cooktops, and wall ovens. Other major brands include Frigidaire, Jenn-Air, Kenmore (Sears), KitchenAid, and Maytag. Mainstream brands have established high-end offshoots, such as GE Profile, Kenmore Elite, and Whirlpool Gold. High-end, pro-style brands include Bosch, Dacor, DCS, GE Monogram, Thermador, Viking, and Wolf.

SHOP SMART
Porcelain-coated oven racks ease cleanup compared with bare metal.

Freestanding, slide-in, and drop-in ranges. Freestanding ranges can fit in the middle of a kitchen counter or at the end. Widths are usually 20 to 40 inches, although most are 30 inches wide. They typically have oven controls on the vertical backguard. Slide-in models eliminate the side panels to blend into the countertop, with their controls up front, below the cooktop surface. Drop-in ranges are similar, but they rest atop a toe-kick-level cabinet and typically lack a storage drawer. Ovens can be self-cleaning or require manual cleaning, although most mainstream ranges and a growing number of pro-style models now come with a self-cleaning feature.

Price range: $400 to $1,500.

Pro-style ranges. Larger than freestanding ranges, these can be anywhere from 30 to 60 inches wide. The biggest include six or eight burners, a grill or griddle, and a double oven. Many have a convection feature, and some have an infrared gas broiler. You usually don't get a storage drawer, and some lack sealed burners, which keep crumbs from falling beneath the cooktop.

Price range: $2,500 to $8,000.

Cooktops. You can install a cooktop on a kitchen island or anywhere else counter space allows. As with freestanding ranges, cooktops can be electric coil, electric smoothtop, or gas. Paired with a wall oven, a cooktop adds flexibility, since it can be located separately. Most cooktops are 30 inches wide and are made of porcelain-coated steel or ceramic glass, with four elements or burners. Some are 36 or 48 inches wide and have space for an extra burner or two.

Modular cooktops let you mix and match parts any time you choose at home—removing burners and adding a grill, say—although you'll pay more for that added flexibility. Preconfigured cooktops are less expensive.

Price range: $200 to $1,300 (electric); $300 to $1,800 (gas).

Wall ovens. These are mostly electric and usually offer a convection setting (this usually adds $300 to the price). Width is typically 24, 27, or 30 inches. Best of all, you can eliminate having to bend to put things in or take things out by installing the oven at waist or eye level—although you can also nest it under a countertop if that suits your needs.

Price range: $400 to more than $3,500 for double-oven models.

KEY FEATURES

On all ranges: Look for easy-cleaning features such as a **glass** or **porcelain backguard** instead of a painted one; **seamless corners** and **edges**, especially where the cooktop joins the backguard; and a **raised edge** around the cooktop to contain spills.

On electric ranges and cooktops: Freestanding ranges typically locate controls on the backguard, with burner controls to the left and right, and oven controls in between, giving you a quick sense of which control operates which element. Backguard controls clustered in the center offer the advantage of being visible when tall pots sit on the rear heating elements. On most electric cooktops, controls take up room on the surface; some models, however, have electronic touchpads that allow the entire cooktop to be flush with the counter.

Coil elements, the most common and least expensive electric option, are easy to replace if they break. On an electric range with coil elements, look for a **prop-up top** for easier cleaning. Deep **drip pans** made of porcelain can better contain spills and ease cleaning.

Smoothtop models generally use radiant heat, although some halogen units are available. **Radiant elements** take about six seconds to redden when first turned on; **halogen elements** redden immediately. Some smoothtops have **expandable elements,** which let you switch between a large, high-power element and a small, low-power element contained within it. Some smoothtops also include a **low-wattage element** for warming plates or keeping just-cooked food at the optimal temperature.An elongated **"bridge" element** spans two burners—a nicety for accommodating rectangular or odd-shaped cookware, such as a large roasting pan or a fish poacher. Many have at least one **hot-surface light**—a key safety feature, since the surface can remain hot long after the elements have been turned off. The safest setup includes a dedicated, prominently placed "hot" light for each element.

Most electric ranges and cooktops have one large **higher-wattage burner** in front and one in back. An **expanded simmer setting** in some electric models lets you fine-tune the simmer setting on one burner for, say, melting chocolate or keeping a sauce from getting too hot.

On gas ranges and cooktops: Most gas ranges have four **burners** in three sizes, measured in British thermal units per hour (Btu/hr.): one or two medium-power burners (about 9,000 Btu/hr.), a small burner (about 5,000 Btu/hr.), and one or two large ones (about 12,000 Btu/hr.). We recommend a model with one or more burners of about 12,000 Btu/hr. for quick heating. On a few models, the burners automatically reignite if the flame goes out for any reason.

For easier cleaning, look for **sealed burners** and **removable burner pans** and **caps.** Gas ranges typically have **knob controls;** the best rotate 180 degrees or more for flame adjustment. Try to avoid knobs that have adjacent "off" and "low" settings and those that rotate no more than 90 degrees between High and Low.

Spending more on a gas stove or cooktop gets you heavier **grates** made of porcelain-coated cast iron, multiple high-power burners, and **stainless-steel accents.**

On pro-style ranges: These models have brass or cast-iron burners, all of which offer very high output (usually about 15,000 Btu/hr.). The burners are sometimes nonsealed, with hard-to-clean crevices, though sealed burners are appearing on some models. Large knobs are another typical pro-style feature, as are continuous grates designed for heavy-duty use. The latter, however, can be unwieldy to remove for cleaning.

On ovens: Electric-range ovens used to have an edge over gas ovens in roominess, but we've recently found roomy ovens among both types. Note, though, that an oven's usable **capacity** may be less than what manufacturers claim, because they don't take protruding broiler elements and other features into account.

A **self-cleaning cycle** uses high heat to burn off spills and splatters. Most ranges have it, although some pro-style gas models still don't. An **automatic door lock** on most self-cleaning models is activated during the cleaning cycle, then unlocks when the oven has cooled. Also useful is a **self-cleaning countdown** display, which shows the time left in the cycle.

Higher-priced ranges and wall ovens often include a **convection mode,** which uses a fan and, sometimes, an electric element to circulate heated air. In our tests, the convection mode usually shaved cooking time for a large roast and, in some cases, baked large cookie batches more evenly because of the circulating air. But the fan can take up valuable oven space. Another cooking technology, found in the GE Advantium over-the-range oven, uses a **halogen heating bulb** as well as microwaves.

A **variable-broil** feature in most electric ovens offers adjustable settings for foods such as fish or thick steaks that need slower or faster cooking. Ovens with **12-hour shutoff** turn off automatically if you leave the oven on for that long; most models allow you to disable this feature. A **child lockout** lets you disable oven controls.

Manufacturers are updating oven controls across the price spectrum. **Electronic touchpad controls** are a high-end feature now showing up in more lower-priced ranges. A **digital display** makes it easier to set the temperature and keep track of it. A **cook time/delay start** lets you set a time for the oven to start and stop cooking; remember, however, that you shouldn't leave most foods in a cold oven very long. An **automatic oven light** comes on when the door opens, although some ovens have a switch-operated light. A **temperature probe,** to be inserted into meat or poultry, indicates when you've obtained a precise internal temperature.

Oven **windows** come in various sizes. Those without a decorative grid usually offer the clearest view, although some cooks may welcome the grid to hide pots, pans, and other cooking utensils sometimes stored inside the oven.

HOW TO CHOOSE

Performance differences. Almost every range, cooktop, or wall oven we've tested cooks well. Differences are in the details. An electric range may boil a pot of water a bit more quickly than a gas range, while a gas model can sometimes be adjusted with more precision. Our tests have also shown that the powerful burners on some pro-style gas ranges may not be able to simmer some foods without scorching them. Among electric ranges, smoothtops are displacing coil-tops, but they aren't necessarily better or more reliable. A smoothtop's glass surface can ease cleaning. However, you need to wipe up sugary spills immediately to avoid pitting the surface; also, fussy people may find themselves spending extra time keeping the top clean and free of streaks. Be aware that the doors and windows of some ovens can become fairly hot during self-cleaning, while others are left with a permanent residue.

Recommendations. Decide on the type you want, then consider the features, price, and brand reliability. You must also factor in your cabinetry and floor plan, and whether or not you have access to a gas hookup. A freestanding range generally offers the best value; a very basic electric or gas model costs $400 or less. Smoothtop electric ranges cost $100 to $200 more than those with coil elements. Spending more than $1,000 buys lots of extras, including electronic controls and pro-style touches such as stainless-steel trim. Expect to pay thousands for a real pro-style model. In wall ovens, the convection feature adds hundreds of dollars to the price.

Related CR Report: March 2003, September 2003
Ratings: page 304, 255, 334
Reliability: page 30

REFRIGERATORS

Top-freezer and bottom-freezer fridges generally give you more for your money than their side-by-side siblings—and cost less to run.

If you're shopping for a new refrigerator, you're probably considering models that are fancier than your current fridge. The trend is toward spacious models with flexible, more efficiently used storage space. Useful features such as spillproof, slide-out glass shelves and temperature-controlled compartments, once only in expensive refrigerators, are now practically standard in midpriced models. Stainless-steel doors are a stylish but costly extra. Built-in refrigerators appeal to people who want to customize their kitchens, but they're expensive. Some mainstream models offer a built-in-style look for less.

Replacing an aging refrigerator may save you in electric bills, since refrigerators are more energy efficient now than they were a decade ago. The Department of Energy toughened its rules in the early 1990s and imposed even stricter requirements in July 2001 for this appliance, which is among the top electricity users in the house.

WHAT'S AVAILABLE

Only a handful of companies actually manufacture refrigerators. The same or very similar units may be sold under several brand names. Frigidaire, General Electric, Kenmore, and Whirlpool account for about three-quarters of top-freezer sales. For side-by-side models, these brands and Maytag account for more than 80 percent of sales. Brands offering bottom-freezers include Amana, GE, Jenn-Air, Kenmore, Kitchen Aid, LG, Maytag, Samsung, and Whirlpool. Mainstream manufacturers have introduced high-end sub-brands such as GE Profile and Kenmore Elite. Five brands specialize in built-ins: Sub-Zero, Viking, GE Monogram, Jenn-Air, and KitchenAid. Amana, GE, Jenn-Air, KitchenAid, LG, and Whirlpool offer built-in-style, or "cabinet depth" models. LG and Samsung, brands new to the U.S. market, offer side-by-side, top-freezer, and bottom-freezer types.

Top-freezer models. Accounting for almost two-thirds of models sold, these are generally less expensive to buy and run—and more space efficient—than comparably sized side-by-side models. Width ranges from about 24 to 36 inches. The eye-level freezer offers easy access. Fairly wide refrigerator shelves make it easy to reach the back, but you have to bend to reach the bottom shelves. Nominal, labeled capacity ranges from about 10 to almost 27 cubic feet. (Our measurements show that a refrigerator's usable capacity is typically about 60 to 80 percent of its nominal capacity.)

Price range: $450 to more than $1,200, depending on size and features.

Side-by-side models. These are by far the most fully featured fridges, and are where you'll most often find through-the-door ice and water dispensers—among the most requested consumer feature—as well as temperature-controlled bins and rapid ice-making cycles. Their narrow doors are handy in tight spaces. High, narrow compartments make finding stray items easy in front (harder in the back); they may not hold such items as a sheet cake or a large turkey. Compared with top- and bottom-freezer models, a higher proportion of capacity goes to freezer space. Side-by-sides are typically large—30 to 36 inches wide, with nominal capacity of 19 to 30 cubic feet. They're much more expensive than similar-sized top-freezer models and are less efficient in terms of space and energy use.

SHOP SMART
What you gain in style with built-ins and cabinet-depth models you lose in convenience. Because they are shallow, they have less usable space than comparable refrigerators.

Price range: $800 to more than $2,400.

Bottom-freezer models. A small but growing part of the market, these put frequently used items at eye level. Fairly wide refrigerator shelves provide easy access. Though you must bend to locate items in the freezer, even with models that have a pull-out basket, you will probably do less bending overall because the refrigerator is at eye level. Bottom-freezers are a bit pricier than top-freezers and offer less capacity (up to 25 cubic feet) relative to their external dimensions because of the inefficiency of the pull-out bin.

Price range: $700 to $1,800.

Built-in models. These are generally side-by-side and bottom-freezer models. They show their commercial heritage, often having fewer standard amenities and less soundproofing than lower-priced "home" models. Usually 25 to 26 inches front to back, they fit nearly flush with cabinets and counters. Their compressor is on top, making them about a foot taller than regular refrigerators. Most can accept a front panel that matches the kitchen's décor. Side-by-side models in this style are available in 42-inch and 48-inch widths (vs. the more typical 36-inch width). You can even obtain a built-in pair: a separate refrigerator and freezer mounted together in a 72-inch opening.

Price range: $4,000 to over $6,000.

Built-in-style, or cabinet-depth models. These freestanding refrigerators offer the look of a built-in for less money. These are available mostly in side-by-side and bottom-freezer styles, with a few top-freezers. Many accept panels for a custom look.

Price range: $1,500 to $2,500.

KEY FEATURES

Interiors are ever more flexible. Adjustable door bins and shelves can be moved to fit tall items. Some shelves can be cranked up and down without removing the contents. Some split shelves can be adjusted to different heights independently. With other shelves, the front half of the shelf slides under the rear portion to provide clearance.

Shelf snuggers—sliding brackets on door shelves—secure bottles and jars. A few models have a wine rack that stores a bottle horizontally.

Glass shelves are easier to clean than wire racks. Most glass shelves have a raised, sealed rim to keep spills from dripping over. Some slide out. Pull-out freezer shelves or bins give easier access. An alternative is a bottom-freezer with a sliding drawer.

A **temperature-controlled drawer** can be set to be several degrees cooler than the rest of the interior, useful for storing meat or fish. Crispers have controls to maintain humidity. Our tests have shown that, in general, temperature-controlled drawers work better than plain drawers; results for humidity controls are less clear-cut. See-through drawers let you see at a glance what's inside.

Curved doors give the refrigerator a distinctive profile and retro look. Most manufacturers have at least one curved-door model in their lineups.

Step-up features include a variety of finishes and colors. Every major manufacturer has a stainless-steel model that typically costs significantly more than one with a standard pebbled finish. Another alternative is a smooth, glass-like finish.

Novel color choices include biscuit, bisque, or linen instead of almond. Several lines include black models, and KitchenAid has a cobalt-blue finish to match its small appliances. Kenmore, LG, Samsung, and Whirlpool have models with a stainless-steel look that unlike stainless resists fingerprints and accepts magnets.

Most models have an **icemaker** in the freezer (or give you the option of installing one yourself). Typically producing 3 or 4 pounds of ice per day, an icemaker reduces freezer space by about a cubic foot. The ice bin is generally located below the icemaker, but some new models have it on the inside of the freezer door, providing a bit more usable volume. A through-the-door ice-and-water dispenser is common in side-by-side refrigerators. Top- and bottom-freezer refrigerators don't offer through-the-door **ice-and-water dispensers,** but alternatively, some models have water dispensers inside the main compartment.

With many models, the icemaker and/or water dispenser includes a **water filter,** designed to reduce lead, chlorine, and other impurities, a capability you may or may not need. An icemaker or water dispenser will work without one. You can also have a filter installed in the tubing that supplies water to the refrigerator.

Once a refrigerator's controls are set, there should be little need to adjust temperature. Still, accessible controls are an added convenience.

HOW TO CHOOSE

Performance differences. Most refrigerators—even the least expensive—keep things cold very well. Many models are fairly quiet, and some are very quiet. But configurations and convenience features vary considerably. Less expensive models usually lack spillproof glass shelves, large bins, and easily arranged shelves.

Energy efficiency does vary, according to CONSUMER REPORTS tests. An efficient model that costs more may be a better buy in the long run than a cheaper but less-efficient model.

Refrigerators made as of July 2001 were required to meet efficiency standards up to 30 percent more stringent than those in place before. Some models on the market have an Energy Star designation; that means they're at least 10 percent more efficient than what the 2001 regulations require. Yellow EnergyGuide stickers, which include information on energy usage, are required on all refrigerators. As of 2003, new models must be made without hydrochlorofluorocarbons, which can harm the earth's ozone layer.

Recommendations. Top-freezer models give you the most refrigerator for the money. But kitchen layout or personal preference may necessitate another type. Most built-in models offer no performance or efficiency advantages. In general, larger refrigerators have more features. An icemaker adds $50 to $75 to the price; a through-the-door water dispenser adds about $100. Models with an interior water dispenser are increasingly common, as are models with a built-in filtration system.

Some refrigerators can be placed flush against a side wall; others need space for doors to swing open. Top- and bottom-freezer models have reversible hinges so they can open to either side. The doors on side-by-side models require the least amount of front clearance space.

CONSUMER REPORTS surveys show that the presence of an icemaker or a water dispenser tends to increase the chances of needing a repair. A recent survey of refrigerators found that almost 25 percent of 5-year-old side-by-side models with an icemaker and a water dispenser had needed a repair, compared with almost 15 percent for top-freezer models of the same age with an icemaker and just 10 percent for top-freezer models without an icemaker.

TECH TIP
To increase your refrigerator's efficiency and cut down on energy costs, clean the condenser coil once or twice a year.

Considering cost of repair, cost of replacement, and technology improvements, you'll probably want to fix a broken top-freezer that's less than five years old or a side-by-side that's less than six years old. You may want to consider repairing a model up to eight years old if you're satisfied with its performance. You'll probably want to replace an older model that's broken to take advantage of a new model's features and reduced energy costs.

Related CR Report: July 2003
Ratings: page 312
Reliability: page 31

TOASTING APPLIANCES

Some people like the straightforwardness of a basic toaster. Others prefer an appliance that toasts, bakes, and more. Either way, you can get good performance without spending a lot.

Piggybacking on the popularity of bagels, toaster pastries, and frozen, ready-to-heat omelets, manufacturers are redesigning the basic toaster for improved functionality. What's more, new models have styling and cachet that can make them the sharpest-looking appliance on the counter.

Developments in toaster functionality include a setting for bagels, which browns only a single side; a cancel mode to interrupt the toast cycle; and nonstick slots. "Smart" toasters with microchips and heat sensors promise perfect doneness from first batch to last (they don't always deliver, we've found). Some models incorporate an LED indicator to show the darkness selection and to count down the time remaining in a particular cycle.

You'll see more toasters with rounded sides and that retro look, and more extra-wide and long-slot models. Black & Decker has introduced a toaster with clear glass sides that let you watch the browning. West Bend has the unorthodox Slide Thru toaster: You insert the bread in the slot and remove it through a door at the base. The door doubles as a "dressing table" for spreading butter or jam.

You don't need a $100 or $200 toaster to get perfectly browned bread. For $20 or less, you can buy a competent product that will make decent toast, two slices at a time, with all the basics: a darkness control to adjust doneness, a push-down lever to raise or lower the bread, and cool-touch housing to keep you from burning your fingers.

And of course there's life beyond the toaster. With increased demand for multifunction appliances—and the space savings that result from having one machine that can do the work of two—many people opt for a hybrid appliance that can not only toast but also bake muffins, heat frozen entrées, or broil a small batch of burgers or a small chicken.

WHAT'S AVAILABLE

Toastmaster invented the pop-up toaster in the 1920s and now shares shelf space with other venerable brands of toasters and toaster ovens such as Black & Decker, Hamilton Beach, and Sunbeam, plus players such as Cuisinart, DeLonghi, Kenmore (Sears), KitchenAid, Krups, Rival, T-Fal, and West Bend. Dualit makes old-fashioned, commercial-style, heavy-gauge stainless-steel toasters.

Toasters come in a variety of exterior finishes, such as chrome and brushed metal. Of the 12 million toasters sold annually, two-slice models outsell four-slicers 4 to 1. Nearly three-quarters of toaster ovens sold are equipped with a broiler function. Most toaster ovens are countertop models, though a few under-the-cabinet models are sold.

Price range: $20 to $100 and up (toasters); $30 to $100 and up (toaster ovens and broilers).

KEY FEATURES

For all the bells and whistles on today's toasters, a simple **dial** or **lever** to set for darkness is sufficient. **Electronic controls** regulate shadings and settings with a touchpad instead. A **pop-up control** lets you eject a slice early if you think it's done. A **toast boost,** or **manual lift,** lets you raise smaller items such as English muffins above the slots so there's no need to fish around with a fork, a potentially dangerous exercise if you don't unplug the toaster. Another safety note: Underwriters Laboratory (UL) now requires that toasters shut off at the end of the toasting cycle even if a piece of bread is stuck in the carriage.

A few models offer an astounding (and unnecessary) 63 time and temperature toasting options. Recent toaster-oven innovations include a **liner** that can be removed for cleaning, and various ways to speed up the cooking process, including use of a **convection fan** or **infrared heat.**

A **removable crumb tray** facilitates cleaning. **Nonstick slots** also make it easy to remove baked-on goop left by toaster pastries. More and more models incorporate a control that automatically defrosts and toasts in a single step, nice if you regularly prepare items such as frozen hash-brown patties. With toaster ovens, a **removable cooking cavity** makes cleaning easier.

HOW TO CHOOSE

Performance differences. Most toasters make respectable toast. But few models, including those with microchips and heat sensors, toast to perfection. In our tests, problems included toast that came out darker on one side than the other and successive batches that were inconsistently browned.

As in the past, toaster ovens as a group were not as good as their plainer cousins at making toast—though they do let you keep an eye on the browning process. Their ability to bake and broil does make them more versatile than toasters. Elegant styling and a sleek design can carry a high price tag, but may offer little else.

Recommendations. If all you want is toast, a $20 toaster will do the job just fine. Toaster ovens and broilers offer versatility so you needn't, for example, heat up your big oven to warm leftovers or use the stove to melt a grilled-cheese sandwich.

Related CR Report: December 2001

WASHING MACHINES

Nearly all do a fine job of washing. Top-loaders are usually less expensive, but front-loaders cost less to operate because they use less water and energy.

Virtually any washing machine will get your clothing clean. Front-loaders do the job using less water, including hot water, and thus less energy than most top-loaders. But top-loading washing machines are becoming more energy efficient. New, stricter Department of Energy standards regarding energy and hot-water use and water extraction become effective as of January 2004, and standards will become even more stringent in 2007. (Front-loaders already meet the tougher requirements, as do some top-loaders.)

Two top loading designs—the Calypso from Whirlpool and Kenmore, and one Fisher & Paykel model—work somewhat like front-loaders. They fill partially with water and spray clothes with a concentrated detergent solution. They outscored other top-loaders in our tests of water and energy efficiency.

In the past few years, front-loading washers, which you load the same way you would a dryer, have gained in popularity. Today about 15 percent of newly purchased washing machines are front-loaders, up from less than 5 percent several years ago.

WHAT'S AVAILABLE

The top four brands—GE, Maytag, Kenmore (Sears), and Whirlpool—account for just over 80 percent of washing machine sales. Other brands include Amana (owned by Maytag), Frigidaire (owned by Electrolux), Hotpoint (made by GE), and KitchenAid and Roper (both made by Whirlpool). You may also run across smaller brands such as Crosley, Gibson, and White-Westinghouse, all of which are made by the larger brands. Asko, Bosch, and Miele are European brands. Fisher-Paykel is imported from New Zealand, LG from Korea, and Haier from China.

Top-loaders. Most top-loaders fill the tub with enough water to cover the clothing, then agitate it. Because they need to move the laundry around to ensure thorough cleaning, these machines have a smaller effective load capacity than front-loaders—generally about 12 to 16 pounds. The Calypso models from Kenmore and Whirlpool are unusual in that they have a "wash plate," rather than an agitator, to move clothes around. That enables them to hold 18-pound loads and makes them gentler on clothing.

It's easier to load laundry and to add items midcycle to a top-loader. But top loaders are also noisier than front-loaders. Top-loaders are generally 27 to 29 inches wide.

Price range: $200 to $1,000.

Front-loaders. Front-loaders get clothes clean by tumbling them in the water. Clothes are lifted to the top of the tub, then dropped into the water below. The design usually makes front-loaders gentler on clothing and more adept at handling unbalanced loads. They can typically handle 12 to 20 pounds of laundry. Front-loading washing machines perform best with front-loader detergent, which doesn't produce as many suds as detergent intended for top-loaders. Like top-loaders, they're typically 27 to 29 inches wide.

Price range: $600 to $1,500.

Space-saving options. Compact models are typically 24 inches wide or less and wash 8 to 12 pounds of laundry. A compact front-loader can be stacked with a compact dryer. (Many full-sized front-loaders can also be stacked with a matching dryer.) Some compact models can be stored in a closet and rolled out to be hooked up to the kitchen sink.

Price range: $450 to $1,700.

Washer-dryer laundry centers combine a washer and dryer in one unit, with the dryer located above the washer. These can be full-sized (27 inches wide) or compact (24 inches wide). The full-sized models hold about 12 to 14 pounds, the compacts a few pounds less. Performance is generally comparable to that of full-sized machines.

Price range: $700 to $1,900.

KEY FEATURES

A porcelain-coated steel **inner tub** can rust if the porcelain is chipped. Stainless-steel or plastic tubs won't rust. A porcelain top/lid resists scratching better than a painted one.

High-end models often have **touchpad controls;** others have traditional **dials.** Controls should be legible, easy to push or turn, and logically arranged. A plus: **lights** or **signals** that indicate the cycle. On some top-loaders, an **automatic lock** during the spin cycle keeps children from opening the lid. Front-loaders lock at the beginning of a cycle but can usually be opened by interrupting the cycle, although some doors remain shut briefly after the machine stops.

Front-loaders automatically set wash speed according to the **fabric cycle** selected, and some also automatically set the spin speed. Top-loaders typically provide **wash/spin speed combinations,** such as Regular, Permanent Press, and Delicate (or Gentle). A few models also allow an **extra rinse** or **extended spin.**

Front-loaders and some top-loaders set water levels automatically, ensuring efficient use of water. Some top-loaders can be set for four or more levels; three or four are probably as many as you would need.

Most machines establish wash and rinse temperatures by mixing hot and cold water in preset proportions. For incoming cold water that's especially cold, an **automatic temperature control** adjusts the flow for the correct wash temperature. A **time-delay feature** lets you program the washer to start at a later time, such as at night, when your utility rates are low. **Automatic bleach, detergent,** and **fabric-softener dispensers** release powder or liquid at the appropriate time. Bleach dispensers also prevent spattering. Some machines offer a **hand-washing cycle.**

TECH TIP
Chlorine bleach loses effectiveness if added to the wash too soon, so wait 5 minutes or so into the wash cycle. Consider a washer with an automatic bleach dispenser that will release the bleach at the proper time.

HOW TO CHOOSE

Performance differences. All washing machines get clothes clean. In our tests, differences in washing ability tended to be slight. Differences were more apparent in water and energy efficiency and in noisiness. Front-loaders have the edge on all counts.

The water efficiency of any washing machine rises with larger loads, but overall, front-loaders use far less water per pound of laundry and excel in energy efficiency.

Washing six loads of laundry per week, the most water-efficient front-loaders can save almost 6,000 gallons of water a year.

Using electricity to heat the water, and using an electric dryer, the most energy-efficient front-loaders can save you about $60 worth of electrical energy annually compared with the least efficient top-loader. (Costs are based on 2003 national average utility prices; differences would narrow with a gas water heater, gas dryer, full loads, or carefully set water levels.) Front-loaders are generally quieter than top-loaders except when draining or spinning, and they are usually gentler on your laundry.

Recommendations. Top-loaders generally cost less than front-loaders and do a fine job. Best values: midpriced top-loaders with few features, which you can usually find for less than $500. Bells and whistles such as extra wash/spin options or time delay don't necessarily improve performance. While front-loaders are usually more expensive to buy, they can cost significantly less to operate, especially in areas where water or energy rates are very high. In general, though, the savings are not likely to make up the price difference over a washer's typical life span.

Buying one of the more expensive top-loading or front-loading models can get you larger capacity and features that give you more flexibility, such as programming frequently used settings.

Related CR Report: August 2003
Ratings: page 335
Reliability: page 34

HOME & YARD

What's New in Home & Yard Equipment

Innovations, often prompted by tougher state and federal environmental regulations, are making home and yard gear easier and safer to use, as well as friendlier to the environment. So buying a new piece of equipment rather than nursing along an old one may be a good move. Here are trends you'll see this year:

"Greener" products. Stricter Department of Energy (DOE) rules have made today's room air conditioners more efficient. Government rules for emissions by lawn mowers and other gasoline-powered yard tools are designed to reduce emissions by hundreds of thousands of tons per year. Emissions aren't the only type of pollutant; dozens of towns and cities have enacted laws designed to quiet leaf blowers. Manufacturers are equipping a growing number of cordless drills and other tools with nickel-metal hydride batteries that can be safely thrown away with ordinary refuse. "Green" and "healthy" claims turn up in ads for vacuum cleaners, some of which have a high-efficiency particulate-air (HEPA) filter, designed to trap dust and allergens sucked up by vacuuming. But CONSUMER REPORTS tests have shown that many models without a HEPA filter can keep the air as free of potentially irritating particles.

Friendlier, safer controls. Many room air conditioners now have touchpad controls instead of traditional mechanical dials. Out in the yard, clutchless hydrostatic transmissions on a growing number of ride-on mowers and tractors make mowing go more smoothly. All these machines stop the engine and blade when you leave the seat. And even the least expensive push and self-propelled power mowers stop the blade when you release the safety handle. Some higher-priced models stop the blade but not the engine, eliminating the need to restart the mower.

More capability—and more luxury. Lawn and garden tractors can power extra-cost accessories that let you plow and tow, as well as throw snow. Many models have become the backyard equivalent of sport-utility vehicles with their large engines and ever-wider cutting swaths. You'll also find a growing number of "zero-turn-radius" mowers and tractors that can turn 360 degrees in one spot to better maneuver around obstacles.

Built-in gas barbecue grills with stainless-steel finishes now rival multithousand-dollar, professional-style kitchen ranges in size and price. You'll also find stainless-steel stand-alone grills priced at $1,000 and beyond—though increasingly, you can get grills with a thousand-dollar look for about $500.

More shopping options. Home and yard products are sold over the Internet through sites such as Amazon.com, Home-depot.com, Lowes.com, and Sears.com. Such online sites can be useful, especially as research tools, but there's still a lot to be said for the local hardware store or home center. You can't beat hefting a vacuum or rolling a mower to see if it feels right in your hands.

Large chains such as Sears and Wal-Mart usually have the best selection of lower-priced brands. Home centers such as Home Depot and Lowe's offer a mix of low-priced, midpriced, and upscale brands. Local hardware stores and other independent dealers tend to carry midpriced and upscale brands. Such stores often offer service that mass merchandisers and home centers don't.

More ways to hire a contractor. A growing number of manufacturers and retailers are providing roofing, siding, and other home-product installers as well as the products themselves, typically by referral. That may reduce the risk of shoddy work as some of these retailers and manufacturers screen and even certify the installers they suggest. Industry associations such as the Vinyl Siding Institute are also raising the bar for pros; the industry offers training programs and is developing an installer certification program.

AIR CLEANERS

Whole-house and single-room air cleaners have limitations, but both can provide significant relief from some indoor pollutants when other measures don't work.

Indoor air is more polluted than the air on the other side of the window, according to estimates by the U.S. Environmental Protection Agency. Further, the American Lung Association cites indoor pollution as a health hazard for millions of Americans with asthma or allergies. Indoor pollutants may include visible particles of dust, pollen, and smoke as well as invisible combustion by-products such as carbon monoxide and nitrous oxide, along with other gaseous invaders such as fumes from carpet adhesives and upholstery.

Two commonsense solutions are insuring proper ventilation and controlling the pollutant at the source. If dust is a problem, you might want to replace wall-to-wall carpeting with bare floors or area rugs. Frequent vacuuming may help, though some vacuum cleaners stir up dust. You can lessen the effects of pet dander by designating pet-free rooms, particularly bedrooms. A properly vented range hood can rid kitchen air of smoke and odor, while an exhaust fan in a bathroom can help squelch mold, mildew, and odor.

Air cleaners may be the next step when those measures aren't enough. But only people with respiratory problems are likely to benefit from using such devices. Even then, experts say, air cleaners may not be consistently effective.

If your house has forced-air heating and cooling, choose an appropriate whole-house furnace filter or professionally installed cleaner for your system. If your house doesn't have forced-air heating and cooling, your only option is a room air cleaner.

WHAT'S AVAILABLE

Whole-house air cleaners. Major brands include Aprilaire, Honeywell, Lennox, Trane, and Trion. Whole-house cleaners range from inexpensive fiberglass furnace filters to electronic precipitators, which must be installed professionally in a home's duct system.

Furnace filters range from plain matted-fiberglass (about $1), meant to trap large particles of dust and lint, up to electrostatically charged filters ($15 to $25) designed to attract pollen, lint, pet dander, and dust.

Electronic-precipitator air cleaners impart an electrical charge to particles flowing through them, then collect the particles on oppositely charged metal plates or filters. These more elaborate systems must be fitted into ductwork and wired into the house's current. Most have a collector-plate assembly that must be removed and washed every one to two months.

Price: about $400, plus $200 or more for installation.

Room air cleaners. Sharper Image has surpassed other brands as the market leader. Other notable brands include Bionaire, Friedrich, Holmes, Honeywell, Hunter, and Whirlpool. Most room air cleaners weigh between 10 and 20 pounds. They can be round or boxy, and can stand on the floor or on a table.

Room air cleaners can work quite well, even on dust and cigarette-smoke particles, which are much smaller and harder to trap than pollen and mold spores. They aren't good at trapping gases, however.

Two technologies predominate. The most common is a filter system in which a high-efficiency particulate air (HEPA) filter mechanically strains the air of fine particles. The other dominant technology uses an electronic precipitator that works like those in some whole-house systems, with a fan to move air through them. Honeywell, Hoover, and Sharper Image sell a type of electrostatic precipitator. It typically has no fan or has one that is not effective.

The Association of Home Appliance Manufacturers (AHAM), a trade group, tests and rates room air cleaners using a measurement known as clean air delivery rate (CADR), which is determined by how well a filter traps particles and how much air the unit moves. Separate CADRs are listed for dust, tobacco smoke, and pollen. (While most manufacturers participate in this voluntary program, some models do not have an AHAM-certified performance rating.) We've typically found the AHAM-certified CADRs to be accurate. If whole-house air cleaners and filters are labeled, they carry a minimum efficiency reporting value (MERV). The higher the MERV, the better for trapping small particles.

Price range: $110 to $600. Annual filter cost: $30 to $220.

KEY FEATURES

Whole-house air cleaners are generally available in a range of standard sizes or can be adapted to fit the space. Some manufacturers say their filters are treated with a special antimicrobial agent, presumably to prevent bacterial growth on the filter. We've not evaluated those claims.

Room air cleaners typically use a **fan** to pull air into the unit for filtration. Some models with an electronic precipitator or a HEPA filter incorporate **ionizing circuitry** that uses powered needles or wires to charge particles, which are then more easily trapped by the filter. But this ionization may also make the particles stick to walls or furnishings, possibly soiling them. An **indicator** in most models let you know when to change the filter.

HEPA filters are supposed to be replaced annually and can cost more than $100—sometimes as much as the room air cleaner itself. **Prefilters,** which are designed to remove odors and/or larger particles, are generally changed quarterly, while washable prefilters should be cleaned monthly. An electronic precipitator's **collector-plate assembly** must be removed and washed every month or so; it slides out like a drawer, and you can put it in a dishwasher or rinse it in a sink.

Most room air cleaners have a **handle,** while some heavier models have **wheels. Fan speeds** usually include low, medium, and high. A few cleaners use a **dust sensor** and an **air-quality monitor** designed to raise or lower the fan speed automatically, depending on conditions. Our tests of one model with this feature found that it did not respond well to very small particles in the air.

HOW TO CHOOSE

Performance differences. CONSUMER REPORTS tests of furnace filters and whole-house air cleaners found that the better ones were effective with dust but not smoke. The filters may also restrict air flow through the system, adversely affecting the performance of your furnace or air conditioner. Electronic-precipitator filters were most effective against dust and smoke, and they restrict airflow much less.

Room air cleaners provided varying levels of performance in our tests, with no one type—HEPA filter or electronic precipitator—clearly outdoing the others. When set at high, the best did a very good job of clearing a room of dust and smoke; other models were only good or fair. Most of the room air cleaners were easy to use, we found. Electronic-precipitator models cost less to run than HEPA units because they don't require you to replace an expensive filter. The Sharper Image Ionic Breeze, Honeywell Environizer, and Hoover Silent Air were far less effective than any other air cleaner tested.

Recommendations. Choose an air cleaner based on the size of your air-quality problem. Among whole-house models, one of the better pleated electrostatic filters may be all you need; consider an electronic precipitator if someone in your home smokes or has a chronic respiratory problem. Also be sure a whole-house filter fits snugly in its mount, since leaks can make it less effective. (You can seal gaps with weather stripping.)

If you decide to get a room air cleaner, choose one that's appropriately sized for the room. We suggest looking for a model with a clean air delivery rate of at least two-thirds of the room's area, assuming an 8-foot ceiling. For example, a 12x15-foot room—180 square feet—needs a model with a CADR of at least 120 for the contaminant you want to remove (dust, smoke, or pollen, for example).

The CADR printed on the packaging assumes you'll run the air cleaner at high speed. If you think you'll use medium or low speed to cut noise, compensate by getting a model with a CADR that is a bit higher than suggested for the room size. Also note that a room with a high ceiling requires a model with a correspondingly higher CADR. Follow instructions when placing a room air cleaner to ensure it will work effectively. Some models can sit against a wall; others need to go in the middle of the room.

Related CR Report: October 2003
Ratings: page 235, 237

AIR CONDITIONERS

Falling prices make individual room air conditioners an inexpensive alternative to central-air systems for cooling one or two rooms.

Once a high-priced convenience, relatively precise electronic controls with digital temperature readouts have replaced vague "warmer" and "cooler" settings on a growing number of lower-priced air conditioners. Added efficiency is also trickling down the price scale. Many models have a higher Energy Efficiency Rating (EER) than the federal government requires: The minimum EER for air conditioners below 8,000 British thermal units per hour (Btu/hr.) is 9.7; it's 9.8 for those with 8,000 to 13,999 Btu/hr.

WHAT'S AVAILABLE

Fedders, GE, Kenmore (Sears), and Whirlpool are the leading brands of room air conditioners. You'll find cooling capacities that range from 5,000 Btu/hr. to more than 30,000 Btu/hr. The majority of room air conditioners in stores are small and midsized units from 5,000 to 9,000 Btu/hr. Price range: about $100 to more than $600, depending mostly on cooling capacity.

KEY FEATURES

An air conditioner's exterior-facing portion contains a **compressor, fan,** and **condenser,** while the part that faces a home's interior contains a **fan** and an **evaporator**. Most room models are designed to fit **double-hung windows,** though some are built for **casement** and **slider windows** and others for **in-wall installation.**

Most models have **adjustable vertical and horizontal louvers** to direct airflow. Many offer a **fresh-air intake** or **exhaust setting** for ventilation, although this feature moves a relatively small amount of air. An **energy-saver setting** on some units stops the fan when the compressor cycles off. **Electronic controls** and **digital temperature readouts** are becoming common. A **timer** lets you program the unit to switch on (say, half an hour before you get home) or off at a given time. More and more models also include a **remote control.** Some models install with a **slide-out chassis**—an outer cabinet that anchors in the window, into which you slide the unit.

HOW TO CHOOSE

Performance differences. Most room air conditioners we've tested do a fine job of cooling. But we've found wide variations in quietness. We've also found significant differences in how well models direct airflow to the left or right. That's important if the mounting window is off to one side, rather than centered in the wall, so you can direct cool air toward the room's center.

Recommendations. Start by determining the right size air conditioner for the room: One that's too large may not dehumidify properly, while one that's too small may not adequately cool the space. Then check the unit's EER on the yellow EnergyGuide tag to see how efficient it is compared with other models.

A typical room air conditioner can weigh anywhere from 40 to 100 pounds, making installation a two-person job. Once the air conditioner is in, maintain it by cleaning its air filter every few weeks; some units have an indicator that tells you when it's time to clean or change the filter.

Related CR Report: July 2003

CHAIN SAWS

They're still noisy, but many of the latest are safer and cleaner. Gasoline-powered saws still outperform electrics, although plug-ins can be fine for light-duty use.

Chain saws are inherently dangerous and noisy, though modern designs attempt to improve usability on both counts. Nearly all chain saws now have multiple features aimed at minimizing "kickback," which occurs when the saw snaps up and back toward the operator.

Electric models are quieter and cleaner than gasoline-powered ones. Gasoline-powered saws are cleaning up their act, however, as tougher federal standards reduce allowable emissions for these machines.

WHAT'S AVAILABLE

You'll find gasoline- and electric-powered chain saws at home centers, discount stores, and lawn-and-garden shops. Major brands include Craftsman (Sears), Homelite, Husqvarna, Poulan, Remington, and Stihl. Gas-powered saws use a small two-stroke engine that requires a mixture of gasoline and oil. Nearly all electric saws plug into an outlet and run off an electric motor. A few rechargeable, battery-powered chain saws are available, but they tend to be underpowered for most jobs.

As with most outdoor tools, the gas-powered versions tend to offer the most power and mobility. But plug-in electrics compensate somewhat with lighter weight, less noise, and trigger starting. They also emit no exhaust, don't need engine tune-ups, and typically cost less.

Price range: $100 to $300 (gas); less than $100 (electrics).

KEY FEATURES

Chain saws are typically marketed by the size of the **bar** (the metal extension that supports the chain—usually between 14 and 20 inches long) as well as the **engine** or **motor** (measured in cubic centimeters for gas saws, amps for electrics). Usually, the larger the saw, the more you'll pay, though smaller models from high-end brands such as Husqvarna and Stihl can cost more than larger ones from Craftsman, Homelite, and other lower-priced brands.

Other features are aimed mainly at safety and convenience. Major kickback-reducing devices include a **reduced-kickback chain** with added guard links to keep the cutters from taking too large a bite, along with a narrow-tipped, **reduced-kickback bar** that limits the contact area where kickback occurs. All saws also have a **chain catcher**—an extension under the guide bar that keeps a broken chain from flying rearward. Some saws have a **chain brake,** which stops the chain almost instantly when activated, or a **bar-tip guard,** which prevents kickback by covering the bar's tip, or "nose."

WORK SMART

Never use a chain saw while on a ladder or perched in a tree. And don't cut anything above shoulder height, except with a pole pruner.

Other safety features for most chain saws include a **trigger lockout switch** that must be pressed for the throttle trigger to operate and, for gas saws, a **shielded muffler** designed to prevent burns from accidental contact.

Common labor-saving features include an **automatic chain oiler,** which eliminates the need to periodically push a plunger to lubricate the chain and bar. Metal **bucking spikes** act as a pivot point when cutting larger logs. Some saws have a **chain-adjuster screw** mounted on the side of the bar. A few Stihl models feature a **tools-free adjuster** that lets you loosen or tighten the chain by turning a wheel.

Visible bar-oil and **fuel levels** are also convenient, as is a **wide rear handle** that eases gas-saw starts by allowing room for the toe of a boot to secure the saw on the ground. Also look for **antivibration bushings** or **springs** between the handles and the engine, bar, and chain, along with a combined **choke/on-off switch** that activates a gas saw's ignition while closing off air to its carburetor for easier starting.

HOW TO CHOOSE

Performance differences. CONSUMER REPORTS tests confirm that gas saws cut faster than electrics. More saws we've tested now have useful and important safety features—but any chain saw should still be handled with care. And even quieter electric saws remain noisy enough for us to recommend ear protection.

Recommendations. Buy a gasoline-powered saw if you need go-anywhere mobility. The best electrics, which cost less than $100, are fine for small branches and other light-duty cutting. In either case, you'll find a light saw (less than 14 pounds for gas models, less than 10 pounds for electrics) easier to use for longer periods. Unless you're felling large trees, a 14- or 16-inch bar should be more than adequate.

Related CR Report: May 2001

CIRCULAR SAWS

Circular saws are a mainstay for cutting the two-by-fours and plywood used in many home-improvement projects.

A circular saw is an essential tool for any but the most rudimentary workshop. Most have a power cord, but there are some cordless saws on the market.

WHAT'S AVAILABLE

Black & Decker, Craftsman (Sears), DeWalt, Makita, Milwaukee, Porter-Cable, and Skil brands account for most of the circular saws sold.

Corded models. These models run on an electric motor that can range from 10 to 15 amps. The higher the amps, the more power you can expect. Most models are oriented so the motor is perpendicular to the blade. Another type uses a "worm drive" design in which the motor is parallel to the blade; that gives a saw a lot of power, but at the expense of speed.

Price range: $40 to $140.

Cordless models. These range from 14.4 to 24 volts. They usually have a smaller blade and a shorter run time than corded models.

Price range: $60 to $260.

KEY FEATURES

Every saw has a big main **handle** and a stubby auxiliary handle; the former incorporates the saw's **on/off switch**. Some saws include an **interlock** you have to press before the on/off switch will work. This adds a level of safety, but can make the saw awkward to use.

Inexpensive saws have a stamped-steel **base** and thin housing; pricier models use thick, rugged material, such as plastic or cast aluminum, that stands up to hard use. A **blade** with two dozen large teeth cuts fast but can splinter the wood; a blade with 40 or more teeth gives a cleaner cut. The thinner the blade, the faster the cut and the less wasted wood. Typically, slower saws come with a steel blade while the fastest models have a carbide-tipped blade.

Bevel adjustment is used to change the angle of the cut from 0 to 45 degrees. The **depth adjustment** changes the blade's cutting depth. A circular saw works best when the teeth just clear the bottom of the wood. The **cutting guide**—the notch in the base plate that's aligned with the saw blade—helps you follow the cutting line you've drawn on the wood.

A **blade-lock button** keeps the blade from turning when you change blades. The **dust chute** directs the sawdust away so you can see what you're doing.

HOW TO CHOOSE

Performance differences. Seconds count if you have a lot of wood to cut. Speed also affects safety; you're more likely to push a slow saw, dulling the blade quickly and overheating the motor, or making the saw jam or kick back. CONSUMER REPORTS tests found that most corded saws have adequate torque for any typical home-workshop job. Battery-powered saws are much weaker. A weak saw could have trouble when used on thick hardwood or for other tough work.

Design points that can make a saw easy to use include a visible cutting guide, a blade that's simple to change and to adjust for depth and angle, good balance, a comfortable handle, and a handy on/off switch. How well the saw is constructed impacts its potential for a long, trouble-free life. It should have durable bearings, motor brushes that are accessible for servicing or replacement, a heavy-duty base, and rugged blade-depth and cutting-angle adjustments.

Recommendations. Judging from our tests, you can get a fine corded saw for as little as $60; for $120 to $160, you can get an excellent model. A cordless saw lacks the might for tough jobs but might do for occasional light work.

Whichever you buy, if it comes with a steel blade, replace it with a carbide-tipped one. Be sure to match the number of teeth with the material you want to cut; a blade for plywood, say, has more teeth than one for rough cutting.

All the saws are loud enough when cutting to warrant hearing protection. All kick up a lot of chips and dust, so safety glasses or goggles are a must. You may also want to wear a dust mask, especially when cutting pressure-treated lumber.

Related CR Report: August 2002
Ratings: page 250

CORDLESS DRILLS

Many of the latest models are powerful enough to handle construction and repair chores formerly reserved for corded models.

Better battery packs let today's cordless drills run longer and more powerfully per charge. The best can even outperform corded drills and handle deck construction and other big jobs before their batteries need to be recharged. Much of the credit goes to nickel-cadmium (NiCad) batteries, which can be charged hundreds of times. NiCads must be recycled, however, since the cadmium is toxic and can leach out of landfills to contaminate groundwater if disposed of improperly. Incineration can release the substance into the air and pose an even greater hazard. Some cordless drills have nickel-metal-hydride (NiMH) batteries, which don't contain cadmium and are safer for the environment.

WHAT'S AVAILABLE

Black & Decker and Craftsman (Sears) along with Ryobi and Skil are aimed primarily at do-it-yourselfers. Bosch, Craftsman Professional, DeWalt, Hitachi, Makita, Milwaukee, and Porter-Cable offer pricier drills with professional-style features.

Cordless drills come in several sizes, based on battery voltage. In general, the higher the voltage, the greater the drilling power. The most potent models pack 18 to 24 volts, while the 6- to 9.6-volt models are usually limited to light-duty use. In between are the 12- and 14.4-volt drills that often provide the best balance of high performance and affordability. There may still be some 24-volt models available online.

Sometimes, you'll also find a flashlight

or a cordless saw bundled with a drill and sold as a kit. For the first time last year, sales of individual drills were flat, while the sale of drill kits grew.

Price range: $30 to $130 (6- to 9.6-volt); $50 to $190 (12-volt); $60 to $270 (14.4- and 18-volt); $300 to $370 (24-volt, available online).

KEY FEATURES

Most cordless drills 12 volts and higher have **two speed ranges:** low for driving screws and high for drilling. Low speed provides much more torque, or turning power, than the high-speed setting, which is useful for drilling and boring holes. Most drills have a **variable speed trigger,** which can make starting a hole easier. An **adjustable clutch** is used to lower maximum torque, which can help you avoid driving a screw too far into soft wallboard or mangling the screw's head or threads once it's in. Most of today's models are also **reversible,** letting you easily remove a screw or back a drill bit out of a hole.

TECH TIP
Recycle used rechargeable batteries in bins at participating retailers such as RadioShack and Wal-Mart. To find one near you, call 800-8-BATTERY.

Most drills have a **⅜-inch chuck** (the attachment that holds the drill bit), though some high-voltage, professional-grade models have a **½-inch chuck.** In either case, most drills have replaced the little key needed to loosen and tighten the chuck with a **keyless chuck.**

Still other features make some drills easier to use. A **T-handle** in the center of the motor housing provides better balance than a pistol grip on the back, although a **pistol grip** lets you slide your hand up in line with the bit to better apply pressure. Models with **two batteries** let you use one while the other is charging. A **smart charger** charges the battery in an hour or less, rather than three hours or more for a conventional charger. Some smart chargers also extend battery life by adjusting the charge as needed. Many switch into a **maintenance** or **"trickle-charge"** mode after the battery is fully charged.

An **electric brake** stops a drill instantly when you release the trigger—a handy feature that helps you avoid damaging the workpiece and allows you to resume drilling or driving without waiting. Some models also include a **built-in bubble level;** others feature a **one-handed chuck** for easier bit changes.

HOW TO CHOOSE

Performance differences. In our recent tests, a 15.6-volt NiMH-powered drill ran longer than many 18-volt NiCad-powered models, yet weighed less. What's more, some 18-volt models can nearly equal a 24-volt drill's performance with less weight and a lower price tag. While higher voltage equals greater power, it also tends to mean added weight. That can make it tiring to hold a drill for any length of time, especially overhead.

Recommendations. A 24-volt cordless drill delivers power and endurance, but it can weigh up to 8 pounds and cost more than $300. If you're a contractor or serious do-it-yourselfer, you'll find plenty of power and endurance in a 14.4- or 18-volt model. The best selection is available in those sizes. They're also the best value. Drills with 12 volts or less are a dubious choice; although they are lightweight, many are suitable only for light-duty chores. What's more, recharging many of the least expensive models can take anywhere from 3 to 16 hours.

Look for a smart charger and two batteries, which often come with the better models. Whichever size drill you choose, make sure you're comfortable with its weight and ergonomics. And, if possible, try before buying.

Related CR Report: January 2003
Ratings: page 264

GAS GRILLS

Many people are choosing models that do more than just grill. Go high-end, and you can pay as much as you would for a pro-style kitchen range.

A $15 charcoal hibachi is all it takes to give burgers that outdoorsy barbecue taste. But a gas or electric grill offers flexible controls and spares you the hassle of starting the fire and getting rid of the ashes when you're done. Most grills have extras such as a warming rack for rolls; some have an accessory burner for, say, boiling corn on the cob. Shoppers looking for a backyard statement will find models that cost thousands of dollars and have stainless-steel exteriors and grates, porcelain-coated steel and aluminum lids, separately controlled burners, utensil holders, and other perks. You'll also find more modest grills that can serve up flavor and convenience for $200 or so.

WHAT'S AVAILABLE

Char-Broil, Coleman, Kenmore (Sears), and Weber account for more than 60 percent of gas-grill sales. Char-Broil is a mass-market brand, with both gas and electric models available. Weber is a high-end brand that also markets its classic dome-top charcoal grills. Sears covers the entire spectrum under its Kenmore name.

Gas. These grills are easy to start, warm up quickly, and usually cook predictably, giving meat a full, browned flavor. Step-up features include shelves and side burners. Better models offer added sturdiness and more even cooking.

Price range: $100 to more than $2,000.

Electric. Easy to start, they offer precise temperature control and let you grill with nonstick cookware. But they take a bit longer than gas models to warm up and be ready to grill.

Price range: about $100 to $300.

Charcoal. These provide an intense, smoky flavor prized by many. But they don't always light easily (using a chimney-style starter can help remedy that). They also burn less cleanly than gas, their heat is harder to regulate, and cleanup can be messy—major reasons why charcoal models are no longer the top-selling type.

Price range: usually $100 or less.

KEY FEATURES

Most cooking **grates** are made of porcelain-coated steel, with others made of the somewhat sturdier porcelain-coated cast iron, bare cast iron, or stainless steel. A porcelain-coated grate is rustproof and easy to clean, but it can eventually chip. Bare cast iron is sturdy and sears beautifully, but you have to season it with cooking oil to fend off rust.

The best of both worlds: stainless steel, which is sturdy, heats quickly, and resists rust without a porcelain coating. Cooking grates with wide, closely spaced bars tend to provide better searing than grates with thin, round rods, which may allow more food to fall to the bottom of the grill.

Both gas and electric grills are mounted on a **cart,** usually of painted steel tubing assembled with nuts and bolts. Higher-priced grills have welded joints, and a few have a cart made of stainless steel. Carts with two wheels and two feet must be lifted at one end to move; better are two large wheels and two casters or four casters, which make moving easier. Wheels with a full axle are better than those bolted to the frame, which can bend over time.

Gas and electric grills generally have one or more **exterior shelves,** which flip up from the front or side or are fixed on the side. Shelves are usually made of plastic, though some are made of cast aluminum or stainless steel, which is more durable. (Wood shelves are the least sturdy and tend to deteriorate over time.) Most grills have **interior racks** for keeping food warm without further cooking. Another plus for gas or electric grills is a **lid** and **firebox** made of stainless steel or porcelain-coated steel, both of which are more durable than cast aluminum.

Still other features help a gas grill start more easily and cook more evenly. An example is the **igniter,** which works via a knob or a push button. Knobs emit two or three sparks per turn, while push buttons emit a single spark per push. Better are **battery-powered electronic igniters,** which produce continuous sparks as long as the button is held down. Also look for **lighting holes** on the side of or beneath the grill, which are handy if the igniter fails and you need to use a wooden match to start the fire.

Most gas grills have steel **burners,** though some are stainless steel, cast iron, or cast brass. Those premium burners typically last longer and carry warranties of 10 years or more. Most grills have two burners, or one with two independent halves. A few have three or four, which can add cooking flexibility. A **side burner,** which resembles a gas-stove burner and has its own heat control, is handy for cooking vegetables or sauce without leaving the grill. Other step-up features include an **electric rotisserie,** a **fuel gauge,** a **smoker drawer,** a **wok,** a **griddle pan,** a **steamer pan,** a **deep fryer,** a **nonstick grill basket,** and one or more high-heat **infrared burners** in lieu of the conventional type.

Most gas grills also use a **cooking medium**—a metal plate or metal bars, ceramic or charcoal-like briquettes, or lava rocks—between the burner and grates to distribute heat and vaporize juices, flavoring the food. Our tests have shown that no one type is better at ensuring even heating. But grills with nothing between the burner and the cooking grates typically cook less evenly.

Gas grills sometimes include a **propane tank;** buying a tank separately costs about $25. Some grills can be converted to run on natural gas or come in a natural-gas version. Tanks usually sit next to or on the base of the grill and attach to its gas line with a handwheel. All tanks must now comply with upgraded National Fire Protection Association standards for **overfill protection.** Noncompliant tanks have a circular or five-lobed valve and aren't refillable, although they can be retrofitted with a three-lobed valve or swapped for a new tank at a hardware store or other refilling facility.

HOW TO CHOOSE

Performance differences. Most gas or electric grills do a good job at grilling hotly and evenly. Salespeople might tell you that more Btus (British thermal units) mean faster warm-up, but that's not always true.

Assembling one of these grills can take anywhere from 30 minutes to 3 hours; some stores include assembly and delivery in the price, while others charge for that service. Some minor safety problems have turned up in our tests. Typically they involved handles, knobs, or thermometers that got too hot to handle without pot holders. Also, grills without a grease cup or another means of catching and draining grease from the burners can flare up if the grease catches fire.

Recommendations. Consider how often you cook outdoors and how many people you typically feed. While price and performance don't track precisely, our tests have shown that some lower-priced gas grills ($275 or less) are particularly good values. Gas models priced at $350 to $600 have more features—grates with wide bars, ample warming shelves, stainless-steel burners and grates, electronic igniters, longer warranties, and sturdier carts. Spending thousands of dollars gets you many or all of those features plus more burners and mostly stainless-steel construction, but few consumers spend that much on a grill.

An electric grill can be a good, inexpensive option for places where gas grills aren't allowed. Charcoal grills cost the least overall, but they require the most preparation and cleanup work.

Related CR Report: June 2003
Ratings: page 271

HEDGE TRIMMERS

A good electric trimmer is all most people need to keep greenery shapely. Gasoline- or battery-powered models free you from a cord, but you pay for that convenience.

A gas or electric hedge trimmer can be a useful addition to your tool shed if your property includes lots of shrubs. Both types of trimmer can save you some of the physical effort hand clippers require, since an engine or motor—rather than elbow grease—powers their blades. But using any powered hedge trimmer can still be hard work, since you're holding the device in midair for extended periods. That can make a trimmer's weight, balance, and vibration as important as its cutting power.

WHAT'S AVAILABLE

Black & Decker makes electric-powered models and sells more than half of all hedge trimmers. Craftsman (Sears) is Black & Decker's largest competitor, and sells electric plug-in and battery-powered trimmers as well as gas-powered models. Other brands include Echo, Homelite, Husqvarna, Little Wonder, Stihl, Ryobi, Toro, and Weed Eater.

Electric corded hedge trimmers. Most consumers prefer plug-in electric trimmers, which are relatively light and quiet, start with the push of a button, produce no exhaust, and require little maintenance. The best electrics can also perform comparably to gasoline-powered models—provided you're within 100 feet of a power outlet.

Price range: $30 to $100.

Gasoline-powered hedge trimmers. Commercial landscapers favor gas-powered models for their power and mobility. Indeed, a gas-powered, long-reach trimmer can provide access to remote spots a corded electric trimmer can't reach. But their two-stroke engines entail the fuel-mixing, pull-starting, noisiness, maintenance, and exhaust emissions of other gas-powered, handheld yard tools. Gas trimmers can also be expensive.

Price range: $120 to $450.

Electric battery-powered hedge trimmers. Cordless trimmers combine the mobility of gas models with the convenience, clean running, and easy maintenance of plug-in electrics, courtesy of an onboard battery. On the downside, battery-powered trimmers offer relatively little cutting power, along with a short running time before the battery must be recharged. They can also cost as much as some gas-powered models.

Price range: $80 to $120.

KEY FEATURES

A hedge trimmer's **blades** are simply two flat metal plates with tooth-lined edges. Blade length typically ranges from 13 to 30 inches, although most are between 16 and 24 inches long. **Blade gap**—the distance between teeth—is also important, since it helps determine how large a branch the trimmer can cut. In general, the wider the gap, the larger the branch a trimmer can handle and the easier it is to push the machine through a hedge.

Gasoline-powered, professional-grade trimmers have blade gaps of 1 inch or more, while homeowner-grade models typically have ⅜- to ¾-inch gaps—narrow enough to help keep fingers safe.

Still other factors make some blades more effective than others. **Double-sided blades** allow cutting in both directions, letting you stand in one position longer than you can with **single-sided blades,** which cut in one direction only. Pricier trimmers also tend to use **dual-action blades,** where both the top and bottom blade plates move back and forth, reducing vibration. With **single-action blades,** only the top blade moves.

Handle designs also vary. Trimmers with a **wrap-around front handle** let you keep your hands in a comfortable position as you pivot the trimmer to cut vertically or at odd angles. Safety features include **tooth extensions,** which are designed to prevent thighs and other body parts from contacting the blades' teeth. Some tooth extensions are part of the blades and move with them; Consumer Reports thinks separate, stationary tooth extensions provide better protection. Trimmers also have a **front-handle shield** designed to prevent your forward hand from touching the blade.

HOW TO CHOOSE

Performance differences. Any powered hedge trimmer should be up to light-duty tidying. The best can cut branches just shy of ⅝ inches in diameter, while dense, ¼-inch-thick branches were enough to stop the battery-powered trimmers we tested.

Recommendations. Begin by deciding which type of trimmer matches the trimming chores you do. Electric corded models are relatively quiet and inexpensive. They also deliver the best combination of cutting power, maneuverability, and ease—provided you stay within range of a power outlet. Battery-powered trimmers offer cord-free convenience, but their lack of cutting power and limited running time between charges make them best suited to touchups and other light-duty work. In either case, look for an Underwriters Laboratories (UL) seal, which requires trimmers to have crucial safety features. Gasoline-powered models are best for heavier-duty trimming beyond the range of a cord. Wear hearing protection when using a gas-powered trimmer. And make sure you wear protective work gloves, safety glasses or goggles, and nonskid shoes when using any powered trimmer. Also be sure to do your trimming on firm footing or on a steady ladder. And if you're using an electric trimmer, make sure the cord trails away from the blades.

Related CR Report: May 2000

LAWN MOWERS AND TRACTORS

Practically any mower—even an inexpensive one—will cut your grass. But you can get better results with less effort by choosing a machine

based on your lawn size and shape and your mowing preferences.

Mowing options range anywhere from $100 manual-reel mowers to tractors that can cost $4,000 and beyond. Manual-reel and electric walk-behind mowers are appropriate for people with a small yard, while gasoline-powered walk-behind mowers are fine for most lawns up to about a half-acre. Those with lawns larger than that will appreciate the ease and speed of a riding mower or a lawn tractor.

Gasoline-powered mowers produce a disproportionate amount of air pollution compared with cars. Federal regulations aimed at reducing smog-producing lawnmower emissions by 390,000 tons annually are being phased in over the next few years.

WHAT'S AVAILABLE

Manual-reel mowers are still made by a few companies, such as Great States and Scotts, while major electric-mower brands include Black & Decker and Craftsman (Sears). Craftsman is also the largest-selling brand of gasoline-powered walk-behind mowers, riding mowers, and lawn tractors. Other less-expensive, mass-market brands of gas-powered mowers and tractors include Bolens, Murray, Troy-Bilt, Yard Machines, and Yard-Man. Pricier brands, traditionally sold at outdoor power-equipment dealers include Ariens, Cub Cadet, Honda, Husqvarna, John Deere, Kubota, Lawn Boy, Poulan, Simplicity, Snapper, and Toro, although models from several of these brands are now available at large retailers.

Which type is best for your lawn? Here's what to consider:

Manual-reel mowers. Pushing these simple mowers rotates a series of curved blades that spin in conjunction with the wheels. Reel mowers are quiet, inexpensive, and nonpolluting. They're also relatively safe to operate and require little maintenance other than periodic blade adjustment and sharpening. On the downside, our tests have shown that most can't cut grass higher than 1½ inches or trim closer than 3 inches around obstacles. Cutting swaths of just 14 to 18 inches wide is also a drawback if you have a decent-sized yard. Consider a manual mower for a small, flat lawn of one-quarter acre or less.

Price range: $100 to about $250.

Electric mowers. These push-type walk-behind mowers use an electric motor to drive a rotating blade. Both corded and cordless versions start with the push of a button, produce no exhaust, and, like reel mowers, require little maintenance aside from sharpening. Most offer a side or rear grass catcher, and many can mulch—a process in which clippings are recut until they're small enough to hide unobtrusively within the lawn. But electrics tend to be less powerful than gas mowers and less adept at tackling tall or thick grass and weeds. What's more, their narrow, 18- to 19-inch swaths take a smaller bite than most gas-powered mowers.

Both corded and cordless electrics have other significant drawbacks. Corded mowers limit your mowing to within 100 feet of a power outlet—the typical maximum length for an extension cord. Cordless versions, while more versatile, weigh up to 30 pounds more than corded models and typically mow just one-quarter to one-third acre before their sealed lead-acid batteries need recharging. That makes both types of electrics suitable mainly for small, flat lawns of one-quarter acre or less.

Price range: $125 to $250 (corded); $300 to $400 (cordless).

Gasoline-powered walk-behind mowers. These include push as well as self-propelled models. Most have a 3.5- to 6.5-hp four-stroke engine and a cutting swath 20 to 22 inches wide, allowing them to do more work with each pass and handle long or thick grass and weeds. And all can keep mowing as long as there's fuel in the tank. But gas mowers are relatively noisy and require regular maintenance.

Most gas mowers provide three cutting modes: bagging, which gathers clippings in a removable catcher; side-discharging, which dispenses clippings onto the lawn; and mulching. Consider a push-type model for lawns of about one-quarter acre that are relatively flat or for trimming larger lawns, and a self-propelled model for lawns of a half-acre or more or those that are hilly.

Price range: $100 to more than $400 (push-type); $250 to $900 (self-propelled).

Riding mowers and tractors. These are suitable for lawns of a half-acre or larger. Riding mowers have their engine in back and tend to be smaller, simpler, and easier to maneuver than tractors. While their 28- to 33-inch mowing swath is larger than a walk-behind mower's, it's far smaller than the 38 to 48 inches offered by lawn tractors and the 60 inches available with some larger garden tractors.

Lawn and garden tractors have a large engine mounted in front for better weight distribution. Both can also accept attachments that let them plow and tow a cart as well as clear snow; garden tractors accept soil-tilling equipment. Lawn tractors have become far more popular than garden tractors, although even these usually can't mulch or bag without accessories. Figure on another $25 to $150 for a mulching kit and $200 to $450 for a bagging system.

Zero-turn-radius ride-ons and tractors are also gaining ground in the marketplace. With most, you steer by pushing or pulling control levers, each controlling a driven rear wheel, although John Deere manufactures a zero-turn lawn tractor that uses a conventional steering wheel. The payoff for these tight-turning machines is added maneuverability in tight spots and around obstacles, but you can experience less steering control on hills. You pay a premium for the agility of a zero-turning-radius mower.

Price range: $700 to $2,000 (riding mowers); $800 to $3,500 (lawn tractors); $2,000 to $6,000 (garden tractors); $3,000 to $7,000 (zero-turning-radius mowers).

KEY FEATURES

For electric mowers: A **sliding clip** helps ease turns with corded mowers by letting the cord move from side to side. Some mowers have a **flip-over handle** you move from one end of the machine to the other as you reverse direction, say, at the end of a row.

For gas-powered mowers: Some high-end models have a **blade-brake clutch system** that stops the blade but lets the engine keep running when you release the handlebar safety bail. This is more convenient than the usual **engine-kill system,** which stops the engine and blade and requires you to restart the engine. A **four-stroke engine,** which burns gasoline alone, runs more cleanly than a **two stroke engine,** which runs on a mixture of oil and gasoline. An **overhead-valve** four-stroke engine tends to pollute less than a traditional **side-valve** four-stroke engine.

Replacing the traditional choke on most gas mowers is a small rubber bulb called a **primer,** which you press to supply extra fuel for cold starting. An **electric starter** is easier to use than a pull starter, though it typically adds $50 to $100 to the price. Most mowers with a **recoil starter** are easier to start than they once were, however. Some models from MTD-made Cub Cadet, White, and Yard-Man now have a spring-powered **self-starter,** which uses energy generated as the engine is shut off to provide push-button starts without a battery or outlet. CONSUMER REPORTS tests have found the device effective, provided you don't attempt starts in thick grass.

Some self-propelled mowers have just **one speed,** usually about 2½ mph; others have **several speeds** or a **continuous range,** typically from 1 to 3½ mph. Self-propelled mowers also include front-drive and rear-drive models. Front-drive mowers tend to be easier to maneuver and turn, although rear-wheel-drive models generally have better traction on hills and can maintain traction even with a full grass bag. Mowers with **swivel front wheels** offer the most maneuverability by allowing easy 180-degree turns. But, on many, each front casterlike wheel must be removed to adjust cutting height.

You'll also find several different **deck** choices. Most decks are steel, although some mowers have an **aluminum** or **plastic** deck, which is rustproof; plastic also resists dents and cracks. Even many lower-priced mowers now have **tools-free cutting-height adjusters,** which raise and lower the deck with one or two levers. Most models also let you change mowing modes without tools, although a few still require wrenches and, sometimes, a blade change. Some mowers use a **side-bagging deck design,** in which a side-exit chute routes clippings into a side-mounted bag or out onto the lawn—or is blocked with a plate or plug for mulching.

Mowers with a **rear-bagging deck** tend to cost more, but their rear-mounted bag holds more than side bags and eases maneuvering by hanging beneath the handlebar, rather than out to the side. The rearward opening is fitted with a chute for side discharging or a plug for mulching. Some **"hybrid" rear-baggers** have a discharge port for clippings on the side of the deck as well as one for the bag in back.

For riding mowers and tractors: Some are gear-driven and require a lever and combination brake/clutch to change speed. Some gear-drive models use foot pedals with a pulley that allows continuously variable speed changes without the usual shifting. Spending more will buy you a model with a clutchless **hydrostatic drive,** which allows even more convenient continuously variable speed changes. Most models have a **translucent fuel tank,** making it easy to check the fuel level. Some have a **fuel gauge.** Still others let you remove the collection bag without flipping the seat forward.

HOW TO CHOOSE

Performance differences. Nearly all gas-powered push and self-propelled walk-behind mowers now handle mulching, bagging, and side discharging. In our tests, we've found that most do at least a good job at mulching, which is the fastest and easiest way to dispose of clippings. All but the best mulchers leave a few visible clippings on the lawn, while the worst leave enough clippings to require raking. Even the best mulchers won't work well if the grass is too tall or wet, however.

Our tests also found that a mower's horsepower rating tends to have little bearing on mowing performance. Rear-bagging mowers, whether gas or electric, tend to perform better than side-baggers. Electric models do a decent job at mulching, bagging, and side discharging, but they struggle with tall grass or weeds. And they take a relatively narrow bite with each pass.

Virtually all riding mowers and tractors can handle all three mowing modes. In tests, most did a thorough job of vacuuming up clippings when bagging, although some clogged before their bags were full. The best held more than twice as many clippings as the best push mowers.

Recommendations. Balance the size of your yard with how much you want to spend. Gas-powered push and self-propelled mowers are appropriate for many lawns. Electric mowers offer cleaner, quieter running and easy maintenance—but they're limited by a cord or, for cordless models, the relatively short mowing time between charges.

Homeowners with a small lawn can also consider a manual-reel mower. Just be sure that your lawn isn't too thick and that you don't skip a week. If you decide to ride, you'll probably want a lawn tractor unless your lawn has lots of tight areas and obstacles; then the smaller size of a riding mower is an advantage. You can also opt for a zero-turn mower or tractor, which combines a wide deck with tight turning. But, at $3,000 and beyond, it's an expensive option.

Related CR Report: May 2003, June 2003
Ratings: page 278, 280
Reliability: page 29

PAINT, EXTERIOR

The best paint can improve your home's appearance and protect it from the weather for up to 10 years.

While a fresh coat of paint on the siding and trim will give your house curb appeal, exterior paint isn't just for show. It provides an important layer of protection against moisture, mildew, and the drying effects of the sun.

WHAT'S AVAILABLE

Major brands include Ace, Behr (sold at Home Depot), Benjamin Moore, Dutch Boy, Glidden, Sears, Sherwin-Williams, True Value, and Valspar (sold at Lowe's). You'll also see many brands of paint sold regionally.

Exterior paints come in a variety of sheens. The dullest is flat, followed by low-luster (often called eggshell or satin), semi-gloss, and gloss. The flatter finishes are best for siding, with the lowest-sheen variety the best choice if you need to mask imperfections. Glossy paint is most often used for trim because it highlights the details of the woodwork and the paint is easy to clean.

Price range: $15 to $30 a gallon.

KEY FEATURES

The choice of **color** affects a paint's longevity. Some pigments are inherently more vulnerable to the damaging effects of sunlight. Blues are the most likely to change color by fading or turning a greenish yellow. Yellowish-tan paints are also subject to color change.

Most brands of paint come in different **grades,** such as "good," "better," and "best." You'll also find "contractor" grades that, despite their names, are relatively low quality.

HOW TO CHOOSE

Performance differences. Our tests of exterior paints are very severe, exposing painted panels on outdoor racks angled to catch the maximum amount of sun. One year of testing is about the equivalent of three years of extreme weather on a typical house.

CONSUMER REPORTS tests have found that the grade of paint matters. "Good" or "economy" grades don't weather as well as the top-of-the-line products. Using a cheaper grade of paint means you'll spend more time and money in the long run because you'll need to repaint more often. "Contractor" grades of paint that we've tested also tend to be mediocre.

Generally, most paints will look good for at least three years, and some should look good for about six. Most also do a good job of resisting the buildup of mildew and preventing the wood from cracking.

Recommendations. Only a few brands consistently perform well no matter what the color. They include M.A. Bruder and California, both sold mainly in the East, and the Glidden Endurance and Glidden Spred Dura national brands.

Related CR Report: August 2003

Ratings: page 287

PAINT, INTERIOR

Plenty of high-quality, durable wall paints are available to brighten your rooms. And you won't need to endure as many fumes as in years past.

A fresh coat of paint is an easy, inexpensive way to freshen a room. Today's paints are significantly better than their predecessors of even a few years ago in several important respects: They spatter less, keep stains at bay, and have ample tolerance for scrubbing. They also resist the buildup of mildew (important if you're painting a kitchen, a bath, or a basement room that tends to be damp). Further, paints today have reduced amounts of volatile organic compounds (VOCs), which improves air quality while painting. Some are labeled low-VOC.

WHAT'S AVAILABLE

Major brands include Ace, Behr (sold at Home Depot), Benjamin Moore, Dutch Boy, Glidden, Sears, Sherwin-Williams, True Value, and Valspar (sold at Lowe's). You'll also see designer names such as Martha Stewart, Bob Vila, and Ralph Lauren, as well as many brands of paint sold regionally.

You'll find several types of paints for interior use. Wall paints can be used in just about any room. Glossier trim enamels are used for windowsills, woodwork, and the like. Kitchen and bath paints are usually fairly glossy and formulated to hold up to water and scrubbing and to release stains.

Price range: $15 to $30 per gallon.

KEY FEATURES

Paint typically comes in a variety of **sheens**—flat, low luster, and semigloss. The degree of glossiness can be different from one manufacturer to another. **Flat** paint, with the dullest finish, is the best at hiding surface imperfections, but it also tends to pick up stains and may be marred by scrubbing. It's well suited for formal living rooms, dining rooms, and other spaces that don't see heavy use.

A **low-luster** finish (often called **eggshell** or **satin**) has a slight sheen and is good for family rooms, kids' rooms, hallways, and the like. **Semigloss,** shinier still, usually works best on kitchen and bathroom walls and on trim because it's generally easier to clean. Low-luster and semigloss paints look best on smooth, well-prepared surfaces, since the paint's shine can accentuate imperfections on the wall.

Most brands come in several **tint bases**—the uncolored paint that forms the foundation for the specific color you choose. The tint base largely determines the paint's toughness, resistance to dirt and stains, and ability to withstand scrubbing. The **colorant** determines how much the paint will fade. Whites and browns tend not to fade; reds and blues fade somewhat; bright greens and yellows tend to fade a lot.

HOW TO CHOOSE

Performance differences. CONSUMER REPORTS tests have shown that few paints hide the old color in one coat, so plan on applying two coats. Regular semigloss paints designed for kitchens and baths are formulated to be easy to clean; our tests show that some brands are especially stain resistant and handle scrubbing extremely well. Some semigloss paints can remain sticky even after they've dried, however, meaning flowerpots or other windowsill knick-knacks can get stuck to the surface.

SHOP SMART
If an exact color match is critical, buy a quart of the paint you think you want and try it out on the wall first.

Drying time is the biggest difference we've discovered between regular paints and those specifically labeled low-VOC. Low-VOC paints dry very fast. You have to work quickly to avoid marks from overlapping roller strokes as well as brush marks around trim. Brushes and rollers may be harder to clean after applying a low-VOC paint.

Recommendations. Most paint manufacturers offer three levels of quality—essentially, good, better, and best.

Decades of CONSUMER REPORTS tests have clearly shown that it makes sense to buy top-of-the-line paints. Many of the leading brands produce paints that have delivered very good or excellent performance in our tests. The Behr and Valspar paints sold at Home Depot and Lowe's, respectively, make good all-around choices.

Related CR Report: September 2003
Ratings: page 290

POWER BLOWERS

The best electric handheld blowers outperform their gas counterparts and cost less. But they aren't any quieter, and the power cord can be a hassle.

These miniature wind machines take some of the effort out of sweeping and cleaning fallen leaves and other small yard and driveway debris. Many can also vacuum and shred what they pick up. But practically all available models still make enough noise to annoy the neighbors. Indeed, some localities have ordinances restricting or forbidding their use.

WHAT'S AVAILABLE

Mainstream brands include Black & Decker, Craftsman (Sears), Homelite, Ryobi, Toro, and Weed Eater. Pricier brands of gas-powered blowers include Echo, Husqvarna, John Deere, and Stihl. As with other outdoor power tools, gas and electric blowers have their pros and cons. You'll also find variations among gas-powered models. Here are your choices:

Electric handheld blowers. Designed for one-handed maneuvering, these are light (about 7 pounds or less). Many are also relatively quiet, produce no exhaust emissions, and can vacuum and shred. Some perform better than handheld gas-powered models, although mobility and range are limited by the power cord.

Price range: $30 to $100.

Gasoline handheld blowers. These perform like the best electrics but can go anywhere. As with other gas-powered equipment, tougher regulations have reduced allowable emissions. Manufacturers have also quieted some of models in response to new noise ordinances. Most blowers, however, are still loud enough to warrant hearing protection. Other drawbacks include added weight (most weigh 7 to 12 pounds) and the fuel-and-oil mixing that is required by the two-stroke engines most models use. A few blowers, notably from Ryobi, have a four-stroke engine that burns gasoline only.

Price range: $75 to $225.

Gasoline backpack blowers. At 16 to 25 pounds, these are double the weight of handheld blowers, which is why you wear them instead of carry them. But the payoff with most is added power and ease of use for extended periods, since your shoulders support their weight. Hearing protection is recommended. Backpack blowers don't vacuum. And they can be expensive.

Price range: $300 to $420.

Gasoline rolling blowers. These offer enough oomph to sweep sizable areas quickly. All use a four-stroke engine that requires no fuel mixing. But these machines are large and heavy, requiring some effort to push them around. They also cost the most and tend to be hard to maneuver, which can make it difficult to precisely direct leaves and other yard waste. Count on using hearing protection.

Price range: $400 to $600.

KEY FEATURES

Look for an easy-to-use **on-off switch** on electric blowers, a **variable throttle** you can preset on electric and gasoline-powered models, and a convenient **choke** on gas-powered units. Blowers that excel at cleaning usually have **round-nozzle blower tubes; oblong** and **rectangular nozzles** are better for moving leaves. A **control stalk** attached to the blower tube of backpack models improves handling, while an **auxiliary handle** on the engine or motor housing of a handheld blower makes it to easier to use—provided the handle is comfortable. Other useful features on gas-powered models include a **wide fuel fill** and a **translucent fuel tank**, which shows the level inside.

HOW TO CHOOSE

Performance differences. In Consumer Reports tests, the strongest blowers could push leaves into piles 20 inches high, while the weakest had trouble building 12-inch piles. The best electric blowers are better than most gasoline-powered models and tend to be lighter and easier to handle. Backpack blowers, while heavy, tend to be easiest to use for extended periods, since the blower tube is all you hold in your hands.

SHOP SMART
Models with a T-handle let you set air speed and control its direction with one hand.

Recommendations. Begin by matching the blower to your needs. The smaller the leaf-clearing job, the less blowing power you'll require. You can also get by with less power if you'll be clearing mostly hard surfaces such as a driveway—jobs for which relatively quiet, light, and inexpensive handheld electric machines may suffice. Models that vacuum can be handy for sucking leaves out of corners and from beneath shrubs. Whichever power blower you're considering, find out about any local noise restrictions before buying.

Related CR Report: September 2003
Ratings: page 297

STAIN, EXTERIOR

You may like the look that exterior stain gives your house, but it doesn't protect as well as paint.

Exterior stains for clapboard and cedar-shake siding come in solid and semitransparent formulations. Opaque (solid-color) finishes look almost paintlike, covering the wood completely so the grain doesn't show. Semitransparent stains add color to the wood but let the grain show. Either type soaks into the wood, leaving a flat dull, finish.

WHAT'S AVAILABLE

The major brands include Ace, Behr (sold at Home Depot), Benjamin Moore, Cabot, Olympic, Sherwin Williams, and True Value.

Stains come in a fairly limited range of basic colors: reds, greens, blues, grays, browns, and whites. Whether solid or semitransparent, stains come in water-based and oil-based formulations.

Price range: about $25 to $165 per gallon.

KEY FEATURES

Pigment is a key factor in the coverage ability of a stain and in the durability of the finish. Colors with yellow pigments—mainly greens and blues—are more prone to fading in bright sunlight. Solid stains provide better protection against degradation by ultraviolet light.

SHOP SMART
White stains tend to be most susceptible to dirt and mildew; reds tend to be most resistant.

HOW TO CHOOSE

Performance differences. Our tests have shown that water-based stains keep looking good the longest. Opaque stains are the most like paint and offer more protection and durability than semitransparent stains. In real life, that can mean going as long as nine years between paint jobs with solid stains, as opposed to about six years with semitransparent stains.

Recommendations. When aesthetics call for a stain instead of paint, consider an opaque. Whichever brand you choose, plan to apply two coats. We recommend painting with a brush to thoroughly work the stain into the wood.

Related CR Report: August 2003
Ratings: page 322

STRING TRIMMERS

An electric model can do a good job for many trimming tasks. But for strong all-around performance, you'll need a gasoline-powered string trimmer.

A string trimmer can pick up where a lawn mower leaves off. It provides the finishing touches, slicing through tufts of grass around trees and flower beds, straightening uneven edges along a driveway, and trimming stretches of lawn your mower or tractor can't reach. Gasoline-powered models can also whisk away tall grass and weeds.

Thanks to their flexible plastic lines, all string trimmers can venture into rock-strewn areas that would destroy a mower's metal blades. Some, however, are less capable and convenient at those tasks.

WHAT'S AVAILABLE

Black & Decker, Craftsman (Sears), Homelite, Ryobi, Toro, and Weed Eater are the major mainstream brands, with Weed Eater selling the most. Leading high-end brands include Echo, Husqvarna, and Stihl.

Gasoline-powered trimmers. These are better than electrics at cutting heavy weeds and brush, and are often better at edging—turning the trimmer so its spinning line cuts vertically along a walk or garden border. They also go anywhere and cut relatively large swaths up to 18 inches wide. Some accept a metal blade (usually an option) that can cut branches up to about ¾-inch thick. On the downside, gas trimmers can be heavy, weighing from about 10 to 16 pounds. Most have a two-stroke engine that requires a mixture of gas and oil. These tend to pollute more than a four-stroke engine that uses gasoline only, and entails pull-starting and regular maintenance.

Price range: less than $100 to more than $300. Most models, however, cost from $100 to $200.

Electric-corded trimmers. These are the least expensive and lightest; many weigh only about 5 pounds. Some work nearly as well as gas trimmers for most trimming. All are quieter and easier to start than gas trimmers—you simply pull a trigger rather than a starter cord. The power cord does limit your range to about 100 feet from an outlet. Many electrics have the motor at the bottom of the shaft, rather than at the top, making them harder to handle. And even the most powerful models are unlikely to handle the tall grass and weeds that the best gas-powered trimmers can tackle.

Price range: $25 to $75.

Electric battery-powered trimmers. Cordless trimmers combine the free range of gas trimmers with the convenience of corded electrics: less noise, easy starting and stopping, no fueling, and no exhaust emissions. But they're weak at cutting and run only about 15 to 30 minutes before the onboard battery needs recharging, which can take a day. They also tend to be pricey and heavy for their size (about 10 pounds). Models with the motor at the bottom of the shaft can be even harder to handle than the lighter corded versions.

Price range: $50 to $100.

KEY FEATURES

All trimmers have a **shaft** that connects the engine or motor and controls to the **trimmer head,** where the plastic lines revolve. **Curved-shaft trimmers** are the most common and can be easier to handle when trimming up close. **Straight-shaft trimmers** tend to be better for reaching beneath bushes and other shrubs. Some models have a **split shaft** that comes apart so you can replace the trimmer head with a leaf blower, edging blade, or other yard tool, though we've found that some of these attachments aren't very effective.

Most gas-powered trimmers have two **cutting lines,** while many electrics use just one, which means they cut less with each revolution. Most gas and electric trimmers have a **bump-feed line advance** that feeds out more line when you bump the trimmer head on the ground; a blade on the safety shield cuts it to the right length.

Auto-feed systems add convenience by automatically feeding out new line as they sense a change in the centrifugal force exerted by a shortened line. But some auto-feed systems don't work very well and may compromise cutting performance. In either case, replacing the line usually involves removing and rethreading the empty spool. With some trimmers, you simply pull off the old spool and push on a new one.

Most gasoline models use **two-stroke engines,** which burn lubricating oil with the gasoline. Federal law requires manufacturers to slash exhaust emissions for new gas-powered trimmers by 70 percent by 2005, while California has required that emissions reduction since 2000. Some trimmers use inherently cleaner **four-stroke engines,** but these tend to weigh and cost more. Corded and battery models typically use a 1.8- to 5-amp **motor**.

To start most gas trimmers, you set a **choke** and push a **primer bulb,** then pull a rope. On most, a **centrifugal clutch** allows the engine to idle without spinning the line—safer and more convenient than models where the line continues to turn. On models without a clutch, the string is spinning while the engine is running. Electric-trimmer lines don't spin until you press the switch.

Some models make edging more convenient with a **rotating head, shaft,** or **handle** that makes the trimmer head easier to move to the vertical position. Heavier-duty models often offer a **shoulder harness,** which can ease handling and reduce fatigue. Other convenient features include easy-to-reach and easy-to-adjust **switches,** comfortable **handles,** and—on gas models—a **translucent fuel tank.**

HOW TO CHOOSE

Performance differences. While almost any machine can trim a small, well-maintained lawn, some corded electric trimmers and all the battery-powered models in our most recent tests proved weak. As a rule with electric trimmers, the higher the amps, the better they cut. Slicing through tall grass and weeds generally requires a gasoline-powered trimmer, although our tests have shown no correlation between engine size and performance with these units.

Recommendations. Look for a trimmer that fits your physique, letting you work without stooping and maintain good balance so that your arms don't tire before the job is done. For competent performance on a range of trimming and edging tasks, you'll probably prefer a gas-powered model. Look for a cutting head with two strings for better performance. For smaller spaces and lighter-duty trimming, consider a corded electric trimmer. Look for one with the motor on top of the shaft for better balance and easier handling. Consider a cordless electric model only for the lightest of trimming chores.

Related CR Report: May 2002

VACUUM CLEANERS

Fancy features and a hefty price don't necessarily mean improved cleaning ability. You'll find lots of competent models at a reasonable price.

Which type of vacuum cleaner to buy was once a no-brainer. Uprights were better for carpets, canisters for bare floors. Period. Now that distinction has been blurred, as more uprights can clean bare floors without scattering dust and more canisters do a very good job on carpeting.

You'll also see a growing number of features such as dirt sensors and bagless dirt bins as manufacturers attempt to boost convenience. Some of those features, however, may contribute more to price than function. Other, more essential features may not be found on the least-expensive models.

WHAT'S AVAILABLE

Hoover, the oldest and largest vacuum manufacturer, is a division of Maytag and offers roughly 50 models priced from $50 to $500. Many of the Hoover models are similar, with minor differences in features. And some Hoover machines are made exclusively for retail chain stores. Kenmore accounts for about 25 percent of all canister vacuums sold in the U.S.

Other players include Dirt Devil (made by Royal Appliance), which sells uprights and canisters as well as stick brooms and hand vacuums; Eureka, which offers low-priced models; and other brands such as Miele, Panasonic, Samsung, Sanyo, Sharp, and Simplicity, which are more likely to be sold at specialty stores. Upscale Aerus (formerly Electrolux) and Oreck vacs are sold in their own stores and by direct mail. Kirby and Rainbow models are still sold door-to-door.

Uprights. These tend to be less expensive and easier to store than canister models. A top-of-the-line upright may have a wider cleaning path, be self-propelled, and have a HEPA filter, dirt sensor, and full-bag indicator.

Price range: $50 to $1,300.

Canister vacuums. These tend to do well on bare floors because they let you turn off the brush or use a specialized tool to avoid scattering dirt. Most are quieter than uprights and more adept at cleaning on stairs and in hard-to-reach areas. You'll also find a growing number of models at the lower end of the price scale.

Price range: $150 to $1,500.

Stick vacs and hand vacs. Whether corded or cordless, these lack the power of a full-sized vacuum cleaner but can be handy for small, quick jobs.

Price range: $20 to $75.

KEY FEATURES

Typical attachments include **crevice** and **upholstery tools.** Most vacuums also include an **extension wand** for reaching high places. A **full-bag alert** can be handy, since an overstuffed bag impairs a vacuum's ability to clean. Lately, many uprights have adopted a **bagless** configuration with a **see-through dirt bin** that replaces the usual bag. But we've found that emptying the bins can raise enough dust to concern even people without allergies.

The canister vacuums we've tested have a **power nozzle** that cleans carpets more thoroughly than a simple suction nozzle can. Also look for a **suction control** feature; found on most canisters and some uprights, it lets you reduce airflow for drapes and other delicate fabrics. When you're using an upright with attachments, having an **on-off switch** for the brush is a real plus; it protects you from injury, the power cord from damage, and furnishings from undue wear.

Generally, a vacuum cleaner cord is 20 to 30 feet long. While most uprights require you to manually wrap the cord for storage, canisters typically have a **retractable cord** that rewinds with a tug or push of a button.

Another worthwhile feature is **manual pile-height adjustment,** which can improve cleaning by letting you match the vacuum's height to the carpet pile more effectively than machines that adjust automatically. You'll also find more uprights with a **self-propelled feature** to make pushing easy, although that can also make them heavier and harder to carry up or down the stairs.

Some models have a **dirt sensor** that triggers a light indicator when the concentration of dirt particles in the machine's air stream reaches a certain level. But the sensor signals only that the vacuum is no longer picking up dirt—not whether there's dirt left in your rug. Result: You keep vacuuming longer, working harder and gaining little in cleanliness.

WORK SMART

A regular vacuum has no tolerance for wetness and should never be used outdoors. Even moisture from a recently shampooed rug can damage the motor.

In the normal process of vacuuming, fine particles may pass through a vacuum's bag or filter and escape into the air through the exhaust. Many models are being marketed with the claim of **microfiltration** capabilities, which entails using a bag with smaller pores or a second, electrostatic filter in addition to the standard motor filter. Some vacuums have a **HEPA filter,** which may benefit someone with asthma. But many models without a HEPA filter performed just as well in CONSUMER REPORTS emissions tests as those with the special filters, because the amount of dust emitted depends as much on the design of the entire machine as on its filter.

A vacuum's design can also affect how long it lasts. With some uprights, for example, dirt sucked into the machine passes through the blower fan before entering the bag–a potential problem, because most fans are plastic and vulnerable to damage from hard objects. Better systems filter dirt through the bag before it reaches the fan; while hard objects can lodge in the motorized brush, they're unlikely to break the fan.

Like bagless uprights and canisters, stick vacs and hand vacs typically have a messy dirt-collection bin. Some have a **revolving brush,** which may help remove surface debris from a carpet. Stick vacs can hang on a hook or, if they're cordless, on a wall-mounted charger base.

HOW TO CHOOSE

Performance differences. Better uprights and canisters clean carpet very well, although uprights still outperform canisters in this area. Uprights can also do an excellent job on bare floors, thanks in part to an on-off switch for the brush. We've found greater differences in overall performance among uprights than among canisters. Bagless vacs filter dust as well as bag-equipped models overall, but emptying their bins releases enough dust to make wearing a mask a consideration.

We have found stick vacs less impressive, with few excelling at all types of cleaning. Overall, hand vacs do a better job along wall edges than stick vacs because they come closer to the moldings and can angle into nooks and crannies.

High-end features such as dirt sensors don't necessarily improve performance. And ignore claims about amps and suction. Amps are a measure of running current, not cleaning power, and suction alone doesn't determine a vacuum's ability to lift dirt from carpeting. Some vacuums are extremely expensive—anywhere from $700 to $1,500 and more. CONSUMER REPORTS tests have shown that high-priced brands such as Aerus, Kirby, and Miele perform no better than many models that cost $150 to $300. Many of the least expensive uprights, however, sacrifice key features as well as performance.

Recommendations. Decide whether you prefer an upright or a canister. Then choose a model that performs well and has the right features for your kind of cleaning. If you have a variety of cleaning needs, you may want to consider getting more than one vacuum cleaner—an upright for carpets, a compact canister for when tool use is important, and a hand vac or stick vac for quick touch-ups around the kitchen and family room.

Related CR Report: November 2003
Ratings: page 328
Reliability: page 34

HOME OFFICE

What's New in Home-Office Gear

Computer gear continues to be ever easier to use, with the emphasis on multimedia fun. Much of the new hardware meant for home use emphasizes listening to online music, editing digital photos as well as home movies downloaded from a camcorder, creating your own CDs and DVDs, playing games, and pursuing hobbies from genealogy to collecting baseball cards.

Meanwhile, computers and telephones have merged, in the form of cell phones that can access the Internet and personal digital assistants that can act as phones. Other trends that have affected computers, phones, and related gear:

Faster, cheaper, better products. Processors, which serve as the brains of a computer, have reached speeds of nearly 3 gigahertz, or 3 billion cycles per second. That's nearly 1,000 times the speed of the earliest personal computers. Laser and photo-quality color inkjet printers are fast and affordable. Scanners for photos and text are also inexpensive and produce excellent results. PDAs with a color screen continue to come down in price, though they still cost more than a black-and-white model.

Telephone answering machines have pretty much disappeared as a stand-alone product, as faster, cheaper computer chips have allowed the function to be inexpensively added to cordless and corded phones.

Smaller products. Desktop computer manufacturers have developed interesting alternatives to the familiar beige box. Apple's iMac, for example, puts an entire computer into a small hemisphere from which sprouts a stalk holding the svelte flat-panel display. Such displays are becoming the norm for all desktop systems, as they continue to drop in price. Computer users on the go can take advantage of laptops that are as thin as a couple of magazines. Cell phones are tiny, easily fitting into a pocket.

More ways to buy. Nearly all major computer manufacturers sell their wares directly, through the Web, telephone orders, and factory stores. They offer financing programs that let you make monthly payments, as well as leasing programs for home-based businesses. Retail venues include computer superstores such as CompUSA and PC Warehouse, electronics superstores like Best Buy and Circuit City, home-office superstores such as Office Depot and Staples, and warehouse clubs like Costco and Sam's Club. At some stores, you can custom-design your own computer at an interactive kiosk. According to the most recent CONSUMER REPORTS survey, you're likely to be better satisfied if you buy directly from the manufacturer than if you buy through a retail store.

The new sell in cellular. More than 150 million cell phones are now in use, increasingly as a household's main phone. A cell phone offers undeniable convenience as well as some inescapable shortcomings. The phones themselves employ sophisticated digital technology that allows them to access the Internet and e-mail, send short text messages to other phones, even take low-resolution digital photos. Problems with service—"dead zones," where calls can't be made; dropped calls; poor connections—continue to plague all the major carriers. And while the cost of a cell-phone call continues to drop, it's still an expensive way to keep in touch. Most carriers offer a variety of often-confusing calling plans, most requiring a one- or two-year commitment.

Online access speeds up. More people are getting high-speed Internet access. Broadband options that let you speed up your Web connection include a cable modem, available through a cable television provider; digital subscriber line (DSL), available through an Internet service provider in conjunction with either a phone company or a third party; and two-way satellite via a rooftop dish.

Wi-fi gains popularity. Wireless has become the new byword for computing, at home and on the road. One in 10 of the people we've surveyed who have linked their computers in a home network did it wirelessly. In addition, more than a million people in North America handle their e-mail and surf the Web wirelessly at more than 28,000 public "hotspots" at airports, hotels, cafes, and more. Some hotspots are free by design—in parks, for instance—others charge for access.

CELL PHONES

Complex pricing schemes and incompatible technologies can make it hard to find the right calling plan and handset. We give you guidelines.

The cell phone is a permanent part of the landscape. There are now more than 145 million subscribers, who spend an average of $47 a month on local service. A small but steadily growing number of people use a cell phone as their only phone. Most major phone manufacturers and cellular-service providers are promoting a new generation of equipment that lets users do much more than merely make phone calls.

Despite its popularity, cellular service has a reputation for problems: dead zones, where you can't get service; calls that inexplicably end in mid-conversation; inadequate capacity, so you can't put a call through when you want; hard-to-fathom calling plans; and errors in bills. Problems like those are why as many as one-third of all cell-phone users say they're ready to switch carriers.

WHAT'S AVAILABLE

The cell phone itself is only half of what you need for wireless calling. You also have to sign up for service with a cellular provider and choose a calling plan. You can find phones in many outlets, including independent wireless retailers, electronics stores, and cellular-provider stores and Web sites.

The providers. The major national companies are AT&T Wireless, Cingular, Nextel, Sprint PCS, T-Mobile, and Verizon Wireless. There are also numerous local or regional providers.

What distinguishes one provider from another is not necessarily the level of service—surveys done by CONSUMER REPORTS, among others, indicate that every major carrier suffers from some significant problems—but the type of wireless technology used. Most carriers use one of three digital technologies, often with analog calling as a backup. Among the major national providers, only Nextel and T-Mobile are all-digital, with no analog capability. CONSUMER REPORTS believes that analog capability is essential in a cell phone. Not only does it improve coverage in general, it also betters the chances that an emergency call to 911 can get through. That's because analog is a common cellular language; the digital technologies are mostly incompatible with one another.

TECH TIP
Many states prohibit drivers from using hand-held cell phones, so use a hands-free kit if you absolutely must talk and drive at the same time. Better still, pull off the road to make the call that can't wait.

The calling plans. Most providers offer a range of plans based around a "bucket" of minutes of calling time. The more minutes in the bucket, the more the plan costs you each month. However, the total number of minutes isn't the most important figure. Some of those minutes may be good anytime, others available only on nights and weekends; if you exceed the allotment of minutes, you'll be charged 20 to 60 cents per minute, depending on the plan. Cingular, alone among the major carriers, lets customers roll over unused minutes to the next month. You need to determine when and where you'll be using a cell phone most in order to select a plan that's right for you. Most plans require you to sign a one- or two-year contract and levy a hefty fee if you want to cancel before the contract expires.

Prepaid plans are a good alternative if you're averse to a long-term contract. Many cellular providers as well as a service called Tracfone offer prepaid calling. You pay in advance for airtime minutes, which typically last 45 to 60 days before they expire. GoPhone, a new service from AT&T wireless, works like the automated highway-toll services. You set up an account with no long-term contract and an opening balance posted to a credit card. Calls debit the account, which is automatically replenished every 30 days or when the balance drops below $5. You have 30 days to use the calling time you've bought or replenish the account.

There are also different types of calling plans. Local plans, the most limited, typically encompass a metropolitan area and its environs; calls outside that area entail extra roaming charges, long-distance charges, or both. Regional plans take in a wider area, sometimes all or part of several states. Roaming and long-distance charges apply outside the main calling area. National plans, as their name implies, take in the widest area and usually involve no long-distance or roaming charges. Family plans (which can be local, regional, or national in scope) allow family members to pool their monthly minutes for use on several phones.

The phones. Some are simple rectangles with a display window and keypad on the front. Others are curvaceous or have a flip-open cover to protect the keys. Sony-Ericsson, Kyocera, LG, Motorola, Nokia, Panasonic, Samsung, and Sanyo are the major phone manufacturers. Light weight is pretty much standard. All the newer phones can send and receive text messages up to 160 characters long to or from any other cell-phone user. You'll also see phones that can access popular computer games, are integrated with a digital camera, offer wireless Internet access, or are combined with a personal digital assistant (PDA). All of those applications carry an additional cost.

KEY FEATURES

Cell-phone makers and service providers are beginning to offer so-called **3G service,** which enhances the speed of data transfer. At this point, 3G is the frosting, not the cake. Its main benefit at present: allowing users to e-mail photos and download games. Finding the right service and calling plan is still more important. Among basic cell-phone features, look for a **liquid-crystal display (LCD) screen** that is readable in both low- and bright-light conditions. The **keypad** should be clearly marked and easy to use. **Programmable speed dial** lets you store the names and numbers of the people you most frequently call. **Single-key last-number redial** is useful for dropped calls or when you're having trouble connecting. Some providers offer **caller ID, voice mail**, and **messaging,** often for an extra charge.

Instead of ringing, some handsets have a **vibrating alert** or a flashing light-emitting diode to let you know about an incoming call, useful when you're in a meeting or at the movies. An **any-key answer** feature lets you answer the phone by pressing any key rather than the Talk or Send key. Many folding phones answer the call when you open the mouthpiece flap.

The **battery** offered with the phone you buy won't necessarily give you the best service—and it's not your only option. There are several choices of battery size, each offering different amounts of talk time and standby time.

The base of some phones has an extra battery that can be kept charged while the handset is in use; you don't lose any time waiting for a recharge, which can take 6 to 24 hours in some "trickle" chargers. An **automobile adapter** lets you power the phone by plugging it into your car's cigarette lighter. Some cell-phone models include a **headset.** That capability is increasingly demanded by various states' laws for drivers using cell phones.

Phones vary widely in keypad design, readability of displays, and ease of using the function menu or performing such basic tasks as one-button redial and speed dial for frequently called numbers.

HOW TO CHOOSE

Ask friends who use a cell phone in the same areas that you do whether they're satisfied with their service. That will increase the odds that you'll have service where you need it. Carefully compare calling plans from competing carriers. Once you've selected a carrier and a plan, select a phone. Be sure the phone is the right size for your hands, and that the keypad buttons aren't too small for your fingers. If possible, have a clerk maneuver the phone through several functions, so you can see how easy it is to program the phone for common settings and tasks—setting the ring volume, say, or retrieving text messages.

Rebates and special promotions, common these days, can drastically reduce the price of the phone.

Related CR Report: February 2003

DESKTOP COMPUTERS

Even the least-expensive desktop machines deliver impressive performance. The quality of technical support may be the deciding factor.

The desktop computer has become just another appliance you use every day.

Replacement sales—not first-time purchases—now drive the computer market. Prices continue to drop. Fully loaded desktop systems selling for less than $1,000, a novelty a few years ago, are now common, even among established brands.

WHAT'S AVAILABLE

There are dozens of companies vying to put a new desktop in your home. Dell, Gateway, Hewlett-Packard (which merged with Compaq in 2002), IBM, and Sony all make Windows machines. Another contender, eMachines, has emerged as a player with a series of budget-priced Windows systems. Apple is the sole maker of Macintosh models. Small mail-order and store brands cater to the budget-minded.

Price range: $400 to $2,500. (The monitor is often extra.)

KEY FEATURES

The **processor** houses the "brains" of a computer. Its clock speed, measured in megahertz (MHz), determines how fast the chip can process information. In general, the higher the clock speed, the faster the computer. But not always. In our tests, one computer with a 1.4-gigahertz (GHz) Pentium M chip outperformed a machine driven by a 2.4-GHz Pentium 4 chip. Manufacturers of Windows machines generally use 2.2- to 3.2-GHz processors with one of the following names: Intel's Pentium 4 or Celeron or AMD's Athlon XP or Duron. Celeron and Duron are lower-priced processors that are equal to higher-priced chips in many respects. Apple's Macintosh machines use 800-MHz to 2.0-GHz PowerPC G5 processors, which are manufactured by IBM. Apple and AMD have maintained that the system architecture of their chips makes them as fast as or faster than Pentium 4s with higher clock speeds.

TECH TIP

Features you might want when buying a desktop are a FireWire port, which is useful for connecting peripherals like camcorders and external hard drives, and separate CD-RW and DVD drives, which let you copy directly from one CD to another.

All name-brand computers sold today have at least 128 megabytes (MB) of **RAM,** or **random access memory,** the memory that the computer uses while in operation. **Video RAM,** also measured in megabytes, is secondary RAM essential for smooth video imaging and game play.

The **hard drive** is your computer's long-term data storage system. Given the disk-space requirements of today's multimedia games and video files, bigger is better. You'll find hard drives ranging in size from 20 to 200 gigabytes (GB).

A **CD-ROM** drive has been standard on most desktops for a number of years. Fast replacing it is **CD-RW** (CD-rewriteable), which lets you create backup files or make music compilations. **DVD-ROM** brings full-length movies or action-packed multimedia games complete with full-motion video to the desktop. It complements the CD-RW drive on midline and higher-end systems, letting you copy CDs directly between the two. A DVD drive will also play CD-ROMs. Combo drives combine CD-writing and DVD-playing in a single drive, saving space. The newest in this family is the **DVD-writer,** which lets you transfer home-video footage to a DVD disk. There are three competing, incompatible formats: DVD-RW, DVD+RW, and DVD-RAM.

The **diskette drive** is where 3.5 inch diskettes are inserted, letting you read or store relatively small amounts of data. Apple Macintoshes and a growing number of PCs don't have a diskette drive built in. The traditional capacity of a 3.5-inch diskette is 1.4 MB. That's too small for many purposes today, so many people use a CD-RW as a large "diskette" drive to transport files. You can also get external drives or use a USB memory module that holds much more than a diskette.

The computer's **cathode ray tube (CRT)** or flat-panel **liquid crystal display (LCD)** monitor contains the screen and displays the images sent from the graphics board—internal circuitry that processes the images. Monitors come in sizes (measured diagonally) ranging from 15 inches to 21 inches and larger. Seventeen-inch monitors are the most common. Apple's iMac comes with a built-in monitor.

The critical components of a desktop computer are usually housed in a case called a **tower.** A **minitower** is the typical configuration. More expensive machines have a **midtower,** which has extra room for upgrades. A **microtower** is a space-saving alternative that is usually less expensive. The Apple iMac has no tower; everything but the keyboard and mouse is built into a small case that supports the monitor. Apple's Power Mac line of computers has a tower.

A **mouse,** the small device that fits in your hand and has a "tail" of wire that connects to the computer, moves the cursor (the pointer on the screen) via a rolling ball on its underside. Alternatives include a mouse that replaces the ball with a light sensor; a trackball, which is rolled with the fingers or palm in the direction you want the cursor to go; a pad, which lets you move the cursor by sliding a finger; a tablet, which uses a penlike stylus for input; and a joystick, used to play computer games.

All computers come with a **standard keyboard,** although you can also buy one separately. Many keyboards have **CD (or DVD) controls** to pause playback, change tracks, and so on. Many also have keys to facilitate getting online, starting a search, controlling a DVD movie, or retrieving e-mail.

Multimedia computers for home use feature a **high-fidelity sound system** that can play music from CDs or downloaded music files, synthesized music, game sounds, and DVD-movie soundtracks. **Speaker systems** with a subwoofer have deeper, more powerful bass. Surround-sound systems can turn a PC into a home theater. Some computers come with a **microphone** for recording, or one can be added.

PCs usually come with a modem to allow a dial-up Internet connection. A V.90 modem provides the fastest downloading supported by dial-up providers. A V.92 modem can speed up connection and uploading if the Internet provider supports it.

Parallel and **serial ports** are the traditional connection sites for printers and scanners. **Universal Serial Bus (USB) ports,** seen on all new computers, are designed to replace parallel and serial ports. **FireWire** or **IEEE 1394 ports** are used to capture video from digital camcorders and other electronic equipment. An Ethernet, or wireless, **network** lets you link several computers in the household to share files, a printer, or an Internet connection. An **S-video output jack** lets you run video cables from the computer to a TV, which lets you use the computer's DVD drive and view a movie on a TV instead of on the computer monitor.

HOW TO CHOOSE

Performance differences. Judged on performance alone in CONSUMER REPORTS tests, most desktop computers are closely matched and extremely good overall. But there are some differences in connectivity, expandability, the design of the keyboard and controls, and the sound of the loudspeakers. Surveys of users have found differences in reliability (frequency of repair), and survey respondents report that some manufacturers are better than others at providing support to consumers with problems.

Recommendations. You'll have to decide between Windows and Macintosh. Windows has the advantage for its sheer number of compatible software applications and peripheral devices. Macintosh has the edge for its ease of setup and use. Then decide on power, speed, and features that suit your work—or play.

Related CR Report: June 2003
Reliability: page 26

LAPTOP COMPUTERS

A long-time companion at work, school, and on the road, the laptop has finally come into its own as a serious alternative to the desktop computer.

In May 2003, laptop sales outstripped those of desktops for the first time. It's not hard to understand why. Small screens and cramped keyboards have been replaced by bigger displays and more usable key layouts. Processors have caught up in speed, and an innovative new processor provides some real advantages. Fast CD and DVD recording drives are common, as are ample hard drives. And a growing interest in wireless computing plays to the laptop's main strength: its portability. A laptop is the only way you can take full advantage of the growing availability of high-speed wireless Internet access at airports, schools, hotels, and even restaurants and coffee shops.

The Centrino technology that's central to Intel's newest laptop processors has wireless capability built in and delivers considerably longer battery life than comparable chips.

The thinnest laptops on the market are only an inch or so thick and weigh just 3 to 5 pounds. To get these light, sleek models, however, you'll have to pay a premium and make a few sacrifices.

WHAT'S AVAILABLE

Dell, Gateway, HP, Compaq (now owned by HP), IBM, Sony, and Toshiba are the leading Windows laptop brands. Macintosh laptops are made by Apple. Laptops come in two basic configurations:

Desktop replacement. These machines can handle everyday computing just as a desktop can. The hard drive, diskette drive (if included), and optical drive (CD-ROM, CD-RW, DVD-ROM, DVD-RW, or combo drive) reside onboard. These models also have a full complement of jacks, connectors, and expansion slots for PC cards. But they're the biggest and heaviest laptops, measuring 1¾ inches thick and weighing 7 to 8 pounds. The keyboard is full size, and the screen typically measures 15 inches diagonally. (Apple and a few others have laptops with a 17-inch screen.) Some models can hold a second battery for increased running time; most should deliver three to four hours of work on a fresh battery. Others can shed drives to reduce size and weight. With a docking station, you can easily switch from mobile to desktop use.

Price range: About $1,300 to $2,200.

Lightweight. Especially good for traveling, these models measure about 1 inch thick and weigh 4 to 6 pounds. The case contains the hard drive and a smallish battery. The optical drive and the diskette drive are often external, plugged into the laptop when need be. A docking station is a common option. A few lightweights have a screen measuring only 12 inches diagonally, although a 14-inch screen is more common. The keyboard may be small and somewhat hard to use. Battery life should be about the same as with a desktop replacement: three to four hours, possibly longer with some.

Price range: $1,500 to $2,500.

KEY FEATURES

A **diskette drive** is becoming a rarity in all computers. As an alternative, you can use a USB memory drive (about $20 and up), which fits on a keychain and holds as much data as many diskettes. Or you can save files on a writeable CD or an external ZIP drive.

Windows laptops generally have a 1.0 to 3.0-GHz **processor.** Pentium 4 processors have the higher speed ratings; the new Centrino technology has a slower-rated speed but actually performs on a par with other processors. Macintosh Power PC processors are measured on a different basis altogether. In short, the different types of processors make direct speed comparisons difficult. It doesn't pay to try because any processor will deliver all the speed you need.

Laptops come with a 10- to 60-gigabyte **hard drive** and 256 megabytes of **random access memory (RAM)** and can be upgraded to 512 MB or even 1 GB.

Most of today's laptops use a rechargeable **lithium-ion battery.** In CONSUMER REPORTS tests, batteries provided two to five hours of continuous use when running office applications. (Laptops go into sleep mode when used intermittently, extending the time between charges.) You can extend battery life somewhat by dimming the display as you work and by removing PC cards when they aren't needed. Playing a DVD movie uses more battery power than usual, but any laptop should be able to play a movie through to the end.

A laptop's **keyboard** can be quite different from that of a desktop computer. The keys themselves may be full-sized (generally only lightweight models pare them down), but they may not feel as solid. Some laptops have extra buttons to expedite your access to e-mail or a Web browser or to control DVD playback. If your laptop has a USB port you can attach an external keyboard, which you may find easier to use.

A 14- to 15-inch **display,** measured diagonally, should suit most people. A few desktop replacements have a 16- or 17-inch display. With liquid-crystal display (LCD) monitors, the display size represents the actual viewing area you get. By contrast, the viewing area is smaller than the measured display with traditional cathode-ray tube (CRT) monitors. A resolution of 1,280x1,024 pixels (picture elements) or more is better than 1,024x768 for viewing the fine detail in photographs or video, but may shrink objects on the screen. You can use settings in Windows to make them larger.

SHOP SMART

Buy a la carte. Laptops can be tailored to an individual buyer's needs, much like choosing options for a car. Configure-to-order menus show you all the options and let you see how a change in one affects the overall price.

Most laptops use a small **touch-sensitive pad** in place of a mouse—you drag your finger across the pad to move the cursor. You can also program the pad to respond to a "tap" as a "click," or to scroll as you sweep your index finger along the pad's right edge. An alternative pointing system uses a pencil-eraser-sized joystick in the middle of the keyboard.

Laptops include at least one **PC-card slot** for expansion. You might add a **wireless network card** or a **digital-camera memory-card reader,** for example. Many laptops offer a connection for a **docking station,** a $100 or $200 base that makes it easy to connect an external monitor, keyboard, mouse, printer, or phone line. Most laptops let you attach these devices anyway, without the docking station. At least two **USB ports,** for easy hookup of, say, a printer, digital camera, or scanner, is standard. A **wired network (Ethernet) port** is common, as is a **FireWire port** for digital-video transfer. Some models have a standard or optional internal wireless-network adapter. An **infrared port,** used to synchronize data between the computer and a personal digital assistant (PDA), can be useful.

Laptops typically come with far less software than desktop computers, although almost all are bundled with a basic home-office suite (such as Microsoft Works) and a personal-finance package. The small **speakers** built into laptops often sound tinny, with little bass. Headphones or external speakers deliver much better sound.

HOW TO CHOOSE

Performance differences. In our tests, most laptop computers have performed solidly in many ways. Desktop-replacement models pack computing muscle comparable to that of their desktop cousins. Lightweights may sacrifice drive space for easy portability. Aside from size and weight, a major factor distinguishing laptops is battery performance. Some models run longer on a charge and have better power management than others. You can count on Centrino-powered laptops to have the best battery performance, although such machines command a premium price.

Recommendations. Consider buying a little more laptop power than you think you need, since upgrading can be difficult or impossible. While desktop computers often use interchangeable, off-the-shelf components, a laptop's parts are typically proprietary. Adding more RAM might be relatively easy, but installing a larger hard drive or upgrading a video card might be out of the question.

Related CR Report: September 2003

MONITORS

Prices are dropping for larger CRT monitors and flat-panel LCD displays, meaning that a roomier screen—or more space on your desktop—is now within reach.

Deciding whether to buy a flat-panel LCD or a CRT monitor comes down to this: Do you need more space on the surface of your desk or on the screen? If freeing up space on your desk is the priority, an LCD (liquid crystal display) monitor would seem to be the clear choice. But since LCDs are costly, you might still opt for a CRT (cathode ray tube) monitor. Despite price drops for both types, the typical 17-inch LCD costs nearly $600, more than twice the cost of a CRT whose screen is an inch larger.

Desktop computers and monitors are often sold as a package. Still, some people buying a new desktop decide to hold on to their old monitor. Others choose to buy a new monitor for their existing computer.

WHAT'S AVAILABLE

Apple, Dell, eMachines, Gateway, Hewlett-Packard (which merged with Compaq in

2002), IBM, and Sony all market their own brands of monitors for their computers. Other brands of monitors, such as CTX, Envision, Mitsubishi, NEC, Philips, Samsung, and Viewsonic are sold separately. Many brands are manufactured on an outsource basis.

CRTs. Most desktop monitors sold today are CRTs, typically ranging from 17 to 21 inches. To reduce glare, some CRTs have a flattened, squared-off screen (not to be confused with a flat-panel LCD screen). The nominal image size—the screen size touted in ads—is generally based on the diagonal measurement of the picture tube. The image you see, called the viewable image size (VIS), is usually an inch smaller. Thus a 17-inch CRT has a 16-inch VIS. As a result of a class-action lawsuit, ads must state a CRT's VIS as well as its nominal image, but you may have to squint at the fine print to find it.

Generally the bigger the screen, the more room a CRT takes up on your desk, with depth roughly matching nominal screen size. "Short-depth" models shave an inch or more off the depth.

A 17-inch monitor, the most frequent choice these days, has almost one-third more viewable area than the 15-inch version now vanishing from the market. The larger size is especially useful when you're using the Internet, playing video games, watching DVD movies, editing photos, or working in several windows.

If you regularly work with graphics or sprawling spreadsheets, consider a 19-inch monitor. Its viewable area is one-fourth larger than a 17-inch model's. A short-depth 19-inch model doesn't take up much more desktop space than a standard 17-inch.

Aimed at graphics professionals, 21- and 22-inch models provide ample viewing area but gobble up desktop space.

Price range: $150 to $300 (17-inch); $170 to $400 (19-inch); $500 to $1,000 (21- to 22-inch).

Flat-panel LCDs. Because these monitors have a liquid-crystal display rather than a TV-style picture tube, they take up much less desktop space than CRTs. They operate with analog or digital input, or both. Unlike a CRT, the nominal and the viewable image sizes of a flat-panel LCD are the same. Desktop models typically measure 15 inches diagonally and just a few inches deep, and weigh 10 pounds or less (compared with 40 pounds for a 17-inch CRT and 50 pounds for a 19-inch CRT). LCDs with a screen 17 inches or larger are available but are still somewhat pricey. Wide-screen LCDs with a 17-inch VIS, specially designed for watching wide-format videos, are also available. These screens have an aspect ratio of 16:9, like those found on most digital TVs; they're also fairly pricey.

Flat-panel displays deliver a very clear image, but they have some inherent quirks. Their range of color is a bit narrower than that of CRT monitors. And you have to view a flat-panel screen straight on; except for wide-screen models, the picture loses contrast as you move off-center. Fine lines may appear grainy. In analog mode, you have to tweak the controls to get the best picture.

Price range: $270 to $500 (15-inch); $400 and up (17- to 18-inch).

KEY FEATURES

A monitor's **resolution** refers to the number of picture elements, or pixels, that make up an image. More pixels mean finer detail. Most monitors can display at several resolutions, generally ranging from 640x480 to 1,600x1,200, depending on the monitor and the graphics card. An LCD usually displays a sharper image than a CRT of comparable size when both are viewed at identical resolutions. But that's only if the LCD is set to its "native" resolution—1,024x768 pixels for a 15-inch screen; 1,280x1,024 or 1,400x1,050 for a 17-, 18-, or 19-inch model. On both types of monitor, the higher the resolution, the smaller the text and images, so more content fits on the screen. Bigger CRT screens can handle higher resolutions and display more information.

Dot pitch, measured in millimeters, refers to the spacing between a CRT's pixels. All else being equal, a smaller dot pitch produces a more detailed image, though that's no guarantee of an excellent picture. In general, avoid models with a dot pitch higher than 0.28 mm.

A CRT requires a high **refresh rate** (the number of times per second the image is redrawn on the screen) to avoid annoying image flicker. In general, you'll be more comfortable with a 17-inch monitor set at a refresh rate of at least 75 hertz (Hz) at the resolution you want. With a 19-inch monitor, you may need an 85-Hz rate to avoid eyestrain, especially at higher resolutions. While the refresh rate of a flat panel display is 60 or 75 Hz, its native resolution is 1,024x768 unless otherwise specified. Refresh rate isn't an issue with flat-panel displays.

Monitors have controls for **brightness** and **contrast.** Most of them also have controls for **color balance** (usually called color temperature), **distortion,** and such. Buttons activate onscreen controls and menus.

Bigger CRTs use a considerable amount of juice: for example, about 80 watts for a typical 19-inch model, between 65 to 70 watts for a 17-inch model, and about 20 watts for a 15-inch flat-panel LCD. Most monitors have a **sleep mode** that uses less than 3 watts when the computer is on but not in use.

Some monitors include a **microphone,** integrated or separate **speakers,** or **composite-video inputs** for viewing the output of a VCR or camcorder.

Plug-and-play capability makes it relatively simple to add a new monitor to an existing computer.

HOW TO CHOOSE

Performance differences. Most of the larger CRT monitors (16-inch and 18-inch VIS) that CONSUMER REPORTS recently tested have a display we judged very good or excellent. There are some subtle performance differences between the two types of monitor: CRTs respond more quickly than LCDs to videos and fast-action games, and they can provide richer color in a fuller spectrum. CRTs with a flattened, squared-off screen may pick up fewer reflections, but that doesn't necessarily result in better display quality. Some CRTs have control buttons that are poorly labeled or on-screen controls that are difficult to use. Tilting is difficult with some models.

Most of the flat-panel LCDs tested had excellent display quality. Advantages over CRTs include compactness and lower power consumption.

Recommendations. Buy the right size for your task and workspace. You may decide that the slim profile and power savings of a flat-panel monitor make the premium you'll pay worthwhile.

If you're buying a new computer, your best value may well be the monitor the manufacturer bundles with it. Try to view the monitor before buying it. Look at a page of text on screen to be sure both center and edges are bright and clear. Open up a picture file to see whether the colors look natural and clear. Compare monitors side-by-side, if possible, with the same image displayed on each screen.

Of course, buying through mail order or over the Internet doesn't allow you to judge the monitor you're choosing. See if a friend or co-worker has the model you're considering, or try to see it in a store. Wherever you buy, it's wise to get a 30-day money-back guarantee.

On your desk, the new monitor should sit 18 to 30 inches away from you, with the top line of text just below eye level. Good lighting and correct placement of the keyboard and mouse are also critical.

Related CR Report: June 2003
Ratings: page 284

PDAS

Besides serving as an address book, calendar, and to-do list, many personal digital assistants offer multimedia functions and can manage your e-mail. Some even combine a PDA with a cell phone.

PDAs can store thousands of phone numbers, appointments, tasks, and notes. All can exchange, or synchronize, information with a full-sized computer simply by connecting via a cradle or cable. The cradle doubles as a charger for PDAs that run on rechargeable batteries. Infrared and other wireless technologies let you synchronize your PDA with a computer without the use of wires or a cradle.

Most PDAs can be made to work with Windows and Macintosh computers—either with an inexpensive adapter or with third-party software. Many provide access to an abbreviated form of the Internet, most often with the addition of a separately purchased accessory such as a modem. Some PDAs can record your voice, play videos, display digital photos, or hold maps, city guides, or a novel.

WHAT'S AVAILABLE

There are currently more than two dozen models on the market. Most are the familiar tablet-with-stylus types that feature a squarish display screen, a design pioneered by Palm, Inc. Today the main choices are PDAs that use the Palm operating system (OS)—mostly Palm and Sony models—and PocketPC devices from companies such as Casio, Dell, Hewlett-Packard, and Toshiba. The latter use a stripped-down version of Microsoft Windows. A few PDAs use a proprietary operating system. Handspring (due to merge with Palm), Kyocera, Nokia, and Samsung offer units that combine a cell phone and a PDA.

Palm OS systems. Equipped with software to link with Windows and (for Palm-brand units) Macintosh computers, Palm units and their clones have a simple user interface. You use a stylus to enter data on the units by tapping an onscreen keyboard or writing in a shorthand known as Graffiti. Or you can download data from your computer. Most Palm OS-based PDAs can synchronize with a variety of e-mail software programs and include their own basic personal-information-management (PIM) application. These PDAs are easy to use, although navigation between different programs is cumbersome because of the operating system's "single-tasking" nature.

Models with a backlit monochrome display (growing scarce) are easy to read under normal lighting conditions and are very easy on batteries. Our tests have shown that monochrome models can operate continuously with the backlight off for at least 24 hours, the equivalent of seven weeks of use at a half-hour per day. Models with a color display use a rechargeable lithium-ion battery that must be recharged after just a few hours of continuous use. A few models let you replace the old battery once it will no longer hold a charge. But most make it difficult or impossible to replace the battery yourself. And, beyond the warranty period, you can't be sure the manufacturer will do it for you.

The latest Palm OS models typically have expansion slots that let you add memory or attach separately purchased accessories. All Palm-based PDAs can be enhanced by adding third-party software applications—the more free memory that a model comes with, the more software it can accommodate. A large body of Palm OS-compatible freeware, shareware, and commercial software is available for download at such sites as *www.palmgear.com.* Many Palm models come with "Documents to Go," word-processing and spreadsheet software similar to that used in Pocket PCs, but more versatile.

TECH TIP

Test ease of use while shopping for a PDA. Far too many people invest in one only to find its keypad, stylus, or shorthand are hard for them to use.

Price range: about $100 to $800.

Pocket PC systems. These resemble Palm-based models but are more like miniature computers. They have a processor with extra horsepower and come with familiar applications such as a word processor and a spreadsheet. Included is a scaled-down version of Internet Explorer, plus voice-recording and perhaps some financial functions. Also standard is an application that plays MP3 music files, as well as Microsoft Reader, an e-book application.

As you might expect, all the application software included in a Pocket PC integrates well with the Windows computer environment. You need to purchase third-party software to use a Mac. And you'll need Microsoft Office programs such as Word, Excel, and Outlook on your computer to exchange data with a PDA. Most Pocket PCs have a color display that livens up the interface but also quickly drains their rechargeable lithium-ion batteries. As with most Palm-based PDAs, replacing the battery of most Pocket PCs is difficult or impossible.

Price range: $200 to $700.

KEY FEATURES

Whichever operating system your PDA uses, you may need to install some programs in your computer to enable the PDA to synchronize with it. This software lets you swap data with leading PIM programs such as Lotus Organizer and Microsoft Outlook.

Most PDAs have the tools for basic tasks: a **calendar** to keep track of your appointments; **contact/address software** for addresses and phone numbers, **tasks/to-do lists** for reminders and keeping track of errands, and a calculator. A **notes/memo function** lets you make quick notes to yourself. Other capabilities include **word-processing, spreadsheet, database,** and **money-management functions.** A **voice recorder,** which includes a built-in microphone and speaker, works like a tape recorder. **MP3 playback** lets you listen to digital-music files stored in that format, and a **picture viewer** lets you look at **digital photos**. A few models also include a built-in **digital camera.**

A PDA's **processor** is the system's brain. In general, the higher the processing speed of this chip, the faster the PDA will execute tasks—and the more expensive the PDA will be. But higher-speed processors may require more battery power and thus deplete batteries more quickly. Processing speeds are 16 to 400 megahertz (MHz), and models typically have 2 to 64 megabytes (MB) of user memory. Even the smallest amount in that range should be more than enough for most people.

A **backlight** for the display is near-standard. With a monochrome screen, you need the backlight when using the PDA in the dark. The backlight is always used with color screens.

Nearly every PDA offers an **expansion slot** for some form of removable memory card: CompactFlash, MultiMediaCard (slots also accept Secure Digital cards), or Memory Stick. Models with two expansion slots can accommodate a **peripheral device,** such as a **wi-fi wireless networking card,** as well as removable memory. If you plan to transfer photos from a digital camera to your PDA, make sure the two devices use the same type of card.

Some PDAs offer **wireless connectivity.** Models with a capability known as **Bluetooth** can connect wirelessly over short distances to a properly equipped computer or peripheral device such as a printer or modem. Models with "wi-fi" can connect over medium distances to a wi-fi-enabled home network or to the Internet at "hot spots" in certain airports, coffee shops, hotels, and parks. A PDA with a built-in **cell phone** can make voice calls or directly connect to the Internet via a wireless Internet service provider. It's possible for a single PDA to have more than one of these three types of wireless connectivity.

HOW TO CHOOSE

Performance differences. CONSUMER REPORTS tests have shown that Palm OS models are best for basic organizer functions, such as date and address books, and for exchanging documents and e-mail with computers running programs other than Microsoft Office.

Newer, higher-priced models are well suited to multimedia, and all Palm-brand models include software to connect with a Macintosh. (To make a Sony model compatible with a Macintosh running OS X or OS 9, you need third-party software.) Exchanging files and handling e-mail attachments, however, isn't as easy as with Pocket PCs. Also, newer Palm OS models can't accept a CompactFlash card.

Pocket PCs are best for exchanging, reading, and editing word-processing documents, spreadsheets, and other files compatible with Microsoft Office applications running on a PC. The user interface is easy to learn if you're familiar with Windows. Its architecture allows a wider variety of plug-in cards, including CompactFlash, than does Palm OS, and makes it easier to access data stored on them. All models are well-suited to multimedia.

Recommendations. If you're new to PDAs, look for one with a monochrome display and, thus, excellent battery life. While color models are becoming the norm, monochrome PDAs are still available. Color models are coming down in price, but battery life remains an issue. If you're replacing a Palm OS unit with a model with greater capability, look for one with more built-in memory and an expansion slot. If you need power and room for multimedia functions, such as MP3 playback and picture viewing, an increasing number of Palm OS systems and Pocket PCs have a fast processor and expandable memory as well as color display. If you want a computer—that is, a Windows-based computer—in your pocket and regularly run Microsoft applications and need multimedia capability, choose a Pocket PC.

Related CR Report: July 2003
Ratings: page 294

PRINTERS

New, inexpensive inkjets print color superbly. And they do it faster than ever. Laser printers excel at printing black-and-white text.

Inkjet printers are now the standard for home-computer output. They do an excellent job with color—turning out color photos nearly indistinguishable from photographic prints, along with banners, stickers, transparencies, T-shirt transfers, and greeting cards. Many produce excellent black-and-white text. With some very good models going for less than $200, the vast majority of printers sold for home use are inkjets.

Laser printers still have their place in home offices. If you print reams of black-and-white text documents, you probably need the speed and low per-copy cost of a laser printer.

Printers use a computer's microprocessor and memory to process data. The latest models are so fast partly because computers themselves have become more powerful and contain much more memory than before. Unlike the computers they serve, most home printers can't be upgraded—except for adding memory to laser printers. Most people usually get faster or more-detailed output by buying a new printer.

WHAT'S AVAILABLE

The printer market is dominated by a handful of well-established brands. Hewlett-Packard is the market leader. Other brands are Brother, Canon, Epson, Lexmark, and Samsung.

The type of computer a printer can serve depends on its ports. A universal serial bus (USB) port lets a printer connect to Windows or Macintosh computers. Some models have a parallel port, which lets the printer work with older Windows computers. All these printers lack a serial port, which means they won't work with older Macs.

Inkjet printers. Inkjets use droplets of ink to form letters, graphics, and photos. Some printers have one cartridge that holds the cyan (greenish-blue), magenta, and yellow inks, and a second cartridge for the black ink. Others have an individual cartridge for each ink. For photos, many inkjets also have additional cartridges that contain lighter shades of cyan and magenta inks.

Most inkjets print at 2½ to 9½ pages per minute (ppm) for black-and-white text, but are much slower for color photos, taking from 2 to 18 minutes to print a single 8x10. The cost of printing a black-and-white page with an inkjet printer varies considerably from model to model—ranging from 3 to 9 cents. The cost of printing a color photo can range from 70 cents to $1.10.

Price range: $50 to $700.

Laser printers. These work much like plain-paper copiers, forming images by transferring toner (powdered ink) to paper passing over an electrically charged drum. The process yields sharp black-and-white text and graphics. Laser printers usually outrun inkjets, cranking out black-and-white text at a rate of 9 to 15 pages per minute. Black-and-white laser printers generally cost about as much as high-end inkjet models, but they're cheaper to operate. Color laser printers are also available. Laser cartridges, about $100, often contain both the toner and the drum and can print thousands of black-and-white pages for a per-page cost of 2 to 4 cents.

Price range: $200 to $1,000 (black-and-white); $700 and up (color).

KEY FEATURES

Printers differ in the fineness of detail they can produce. **Resolution,** expressed in dots per inch (dpi), is often touted as the main measure of print quality. But other factors, such as the way dot patterns are formed by software instructions from the printer driver, count too. At their default settings—where they're usually expected to run—inkjets currently on the market typically have a resolution of 600x600 dpi.

For color photos, the dots per inch can be increased. Some printers go up to 4,800x1,200 dpi. Laser printers for home use typically offer 600 or 1,200 dpi. Printing color inkjet photos on special paper at a higher dpi setting can produce smoother shading of colors, but can slow printing significantly.

Most inkjet printers have an **ink monitor** to warn when you're running low. Generic ink cartridges and refill kits can cut costs, but think twice about using them: A printer's warranty might not cover repairs if an off-brand cartridge damages the machine.

For **double-sided printing,** you can have printers print the odd-numbered pages of a document first, then flip those pages over to print the even-numbered pages on a second pass through the printer. A few printers can automatically print on both sides, but doing so slows down printing.

HOW TO CHOOSE

Performance differences. When it comes to producing graphics and photos, many inkjets do excellent work. The best in our tests print graphics that are crisp, clean, and vibrant-looking. Photos rival the output of a photofinishing lab, with smooth gradations and deep blacks.

The worst inkjets turn out graphics that are dull, grainy, or banded. Photos may suffer from over-inked dark areas, textures that make skin seem pebbled, and grainy or dull colors.

In recent tests, laser printers had the advantage when it came to producing excellent-quality black-and-white text, though more than half of the inkjets we tested rivaled them. Page for page, laser models are cheaper to operate.

Printing results were sometimes better for one side of the paper than the other. Some brands of paper indicate on the package which side to use. We've found that brand-name paper generally gives better results than low-cost products, especially when used with the same brand of printer.

TECH TIP

To trim costs, print snapshots in 3.5X5-inch size; you'll fit four to a sheet. And crop and edit before printing so you'll get the desired results on the first try.

Recommendations. An inkjet printer is the more versatile choice, and it's inexpensive for both color and black-and-white output. If you plan on printing color graphics and photos, an inkjet is the way to go. Buy a laser printer if you need to turn out a large amount of high-quality black-and-white text.

Depending on the printer and the ports available, you have several connection options. Most printers now support USB connectivity. If you have a parallel port, you should use an IEEE 1284-compliant printer cable.

However, most laser printers now offer a built-in Network Interface Card (NIC) option, for a high-speed Ethernet connection over an office Local Area Network (LAN) or even a home network, allowing multiple users to share a single printer.

Related CR Report: September 2003
Ratings: page 299

SCANNERS

A scanner is a simple, cheap way to digitize images for printing, editing on your computer, or sending via e-mail.

You don't need a digital camera to take advantage of the computer's ability to edit photos. Images captured on film can be digitized by a photo processor and delivered to you on a CD or via the Web. But if you do more than a modest amount of film photography, having a processor digitize your photos—at $5 to $10 per roll—can quickly become expensive. You're also paying for digitizing outtakes as well as winners. A more cost-effective way to digitize selected photographs is with a scanner, which can capture the image of nearly anything placed on its glass surface—even those old photos you've tucked away in a family album or a shoebox.

Most scanners work basically the same way. As with photocopiers, a bar housing a light source and an array of sensors passes beneath a plate of glass on which the document lies facedown. (In the case of a sheet-fed model, the document passes over the scanner.) The scanner transmits data from the sensor to your computer, typically via a USB port. Driver software, working in concert with the hardware, lets you scan at certain settings. Once the image is in the computer, software bundled with the scanner (or purchased separately) lets you crop, resize, or otherwise edit the image to suit your needs. From there, you can print it, attach it to e-mail, or post it on the Web.

WHAT'S AVAILABLE

A number of scanners come from companies, including Microtek and Visioneer, that made their names in scanning technology. Other brands include computer makers and photo specialists such as Canon, Epson, Hewlett-Packard, and Nikon.

Which type of scanner you should consider—flatbed, sheet-fed, or film—depends largely on how you'll use it. If you're short on space, consider a multifunction device.

Flatbed scanners. More than 90 percent of the scanners on the market are flatbeds. They work well for text, graphics, photos, and anything else that is flat, including a kindergartner's latest drawing. Flatbeds include optical-character-recognition (OCR) software, which converts words on a printed page into a word-processing file in your computer. They also include basic image-editing software. Some stores may throw in a flatbed scanner for free, or for a few dollars extra, when you buy a desktop computer.

A key specification for a scanner is its maximum optical resolution, measured in dots per inch (dpi). You'll pay more for greater resolution.

Price range: less than $100 for 600x1,200 dpi; $100 to $500 for models with greater resolution.

Sheet-fed models. Sheet-fed models can automatically scan a stack of loose pages, but they sometimes damage pages that pass through their innards. And they can't scan anything much thicker than a sheet of paper (meaning an old photo might be too thick). This type of scanner is often the one that comes as part of a multifunction device that can also print, send, and receive faxes. An increasing percentage of multifunction devices, however, include a flatbed scanner. Sheet-fed scanners also use OCR software.

Price range: $150 to $600.

Film scanners. Serious photographers may want a film-only model that scans directly from an original slide (transparency) or negative. These offer a higher maximum resolution than you get from an ordinary flatbed or sheet-fed model. Some can accept small prints as well.

Price range: $400 to $800.

KEY FEATURES

While the quality of images a scanner produces depends in part on the software included with it, there are several hardware features to consider.

You start scanning by running **driver software** that comes with the scanner or by pressing a preprogrammed button. Models with buttons automate routine tasks to let you operate your scanner as you would other office equipment. On some models, you can customize the functions of the buttons. Any of these tasks can also be performed through the scanner's software without using buttons. A **copy/print button** initiates a scan and sends a command to print the results on your printer, effectively making the two devices act as a copier. Other button functions found on some models include **scan to a file, scan to a fax modem, scan to e-mail, scan to Web, scan to OCR, cancel scan, power save, start scanner software,** and **power on/off.**

You can also start the driver software from within an application, such as a word processor, that adheres to an industry standard known as "twain." A scanner's driver software lets you **preview** a scan onscreen and crop it or adjust **contrast** and **brightness.** Once you're satisfied with the edited image, you can perform a final scan and pass the image to a running program or save it on your computer. You can make more extensive changes to an image with specialized **image-editing software.** And to scan text from a book or letter into a word-processing file in your computer, you run **OCR software.**

Many documents combine text with graphic elements, such as photographs and drawings. A handy software feature on many scanners, called **multiple-scan mode,** lets you break down such hybrids into different sections that can be processed separately in a single scan. You can designate, for example, that the sections of a magazine article that are pure text go to the OCR software independently of the article's graphic elements. Other scanners would require a separate scan for each section of the document.

Some flatbed models come with a **film adapter** designed to scan film or slides, but if you have this need often, you're better off getting a film scanner.

HOW TO CHOOSE

Performance differences. In recent tests of flatbed scanners, we used the scanner software provided by the manufacturer to print scanned photos on a high-resolution inkjet printer at 150, 300, 600, and (when possible) 1,200 and 2,400 dpi. There was little improvement in the quality of scanned color and black-and-white photographs above 300 dpi. For the flatbed scanners tested, the manufacturer's recommended scan ranges were 150 to 300 dpi for photos, text, and line art, and 72 to 96 dpi for e-mail, Web sites, and onscreen viewing. Unless you plan to regularly scan line drawings or graphics rich in pastels, taking the time and trouble to do high-resolution scans is worse than unnecessary. It results in scans that take two to four times longer and creates files that are much larger.

The OCR software that came with our test models did a nearly error-free job of converting a typewritten memo. The scanners made more errors processing a page from CONSUMER REPORTS magazine, but still few enough that our testers were able to fix those mistakes with minimal effort.

Images produced with film-scanning adapters that come with some flatbed scanners aren't really worth the effort. The adapters weren't very effective at flattening the film in our tests and have no focus adjustment to control the distance between the scan head and the film. The resulting images were usually slightly fuzzy. Worse, they were off in color or contrast; some even looked grainy. If you frequently need to scan film or slides, it's generally worth buying a dedicated film scanner.

Matching the original version of a color photo is the most demanding of a scanner's functions. You'll sometimes need to use image-editing software to get a printed version that's faithful to the original.

Recommendations. For most home users, a flatbed scanner offers the best combination of versatility, performance, and price. Most consumers don't need a high-resolution scanner with considerably more than 300 dpi. Look instead for features and conveniences you can use, such as photo-editing software or one-button functions.

Related CR Report: May 2003

TELEPHONES

Cordless phones

Newer, higher-frequency cordless phones are available, but they aren't necessarily better than the earlier 900-MHz phones.

If you have a cordless phone that's several years old, it's probably a 900-megahertz (MHz) phone. Newer phones use higher frequencies, namely 2.4 or 5.8 gigahertz (GHz).

WHAT'S AVAILABLE

A few brands—AT&T, Bell South, GE, Panasonic, Uniden, and VTech—account for more than 70 percent of the market. VTech owns the AT&T Consumer Products Division and now makes phones under the AT&T brand as well as its own name.

The current trends include multiple-handset-capable phones, which support two or more handsets with one base, less expensive 2.4-GHz analog phones, and high frequency 5.8 GHz phones. Some of the multiple-handset-capable phones now include an additional handset with a charging cradle. About a third of the cordless phones sold include a digital answering machine(see sidebar, page 156).

A main distinction among cordless phones is the way they transmit their signals. The major types are:

Analog. These phones are the least expensive type available now, offering enough range to let you chat anywhere in your house and yard, or even a little beyond. But analog transmission isn't very secure if the phone doesn't have voice-scrambling capability; anyone with an RF scanner or comparable wireless device might be able to listen in. Analog phones are also more likely than digital phones to suffer occasional static and RF interference from other wireless products.

Price range: $15 to $100.

Digital. These offer about the same range as analog phones, but with better security. They're less prone to RF interference than analog phones. Price range: $50 to $130.

Digital spread spectrum (DSS). With these phones, a call is distributed across a number of frequencies, providing still tighter security. And this technology is even more immune to RF interference. The range may be slightly better than that of analog or digital phones. Note that some DSS phones—usually the multiple-handset-capable phones with handset-to-handset talk capabilities—use such a wide swath of the spectrum even in standby mode that they may interfere with baby monitors and other wireless products operating in the same frequency band.

Price range: $75 to $225 (for multiple handset systems).

Another distinguishing factor is the frequency band in which cordless phones operate. Manufacturers are phasing out 900-MHz phones in favor of higher-frequency phones, so expect to find fewer of the former on the market in the future. Most phones currently sold are 2.4-GHz models. Unfortunately, many other electronic products—baby monitors, wireless computer networks, microwaves ovens—use the same band. Newer phones use the 5.8-GHz band. Its main advantage: less chance of RF interference because few other products use this band at present. Some phones are dual-band, but that only means they transmit between base and handset in one band and receive in another; you can't switch from one band to another.

KEY FEATURES

Standard features on most cordless phones include **handset volume control, last-number redial,** a **pager** to locate the handset, a **flash** button to answer call waiting, and a **low-battery indicator.**

A phone that supports **two lines** can receive calls for two phone numbers—useful if you have, say, a business line and a personal line that you'd like to use from a single phone. Some of the phones have **two ringers**, each with a distinctive pitch to let you know which line is ringing. The two-line feature also facilitates conferencing two callers in three-way connections.

Some phones let you support **two or more handsets** with just one base without the need for extra phone jacks. Additional handsets including the charging cradle are usually sold separately.

An **LCD screen**, found on many handsets and on some bases, can display a personal phone directory and useful information such as the name and/or number dialed, caller ID, battery strength, or how long you've been connected. **Caller ID** displays the name and number of a caller and the date and time of the call if you use your phone company's caller ID service. If you have caller ID with call waiting, the phone will display data on a second caller when you're already on the phone.

MORE INFO
Americans spend billions on directory assistance. These five Web-based services give you listings for free:
- *www.anywho.com*
- *www.infospace.com*
- *www.infousa.com*
- *www.switchboard.com*
- *www.whowhere.com*

A **speakerphone** offers a hands-free way to converse or wait on hold and lets others chime in as well. A base speakerphone lets you answer a call without the handset; a handset speakerphone lets you chat hands-free anywhere in the house as long as you stay within a few feet of the handset.

Many cordless phones have a **headset jack** on the handset and include a belt clip for carrying the phone. This allows hands-free conversation anywhere in the house. Some phones have a headset jack on the base, which allows hands-free conversation without any drain on the handset battery. Headsets are usually sold separately for about $20.

A **base keypad** supplements the keypad on the handset. It's handy for navigating menu-driven systems, since you don't have to take the phone away from your ear to punch the keys. Some phones have a **lighted keypad** that either glows in the dark or lights up when you press a key, or when the phone rings. This makes the phone easier to use in low-light conditions. All phones have a handset **ringer**, and many phones have a base ringer. Some let you turn them on or off, adjust the volume, or change the auditory tone.

Other convenient features include **auto talk**, which lets you to lift the handset off the base for an incoming call and start talking without having to press a button, and **any key answerer**. An **auxiliary jack data port** to plug in a fax, modem, or other phone device can also be useful.

Phones that have earned the **Energy Star** designation use somewhat less electricity than others.

Some phones provide a **battery holder for battery backup**—a compartment in the base to charge a spare handset battery pack or to hold alkaline batteries for base-power backup, either of which can enable the phone to work if you lose power. Still, it's wise to keep a corded phone somewhere in your home

Some multiple-handset-capable phones allow conversation between handsets and facilitate **conferencing** handsets with an outside party. For some phones with this capability, the handsets have to be within range of the base for handset-to-handset use; others also allow direct communication between handsets, so you can use them like walkie-talkies.

Multiple handsets supported represents the maximum number of handsets that can be registered to a phone's base. A phone that can support up to eight hand-

MESSAGE CENTERS

Answering machines

Digital answering machines come as stand-alone devices or as part of a phone/answerer combo unit. The main advantage of a combo unit–less clutter–has to be weighed against the loss of one part of the combo if the other goes bad.

Answerers usually have standard features and capabilities such as a selectable number of rings and a toll-saver, answerer on/off control, call screening, remote access from a touch-tone phone, and a variety of ways to navigate through your messages. Most have a message day/time stamp, can delete all messages or just individual ones, allow you to adjust the speaker volume, and can retain messages and greeting after a momentary power outage.

Other answerer features you may want to consider are several mailboxes, advanced playback controls, remote handset access, conversation recording, a message counter display that indicates the number of messages received, and a visual indicator or audible message alert that lets you know when you have new messages.

In Consumer Reports tests, most answerers delivered very good voice quality for recorded messages and good quality for the greeting. Phones that let you record your greeting through the handset (i.e., using the remote handset access) usually scored better. Some let you listen to your greeting through the handset, as opposed to listening though the base speakerphone; that gives you a better indication of how the greeting will sound to the calling party.

Price range: $20 to $80 (stand-alone units); $30 to $240 (combos).

sets, for example, can have eight handsets registered to the base, but you may only be able to use four at once. For instance, two handsets can be used for handset-to-handset intercom, while two others conference with an outside party. Other phones may allow only one handset to be used at a time.

HOW TO CHOOSE

Performance differences. CONSUMER REPORTS tests show that most new cordless phones have very good voice quality. Some are excellent, approaching the voice quality of the best corded phones. In our latest tests, most fully charged nickel-cadmium (Ni-Cd) or nickel-metal hydride (Ni-MH) batteries handled eight hours of continuous conversation before they needed recharging.

Most manufacturers claim that a fully charged battery will last at least a week in standby mode. When they can no longer hold a charge, a replacement battery costs about $10 to $20. (To find a store that will recycle a used battery, call 800-822-8837.)

Some phones offer better surge protection than others against damage from lightning or faulty wiring.

Recommendations. A 900-MHz phone should suit most users. There are fewer new 900-MHz phones being manufactured, however, as the technology is being replaced by higher-frequency 2.4-MHz and 5.8-MHz phones. Analog phones, apt to be less expensive than digital, are fine for many people. But if privacy is important, choose a digital or DSS phone. Once you decide on a phone and the features you want, stick with what you need. Shop around or check online, as some retailers or manufacturers may have the lower-priced phones with fewer features in stock.

If you're in a store, ask to look at the manual. (You may also find user manuals online at manufacturers' or retailers' Web sites.) The manual can detail all the available features of a particular model, and give you some sense of how easy those features are to use. It can also show you how the phone is wall mounted—flat against the wall or with an L bracket.

Before you buy, hold the handset to your head to see if it feels comfortable. The handset of a cordless phone should fit the contours of your face. The earpiece should have rounded edges and a recessed center that fits nicely over the middle of your ear. Check the buttons and controls to make sure they're reasonably sized and legible.

Note that ads mentioning the word "digital" may not be referring to the wireless transmission between the base and handset. To ensure voice-transmission security, look for wording such as "digital phone," "digital spread spectrum," or "phone with voice scrambling." Phones that aren't secure might have packaging with wording such as "phone with digital security code," "phone with all-digital answerer," or just "spread spectrum technology."

Corded phones

Today's basic phone is sleeker and more versatile than its boxy predecessor.

For $10, you can now buy a corded phone with such features as volume control and speed-dialing for 10 or more numbers. For $50 or more, you get a console with speakerphone or two-line capability, sometimes both.

Every home should have at least one corded phone, if only for emergencies. In an emergency, you can't always rely on a cell phone because circuits fill up quickly or because the signal may not reach your house. A cordless phone may not work if you lose electrical power. Because a corded phone draws its power from the phone system, it will operate even if you lose household AC power.

WHAT'S AVAILABLE

AT&T (currently made by VTech) and GE are the dominant brands. When shopping, you'll find these types:

Console models. These are updated versions of the traditional Bell desk phone.

Price range: $15 to more than $100.

Trim-style models. These space savers have push buttons on the handset, and the base is about half as wide as a console model's. But a trim-style phone can be hard to use when you need to listen and punch buttons at the same time to navigate an unfamiliar voice-mail or automated-banking menu.

Price range: $10 to $30.

Phones with answerers. Combo units can sometimes be less expensive than buying a phone and an answerer separately.

Price range: $50 to $150.

KEY FEATURES

Corded phones tend to be less feature-laden than cordless ones. It's practically standard for any phone to have **handset volume control, last-number redial** and **speed dialing**. Features such as a **speakerphone, two-line capability,** or **caller ID** add to the price.

HOW TO CHOOSE

Performance differences. Most corded phones should perform quite capably, conveying voices intelligibly under normal conditions. The variations in sound quality that we have found in the past are likely to matter only in very noisy environments.

Recommendations. Since good quality is pretty much a given, your main considerations should be features and price. Before you buy, make sure the handset is comfortable in your hand and to your ear. Look for a good-sized, clearly labeled keypad, especially if your eyesight isn't good.

Related CR Report: October 2003
Ratings: page 324

AUTOS

What's New in Autos for 2004

More than 50 new or redesigned models are being introduced for 2004, and this doesn't include those that are appearing as early-2005 entries. These models make their debut against the backdrop of several ongoing trends: more vehicles emphasizing versatility, sportiness, and discounted pricing.

The characteristics that once distinguished cars from trucks and minivans from sport-utility vehicles continue to blur as automakers put the emphasis on versatility, trying to make vehicles that do everything for everybody. The result is more—more power, more sportiness, and more interior space. Midsized SUVs, for example, are increasingly offering third-row seats so they can carry up to seven or eight people. Crewcab pickups, which provide seating for five people, have become a mainstay. There is literally something for everyone.

Discounts, rebates, and low-interest financing have become prevalent even on newly released models. That's generally good for consumers, but it's not all that it appears to be. The Big Three, for instance, have been raising the list prices on certain models, offsetting some of the discounts.

Dealers are also using cheap-financing deals to urge customers to load up on options. So don't be tempted by a low-cost loan into spending more than you intended, or buying a car that's not right for you.

The rebates and special deals on new cars have effectively pushed down prices in the used-car market, which is more than twice the size of the new-car market. This is good news for buyers, but bad news for dealers and for people trying to sell their present car.

The Internet remains an increasingly popular source for automotive research of all kinds, but so far only a small percentage of shoppers actually purchases a vehicle online. To help you find car related information, see our guide to Web sites on page 170.

With more than 220 models from which to choose, consumers looking for a new vehicle now have more choice than ever. Look for full road tests on many of these models in Consumer Reports magazine and online at *www.ConsumerReports.org.*

New & noteworthy

Sedans: More of everything. Sedans are still the largest single segment of the auto market, with more than 80 models available, but the percentage of overall sales has been gradually dropping as more buyers have moved to SUVs, minivans, and other light trucks. To increase their sedans' appeal, automakers are spicing them up with better handling and more performance, and an improved driving position.

Midsized sedans remain the bread-and-butter of the mass market, even with the wide range of new vehicles. For 2004, Chevrolet has redesigned the Malibu. Built on a platform shared with the Saab 9-3, the Malibu sedan looks like a pretty good package, except for an antiquated V6 powertrain and unknown reliability. Its wagon version is called Malibu Maxx.

Mitsubishi's redesigned Galant appears to be competitive with the excellent Toyota Camry and Honda Accord. It has a stronger 230-hp, 3.8-liter V6 and a more stylish interior than the previous version.

Pontiac has redesigned the Grand Prix. The new one is styled like a coupe, which robs head room and inhibits rear access, but the new car could ride and handle reasonably well. GM's pushrod V6 provides decent power but isn't as refined as more advanced designs.

Large sedans may stage something of a comeback, and may get larger, too. Chrysler's big, rear-drive 300C, a 2005 model, is the latest installment in DaimlerChrysler's bid to drive the Chrysler brand upmarket. More mainstream Chrysler Concorde and Dodge Intrepid siblings will follow later.

In the late summer of 2004, Ford is slated to bring out its new Five Hundred, an all-wheel-drive, 2005-model-year sedan larger than the Taurus in all dimensions. A Mercury version is called the Montego.

Kia has brought out the Amanti, an inexpensive ($27,000), Mercedes E-Class knockoff based on the Hyundai XG350. A full slate of safety gear, including eight air bags, is optional. The Hyundai version has good acceleration, brakes, and interior quality, but clumsy handling.

Those who like sporty sedans will find interesting new offerings. The new Acura TSX is marketed as a sports sedan intended to compete with the Audi A4 and BMW 325i. It's based on the four-cylinder Honda Accord currently sold in Europe and Japan. In comparison, the U.S. Accord is larger, its V6 offers more power, and costs less than the TSX. Acura has also redesigned the TL, which is based on the U.S. Accord V6. Besides the prestige name, the extra money the TL costs brings more features, more sound-deadening material, and an upscale decor.

SHOP SMART

Every issue of CONSUMER REPORTS has road tests of selected vehicles. The annual auto issue, in April, provides the latest Ratings and survey results. For all models you can find updates any time at *ConsumerReports.org.*

This past fall BMW introduced a redesigned 2004 5-Series. The new car replaced one of the world's all-around best sedans. It employs a version of the iDrive multifunction control system that uses one knob to control audio, climate, navigation, communications, and other functions. We found the iDrive system on the top-of-the-line 7-Series needlessly complicated and distracting. Hopefully the 5-Series' system will be less challenging.

Small cars: Shedding their econobox image. Mazda has introduced the Mazda3 to replace the Protegé, a car we long liked. The Mazda3 looks to be a cleverly-packaged small sedan and hatchback with a well-laid-out interior.

Toyota has introduced a whole new brand, called Scion, aimed at younger buyers. Scion dealers will be specially trained and the cars sold at a no-haggle price, like Saturns. The first two Scions are both based on the small Toyota Echo. The xA is a conventional five-door hatchback, while the attention-getting xB is like a big square box on wheels and provides the most interior room available at its price.

Sporty cars: Quicker, slicker. Notable new sport coupes include the Chrysler Crossfire, the redesigned 2005 Ford Mustang, and the revived Pontiac GTO.

The Crossfire coupe, based on the previous-generation Mercedes-Benz SLK, has stylish looks but is not especially fun to drive and has a stiff ride.

Judging from auto-show concepts, the redesigned 2005 Mustang is a well-styled and attractive package. It's rumored to share some underpinnings with the good-handling Lincoln LS.

The Pontiac GTO is adapted from an Australian car, the Holden Monaro, which in turn uses a modified version of the discontinued Cadillac Catera's platform. This rear-wheel-drive coupe uses a 350-hp V8 from the Chevrolet Corvette.

The 300-hp Subaru WRX STi is an Impreza souped-up beyond the already sporty 227-hp WRX. The STi is essentially a street-legal rally-racing car with race-car handling and all-wheel drive. Similarly, the AWD, 271-hp Mitsubishi Lancer Evolution is a close copy of the company's entry in international rally races. Both are exceedingly quick and agile.

At the other end of the design spectrum is the Chevrolet SSR, a specialty car hot-rod pickup styled like Chevys of the early '50s. Sharing a chassis with the TrailBlazer SUV, the SSR has a retractable hardtop over its two seats, a big but not very perky V8, and a hard-shell tonneau cover over a pickup-like cargo bed.

SUVs: A wider spectrum. Car-based SUVs and the similar wagonlike "crossover" vehicles make up the fastest-growing segment of the auto market. In our testing, we've found that in typical everyday driving, which is how most owners use their SUVs, the car-based models are notably better than traditional truck-based SUVs in ride comfort, handling, fuel economy, and ease of access. In fact, car-based models occupy all the top spots in our SUV Ratings.

New car-based SUVs include the BMW X3, Cadillac SRX, and Chevrolet Equinox. The X3 is derived from the fine 3-Series sedan, and is a slightly smaller version of the existing BMW X5. The Cadillac SRX is derived from the good CTS sedan and will offer three rows of seats and a Northstar V8 engine. The Chevrolet Equinox, Chevy's first car-based SUV, is related to the Saturn VUE, and will have GM's aging 3.4-liter pushrod V6.

Later in 2004 we'll also see crossovers that are more like all-wheel-drive wagons, including the Chevrolet Malibu Maxx and the Ford Freestyle. The Malibu Maxx is a wagon version of the redesigned Malibu sedan. The somewhat larger Ford Freestyle is a spinoff of the Five Hundred sedan. This is Ford's answer to the Chrysler Pacifica that came out in 2003, a six-passenger wagon with three rows of seats.

Not all SUVs are derived from cars. In September of 2003, Nissan brought out a traditional, truck-based SUV, the Pathfinder Armada, which is derived from its new full-sized pickup, the Titan. The big Pathfinder Armada is an addition to the line, not a replacement for the mid-sized Pathfinder.

Dodge has redesigned the Durango, making it larger to compete with such full-sized models as the Chevrolet Tahoe, Ford Expedition, and GMC Yukon, as well as conventional midsized SUVs.

Minivans: New styling & features. As a whole, minivans are the most versatile vehicles on the market. Nissan's redesigned Quest, which arrived last summer, is now as large as a Dodge Grand Caravan or Honda Odyssey, and uses bold, edgy styling. Part of that is a nearly horizontal control pod for audio and climate systems that isn't very convenient. The Quest rides and handles very well, though.

Now our top-Rated minivan, the redesigned 2004 Toyota Sienna is also much larger than the old one. Available features include a split fold-away third-row seat, optional all-wheel drive, head-protection air bags, run-flat tires, adaptive cruise control, and a rear-mounted video camera to help when backing up.

The Ford Windstar gets a partial redesign and a new name, the Freestar. This reworked model offers a fold-away third row of seats and Ford's "rollover canopy" system, which automatically deploys side-curtain air bags if the vehicle begins to roll over. The Mercury version of the Freestar is called the Monterey.

Pickups: Big and small. There are two new full-sized pickups for 2004: the redesigned Ford F-150 and the all-new Nissan Titan. The new F-150 looks fairly similar to the old truck on the outside, but the interior has been updated a lot, with roomier cabins, a center console-mounted shifter, and adjustable pedals. It's also quieter and better-riding.

Nissan's first full-sized truck, the imposing Titan, will be available at first only with an extended cab, and later with a crew cab. It offers a floor-mounted shifter and a powerful 300-hp, 5.6-liter V8. The extended cab provides a relatively roomy rear-seat area and rear doors.

This past fall Chevrolet brought out the replacement for its aging S10 compact pickup, the all-new Chevrolet Colorado. (The similar GMC is called the Canyon.) The Colorado has a neatly designed interior, but the two engine choices (an inline four and five-cylinder) both look rather weak, and the four-wheel-drive setup is part-time only.

Hybrids and diesels: More on the way. In the next few years, gas/electric hybrid powertrains will begin to show up in a greater range of models. These provide better fuel economy and lower emissions than equivalent gasoline engines. Currently, only the Honda Civic Hybrid and Insight and Toyota Prius offer them.

Toyota is the farthest along in hybrid development. It has already unveiled its second-generation 2004 Prius. The new Prius is a 5-door hatchback that is said to be both quicker and more fuel-efficient. For 2005, Toyota's luxury division, Lexus, will offer a hybrid RX330 SUV. It will use front and rear electric motors to supplement a regular V6 engine propelling the front wheels. That will provide the benefits of all-wheel drive without the weight and drag of conventional AWD systems.

The first hybrid SUV, the Ford Escape Hybrid, is due to go on sale in mid-2004. Ford says the Escape Hybrid will get about 35 to 40 mpg in city driving. But in tests with current hybrids, our fuel-economy figures have been significantly lower than those claimed by the automakers and the Environmental Protection Agency.

General Motors has developed three different hybrid systems, which will be offered first in models such as the 2004 full-sized Chevrolet Silverado and GMC Sierra pickups and the 2005 Saturn VUE SUV.

More diesel-powered cars also arrive for 2004. The Jeep Liberty, Mercedes E-Class, and Volkswagen Passat TDI will all offer a turbocharged diesel engine. These modern diesels are much quicker, cleaner, and quieter than the clattering old-style diesels we're used to. Once low-sulfur fuel becomes the standard in the fall of 2006, new diesels will be able to run cleaner still.

Features & options

Equipping a vehicle only with the options you want is often a juggling act. If you must have a car quickly, you may have to settle for what's on the dealer's lot. Special ordering a car can take weeks or even months, which is fine if you have the time.

Many options are available individually, but often certain items come only as part of an option package, with a name like "convenience group" or "preferred equipment package." If you want most or all of the package's components, then such a package can save you money over buying the options separately. But sometimes you can't get an option you want without buying things you otherwise wouldn't consider.

You can negotiate the price of options. To help, CONSUMER REPORTS offers its New Car Price Report, which includes a complete list of options and packages, with both invoice and retail prices. It also includes CR's equipment recommendations. Call 800-269-1139 or go to *www.ConsumerReports.org* to get the New Car Price Report.

UPGRADES TO CONSIDER

Audio. Many standard audio systems provide good sound and some form of theft protection. Higher-level systems typically improve audio quality and convenience. CD players are usually standard, but you can often upgrade to a multidisc CD changer. Changers mounted in the dash or console are more convenient than changers mounted in the trunk, which used to be the norm.

Comfort and convenience. From leather upholstery to heated seats, sunroofs, roof racks, and navigation systems, the list of small and large conveniences can seem almost endless and maybe irresistible. Be careful, though, because the tally can add up quickly.

A key-fob remote control is a handy addition to power locks. It lets you unlock the vehicle's doors and, often, turn on interior lights from a distance. That's both a convenience and a security consideration.

Engines. If price and fuel economy are more important to you than performance, a vehicle's base engine is likely to be fine. A more powerful engine usually gets you quicker acceleration, better hill-climbing, and quieter operation. Often the model with the larger engine comes with upgraded tires that contribute to better cornering and braking. Larger engines sometimes also boost towing capacity. The trade-off is usually worse fuel economy.

Four-wheel and all-wheel drive. Both maximize traction (as does traction control). Although the terms are often used interchangeably, 4WD systems are generally heavier-duty and equipped with low-range gearing for serious off-road or hazardous-terrain travel. Part-time 4WD systems, the type found on most pickups and less-expensive SUVs, should not be used on dry pavement while in 4WD mode. Full-time 4WD systems are more versatile. All-wheel drive, which usually uses smaller and lighter components, lacks the low-range setting and is intended for all-weather and moderate off-road travel.

Two-wheel drive is enough for most people, especially if the vehicle is front-wheel drive. Modern rear-drive cars (most of which these days are luxury and high-performance models) can provide decent traction in slippery conditions if they're equipped with electronic traction-control and stability-control systems.

Transmission. A manual transmission can provide an edge in fuel economy and performance over an automatic, and some prefer the greater control and sporty feel that a stick shift provides. But automatic transmissions have become much smoother and more responsive and are far more popular, particularly among drivers who have to deal with a lot of traffic congestion.

Tires and wheels. The only parts of a car that actually touch the road, tires can make a big difference in handling, braking, and ride comfort. Upgraded, higher-performance tires improve handling and braking, although they tend to ride more firmly and noisily, and can wear faster. Whatever tires you choose, keeping them inflated to the right pressure optimizes driving dynamics and maximizes tread life.

KEY SAFETY FEATURES

While safety belts remain the most important safety feature, every year new technology shows up to help drivers avoid an accident or help protect passengers during a collision. Here's a rundown of the major features that are available.

Antilock brakes (ABS). Antilock brakes prevent the wheels from locking up during an emergency stop. Locked-up wheels can cause a sideways skid and also impede your steering control. ABS can not only help you stop shorter, particularly on slippery surfaces, but it also helps keep the vehicle heading straight. And it allows the driver to retain steering control while braking, so you can steer around an obstacle if necessary. Consumer Reports strongly recommends ABS when available.

Brake assist. This adjunct to ABS senses the speed or force with which the brake pedal is depressed to determine if the driver is trying to make an emergency stop. If so, it applies greater braking force even if the driver is tentative in pressing the pedal.

Traction control. This system limits wheel-spin during acceleration. It's particularly useful when starting from a standstill in wet or icy conditions. It can serve as a less expensive (though less effective) alternative to all- or four-wheel drive, particularly in rear-wheel-drive cars.

Stability control. This system helps prevent a vehicle from skidding or sliding in a turn. It's especially helpful in slippery conditions, and can help prevent an SUV from getting into a state where it could roll over. Stability control selectively brakes one or more wheels and, if necessary, cuts back engine power if it detects that the vehicle is beginning to slide or skid. Consumer Reports strongly recommends stability control, particularly on SUVs.

Front air bags. All new vehicles come with front air bags. Advanced designs use dual-stage deployment, where the bags may not inflate or may inflate with reduced force in a low-level collision. In a higher-speed collision, the bags inflate with full force. Another enhancement on more models: occupant-sensing systems that adjust the deployment of the air bags to fit the size and position of the occupant, modifying or preventing deployment as appropriate.

Side air bags. Side air bags for the front seats are now common. Some automakers offer side air bags for the rear seats too. Some models provide occupant-sensing systems for side bags. The system in Acura and Honda models, for instance, deactivates the side bags if a front passenger is leaning too close to the door, to prevent possible air-bag injury.

Head-protection side bags. Head-protection side air bags are an important enhancement. The most common are side-curtain air bags, which cover both front and rear side windows to prevent occupants from hitting their head or from being ejected through the window.

Pretensioners and force limiters. These features help safety belts work better. Pretensioners retract the safety belts to remove slack and help place the person in the optimum position for the air bags. Force limiters pay the belt back out slightly following the initial impact. That can help prevent chest and internal injuries caused by the belt.

Rollover-detection system. This new system is now available on the Ford Explorer, Expedition, and Windstar (Freestar); Mercury Mountaineer; Lincoln Aviator and Navigator; Volvo XC90; Lexus LX470; and Toyota Land Cruiser. If sensors determine that the vehicle has leaned beyond a specified angle, indicating that a rollover is imminent, they automatically trigger the side-curtain air bags, and keep them inflated for a time, to help prevent occupants from being injured or ejected.

Child-seat attachments. All new vehicles now must have a LATCH (for Lower Anchors and Tethers for Children) system for attaching compatible child seats. It has anchors for top-tethers and a universal lower mounting system located in the crease between the car's rear-seat backrest and lower cushion.

Smart buying or leasing

To get the vehicle you want at the best price, do your homework. Think about what you need and like and then follow these steps:

STEP 1: NARROW YOUR CHOICES

Consumer Reports can help you get started. Check out the overall Ratings of models that Consumer Reports has recently tested, starting on page 234. Beginning on page 171 are overviews for all the major 2004 and some 2005 models, including predictions on how reliable the model is likely to be. Models that CR recommends are highlighted. The Frequency-of-Repair charts that begin on page 203 detail the reliability histories for more than 200 vehicles.

STEP 2: RESEARCH THE DETAILS

Once you have a short list of cars, gather key details on features, prices, safety equipment, and insurance options. Many sources—both in print and online—offer basic information and specifications. The automakers' own brochures and Web sites can be useful for learning about the various features available and how the vehicles come equipped. You'll find automaker Web addresses on page 170.

STEP 3: BUY OR LEASE?

Most people finance a new vehicle either through a loan or by leasing the vehicle. How you use the car should determine which is best for you.

Leasing generally makes sense only if:

- You don't exceed the annual mileage allowance—typically 12,000 to 15,000 miles per year. Extra miles usually cost 15 to 25 cents each.
- You don't terminate the lease early. You risk thousands of dollars in penalties if you do.
- You keep your vehicle in very good shape. "Excess wear and tear" charges at lease end can run several hundred to a thousand dollars or more.
- You prefer to trade your vehicle in every two or three years. If you keep a car longer, you're probably better off buying it from the start.

STEP 4: NAIL DOWN THE PRICE

The amount of the monthly loan or lease payment hinges on your ability to negotiate the lowest possible price for the vehicle.

Finding the sticker price is easy. It's on the car window and available at many Web sites. You also can find the dealer invoice price on many Web sites and in printed pricing guides.

The dealer-invoice price, however, isn't necessarily what the dealer paid for the vehicle. Behind-the-scenes sales incentives further reduce the dealer's cost. Knowing about these incentives can help you establish an even better place to start your price negotiations. To help you get to the true bottom price, CONSUMER REPORTS provides the CR Wholesale Price. It takes the dealer's invoice price and figures in any sales incentives, holdbacks, and rebates in effect. The CR Wholesale Price is provided as part of the CONSUMER REPORTS New Car Price Service (see the back cover).

Typically, models in ample supply sell for 4 to 8 percent over the CR Wholesale Price. Slow-selling models may sell for less than invoice. High-demand vehicles sell for prices closer to the sticker, or in some cases, over the sticker. But most domestic models, even those just introduced, often sell at a discount right away.

STEP 5: SHOP FOR FINANCING

Check online services, local banks, and your credit union for the best rates. Most automakers have finance arms, such as Ford Motor Credit for Ford products or GMAC for General Motors vehicles. They often offer very favorable financing terms, but don't be drawn into a great deal on a car you don't really want.

Here are some tips:

- Examine the terms. The most attractive rates, like zero-percent financing, often have limitations. They apply only to short-term loans, or only to people with faultless credit histories, or, often, to cars that aren't selling well.
- Know what's really discounted. Make sure that the "great low rate" is available on the car after you bargain down the price. If it applies only to a car selling for full price, then it may not be such a bargain.
- Avoid needless extras. Pass up extras like credit-life and disability insurance, an extended warranty, rustproofing, paint sealant, and so on.

STEP 6: TAKE SOME TEST DRIVES

This important step lets you see how the car fits you. Seat comfort, visibility, roominess, and the ergonomics of the controls can make a big difference in how happy you'll be with a vehicle over the long term.

Test drive the exact version you're considering. Take your time. Get a feel for the ride and noise level by driving the vehicle over different types of roads.

Make sure that the driving position and view out is comfortable, and that the driver's seat accommodates everyone who will be driving the vehicle. The controls should be easy to use and the safety belt should be comfortable.

STEP 7: NEGOTIATE SMARTLY

If you can, visit three or four dealers to see how the cars in stock are typically equipped and to gauge which dealers might be willing to accept a smaller profit margin. Then follow this game plan:

Keep the deal simple. Negotiate the price of the new car or of your trade-in first, but don't do both deals at once. It's simplest to negotiate the price of the new vehicle first, and treat it as if it were a straight-out cash deal. When it's concluded, then discuss the possibility of leasing or the price of the trade-in. Make it clear from the outset you're serious about buying soon but won't sign a contract on the spot. Tell the salesperson you are shopping different dealers and whichever offers the lowest price will get your business.

Don't bid against yourself. Bargain up from your lowest figure a little at a time. Once you've made an offer, say nothing until you receive a counteroffer.

Be prepared to walk. Avoid pinning your hopes on one dealer or one car. There will be other good deals on other cars.

Tips on handling the trade-in. Negotiate a trade-in separately from the purchase or lease deal. You're apt to get the best price for your old car if you can sell it privately, but that's too much trouble for some.

Clean the old car thoroughly inside and out, including the trunk and engine bay. Consider fixing small dings or other flaws. Such measures can improve the resale value substantially. To learn what your old car should net as a trade-in, try shopping it around at local new-dealers' used-car department. That will establish a rock-bottom price. Then check local classified-ad publications and Internet used-car sites to see what dealers and private parties are asking for cars like yours. That establishes the high end of the range. Your trade-in target price is apt to be somewhere in the middle between those extremes.

Special tips for leasing. Proceed with the leasing deal only after you receive a firm price quote for the car. Make sure that the purchase price is the figure used to calculate the lease terms. Other items you can negotiate include the annual mileage limit, the down payment, and the purchase-option price.

Be sure the value of any trade-in is deducted from the "capitalized cost" or selling price, on which the monthly figure is calculated. To figure out what you're really paying in interest, ask the dealer for the "money factor," a four- or five-digit decimal. Multiply that by 2,400 to get an approximate annual interest-rate percentage. For example, a "money factor" of .00375 is about equivalent to a 9 percent annual interest rate (.00375 x 2,400 = 9).

In a typical lease calculation, your monthly payment consists of depreciation, a "lease fee," and applicable taxes. The lease fee is the money factor multiplied by the sum of the capitalized cost and the residual value. Since residual value is already part of the capitalized cost, it may look like it's being counted twice. It isn't. The money factor takes it into account.

Try to avoid a lease that extends past the vehicle's basic warranty. Otherwise you might be saddled with expensive repairs on a vehicle you don't own.

If you might buy the car at lease-end, find out the purchase-option fee and pay it up front. And if you think you'll exceed the annual mileage allowance, buy extra miles up front, too. It's much cheaper that way.

Buying a used car

Used cars are often the best value. With a used car, the original owner pays for the steepest part of the depreciation curve.

Manufacturer-certified used cars are late-model vehicles that have been prescreened, inspected, and, reconditioned as necessary to ensure top-notch condition. They generally come with a manufacturer's warranty lasting from three months to a year or more, but typically cost more than a noncertified car.

Cars from used-car dealers are usually a notch down in price from those available at new-car dealers, but also often a notch down in quality and after-sale care.

You might be able to get the lowest price by buying from a private owner, but you may have little recourse if the car turns out to have problems.

KEY RESEARCH

If buying from a new-car dealer who sells the same make, ask that the car's vehicle identification number (VIN) be run through the dealer's computer and get a printout of any completed warranty repairs. The dealer can also check the status of any federal recalls and service bulletins.

Inspect any used car carefully, top to bottom and inside and out, in broad daylight. The car's overall condition should jibe with its odometer reading. Signs of high mileage include excessive wear on the pedals or brand-new pedal pads; a new set of tires or more than one brand; a well-worn ignition key; a worn or sagging driver's seat; frayed carpeting; and a sagging driver's door.

When you find a good prospect, take it to a mechanic for a thorough inspection—well worth the $100 or so that costs. If you're an American Automobile Association member, consider using an AAA-sanctioned garage.

Consumer Reports can also help. Check the Best and Worst Used Cars lists that start on page 198. The reliability histories beginning on page 203 give you more detailed information about each vehicle's problem areas. For help in determining prices, see the section on trade-ins on page 199 or call the Consumer Reports Used Car Price Service at 800-422-1079.

ONLINE RESEARCH

Using the Web to shop for a car

You can find specs, pictures, and prices online. You can find out what car testers such as Consumer Reports and others have to say, and what sort of financing is available. You can check insurance rates, bank rates, lease deals, and look at your own credit report. It's getting easier to separate good sites from bad ones. Still, you should treat Web-generated information with caution. When it comes to a car, nothing beats seeing it in person.

If you want to buy or lease a car, various services can get the ball rolling for you by quoting a price (either their set price or one from a participating dealership). Or they can handle the entire deal, from arranging financing to delivery of the car.

With a buying site, you are cued to fill out a detailed questionnaire about the car or cars you are looking for. The service then quotes a price (sometimes instantly, sometimes within hours or days), and searches for a dealer who has the car.

Some buying sites essentially put you in touch with a local dealer who has agreed to sell a car at a specified price. But when you visit the dealer you may or may not be pressured to buy more equipment, extended warranties, or other extras. Other buying sites arrange a final, out-the-door price, and you go to a dealer only to write a check and pick up the car.

Used-car buying sites essentially work like extensive classified-ad publications. After you enter the model in which you're interested, they typically list all vehicles that are available within a specified price and distance from your home. You can use them to find a car, or just to get a handle on the going prices, whether you are in the market to sell or buy.

MORE INFO

Online Resource Guide

This list includes major providers of auto information and services. These sites are provided for reference only: CR has not rated and doesn't endorse them. All addresses begin with "www."

CONSUMERREPORTS.ORG

Consumer Reports offers online assistance at *ConsumerReports.org*. Site subscribers get unlimited access to our extensive archives, including full road tests and an interactive vehicle selector for new and used cars. The free area of the Autos section provides articles on buying, safety, and more. CR New Car and Used Car Price Reports, with model-specific information, are designed to help you get the best deal on your vehicle purchase. They can be ordered online.

PRICING: NEW & USED CARS

Provide dealer invoice and incentives on new cars.

AutoSite .... autosite.com
Edmunds .... edmunds.com
Intellichoice .... intellichoice.com
Kelley Blue Book .... kbb.com
National Automobile Dealer Association .... nada.com
VMR (used cars only) .... vmrintl.com

VEHICLE REVIEWS & COMPARISONS

Check several for a range of opinions.

Automobile .... automobilemag.com
Car and Driver .... caranddriver.com
Epinions .... epinions.com
Motor Trend .... motortrend.com
MSN Autos .... autos.msn.com
New Car Test Drive .... nctd.com
Road & Track .... roadandtrack.com

NEW-CAR BUYING

Provide prices and put you in touch with dealerships.

Autobytel .... autobytel.com
Auto Trader .... autotrader.com
AutoVantage .... autovantage.com
Autoweb .... autoweb.com
CarBargains .... checkbook.org
Cars.com .... cars.com
CarsDirect .... carsdirect.com
InvoiceDealers.com .... invoicedealers.com
MSN Autos .... autos.msn.com
StoneAge .... stoneage.com

USED-CAR BUYING & SELLING

Online classified ads that search all areas.

Autobytel .... autobytel.com
Auto Trader .... autotrader.com
Autoweb .... autoweb.com
Cars.com .... cars.com
Dealernet .... dealernet.com
Ebay .... ebaymotors.com
Imotors .... imotors.com
StoneAge .... stoneage.com
Usedcars.com .... usedcars.com
Used Cars Online .... ausedcar.com

LEASING DEALS & INFORMATION

Automotive Lease Guide .... alg.com
Federal Reserve Board .... federalreserve.gov/pubs/leasing
LeaseSource .... leasesource.com
Intellichoice .... intellichoice.com

AUTO LOAN RATES & LENDERS

Bank Rate Monitor .... bankrate.com
E-Loan .... eloan.com
LendingTree .... lendingtree.com
Household Auto .... householdauto.com
Peoplefirst .... peoplefirst.com
VirtualBank .... virtualbank.com

CREDIT REPORTS

Experian .... experian.com
Trans Union .... transunion.com
My Credit .... mycreditfile.com

MAINTENANCE/OWNERSHIP COSTS

Intellichoice .... intellichoice.com

SAFETY/CRASH-TEST RESULTS

National Highway Traffic Safety Administration .... nhtsa.dot.gov
Insurance Institute for Highway Safety .... hwysafety.org

VEHICLE HISTORY REPORTS

Carfax .... carfax.com
Experian .... autocheck.com

FUEL ECONOMY/EMISSIONS

Environmental Protection Agency .... epa.gov/greenvehicles
.... fueleconomy.gov
Ames Awards .... amesaward.com

REVIEWS OF THE 2003-04 MODELS

This rundown of all the major 2003-04 models can start you on your search for a new car. You'll find a capsule summary of each model, as well as the Consumer Reports prediction of how reliable the vehicle will be, and how much it's likely to depreciate in value. Model descriptions in this book are based on recent road tests that pertain to this year's models.

Models with a ✔ are recommended by Consumer Reports. These are models that performed well in Consumer Reports testing, have average or better reliability according to our annual survey, and have not performed poorly in a crash test.

Entries include, where available, the date of the last road test for that model published in Consumer Reports magazine. These road-test reports are also available to subscribers of our Web site, *(www.ConsumerReports.org)*.

The 2003-04 cars, trucks, SUVs & minivans

Predicted reliability is a judgment based on our annual reliability survey data. New or recently redesigned models are marked "New." **Depreciation** predicts how well a new model will keep its value, based on the difference between the original sticker price of a 2000 model and its current resale value. The average depreciation for all vehicles was 43 percent. As a group, full-sized pickup trucks have the lowest depreciation rate. Sporty cars also tend to hold value. Large luxury cars, on the other hand, have a relatively high depreciation rate. Throughout, ✔ indicates a model is recommended by Consumer Reports; NA means data not available.

Better ← → **Worse**
⊜ ⊖ ○ ◒ ●

Model	Predicted reliability	Depreciation	Comments
Acura CL	⊖	NA	This is a two-door version of the Acura TL. The ride is OK and the handling competent, but the CL doesn't feel all that sporty, even in the Type-S higher-performance trim level. The CL is dropped for 2004. **Last road test: --**
✔ **Acura MDX**	⊜	NA	The MDX is a well-designed car-based SUV that can hold seven passengers. The powertrain is strong and refined. Ride and handling are competent. The interior is flexible, with a 50/50-split third-row seat that folds flat into the cargo floor. **Last road test: Sep. 2003**
✔ **Acura RL**	⊜	○	Acura's flagship sedan is quiet, spacious, and impeccably finished, but a bit bland. It handles securely and delivers a smooth, quiet ride. Although comfortable and competent, the RL lacks the superb performance found in its competitors. Expect a redesign in early 2004. **Last road test: Nov. 2000**

Model	Predicted reliability	Depre-ciation	Comments
✔ **Acura RSX**	○	NA	The RSX is a two-door coupe, with two engine choices. Handling is capable but the ride is stiff, choppy, and noisy. The hatchback configuration adds versatility. **Last road test: Dec. 2001**
✔ **Acura TL**	⊜	⊖	This upscale midsized sedan offers a sprightly and quiet V6, sound handling, a comfortable ride, and good reliability. It's a sensible, competitively priced choice. Expect an '04 redesign based on the new Honda Accord. **Last road test: Mar. 2002**
Acura TSX	NEW	NA	The TSX is based on the smaller Honda Accord sold in Japan and Europe. This four-door competes as a less expensive alternative to the Audi A4, BMW 325i, and Lexus IS300. It features a high-revving four-cylinder engine, but ride and handling aren't radically different from the Accord. **Last road test: --**
Audi A4	◒	NA	The A4 handles nimbly and accelerates well, though the ride at low speeds is a bit too firm. The interior is polished and luxurious–comfortable in front, meager in the rear. All-wheel drive is available; a continuously variable transmission is available on front-wheel-drive models. **Last road test: Mar. 2002**
Audi A6/Allroad	◒	○	Audi's refined midsized sedan has a supple ride and handles responsively. The Allroad variant is a good-performing (if pricey) wagon with an adjustable height suspension for moderate off-road use. The 2.7-liter turbo V6 and 4.2-liter V8 are much stronger than the 3.0-liter V6. **Last road test: Nov. 2001**
Audi A8	NEW	NA	Audi's redesigned flagship holds its own with the best. It features a strong V8, AWD, and an aluminum body with a roomy, well-crafted interior. It is quiet and agile, but the ride is unremarkable for a luxury car. **Last road test: Nov. 2003**
Audi TT	●	⊖	This stylish runabout is available in both convertible and coupe versions. A nicely detailed interior and available all-wheel drive offset a character that is less sporty than the Porsche Boxster. The ride is stiff and the engine noisy. An automatic is available with the less powerful engine and a 250 hp, V6 arrives for 2004. **Last road test: June 2002**
BMW 3-Series	◒	⊜	The 3 Series models are an ideal blend of comfort, luxury, sportiness, and safety. They are quiet and refined, yet quick and agile. Coupe, convertible, and wagon models are available, as well as sedan and wagon all-wheel-drive Xi versions. **Last road test: May 2001**
✔ **BMW 5-Series**	○	⊖	These superbly designed rear-wheel-drive luxury sports sedans embody pure precision and nimble, responsive handling. The ride is supple and quiet, with extremely comfortable, supportive seats. Powertrains are smooth and punchy. A redesign is scheduled to arrive in fall 2003. **Last road test: Nov. 2001**
BMW 7-Series	NA	NA	The 7-Series is quick, agile, and roomy, but ultimately fails to deliver as a luxury car. The ride is too firm. The "iDrive" system, shifter, and seat controls are extremely cumbersome and frustrating to use. **Last road test: Nov. 2003**
BMW X5	●	⊜	The X5 drives like a capable sports sedan. The Six performs well, but the V8s are quicker and more stable in emergency maneuvers. Braking is top notch, though the ride is a bit choppy and cargo space is modest. **Last road test: Sep. 2003**

Model	Predicted reliability	Depre-ciation	Comments
BMW Z4	NEW	NA	The Z4 replaced the Z3 roadster, with a roomier cockpit but the same engines. Standard is a punchy 184-hp 2.5-liter, with an optional 225-hp 3.0-liter. Electronic stability control and traction control are both standard. Luggage space is also improved. **Last road test: --**
Buick Century	⊖	●	The Century feels like old technology. The ride is quiet and soft, at least at low speeds, but bumpy roads easily upset its composure. Handling isn't responsive and braking is subpar. The front bench seat is roomy, but the soft seats offer little support. **Last road test: --**
✔ Buick LeSabre	○	◒	The big LeSabre has a roomy interior and a quiet ride. Handling is secure, especially with the Touring suspension, which also makes the ride more settled. The seats are unsupportive. **Last road test: Feb. 2000**
Buick Park Avenue	◒	●	Buick's top-of-the-line sedan rides and handles relatively well. Acceleration is effortless in the supercharged Ultra. The interior is roomy and quiet, and the seats are fairly comfortable. **Last road test: Feb. 2003**
Buick Rainier	NEW	NA	The upscale Buick Rainier is a rebadged Oldsmobile Bravada that goes on sale this fall. It comes with a 4.2-liter Six or a 5.3-liter V8. The permanently engaged AWD system has no low range, making it suited for slippery roads than off-roading. **Last road test: --**
Buick Regal	⊜	◒	This car rides well at low speeds, although handling is a bit cumbersome. Its V6 accelerates adequately and the cabin is quiet. The GS features a supercharged V6. The seats are soft and grow less comfortable on long rides. **Last road test: --**
Buick Rendezvous	◒	NA	This minivan-based SUV has a fairly comfortable ride with secure but not agile handling. Optional AWD and room for seven are pluses. The base V6 struggles to move it and the interior is made with cheap-looking materials. **Last road test: Oct. 2001**
Cadillac CTS	NEW	NA	Built in the U.S., this rear-wheel drive, European-style sports sedan feels agile and taut, but has pesky oversights and a relatively tight rear seat. Power is now provided by a 3.6-liter, 255-hp V6. Acceleration is quick and the transmission is very smooth. **Last road test: July 2003**
Cadillac DeVille	◒	◒	This big, plush freeway cruiser rides comfortably and quietly and handles commendably for such a large car. It offers plenty of refined power and many standard features, including an optional infrared Night Vision system. **Last road test: Nov. 2000**
Cadillac Escalade	●	NA	Essentially a Chevrolet Tahoe, this SUV features powerful engines and a smooth-shifting transmission. Though spacious, the interior isn't very flexible and the third seat is uncomfortable. The EXT is based on the Avalanche, and the ESV is based on the Suburban. **Last road test: --**
Cadillac Seville	●	●	Positioned as an alternative to European and Japanese luxury sedans, the Seville has a sophisticated V8, but lacks the dynamic prowess of most of its competitors. The interior is quiet, but ride and handling are just OK and the rear seat is tight. **Last road test: --**

Model	Predicted reliability	Depre-ciation	Comments
Cadillac SRX	NEW	NA	The upscale 2004 SRX is the first car-based SUV from Cadillac. It is powered by either a V8 or a V6, and comes with a five-speed automatic. An optional power-folding third-row seat pits it against competitors like Acura's MDX and Volvo's XC90. **Last road test: --**
Chevrolet Astro	●	◒	The Astro is seriously outclassed by all modern minivan designs. Handling is ponderous, and the ride is uncomfortable. It can haul lots of cargo or tow a heavy trailer. AWD is optional. **Last road test: --**
✔ **Chevrolet Avalanche**	○	NA	Essentially a crew-cab pickup version of the Suburban, this truck has an innovative "midgate" that allows long items to extend into the rear-passenger compartment. The ride is comfortable and the V8 is strong but not very economical. **Last road test: Sep. 2002**
Chevrolet Blazer	●	●	This dated SUV offers adequate cargo space and a tolerable ride. Emergency handling is subpar. Its replacement, the vastly superior TrailBlazer, has made this model a rental-fleet filler. **Last road test: --**
Chevrolet Cavalier	○	●	The Cavalier has an outdated design and is best for basic transportation. Rough roads make the body bounce. The front seats are uncomfortable, the rear seat low and cramped. **Last road test: Mar. 2003**
Chevrolet Corvette	●	⊜	The Corvette comes as a coupe, fixed hardtop, or convertible. You get muscular V8 performance and well balanced handling. The tires grip tenaciously. The ride is jarring and noisy, and fit and finish are unimpressive for a $50,000 car. **Last road test: June 2002**
✔ **Chevrolet Impala**	○	◒	The Impala is a roomy sedan. Ride and handling are sound, and the powertrain is smooth. The low, short rear seat is uncomfortable, the plastic interior-trim surfaces look and feel cheap, and some of the controls are not well executed. **Last road test: May 2000**
Chevrolet Malibu	NEW	NA	A 2004 redesign has just arrived. It comes with a 4-cyl and an outdated V6. It is roomy and soundly designed. A hatchback arrives this winter. **Last road test: --**
Chevrolet Monte Carlo	○	○	A coupe version of the Impala, the Monte Carlo accelerates well, but road noise is pronounced and rear access is a chore. Overall, it offers an underwhelming driving experience. **Last road test: --**
Chevrolet S-10	●	○	The compact S-10 and its sibling, the GMC Sonoma, ride stiffly and lean a lot in corners. Only the crew-cab body style will be available in 2004, along with a replacement called the Colorado bowing this fall. **Last road test: Aug. 2001**
✔ **Chevrolet Silverado 1500**	○	⊖	The Silverado, a full-sized pickup, drives fairly nicely. The optional four-wheel drive is a selectable full-time system. Quadrasteer is a handy, but expensive, four-wheel-steering option. Extended-cab versions have a usable rear seat, a rarity in this class. **Last road test: Nov. 1999**
Chevrolet SSR	NEW	NA	The SSR (Super Sport Roadster) is a pickup truck with a retractable hardtop. The V8 powers the rear wheels. Evoking the styling of Chevy trucks from the 1950s, this two-seater is about nostalgia and open-topped motoring. **Last road test: --**

Model	Predicted reliability	Depre-ciation	Comments
✔ **Chevrolet Suburban**	○	⊜	One of the largest SUVs, the Suburban can seat nine people, hold their luggage, and tow a heavy trailer. It's quiet, comfortable, and handles fairly well. The GMC Yukon XL is similar. **Last road test: June 2000**
✔ **Chevrolet Tahoe**	○	○	This SUV is similar to the Suburban, but with less cargo room. Eight can ride, but those in the third seat will be very uncomfortable. It boasts an impressive towing capability. **Last road test: Nov. 2002**
Chevrolet Tracker	○	◒	This SUV uses the old truck-based, body-on-frame design. It's slow, noisy, and crude. Built by Suzuki, it shares underpinnings with the Suzuki Vitara. '04 may be its last year. **Last road test: --**
Chevrolet TrailBlazer	●	NA	This SUV is quiet (except for wind noise) and spacious, with a comfortable ride and a spirited inline-Six. Handling is a bit ponderous and can be tricky at its limit. A longer EXT model with a third seat is also available. **Last road test: Aug. 2003**
Chevrolet Venture	◒	◒	This spacious minivan has a responsive powertrain and comfortable seating. Subpar reliability and poor performance in crash tests keep it out of contention. **Last road test: Jan. 2001**
✔ **Chrysler 300M**	○	○	The 300M is a roomier, upscale sibling of the Dodge Intrepid and Chrysler Concorde. Handling is fairly nimble, but the ride is stiff, and the cabin admits too much noise. The front seats are soft and unsupportive. The rear-drive 300C will replace it in 2004. **Last road test: Oct. 1999**
✔ **Chrysler Concorde**	⊜	●	This large, middle-of-the-road sedan handles fairly nimbly and has a supple ride, although both of the available V6 engines lack refinement. Road noise is constant, and rear-seat access is a chore. **Last road test: --**
Chrysler Crossfire	NEW	NA	This rear-drive, two-seater coupe is based on the Mercedes SLK. The engine is strong, but handling lacks finesse. The ride is stiff and visibility poor. **Last road test: Dec. 2003**
Chrysler Pacifica	NEW	NA	The Pacifica combines the characteristics of an SUV, a minivan, and a wagon in an all-wheel-drive package that seats six. Ride and handling are capable, but the powertrain falls a bit short. Access is easy, and the third row folds flat when not needed. **Last road test: Aug. 2003**
✔ **Chrysler PT Cruiser**	⊜	NA	The PT Cruiser is a tall front-drive wagon. It offers a versatile interior and secure handling, but acceleration is languid. A quicker, turbocharged GT version was new for 2003. **Last road test: Oct. 2000**
Chrysler Sebring	○	NA	The Sebring is available in sedan, coupe, and convertible forms. The coupe is derived from the mediocre Mitsubishi Eclipse. The V6 sedan is quick enough, but not agile or smooth-riding. **Last road test: June 2001**
Chrysler Town & Country	◒	◒	This minivan is quiet inside but is falling behind the competition. Engines are lackluster. Ride and handling are ok. Interior flexibility is wanting. All-wheel drive is optional. **Last road test: Oct. 2003**

Model	Predicted reliability	Depre-ciation	Comments
Chrysler Voyager	●	NA	This is a short-wheelbase version of the Town & Country. It rides quietly but interior flexibility is lacking. The third-row bench seat is removable but doesn't fold into the floor. This model will be discontinued for 2004. **Last road test: --**
Dodge Caravan/ Grand Caravan	◒	◒	The Caravan and extended-length Grand Caravan ride quietly though the engines are lackluster. The interior lacks flexibility. The third-row seat doesn't stow into the floor. Overall it's falling behind the competition. **Last road test: Oct. 2003**
Dodge Dakota	○	○	The Dakota handles responsively for a pickup, though the ride is jarring and the V6 and V8s guzzle gas. The brakes are marginal. A spacious four-door crew-cab is available. **Last road test: Aug. 2001**
Dodge Durango	◒	○	This uninspired SUV offers three rows of seats, although the third row is pretty tight. The front seats are uncomfortable, and the ride is stiff and choppy. The 4.7-liter V8 provides good acceleration. A redesign arrives for 2004. **Last road test: Sep. 2001**
✔ **Dodge Intrepid**	○	●	This large and stylish car delivers so-so performance overall. Handling is fairly nimble, and the ride is OK. The 2.7-liter V6 is noisy, and access is a chore. **Last road test: Feb. 2002**
Dodge Neon	◒	●	This small sedan handles securely, brakes well, and has a relatively roomy interior. But the ride is stiff and uncomfortable and the cabin noisy. The four-speed automatic is mediocre. **Last road test: Mar. 2003**
Dodge Ram 1500	●	NA	This pickup was redesigned for 2002 but still falls short of the competition. The handling and powertrain are improved, but the ride is jittery and the cabin noisy. The crew-cab has less rear-seat room than other domestic pickups but a bigger cargo bed. **Last road test: Sep. 2002**
Dodge Stratus	○	NA	The Stratus, available as a sedan or coupe, feels a bit rough and underdeveloped. The sedan offers quick acceleration with the V6, but ride and handling fall short. The cabin is noisy and access is difficult. **Last road test: June 2001**
Ford Crown Victoria	◒	◒	A big, old-fashioned sedan. Jiggly ride and engine noise reveal how dated the car is. Braking and emergency handling are fairly good. Rear leg room is skimpier than you might expect. **Last road test: Feb. 2003**
Ford Escape	◒	NA	The Escape and its cousin, the Mazda Tribute, are small, car-based SUVs with good interior space and fairly nimble handling, but a stiff and noisy ride. The V6 is lively. Some interior appointments look and feel cheap. **Last road test: Mar. 2001**
Ford Excursion	○	○	Designed to be the largest SUV on the road, the Excursion is a clumsy, fuel-guzzling behemoth with a noisy engine, atrocious fuel economy, uncomfortable ride, and marginal brakes. **Last road test: June 2000**
Ford Expedition	NA	NA	This large SUV has a well-designed interior with flexible seating and a handy fold-down split third seat. Ride and handling are commendable, but the available engines are slow and thirsty. **Last road test: Nov. 2002**

Model	Predicted reliability	Depre-ciation	Comments
Ford Explorer	●	NA	The spacious Explorer rides fairly comfortably and quietly and handles securely. A third-row seat adds versatility. Advanced safety gear is another plus. The base V6 is noisy but provides adequate acceleration. **Last road test: Sep. 2001**
Ford Explorer Sport Trac	◒	NA	This crew-cab truck is based on the previous Ford Explorer and features a truncated pickup bed and five-person cabin. The ride is stiff and choppy, but handling is secure and relatively responsive. The V6 is unrefined but powerful enough. **Last road test: Aug. 2001**
Ford F-150	⊖	○	The F-150 feels like an old design, with ride and cabin quietness not up to the level of Toyota or Chevy trucks. The crewcab version is roomy but has a high step-up. A redesigned F-150 is now on sale alongside the old model. **Last road test: Sep. 2002**
Ford Focus	●	○	The Focus sedan, hatchback, and wagon tested very well–it's agile, spacious, and fun to drive–but reliability has been below average. **Last road test: Aug. 2002**
Ford Freestar	NEW	NA	The Freestar is a freshened version of the Windstar minivan. Two V6 engines are available. As is common now, it features a flat-folding third-row seat. **Last road test: --**
Ford Mustang	◒	○	This old-fashioned rear-drive muscle car got its last upgrade in 1999. Ride, handling, and braking are OK, but the car doesn't feel very sporty. Seats aren't especially comfortable. The V8 is the engine of choice. Expect a redesign for 2005. **Last road test: --**
Ford Ranger	◒	◒	The Ranger and similar Mazda B-Series are all-around competent pickup trucks. Handling is fairly responsive, although the ride is stiff and choppy. The Explorer Sport Trac is a crew-cab version of the Ranger. Expect some cosmetic interior and exterior changes for 2004. **Last road test: --**
✔ Ford Taurus	○	●	This is a roomy, comfortable, fairly quiet sedan and wagon. Ride and handling are sound but unimpressive. Choose the uplevel V6. Adjustable pedals could be handy for shorter drivers. **Last road test: May 2000**
Ford Thunderbird	NA	NA	The T-Bird is a retro-revival two-seater that handles well but isn't sporty. Headroom is tight. The soft top is power operated; a removable hard top is also available. Production ceases in 2005. **Last road test: June 2002**
GMC Envoy	●	NA	This midsized SUV twin of the Chevrolet TrailBlazer is spacious, with a comfortable ride. Handling is a bit ponderous and can be tricky at the limit. A longer XL model has a third seat. **Last road test: Sep. 2001**
GMC Safari	●	◒	This outdated minivan can haul lots of cargo or tow a heavy trailer. All-wheel drive is optional. It handles ponderously and feels like a truck. **Last road test: --**
✔ GMC Sierra 1500	○	⊖	The Sierra, a full-sized pickup, drives fairly nicely. The optional four-wheel drive is a selectable full-time system. The Denali version has a handy four-wheel-steer option. Extended-cab versions have a usable rear seat, a rarity in this class. **Last road test: Nov. 1999**

Model	Predicted reliability	Depre-ciation	Comments
GMC Sonoma	●	◒	Like its sibling, the Chevy S-10, the compact Sonoma rides stiffly and lacks agility. Only the four-door, crew-cab model continues for '04 alongside its replacement, the Canyon. The cabin is quiet, and the 4.3-liter V6 accelerates well. **Last road test: Aug. 2001**
✔ **GMC Yukon**	○	⊖	This SUV is similar to the Chevy Suburban in XL trim. The standard length has less cargo room. Eight can ride, but those in the third seat will be very uncomfortable. The Yukon boasts an impressive towing capability. **Last road test: Nov. 2002**
✔ **Honda Accord**	⊜	NA	The redesigned Accord features fairly agile handling and a steady, compliant ride. The cabin is roomy and controls are intuitive. The five-speed automatic shifts very smoothly and responsively. The 160-hp Four is smooth, and the quick V6 is relatively fuel efficient. **Last road test: May 2003**
✔ **Honda Civic**	⊖	⊖	One of the best small sedans, the Civic handles well and gets good fuel economy, though its ride is a bit nervous. The interior is well finished, and controls are excellent. The sporty Si version doesn't drive very sporty. The Hybrid performs similarly to the sedan and provides excellent fuel efficiency. **Last road test: Dec. 2002**
✔ **Honda CR-V**	⊖	⊖	This is one of the better car-based SUVs on the market, with a supple, controlled ride and responsive powertrain. The steering feel is good, but the tires' sideways grip compromises handling a bit. The rear seat is roomy, but road noise is a bit pronounced. **Last road test: May 2002**
✔ **Honda Element**	⊖	NA	This small SUV is based on Honda's very good CR-V. Styling is boxy, with rear doors that are hinged at the rear and no roof pillar between front and rear doors. This creates a huge loading port. The rear seat folds away to create a big cargo area. The ride is choppy and noisy. **Last road test: June 2003**
Honda Insight	NA	⊖	This lightweight two-seater has a three-cylinder engine and a 13-hp electric motor that assists the gas engine. Handling is secure but not nimble. A stiff, uncomfortable ride and intrusive interior noise are major trade-offs for the car's excellent fuel economy **Last road test: Dec. 2000**
✔ **Honda Odyssey**	⊖	⊜	The Odyssey is among our top-rated minivans. It has a sprightly V6, dual sliding rear doors, and a fold-down third row. It handles well and has a steady, supple ride. Road noise is our only gripe. **Last road test: Oct. 2003**
✔ **Honda Pilot**	⊖	NA	The Pilot is a well-designed car-based SUV that can hold eight passengers. Ride and handling are competent. The interior is flexible, with a third-row seat that folds flat into the cargo floor. **Last road test: Nov. 2002**
✔ **Honda S2000**	⊜	⊜	The S2000 is a pure sports car that delivers impressive acceleration, handling, and braking. But it's noisy and hard riding, and feels a bit ordinary in normal driving. A glass rear window is now standard. **Last road test: Aug. 2000**
Hummer H2	NEW	NA	The H2 is based on the Chevy Tahoe and has a more usable interior than the grossly impractical Hummer H1. Ride and handling are fairly civilized, with exceptional off-road ability. With a short windshield and wide roof pillars, the view out is wanting. **Last road test: --**

Model	Predicted reliability	Depreciation	Comments
Hyundai Accent	○	◒	The Accent offers basic transportation. The ride is choppy but relatively quiet, and its 1.6-liter four-cylinder engine accelerates adequately. Antilock brakes are not available. It comes as either a sedan or a hatchback. **Last road test: Mar. 2003**
Hyundai Elantra	○	NA	The Elantra, spacious for a small sedan, rides well and handles securely, making it competitive with other good small sedans. Poor offset-crash-test results is a big minus. Models with the optional antilock brakes are hard to find. **Last road test: Feb. 2001**
✔ Hyundai Santa Fe	⊖	NA	This car-based SUV has a supple, quiet ride and handles securely, if not nimbly. Acceleration and fuel economy are not impressive. A steeply raked windshield makes the cockpit feel a bit confining. **Last road test: Mar. 2001**
✔ Hyundai Sonata	⊖	◒	The midsized Sonata offers good power, comfort, and convenience, up-to-date safety gear, and a long warranty. Emergency handling is clumsy but secure and the brakes perform well. **Last road test: June 2001**
Hyundai Tiburon	NEW	NA	The GT V6 version of this sporty coupe delivers refined power, but handling is not so agile. The ride is stiff. Even moderately tall drivers will have to duck under the low roof. **Last road test: Oct. 2002**
✔ Hyundai XG350	○	NA	This quiet, roomy sedan, a little larger than the Sonata, comes with lots of standard features, like automatic climate control. Handling is short on agility, and the ride floats a bit at highway speeds. **Last road test: May 2003**
✔ Infiniti FX	⊖	NA	The FX is an upscale car-based SUV. This five-seater features AWD, powerful engines, and fairly nimble handling, though the ride is jittery. Visibility is poor, the cabin is snug, and cargo space is modest. **Last road test: Sep. 2003**
✔ Infiniti G35	⊖	NA	The G35 is a rear-wheel-drive sedan also available as a coupe. The 3.5-liter V6 provides abundant power. The ride is firm and steady. Handling is responsive, but not as agile or forgiving as a BMW 3-Series. Many controls are inconvieniently placed and not intuitive. **Last road test: July 2003**
✔ Infiniti I35	○	○	The I35 is essentially a previous generation Nissan Maxima with extra sound-deadening and a plusher interior. The ride is unexceptional. Handling is secure but not inspiring. 2003 may be its last year. **Last road test: Mar. 2002**
Infiniti M45	NEW	NA	Think of the M45 as a slightly smaller, lower-priced Q45, a model with which it shares many components. It has a strong V8, a five-speed automatic transmission, and many luxury appointments, though the interior is quite tight. **Last road test: —**
Infiniti Q45	NA	◒	Nissan's flagship sedan competes against the Lexus LS430. The engine is smooth and quiet. But ride and handling aren't all that impressive, and rear-seat room is relatively cramped. The many high-tech gadgets take some practice to master. **Last road test: —**
Isuzu Ascender	NEW	NA	This midsized SUV is a rebadged Chevy TrailBlazer. It seats seven, or five in the short model. It's quiet (except for wind noise) and spacious, with a comfortable ride and a spirited inline Six, but emergency handling was sloppy and braking mediocre. **Last road test: —**

Model	Predicted reliability	Depreciation	Comments
Isuzu Axiom	NA	NA	Beneath its modern countenance, the Axiom is a traditional body-on-frame SUV that borrows heavily from the discontinued Trooper and aging Rodeo. Pluses include a potent 3.5-liter V6 and selectable full-time 4WD. **Last road test: --**
Isuzu Rodeo	◒	○	This aging truck-based SUV offers a smooth, powerful V6 but has a busy and jittery ride. Handling is clumsy. The Rodeo Sport, previously known as the Amigo, has been dropped. **Last road test: --**
Jaguar S-Type	●	○	The S-Type V8 is strong and smooth, the V6 much less so. The interior is a bit cramped, and the trunk is small. The overall experience is more run-of-the-mill than luxurious. Ride and steering were improved recently. **Last road test: Nov. 2001**
Jaguar XJ8	NEW	NA	The redesigned XJ8 features an aluminum body and offers a bit more interior room. The classy styling remains. The powertrain is strong but the ride isn't luxurious. Handling is nimble, but steering is light. **Last road test: Nov. 2003**
Jaguar X-Type	●	NA	Based on the European Ford Mondeo, this entry-level Jag comes with standard all-wheel drive and a choice of two V6 engines. It aims to compete with the BMW 3-Series and Audi A4 but lacks their refinement, interior quality, and driving enjoyment. **Last road test: Mar. 2002**
Jeep Grand Cherokee	●	◒	Cramped and rough riding by today's standards, the Grand Cherokee is showing its age. Handling is imprecise, and the standard Six is noisy. The 4.7-liter V8 is a better choice. Accommodations are less generous than in its competitors. **Last road test: Sep. 2001**
✔ **Jeep Liberty**	○	NA	The Liberty is good for off-roading and towing. Handling is secure and predictable. The ride is jittery and fuel economy is unimpressiv with the V6. The cockpit is narrow, and access is awkward. **Last road test: May 2002**
Jeep Wrangler	●	⊜	The Wrangler is the smallest and crudest Jeep. The ride is hard and noisy, handling is primitive, and the driving position is unpleasant. Nevertheless, it remains popular with off-road enthusiasts. A four-speed automatic was new for 2003. **Last road test: --**
Kia Optima	NA	NA	This midsized sedan is essentially a Hyundai Sonata with less-adventurous styling. The interior is fairly spacious and quiet, and the V6 powertrain reasonably refined. Handling is not the Optima's forte. **Last road test: --**
Kia Rio	NA	NA	The Rio sedan is one of the lowest-priced cars sold in the U.S. Expect to get what you pay for. It's based on the dreadful Ford Aspire, which was made for Ford by Kia in the mid-1990s. A wagon, the Cinco, is also available. **Last road test: --**
Kia Sedona	○	NA	The Sedona is the first Korean minivan to be sold in the U.S. It's relatively refined, with good fit and finish, but it's not very nimble. The Sedona corners reluctantly. The ride is stiff and jiggly, and the van's heavy weight hinders acceleration. **Last road test: Oct. 2003**
Kia Sorento	NEW	NA	Relatively roomy and well-equipped for the price, this body-on-frame SUV is good off-road. Handling is secure, though the ride is awful and fuel economy is abysmal. **Last road test: June 2003**

Model	Predicted reliability	Depreciation	Comments
Kia Spectra	NA	NA	Available as a sedan or hatchback, the Spectra trails the competition in just about every way. It suffers from a noisy cabin, a poor ride, an unrefined powertrain, and clumsy handling. Cabin materials feel cheap and insubstantial. **Last road test: --**
Land Rover Discovery	NA	○	The Discovery is designed primarily for off-road use, compromising its on-road handling. The steering is imprecise, and the ride is stiff and choppy. Access is difficult, and controls are not intuitive. For 2003, a 4.6-liter V8 replaced the lackluster and thirsty 4.0-liter. **Last road test: --**
Land Rover Freelander	NA	NA	The Freelander offers full-time AWD and fully independent suspension, and ride and handling are commendable. The V6 is neither energetic nor fuel-efficient. Off-road performance is capable. **Last road test: May 2002**
Land Rover Range Rover	NEW	NA	The redesigned Range Rover delivers smooth, strong acceleration, powertrain refinement, and a very comfortable ride. It features a height-adjustable air-spring suspension and luxury-car amenities. **Last road test: --**
✔ Lexus ES300	⊖	⊖	The ES300 is a quiet, comfortable, easy-going car with a nicely trimmed interior. The V6 is smooth and powerful. Handling is a bit lucklaster. A 3.3-liter V6 engine arrives for 2004. **Last road test: Mar. 2002**
✔ Lexus GS300/GS430	⊖	⊖	The GS is sportier and less expensive than the flagship LS430. Ride and handling are competent but unexceptional. Seating is comfortable, but the rear is tight for three. Expect a redesigned model with all-wheel drive to arrive in 2004. **Last road test: --**
Lexus GX470	NEW	NA	The GX470 is a Lexus version of the redesigned Toyota 4Runner. It's smaller than the huge LX470 but also offers a third seat. It shares a powertrain and many of the LX470's luxury appointments, and is also quite competent off-road. **Last road test: --**
✔ Lexus IS300	⊜	NA	This rear-drive sedan has a smooth, powerful inline Six and handles and brakes very capably. The IS300's ride is firm but a bit jittery, and it lacks the ride compliance found in its German competitors. The trunk is small and the rear seat tight. **Last road test: May 2001**
✔ Lexus LS430	⊜	○	The LS430 is among the world's best. The engine and transmission are extremely smooth, and passengers are pampered with many standard convenience and safety features. The ride is smooth and quiet, but the LS isn't very agile. **Last road test: Nov. 2003**
Lexus LX470	NA	○	This luxury SUV, based on the Toyota Land Cruiser, features a height-adjustable suspension and a well-equipped interior. Like the Cruiser, it has a smooth engine and transmission, full-time four-wheel drive, and a comfortable, quiet ride. It's capable off-road and civilized on pavement. **Last road test: --**
✔ Lexus RX330	⊜	NA	Our top-rated SUV, the RX330 delivers a comfortable, very quiet ride, and AWD that provides good traction for bad weather and light off-road use. The V6 is smooth and responsive. Handling is responsive and secure. Attention to detail is impressive. **Last road test: Sep. 2003**
Lexus SC430	○	NA	The SC430 convertible features an electrically operated hard top. Power comes from the potent and refined V8 used in the GS and LS sedans. Handling is less sporty than in some competing models. **Last road test: --**

Model	Predicted reliability	Depreciation	Comments
Lincoln Aviator	NEW	NA	The Aviator is a Lincoln version of the Mercury Mountaineer/Ford Explorer. It has a big V8, many luxury features, and styling similar to the Lincoln Navigator. A standard third row expands seating to seven and folds flat into the floor when not needed. **Last road test: —**
Lincoln LS	●	○	The LS is a capable rear-drive sedan with a smooth powertrain, agile handling, and a firm, comfortable ride. The optional V8 and standard V6 both received more power for 2003. Some recent tweaks yielded much needed in-cabin storage space and less road noise. **Last road test: July 2003**
Lincoln Navigator	NEW	NA	The redesigned Navigator features a fully independent suspension and a comfortable, power-operated split third-row seat that folds flat into the floor. The cabin is quiet, steering is responsive, and ride and handling are improved over the old version. **Last road test: —**
✔ **Lincoln Town Car**	○	●	The last of the domestic rear-wheel-drive luxury cruisers, the Town Car's ride is too jiggly for a luxury car and handling is clumsy, but secure. The front seats are soft but poorly shaped. The rear seats three with ease, and the trunk is very large. **Last road test: Feb. 2003**
Mazda B-Series	◒	◒	This is a compact Ford Ranger pickup with a Mazda nameplate. Handling is quite good for a truck, but the ride is stiff and jiggly. The 4.0-liter SOHC V6 is a welcome option. The rear seats in the extended-cab version are tight. **Last road test: —**
✔ **Mazda MPV**	⊜	○	The MPV minivan is smaller and narrower than most competitors but has some clever interior details, such as a fold-flat third-row seat. Handling is secure but the ride is stiff. The 3.0-liter, 200-hp V6 feels lethargic. **Last road test: Oct. 2003**
✔ **Mazda MX-5 Miata**	⊜	○	Zesty performance, nimble handling, and precise steering make this a fun but noisy car to drive. The interior, though, is cramped for tall people. **Last road test: Aug. 1998**
✔ **Mazda Protegé**	⊖	○	This small sedan has fallen behind the Honda Civic and Toyota Corolla. Handling is secure, but the ride is stiff and choppy. Interior room is relatively spacious. The Protegé5 four-door hatchback/wagon offers cargo versatility. A redesign for 2004 arrives in late fall '03. **Last road test: July 2002**
Mazda RX-8	NEW	NA	The new RX-8 revives the rotary-engine in Mazda sports cars. It is a nimble coupe that revs exceptionally smoothly. The ride is more than tolerable. The four-seater has rear-hinged rear doors, which improves access. **Last road test: Dec. 2003**
Mazda Tribute	◒	NA	The car-based Tribute is a mechanical twin of the Ford Escape. The Tribute is slightly nimbler but has a stiffer ride. It offers good interior space and a powerful V6, but wind noise penetrates the cabin. **Last road test: Mar. 2001**
✔ **Mazda6**	⊖	NA	The new Mazda6 offers fairly nimble handling and a firm, but compliant ride. A five-speed automatic transmission is available only with the V6. The Four doesn't feel as punchy or refined as those in the Accord or Camry. Wagon and hatchback versions arrive for 2004. **Last road test: May 2003**

Model	Predicted reliability	Depreciation	Comments
Mercedes-Benz C-Class	●	⊖	The C-Class comes as a coupe, wagon, and sedan. These models offer quick acceleration, a quiet, comfortable ride, and agile, secure handling. The seats are exceptionally comfortable and supportive, but the rear is tight. **Last road test: May 2001**
Mercedes-Benz CLK	NEW	NA	The redesigned CLK accelerates quickly, handles well with more precise steering, and rides comfortably. It is powerful, with three engines available. Rear seating is reasonably hospitable for a coupe. A convertible version is available. **Last road test: —**
Mercedes-Benz E-Class	NEW	NA	The E-Class was redesigned for 2003, and offers V6 and V8 engines and a smooth automatic transmission. Seat comfort and driving position are first-class. Wagon and all-wheel-drive 4Matic models will arrive for 2004. **Last road test: —**
Mercedes-Benz M-Class	●	⊖	Civilized on the road and relatively capable off-road initially, the so-so ride and awkward controls show its age. Both engines are smooth and powerful. The cabin is spacious, and the seats are comfortable. Reliability is poor. **Last road test: June 2000**
Mercedes-Benz S-Class	●	⊖	The stately S-Class keeps company with the world's most expensive luxury cars. The ride is supremely comfortable and quiet, with a roomy rear seat. Handling is suprisingly agile. All-wheel drive is optional. **Last road test: Nov. 2003**
Mercedes-Benz SLK	◒	⊖	This two-seat convertible has an electrically retractable hardtop, which makes it feel almost as solid as a fixed-roof coupe. The SLK's chief liability is its imprecise and not overly quick steering, which makes the driving experience less sporty than some might expect. **Last road test: June 2002**
Mercury Grand Marquis	◒	◒	A big, old-fashioned sedan, the Grand Marquis' ride is jiggly and engine noise is pronounced. Braking and emergency handling are fairly good. Rear leg room is skimpier than you might expect. **Last road test: Feb. 2003**
Mercury Monterey	NEW	NA	This upscale version of the Ford Freestar debuts in the fall with a standard 4.2-liter V6. It features a flat-folding third-row seat. The side-curtain air-bag system protects occupants in all three rows in the event of a rollover. **Last road test: —**
Mercury Mountaineer	●	NA	The much-improved Mountaineer has an independent suspension, an optional third-row seat, and up-to-date safety gear. The all-wheel-drive system is permanent and lacks a low range, differentiating it from the Ford Explorer. **Last road test: —**
✔ **Mercury Sable**	○	●	This sedan is showing its age. The ride is firm and well controlled. The front seat is available as a bench. The rear seat can hold three adults comfortably, but access is difficult. The Sable is also available as a wagon with three rows of seats. **Last road test: May 2000**
Mini Cooper	NA	NA	The Mini, from BMW, blends much of the old model's rakish charm with modern levels of creature comforts and safety. Handling is extremely agile, but the ride is choppy. Even tall people will find the cockpit adequately roomy, but the rear is very tight. **Last road test: Oct. 2002**

Model	Predicted reliability	Depreciation	Comments
Mitsubishi Diamante	NA	◒	This sedan doesn't measure up to luxury competitors. Its strongest assets are a lively engine and a nifty sound system, but ride, handling, and interior room are all unimpressive. A face-lift marks the 2004 model. **Last road test: Oct. 1999**
✔ Mitsubishi Eclipse	○	○	A powerful engine in the GT version is the coupe's major appeal. The cockpit is cramped. Handling and braking are nothing special, and the ride is stiff and busy. **Last road test: Aug. 2000**
Mitsubishi Endeavor	NEW	NA	The Endeavor is Mitsubishi's midsized car-based SUV. Power comes from a 3.8-liter V6, which it shares with the Montero. Front-wheel-drive and all-wheel-drive versions are available. The Endeavor rides reasonably well, but cornering isn't particularly agile. **Last road test: Aug. 2003**
✔ Mitsubishi Galant	○	◒	This sedan's high points include smooth V6 power and a competitive price. Handling is fairly nimble, but the ride is a little choppy. The front seats aren't very comfortable, and the rear is cramped. A redesigned larger, more powerful 2004 model arrives this fall. **Last road test: July 2000**
Mitsubishi Lancer	NA	NA	Mitsubishi's entry in the small sedan category falls short of the competition–and offers no price advantage, either. Handling is clumsy, the ride unsettled, and the interior noisy. A wagon arrives for 2004, and an AWD Evolution model competes with the Subaru WRX STi. **Last road test: July 2002**
Mitsubishi Montero	NA	NA	We rated the 2001 Montero Limited Not Acceptable after it exhibited repeated tip-ups in our avoidance maneuver test. The new standard stability-control system improved matters but it still feels tippy and unpredictable. Therefore it earned a poor rating in our emergency-handling test. **Last road test: Aug. 2003**
Mitsubishi Montero Sport	○	●	The Montero Sport is very trucklike. Common road bumps deliver stiff, rubbery kicks, and even the highway ride is jittery. Handling is rather cumbersome, and access is awkward. **Last road test: --**
Mitsubishi Outlander	NEW	NA	The new-for-2003 Outlander is based on the Lancer. Available with either front- or all-wheel drive, it's powered by a 2.4-liter Four. The ride is reasonably comfortable. Handling is secure but clumsy, with pronounced body lean and imprecise steering. **Last road test: June 2003**
Nissan 350Z	NEW	NA	The 350Z is a two-seat coupe sharing underpinnings with the Infiniti G35. It uses a smooth-revving 3.5-liter V6. The manual gearbox has six speeds and the shifter feels slightly notchy. Handling is capable, but the stiff ride is awful. A convertible arrived this summer. **Last road test: Dec. 2003**
✔ Nissan Altima	○	NA	The Altima is roomy, with strong engines and secure handling. But the ride is stiff and jittery, especially in the V6 model. Interior trim is cheap. The front seats are fairly comfortable, and the low rear bench offers plenty of leg room. A wide turning circle hampers maneuverability. **Last road test: Feb. 2002**
Nissan Frontier	○	⊖	This compact pickup is fairly crude. An optional supercharged V6 adds some oomph but whines annoyingly and guzzles fuel. Handling is cumbersome and the ride awful. **Last road test: Aug. 2001**

Model	Predicted reliability	Depreciation	Comments
✔ Nissan Maxima	⊖	NA	The redesigned 2004 Maxima is larger than the old model and powered by a 265-hp V6. The spacious, airy cabin and handling are improved from the outgoing model. The ride is stiff and the automatic isn't as smooth as in the previous model. The wide turning circle is a nuisance. **Last road test: July 2003**
Nissan Murano	NEW	NA	The Murano is stylish and quick, with nimble handling. Its V6 delivers strong performance and respectable fuel economy, but the ride is stiff. The spring-loaded rear seat can be folded by flipping a lever. Visibility is poor. **Last road test: Aug. 2003**
✔ Nissan Pathfinder	⊜	○	This midsized SUV has a tolerable ride and handles securely. Cargo space is modest. A powerful V6 and outstanding reliability are pluses. Four-wheel drive is part-time on all trim lines except the LE. **Last road test: Sep. 2001**
Nissan Pathfinder Armada	NEW	NA	The Pathfinder Armada is a large SUV with seating for up to eight passengers. It is powered by a 5.6-liter V8 engine with a five-speed automatic and has an independent rear suspension. It comes in both two- and four-wheel drive. **Last road test: --**
✔ Nissan Quest	○	NA	The redesigned Nissan Quest is a capable, competitively priced minivan powered by a 240-hp, 3.5-liter V6. Both the second- and third-row seats fold flat and out of the way. Ride and handling are good. The center mounted gauges are a nuisance. **Last road test: Oct. 2003**
✔ Nissan Sentra	○	○	The Sentra is a worthy small sedan with a refined, efficient powertrain, decent handling, and a well-designed interior. But ride comfort, braking, and rear-seat room fall a bit short. **Last road test: Sep. 2000**
Nissan Titan	NEW	NA	The Titan is Nissan's first full-sized pickup, powered by a 5.6-liter V8 engine. It will come with two- or four-wheel drive. Extended-cab models will feature a rear door that opens flat against the body. A crew-cab model will also be available. **Last road test: --**
Nissan Xterra	○	⊖	The truck-based Xterra has good cargo space, towing capacity, and off-road capability, but also clumsy handling, an uncomfortable ride, leisurely acceleration, and poor fuel economy. Stability control and head-protection air bags were new for 2003. **Last road test: Oct. 2000**
Oldsmobile Alero	◒	●	A cousin of the Pontiac Grand Am, the Alero comes as a sedan or coupe. Handling is secure and fairly agile in V6 models. The ride is a bit jittery. The interior is cheap, and rear head room is tight. 2004 is this model's last year. **Last road test: June 2001**
Oldsmobile Silhouette	◒	◒	This minivan, like Chevy Venture cousin, has a responsive powertrain and comfortable seating. Subpar reliability and poor performance in offset-crash tests keep it out of contention. **Last road test: Jan. 2001**
Pontiac Aztek	○	NA	The minivan-derived Aztek includes some innovative interior touches and lots of neat storage nooks. The rear seat is too low and the rear gate is a nuisance. All-wheel drive is available. The lack of a rear wiper exacerbates the poor rear visibility in inclement weather. **Last road test: June 2003**

Model	Predicted reliability	Depreciation	Comments
Pontiac Bonneville	◒	○	Pontiac's flagship offers lots of gadgets and frills. The SE has a supple, well-controlled ride. Handling is taut though not sporty. The front seats lack support, and the seat-mounted shoulder belts may be uncomfortable for some. The rear seat is both too low and too soft. **Last road test: Feb. 2000**
Pontiac Grand Am	◒	●	Pontiac's best-selling model has little to recommend it. The Grand Am's handling is adequate but not very crisp, and its ride is unremarkable. Wind noise is quite pronounced. The cabin offers plenty of headroom, but the front seats are soft and unsupportive. **Last road test: Jan. 1999**
Pontiac Grand Prix	NEW	NA	The redesigned 2004 Grand Prix is available with a carryover push-rod 3.8-liter, 200-hp V6 or a supercharged 260-hp version. The rear seatbacks fold flat, as does the front passenger seat, to allow the transport of very long objects. **Last road test: —**
Pontiac GTO	NEW	NA	The new Pontiac GTO is a slightly modified Holden Monaro, a car produced by GM's Australian subsidiary. The rear drive coupe will feature a 340-hp version of the Corvette's 5.7-liter V8, and offers seating for four. **Last road test: —**
Pontiac Montana	◒	◒	This minivan is competitive in most ways, but its below par reliability and poor offset-front-crash-test performance keep it out of contention. The third-row seat folds flat into the cargo floor. All-wheel drive is optional. **Last road test: Jan. 2001**
Pontiac Sunfire	○	●	The Sunfire coupe, cousin of the Chevy Cavalier, is basic transportation only—crude and outdated. The ride is noisy and hard. Seats are uncomforatble, and interior fit and finish are subpar. ABS is no longer standard. **Last road test: —**
✓ Pontiac Vibe	⊖	NA	The Vibe, cousin of the Toyota Matrix, is a roomy small wagon with easy access for people and cargo. Handling and ride are OK, but the engine is noisy and the driving position is not ideal. All-wheel drive is optional. **Last road test: Aug. 2002**
✓ Porsche Boxster	⊖	⊜	This roadster is everything a sports car should be. With front and rear storage compartments, it's almost practical. Handling and braking are superb, and the ride is firm yet not punishing. Lowering the top is very easy. A glass rear window arrived for 2003. **Last road test: June 2002**
Porsche Cayenne	NEW	NA	Porsche's first SUV is about the size of a BMW X5. Made mainly for road use, low-range gearing, and advanced electronics lend it considerable off-road capability. It comes with a choice of engines and an available air suspension. **Last road test: —**
Saab 9-3	NEW	NA	The redesigned 9-3 sedan is available with two turbocharged engines. Handling is significantly improved, with quick, direct steering and taut body control. The rear seat is cramped and the ride is stiff. A convertible, based on the redesign, has just been introduced. **Last road test: July 2003**
✓ Saab 9-5	⊖	○	The 9-5 is competent and pleasant to drive, with a firm, compliant ride. Front seats are comfortable, and the rear is relatively roomy. The wagon is competent well designed but has no third-row seat option. **Last road test: —**

Model	Predicted reliability	Depreciation	Comments
Saturn Ion	NEW	NA	The disappointing Ion replaced Saturn's long-running S-Series. Roomier and with a more refined engine, it's still a noisy and cramped small car. The ride is OK but bounding. Fit and finish are inferior. **Last road test: Mar. 2003**
Saturn L-Series	◒	◒	The midsized L-Series tries to compete with the VW Passat, Toyota Camry, and Honda Accord. The strong V6 and automatic work very well. Handling is competent and secure, but not nimble, and the ride is a bit stiff and noisy. **Last road test: Jan. 2003**
✔ **Saturn VUE**	○	NA	This SUV, like the Ford Escape and Toyota RAV4, uses a unibody platform. Handling is carlike and secure, but the steering is too light at low speeds, and the AWD system is slow to respond. Interior fit and finish are subpar, the front seats lack support, and the rear bench is too low. **Last road test: May 2002**
Scion xA	NEW	NA	The xA is a small four-door hatchback powered by a 1.5-liter, 108-hp Four. It is expected to be available nationwide by the summer of 2004, and includes standard amenities such as antilock brakes and air conditioning. The 60/40-split rear seat folds to increase cargo room. **Last road test: —**
Scion xB	NEW	NA	The xB is a small, tall, slab-sided wagon powered a 1.5-liter, 108-hp Four. It offers an enormous amount of room. Standard equipment includes antilock brakes, stability control, and air conditioning. The rear seat can be removed in sections for a flat load floor. **Last road test: —**
✔ **Subaru Baja**	⊖	NA	The Baja is essentially a Subaru Legacy with a rear roof section chopped off to form a small pickup with four full-sized doors. A folding hatch between cabin and cargo bed adds to its versatility. A 210-hp turbocharged model will be available for 2004. **Last road test: June 2003**
✔ **Subaru Forester**	⊖	⊖	Our top-rated small SUV, the Forester has a tall and roomy cargo area and a controlled, compliant ride. Handling is relatively responsive and acceleration and rear seat room have improved. **Last road test: June 2003**
✔ **Subaru Impreza/ Outback Sport**	○	⊖	The small Impreza delivers good handling and a quiet, comfortable ride. The line includes an Outback Sport, a small wagon, and the sporty WRX, available as sedan or wagon. A 300 hp WRX STi is now available. **Last road test: July 2002**
✔ **Subaru Legacy/Outback**	⊖	○	The all-wheel-drive Legacy is agile with good steering feel, but can get twitchy at its limits. The ride is firm but supple. It's also available in wagon models, including the Outback, which is a plausible alternative to an SUV. **Last road test: Jan. 2003**
Suzuki Aerio	NA	NA	The Aerio replaced the unimpressive Esteem. It features a tall roofline designed to increase head room and improve outward visibility. The ride is very stiff and the engine noisy. Sedan and wagon versions are available. **Last road test: Mar. 2003**
✔ **Suzuki Vitara/XL-7**	○	◒	This small, truck-based SUV is hampered by a crude, unresponsive automatic and a stiff ride. Handling is vague but secure. The driver's seat lacks support, and the cockpit feels narrow. The extended-length XL-7 has a small third-row seat. **Last road test: May 2002**

Model	Predicted reliability	Depreciation	Comments
✔ **Toyota 4Runner**	⊖	NA	The redesigned 4Runner is available with strong and refined V8 and V6 engines. It rides relatively comfortably and is very quiet. Handling is sound and secure. This credible off-roader offers hill-descent control and a system that prevents roll-back on slow, steep ascents. **Last road test: Aug. 2003**
✔ **Toyota Avalon**	⊜	○	The Avalon is an upscale Camry with an extra-roomy rear seat and trunk. It features interior ambience similar to that of a Lexus, along with a smooth V6 and a quiet cabin. The seats are large and comfortable. **Last road test: Feb. 2003**
✔ **Toyota Camry**	○	NA	The Camry remains an excellent sedan–quiet, refined, and roomy. Both the Four and V6 are smooth and responsive. Cabin controls are logical. Limited front-seat thigh support and the lack of a telescoping wheel compromise the driving position. **Last road test: Feb. 2002**
✔ **Toyota Camry Solara**	⊜	○	The Solara is a sportier two-door version of the last Camry design. The ride is well controlled, handling is fairly nimble, and the cabin is hushed. A convertible is available. A redesigned 2004 model based on the new Camry arrives in the fall of 2003. **Last road test: --**
✔ **Toyota Celica**	⊜	⊜	The Celica is a fun-to-drive sporty coupe that handles nimbly. The ride is pretty good for a sporty car. The budget-minded may prefer the plain GT, which isn't as quick or agile as the high-revving GT-S, but is about $4,500 cheaper. **Last road test: Aug. 2000**
✔ **Toyota Corolla**	⊜	NA	The redesigned Corolla is one of the better small sedans, with good room inside and a quality interior. It handles and rides better than the previous version. The standard engine delivers good performance and excellent fuel economy even with the optional automatic. **Last road test: July 2002**
✔ **Toyota Echo**	⊜	⊖	The Echo is a surprisingly roomy small runabout. The driving position is fairly high, and it's easy to get in and out. The 1.5-liter 108-hp engine provides good fuel economy. Handling is fairly responsive and secure, but body roll is pronounced. **Last road test: Dec. 2000**
✔ **Toyota Highlander**	⊜	NA	This Camry-derived all-wheel-drive SUV has a punchy V6 powertrain and is roomy, quiet, comfortable, and well designed. One of our top-rated SUVs, it scored close to the Honda Pilot. A third-row seat and new 3.3-liter V6 debut for 2004. **Last road test: Oct. 2001**
✔ **Toyota Land Cruiser**	⊜	⊖	This big, expensive SUV sports a smooth, quiet 4.7-liter V8 and rides smoothly and quietly. The interior offers lots of room and a third seat. Permanent four-wheel-drive and stability control are both standard and make handling secure. **Last road test: Mar. 2001**
✔ **Toyota Matrix**	⊖	NA	The Matrix is a roomy small wagon with easy access for people and cargo. Handling and ride are OK, but the engine is noisy and the driving position is not ideal. All-wheel drive is optional. **Last road test: Aug. 2002**
✔ **Toyota MR2**	⊜	⊜	Think of this unadulterated roadster as a scaled-down Porsche Boxster. It offers impressive steering and acceleration, precise shifting, and excellent brakes. Luggage space is close to zero making this car primarily a fun-to-drive toy rather than a long-haul companion. **Last road test: Aug. 2000**

Model	Predicted reliability	Depreciation	Comments
✔ Toyota Prius	⊜	NA	The Prius managed 41 mpg in our tests, thanks to its gas-electric hybrid powerplant. It seats five and provides adequate acceleration, secure handling, and a comfortable ride. An '04 redesign in the form of a bigger hatchback arrives this fall. **Last road test: Dec. 2000**
✔ Toyota RAV4	⊖	⊖	The RAV4 is one of our highly-rated small SUVs. It has a flexible interior layout, easy access, nimble handling, and excellent brakes. There's no V6, but the improved Four accelerates adequately. **Last road test: Mar. 2001**
✔ Toyota Sequoia	⊜	NA	The Sequoia competes against the Ford Expedition and Chevy Tahoe. It's roomier than the Land Cruiser, but doesn't ride nearly as comfortably, and its four-wheel-drive system is less sophisticated. It boasts a V8 powertrain and a third-row seat. **Last road test: Nov. 2002**
✔ Toyota Sienna	⊜	NA	The redesigned Sienna is our top-rated minivan. The spacious interior features a third seat that folds into the floor in sections. It rides very comfortably and quietly. The sliding doors have windows that can be opened. **Last road test: Oct. 2003**
✔ Toyota Tacoma	⊖	⊖	The compact, utilitarian Tacoma pickup is a super off-roader but rides uncomfortably and handles ponderously. Acceleration is adequate. The seats are low and flat, making for an uncomfortable driving position. **Last road test: Aug. 2001**
✔ Toyota Tundra	⊜	⊖	The Tundra is one of our top-rated full-sized pickups. The V8 is smooth and powerful, the cabin is quiet. The ride is pleasant. The rear seat in extended-cab versions is very cramped. A crew-cab model is new for 2004. **Last road test: Nov. 1999**
Volkswagen EuroVan	NA	◒	The EuroVan is being discontinued for 2004. It lacks the interior flexibility of most modern minivans, but offers a dedicated Camper version. The V6 is smooth and torquey. Handling is commendable, and the ride is well controlled. **Last road test: —**
Volkswagen Golf	●	⊖	The Golf's responsive but noisy 2.0-liter Four and easy-shifting manual perform well together. You can also get a smooth, powerful V6, a 1.8-liter turbo Four, or a diesel engine. The ride is supple. The front seats offer good, firm support, but the rear is cramped. **Last road test: Dec. 2000**
Volkswagen Jetta	●	⊖	The Jetta shares underpinnings with the Golf and boasts many thoughtful details, a comfortable ride, and responsive handling. The front seats are supportive; the rear is cramped. The standard 2.0-liter Four is noisy, the diesel economical. **Last road test: Dec. 2002**
Volkswagen New Beetle	◒	⊖	The modern, well-equipped New Beetle rides and handles well. The front seats are supportive, but the rear is cramped. A 180-hp Turbo S model is quick but handling is not very sporty. A convertible debuted for spring 2003. **Last road test: Oct. 2002**
✔ Volkswagen Passat	○	⊖	One of our top-picks for family sedans, the Passat is roomy and comfortable. It handles precisely and delivers a firm yet supple ride. The interior is roomy and its appointments have a high-quality feel. AWD is available in sedans and wagons. **Last road test: May 2003**

Model	Predicted reliability	Depre-ciation	Comments
Volkswagen Phaeton	NEW	NA	The Phaeton, due to go on sale in the U.S. in fall 2003, is Volkswagen's first large, premium-luxury cruiser. Engines include a 4.2-liter V8 and an optional 6.0-liter 12-cylinder. All-wheel drive is standard. This heavy sedan rides on an adjustable air suspension. **Last road test: —**
Volkswagen Touareg	NEW	NA	Volkswagen's first SUV has off-road features such as low-range gearing and a locking center differential. It is one of the only car-based SUVs that's capable off road. The V6 is thirsty and underpowered. The $45,000 V8 is stronger. The interior is elegant but not so roomy. **Last road test: Sep. 2003**
Volvo C70	NA	○	A convertible based on the old Volvo S70 sedan. Handling is capable but not sporty, and the brakes work well. The high pressure turbocharged Five doesn't feel very responsive. The light pressure engine is a better choice. **Last road test: –**
Volvo S40/V40	◒	○	The S40 sedan and V40 wagon are cramped and a bit noisy. Handling is secure and the brakes are excellent, but the ride is stiff. The engine is responsive, and the wagon offers optional built-in booster seats. Expect a redesign in 2004. **Last road test: Jan. 2000**
✔ **Volvo S60**	○	NA	The S60 isn't not as sporty or comfortable as the BMW 3-Series. It comes with a plethora of advanced safety gear, and all-wheel-drive is available. The seats are very comfortable, but the rear is cramped and visibility poor. **Last road test: May 2001**
Volvo S80	●	○	Volvo's front-drive flagship performs well in its class. It's roomy, quiet, and comfortable. The base engine is a lively straight Six; the turbocharged T6 version offers effortless acceleration. An all-wheel-drive version arrives for 2004. **Last road test: —**
✔ **Volvo V70/XC70**	○	○	The V70 is a spacious, comfortable wagon. The all-wheel drive XC70 Cross Country model is an SUV alternative that doesn't ride and handle as well as the V70. All-wheel drive is also available on the V70. Horsepower was increased for 2003. **Last road test: July 2001**
Volvo XC90	NEW	NA	This seven-seater SUV has AWD and a comfortable, flexible interior. Handling is secure but acceleration and fuel-economy are so-so. The ride is more comfortable than in the XC70. Power comes from either a five- or six-cylinder turbo engine. **Last road test: Sep. 2003**

RATINGS OF THE 2003-04 MODELS

Which cars are best? This section can give you a head start in answering that question. Included here are overall Ratings on 190 vehicles from Consumer Reports extensive testing program. Though most tests were conducted on 2003 or slightly earlier models, results still apply since cars typically change little from year to year. Recommended models are indicated with a ✔. They performed competently in our tests; our survey data indicate they should have at least average reliability; and they have not performed poorly in any crash tests. Twins and triplets (similiar models sold under different nameplates) are grouped together in the chart below and marked with ▪ symbols when only one version has been tested. Overall mpg is based on our tests in a range of mixed highway and city driving conditions.

Recommendations reflect results from our latest reliability survey.

Listed within type in order of performance.

Make and Model	Overall score (P F G VG E)	Overall mpg	Tested model
SMALL SEDANS			
✔ Ford Focus		25	ZTS 2.0 Four; auto 4
✔ Honda Civic		29	EX 1.7 Four; auto 4
✔ Honda Civic		36	Hybrid 1.3 Four; CVT
Volkswagen Jetta		32	GLS 1.9 Four turbodiesel; auto 4
✔ Toyota Prius		41	1.5 Four; CVT
✔ Toyota Corolla		29	LE 1.8 Four; auto 4
Hyundai Elantra		25	GLS 2.0 Four; auto 4
✔ Subaru Impreza		22	2.5 RS 2.5 Four; auto 4
✔ Mazda Protegé		26	LX 2.0 Four; auto 4
Nissan Sentra		26	GXE 1.8 Four; auto 4
Suzuki Aerio		25	GS 2.0 Four; auto 4
Mitsubishi Lancer		26	LS 2.0 Four; auto 4
Hyundai Accent		26	GL 1.6 Four; auto 4
Saturn Ion		24	3 2.2 Four; auto 5
Dodge Neon		24	SXT 2.0 Four; auto 4
Chevrolet Cavalier		26	LS 2.2 Four; auto 4

Make and Model	Overall score P F G VG E	Overall mpg	Tested model
FUEL-EFFICIENT CARS			
Volkswagen Golf		41	GLS 1.9 Four turbodiesel; man 5
✔ Honda Civic		36	Hybrid 1.3 Four; CVT
Volkswagen Jetta		32	GLS 1.9 Four turbodiesel; auto 4
✔ Toyota Prius		41	1.5 Four; CVT
✔ Toyota Echo		38	1.5 Four; man 5
Honda Insight		51	1.0 Three; man 5
FAMILY SEDANS			
✔ Volkswagen Passat		21	GLX 2.8 V6; auto 5
✔ Toyota Camry		20	XLE 3.0 V6; auto 4
✔ Honda Accord		23	EX 3.0 V6; auto 5
✔ Honda Accord		24	EX 2.4 Four; auto 4
Volkswagen Passat		23	GLS 1.8 Four turbo; auto 5
✔ Toyota Camry		24	LE 2.4 Four; auto 4
✔ Nissan Maxima		21	3.5 SE 3.5 V6; auto 5
✔ Nissan Altima		20	3.5 SE 3.5 V6; auto 4
✔ Mazda6		23	i 2.3 Four; auto 4
✔ Mazda6		20	s 3.0 V6; auto 5
✔ Nissan Altima		22	2.5 S 2.5 Four; auto 4
✔ Volvo S40		22	1.9 Four turbo; auto 4
✔ Subaru Legacy		21	L Special Edition 2.5 Four; auto 4
✔ Hyundai Sonata		21	GLS 2.5 V6; auto 4
✔ Mitsubishi Galant		22	ES 3.0 V6; auto 4
✔ Chevrolet Malibu		22	LS 3.1 V6; auto 4
✔ Chevrolet Impala		20	LS 3.8 V6; auto 4
✔ ■ Ford Taurus		21	SE 3.0 V6; auto 4
✔ ■ Mercury Sable		21	Ford Taurus SE 3.0 V6; auto 4
Oldsmobile Alero		20	GL 3.4 V6; auto 4
✔ Hyundai XG350		19	L 3.5 V6; auto 5
✔ Dodge Intrepid		19	ES 3.5 V6; auto 4
■ Chrysler Sebring		21	LX 2.7 V6; auto 4
■ Dodge Stratus		21	Chrysler Sebring LX 2.7 V6; auto 4
Pontiac Grand Am		23	SE 2.4 Four; auto 4
Saturn L-Series		24	L200 2.2 Four; auto 4

Make and Model	Overall score (P F G VG E)	Overall mpg	Tested model
UPSCALE SEDANS			
✔ BMW 3-Series		22	330i 3.0 Six; auto 5
✔ Lexus IS300		21	3.0 Six; auto 5
✔ Lincoln LS		19	Premium 3.0 V6; auto 5
Mercedes-Benz C-Class		21	C320 3.2 V6; auto 5
✔ Lexus ES300		21	3.0 V6; auto 5
Audi A4		20	Quattro 3.0 V6; auto 5
Cadillac CTS		20	3.2 V6; auto 5
✔ Acura TL		22	Type-S 3.2 V6; auto 5
✔ Infiniti I35		20	3.5 V6; auto 4
✔ Infiniti G35		20	3.5 V6; auto 5
Jaguar X-Type		19	3.0 V6; auto 5
✔ Volvo S60		21	2.4T 2.4 Five turbo; auto 5
Oldsmobile Aurora		19	4.0 V8; auto 4
Saab 9-3		21	Vector 2.0 Four turbo; auto 5
✔ Chrysler 300M		21	3.5 V6; auto 4
Mitsubishi Diamante		20	3.5 V6; auto 4
LARGE SEDANS			
✔ Toyota Avalon		21	XLS 3.0 V6; auto 4
✔ Buick Park Avenue		21	Ultra 3.8 V6 supercharged; auto 4
✔ Lincoln Town Car		17	Signature 4.6 V8; auto 4
Pontiac Bonneville		20	SE 3.8 V6; auto 4
✔ Buick LeSabre		20	Limited 3.8 V6; auto 4
■ Ford Crown Victoria		16	Mercury Grand Marquis LSE 4.6 V8; auto 4
■ Mercury Grand Marquis		16	LSE 4.6 V8; auto 4
LUXURY SEDANS			
✔ BMW 5-Series		20	530i 3.0 Six; auto 5
✔ Lexus LS430		19	4.3 V8; auto 5
Mercedes-Benz S-Class		18	S430 4.3 V8; auto 5
Audi A6		18	2.7T 2.7 V6 turbo; auto 5
Cadillac DeVille		19	DHS 4.6 V8; auto 4
Audi A8		17	L 4.2 V8; auto 6
✔ Acura RL		21	3.5 V6; auto 4
Jaguar XJ8		19	Vanden Plas 4.2 V8; auto 6
BMW 7-Series		18	745Li 4.4 V8; auto 6
Jaguar S-Type		20	3.0 V6; auto 5

Make and Model	Overall score (P F G VG E)	Overall mpg	Tested model
SPORTY CARS			
✔ Ford Focus		24	SVT 2.0 Four; man 6
✔ Subaru Impreza		21	WRX 2.0 Four turbo; man 5
✔ Toyota Celica		28	GT-S 1.8 Four; man 6
Mini Cooper		30	Base 1.6 Four; man 5
Volkswagen New Beetle		25	Turbo S 1.8 Four turbo; man 6
✔ Honda Civic		26	Si 2.0 Four; man 5
✔ Acura RSX		26	Type-S 2.0 Four; man 6
Hyundai Tiburon		22	GT 2.7 V6; man 6
✔ Mitsubishi Eclipse		24	GT 3.0 V6; man 5
ROADSTERS			
✔ Honda S2000		27	2.0 Four; man 6
Chevrolet Corvette		21	Base conv. 5.7 V8; man 6
✔ Porsche Boxster		22	Base 2.7 Six; man 5
✔ Toyota MR-2		31	1.8 Four; man 5
Mercedes-Benz SLK		23	SLK 320 3.2 V6; man 6
Audi TT		22	Conv. AWD 1.8 Four turbo; man 6
✔ Mazda MX-5 Miata		27	1.8 Four; man 5
✔ Ford Thunderbird		17	Premium 3.9 V8; auto 5
MINIVANS			
✔ Toyota Sienna		21	LE 3.3 V6; auto 5
✔ Honda Odyssey		18	EX 3.5 V6; auto 5
✔ Mazda MPV		19	ES 3.0 V6; auto 5
✔ Nissan Quest		18	3.5 SL 3.5 V6; auto 4
▪ Chrysler Town & Country		17	Dodge Grand Caravan eX 3.8 V6; auto 4
▪ Dodge Grand Caravan		17	eX 3.8 V6; auto 4
▪ Chevrolet Venture		19	LS 3.4 V6; auto 4
▪ Oldsmobile Silhouette		19	Chevrolet Venture LS 3.4 V6; auto 4
▪ Pontiac Montana		19	Chevrolet Venture LS 3.4 V6; auto 4
Ford Windstar		17	SE Sport 3.8 V6; auto 4
Kia Sedona		17	EX 3.5 V6; auto 5
WAGONS & HATCHBACKS			
✔ Volkswagen Passat		18	GLX 4Motion 2.8 V6; auto 5
Volkswagen Passat		21	GLS 1.8 Four turbo; auto 5
Audi Allroad		16	2.7 V6 turbo; auto 5
✔ Ford Focus Wagon		23	SE 2.0 Four; auto 4

Make and Model	Overall score (P F G VG E)	Overall mpg	Tested model
WAGONS & HATCHBACKS *continued*			
Volkswagen Jetta Wagon		23	GLS 1.8 Four turbo; auto 5
✔ Subaru Legacy Outback		20	H6 VDC 3.0 Six; auto 4
✔ Volvo V70		18	XC 2.4 Five turbo; auto 5
✔ Subaru Legacy Outback		20	Limited 2.5 Four; auto 4
✔ ■ Toyota Matrix		24	XR AWD 1.8 Four; auto 4
✔ ■ Pontiac Vibe		26	Base 1.8 Four; auto 4
✔ Ford Focus Hatchback		24	ZX5 2.0 Four; auto 4
✔ Volvo V40		21	1.9 Four turbo; auto 4
✔ Chrysler PT Cruiser		18	Limited 2.4 Four; auto 4
✔ Mazda Protégé		25	Protege5 2.0 Four; auto 4
Saturn L-Series		21	LW2 3.0 V6; auto 4
✔ Subaru Impreza		22	Outback Sport 2.5 Four; auto 4
SMALL SPORT-UTILITY VEHICLES			
✔ Subaru Forester		21	2.5 X 2.5 Four; auto 4
✔ Toyota RAV4		22	Base 2.0 Four; auto 4
✔ ■ Pontiac Vibe		24	Toyota Matrix XR AWD 1.6 Four; auto 4
✔ ■ Toyota Matrix		24	XR AWD 1.6 Four; auto 4
✔ Subaru Baja		20	2.5L 2.5 Four; auto 4
✔ Honda CR-V		21	EX 2.4 Four; auto 4
✔ Hyundai Santa Fe		18	GLS 2.7 V6; auto 4
✔ Ford Escape		17	XLT 3.0 V6; auto 4
✔ Honda Element		20	EX 2.4 Four; auto 4
Mitsubishi Outlander		20	XLS 2.4 Four; auto 4
Mazda Tribute		18	LX 3.0 V6; auto 4
✔ Saturn VUE		18	3.0 V6; auto 5
Land Rover Freelander		17	SE 2.5 V6; auto 5
✔ Suzuki XL-7		17	Touring 2.7 V6; auto 4
✔ Jeep Liberty		15	Sport 3.7 V6, auto 4
Kia Sorento		15	EX 3.5 V6; auto 4
Pontiac Aztek		17	3.4 V6; auto 4
Nissan Xterra		15	SE 3.3 V6; auto 4
SPORT-UTILITY VEHICLES			
Audi Allroad		16	2.7 V6 turbo; auto 5
✔ Lexus RX330		18	3.3 V6; auto 5
BMW X5		15	4.4i 4.4 V8; auto 5

Make and Model	Overall score (P F G VG E)	Overall mpg	Tested model
SPORT-UTILITY VEHICLES *continued*			
✔ Honda Pilot		19	EX 3.5 V6; auto 5
✔ Nissan Murano		19	SL 3.5 V6; CVT
✔ Toyota Highlander		18	Limited 3.0 V6; auto 4
✔ Subaru Legacy Outback		20	H6 VDC 3.0 Six; auto 4
✔ Acura MDX		17	Touring 3.5 V6; auto 5
✔ Volvo V70		18	XC 2.4 Five turbo; auto 5
✔ Infiniti FX		18	FX35 3.5 V6; auto 5
BMW X5		17	3.0i 3.0 Six; auto 5
✔ Toyota Land Cruiser		14	4.7 V8; auto 4
Mitsubishi Endeavor		17	XLS 3.8 V6; auto 4
✔ Toyota 4Runner		16	SR5 4.0 V6; auto 4
Chrysler Pacifica		16	3.5 V6; auto 4
Volvo XC90		15	T6 2.9 Six twin-turbo; auto 4
Mercedes-Benz M-Class		15	ML430 4.3 V8; auto 5
✔ Toyota Sequoia		15	Limited 4.7 V8; auto 4
✔ ▪ Chevrolet Suburban		13	LT 5.3 V8; auto 4
✔ ▪ GMC Yukon XL		13	Chevrolet Suburban LT 5.3 V8; auto 4
Volkswagen Touareg		15	3.2 V6; auto 6
Ford Explorer		16	XLT 4.0 V6; auto 5
Ford Expedition		12	Eddie Bauer 5.4 V8; auto 4
✔ Nissan Pathfinder		16	LE 3.5 V6; auto 4
Buick Rendezvous		16	CXL 3.4 V6; auto 4
✔ ▪ Chevrolet Tahoe		13	LT 5.3 V8; auto 4
✔ ▪ GMC Yukon		13	Chevrolet Tahoe LT 5.3 V8; auto 4
Mitsubishi Montero		14	Limited 3.8 V6; auto 5
▪ Chevrolet TrailBlazer		15	GMC Envoy SLE 4.2 Six; auto 4
▪ GMC Envoy		15	SLE 4.2 Six; auto 4
▪ Chevrolet TrailBlazer		13	EXT LT 4.2 Six; auto 4
▪ GMC Envoy		13	Chevrolet TrailBlazer EXT LT 4.2 Six; auto 4
Dodge Durango		13	SLT Plus 4.7 V8; auto 4
Jeep Grand Cherokee		16	Laredo 4.0 Six; auto 4
Ford Excursion		10	XLT 6.8 V10; auto 4
COMPACT PICKUP TRUCKS - CREW CAB V6 4WD			
Ford Explorer Sport Trac		15	4.0 V6; auto 5
Dodge Dakota Quad Cab		13	SLT Plus 4.7 V8; auto 4

Make and Model	Overall score (P F G VG E)	Overall mpg	Tested model
COMPACT PICKUP TRUCKS - CREW CAB V6 4WD *continued*			
✔ Toyota Tacoma Double Cab		16	TRD 3.4 V6; auto 4
▪ Chevrolet S-10 Crew Cab		15	LS 4.3 V6; auto 4
▪ GMC Sonoma Crew Cab		15	Chevrolet S-10 LS 4.3 V6; auto 4
Nissan Frontier Crew Cab		14	SC 3.3 V6 supercharged; auto 4
LARGE PICKUP TRUCKS - V8 4WD			
✔ Chevrolet Avalanche 1500		13	5.3 V8; auto 4
✔ Toyota Tundra extended		15	SR5 4.7 V8; auto 4
✔ ▪ Chevrolet Silverado 1500 ext.		15	LS 5.3 V8; auto 4
✔ ▪ GMC Sierra 1500 extended		15	Chevrolet Silverado LS 5.3 V8; auto 4
Ford F-150 Supercrew		14	XLT 5.4 V8; auto 4
Dodge Ram 1500 Quad cab		12	SLT 4.7 V8; auto 4

THE BEST AND WORST USED CARS

Long-term reliability is a key consideration for the used-car shopper, and yet it's one of the hardest aspects of a vehicle to discern. CONSUMER REPORTS reliability surveys have shown that the combined experience of many other owners in the recent past is the best guide to how you can expect a particular vehicle to fare.

Every year, CONSUMER REPORTS conducts an extensive survey of car owners, asking them about serious problems that have cropped up in the past 12 months. The survey generates more than half a million responses, which together paint a detailed picture of how cars up to eight years old are holding up.

Vehicles with consistently high reliability year after year that have also done well in CONSUMER REPORTS performance tests are named "CR Good Bets." Most have Japanese nameplates. That's because Japanese cars, whether they're assembled in this country or overseas, have the most consistent records of above-average reliability.

The list of "Reliable used cars by price," on the following two pages, highlights all the cars in the survey that racked up better-than-average reliability scores. They may or may not have done especially well in performance tests. We also list the models to avoid starting on page 201.

WHAT WE RECOMMEND

CR Good Bet

The best used cars

You can increase your odds of getting a reliable used car by choosing one of the models listed below.

Acura Integra	Lexus GS300/GS400, GS430	Subaru Legacy
Acura RL	Lexus LS400, LS430	Subaru Outback
Acura TL	Lexus RX300	Toyota 4Runner
Ford Escort	Mazda Millenia	Toyota Avalon
Geo/Chevrolet Prizm	Mazda MX-5 Miata	Toyota Camry
Honda Accord	Mazda Protegé	Toyota Camry Solara
Honda Civic	Mercury Tracer	Toyota Celica
Honda CR-V	Nissan Altima	Toyota Corolla
Honda Odyssey	Nissan Maxima	Toyota Echo
Infiniti G20	Nissan Pathfinder	Toyota RAV4
Infiniti I30	Saab 9-5	Toyota Sienna
Isuzu Oasis	Subaru Forester	Toyota Tacoma
Lexus ES300	Subaru Impreza	Toyota Tundra

CR Good Bets These models have performed well in CONSUMER REPORTS road tests and have proved to be better than average in overall reliability for the model years 1995 to 2002. Models are listed alphabetically. Some are twins, essentially similar models sold under different nameplates. We've included only the models for which we have sufficient data for at least three model years. Problems with the engine, cooling system, transmission, and driveline are weighted more heavily than other problems in calculating the overall reliability scores for both the best- and worst-car lists.

Reliable used cars by price

These are models that have had above-average reliability in one or more model years. Listed by price group, and alphabetically within groups. Price ranges are what you'd pay for a typically equipped base trimline car with average mileage

LESS THAN $6,000

Acura Integra '95
Buick Century '98
Chevrolet Prizm '98-00
Ford Crown Victoria '97 · **Escort** '97-98, '01 · **Explorer (2WD)** '95-96 · **F-150** '95
Geo Metro '95 · **Prizm** '95-97 · **Tracker** '95
Honda Accord '95-96 · **Civic** '97
Infiniti G20 '95-96
Mazda B-Series (2WD) '95-98 · **Miata** '95 · **Protegé** '96-98
Mercury Marquis '97-98 · **Tracer** '97-99
Nissan Altima '96 · **Sentra** '97 · **Pickup** '95
Saturn SL/SW '98-99
Subaru Impreza '95 · **Legacy** '95
Suzuki Sidekick '95 · **Swift** '95
Toyota Corolla '95-97 · **RAV-4** '97 · **T-100** '95 · **Tercel** '95-97

$6,000-$8,000

Acura CL '97-'98 · **Integra** '96-98 · **TL** '96-97
BMW 3-Series '95
Buick Century '01
Chevrolet Prizm '01-02
Ford Crown Victoria '98-99 · **Escort** '99-00 · **F-150 (2WD)** '97-98 **(4WD)** '97 · **Ranger (2WD)** '95-97
Honda Accord '97-98 · **Civic** '95-96 · **Odyssey** '95-97
Hyundai Sonata '01
Infiniti I30 '96-97
Isuzu Oasis '96-97
Lincoln Continental '96 · **Town Car** '95-97
Mazda 626 '98-99 · **Miata** '96-97 · **Millenia** '98 · **Protegé** '99-00
Nissan Altima '97-99 · **Frontier** '98-99 · **Maxima** '95-98 · **Pathfinder** '95 · **Pickup** '99 · **Sentra** '99
Subaru Impreza '96-98 · **Legacy/Outback** '98
Toyota 4Runner '96 · **Avalon** '95-97 · **Camry** '95-98 · **Celica** '95-96 · **Corolla** '98-99 · **Echo** '00-01 · **Previa** '95 · **RAV-4** '96, '98 · **T100** '96-97 · **Tacoma** '95-96, '99

$8,000-$10,000

Acura 3.5 RL '96-97 · **CL** '99 · **Integra** '99 · **Legend** '95 · **TL** '98
Buick Century '02 · **Regal** '00-01
Chevrolet Impala '02
Ford Expedition (2WD) '97 · **F-150 (2WD)** '02, **(4WD)** '98 · **Ranger** '98
Honda Accord '99 · **Civic** '00 · **CR-V** '97-99 · **Odyssey** '98
Hyundai Sonata '02
Infiniti G20 '99 · **Infiniti** I30 '98-99 · **QX4** '97
Isuzu Oasis '98
Lexus ES300 '95-97
Lincoln Town Car '98
Mazda 626 '00 · **Miata** '99 · **Millenia** '99-00 · **Protegé** '01-02
Mercury Grand Marquis '99-00
Nissan Altima '00-01 · **Maxima** '99 · **Pathfinder** '96-98
Saturn SL/SW '01
Subaru Forester '98-99 · **Impreza** '00 · **Legacy/Outback** '97, '99
Toyota 4Runner '95 · **Avalon** '98-99 · **Camry** '99 · **Celica** '97 · **Corolla** '02 · **Echo** '02 · **Sienna** '98 · **Tacoma** '00

$10,000-$12,000

Acura Integra '00-01 · **TL** '99
BMW Z3 '97

Buick Regal '02
Chrysler PT Cruiser '01-02
Ford Expedition (2WD) '98 • **F-150 (2WD)** '99
Honda Accord '01-02 • **CR-V** '00
Infiniti G20 '00-01
Lexus ES300 '98 • **SC300/SC400** '95
Mazda MPV '00-01
Mercedes-Benz C-Class '00
Nissan Frontier '00-01 • **Maxima** '00-01 • **Pathfinder** '99
Saturn SL/SW '02
Subaru Impreza '01
Toyota 4Runner '97-98 • **Camry** '00-01 • **Camry Solara** '99-00 • **Celica** '99-01 • **RAV4** '99-00 • **Sienna** '99 • **Tundra** '00

$12,000-$14,000

Acura CL '01 • **3.5RL** '98
Ford F-150 (2WD) '00
Honda Accord '02 • **CR-V** '01-02
Hyundai Santa Fe '02
Infiniti G20 '02 • **QX4** '98-99
Lexus LS400 '95-96
Lincoln Continental '00
Mazda Miata '00-01 • **Millenia** '01 • **MPV** '02
Nissan Maxima '02 • **Pathfinder** '00-01
Subaru Legacy, Outback '00-02
Toyota 4Runner '99 • **Avalon** '00 • **Camry Solara Coupe** '02 • **RAV4** '02 • **Sienna** '00 • **Tacoma** '97-98

$14,000-$16,000

Acura 3.5RL '99 • **TL** '00-01
BMW Z3 '98
Ford F-150 (2WD) '99
Infiniti QX4 '00
Lexus ES300 '99 • **LS400** '97
Saab 9-5 '00
Subaru Forester '01-02
Toyota Camry Solara Convertible '01 • **Celica** '02 • **Sienna** '01-02 • **Tacoma** '97-98

$16,000-$18,000

Ford Expedition '02 • **F-150 (2WD)** '00-02
Infiniti QX4 '01
Lexus ES 300 '00 • **GS300/GS400** '98 • **IS300** '02 • **RX300** '99
Lincoln Town Car '00
Nissan Pathfinder '02
Toyota 4Runner '00-01 • **Avalon** '01-02 • **Camry Solara Convertible** '02 • **Highlander** '01 • **Prius** '01-02

$18,000-$20,000

Acura 3.5RL '00 • TL '02
BMW 5-Series '99 • Z3 '01
Honda Odyssey '01-02 • **S2000** '00-01
Lexus ES300 '01 • **GS300/GS400** '99
Mercedes-Benz C-Class '97
Toyota 4Runner '02 • **Highlander** '02 • **Tacoma** '01-02

$20,000-$26,000

Acura 3.5RL '02
Ford F-150 (4WD) '02
Lexus ES300 '02 • **GS300** '00 • **GS300/GS430** '01 • **LS400** '98-99
Porsche Boxster '00
Saab 9-3 Convertible '01
Toyota Tundra '01-02

$26,000 AND UP

Acura MDX '01-02
BMW 7-Series '01
Lexus LS430 '01-02 • **RX300** '00-02
Saab 9-5 '01-02
Toyota Land Cruiser '00 • **Sequoia** '01-02

WHAT TO WATCH OUT FOR

The worst used cars

Some cars have a bad year, while others trail the pack consistently. The vehicles on this list have had more problems than average over multiple years. Buying one could be asking for trouble.

Cadillac Catera
Cadillac Seville
Chevrolet Astro
Chevrolet Blazer
Chrysler New Yorker, LHS
Chrysler Town & Country (AWD)
Dodge Caravan (4-cyl.)
Dodge Dakota (4WD)
Dodge Durango
Dodge Grand Caravan (AWD)
Dodge Neon
Ford Focus
Ford Windstar
GMC Jimmy
GMC Safari
Jeep Grand Cherokee
Lincoln LS
Mercedes-Benz M-Class
Oldsmobile Alero
Oldsmobile Bravada
Oldsmobile Cutlass
Plymouth Grand Voyager
Plymouth Neon
Plymouth/Chrysler Voyager (4-cyl.)
Pontiac Grand Am
Volkswagen Jetta
Volkswagen New Beetle
Volvo S80

Reliability risks The models on this list have been consistently risky buys. They have exhibited multiple years of much worse than average overall reliability for the model years 1995 to 2002. Some are twins or triplets, essentially similiar models sold under different nameplates. Models are listed alphabetically.

Used cars to avoid by make and year

Models on this list have shown below-average reliability for the model years indicated. They are listed alphabetically by make, model and year.

Audi A4 '97, '00, '02 • **A6** (V6) '97-99 • **A6 (V6, Turbo)** '00 • **TT** '00-01

BMW 3-Series '00-01 • **X5** '01-02

Buick Park Avenue '97-98, '01-02 • **Rendezvous** '02 • **Riviera** '95 • **Roadmaster** '95-96

Cadillac Catera '97-01 • **DeVille** '95-98, '00-01 • **Escalade** '02 • **Seville** '95-02

Chevrolet Astro '95-02 • **Blazer** '95-02 • **C1500** '96-97 • **Camaro** '96-00 • **Caprice** '96 • **Cavalier** '96-97, '02 • **Corsica, Beretta** '95 • **Corvette** '00-01 • **Express 1500** '96-01 • **K1500** '96-99 • **Lumina Minivan** '95 • **Malibu** '97-00 • **Monte Carlo** '95 • **S-10 (4-cyl.)** '95 • **S-10 (V6)** '96-02 • **Silverado 1500 (4WD)** '99-02 • **Suburban** '96-00 • **Tahoe** '96-98, '00 • **Tracker** '00 • **TrailBlazer** '02 • **Venture (ext.)** '97-00, '02 • **Venture (reg.)** '99-00

Chrysler 300M '99, '02 • **Cirrus (V6)** '99 • **Concorde** '95-99 • **New Yorker, LHS** '95-97, '99 • **Sebring Convertible** '98, '00, '02 • **Sebring (V6)** '01 • **Town & Country (reg.)** '96-97, '99 • **Town & Country (ext.) (2WD)** '95-97, '00-01 • **Town & Country (ext.) (AWD)** '97, '99-01 • **Voyager** '01-02

Dodge Caravan (4-cyl.) '95-98, '01-02 • **Caravan (V6)**

'95-97, '99, '01-02 • **Dakota (2WD)** '98-99, '02 • **Dakota (4WD)** '96-01 • **Durango** '98-02 • **Grand Caravan (V6, 2WD)** '95-97, '00-01 • **Grand Caravan (V6, AWD)** '97, '99-01 • **Intrepid** '95-99 • **Neon** '95-00 • **Ram 1500 (2WD)** '97-98, '01-02 • **Ram 1500 (4WD)** '96-00, '02 • **Stratus (4-cyl.)** '96-98 • **Stratus (V6)** '99, '01

Ford Contour '95-96 • **Contour (V6)** '97-98 • **Crown Victoria** '02 • **Econoline E-150 wagon** '96-97 • **Escape (V6)** '01-02 • **Expedition (4WD)** '99 • **Explorer** '98-02 • **Explorer Sport Trac** '01-02 • **Focus** '00-01 • **Mustang** '01-02 • **Probe** '95-96 • **Ranger (4WD)** '97-01 • **Ranger** '02 • **Taurus** '95 • **Windstar** '95-02

GMC Envoy '02 • **Jimmy** '95-'01 • **S-15 Sonoma (4-cyl.)** '95 • **S-15 Sonoma (V6)** '96-02 • **Safari** '95-02 • **Savana Van 1500** '96-01 • **Sierra 1500 (2WD)** '96-97 • **Sierra 1500 (4WD)** '96-02 • **Suburban** '96-99 • **Yukon** '96-98, '00 • **Yukon XL** '00

Honda Passport '96-97, '99-01

Isuzu Rodeo '96-97, '99-01

Jaguar S-Type '00-01 • **X-Type** '02

Jeep Cherokee '00-01 • **Grand Cherokee** '95-02 • **Wrangler** '97-02

Lincoln LS '00-02 • **Town Car** '01

Mazda B-Series (4WD) '97-01 • **B-Series** '02 • **Tribute (V6)** '01-02

Mercedes-Benz C-Class '95, '01 • **CLK** '00-02 • **E-Class** '98, '00 • **M-Class** '98-02 • **S-Class** '00-01 • **SLK** '01

Mercury Cougar '99 • **Grand Marquis** '02 • **Mountaineer** '98-02 • **Mystique** '95-96 • **Mystique (V6)** '97-98 • **Sable** '95

Mitsubishi Eclipse '01 • **Galant** '01

Nissan Sentra '00

Oldsmobile 88 '97 • **Alero** '99-01 • **Aurora** '95-98, '01-02 • **Bravada** '97-99, '02 • **Cutlass** '97-99 • **Intrigue** '02 • **Silhouette (ext.)** '97-00, '02 • **Silhouette (reg.)** '95, '99-00

Plymouth Breeze '96-98 • **Grand Voyager (V6)** '95-97, '00 • **Neon** '95-00 • **Voyager (4-cyl.)** '95-98 • **Voyager (V6)** '95-97, '99

Pontiac Bonneville '95, '97, '00-02 • **Firebird** '96-00 • **Grand Am** '95-02 • **Grand Prix** '97 • **Montana (ext.)** '97-00, '02 • **Montana (reg.)** '99-00 • **Sunfire** '96-97, '02 • **Trans Sport** '95 • **Trans Sport (ext.)** '97-98

Saturn L-Series '00-01

Suzuki Vitara '00

Volkswagen Golf '99-01 • **Jetta** '95-02 • **New Beetle** '98-01 • **Passat (4-cyl.)** '98 • **Passat (V6, AWD)** '00, '02

Volvo 960 '96-97 • **S40/V40** '00 • **S80** '99-01 • **S90/V90** '98 • **V70 (except XC)** '01 • **V70 Cross Country** '98-99

AUTO RELIABILITY

For any car shopper, whether you're buying new or used, reliability is one of the key considerations. To gauge reliability, Consumer Reports asks readers every year to tell us about any serious problems they've experienced in the last year with the cars they own.

That survey information enables us to predict the reliability of new cars and to zero in on trouble spots found in older cars, trucks, minivans, and SUVs. See the reviews beginning on page 171 for the results as they apply to new models. The histories on the following pages can help you shop for a used car.

The most common complaints across all model years continue to involve the electrical system, power equipment, body hardware and integrity (squeaks and rattles). Problems with engine, cooling, and fuel have been less worrisome in recent years. Rust problems have almost vanished, and complaints about the driveline, exhaust system, and the paint and trim have fallen significantly.

How to use the CR Reliability Histories

ZERO IN ON A SPECIFIC MODEL

Find the make, model, and year for the vehicle you're interested in. For an overall idea of how its reliability stacks up, check the Reliability Verdict. Models with a ✓ have proved more trouble-free than the average. They're the same models you'll find on the list of "Reliable Used Cars" on page 199.

WHAT'S THE TROUBLE?

Use the specific trouble-spot scores to determine whether the vehicle you're interested in is likely to have problems that you need to check out. What's covered in each score is explained on page 204.

COMPARE TO THE AVERAGE

Use the chart for "The Average Model" on the next page as a benchmark to determine if the problems with the model and year you're considering are unusually extensive or are just related to normal aging.

Every model experiences troubles as it ages. "The Average Model" shows the overall average for all models for each model year. To see if the car you're considering might be unusually troublesome in some area, compare its score with the average model. If you look up the 1995 Dodge Intrepid, for instance, you'll see that it gets a ● for transmission problems—more than its share, even for a car that old. With older models, a score of ◒ is not unusual for categories such as electrical, brakes, and air conditioning (A/C). On newer models, even a score of ○ or ⊖ warrants caution. Have those components carefully checked before you buy.

WHY A CAR MIGHT GET NO CHECK

Sometimes a vehicle (especially a 2002 model) with mostly high scores in the 14 trouble spots gets an average or below-average Reliability Verdict. That's because it didn't compare well with the average for that model year (see chart next page). For example, the 2002 Ford Explorer 4WD scored ◒ in eight categories and ◒ - ⊜ in six others. Its scores were worse than the 2002 average in four areas, including transmission, which was weighted more heavily than others in calculating the Reliability Verdict. The result: worse-than-average overall reliability (no check). By contrast, the Honda Accord got ⊜ in all but one category. It earned a "for better-than-average" reliability.

RELIABILITY HISTORY

TROUBLE SPOTS	The Average Model							
	95	96	97	98	99	00	01	02
Engine	○	○	⊖	⊖	⊖	⊜	⊜	⊜
Cooling	○	○	⊖	⊖	⊜	⊜	⊜	⊜
Fuel	○	○	○	⊖	⊖	⊖	⊖	⊜
Ignition	⊖	⊖	⊖	⊜	⊜	⊜	⊜	⊜
Transmission	○	○	⊖	⊖	⊖	⊖	⊜	⊜
Electrical	◒	◒	◒	◒	○	○	⊖	⊜
Air conditioning	◒	○	○	⊖	⊖	⊜	⊜	⊜
Suspension	○	○	○	⊖	⊖	⊖	⊖	⊜
Brakes	◒	◒	◒	○	○	⊖	⊖	⊜
Exhaust	⊖	⊖	⊜	⊜	⊜	⊜	⊜	⊜
Power equipment	○	○	○	○	○	○	⊖	⊜
Paint/trim/rust	○	⊖	⊖	⊖	⊖	⊖	⊜	⊜
Body integrity	○	○	○	○	○	○	○	⊖
Body hardware	○	○	○	○	○	○	○	⊖
RELIABILITY VERDICT	✔	✔	✔	✔	✔	✔	✔	✔

Key to trouble spots

⊜ 2.0% or less
⊖ 2.0% to 5.0%
○ 5.0% to 9.3%
◒ 9.3% to 14.8%
● More than 14.8%

Reliability Verdict

✓ = better than average overall reliability
✔ = average overall reliability
no check = worse than average overall reliability

What the trouble spots include

Scores for the individual trouble spots represent the percentage of respondents to CR's 2002 survey who reported problems occurring in the 12 months from April 1, 2001, through March 31, 2002, that they deemed serious on account of cost, failure, compromised safety, or downtime.

ENGINE Pistons, rings, valves, block, heads, bearings, camshafts, gaskets, supercharger, turbocharger, cam belts and chains, oil pump.

COOLING Radiator, heater core, water pump, thermostat, hoses, intercooler, and plumbing.

FUEL Fuel injection, computer and sensors, fuel pump, tank, emission controls, check-engine light.

IGNITION Spark plugs, coil, distributor, electronic ignition, sensors and modules, timing.

TRANSMISSION Transaxle, gear selector and linkage, coolers and lines. (We no longer provide separate data for manual transmissions, since survey responses in this area are few.)

ELECTRICAL Starter, alternator, battery, horn, gauges, lights, wiring, and wiper motor.

AIR CONDITIONING Compressor, condenser, evaporator, expansion valves, hoses, fans, electronics.

SUSPENSION Steering linkage, power-steering gear, pump, coolers and lines, alignment and balance, springs and torsion bars, ball joints, bushings, shocks and struts, electronic or air suspension.

BRAKES Hydraulic system, linings, rotors and drums, power boost, antilock brake system, parking brake, and linkage.

EXHAUST Manifold, muffler, catalytic converter, pipes.

POWER EQUIPMENT Electronically operated accessories such as mirrors, sunroof, windows, door locks and seats, cruise control, audio system, navigational system.

PAINT/TRIM/RUST Fading, discoloring, chalking, peeling, cracking paint; loose trim or moldings; rust.

BODY INTEGRITY Seals, weather stripping, air and water leaks, wind noise, rattles and squeaks.

BODY HARDWARE Manual mirrors, sunroof; window, door, and seat mechanisms; locks; safety belts; loose interior trim; glass defects.

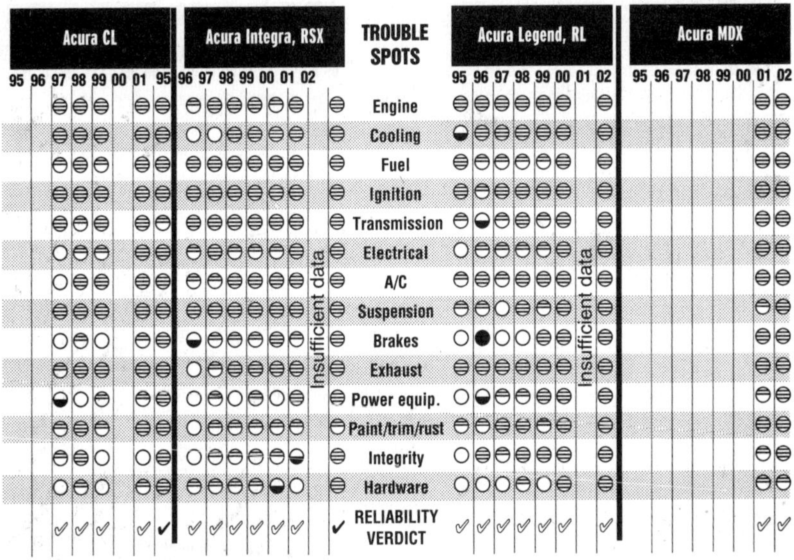
Acura CL
Acura Integra, RSX
TROUBLE SPOTS
Acura Legend, RL
Acura MDX
95 96 97 98 99 00 01
95 96 97 98 99 00 01 02
95 96 97 98 99 00 01 02
95 96 97 98 99 00 01 02
Engine
Cooling
Fuel
Ignition
Transmission
Electrical
A/C
Suspension
Brakes
Exhaust
Power equip.
Paint/trim/rust
Integrity
Hardware
RELIABILITY VERDICT
Insufficient data
Insufficient data

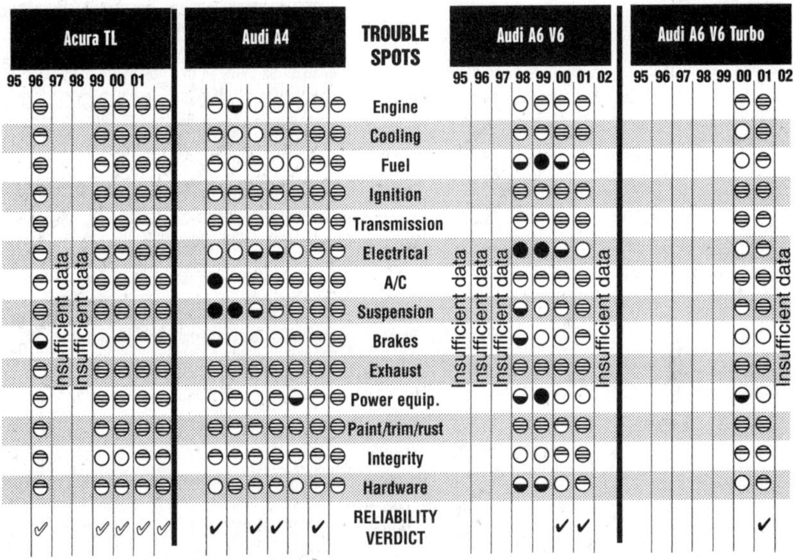
Acura TL
Audi A4
TROUBLE SPOTS
Audi A6 V6
Audi A6 V6 Turbo
95 96 97 98 99 00 01
95 96 97 98 99 00 01 02
95 96 97 98 99 00 01 02
Engine
Cooling
Fuel
Ignition
Transmission
Electrical
A/C
Suspension
Brakes
Exhaust
Power equip.
Paint/trim/rust
Integrity
Hardware
RELIABILITY VERDICT
Insufficient data
Insufficient data
Insufficient data
Insufficient data
Insufficient data
Insufficient data
Insufficient data

Audi TT

TROUBLE SPOTS	95	96	97	98	99	00	01	02
Engine						Insufficient data	⊜	Insufficient data
Cooling							⊜	
Fuel							⊖	
Ignition							⊜	
Transmission							⊜	
Electrical							◒	
A/C							⊜	
Suspension							⊜	
Brakes							⊜	
Exhaust							⊜	
Power equip.							⊖	
Paint/trim/rust							⊜	
Integrity							◒	
Hardware							○	
RELIABILITY VERDICT								

BMW 3-Series

TROUBLE SPOTS	95	96	97	98	99	00	01	02
Engine	⊖	⊖	⊖	⊜	⊜	⊜	⊜	⊜
Cooling	◒	◒	○	⊜	⊖	○	○	⊜
Fuel	⊖	◒	◒	⊖	○	⊖	⊜	⊜
Ignition	⊜	⊜	⊜	⊜	⊖	⊜	⊜	⊜
Transmission	⊖	⊜	⊜	⊖	⊜	⊜	⊜	⊜
Electrical	◒	●	◒	◒	○	⊖	⊖	⊖
A/C	○	⊖	⊖	⊖	⊖	⊖	⊖	⊜
Suspension	⊖	○	⊖	⊖	⊖	⊖	⊜	⊜
Brakes	○	○	⊖	○	◒	⊖	⊖	⊜
Exhaust	⊜	⊖	○	⊜	⊜	⊜	⊜	⊜
Power equip.	◒	○	○	◒	○	◒	⊖	⊜
Paint/trim/rust	⊖	⊜	⊖	⊜	⊜	⊜	⊜	⊜
Integrity	○	○	⊖	○	⊖	○	○	⊖
Hardware	○	○	◒	◒	○	◒	○	⊖
RELIABILITY VERDICT	✓	✔	✔	✔	✔			✔

BMW 5-Series

TROUBLE SPOTS	95	96	97	98	99	00	01	02
Engine	○		○	⊜	⊜	⊖	⊜	⊜
Cooling	●		●	○	⊖	○	⊖	⊜
Fuel	○		○	⊖	⊜	⊖	⊜	⊜
Ignition	⊜		⊜	⊖	⊜	⊜	⊜	⊜
Transmission	⊖		⊜	⊜	⊜	⊜	⊜	⊜
Electrical	◒		◒	○	○	⊖	⊖	⊖
A/C	○		⊖	⊖	⊜	○	⊖	⊜
Suspension	○		○	⊖	⊜	⊜	⊜	⊖
Brakes	○		⊖	⊖	○	⊜	⊜	⊜
Exhaust	⊜		⊖	⊜	⊜	⊜	⊜	⊜
Power equip.	◒		◒	◒	⊜	⊖	⊖	⊜
Paint/trim/rust	⊖		⊖	⊜	⊜	⊜	⊜	⊜
Integrity	⊖		○	○	○	⊖	⊖	⊜
Hardware	○		◒	◒	⊜	○	⊖	⊖
RELIABILITY VERDICT	✔			✔	✓	✔	✔	✔

BMW 7-Series

TROUBLE SPOTS	95	96	97	98	99	00	01	02
Engine	Insufficient data	Insufficient data	Insufficient data	⊖	Insufficient data	Insufficient data	⊜	Insufficient data
Cooling				◒			⊜	
Fuel				⊖			⊜	
Ignition				⊜			⊜	
Transmission				⊜			⊜	
Electrical				○			⊖	
A/C				⊖			⊜	
Suspension				○			⊜	
Brakes				◒			⊜	
Exhaust				⊖			⊜	
Power equip.				○			⊖	
Paint/trim/rust				⊖			⊜	
Integrity				⊖			⊖	
Hardware				◒			○	
RELIABILITY VERDICT				✔			✓	

BMW X5

TROUBLE SPOTS	95	96	97	98	99	00	01	02
Engine						Insufficient data	⊜	⊜
Cooling							○	⊜
Fuel							⊖	⊜
Ignition							⊜	⊜
Transmission							⊜	⊖
Electrical							◒	⊖
A/C							○	⊜
Suspension							⊖	⊜
Brakes							⊜	⊜
Exhaust							⊜	⊜
Power equip.							◒	○
Paint/trim/rust							⊜	⊜
Integrity							○	⊖
Hardware							◒	⊖
RELIABILITY VERDICT								

BMW Z3

TROUBLE SPOTS	95	96	97	98	99	00	01	02
Engine		Insufficient data	⊖	⊜	Insufficient data	⊜	⊜	Insufficient data
Cooling			⊖	⊖		⊖	⊜	
Fuel			⊖	◒		⊜	○	
Ignition			⊜	⊜		⊜	⊜	
Transmission			⊜	⊜		⊜	⊖	
Electrical			○	⊖		◒	○	
A/C			○	⊖		⊜	⊜	
Suspension			⊖	⊖		⊜	⊜	
Brakes			⊖	○		⊜	⊜	
Exhaust			⊜	⊖		⊜	⊜	
Power equip.			⊜	⊖		○	○	
Paint/trim/rust			⊜	⊖		⊖	⊜	
Integrity			●	●		●	⊖	
Hardware			◒	○		◒	○	
RELIABILITY VERDICT			✓	✓		✔	✓	

Buick Century

TROUBLE SPOTS	95	96	97	98	99	00	01	02
Engine	◒	◒	○	⊖	⊜	⊖	⊜	⊜
Cooling	○	◒	⊖	⊜	⊖	⊜	⊜	⊜
Fuel	○	◒	⊖	⊖	⊖	⊖	⊜	⊜
Ignition	⊖	⊖	⊖	⊜	⊖	⊜	⊜	⊜
Transmission	◒	⊖	⊖	⊖	⊖	⊖	⊜	⊜
Electrical	●	●	◒	○	○	○	⊖	⊖
A/C	○	⊖	⊖	⊜	⊖	⊜	⊜	⊜
Suspension	○	⊖	⊖	⊖	⊖	⊖	⊜	⊜
Brakes	●	●	○	○	○	⊖	⊜	⊜
Exhaust	◒	⊖	⊖	⊜	⊜	⊜	⊜	⊜
Power equip.	○	○	○	○	○	⊖	⊖	⊜
Paint/trim/rust	◒	○	⊖	⊜	⊖	⊖	⊜	⊜
Integrity	○	○	◒	⊖	○	○	⊖	⊖
Hardware	◒	◒	○	○	○	○	⊖	⊜
RELIABILITY VERDICT		✔	✔	✓	✔	✔	✓	✓

Buick LeSabre

TROUBLE SPOTS	95	96	97	98	99	00	01	02
Engine	○	○	○	○	⊖	⊜	⊜	⊜
Cooling	○	○	◒	○	⊖	⊜	⊜	⊜
Fuel	○	○	○	○	○	⊖	⊜	⊜
Ignition	○	⊖	⊖	⊖	⊖	○	⊖	⊖
Transmission	○	⊖	○	○	⊖	⊖	⊜	⊜
Electrical	◒	○	◒	◒	◒	○	○	⊜
A/C	◒	◒	⊖	⊖	⊜	⊜	⊜	⊜
Suspension	⊖	○	⊖	⊖	⊖	○	⊖	⊜
Brakes	●	◒	◒	◒	○	○	⊖	⊜
Exhaust	⊜	⊜	⊜	⊜	⊜	⊜	⊜	⊜
Power equip.	◒	◒	○	⊖	⊖	◒	⊖	⊖
Paint/trim/rust	○	⊜	⊖	⊖	⊖	⊜	⊜	⊜
Integrity	⊖	○	○	○	○	○	○	⊖
Hardware	○	○	○	⊖	⊖	○	⊖	⊜
RELIABILITY VERDICT	✔	✔	✔	✔	✔	✔	✔	✔

Buick Park Avenue

TROUBLE SPOTS	95	96	97	98	99	00	01	02
Engine	○	⊖	○	○	⊜	⊜	⊜	⊜
Cooling	◒	⊖	●	⊖	⊜	⊖	⊜	⊜
Fuel	○	⊖	○	○	⊖	⊜	⊜	⊜
Ignition	○	⊖	⊖	⊖	⊖	⊜	⊜	⊜
Transmission	○	○	◒	○	⊖	⊜	⊜	⊜
Electrical	●	◒	●	◒	◒	◒	○	⊖
A/C	◒	○	○	⊜	⊖	⊜	⊜	⊜
Suspension	○	○	○	⊖	○	⊖	◒	⊜
Brakes	●	○	◒	◒	○	○	○	⊜
Exhaust	⊜	⊜	⊜	⊜	⊜	⊜	⊜	⊜
Power equip.	●	◒	◒	◒	○	○	⊖	○
Paint/trim/rust	◒	⊖	⊖	⊖	⊜	⊜	⊖	⊜
Integrity	○	○	○	⊖	○	⊖	○	⊖
Hardware	◒	○	●	◒	◒	○	○	⊖
RELIABILITY VERDICT	✔	✓			✔	✔		

Buick Regal

TROUBLE SPOTS	95	96	97	98	99	00	01	02
Engine	◒	○	⊖	⊖	⊜	⊜	⊜	⊜
Cooling	◒	◒	◒	⊖	⊜	⊜	⊜	⊜
Fuel	⊖	○	⊜	⊖	⊜	⊖	⊜	⊜
Ignition	⊖	⊖	⊖	⊜	⊜	⊜	⊜	⊜
Transmission	○	⊖	⊖	⊖	○	⊖	⊜	⊜
Electrical	●	◒	◒	○	○	○	⊖	⊜
A/C	◒	⊖	○	⊖	⊖	⊜	⊜	⊜
Suspension	○	○	○	⊖	⊖	⊖	⊖	⊜
Brakes	●	●	○	○	○	⊖	⊜	⊜
Exhaust	⊜	⊜	⊜	⊜	⊜	⊜	⊜	⊜
Power equip.	○	⊜	○	○	◒	⊖	⊜	⊜
Paint/trim/rust	○	○	⊖	⊖	⊖	⊜	⊜	⊜
Integrity	○	○	○	○	◒	○	⊖	⊜
Hardware	◒	○	○	◒	○	○	⊜	⊜
RELIABILITY VERDICT	✔	✔	✔	✔	✔	✓	✓	✓

Buick Rendezvous

TROUBLE SPOTS	95	96	97	98	99	00	01	02
Engine								⊜
Cooling								⊜
Fuel								⊜
Ignition								⊜
Transmission								⊜
Electrical								⊖
A/C								⊜
Suspension								⊜
Brakes								⊜
Exhaust								⊜
Power equip.								○
Paint/trim/rust								⊜
Integrity								⊖
Hardware								⊖
RELIABILITY VERDICT								

Cadillac Catera

TROUBLE SPOTS	95	96	97	98	99	00	01	02
Engine			●	○	Insufficient data	⊖	Insufficient data	
Cooling			●	●		●		
Fuel			◒	○		◒		
Ignition			○	⊖		○		
Transmission			⊖	○		⊜		
Electrical			●	●		●		
A/C			◒	○		○		
Suspension			○	◒		⊖		
Brakes			◒	◒		○		
Exhaust			⊜	⊖		⊜		
Power equip.			◒	●		○		
Paint/trim/rust			○	○		⊜		
Integrity			○	○		⊜		
Hardware			●	●		⊜		
RELIABILITY VERDICT								

Cadillac DeVille

TROUBLE SPOTS	95	96	97	98	99	00	01	02
Engine	◒	◒	○	⊖	⊖	⊖	⊖	⊜
Cooling	◒	○	○	⊜	⊜	⊖	⊖	⊜
Fuel	◒	●	○	○	○	○	⊖	⊜
Ignition	○	○	⊖	⊖	⊜	○	⊖	⊜
Transmission	○	◒	⊜	⊖	⊜	⊖	⊖	⊜
Electrical	◒	●	●	●	◒	◒	○	⊖
A/C	●	●	◒	◒	⊖	⊖	⊜	⊜
Suspension	◒	○	○	○	○	⊖	○	⊖
Brakes	●	○	●	●	◒	○	⊖	⊜
Exhaust	⊖	⊜	⊜	⊜	⊜	⊖	⊜	⊜
Power equip.	◒	◒	○	◒	○	◒	○	⊖
Paint/trim/rust	⊖	⊖	⊖	○	⊖	⊖	⊜	⊜
Integrity	⊖	⊖	○	○	○	⊖	⊜	⊖
Hardware	○	◒	◒	○	◒	○	⊖	⊜
RELIABILITY VERDICT					✔			✔

Cadillac Escalade

TROUBLE SPOTS	95	96	97	98	99	00	01	02
Engine					Insufficient data	Insufficient data		⊜
Cooling								⊜
Fuel								⊜
Ignition								⊜
Transmission								⊜
Electrical								⊖
A/C								⊜
Suspension								⊜
Brakes								⊜
Exhaust								⊜
Power equip.								○
Paint/trim/rust								⊖
Integrity								○
Hardware								○
RELIABILITY VERDICT								

Cadillac Seville

TROUBLE SPOTS	95	96	97	98	99	00	01	02
Engine	◒	○	●	○	⊖	○	⊖	Insufficient data
Cooling	○	○	○	○	⊖	⊜	⊜	
Fuel	◒	●	○	⊖	○	○	○	
Ignition	○	◒	◒	⊖	⊖	⊖	⊖	
Transmission	◒	⊖	⊜	⊖	⊖	⊖	⊖	
Electrical	●	●	●	◒	◒	○	●	
A/C	●	●	◒	⊖	⊖	⊜	⊖	
Suspension	○	○	○	○	○	○	◒	
Brakes	○	⊖	◒	◒	◒	○	⊖	
Exhaust	⊖	⊜	⊜	⊜	⊜	⊜	⊜	
Power equip.	◒	◒	◒	◒	◒	○	◒	
Paint/trim/rust	⊖	⊖	⊖	⊖	⊖	⊖	⊖	
Integrity	⊖	○	○	◒	○	◒	◒	
Hardware	○	◒	◒	●	◒	◒	○	
RELIABILITY VERDICT								

Chevrolet Astro

TROUBLE SPOTS	95	96	97	98	99	00	01	02
Engine	○	○	○	○	⊖	⊜	⊜	Insufficient data
Cooling	○	◒	○	⊖	⊖	⊜	⊜	
Fuel	◒	●	●	○	○	⊖	⊖	
Ignition	⊖	⊖	⊖	⊖	⊖	⊜	⊜	
Transmission	○	◒	◒	○	○	⊖	⊖	
Electrical	●	●	●	◒	◒	○	⊖	
A/C	●	●	◒	○	○	⊖	⊜	
Suspension	◒	●	◒	◒	○	○	⊖	
Brakes	●	◒	●	●	●	◒	◒	
Exhaust	◒	⊖	⊖	⊜	⊜	⊖	⊜	
Power equip.	◒	●	●	◒	◒	◒	⊖	
Paint/trim/rust	○	◒	○	⊖	⊖	⊖	⊖	
Integrity	◒	●	●	◒	●	●	●	
Hardware	◒	●	●	●	●	●	◒	
RELIABILITY VERDICT								

Chevrolet Avalanche

TROUBLE SPOTS	95	96	97	98	99	00	01	02
Engine								⊜
Cooling								⊜
Fuel								⊜
Ignition								⊜
Transmission								⊜
Electrical								⊜
A/C								⊜
Suspension								⊖
Brakes								⊜
Exhaust								⊜
Power equip.								⊜
Paint/trim/rust								⊖
Integrity								⊖
Hardware								⊖
RELIABILITY VERDICT								✓

Chevrolet Blazer

TROUBLE SPOTS	95	96	97	98	99	00	01	02
Engine	◒	◒	○	⊖	○	○	⊖	⊜
Cooling	◒	●	◒	○	⊖	⊜	⊜	⊜
Fuel	●	◒	●	⊖	○	⊖	⊖	⊜
Ignition	○	⊖	⊖	⊖	⊜	⊖	⊜	⊜
Transmission	◒	○	◒	◒	○	⊖	⊖	⊜
Electrical	●	●	●	●	◒	●	●	⊖
A/C	○	●	◒	○	⊜	⊜	⊜	⊜
Suspension	◒	◒	◒	○	○	○	⊖	⊜
Brakes	●	●	◒	○	○	○	⊖	⊖
Exhaust	◒	⊖	⊜	⊖	⊖	⊜	⊜	⊜
Power equip.	◒	⊖	○	○	○	○	⊖	⊖
Paint/trim/rust	○	○	⊖	⊖	⊖	⊖	⊜	⊜
Integrity	◒	◒	○	◒	◒	○	◒	◒
Hardware	◒	◒	○	◒	●	◒	○	○
RELIABILITY VERDICT								

Chevrolet C1500, Silverado 2WD

TROUBLE SPOTS	95	96	97	98	99	00	01	02
Engine	⊖	○	○	⊖	⊜	⊜	⊜	⊜
Cooling	○	◒	○	○	⊜	⊜	⊜	⊜
Fuel	⊖	◒	◒	○	○	⊖	⊜	⊜
Ignition	⊖	⊖	⊖	⊖	⊜	⊜	⊜	⊜
Transmission	○	○	◒	⊖	⊜	⊖	⊖	⊜
Electrical	●	●	●	◒	○	○	⊖	⊜
A/C	◒	●	○	⊖	⊜	⊜	⊜	⊜
Suspension	○	⊖	◒	⊖	⊖	○	⊖	⊜
Brakes	◒	◒	○	○	◒	⊖	⊜	⊜
Exhaust	◒	⊖	⊖	⊖	⊜	⊜	⊜	⊜
Power equip.	⊖	⊖	⊖	⊖	○	⊖	⊖	⊜
Paint/trim/rust	○	⊖	⊜	⊖	⊖	⊜	⊜	⊜
Integrity	○	○	○	○	●	◒	○	⊖
Hardware	◒	○	○	◒	●	○	⊖	⊖
RELIABILITY VERDICT	✓			✓	✓	✓	✓	✓

Chevrolet Camaro

TROUBLE SPOTS	95	96	97	98	99	00	01	02
Engine	◒	◒	○	⊜	○	⊖	Insufficient data	Insufficient data
Cooling	○	◒	○	⊜	○	⊜		
Fuel	○	◒	○	○	○	⊜		
Ignition	○	◒	○	⊖	⊖	⊜		
Transmission	⊖	⊖	⊖	○	⊖	⊖		
Electrical	●	●	●	●	◒	⊖		
A/C	○	○	⊖	⊜	⊖	⊖		
Suspension	⊖	○	⊖	⊖	⊖	⊜		
Brakes	●	◒	⊖	●	◒	○		
Exhaust	⊖	⊖	⊜	⊖	⊜	○		
Power equip.	●	●	●	◒	◒	○		
Paint/trim/rust	○	⊖	○	⊜	⊖	⊜		
Integrity	◒	◒	◒	◒	◒	●		
Hardware	●	○	◒	○	◒	◒		
RELIABILITY VERDICT	✓							

Chevrolet Cavalier

TROUBLE SPOTS	95	96	97	98	99	00	01	02
Engine	◒	○	○	⊖	⊖	⊖	⊜	⊜
Cooling	◒	◒	◒	○	⊖	⊖	⊜	⊜
Fuel	⊖	○	○	⊖	⊖	⊖	⊖	⊖
Ignition	○	○	○	⊖	○	⊜	⊜	⊜
Transmission	○	⊖	⊖	⊖	⊜	⊜	⊜	⊜
Electrical	●	●	●	◒	○	○	⊖	⊖
A/C	◒	◒	○	⊖	⊜	⊖	⊜	⊜
Suspension	○	○	○	⊖	○	⊖	⊖	⊜
Brakes	◒	◒	◒	●	◒	◒	○	⊜
Exhaust	⊜	⊖	⊖	⊜	⊜	⊜	⊜	⊜
Power equip.	⊖	⊖	○	⊖	⊖	⊖	⊖	⊜
Paint/trim/rust	◒	○	⊜	○	⊖	⊖	⊖	⊖
Integrity	◒	◒	◒	○	◒	◒	○	⊖
Hardware	◒	◒	◒	◒	○	○	⊜	○
RELIABILITY VERDICT	✓			✓	✓	✓	✓	

Chevrolet Corvette

TROUBLE SPOTS	95	96	97	98	99	00	01	02
Engine	Insufficient data	Insufficient data	Insufficient data	⊜	⊜	○	⊖	⊜
Cooling				⊜	⊜	○	⊜	⊜
Fuel				◒	⊖	○	⊖	⊜
Ignition				⊖	⊜	⊜	⊖	⊖
Transmission				⊖	⊜	⊜	⊖	⊜
Electrical				●	⊖	◒	○	⊖
A/C				⊜	⊜	○	⊖	⊖
Suspension				⊖	⊖	◒	⊜	⊜
Brakes				⊖	⊖	◒	⊖	⊜
Exhaust				⊖	⊜	⊜	⊜	⊜
Power equip.				◒	⊖	◒	○	⊜
Paint/trim/rust				⊖	⊜	⊜	⊜	⊖
Integrity				⊖	⊖	◒	⊖	⊖
Hardware				◒	◒	◒	○	⊖
RELIABILITY VERDICT				✓	✓			✓

Chevrolet Express 1500

TROUBLE SPOTS	95	96	97	98	99	00	01	02
Engine		Insufficient data	⊖	○	⊖	⊖	Insufficient data	Insufficient data
Cooling			⊜	◒	⊜	⊜		
Fuel			●	○	○	⊖		
Ignition			⊖	⊖	⊖	⊜		
Transmission			●	◒	○	⊖		
Electrical			●	●	◒	◒		
A/C			●	◒	○	○		
Suspension			○	○	⊖	○		
Brakes			●	●	◒	●		
Exhaust			⊖	⊜	⊜	⊜		
Power equip.			●	○	○	◒		
Paint/trim/rust			○	⊖	⊖	⊖		
Integrity			◒	●	●	◒		
Hardware			●	●	◒	●		
RELIABILITY VERDICT								

Chevrolet Impala

TROUBLE SPOTS	95	96	97	98	99	00	01	02
Engine						⊜	⊜	⊜
Cooling						⊜	⊜	⊜
Fuel						⊖	⊜	⊖
Ignition						⊜	⊜	⊜
Transmission						⊜	⊜	⊜
Electrical						○	⊖	⊜
A/C						⊖	⊜	⊜
Suspension						○	⊖	⊜
Brakes						○	⊖	⊜
Exhaust						⊜	⊜	⊜
Power equip.						⊖	⊜	⊜
Paint/trim/rust						⊜	⊖	⊜
Integrity						○	⊖	⊜
Hardware						⊖	⊜	⊜
RELIABILITY VERDICT						✓	✓	✓

Trouble spots	Chevrolet K1500, Silverado 4WD 95	96	97	98	99	00	01	02
Engine	○	○	○	○	⊖	⊜	⊜	⊜
Cooling	⊖	◒	○	○	⊜	⊜	⊜	⊜
Fuel	⊖	●	◒	○	○	⊖	⊜	⊜
Ignition	⊖	⊖	⊜	⊖	⊜	⊜	⊜	⊜
Transmission	○	○	○	⊖	○	⊖	⊖	⊜
Electrical	●	●	●	○	◒	⊖	⊖	⊜
A/C	○	○	○	⊖	⊜	⊜	⊜	⊜
Suspension	⊖	○	○	○	○	○	⊖	⊜
Brakes	◒	●	◒	●	◒	○	⊜	⊜
Exhaust	◒	⊜	⊜	⊜	⊜	⊜	⊜	⊜
Power equip.	⊖	⊖	⊖	⊜	○	⊖	⊖	⊜
Paint/trim/rust	○	⊖	⊜	⊖	⊖	⊖	⊜	⊜
Integrity	○	○	⊖	○	●	◒	○	⊖
Hardware	○	○	○	⊖	●	○	⊖	⊜
RELIABILITY VERDICT	✓							

Trouble spots	Chevrolet Lumina 95	96	97	98	99	00	01	02
Engine	◒	○	○	⊖	○	Insufficient data		
Cooling	○	◒	⊖	⊖	⊖			
Fuel	○	◒	◒	○	⊖			
Ignition	⊖	⊖	⊖	⊜	⊜			
Transmission	○	⊖	⊖	⊖	⊜			
Electrical	●	◒	●	○	○			
A/C	○	○	⊖	⊖	⊜			
Suspension	⊖	⊖	○	⊜	⊖			
Brakes	●	◒	◒	◒	○			
Exhaust	⊜	⊜	⊜	⊜	⊜			
Power equip.	◒	⊖	⊖	○	⊖			
Paint/trim/rust	○	○	⊖	⊜	⊖			
Integrity	○	⊖	⊖	⊖	○			
Hardware	◒	○	○	○	○			
RELIABILITY VERDICT	✓	✓	✓	✓	✓			

Trouble spots	Chevrolet Lumina Van, Venture (reg.) 95	96	97	98	99	00	01	02
Engine	◒	⊜	○	⊖	○	⊖	⊜	Insufficient data
Cooling	◒	◒	○	⊖	○	⊖	⊜	
Fuel	○	⊜	○	○	○	⊖	⊖	
Ignition	○	⊜	⊜	⊖	⊖	⊜	⊜	
Transmission	◒	○	○	⊖	◒	⊖	⊜	
Electrical	●	●	◒	●	◒	○	○	
A/C	○	⊖	⊖	⊖	⊜	⊜	⊜	
Suspension	◒	◒	○	⊖	⊖	⊖	⊜	
Brakes	●	●	◒	◒	◒	○	⊖	
Exhaust	⊖	⊜	⊜	⊜	⊜	⊜	⊜	
Power equip.	◒	◒	◒	◒	◒	○	⊖	
Paint/trim/rust	◒	◒	⊜	⊖	⊖	⊖	⊜	
Integrity	◒	○	○	○	○	○	○	
Hardware	●	◒	◒	●	●	●	○	
RELIABILITY VERDICT		✓	✓	✓			✓	

Trouble spots	Chevrolet Malibu 95	96	97	98	99	00	01	02
Engine			○	◒	○	⊖	⊖	⊜
Cooling			◒	◒	○	⊖	⊜	⊜
Fuel			○	⊖	⊖	○	⊖	⊜
Ignition			⊖	⊖	⊖	⊜	⊖	⊜
Transmission			⊜	⊜	⊖	⊜	⊜	⊜
Electrical			●	●	●	○	○	⊖
A/C			○	◒	○	⊖	⊖	⊜
Suspension			○	○	⊖	○	⊜	⊜
Brakes			●	●	●	●	○	⊜
Exhaust			⊜	⊜	⊜	⊜	⊜	⊜
Power equip.			⊖	○	○	⊖	⊜	⊜
Paint/trim/rust			⊖	⊜	⊖	⊖	⊖	⊜
Integrity			○	◒	○	○	⊖	⊖
Hardware			○	○	○	⊜	○	⊖
RELIABILITY VERDICT							✓	✓

Trouble spots	Chevrolet Monte Carlo 95	96	97	98	99	00	01	02
Engine	●	Insufficient data	Insufficient data	Insufficient data	⊜	⊜	⊜	Insufficient data
Cooling	○				⊖	⊖	⊜	
Fuel	◒				○	⊖	⊖	
Ignition	⊖				⊖	⊖	⊜	
Transmission	○				⊜	⊖	⊜	
Electrical	●				○	○	○	
A/C	◒				⊜	⊜	⊜	
Suspension	○				⊖	○	⊖	
Brakes	●				◒	○	⊖	
Exhaust	⊖				⊜	⊜	⊜	
Power equip.	◒				⊜	⊖	⊖	
Paint/trim/rust	●				⊜	⊖	⊖	
Integrity	◒				○	○	⊖	
Hardware	●				○	○	○	
RELIABILITY VERDICT					✓	✓	✓	

Trouble spots	Chevrolet S-10 4 cyl. 95	96	97	98	99	00	01	02
Engine	●	◒	○	○	○	⊖	⊖	Insufficient data
Cooling	○	◒	○	⊖	⊖	⊖	⊖	
Fuel	○	○	○	○	⊜	⊖	⊖	
Ignition	⊖	⊖	⊖	○	⊖	⊜	⊜	
Transmission	○	○	⊖	○	⊖	⊜	⊜	
Electrical	●	●	◒	●	◒	○	○	
A/C	●	●	○	⊖	○	⊜	⊖	
Suspension	⊖	○	⊖	⊖	⊖	⊖	⊜	
Brakes	◒	◒	◒	◒	○	○	⊖	
Exhaust	●	⊖	⊜	⊖	⊖	⊜	⊜	
Power equip.	⊖	⊜	⊜	⊜	⊜	⊖	⊜	
Paint/trim/rust	⊖	⊖	⊖	⊖	⊖	⊖	⊖	
Integrity	○	◒	◒	○	●	○	○	
Hardware	○	●	●	●	◒	◒	⊖	
RELIABILITY VERDICT						✓		

Trouble spots	Chevrolet S-10 V6 2WD 95	96	97	98	99	00	01	02
Engine	⊖	◒	⊖	⊖	⊜	⊖	⊖	Insufficient data
Cooling	⊖	●	○	⊖	⊖	⊜	⊜	
Fuel	◒	●	●	⊖	⊖	⊖	⊖	
Ignition	⊖	○	⊖	⊜	⊜	⊜	⊜	
Transmission	○	◒	○	○	○	⊜	⊜	
Electrical	●	●	●	○	◒	○	⊖	
A/C	○	●	●	○	⊜	⊜	⊜	
Suspension	○	◒	⊖	⊖	⊖	○	⊖	
Brakes	●	●	●	○	◒	◒	⊖	
Exhaust	○	⊖	⊜	⊜	⊖	⊖	⊜	
Power equip.	○	⊜	⊖	⊖	⊜	⊖	⊜	
Paint/trim/rust	○	○	⊖	⊜	○	⊜	⊜	
Integrity	○	◒	◒	◒	○	◒	○	
Hardware	◒	●	◒	●	●	●	○	
RELIABILITY VERDICT	✓						✓	

Trouble spots	Chevrolet S-10 V6 4WD 95	96	97	98	99	00	01	02
Engine	Insufficient data	Insufficient data	Insufficient data	Insufficient data	Insufficient data	⊖	⊖	Insufficient data
Cooling						⊜	⊜	
Fuel						⊖	⊖	
Ignition						⊜	⊜	
Transmission						⊖	⊜	
Electrical						⊖	⊖	
A/C						⊜	⊜	
Suspension						⊖	⊖	
Brakes						○	⊜	
Exhaust						⊜	⊜	
Power equip.						⊜	⊜	
Paint/trim/rust						⊖	⊖	
Integrity						○	○	
Hardware						●	⊖	
RELIABILITY VERDICT								

Chevrolet Suburban

TROUBLE SPOTS	95	96	97	98	99	00	01	02
Engine	⊖	○	○	○	⊖	⊜	⊖	⊜
Cooling	○	●	◒	◒	⊖	⊜	⊜	⊜
Fuel	○	◒	◒	⊖	⊖	⊖	⊜	⊜
Ignition	⊖	⊖	⊜	⊜	⊜	⊜	⊜	⊜
Transmission	○	○	◒	○	⊖	⊖	⊜	⊜
Electrical	●	●	●	●	◒	○	⊖	⊖
A/C	●	◒	○	○	⊖	⊜	⊜	⊜
Suspension	○	○	○	○	○	○	⊖	⊜
Brakes	●	●	●	●	●	⊖	⊜	⊜
Exhaust	◒	⊖	⊖	⊜	⊜	⊜	⊜	⊜
Power equip.	○	○	○	⊖	○	●	○	⊜
Paint/trim/rust	○	⊜	⊖	⊜	⊖	⊜	⊖	⊜
Integrity	○	⊖	○	○	○	○	○	⊖
Hardware	●	◒	○	○	◒	●	○	⊖
RELIABILITY VERDICT	✔						✔	✔

Chevrolet Tahoe

TROUBLE SPOTS	95	96	97	98	99	00	01	02
Engine	○	○	○	○	⊖	⊜	⊜	⊜
Cooling	◒	◒	○	○	⊖	⊜	⊜	⊜
Fuel	⊖	◒	◒	⊖	○	⊖	⊜	⊜
Ignition	○	⊖	⊖	⊜	⊜	⊜	⊜	⊜
Transmission	⊖	◒	◒	○	⊖	⊖	⊜	⊜
Electrical	●	●	●	○	○	◒	⊖	⊖
A/C	◒	◒	○	⊖	⊖	⊜	⊜	⊜
Suspension	○	○	○	○	○	○	⊖	⊜
Brakes	●	●	●	●	●	○	⊜	⊜
Exhaust	○	⊜	⊜	⊜	⊜	⊜	⊜	⊜
Power equip.	○	○	⊖	⊖	○	◒	⊖	⊜
Paint/trim/rust	○	⊖	⊖	⊜	⊖	⊜	⊖	⊜
Integrity	○	○	○	⊖	○	◒	○	⊖
Hardware	●	○	○	⊖	○	◒	○	⊖
RELIABILITY VERDICT	✔				✔		✔	✔

Chevrolet TrailBlazer

TROUBLE SPOTS	95	96	97	98	99	00	01	02
Engine								⊜
Cooling								⊜
Fuel								⊜
Ignition								⊜
Transmission								⊖
Electrical								⊖
A/C								⊜
Suspension								⊖
Brakes								⊜
Exhaust								⊜
Power equip.								⊖
Paint/trim/rust								⊖
Integrity								○
Hardware								⊖
RELIABILITY VERDICT								

Chevrolet Venture (ext.)

TROUBLE SPOTS	95	96	97	98	99	00	01	02
Engine			○	○	○	⊜	⊜	⊜
Cooling			○	⊖	○	⊖	⊜	⊜
Fuel			○	⊖	⊖	⊖	⊖	⊜
Ignition			⊜	⊜	⊖	⊜	⊜	⊜
Transmission			⊖	⊖	○	⊖	⊜	⊜
Electrical			◒	◒	◒	◒	⊖	⊜
A/C			⊖	⊖	⊖	⊜	⊖	⊜
Suspension			○	⊖	⊖	⊖	⊖	⊜
Brakes			◒	◒	◒	○	⊜	⊜
Exhaust			⊜	⊜	⊜	⊜	⊜	⊜
Power equip.			●	●	●	◒	○	⊖
Paint/trim/rust			⊖	⊜	⊖	⊖	⊜	⊜
Integrity			●	◒	◒	◒	○	⊖
Hardware			●	●	●	●	◒	⊖
RELIABILITY VERDICT							✔	

Chevrolet/Geo Prizm

TROUBLE SPOTS	95	96	97	98	99	00	01	02
Engine	⊜	⊜	⊜	⊜	⊜	⊜	⊜	⊜
Cooling	⊜	⊜	⊜	⊜	⊜	⊜	⊜	⊜
Fuel	⊜	⊜	⊖	⊜	⊖	⊜	⊜	⊜
Ignition	⊖	⊜	⊜	⊜	⊜	⊜	⊜	⊜
Transmission	⊜	⊜	⊜	⊜	⊜	⊜	⊜	⊜
Electrical	●	○	○	⊖	⊖	⊜	⊜	⊜
A/C	⊖	⊜	⊜	⊖	⊜	⊜	⊜	⊜
Suspension	⊖	⊖	⊖	⊖	⊖	⊜	⊜	⊜
Brakes	○	○	⊖	⊖	⊖	⊜	⊜	⊜
Exhaust	⊖	⊜	⊜	⊜	⊜	⊜	⊜	⊜
Power equip.	⊜	⊜	⊜	⊖	⊜	⊜	⊜	⊜
Paint/trim/rust	○	⊖	⊖	⊜	⊜	⊖	⊜	⊜
Integrity	⊖	⊖	⊖	⊖	⊖	⊖	⊖	⊜
Hardware	○	⊖	○	⊖	⊖	⊖	⊖	⊜
RELIABILITY VERDICT	✓	✓	✓	✓	✓	✓	✓	✓

Chevrolet/Geo Tracker

TROUBLE SPOTS	95	96	97	98	99	00	01	02
Engine	⊖	◒	Insufficient data	Insufficient data	Insufficient data	⊖	⊜	Insufficient data
Cooling	○	⊖				○	⊜	
Fuel	○	○				⊖	⊜	
Ignition	⊖	⊖				⊜	⊜	
Transmission	⊖	⊖				⊖	⊜	
Electrical	◒	○				○	⊖	
A/C	◒	◒				⊖	⊜	
Suspension	⊖	⊜				⊖	⊜	
Brakes	⊖	○				⊖	⊜	
Exhaust	○	⊖				⊜	⊜	
Power equip.	⊖	⊖				○	⊖	
Paint/trim/rust	⊖	○				⊖	⊜	
Integrity	●	○				◒	⊖	
Hardware	○	○				◒	⊖	
RELIABILITY VERDICT	✓	✔					✓	

Chrysler 300M

TROUBLE SPOTS	95	96	97	98	99	00	01	02
Engine					⊖	⊜	⊜	⊜
Cooling					⊜	⊜	⊜	⊜
Fuel					⊖	⊜	⊜	⊜
Ignition					⊜	⊜	⊜	⊜
Transmission					◒	⊖	⊜	⊜
Electrical					◒	⊖	○	⊜
A/C					○	⊜	⊜	⊜
Suspension					○	⊖	⊜	⊜
Brakes					○	⊖	⊖	⊖
Exhaust					⊜	⊜	⊜	⊜
Power equip.					●	○	⊖	⊖
Paint/trim/rust					⊖	⊖	⊜	⊜
Integrity					○	◒	⊖	○
Hardware					◒	○	⊜	⊜
RELIABILITY VERDICT						✔	✓	

Chrysler Cirrus V6

TROUBLE SPOTS	95	96	97	98	99	00	01	02
Engine	○	○	⊜	⊖	⊖	⊜		
Cooling	○	⊖	⊖	⊖	⊜	⊜		
Fuel	○	◒	○	⊖	○	○		
Ignition	○	⊖	⊖	⊜	⊖	⊖		
Transmission	◒	○	◒	⊖	◒	○		
Electrical	○	○	○	⊜	⊖	⊖		
A/C	◒	◒	○	⊜	⊖	⊜		
Suspension	◒	◒	◒	⊖	⊖	⊖		
Brakes	●	●	●	◒	○	○		
Exhaust	⊜	⊖	⊜	⊜	⊜	⊜		
Power equip.	◒	○	⊖	○	○	⊖		
Paint/trim/rust	◒	⊖	⊖	⊖	⊖	⊖		
Integrity	◒	○	⊖	⊖	○	⊖		
Hardware	○	⊖	⊖	⊜	○	⊖		
RELIABILITY VERDICT	✔	✔	✔	✓		✔		

Chrysler Concorde

TROUBLE SPOTS	95	96	97	98	99	00	01	02
Engine	○	○	○	⊖	⊖	⊜	⊜	⊜
Cooling	●	●	●	⊖	⊖	⊜	⊜	⊜
Fuel	○	○	○	⊖	⊜	⊖	⊖	⊜
Ignition	○	⊖	⊖	⊜	⊜	⊜	⊜	⊜
Transmission	●	⊖	○	○	◒	⊜	⊜	⊜
Electrical	◒	⊖	○	◒	○	⊖	⊖	⊖
A/C	●	●	◒	◒	○	⊖	⊜	⊜
Suspension	●	●	◒	○	○	⊖	⊜	⊜
Brakes	◒	○	○	○	⊖	⊜	⊖	⊜
Exhaust	⊜	⊜	⊜	⊖	⊜	⊜	⊜	⊜
Power equip.	○	⊖	⊖	◒	●	⊖	⊖	⊜
Paint/trim/rust	○	○	⊖	○	⊖	⊖	⊜	⊜
Integrity	◒	○	○	◒	○	○	○	⊜
Hardware	○	○	○	◒	◒	⊖	⊜	⊖
RELIABILITY VERDICT						✓	✓	✓

Chrysler New Yorker, LHS

TROUBLE SPOTS	95	96	97	98	99	00	01	02
Engine	○	◒	○		⊜	⊜	Insufficient data	
Cooling	●	●	●		⊖	⊜		
Fuel	◒	○	○		⊖	⊜		
Ignition	○	○	⊖		⊖	⊜		
Transmission	●	○	⊖		◒	⊖		
Electrical	◒	○	○		○	⊖		
A/C	●	●	●		○	⊜		
Suspension	●	●	○		○	⊖		
Brakes	●	◒	◒		⊖	⊖		
Exhaust	⊜	⊜	⊜		⊜	⊜		
Power equip.	○	○	⊖		◒	○		
Paint/trim/rust	⊖	○	○		○	⊖		
Integrity	◒	○	◒		○	◒		
Hardware	○	○	○		◒	○		
RELIABILITY VERDICT						✓		

Chrysler PT Cruiser

TROUBLE SPOTS	95	96	97	98	99	00	01	02
Engine							⊜	⊜
Cooling							⊜	⊜
Fuel							⊜	⊜
Ignition							⊜	⊜
Transmission							⊜	⊜
Electrical							⊖	⊜
A/C							⊜	⊜
Suspension							⊖	⊜
Brakes							⊖	⊜
Exhaust							⊜	⊜
Power equip.							⊜	⊜
Paint/trim/rust							⊜	⊜
Integrity							⊖	⊜
Hardware							⊖	⊜
RELIABILITY VERDICT							✓	✓

Chrysler Sebring Convertible

TROUBLE SPOTS	95	96	97	98	99	00	01	02
Engine		○	⊖	⊜	⊜	⊜	⊜	⊜
Cooling		⊖	⊖	⊖	⊜	⊜	⊜	⊜
Fuel		⊖	⊖	○	○	⊖	⊜	⊜
Ignition		○	⊜	⊖	⊖	⊖	⊜	⊜
Transmission		○	○	⊜	○	⊖	⊜	⊖
Electrical		◒	●	●	○	◒	○	○
A/C		○	○	○	⊜	⊜	⊜	⊜
Suspension		◒	○	○	⊖	⊖	⊖	⊜
Brakes		●	●	◒	◒	◒	⊖	⊜
Exhaust		⊖	⊜	⊜	⊜	⊜	⊜	⊜
Power equip.		◒	⊖	⊖	○	⊖	⊖	⊖
Paint/trim/rust		⊖	○	○	⊖	⊜	⊜	⊜
Integrity		●	◒	◒	◒	◒	◒	○
Hardware		◒	○	○	○	○	○	⊖
RELIABILITY VERDICT		✓	✓		✓		✓	

Chrysler Sebring V6

TROUBLE SPOTS	95	96	97	98	99	00	01	02
Engine	Insufficient data	Insufficient data	Insufficient data	Insufficient data	Insufficient data	Insufficient data	⊜	⊜
Cooling							⊜	⊜
Fuel							⊖	⊖
Ignition							⊜	⊜
Transmission							⊖	⊜
Electrical							○	⊖
A/C							⊖	⊜
Suspension							⊖	⊜
Brakes							⊜	⊜
Exhaust							⊜	⊜
Power equip.							⊜	⊜
Paint/trim/rust							⊖	⊖
Integrity							○	⊖
Hardware							⊖	⊜
RELIABILITY VERDICT								✓

Chrysler Town & Country 2WD

TROUBLE SPOTS	95	96	97	98	99	00	01	02
Engine	○	◒	○	○	⊖	⊖	⊜	⊜
Cooling	◒	◒	◒	⊖	⊖	⊖	⊜	⊜
Fuel	○	●	◒	⊖	⊖	⊖	⊖	⊜
Ignition	⊖	⊖	⊜	⊜	⊜	⊜	⊜	⊜
Transmission	●	●	○	○	◒	◒	⊖	⊜
Electrical	◒	●	●	◒	○	○	⊜	⊖
A/C	●	●	○	⊖	⊖	⊖	○	⊖
Suspension	○	○	○	⊖	⊖	⊖	⊜	⊜
Brakes	◒	●	◒	◒	◒	○	○	⊜
Exhaust	⊜	⊜	⊜	⊜	⊜	⊜	⊜	⊜
Power equip.	◒	●	◒	○	○	○	○	⊖
Paint/trim/rust	◒	○	⊜	⊖	⊜	⊖	⊖	⊜
Integrity	◒	◒	◒	○	○	○	○	⊖
Hardware	◒	●	◒	○	○	○	○	⊖
RELIABILITY VERDICT				✓	✓			✓

Chrysler Town & Country AWD

TROUBLE SPOTS	95	96	97	98	99	00	01	02
Engine	Insufficient data	Insufficient data	○	⊖	⊖	○	⊜	⊜
Cooling			⊖	⊖	⊖	○	⊖	⊜
Fuel			○	⊖	○	⊖	⊖	⊖
Ignition			⊜	⊜	⊖	⊜	⊜	⊜
Transmission			◒	⊖	◒	◒	○	⊜
Electrical			◒	○	○	⊖	○	⊜
A/C			○	⊖	⊖	⊜	○	⊜
Suspension			◒	⊖	⊜	⊖	○	⊜
Brakes			◒	●	●	○	○	⊜
Exhaust			⊜	⊜	⊜	⊜	⊖	⊜
Power equip.			◒	○	○	◒	◒	○
Paint/trim/rust			⊜	⊜	⊜	⊖	⊖	⊜
Integrity			◒	○	○	○	◒	⊜
Hardware			◒	○	○	○	○	⊖
RELIABILITY VERDICT				✓				✓

Dodge Caravan 4 cyl.

TROUBLE SPOTS	95	96	97	98	99	00	01	02
Engine	●	●	●	●	○	⊖	Insufficient data	Insufficient data
Cooling	◒	○	○	⊖	⊖	⊜		
Fuel	◒	○	◒	⊖	⊖	⊜		
Ignition	○	⊖	⊖	⊖	⊜	⊜		
Transmission	●	●	○	◒	⊖	⊖		
Electrical	◒	◒	◒	○	⊖	⊖		
A/C	●	●	○	○	⊜	⊜		
Suspension	○	⊖	◒	⊖	○	⊖		
Brakes	○	◒	●	●	●	○		
Exhaust	⊖	○	⊜	⊖	⊜	⊜		
Power equip.	⊖	⊖	⊖	⊖	⊜	⊜		
Paint/trim/rust	◒	⊖	⊜	⊖	⊖	⊜		
Integrity	◒	◒	○	○	○	⊖		
Hardware	●	◒	⊜	○	○	○		
RELIABILITY VERDICT					✓	✓		

Dodge Caravan V6

TROUBLE SPOTS	95	96	97	98	99	00	01	02
Engine	◒	◒	◒	○	⊖	⊖	⊜	⊜
Cooling	○	◒	○	⊖	⊜	⊜	⊜	⊜
Fuel	○	◒	○	⊖	⊖	⊜	⊜	⊜
Ignition	⊖	⊖	⊜	⊜	⊜	⊜	⊜	⊜
Transmission	●	●	◒	○	◒	◒	⊜	⊖
Electrical	◒	●	●	◒	○	⊖	○	⊜
A/C	●	●	◒	○	⊖	⊜	⊖	⊜
Suspension	○	○	○	⊖	○	⊖	⊖	⊜
Brakes	◒	●	◒	◒	○	○	⊖	⊜
Exhaust	⊜	⊜	⊜	⊜	⊜	⊜	⊜	⊜
Power equip.	○	◒	○	⊖	⊜	⊖	○	⊜
Paint/trim/rust	◒	○	⊖	⊖	⊜	⊜	⊖	⊜
Integrity	◒	◒	○	○	○	⊖	○	⊖
Hardware	◒	◒	○	○	○	○	◒	⊖
RELIABILITY VERDICT				✓		✓		

Dodge Dakota 2WD

TROUBLE SPOTS	95	96	97	98	99	00	01	02
Engine	○	○	○	⊖	⊖	⊜	⊜	⊜
Cooling	●	○	⊖	○	○	⊜	⊜	⊜
Fuel	○	◒	○	○	⊖	⊖	⊖	⊜
Ignition	⊖	○	⊖	⊜	⊖	⊜	⊜	⊜
Transmission	○	○	○	○	⊖	⊜	⊖	⊜
Electrical	◒	●	○	⊖	○	○	⊖	⊜
A/C	●	◒	◒	○	⊜	⊜	⊖	⊖
Suspension	⊖	⊜	○	○	○	⊖	⊖	⊜
Brakes	◒	●	◒	◒	○	◒	⊖	⊜
Exhaust	⊖	⊖	○	○	○	⊜	⊜	⊜
Power equip.	⊖	⊖	⊖	⊖	⊖	⊖	⊜	⊜
Paint/trim/rust	◒	◒	○	⊖	⊖	⊜	⊜	⊖
Integrity	○	◒	○	⊖	⊖	⊖	⊖	⊜
Hardware	○	◒	⊖	○	⊖	○	⊜	⊖
RELIABILITY VERDICT	✓	✓	✓			✓	✓	

Dodge Dakota 4WD

TROUBLE SPOTS	95	96	97	98	99	00	01	02
Engine	Insufficient data	Insufficient data	○	○	○	⊖	⊜	⊜
Cooling			○	○	◒	⊖	⊜	⊜
Fuel			◒	◒	○	○	⊖	⊖
Ignition			⊖	⊖	⊖	⊜	⊜	⊜
Transmission			◒	○	○	⊜	⊖	⊖
Electrical			◒	○	○	⊖	○	⊜
A/C			◒	○	⊜	⊖	⊖	⊜
Suspension			◒	◒	○	○	⊖	⊜
Brakes			●	◒	◒	●	○	⊜
Exhaust			○	○	◒	⊜	⊜	⊜
Power equip.			○	⊖	⊖	⊖	⊜	⊜
Paint/trim/rust			○	○	⊜	⊖	⊖	⊜
Integrity			○	⊜	⊖	⊖	⊖	⊜
Hardware			○	○	⊖	○	⊖	⊜
RELIABILITY VERDICT								✓

Dodge Durango

TROUBLE SPOTS	95	96	97	98	99	00	01	02
Engine				⊖	○	⊖	⊖	⊜
Cooling				○	○	⊜	⊖	⊜
Fuel				⊖	⊖	⊖	⊖	⊜
Ignition				⊖	⊖	⊜	⊜	⊜
Transmission				○	○	⊖	⊖	⊜
Electrical				◒	◒	○	○	⊖
A/C				○	⊖	⊜	⊖	⊜
Suspension				○	○	○	⊖	⊜
Brakes				◒	○	○	⊖	⊜
Exhaust				⊜	⊜	⊜	⊜	⊜
Power equip.				◒	◒	○	⊖	⊖
Paint/trim/rust				○	⊖	⊜	⊖	⊖
Integrity				○	○	○	○	⊖
Hardware				◒	◒	○	○	⊜
RELIABILITY VERDICT								

Dodge Grand Caravan V6 2WD

TROUBLE SPOTS	95	96	97	98	99	00	01	02
Engine	○	◒	○	○	⊖	⊖	⊜	⊜
Cooling	◒	◒	◒	⊖	⊖	⊖	⊜	⊜
Fuel	○	●	◒	⊖	⊖	⊖	⊖	⊜
Ignition	⊖	⊖	⊜	⊜	⊜	⊜	⊜	⊜
Transmission	●	●	○	○	◒	◒	⊖	⊜
Electrical	◒	●	●	◒	○	○	⊖	⊖
A/C	●	●	○	⊖	⊖	⊖	○	⊖
Suspension	○	○	○	⊖	⊖	⊖	⊖	⊜
Brakes	◒	●	◒	◒	◒	○	○	⊜
Exhaust	⊜	⊜	⊜	⊜	⊜	⊜	⊜	⊜
Power equip.	◒	●	◒	○	○	○	○	⊖
Paint/trim/rust	◒	○	⊜	⊜	⊜	⊖	⊖	⊜
Integrity	◒	◒	◒	○	○	○	○	⊖
Hardware	◒	●	◒	○	○	○	○	⊖
RELIABILITY VERDICT				✓	✓			✓

Dodge Intrepid

TROUBLE SPOTS	95	96	97	98	99	00	01	02
Engine	◒	○	○	⊖	⊜	⊜	⊜	⊖
Cooling	◒	●	◒	⊖	⊖	⊖	⊜	⊜
Fuel	○	○	○	⊖	⊖	⊖	⊜	⊖
Ignition	○	○	○	⊖	⊖	⊜	⊜	⊜
Transmission	●	○	○	◒	◒	⊖	⊖	⊜
Electrical	●	◒	○	◒	○	⊖	⊜	⊜
A/C	●	●	○	○	○	⊖	⊜	⊜
Suspension	●	●	◒	○	⊖	⊖	⊜	⊜
Brakes	●	●	◒	◒	○	⊖	⊜	⊜
Exhaust	⊜	⊜	⊜	⊖	⊜	⊜	⊜	⊜
Power equip.	○	○	⊖	◒	●	○	⊖	⊜
Paint/trim/rust	◒	◒	◒	○	⊖	⊖	⊜	⊜
Integrity	●	◒	◒	○	⊖	○	⊖	⊜
Hardware	◒	◒	○	○	◒	○	⊖	⊜
RELIABILITY VERDICT						✓	✓	✓

Dodge Ram 1500 2WD

TROUBLE SPOTS	95	96	97	98	99	00	01	02
Engine	○	○	○	⊖	⊖	Insufficient data	⊖	⊜
Cooling	○	○	○	⊖	○		⊜	⊜
Fuel	◒	○	○	○	⊖		⊜	⊜
Ignition	⊖	⊜	⊖	⊖	⊖		⊜	⊜
Transmission	◒	◒	◒	○	○		○	⊖
Electrical	◒	○	○	○	○		⊖	⊜
A/C	◒	○	○	⊖	⊖		⊜	⊜
Suspension	○	○	⊖	⊖	⊖		⊜	⊖
Brakes	◒	○	○	◒	◒		⊖	⊜
Exhaust	○	○	○	⊜	⊖		⊜	⊜
Power equip.	○	○	○	⊖	⊜		⊖	⊜
Paint/trim/rust	●	◒	○	○	⊖		⊜	⊜
Integrity	○	○	⊖	○	⊖		○	⊖
Hardware	◒	○	○	○	⊖		⊖	⊜
RELIABILITY VERDICT	✓	✓			✓			

Dodge Ram 1500 4WD

TROUBLE SPOTS	95	96	97	98	99	00	01	02
Engine	⊖	⊖	○	○	○	⊖	⊜	⊜
Cooling	⊖	⊖	⊖	⊖	⊖	⊜	⊜	⊜
Fuel	○	◒	○	○	⊖	⊜	⊖	⊜
Ignition	○	⊖	⊜	⊖	⊖	⊖	⊜	⊜
Transmission	◒	●	◒	○	◒	◒	⊖	⊖
Electrical	○	◒	○	⊖	○	⊜	⊖	⊖
A/C	○	○	⊖	⊖	⊖	⊜	⊜	⊜
Suspension	◒	◒	◒	○	○	○	⊖	⊜
Brakes	◒	◒	◒	◒	●	○	⊜	⊜
Exhaust	○	⊖	○	⊜	⊖	⊜	⊜	⊜
Power equip.	○	⊖	⊖	⊖	⊜	⊖	⊜	⊖
Paint/trim/rust	◒	○	○	○	⊖	⊖	⊖	⊜
Integrity	○	◒	○	○	○	○	⊖	⊖
Hardware	○	○	○	○	⊖	○	⊖	⊜
RELIABILITY VERDICT	✓						✓	

Dodge Stratus V6

TROUBLE SPOTS	95	96	97	98	99	00	01	02
Engine	○	○	⊜	⊖	⊖	⊜	⊜	⊜
Cooling	○	⊖	⊖	⊖	⊜	⊜	⊜	⊜
Fuel	○	◒	○	⊖	○	○	⊖	⊖
Ignition	○	⊖	⊖	⊜	⊖	⊖	⊜	⊜
Transmission	◒	○	◒	⊖	◒	○	⊖	⊜
Electrical	○	○	○	⊜	⊖	⊖	○	⊖
A/C	◒	◒	○	⊜	⊖	⊜	⊖	⊜
Suspension	◒	◒	◒	⊖	⊖	⊖	⊖	⊜
Brakes	●	●	●	◒	○	○	⊜	⊜
Exhaust	⊜	⊖	⊜	⊜	⊜	⊜	⊜	⊜
Power equip.	◒	○	⊖	○	○	⊖	⊜	⊜
Paint/trim/rust	◒	⊖	⊖	⊖	⊖	⊖	⊖	⊖
Integrity	◒	○	⊖	⊖	○	⊖	○	⊖
Hardware	○	⊖	⊖	⊜	○	⊖	⊖	⊜
RELIABILITY VERDICT	✔	✔	✔	✓		✔		✔

Dodge/Plymouth Neon

TROUBLE SPOTS	95	96	97	98	99	00	01	02
Engine	●	●	●	●	●	⊖	Insufficient data	Insufficient data
Cooling	◒	○	○	○	⊜	⊖		
Fuel	◒	○	◒	◒	◒	⊖		
Ignition	○	○	○	○	○	⊖		
Transmission	○	○	◒	○	○	⊖		
Electrical	◒	●	◒	◒	◒	◒		
A/C	●	●	◒	○	○	⊖		
Suspension	○	○	○	○	⊖	⊖		
Brakes	◒	◒	◒	○	○	◒		
Exhaust	⊖	⊖	⊖	⊖	⊜	⊜		
Power equip.	⊖	⊖	⊖	◒	○	○		
Paint/trim/rust	●	●	◒	⊖	○	⊖		
Integrity	●	●	●	◒	◒	○		
Hardware	◒	○	○	◒	◒	○		
RELIABILITY VERDICT								

Ford Aerostar

TROUBLE SPOTS	95	96	97	98	99	00	01	02
Engine	⊖	⊖	○					
Cooling	○	○	○					
Fuel	⊖	○	◒					
Ignition	⊖	⊖	⊖					
Transmission	⊖	○	○					
Electrical	◒	◒	○					
A/C	○	○	⊖					
Suspension	◒	○	○					
Brakes	●	◒	◒					
Exhaust	○	⊜	⊖					
Power equip.	○	⊖	⊜					
Paint/trim/rust	○	⊖	⊖					
Integrity	◒	◒	◒					
Hardware	◒	○	○					
RELIABILITY VERDICT	✔	✔	✔					

Ford Contour 4 cyl.

TROUBLE SPOTS	95	96	97	98	99	00	01	02
Engine	◒	○	⊖	⊖	⊜			
Cooling	●	◒	○	○	⊜			
Fuel	◒	◒	○	○	○			
Ignition	○	○	⊖	⊜	⊜			
Transmission	○	○	⊖	⊖	⊖			
Electrical	◒	●	●	◒	○			
A/C	◒	○	○	○	⊖			
Suspension	◒	○	○	◒	⊖			
Brakes	◒	◒	○	◒	○			
Exhaust	⊖	⊖	⊜	⊜	⊜			
Power equip.	○	⊖	⊖	⊖	○			
Paint/trim/rust	⊖	○	○	○	⊜			
Integrity	◒	○	○	○	◒			
Hardware	◒	◒	○	○	◒			
RELIABILITY VERDICT			✔	✔	✔			

Ford Crown Victoria

TROUBLE SPOTS	95	96	97	98	99	00	01	02
Engine	⊖	⊖	⊖	⊜	⊜	⊜	⊖	⊜
Cooling	⊜	⊖	⊖	⊜	⊜	⊜	⊜	⊜
Fuel	◒	○	○	⊖	⊖	⊜	⊖	⊜
Ignition	○	○	⊖	⊜	⊜	⊜	⊜	⊜
Transmission	○	⊖	⊖	⊜	⊜	⊜	⊜	⊜
Electrical	◒	○	○	⊖	⊖	○	⊖	⊖
A/C	○	○	⊖	⊜	⊜	⊜	⊜	⊜
Suspension	◒	○	⊖	⊖	⊖	⊖	⊖	⊖
Brakes	●	◒	◒	⊖	○	⊖	⊖	⊜
Exhaust	⊜	⊖	⊖	⊜	⊜	⊜	⊜	⊜
Power equip.	●	◒	○	⊖	⊖	⊖	⊖	⊖
Paint/trim/rust	⊖	⊖	⊖	⊜	⊜	⊖	⊜	⊜
Integrity	⊖	○	⊖	○	⊖	◒	○	○
Hardware	●	◒	○	⊖	⊖	⊖	○	⊖
RELIABILITY VERDICT	✔	✔	✓	✓	✓	✔	✔	

Ford Econoline Wagon, Van 150

TROUBLE SPOTS	95	96	97	98	99	00	01	02
Engine	⊖	○	⊖	⊖	⊖	⊜	Insufficient data	Insufficient data
Cooling	◒	◒	⊖	⊖	⊜	⊜		
Fuel	○	●	○	⊜	⊜	⊖		
Ignition	⊖	⊖	⊖	⊜	⊜	⊖		
Transmission	○	○	⊖	⊖	○	⊖		
Electrical	○	◒	○	○	⊖	○		
A/C	◒	◒	○	○	⊖	⊜		
Suspension	◒	○	◒	○	○	⊖		
Brakes	●	●	●	◒	●	○		
Exhaust	⊖	⊖	⊜	⊖	⊜	⊜		
Power equip.	⊖	○	⊖	○	⊖	⊜		
Paint/trim/rust	○	◒	○	⊖	⊖	⊜		
Integrity	○	○	○	○	○	○		
Hardware	○	○	◒	◒	◒	○		
RELIABILITY VERDICT	✔			✔	✔	✔		

Ford Escape V6

TROUBLE SPOTS	95	96	97	98	99	00	01	02
Engine							⊜	⊜
Cooling							⊖	⊜
Fuel							○	⊜
Ignition							⊜	⊜
Transmission							⊖	⊜
Electrical							○	⊜
A/C							⊜	⊜
Suspension							⊖	⊜
Brakes							⊖	⊜
Exhaust							⊜	⊜
Power equip.							⊜	⊖
Paint/trim/rust							⊜	⊜
Integrity							◒	○
Hardware							○	⊖
RELIABILITY VERDICT								

Ford Escort

TROUBLE SPOTS	95	96	97	98	99	00	01	02
Engine	◒	◒	⊖	⊖	⊜	⊜	Insufficient data	Insufficient data
Cooling	◒	◒	○	⊖	⊜	⊜		
Fuel	⊖	◒	⊖	⊖	⊖	⊖		
Ignition	⊖	⊖	⊖	⊜	⊜	⊖		
Transmission	⊖	⊖	⊖	⊖	⊜	⊖		
Electrical	◒	◒	○	○	⊖	⊖		
A/C	○	○	⊖	⊖	⊜	⊜		
Suspension	○	○	○	○	○	⊖		
Brakes	◒	○	○	○	○	⊖		
Exhaust	⊖	⊖	⊜	⊜	⊜	⊜		
Power equip.	⊖	⊜	⊜	⊜	⊖	⊖		
Paint/trim/rust	○	○	⊖	⊖	⊖	⊜		
Integrity	○	○	⊖	○	○	○		
Hardware	◒	○	⊖	⊖	⊖	⊖		
RELIABILITY VERDICT	✔	✔	✓	✓	✓	✓		

Ford Excursion V10

TROUBLE SPOTS	95	96	97	98	99	00	01	02
Engine						⊖	Insufficient data	Insufficient data
Cooling						⊜		
Fuel						⊜		
Ignition						⊜		
Transmission						⊜		
Electrical						⊖		
A/C						⊖		
Suspension						○		
Brakes						◒		
Exhaust						⊖		
Power equip.						○		
Paint/trim/rust						⊜		
Integrity						⊖		
Hardware						○		
RELIABILITY VERDICT						✔		

Ford Expedition 2WD

TROUBLE SPOTS	95	96	97	98	99	00	01	02
Engine			⊜	⊖	○	⊖	⊜	⊜
Cooling			⊜	⊜	⊜	⊜	⊜	⊜
Fuel			⊜	⊜	⊖	⊖	⊜	⊜
Ignition			○	⊜	⊜	⊖	⊜	⊜
Transmission			○	⊜	⊜	⊜	⊜	⊜
Electrical			◒	◒	◒	◒	⊖	⊜
A/C			⊖	⊖	⊖	⊜	⊜	⊜
Suspension			○	⊜	⊜	⊖	⊜	⊜
Brakes			⊖	○	⊖	⊜	⊜	⊜
Exhaust			⊜	⊜	⊜	⊜	⊜	⊜
Power equip.			⊖	○	◒	○	⊖	⊜
Paint/trim/rust			○	⊜	⊜	⊖	⊖	⊜
Integrity			⊜	⊜	○	⊖	○	⊖
Hardware			⊖	○	○	○	◒	⊖
RELIABILITY VERDICT			✓	✓	✔	✔	✔	✓

Ford Expedition 4WD

TROUBLE SPOTS	95	96	97	98	99	00	01	02
Engine			⊜	⊖	◒	⊜	⊜	⊜
Cooling			⊜	⊜	⊜	⊜	⊜	⊜
Fuel			○	⊜	⊖	⊜	⊖	⊜
Ignition			⊖	⊖	⊖	⊜	⊜	⊜
Transmission			○	⊖	⊖	⊖	⊖	⊜
Electrical			○	◒	●	◒	○	⊜
A/C			⊜	⊖	⊖	⊜	⊜	⊜
Suspension			◒	○	⊖	⊜	⊖	⊜
Brakes			◒	○	○	⊖	⊜	⊖
Exhaust			⊜	⊜	⊜	⊜	⊜	⊜
Power equip.			○	○	○	○	○	⊜
Paint/trim/rust			○	○	○	⊖	⊜	⊜
Integrity			○	○	○	⊖	○	⊖
Hardware			⊖	○	○	⊖	○	⊜
RELIABILITY VERDICT			✔	✔		✔	✔	✓

Ford Explorer 2WD

TROUBLE SPOTS	95	96	97	98	99	00	01	02
Engine	⊜	⊜	○	○	○	⊖	⊜	⊜
Cooling	○	○	○	⊖	⊖	⊖	⊜	⊜
Fuel	○	◒	○	○	○	⊖	⊖	⊜
Ignition	⊖	⊖	⊜	⊖	⊖	⊖	⊜	⊜
Transmission	○	⊜	⊖	⊖	⊖	⊜	⊖	⊖
Electrical	◒	◒	○	◒	●	◒	○	⊖
A/C	◒	○	●	○	⊖	⊖	⊜	⊜
Suspension	⊖	⊖	○	○	⊖	⊖	⊜	⊜
Brakes	○	○	○	○	⊖	⊖	⊜	⊜
Exhaust	⊜	⊖	⊖	⊜	⊜	⊜	⊜	⊜
Power equip.	◒	○	○	◒	○	○	○	⊜
Paint/trim/rust	⊖	⊖	○	⊖	⊖	⊖	⊜	⊜
Integrity	⊖	○	○	○	○	◒	○	⊖
Hardware	◒	○	◒	◒	○	◒	⊖	○
RELIABILITY VERDICT	✓	✓	✔				✔	

Ford Explorer 4WD

TROUBLE SPOTS	95	96	97	98	99	00	01	02
Engine	⊖	⊖	○	○	⊜	⊖	⊜	⊜
Cooling	○	○	○	⊖	⊖	⊖	⊜	⊜
Fuel	○	○	○	○	○	⊖	⊖	⊜
Ignition	⊖	⊖	⊖	⊖	⊖	⊜	⊜	⊜
Transmission	◒	○	⊜	⊖	⊖	⊖	⊖	⊖
Electrical	◒	○	○	◒	◒	◒	○	⊖
A/C	○	○	◒	⊖	⊜	⊜	⊜	⊜
Suspension	○	○	○	○	⊖	⊖	⊖	⊜
Brakes	◒	◒	◒	○	○	○	⊖	⊜
Exhaust	⊜	⊖	⊖	⊜	⊜	⊜	⊜	⊜
Power equip.	○	○	○	◒	○	○	⊖	⊖
Paint/trim/rust	⊖	⊖	⊖	⊖	⊖	⊖	⊖	⊖
Integrity	○	○	⊖	○	○	○	○	⊖
Hardware	○	○	○	○	○	○	○	⊖
RELIABILITY VERDICT	✔	✔	✔					

Ford Explorer Sport Trac

TROUBLE SPOTS	95	96	97	98	99	00	01	02
Engine							⊜	⊜
Cooling							⊜	⊜
Fuel							⊖	⊖
Ignition							⊜	⊜
Transmission							⊜	⊜
Electrical							○	⊜
A/C							⊜	⊜
Suspension							⊖	⊜
Brakes							⊖	⊜
Exhaust							⊜	⊜
Power equip.							⊖	⊜
Paint/trim/rust							⊖	⊖
Integrity							◒	⊖
Hardware							○	○
RELIABILITY VERDICT								

Ford F-150 2WD

TROUBLE SPOTS	95	96	97	98	99	00	01	02
Engine	⊖	⊖	⊖	⊜	⊖	⊜	⊜	⊜
Cooling	○	⊖	⊖	⊜	⊜	⊜	⊜	⊜
Fuel	⊖	◒	⊖	⊖	⊖	⊜	⊖	⊜
Ignition	⊜	⊖	⊖	⊖	⊖	⊜	⊜	⊜
Transmission	○	○	⊜	⊜	⊖	⊖	⊖	⊜
Electrical	○	○	○	○	⊜	○	⊖	⊖
A/C	⊖	⊖	⊖	⊖	⊖	⊖	⊜	⊜
Suspension	◒	○	○	⊖	⊖	⊜	⊜	⊜
Brakes	◒	◒	○	⊖	⊜	⊖	⊜	⊜
Exhaust	⊜	⊖	⊜	⊜	⊜	⊜	⊜	⊜
Power equip.	⊜	⊜	○	⊖	⊜	⊜	⊖	⊜
Paint/trim/rust	⊖	⊖	⊖	⊖	⊜	⊖	⊖	⊜
Integrity	○	○	○	⊖	○	○	⊖	⊖
Hardware	⊖	○	⊜	⊖	○	⊖	○	⊜
RELIABILITY VERDICT	✓	✔	✓	✓	✓	✓	✔	✓

Ford F-150 4WD

TROUBLE SPOTS	95	96	97	98	99	00	01	02
Engine	○	○	⊜	⊖	○	⊖	⊜	⊜
Cooling	⊖	○	⊜	⊜	⊜	⊜	⊜	⊜
Fuel	○	◒	⊜	⊖	⊖	⊜	⊜	⊜
Ignition	⊖	⊖	⊖	⊖	⊖	⊜	⊜	⊜
Transmission	○	⊜	⊜	⊜	⊖	⊜	⊜	⊜
Electrical	○	○	◒	○	○	⊖	⊖	⊜
A/C	⊖	⊜	⊜	⊖	⊜	⊖	⊜	⊜
Suspension	◒	◒	○	○	⊖	⊖	⊖	⊜
Brakes	◒	◒	○	○	◒	○	⊜	⊜
Exhaust	⊜	⊜	⊜	⊜	⊜	⊜	⊜	⊜
Power equip.	⊜	⊜	⊖	⊖	⊖	⊜	⊜	⊜
Paint/trim/rust	○	⊖	⊖	⊖	⊖	⊖	⊜	⊜
Integrity	○	◒	○	⊖	○	⊖	○	⊖
Hardware	○	⊖	⊜	○	○	⊜	⊖	⊖
RELIABILITY VERDICT	✔	✔	✓	✓	✔	✓	✔	✓

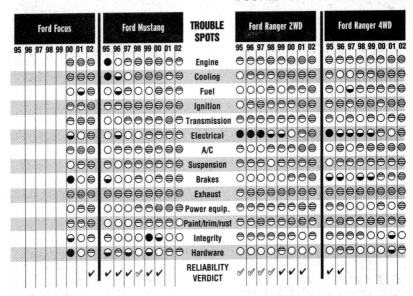

Ford Focus 95	96	97	98	99	00	01	02	Ford Mustang 95	96	97	98	99	00	01	02	TROUBLE SPOTS
					⊜	⊜	⊜	●	○	⊖	⊜	⊜	⊜	⊖	⊖	Engine
					⊜	⊜	⊜	●	◒	○	⊜	⊜	⊜	⊖	⊜	Cooling
					○	◒	⊜	○	◒	⊖	○	○	⊜	⊖	⊖	Fuel
					⊖	⊖	⊜	⊖	⊖	⊜	⊜	⊜	⊜	⊜	⊜	Ignition
					⊖	⊜	⊜	○	○	⊖	⊜	⊖	⊖	⊜	⊖	Transmission
					◒	○	⊜	○	◒	○	○	⊖	⊖	⊖	⊖	Electrical
					⊖	⊜	⊜	○	⊖	⊖	⊖	⊜	⊖	⊜	⊜	A/C
					○	⊖	⊜	⊖	○	⊖	⊖	⊖	⊖	⊖	⊜	Suspension
					●	○	⊜	◒	○	○	⊖	○	⊖	⊜	⊜	Brakes
					⊜	⊜	⊜	⊜	⊜	⊜	⊜	⊜	⊜	⊜	⊜	Exhaust
					○	⊖	⊜	○	○	○	⊖	⊖	⊜	⊜	⊜	Power equip.
					⊖	⊖	⊜	○	○	○	⊖	⊖	⊖	⊖	○	Paint/trim/rust
					◒	○	⊖	⊖	○	○	○	●	◒	○	○	Integrity
					●	○	⊖	◒	⊖	◒	○	◒	○	⊖	⊖	Hardware
							✔	✔	✔	✔	✓	✔	✔			RELIABILITY VERDICT

TROUBLE SPOTS	Ford Ranger 2WD 95	96	97	98	99	00	01	02	Ford Ranger 4WD 95	96	97	98	99	00	01	02
Engine	⊖	⊖	⊖	⊜	⊖	⊜	⊜	⊜	⊜	⊖	⊖	⊖	⊖	⊖	⊜	⊜
Cooling	○	⊖	⊖	⊖	⊜	⊜	⊜	⊜	⊖	○	○	⊖	⊖	⊜	⊜	⊜
Fuel	○	○	○	⊖	○	⊖	⊖	⊜	⊖	○	◒	⊖	⊖	⊖	⊖	⊜
Ignition	○	⊖	⊜	⊖	⊖	⊖	⊜	⊜	⊖	⊜	⊖	⊜	⊜	⊖	⊜	⊜
Transmission	⊖	⊖	⊖	⊖	⊖	⊖	⊖	⊜	⊖	○	⊖	○	⊖	○	⊖	⊜
Electrical	●	●	●	◒	◒	○	⊖	⊜	●	◒	◒	◒	◒	⊖	○	⊜
A/C	⊖	○	○	⊖	⊖	⊖	⊜	⊜	○	⊜	○	⊖	⊜	⊜	⊜	⊜
Suspension	⊖	⊖	⊖	○	⊖	⊖	⊖	⊜	○	⊖	⊖	⊖	⊖	⊖	⊖	⊜
Brakes	○	○	○	○	○	⊖	⊖	⊜	◒	◒	○	◒	◒	⊖	⊖	⊜
Exhaust	⊖	⊜	⊜	⊜	⊜	⊜	⊜	⊜	⊜	⊜	⊜	⊜	⊜	⊜	⊜	⊜
Power equip.	⊖	⊖	⊖	⊖	⊖	⊖	⊜	⊜	⊖	⊖	○	○	○	⊖	○	⊜
Paint/trim/rust	⊖	⊖	⊜	⊖	⊖	⊜	⊜	⊖	⊖	⊜	⊖	⊖	⊜	⊜	⊖	⊜
Integrity	⊖	⊖	⊖	⊖	⊖	⊖	○	⊖	⊖	⊖	⊖	⊖	○	○	◒	○
Hardware	○	○	○	○	⊖	○	○	○	○	⊖	⊖	○	○	○	◒	⊖
RELIABILITY VERDICT	✓	✓	✓	✓	✔	✔	✔		✔	✔						

Ford Taurus 95	96	97	98	99	00	01	02	Ford Thunderbird 95	96	97	98	99	00	01	02	TROUBLE SPOTS
◒	○	⊖	⊜	⊖	⊖	⊖	⊜	○	○	⊖						Engine
●	○	⊖	⊖	⊜	⊜	⊜	⊜	○	●	◒						Cooling
○	○	○	⊖	⊖	○	⊖	⊜	◒	○	⊖						Fuel
⊖	⊖	⊖	⊖	⊜	⊖	⊜	⊜	◒	⊖	⊖						Ignition
◒	◒	○	○	⊜	⊜	⊖	⊜	●	○	○						Transmission
●	◒	◒	◒	○	◒	⊖	⊖	◒	○	○	Insufficient data					Electrical
◒	⊖	⊖	⊖	⊖	⊖	⊜	⊜	○	⊖	○						A/C
◒	○	○	⊖	○	○	⊖	⊜	⊖	⊖	⊖						Suspension
◒	◒	◒	◒	◒	◒	⊖	⊜	◒	◒	◒						Brakes
⊖	⊜	⊜	⊜	⊜	⊜	⊜	⊜	⊜	⊜	⊜						Exhaust
○	○	○	○	⊖	⊖	⊜	⊜	○	⊖	⊖						Power equip.
○	⊖	⊖	⊖	⊖	⊖	⊜	⊜	◒	⊖	⊖						Paint/trim/rust
●	◒	○	⊖	⊖	○	○	⊖	◒	○	○						Integrity
◒	○	○	○	○	○	⊖	⊖	◒	⊖	○						Hardware
	✔	✔	✔	✔	✔	✔	✔	✔	✔	✔						RELIABILITY VERDICT

TROUBLE SPOTS	Ford Windstar 95	96	97	98	99	00	01	02	GMC Jimmy, Envoy 95	96	97	98	99	00	01	02
Engine	●	◒	○	⊖	⊖	⊖	⊜	⊜	◒	◒	○	⊖	○	○	⊖	⊜
Cooling	◒	○	⊖	⊜	⊜	⊜	⊜	⊜	◒	●	◒	○	⊖	⊜	⊜	⊜
Fuel	○	◒	○	○	◒	⊜	⊜	⊖	●	◒	●	⊖	○	⊖	⊖	⊜
Ignition	○	○	⊖	⊖	⊖	⊖	⊜	⊜	○	⊖	⊖	⊖	⊖	⊖	⊜	⊜
Transmission	●	○	○	○	◒	○	⊜	⊜	◒	○	◒	◒	○	⊖	⊖	⊖
Electrical	●	●	●	◒	●	◒	◒	⊖	●	●	●	●	◒	●	●	⊖
A/C	○	○	○	⊖	⊖	⊖	⊖	⊜	○	●	◒	○	⊜	⊜	⊜	⊜
Suspension	○	◒	◒	●	◒	○	⊖	⊜	◒	◒	◒	○	○	○	⊖	⊖
Brakes	●	●	●	◒	⊖	⊖	⊖	⊜	●	●	◒	○	○	○	⊖	⊜
Exhaust	⊖	⊖	⊜	⊜	⊜	⊜	⊜	⊜	◒	⊖	⊜	⊖	⊖	⊜	⊜	⊜
Power equip.	◒	◒	◒	○	◒	○	○	⊖	◒	⊖	○	○	○	○	⊖	⊖
Paint/trim/rust	⊖	⊖	⊖	⊖	○	○	⊖	⊜	○	○	⊖	⊜	⊜	⊖	⊜	⊖
Integrity	◒	○	◒	○	○	◒	◒	○	◒	◒	○	◒	◒	○	◒	○
Hardware	◒	◒	○	◒	◒	◒	◒	⊖	◒	◒	○	◒	●	◒	○	⊖
RELIABILITY VERDICT																

GMC S-15 Sonoma V6 2WD

TROUBLE SPOTS	95	96	97	98	99	00	01	02
Engine	⊖	◒	⊖	⊖	⊜	⊖	⊖	Insufficient data
Cooling	⊖	●	○	⊖	⊖	⊜	⊜	
Fuel	◒	●	●	⊖	⊖	⊖	⊖	
Ignition	⊖	○	⊖	⊜	⊜	⊜	⊜	
Transmission	○	◒	○	○	○	⊜	⊜	
Electrical	●	●	●	○	◒	○	⊖	
A/C	○	●	●	○	⊜	⊜	⊜	
Suspension	○	◒	⊖	⊖	⊖	○	⊖	
Brakes	●	●	●	○	◒	◒	⊖	
Exhaust	○	⊖	⊜	⊜	⊖	⊖	⊜	
Power equip.	○	⊜	⊖	⊖	⊜	⊖	⊜	
Paint/trim/rust	○	○	⊖	⊜	○	⊜	⊜	
Integrity	○	◒	◒	◒	○	◒	○	
Hardware	◒	●	◒	●	●	●	○	
RELIABILITY VERDICT	✔						✔	

GMC S-15 Sonoma V6 4WD

TROUBLE SPOTS	95	96	97	98	99	00	01	02
Engine	Insufficient data	Insufficient data	Insufficient data	Insufficient data	Insufficient data	⊖	⊖	Insufficient data
Cooling						⊜	⊜	
Fuel						⊖	⊖	
Ignition						⊜	⊜	
Transmission						⊜	⊜	
Electrical						⊖	⊖	
A/C						⊜	⊜	
Suspension						⊖	⊖	
Brakes						○	⊜	
Exhaust						⊜	⊜	
Power equip.						⊜	⊜	
Paint/trim/rust						⊖	⊖	
Integrity						○	○	
Hardware						●	⊖	
RELIABILITY VERDICT								

GMC Safari

TROUBLE SPOTS	95	96	97	98	99	00	01	02
Engine	○	○	○	○	⊖	⊜	⊜	Insufficient data
Cooling	○	◒	○	⊖	⊖	⊜	⊜	
Fuel	◒	●	●	○	○	⊖	⊖	
Ignition	⊖	⊖	⊖	⊖	⊖	⊜	⊜	
Transmission	○	◒	◒	○	○	⊖	⊖	
Electrical	●	●	●	◒	◒	○	⊖	
A/C	●	●	◒	○	○	⊖	⊜	
Suspension	◒	●	◒	◒	○	○	⊖	
Brakes	●	◒	●	●	●	◒	◒	
Exhaust	◒	⊖	⊖	⊜	⊜	⊖	⊜	
Power equip.	◒	●	●	◒	◒	◒	⊖	
Paint/trim/rust	○	◒	○	⊖	⊖	⊖	⊖	
Integrity	◒	●	●	◒	●	●	●	
Hardware	◒	●	●	●	●	●	◒	
RELIABILITY VERDICT								

GMC Savana Van 1500

TROUBLE SPOTS	95	96	97	98	99	00	01	02
Engine		Insufficient data	⊖	○	⊖	⊖	Insufficient data	Insufficient data
Cooling			⊜	◒	⊜	⊜		
Fuel			●	○	○	⊖		
Ignition			⊖	⊖	⊖	⊜		
Transmission			●	◒	○	⊖		
Electrical			●	●	◒	◒		
A/C			●	◒	○	○		
Suspension			○	○	⊖	○		
Brakes			●	●	◒	●		
Exhaust			⊖	⊜	⊜	⊜		
Power equip.			●	○	○	◒		
Paint/trim/rust			○	⊖	⊖	⊖		
Integrity			◒	●	●	◒		
Hardware			●	●	◒	●		
RELIABILITY VERDICT								

GMC Sierra 1500 2WD

TROUBLE SPOTS	95	96	97	98	99	00	01	02
Engine	⊖	○	○	⊖	⊜	⊜	⊜	⊜
Cooling	○	◒	○	○	⊜	⊜	⊜	⊜
Fuel	⊖	◒	◒	○	○	⊖	⊜	⊜
Ignition	⊖	⊖	⊖	⊖	⊜	⊜	⊜	⊜
Transmission	○	○	◒	⊖	⊖	⊖	⊖	⊜
Electrical	●	●	●	◒	○	○	⊖	⊜
A/C	◒	●	○	⊖	⊜	⊜	⊜	⊜
Suspension	○	⊖	◒	⊖	⊖	○	⊖	⊜
Brakes	◒	◒	○	○	◒	⊖	⊜	⊜
Exhaust	◒	⊖	⊖	⊖	⊜	⊜	⊜	⊜
Power equip.	⊖	⊖	⊖	⊖	○	⊖	⊖	⊜
Paint/trim/rust	○	⊖	⊜	⊖	⊖	⊜	⊜	⊜
Integrity	○	○	○	○	●	◒	○	⊖
Hardware	◒	○	○	◒	●	○	⊜	⊜
RELIABILITY VERDICT	✔			✔	✔	✔	✔	✔ (outline)

GMC Sierra 1500 4WD

TROUBLE SPOTS	95	96	97	98	99	00	01	02
Engine	○	○	○	○	⊖	⊜	⊜	⊜
Cooling	⊖	◒	○	○	⊜	⊜	⊜	⊜
Fuel	⊖	●	◒	○	○	⊖	⊜	⊜
Ignition	⊖	⊖	⊜	⊖	⊜	⊜	⊜	⊜
Transmission	○	○	○	⊖	○	⊖	⊖	⊜
Electrical	●	●	●	○	◒	⊖	⊖	⊜
A/C	○	○	○	⊖	⊜	⊜	⊜	⊜
Suspension	⊖	○	○	○	○	○	⊖	⊜
Brakes	◒	●	◒	●	◒	○	⊜	⊜
Exhaust	◒	⊜	⊜	⊜	⊜	⊜	⊜	⊜
Power equip.	⊖	⊖	⊖	⊜	○	⊖	⊖	⊜
Paint/trim/rust	○	⊖	⊜	⊖	⊖	⊖	⊜	⊜
Integrity	○	○	⊖	○	●	◒	○	⊖
Hardware	○	○	○	⊖	●	○	⊜	⊜
RELIABILITY VERDICT	✔							

GMC Suburban, Yukon XL

TROUBLE SPOTS	95	96	97	98	99	00	01	02
Engine	⊖	○	○	○	⊖	⊜	⊖	⊜
Cooling	○	●	◒	◒	⊖	⊜	⊜	⊜
Fuel	○	◒	◒	⊖	⊖	⊖	⊜	⊜
Ignition	⊖	⊖	⊜	⊜	⊜	⊜	⊜	⊜
Transmission	○	○	◒	○	⊖	⊖	⊜	⊜
Electrical	●	●	●	●	◒	○	⊖	⊖
A/C	●	◒	○	○	⊖	⊜	⊜	⊜
Suspension	○	○	○	○	○	○	⊖	⊜
Brakes	●	●	●	●	●	⊖	⊜	⊜
Exhaust	◒	⊖	⊖	⊜	⊜	⊜	⊜	⊜
Power equip.	○	○	○	⊖	○	●	○	⊜
Paint/trim/rust	○	⊜	⊖	⊜	⊖	⊜	⊖	⊜
Integrity	○	⊖	○	○	○	○	○	⊖
Hardware	●	◒	○	○	◒	●	○	⊖
RELIABILITY VERDICT	✔						✔	✔

GMC Yukon

TROUBLE SPOTS	95	96	97	98	99	00	01	02
Engine	○	○	○	○	⊖	⊜	⊜	⊜
Cooling	◒	◒	○	○	⊖	⊜	⊜	⊜
Fuel	⊖	◒	◒	⊖	○	⊖	⊜	⊜
Ignition	○	⊖	⊖	⊜	⊜	⊜	⊜	⊜
Transmission	⊖	◒	◒	○	⊖	⊖	⊜	⊜
Electrical	●	●	●	○	○	◒	⊖	⊖
A/C	◒	◒	○	⊖	⊖	⊜	⊜	⊜
Suspension	○	○	○	○	○	○	⊖	⊜
Brakes	●	●	●	●	●	○	⊜	⊜
Exhaust	○	⊜	⊜	⊜	⊜	⊜	⊜	⊜
Power equip.	○	○	⊖	⊖	○	◒	⊖	⊜
Paint/trim/rust	○	⊖	⊖	⊜	⊖	⊜	⊖	⊜
Integrity	○	○	○	⊖	○	◒	○	⊖
Hardware	●	○	○	⊖	○	◒	○	⊖
RELIABILITY VERDICT	✔				✔		✔	✔

Honda Accord

TROUBLE SPOTS	95	96	97	98	99	00	01	02
Engine	⊖	⊖	⊜	⊜	⊜	⊜	⊜	⊜
Cooling	⊖	⊜	⊜	⊜	⊜	⊜	⊜	⊜
Fuel	⊜	⊜	⊜	○	⊖	⊜	⊜	⊜
Ignition	⊜	⊜	⊜	⊜	⊜	⊜	⊜	⊜
Transmission	⊜	⊜	⊜	⊜	⊜	⊜	⊜	⊜
Electrical	○	⊖	⊖	⊖	⊖	⊜	⊜	⊜
A/C	◒	○	⊖	⊜	⊜	⊜	⊜	⊜
Suspension	⊖	⊜	⊜	⊜	⊜	⊜	⊜	⊜
Brakes	◒	○	⊖	⊖	⊖	⊜	⊜	⊜
Exhaust	○	⊖	⊖	⊜	⊜	⊜	⊜	⊜
Power equip.	○	○	○	⊖	⊜	⊜	⊜	⊜
Paint/trim/rust	⊖	⊖	⊖	⊜	⊜	⊜	⊜	⊜
Integrity	⊖	⊖	⊖	⊖	⊖	⊖	⊖	⊖
Hardware	○	⊖	⊖	⊖	⊖	⊖	⊖	⊜
RELIABILITY VERDICT	✓	✓	✓	✓	✓	✓	✓	✓

Honda Civic

TROUBLE SPOTS	95	96	97	98	99	00	01	02
Engine	⊖	⊜	⊜	⊜	⊜	⊜	⊜	⊜
Cooling	⊖	⊜	⊜	⊜	⊜	⊜	⊜	⊜
Fuel	⊜	⊜	⊖	⊜	⊜	⊜	⊖	⊜
Ignition	⊜	⊖	⊜	⊜	⊜	⊜	⊜	⊜
Transmission	⊜	⊜	⊜	⊖	⊜	⊜	⊜	⊜
Electrical	⊖	⊖	⊖	⊖	⊜	⊜	⊜	⊜
A/C	○	⊖	⊜	⊜	⊜	⊜	⊜	⊜
Suspension	⊖	⊜	⊜	⊜	⊜	⊜	⊖	⊜
Brakes	⊖	⊖	⊖	⊖	⊖	⊜	⊜	⊜
Exhaust	○	○	○	⊖	⊜	⊜	⊜	⊜
Power equip.	⊜	⊖	⊖	⊜	⊜	⊜	⊖	⊜
Paint/trim/rust	⊖	⊖	⊖	⊖	⊜	⊜	⊖	⊜
Integrity	⊖	○	⊖	⊖	⊖	⊖	○	⊖
Hardware	⊖	○	⊖	⊖	⊖	⊖	○	⊖
RELIABILITY VERDICT	✓	✓	✓	✓	✓	✓	✔	✓

Honda CR-V

TROUBLE SPOTS	95	96	97	98	99	00	01	02
Engine			⊜	⊜	⊜	⊜	⊜	⊜
Cooling			⊜	⊜	⊜	⊜	⊜	⊜
Fuel			⊜	⊜	⊜	⊜	⊜	⊖
Ignition			⊜	⊜	⊜	⊜	⊜	⊜
Transmission			⊜	⊜	⊜	⊜	⊜	⊜
Electrical			⊜	⊜	⊜	⊜	⊜	⊜
A/C			⊜	⊜	⊜	⊜	⊜	⊜
Suspension			⊖	⊜	⊜	⊜	⊜	⊜
Brakes			⊜	⊜	⊜	⊜	⊜	⊜
Exhaust			⊜	⊜	⊜	⊜	⊜	⊜
Power equip.			⊜	⊖	⊜	⊜	⊜	⊜
Paint/trim/rust			⊖	⊖	⊜	⊜	⊜	⊜
Integrity			⊜	⊖	⊖	⊜	⊜	⊖
Hardware			⊖	⊜	⊜	⊜	⊖	⊖
RELIABILITY VERDICT			✓	✓	✓	✓	✓	✓

Honda Odyssey

TROUBLE SPOTS	95	96	97	98	99	00	01	02
Engine	⊖	○	⊜	⊜	⊜	⊜	⊜	⊜
Cooling	⊖	⊜	⊜	⊜	⊜	⊜	⊜	⊜
Fuel	⊜	⊜	⊜	⊖	⊖	⊜	⊜	⊜
Ignition	⊜	⊜	⊜	⊜	⊜	⊜	⊜	⊜
Transmission	⊜	⊜	⊜	⊖	⊖	⊜	⊜	⊜
Electrical	⊖	⊖	⊖	⊜	○	⊖	⊖	⊜
A/C	○	⊖	⊜	⊜	⊜	⊜	⊜	⊜
Suspension	⊖	⊜	⊖	⊜	⊖	⊜	⊜	⊜
Brakes	●	◒	○	○	○	⊖	⊖	⊜
Exhaust	○	⊖	⊜	⊜	⊜	⊜	⊜	⊜
Power equip.	○	⊖	⊜	⊜	◒	◒	○	⊜
Paint/trim/rust	⊖	⊖	⊜	⊜	⊜	⊖	⊜	⊜
Integrity	⊖	⊖	⊖	⊖	○	○	⊖	⊖
Hardware	○	⊖	⊖	⊜	◒	◒	○	⊜
RELIABILITY VERDICT	✓	✓	✓	✓	✔	✔	✓	✓

Honda Passport

TROUBLE SPOTS	95	96	97	98	99	00	01	02
Engine	●	Insufficient data	Insufficient data	○	○	⊖	⊜	Insufficient data
Cooling	⊖			⊜	⊜	⊜	⊜	
Fuel	⊖			○	○	○	⊖	
Ignition	○			⊖	○	⊜	⊜	
Transmission	⊖			⊜	⊖	⊜	⊖	
Electrical	●			◒	○	○	⊖	
A/C	○			○	⊖	⊖	⊜	
Suspension	⊖			○	⊖	○	○	
Brakes	◒			◒	●	○	⊜	
Exhaust	⊖			⊖	⊜	⊜	⊜	
Power equip.	●			⊖	⊖	⊖	⊖	
Paint/trim/rust	○			○	⊖	⊖	⊖	
Integrity	◒			◒	◒	●	◒	
Hardware	●			○	○	○	○	
RELIABILITY VERDICT	✔			✔				

Honda S2000

TROUBLE SPOTS	95	96	97	98	99	00	01	02
Engine						⊜	⊜	Insufficient data
Cooling						⊜	⊜	
Fuel						⊜	⊜	
Ignition						⊜	⊜	
Transmission						⊜	⊖	
Electrical						⊜	⊜	
A/C						⊜	⊜	
Suspension						⊖	⊜	
Brakes						⊜	⊜	
Exhaust						⊜	⊜	
Power equip.						○	⊖	
Paint/trim/rust						⊖	⊜	
Integrity						⊜	⊜	
Hardware						⊖	⊜	
RELIABILITY VERDICT						✓	✓	

Hyundai Accent

TROUBLE SPOTS	95	96	97	98	99	00	01	02
Engine	Insufficient data	Insufficient data	Insufficient data	Insufficient data	Insufficient data	Insufficient data	⊜	Insufficient data
Cooling							⊜	
Fuel							○	
Ignition							⊜	
Transmission							⊖	
Electrical							⊖	
A/C							⊜	
Suspension							⊖	
Brakes							⊖	
Exhaust							⊜	
Power equip.							⊜	
Paint/trim/rust							⊜	
Integrity							◒	
Hardware							○	
RELIABILITY VERDICT							✔	

Hyundai Elantra

TROUBLE SPOTS	95	96	97	98	99	00	01	02
Engine	Insufficient data	Insufficient data	Insufficient data	Insufficient data	Insufficient data	⊜	⊜	⊜
Cooling						⊜	⊜	⊜
Fuel						⊖	⊖	⊜
Ignition						⊖	⊖	⊜
Transmission						○	⊖	⊖
Electrical						○	⊖	⊜
A/C						⊖	⊜	⊜
Suspension						⊜	⊖	⊜
Brakes						⊜	⊜	⊜
Exhaust						⊖	⊜	⊜
Power equip.						○	⊖	⊜
Paint/trim/rust						⊖	⊖	⊜
Integrity						⊜	○	⊖
Hardware						○	⊖	⊖
RELIABILITY VERDICT						✔	✔	✔

Hyundai Santa Fe

TROUBLE SPOTS	95	96	97	98	99	00	01	02
Engine							⊖	⊜
Cooling							⊜	⊜
Fuel							○	⊜
Ignition							⊜	⊜
Transmission							⊖	⊜
Electrical							⊖	⊜
A/C							⊜	⊜
Suspension							⊖	⊜
Brakes							⊖	⊜
Exhaust							⊜	⊜
Power equip.							⊖	⊜
Paint/trim/rust							⊖	⊜
Integrity							○	⊜
Hardware							⊖	⊜
RELIABILITY VERDICT							✔	✓

Hyundai Sonata

TROUBLE SPOTS	95	96	97	98	99	00	01	02
Engine	Insufficient data	Insufficient data	Insufficient data	Insufficient data	Insufficient data	⊜	⊜	⊜
Cooling						⊜	⊜	⊜
Fuel						⊖	⊖	⊜
Ignition						⊖	⊜	⊜
Transmission						○	⊜	⊜
Electrical						◒	⊖	⊜
A/C						⊜	⊜	⊜
Suspension						⊜	⊜	⊜
Brakes						⊖	⊖	⊜
Exhaust						⊜	⊜	⊜
Power equip.						◒	⊜	⊜
Paint/trim/rust						○	⊜	⊜
Integrity						⊖	⊖	⊖
Hardware						⊖	⊖	⊜
RELIABILITY VERDICT						✔	✓	✓

Hyundai XG300, XG350

TROUBLE SPOTS	95	96	97	98	99	00	01	02
Engine							⊜	Insufficient data
Cooling							⊜	
Fuel							⊖	
Ignition							⊜	
Transmission							⊜	
Electrical							⊖	
A/C							⊜	
Suspension							⊖	
Brakes							⊜	
Exhaust							⊜	
Power equip.							⊖	
Paint/trim/rust							⊖	
Integrity							○	
Hardware							○	
RELIABILITY VERDICT							✔	

Infiniti G20

TROUBLE SPOTS	95	96	97	98	99	00	01	02
Engine	⊖	⊖			⊜	Insufficient data	Insufficient data	Insufficient data
Cooling	⊖	⊜			⊜			
Fuel	⊖	⊖			⊜			
Ignition	⊜	⊜			⊜			
Transmission	⊖	⊜			⊜			
Electrical	◒	○			⊖			
A/C	○	○			⊜			
Suspension	○	⊖			⊖			
Brakes	⊖	○			⊖			
Exhaust	○	⊜			⊜			
Power equip.	⊖	⊖			⊜			
Paint/trim/rust	⊜	⊖			⊖			
Integrity	○	⊖			⊜			
Hardware	⊖	⊖			⊜			
RELIABILITY VERDICT	✓	✓			✓			

Infiniti I30, I35

TROUBLE SPOTS	95	96	97	98	99	00	01	02
Engine		⊜	⊜	⊜	⊜	⊜	⊜	⊜
Cooling		⊜	⊜	⊜	⊜	⊜	⊜	⊜
Fuel		○	⊜	⊜	⊖	⊜	⊜	⊜
Ignition		⊖	⊖	⊜	⊖	⊜	⊜	⊖
Transmission		⊖	⊜	⊜	⊜	⊜	⊜	⊜
Electrical		○	⊖	⊖	⊖	⊖	⊜	⊜
A/C		⊜	⊖	⊖	⊜	⊖	⊜	⊜
Suspension		⊜	⊜	⊜	⊖	⊜	⊜	⊜
Brakes		⊖	⊖	○	⊖	⊖	⊖	⊜
Exhaust		⊜	⊜	⊜	⊜	⊜	⊜	⊜
Power equip.		⊖	⊖	⊖	⊖	⊖	⊜	⊖
Paint/trim/rust		⊖	⊖	⊖	⊜	⊜	⊜	⊜
Integrity		⊖	⊜	○	⊜	⊖	⊖	⊖
Hardware		⊖	⊜	⊜	⊜	⊖	⊜	⊖
RELIABILITY VERDICT		✓	✓	✓	✓	✓	✓	✔

Isuzu Oasis

TROUBLE SPOTS	95	96	97	98	99	00	01	02
Engine		○	⊜	⊜	Insufficient data			
Cooling		⊜	⊜	⊜				
Fuel		⊜	⊜	⊖				
Ignition		⊜	⊜	⊜				
Transmission		⊜	⊜	⊖				
Electrical		⊖	⊖	⊜				
A/C		⊖	⊜	⊜				
Suspension		⊜	⊖	⊜				
Brakes		◒	○	○				
Exhaust		⊖	⊜	⊜				
Power equip.		⊖	⊜	⊜				
Paint/trim/rust		⊖	⊜	⊜				
Integrity		⊖	⊖	⊖				
Hardware		⊖	⊖	⊜				
RELIABILITY VERDICT		✓	✓	✓				

Isuzu Rodeo

TROUBLE SPOTS	95	96	97	98	99	00	01	02
Engine	●	Insufficient data	Insufficient data	○	○	⊖	⊜	Insufficient data
Cooling	⊖			⊜	⊜	⊜	⊜	
Fuel	⊖			○	○	○	⊖	
Ignition	○			⊖	○	⊜	⊖	
Transmission	⊖			⊜	⊖	⊜	⊖	
Electrical	●			◒	○	○	⊖	
A/C	○			○	⊖	⊖	⊜	
Suspension	⊖			○	⊖	○	○	
Brakes	◒			◒	●	○	⊜	
Exhaust	⊖			⊖	⊜	⊜	⊜	
Power equip.	●			⊖	⊖	⊖	⊖	
Paint/trim/rust	○			○	⊜	⊜	⊖	
Integrity	◒			◒	◒	●	◒	
Hardware	●			○	○	○	○	
RELIABILITY VERDICT	✔			✔				

Jaguar S-Type

TROUBLE SPOTS	95	96	97	98	99	00	01	02
Engine						⊜	⊜	Insufficient data
Cooling						⊖	⊜	
Fuel						⊖	⊜	
Ignition						⊜	⊜	
Transmission						⊖	○	
Electrical						○	○	
A/C						⊖	⊖	
Suspension						○	○	
Brakes						○	⊖	
Exhaust						⊜	⊜	
Power equip.						○	◒	
Paint/trim/rust						⊖	⊜	
Integrity						○	○	
Hardware						○	○	
RELIABILITY VERDICT								

Jaguar X-Type

TROUBLE SPOTS	95	96	97	98	99	00	01	02
Engine								⊜
Cooling								⊜
Fuel								⊖
Ignition								⊜
Transmission								⊖
Electrical								⊜
A/C								⊜
Suspension								⊜
Brakes								⊜
Exhaust								⊜
Power equip.								⊖
Paint/trim/rust								⊜
Integrity								⊖
Hardware								○
RELIABILITY VERDICT								

Jeep Cherokee

TROUBLE SPOTS	95	96	97	98	99	00	01	02
Engine	⊖	⊖	⊜	⊜	⊜	⊖	⊜	
Cooling	◒	○	⊖	⊖	⊜	⊜	⊜	
Fuel	⊖	○	◒	○	⊜	⊖	⊖	
Ignition	⊖	⊜	⊜	⊖	⊜	⊜	⊖	
Transmission	⊖	⊖	○	○	⊖	⊖	⊖	
Electrical	◒	○	◒	○	○	⊖	⊖	
A/C	◒	⊖	◒	○	⊖	⊖	⊜	
Suspension	⊖	⊖	⊖	⊖	⊖	⊖	○	
Brakes	◒	○	◒	◒	◒	○	○	
Exhaust	⊖	○	⊜	⊖	⊜	⊖	⊜	
Power equip.	○	⊖	⊖	○	○	○	⊖	
Paint/trim/rust	○	○	○	⊖	⊖	⊖	⊖	
Integrity	◒	◒	○	○	○	◒	⊖	
Hardware	○	○	○	○	◒	○	⊜	
RELIABILITY VERDICT	✔	✓	✔	✔	✔			

Jeep Grand Cherokee

TROUBLE SPOTS	95	96	97	98	99	00	01	02
Engine	○	○	○	⊖	⊖	⊖	⊜	⊜
Cooling	◒	◒	○	⊖	⊖	⊜	⊜	⊜
Fuel	○	◒	◒	○	○	○	⊖	⊖
Ignition	⊖	⊖	⊖	⊜	⊖	⊖	⊜	⊜
Transmission	◒	◒	○	◒	●	○	⊖	⊜
Electrical	◒	●	◒	◒	◒	○	⊖	⊜
A/C	●	◒	○	○	⊖	⊖	⊜	⊜
Suspension	○	○	○	◒	○	⊖	⊖	⊜
Brakes	◒	◒	●	●	●	●	◒	⊖
Exhaust	◒	○	⊜	⊜	⊜	⊜	⊜	⊜
Power equip.	◒	◒	○	○	●	○	⊖	⊜
Paint/trim/rust	⊖	⊖	⊖	⊜	⊖	⊖	⊜	⊜
Integrity	○	○	○	○	◒	○	○	⊖
Hardware	○	◒	○	○	◒	○	⊖	⊖
RELIABILITY VERDICT								

Jeep Liberty V6

TROUBLE SPOTS	95	96	97	98	99	00	01	02
Engine								⊜
Cooling								⊜
Fuel								⊜
Ignition								⊜
Transmission								⊜
Electrical								⊖
A/C								⊜
Suspension								⊜
Brakes								⊜
Exhaust								⊜
Power equip.								⊖
Paint/trim/rust								⊜
Integrity								⊖
Hardware								⊖
RELIABILITY VERDICT								✔

Jeep Wrangler

TROUBLE SPOTS	95	96	97	98	99	00	01	02
Engine	Insufficient data		⊖	⊖	⊖	⊜	⊜	Insufficient data
Cooling			○	○	⊖	⊜	⊜	
Fuel			◒	⊖	⊖	⊜	⊜	
Ignition			⊖	⊜	⊜	⊖	⊖	
Transmission			○	○	⊖	⊖	⊖	
Electrical			○	◒	●	⊖	○	
A/C			○	⊖	⊜	⊖	⊜	
Suspension			○	○	⊖	⊖	⊜	
Brakes			○	⊖	⊖	⊖	⊖	
Exhaust			◒	○	○	⊜	⊜	
Power equip.			⊜	⊜	⊜	⊖	⊜	
Paint/trim/rust			◒	○	○	○	⊖	
Integrity			◒	◒	◒	○	○	
Hardware			◒	○	○	○	⊖	
RELIABILITY VERDICT								

Kia Sedona

TROUBLE SPOTS	95	96	97	98	99	00	01	02
Engine								⊜
Cooling								⊜
Fuel								⊖
Ignition								⊜
Transmission								⊜
Electrical								⊜
A/C								⊜
Suspension								⊜
Brakes								⊜
Exhaust								⊜
Power equip.								○
Paint/trim/rust								⊖
Integrity								⊖
Hardware								⊖
RELIABILITY VERDICT								✔

Lexus ES300

TROUBLE SPOTS	95	96	97	98	99	00	01	02
Engine	○	⊖	○	⊜	⊜	⊜	⊜	⊜
Cooling	⊜	⊜	⊜	⊜	⊜	⊜	⊜	⊜
Fuel	⊖	⊜	⊜	⊖	⊜	⊜	⊜	⊜
Ignition	⊜	⊜	⊜	⊜	⊜	⊜	⊜	⊜
Transmission	⊜	⊜	⊜	⊜	⊜	⊜	⊜	⊖
Electrical	○	⊖	⊖	⊖	⊖	⊖	⊜	⊜
A/C	○	⊖	⊜	⊜	⊜	⊜	⊜	⊜
Suspension	○	⊖	○	⊖	⊜	⊜	⊜	⊜
Brakes	⊖	○	⊜	⊖	⊜	⊖	⊖	⊜
Exhaust	⊜	⊜	⊜	⊜	⊜	⊜	⊜	⊜
Power equip.	○	⊖	⊖	⊖	⊜	⊜	⊜	⊜
Paint/trim/rust	⊜	⊜	⊖	⊜	⊜	⊜	⊜	⊜
Integrity	⊖	⊖	⊖	⊜	⊖	⊖	⊖	⊖
Hardware	⊖	⊖	⊖	⊖	⊖	⊜	⊜	⊜
RELIABILITY VERDICT	✓	✓	✓	✓	✓	✓	✓	✓

Lexus GS300/GS400, GS430

TROUBLE SPOTS	95	96	97	98	99	00	01	02
Engine	Insufficient data	Insufficient data	Insufficient data	⊜	⊜	⊜	⊜	⊜
Cooling				⊜	⊜	⊜	⊜	⊜
Fuel				⊜	⊜	⊜	⊜	⊜
Ignition				⊜	⊜	⊜	⊜	⊜
Transmission				⊜	⊜	⊜	⊜	⊜
Electrical				○	⊖	⊖	⊜	⊜
A/C				⊜	⊜	⊜	⊜	⊜
Suspension				⊖	⊜	⊖	⊖	⊖
Brakes				⊖	⊖	⊜	⊖	⊜
Exhaust				⊜	⊜	⊜	⊜	⊜
Power equip.				⊖	⊖	⊖	⊜	⊖
Paint/trim/rust				⊖	⊜	⊜	⊜	⊜
Integrity				○	⊖	⊖	⊖	○
Hardware				⊖	⊜	⊜	⊖	⊜
RELIABILITY VERDICT				✓	✓	✓	✓	

Lexus IS300

TROUBLE SPOTS	95	96	97	98	99	00	01	02
Engine							⊜	Insufficient data
Cooling							⊜	
Fuel							⊜	
Ignition							⊜	
Transmission							⊖	
Electrical							⊜	
A/C							⊜	
Suspension							⊜	
Brakes							⊜	
Exhaust							⊜	
Power equip.							⊜	
Paint/trim/rust							⊜	
Integrity							⊖	
Hardware							⊖	
RELIABILITY VERDICT							✓	

Lexus LS400, LS430

TROUBLE SPOTS	95	96	97	98	99	00	01	02
Engine	⊜	⊜	⊜	⊜	⊜	⊜	⊜	⊜
Cooling	⊜	⊜	⊜	⊜	⊜	⊜	⊜	⊜
Fuel	⊜	⊜	⊜	⊜	⊜	⊖	⊜	⊜
Ignition	⊜	⊜	⊜	⊜	⊜	⊜	⊜	⊜
Transmission	⊖	⊜	⊜	⊖	⊜	⊖	⊜	⊜
Electrical	○	⊖	⊖	⊖	⊖	○	⊜	⊜
A/C	⊜	⊖	⊜	⊜	⊜	⊖	⊜	⊜
Suspension	◒	○	⊖	⊖	⊖	○	⊜	⊜
Brakes	○	○	⊖	⊖	⊜	⊖	⊖	⊜
Exhaust	⊖	⊜	⊜	⊜	⊜	⊜	⊜	⊜
Power equip.	○	⊜	⊜	⊜	⊖	○	○	⊜
Paint/trim/rust	⊜	⊜	⊖	⊜	⊜	⊜	⊜	⊜
Integrity	⊖	⊜	⊜	⊖	⊜	⊖	⊖	⊜
Hardware	⊖	⊖	⊜	⊜	⊜	⊖	⊖	⊜
RELIABILITY VERDICT	✓	✓	✓	✓	✓	✔	✓	✓

Lexus RX300

TROUBLE SPOTS	95	96	97	98	99	00	01	02
Engine					⊜	⊜	⊜	⊜
Cooling					⊜	⊜	⊜	⊜
Fuel					⊖	⊜	⊜	⊜
Ignition					⊜	⊜	⊜	⊜
Transmission					⊜	⊜	⊜	⊜
Electrical					⊖	⊖	⊜	⊜
A/C					⊜	⊜	⊜	⊜
Suspension					⊖	⊜	⊜	⊜
Brakes					⊖	⊜	⊜	⊜
Exhaust					⊜	⊜	⊜	⊜
Power equip.					⊖	⊜	⊖	⊜
Paint/trim/rust					⊖	⊜	⊜	⊜
Integrity					⊖	⊖	⊖	⊜
Hardware					○	⊖	⊖	⊜
RELIABILITY VERDICT					✓	✓	✓	✓

Lexus SC300/SC400, SC430

TROUBLE SPOTS	95	96	97	98	99	00	01	02
Engine	⊖	Insufficient data	Insufficient data	Insufficient data	Insufficient data	Insufficient data		⊜
Cooling	⊜							⊜
Fuel	⊜							⊜
Ignition	⊜							⊜
Transmission	⊜							⊜
Electrical	○							⊖
A/C	⊖							⊜
Suspension	○							⊖
Brakes	⊜							⊜
Exhaust	⊜							⊜
Power equip.	○							⊜
Paint/trim/rust	⊜							⊖
Integrity	⊜							⊖
Hardware	⊖							⊖
RELIABILITY VERDICT	✓							✔

Lincoln Continental

TROUBLE SPOTS	95	96	97	98	99	00	01	02
Engine	⊖	⊖	⊜	⊜	⊜	⊜	⊜	Insufficient data
Cooling	⊖	⊖	⊜	⊜	⊜	⊜	⊜	
Fuel	◒	⊖	⊖	⊖	○	⊜	⊖	
Ignition	○	⊜	○	⊖	⊖	⊜	⊖	
Transmission	◒	⊜	⊜	⊖	⊜	⊜	⊜	
Electrical	●	◒	◒	○	○	⊖	⊖	
A/C	○	○	○	⊖	⊜	⊜	⊖	
Suspension	●	◒	●	○	○	⊜	⊖	
Brakes	○	◒	◒	◒	○	⊜	⊜	
Exhaust	⊜	⊜	⊜	⊜	⊜	⊜	⊜	
Power equip.	●	○	◒	◒	○	○	○	
Paint/trim/rust	○	⊜	⊖	⊖	⊜	⊜	⊜	
Integrity	◒	○	◒	⊖	⊜	⊖	○	
Hardware	●	◒	○	○	○	◒	○	
RELIABILITY VERDICT	✔	✓	✔	✔	✓	✓	✔	

Lincoln LS

TROUBLE SPOTS	95	96	97	98	99	00	01	02
Engine						⊜	⊜	⊜
Cooling						⊖	⊜	⊜
Fuel						⊖	⊜	⊜
Ignition						⊖	⊜	⊜
Transmission						⊖	⊜	⊖
Electrical						○	○	⊖
A/C						⊜	⊜	⊖
Suspension						⊖	⊖	⊖
Brakes						⊖	⊜	⊜
Exhaust						⊜	⊜	⊜
Power equip.						◒	○	⊖
Paint/trim/rust						⊖	⊜	⊖
Integrity						○	○	○
Hardware						◒	○	⊜
RELIABILITY VERDICT								

Lincoln Mark VIII

TROUBLE SPOTS	95	96	97	98	99	00	01	02
Engine	Insufficient data	Insufficient data	⊜	⊖				
Cooling			⊖	⊖				
Fuel			○	⊜				
Ignition			○	◒				
Transmission			○	⊜				
Electrical			●	●				
A/C			●	◒				
Suspension			⊖	○				
Brakes			◒	●				
Exhaust			⊜	⊜				
Power equip.			◒	○				
Paint/trim/rust			○	⊖				
Integrity			⊖	⊖				
Hardware			●	○				
RELIABILITY VERDICT			✔	✔				

Lincoln Navigator

TROUBLE SPOTS	95	96	97	98	99	00	01	02
Engine				⊖	Insufficient data	⊜	Insufficient data	Insufficient data
Cooling				⊜		⊜		
Fuel				○		⊜		
Ignition				⊜		⊜		
Transmission				⊖		⊜		
Electrical				◒		⊖		
A/C				⊖		⊜		
Suspension				○		○		
Brakes				⊖		⊖		
Exhaust				⊜		⊜		
Power equip.				○		○		
Paint/trim/rust				○		⊖		
Integrity				○		⊖		
Hardware				○		○		
RELIABILITY VERDICT				✔		✓		

Lincoln Town Car	95	96	97	98	99	00	01	02
Engine	⊖	⊖	⊜	⊜	⊜	⊜	⊜	⊜
Cooling	⊜	⊖	⊖	⊜	⊜	⊜	⊜	⊜
Fuel	○	○	○	⊖	⊖	⊜	⊖	⊜
Ignition	○	⊖	⊜	⊖	⊜	⊜	⊜	⊖
Transmission	○	○	⊖	⊖	⊜	⊜	⊜	⊜
Electrical	◒	○	⊖	○	○	⊖	○	⊖
A/C	○	○	○	⊖	⊖	⊖	⊖	⊜
Suspension	◒	○	○	○	⊖	⊖	⊖	⊜
Brakes	●	◒	◒	○	⊖	⊖	⊖	⊜
Exhaust	⊜	⊖	⊜	⊜	⊜	⊜	⊜	⊜
Power equip.	○	◒	◒	◒	○	○	⊖	⊜
Paint/trim/rust	○	⊖	⊖	⊜	⊖	⊖	⊖	⊜
Integrity	○	○	⊖	○	○	⊖	○	⊜
Hardware	○	○	○	◒	○	○	○	⊜
RELIABILITY VERDICT	✓	✓	✓	✓	✓	✓		✓

Mazda 626	95	96	97	98	99	00	01	02
Engine	◒	○	⊖	⊖	⊜	⊜	⊜	Insufficient data
Cooling	○	○	⊖	⊜	⊖	⊜	⊜	
Fuel	○	○	◒	○	⊖	⊖	⊜	
Ignition	○	⊖	○	⊖	⊜	⊜	⊜	
Transmission	◒	◒	○	⊖	⊜	⊜	⊖	
Electrical	○	○	○	○	⊖	⊖	⊖	
A/C	○	⊖	⊖	⊖	⊖	⊜	⊖	
Suspension	○	○	⊖	⊜	⊖	⊜	⊜	
Brakes	◒	○	⊖	○	○	⊖	⊖	
Exhaust	○	○	◒	⊜	⊜	⊜	⊜	
Power equip.	○	⊜	⊜	⊜	⊖	⊖	⊖	
Paint/trim/rust	○	⊖	⊖	⊖	⊖	⊜	⊜	
Integrity	○	⊖	○	○	⊖	⊜	⊖	
Hardware	○	⊜	⊖	⊖	⊖	⊖	⊖	
RELIABILITY VERDICT	✔	✔	✔	✓	✓	✓	✔	

Mazda B-Series 2WD	95	96	97	98	99	00	01	02
Engine	⊖	⊖	⊖	⊜	⊖	⊜	⊜	⊜
Cooling	○	⊖	⊖	⊖	⊜	⊜	⊜	⊜
Fuel	○	○	○	⊖	○	⊖	⊖	⊜
Ignition	○	⊖	⊜	⊖	⊖	⊖	⊜	⊜
Transmission	⊖	⊖	⊖	⊖	⊖	⊖	⊖	⊜
Electrical	●	●	●	◒	◒	○	⊖	⊜
A/C	⊖	○	○	⊖	⊖	⊖	⊜	⊜
Suspension	⊖	⊖	⊖	○	⊖	⊖	⊖	⊜
Brakes	○	○	○	○	○	⊖	⊖	⊜
Exhaust	⊖	⊜	⊜	⊜	⊜	⊜	⊜	⊜
Power equip.	⊖	⊖	⊖	⊖	⊖	⊖	⊜	⊜
Paint/trim/rust	⊖	⊖	⊜	⊖	⊖	⊜	⊜	⊖
Integrity	⊖	⊖	⊖	⊖	⊖	⊖	○	⊖
Hardware	○	○	○	○	⊖	○	○	○
RELIABILITY VERDICT	✓	✓	✓	✓	✔	✔	✔	

Mazda B-Series 4WD	95	96	97	98	99	00	01	02
Engine	⊜	⊖	⊖	⊖	⊖	⊖	⊜	⊜
Cooling	⊖	○	○	⊖	⊖	⊜	⊜	⊜
Fuel	⊖	○	◒	⊖	⊖	⊖	⊖	⊜
Ignition	⊖	⊜	⊖	⊜	⊜	⊖	⊜	⊜
Transmission	⊖	○	⊖	○	⊖	○	⊖	⊜
Electrical	●	◒	◒	◒	◒	⊖	○	⊜
A/C	○	⊜	○	⊖	⊜	⊜	⊜	⊜
Suspension	○	⊖	⊖	⊖	⊖	⊖	⊖	⊜
Brakes	◒	◒	○	◒	◒	⊖	⊖	⊜
Exhaust	⊜	⊜	⊜	⊜	⊜	⊜	⊜	⊜
Power equip.	⊖	⊖	○	○	○	⊖	○	⊜
Paint/trim/rust	⊖	⊜	⊖	⊖	⊜	⊜	⊖	⊜
Integrity	⊖	⊖	⊖	⊖	○	○	◒	○
Hardware	○	⊖	⊖	○	○	○	◒	⊖
RELIABILITY VERDICT	✔	✔						

Mazda Millenia	95	96	97	98	99	00	01	02
Engine	●	Insufficient data	Insufficient data	⊖	⊜	⊜	Insufficient data	Insufficient data
Cooling	◒			⊜	⊜	⊜		
Fuel	○			◒	⊜	⊜		
Ignition	○			⊖	⊜	⊖		
Transmission	⊖			⊜	⊜	⊖		
Electrical	○			⊖	⊖	⊜		
A/C	○			⊖	⊜	⊜		
Suspension	⊖			○	◒	⊖		
Brakes	⊖			⊜	⊖	⊜		
Exhaust	⊜			⊖	⊜	⊜		
Power equip.	○			○	⊖	⊖		
Paint/trim/rust	○			⊖	⊖	⊜		
Integrity	⊖			⊜	○	○		
Hardware	○			⊖	◒	⊖		
RELIABILITY VERDICT	✔			✓	✓	✓		

Mazda MPV	95	96	97	98	99	00	01	02
Engine	Insufficient data	Insufficient data	Insufficient data	Insufficient data		⊜	⊜	Insufficient data
Cooling						⊜	⊜	
Fuel						⊜	⊜	
Ignition						⊜	⊜	
Transmission						⊜	⊜	
Electrical						⊜	⊜	
A/C						⊜	⊜	
Suspension						⊖	⊜	
Brakes						⊖	○	
Exhaust						⊜	⊜	
Power equip.						⊖	⊜	
Paint/trim/rust						⊖	⊜	
Integrity						⊖	⊖	
Hardware						○	○	
RELIABILITY VERDICT						✓	✓	

Mazda MX-5 Miata	95	96	97	98	99	00	01	02
Engine	◒	⊖	⊜		⊜	⊜	⊜	Insufficient data
Cooling	⊜	⊜	⊜		⊜	⊖	⊜	
Fuel	⊜	⊜	⊜		⊖	⊜	⊜	
Ignition	⊖	⊖	⊜		⊜	⊜	⊜	
Transmission	⊜	⊜	⊜		⊜	⊜	⊜	
Electrical	⊖	⊖	⊖		⊖	⊜	⊜	
A/C	○	⊜	⊖		⊜	⊖	⊖	
Suspension	⊜	⊜	⊜		⊜	⊜	⊖	
Brakes	⊜	⊖	⊖		⊜	⊜	⊜	
Exhaust	⊖	⊜	○		⊜	⊜	⊜	
Power equip.	○	⊖	⊜		⊜	⊜	⊜	
Paint/trim/rust	◒	○	⊖		⊜	⊜	⊜	
Integrity	◒	◒	⊖		⊖	⊖	⊖	
Hardware	⊖	○	⊖		⊖	⊜	○	
RELIABILITY VERDICT	✓	✓	✓		✓	✓	✓	

Mazda Protege	95	96	97	98	99	00	01	02
Engine	○	⊖	○	⊜	⊜	⊜	⊜	⊜
Cooling	⊖	⊜	⊖	⊜	⊜	⊜	⊜	⊜
Fuel	⊖	⊖	○	⊖	○	⊜	⊜	⊜
Ignition	○	⊜	⊜	⊜	○	⊖	⊜	⊜
Transmission	○	⊜	⊜	⊜	⊜	⊜	⊜	⊜
Electrical	◒	○	⊖	⊖	⊖	⊖	⊜	⊜
A/C	○	○	⊖	⊖	⊜	⊜	⊜	⊜
Suspension	○	⊖	⊜	⊜	⊖	⊜	⊜	⊜
Brakes	◒	◒	○	◒	⊖	⊖	⊜	⊜
Exhaust	◒	◒	○	⊖	⊖	⊜	⊜	⊜
Power equip.	⊖	⊜	⊖	⊜	⊖	⊖	⊖	⊜
Paint/trim/rust	○	⊜	⊖	⊖	⊜	⊜	⊜	⊜
Integrity	○	○	⊖	○	○	○	⊖	⊜
Hardware	◒	⊖	○	◒	○	○	⊖	⊜
RELIABILITY VERDICT	✔	✓	✓	✓	✓	✓	✓	✓

Mazda Tribute V6

TROUBLE SPOTS	95	96	97	98	99	00	01	02
Engine							⊜	⊜
Cooling							⊖	⊜
Fuel							○	⊜
Ignition							⊜	⊜
Transmission							⊖	⊜
Electrical							○	⊜
A/C							⊜	⊜
Suspension							⊖	⊜
Brakes							⊖	⊜
Exhaust							⊜	⊜
Power equip.							⊜	⊖
Paint/trim/rust							⊜	⊜
Integrity							◒	○
Hardware							○	⊖
RELIABILITY VERDICT								

Mercedes-Benz C-Class

TROUBLE SPOTS	95	96 (Insufficient data)	97	98	99	00	01	02
Engine	◒		⊖	⊜	⊖	⊜	⊖	⊜
Cooling	◒		⊜	⊖	⊜	⊜	⊜	⊜
Fuel	●		○	○	○	○	○	⊖
Ignition	○		○	⊜	⊖	⊜	⊖	⊜
Transmission	○		⊖	⊖	⊖	⊜	⊜	⊜
Electrical	●		◒	◒	●	◒	●	⊖
A/C	●		○	○	⊖	⊖	⊖	⊜
Suspension	○		⊖	⊖	⊜	⊜	⊜	⊜
Brakes	○		⊖	○	⊖	⊖	⊜	⊜
Exhaust	⊖		⊜	⊜	⊜	⊜	⊜	⊜
Power equip.	○		⊜	○	○	⊖	◒	⊖
Paint/trim/rust	⊖		⊜	⊖	⊜	⊖	⊜	⊜
Integrity	○		⊖	⊖	⊖	⊖	⊖	⊜
Hardware	●		○	◒	○	○	○	⊖
RELIABILITY VERDICT			✓	✓	✓	✓		✓

Mercedes-Benz CLK

TROUBLE SPOTS	95	96	97	98 (Insufficient data)	99	00	01	02 (Insufficient data)
Engine					⊜	⊜	⊜	
Cooling					⊜	⊜	⊜	
Fuel					◒	○	⊜	
Ignition					⊜	⊜	⊜	
Transmission					○	○	⊜	
Electrical					●	◒	◒	
A/C					⊖	⊖	⊖	
Suspension					⊖	⊖	⊜	
Brakes					⊜	⊖	⊜	
Exhaust					⊜	⊜	⊜	
Power equip.					○	●	●	
Paint/trim/rust					⊖	⊜	⊜	
Integrity					○	○	⊖	
Hardware					●	◒	◒	
RELIABILITY VERDICT					✓			

Mercedes-Benz E-Class

TROUBLE SPOTS	95	96	97	98	99	00	01	02
Engine	◒	⊖	◒	⊖	⊖	⊜	⊜	⊜
Cooling	○	⊖	⊜	⊖	⊜	⊜	⊜	⊜
Fuel	○	◒	○	⊖	⊖	○	⊖	⊜
Ignition	⊜	○	⊖	⊖	⊜	⊜	⊜	⊜
Transmission	⊖	⊖	○	○	⊖	⊖	⊜	⊜
Electrical	◒	●	●	●	◒	◒	○	⊜
A/C	○	○	○	⊖	⊖	○	○	⊜
Suspension	⊖	⊖	○	⊖	⊜	○	⊜	⊜
Brakes	◒	○	⊖	⊖	⊜	⊖	⊜	⊜
Exhaust	⊖	⊜	⊖	⊜	⊜	⊜	⊜	⊜
Power equip.	◒	◒	○	●	◒	◒	○	⊖
Paint/trim/rust	⊖	⊖	⊜	⊜	⊖	⊖	⊜	⊜
Integrity	⊖	⊖	⊜	⊖	⊖	⊖	⊖	⊜
Hardware	○	○	◒	◒	◒	◒	○	⊖
RELIABILITY VERDICT	✓	✓	✓		✓		✓	✓

Mercedes-Benz M-Class

TROUBLE SPOTS	95	96	97	98	99	00	01	02
Engine				⊖	⊖	⊜	⊜	⊜
Cooling				⊜	⊜	⊖	⊜	⊜
Fuel				●	◒	⊖	○	⊜
Ignition				⊖	⊜	⊖	⊜	⊜
Transmission				○	⊖	⊜	⊜	⊜
Electrical				●	◒	◒	○	⊖
A/C				⊖	⊖	⊜	⊜	⊖
Suspension				○	⊖	⊖	⊖	⊜
Brakes				○	○	◒	⊖	⊖
Exhaust				⊜	⊜	⊜	⊜	⊜
Power equip.				●	◒	●	●	○
Paint/trim/rust				⊖	⊖	⊖	⊖	⊜
Integrity				●	●	●	◒	○
Hardware				●	●	●	●	○
RELIABILITY VERDICT								

Mercedes-Benz S-Class

TROUBLE SPOTS	95 (Insufficient data)	96 (Insufficient data)	97 (Insufficient data)	98 (Insufficient data)	99 (Insufficient data)	00	01 (Insufficient data)	02 (Insufficient data)
Engine						⊜		
Cooling						⊖		
Fuel						○		
Ignition						⊜		
Transmission						⊜		
Electrical						◒		
A/C						○		
Suspension						◒		
Brakes						⊖		
Exhaust						⊜		
Power equip.						●		
Paint/trim/rust						⊖		
Integrity						⊖		
Hardware						◒		
RELIABILITY VERDICT								

Mercedes-Benz SLK

TROUBLE SPOTS	95	96	97	98	99 (Insufficient data)	00 (Insufficient data)	01	02 (Insufficient data)
Engine				⊖			⊜	
Cooling				⊜			⊜	
Fuel				◒			○	
Ignition				⊜			⊜	
Transmission				⊜			⊜	
Electrical				●			○	
A/C				⊜			⊜	
Suspension				⊖			⊜	
Brakes				○			⊖	
Exhaust				⊜			○	
Power equip.				○			⊖	
Paint/trim/rust				⊜			○	
Integrity				○			◒	
Hardware				◒			○	
RELIABILITY VERDICT				✓				

Mercury Cougar

TROUBLE SPOTS	95	96	97	98	99	00	01 (Insufficient data)	02 (Insufficient data)
Engine	○	○	⊖		⊖	⊜		
Cooling	○	●	◒		⊖	⊜		
Fuel	◒	○	⊖		○	◒		
Ignition	◒	⊜	⊜		⊜	⊖		
Transmission	●	○	○		⊖	⊜		
Electrical	◒	○	○		●	○		
A/C	○	⊖	○		○	⊖		
Suspension	⊖	⊖	⊖		⊖	⊜		
Brakes	◒	◒	◒		◒	○		
Exhaust	⊜	⊜	⊜		⊜	⊜		
Power equip.	○	⊖	⊖		◒	○		
Paint/trim/rust	◒	⊜	⊜		⊖	⊜		
Integrity	◒	○	○		◒	○		
Hardware	◒	⊜	○		●	◒		
RELIABILITY VERDICT	✓	✓	✓			✓		

Mercury Grand Marquis

TROUBLE SPOTS	95	96	97	98	99	00	01	02
Engine	⊖	⊖	⊖	⊜	⊜	⊜	⊖	⊜
Cooling	⊜	⊖	⊖	⊜	⊜	⊜	⊜	⊜
Fuel	◒	○	○	⊖	⊖	⊜	⊖	⊜
Ignition	○	○	⊖	⊜	⊜	⊜	⊜	⊜
Transmission	○	⊖	⊖	⊜	⊜	⊜	⊜	⊜
Electrical	◒	○	○	⊖	⊖	○	⊖	⊖
A/C	○	○	⊖	⊜	⊜	⊜	⊜	⊜
Suspension	◒	○	⊖	⊖	⊖	⊖	⊖	⊖
Brakes	●	◒	◒	⊖	○	⊖	⊖	⊜
Exhaust	⊜	⊖	⊖	⊜	⊜	⊜	⊜	⊜
Power equip.	●	◒	○	⊖	⊖	⊖	⊖	⊖
Paint/trim/rust	⊖	⊖	⊖	⊜	⊜	⊖	⊜	⊜
Integrity	⊖	○	⊖	○	⊖	◒	○	○
Hardware	●	◒	○	⊖	⊖	⊖	○	⊖
RELIABILITY VERDICT	✔	✔	✓	✓	✓	✔	✔	

Mercury Mountaineer 4WD

TROUBLE SPOTS	95	96	97	98	99	00	01	02
Engine			○	○	⊖	⊖	⊜	⊜
Cooling			○	⊜	⊜	⊖	⊜	⊜
Fuel			○	○	○	⊖	⊖	⊜
Ignition			⊜	⊖	⊖	⊜	⊜	⊖
Transmission			⊖	⊖	⊖	⊖	⊖	⊖
Electrical			○	◒	◒	◒	○	⊖
A/C			◒	⊖	⊜	⊜	⊜	⊜
Suspension			○	○	⊜	⊖	⊖	⊜
Brakes			◒	○	○	○	⊖	⊜
Exhaust			⊖	⊜	⊜	⊜	⊜	⊜
Power equip.			○	◒	○	○	⊖	⊖
Paint/trim/rust			⊜	⊜	⊖	⊜	⊖	⊖
Integrity			⊖	○	○	○	○	⊖
Hardware			○	○	○	○	○	⊖
RELIABILITY VERDICT			✔					

Mercury Mystique V6

TROUBLE SPOTS	95	96	97	98	99	00	01	02
Engine	○	○	⊖	⊖	⊖	⊜		
Cooling	●	◒	○	○	⊜	⊜		
Fuel	●	●	●	◒	○	○		
Ignition	○	⊖	⊖	⊖	⊖	⊜		
Transmission	○	○	○	⊖	⊜	⊖		
Electrical	◒	●	●	◒	◒	○		
A/C	◒	⊖	○	⊖	○	⊜		
Suspension	◒	◒	⊖	○	⊖	⊖		
Brakes	◒	◒	●	◒	○	⊖		
Exhaust	⊖	○	○	○	⊖	⊜		
Power equip.	○	◒	◒	⊖	⊖	⊜		
Paint/trim/rust	○	⊖	○	⊖	⊖	⊖		
Integrity	◒	◒	○	○	●	◒		
Hardware	◒	○	⊖	○	◒	◒		
RELIABILITY VERDICT					✔	✔		

Mercury Sable

TROUBLE SPOTS	95	96	97	98	99	00	01	02
Engine	◒	○	⊖	⊜	⊖	⊖	⊖	⊜
Cooling	●	○	⊖	⊖	⊜	⊜	⊜	⊜
Fuel	○	○	○	⊖	⊖	○	⊖	⊜
Ignition	⊖	⊖	⊖	⊖	⊜	⊖	⊜	⊜
Transmission	◒	◒	○	○	⊖	⊖	⊖	⊜
Electrical	●	◒	◒	◒	○	◒	⊖	⊖
A/C	◒	⊖	⊖	⊖	⊖	⊖	⊜	⊜
Suspension	◒	○	○	⊖	○	○	⊖	⊜
Brakes	◒	◒	◒	◒	◒	◒	⊖	⊜
Exhaust	⊖	⊜	⊜	⊜	⊜	⊜	⊜	⊜
Power equip.	○	○	○	○	⊖	⊖	⊜	⊜
Paint/trim/rust	○	⊖	⊖	⊖	⊖	⊖	⊜	⊜
Integrity	●	◒	○	⊖	⊖	○	○	⊖
Hardware	◒	○	○	○	○	○	⊖	⊖
RELIABILITY VERDICT		✔	✔	✔	✔	✔	✔	✔

Mercury Tracer

TROUBLE SPOTS	95	96	97	98	99	00	01	02
Engine	◒	◒	⊖	⊖	⊜			
Cooling	◒	◒	○	⊖	⊜			
Fuel	⊖	◒	⊖	⊖	⊖			
Ignition	⊖	⊖	⊖	⊜	⊜			
Transmission	⊖	⊖	⊖	⊖	⊜			
Electrical	◒	◒	○	○	⊖			
A/C	○	○	⊖	⊖	⊜			
Suspension	○	○	○	○	○			
Brakes	◒	○	○	○	○			
Exhaust	⊖	⊖	⊜	⊜	⊜			
Power equip.	⊖	⊜	⊜	⊜	⊖			
Paint/trim/rust	○	○	⊖	⊖	⊖			
Integrity	○	○	⊜	○	○			
Hardware	◒	○	⊖	⊖	⊖			
RELIABILITY VERDICT	✔	✔	✓	✓	✓			

Mercury Villager

TROUBLE SPOTS	95	96	97	98	99	00	01	02
Engine	○	⊖	⊖	⊖	⊜	⊜	⊜	Insufficient data
Cooling	○	○	⊖	⊜	⊜	⊜	⊜	
Fuel	●	◒	◒	○	○	⊖	⊜	
Ignition	⊖	⊖	⊜	⊜	⊜	⊜	⊜	
Transmission	⊜	⊖	⊖	⊖	⊖	⊜	⊖	
Electrical	●	●	◒	○	◒	○	⊖	
A/C	◒	○	○	○	⊜	⊜	⊜	
Suspension	○	○	⊖	⊖	○	○	⊖	
Brakes	○	◒	○	◒	○	⊖	⊖	
Exhaust	○	⊜	⊖	⊜	⊜	⊜	⊜	
Power equip.	○	●	●	●	◒	○	⊖	
Paint/trim/rust	○	⊖	⊖	⊖	⊖	⊖	⊖	
Integrity	◒	◒	○	○	◒	○	○	
Hardware	●	●	●	◒	◒	◒	○	
RELIABILITY VERDICT	✔	✔	✔	✔	✔	✓	✔	

Mitsubishi Eclipse

TROUBLE SPOTS	95	96	97	98	99	00	01	02
Engine	Insufficient data	Insufficient data	Insufficient data	Insufficient data	Insufficient data	⊜	⊜	Insufficient data
Cooling						⊜	⊜	
Fuel						⊜	⊜	
Ignition						⊜	⊜	
Transmission						⊜	⊖	
Electrical						⊖	⊖	
A/C						⊜	⊜	
Suspension						⊖	⊖	
Brakes						⊖	⊜	
Exhaust						⊜	⊜	
Power equip.						○	○	
Paint/trim/rust						⊖	⊖	
Integrity						⊖	◒	
Hardware						○	○	
RELIABILITY VERDICT						✓		

Mitsubishi Galant

TROUBLE SPOTS	95	96	97	98	99	00	01	02
Engine	○	Insufficient data	Insufficient data	Insufficient data	⊜	⊜	⊜	Insufficient data
Cooling	○				⊜	⊖	⊖	
Fuel	⊖				⊖	⊜	⊖	
Ignition	⊖				⊜	⊜	⊜	
Transmission	○				⊖	⊜	⊖	
Electrical	◒				◒	○	⊖	
A/C	◒				⊜	⊜	⊜	
Suspension	●				⊖	⊖	⊖	
Brakes	◒				●	○	○	
Exhaust	⊖				⊜	⊜	⊜	
Power equip.	○				⊜	⊜	⊜	
Paint/trim/rust	○				◒	○	⊖	
Integrity	◒				◒	○	○	
Hardware	◒				◒	○	○	
RELIABILITY VERDICT	✔				✔	✔		

Nissan Altima

TROUBLE SPOTS	95	96	97	98	99	00	01	02
Engine	◒	○	⊖	⊜	⊜	⊖	⊜	⊜
Cooling	○	⊜	⊜	⊜	⊜	⊜	⊜	⊜
Fuel	○	⊖	⊜	⊖	⊜	⊜	⊜	⊜
Ignition	○	⊜	⊜	⊜	⊜	⊜	⊜	⊜
Transmission	⊖	⊖	⊖	⊜	⊜	⊜	⊜	⊜
Electrical	●	◒	○	⊖	⊖	⊖	⊜	⊜
A/C	○	⊖	⊜	⊖	⊜	⊜	⊜	⊜
Suspension	○	⊖	○	⊜	⊖	⊖	⊖	⊜
Brakes	○	○	○	○	○	⊖	⊜	⊜
Exhaust	○	○	⊖	⊜	⊜	⊜	⊜	⊜
Power equip.	○	⊖	⊖	⊖	⊖	⊖	⊖	⊜
Paint/trim/rust	◒	⊖	○	⊖	⊖	⊖	⊜	⊜
Integrity	◒	⊖	○	◒	○	○	○	⊖
Hardware	○	⊖	⊖	⊖	○	○	⊖	⊖
RELIABILITY VERDICT	✔	✓	✓	✓	✓	✓	✓	✔

Nissan Maxima

TROUBLE SPOTS	95	96	97	98	99	00	01	02
Engine	⊖	⊜	⊜	⊜	⊜	⊜	⊜	⊜
Cooling	⊜	⊜	⊜	⊜	⊜	⊜	⊜	⊜
Fuel	◒	⊖	○	⊖	○	⊖	⊖	⊜
Ignition	○	⊜	⊜	⊖	○	⊖	⊜	⊜
Transmission	⊖	⊜	⊜	⊜	⊜	⊜	⊜	⊜
Electrical	●	○	○	○	○	⊜	⊜	⊜
A/C	⊖	⊖	⊖	⊜	⊜	⊜	⊜	⊜
Suspension	⊖	⊖	⊜	⊖	⊜	⊜	⊜	⊜
Brakes	◒	○	○	○	○	○	⊖	⊜
Exhaust	⊖	⊜	⊜	⊜	⊜	⊜	⊜	⊜
Power equip.	⊖	⊖	⊖	⊜	⊜	⊖	⊜	⊜
Paint/trim/rust	⊖	⊖	⊖	⊖	⊜	⊜	⊜	⊜
Integrity	⊖	⊖	⊖	⊜	⊖	⊖	⊖	⊜
Hardware	⊖	⊖	⊖	⊜	⊜	⊜	⊜	⊜
RELIABILITY VERDICT	✓	✓	✓	✓	✓	✓	✓	✓

Nissan Pathfinder

TROUBLE SPOTS	95	96	97	98	99	00	01	02
Engine	⊖	⊖	⊜	⊜	⊜	⊜	⊜	⊜
Cooling	⊖	⊜	⊜	⊜	⊜	⊜	⊜	⊜
Fuel	⊖	○	○	⊖	⊖	⊜	⊜	⊜
Ignition	⊜	⊜	⊜	⊜	⊜	⊖	⊜	⊜
Transmission	⊖	⊖	⊖	⊜	⊜	⊜	⊜	⊜
Electrical	◒	⊖	⊖	⊖	⊖	⊖	⊜	⊜
A/C	⊜	⊖	⊜	⊜	⊜	⊜	⊜	⊜
Suspension	○	◒	○	○	⊜	⊖	⊜	⊜
Brakes	○	○	⊖	○	⊖	⊖	⊜	⊜
Exhaust	○	●	●	⊜	⊜	⊜	⊜	⊜
Power equip.	⊜	⊜	⊖	⊜	⊜	⊖	⊖	⊖
Paint/trim/rust	○	⊖	⊖	⊖	⊜	⊜	⊜	⊜
Integrity	○	○	⊖	○	⊖	⊖	⊜	⊜
Hardware	○	⊜	⊖	○	⊖	⊖	⊖	⊖
RELIABILITY VERDICT	✓	✓	✓	✓	✓	✓	✓	✓

Nissan Pickup, Frontier

TROUBLE SPOTS	95	96	97	98	99	00	01	02
Engine	⊖	⊜	○	⊖	⊜	⊜	⊜	⊜
Cooling	⊖	⊖	⊜	⊜	⊜	⊜	⊜	⊜
Fuel	⊖	◒	○	⊖	⊖	⊜	⊜	⊖
Ignition	⊖	⊖	⊖	⊜	⊜	⊜	⊜	⊜
Transmission	⊖	⊖	⊜	⊜	⊜	⊜	⊜	⊜
Electrical	◒	○	○	○	⊖	⊖	⊜	⊖
A/C	⊖	⊜	⊜	⊖	⊜	⊖	⊜	⊖
Suspension	⊖	⊜	⊜	⊖	⊖	⊖	⊖	⊜
Brakes	○	⊖	⊖	⊜	⊖	⊖	⊖	⊖
Exhaust	⊖	⊜	⊜	⊜	⊜	⊜	⊜	⊜
Power equip.	⊜	⊜	⊜	⊜	⊜	⊜	⊜	⊜
Paint/trim/rust	○	⊖	⊖	⊖	⊜	⊖	⊖	⊜
Integrity	○	○	○	○	○	○	○	⊖
Hardware	○	⊖	○	○	⊖	⊖	⊖	⊜
RELIABILITY VERDICT	✓	✓	✓	✓	✓	✓	✓	✔

Nissan Quest

TROUBLE SPOTS	95	96	97	98	99	00	01	02
Engine	○	⊖	⊖	⊖	⊜	⊜	⊜	Insufficient data
Cooling	○	○	⊖	⊜	⊜	⊜	⊜	
Fuel	●	◒	◒	○	○	⊖	⊜	
Ignition	⊖	⊖	⊜	⊜	⊜	⊜	⊜	
Transmission	⊖	⊖	⊖	⊖	⊖	⊜	⊖	
Electrical	●	●	◒	○	◒	○	⊖	
A/C	◒	○	○	○	⊖	⊜	⊜	
Suspension	○	○	⊜	⊖	○	○	⊖	
Brakes	○	◒	○	◒	○	⊖	⊖	
Exhaust	○	⊜	⊖	⊜	⊜	⊜	⊜	
Power equip.	○	●	●	●	◒	○	⊖	
Paint/trim/rust	○	⊖	⊖	⊖	⊖	⊖	⊖	
Integrity	◒	◒	○	○	◒	○	○	
Hardware	●	●	●	◒	◒	◒	○	
RELIABILITY VERDICT	✔	✔	✔	✔	✔	✓	✔	

Nissan Sentra

TROUBLE SPOTS	95	96	97	98	99	00	01	02
Engine	○	○	○	○	⊜	○	⊖	⊜
Cooling	⊖	⊜	⊜	⊜	⊜	⊜	⊜	⊜
Fuel	○	○	○	○	⊜	⊖	⊜	⊜
Ignition	◒	⊖	⊖	⊖	⊜	○	⊜	⊜
Transmission	○	⊖	⊜	⊖	⊜	⊜	⊜	⊜
Electrical	●	●	○	○	○	○	⊖	⊜
A/C	◒	○	⊖	○	⊜	⊖	⊜	⊜
Suspension	⊖	○	⊖	⊖	⊖	○	○	⊖
Brakes	◒	◒	○	○	⊖	⊖	⊖	⊜
Exhaust	○	⊖	⊜	⊜	⊜	⊜	⊜	⊜
Power equip.	○	⊖	⊖	⊖	⊖	⊜	⊜	⊖
Paint/trim/rust	◒	◒	⊖	⊖	○	⊖	⊖	⊖
Integrity	○	○	◒	○	⊖	○	⊖	⊖
Hardware	○	○	◒	○	⊖	⊖	⊖	⊖
RELIABILITY VERDICT	✔	✔	✓	✔	✓		✔	✔

Nissan Xterra

TROUBLE SPOTS	95	96	97	98	99	00	01	02
Engine						⊜	⊜	Insufficient data
Cooling						⊜	⊜	
Fuel						⊜	⊜	
Ignition						⊜	⊜	
Transmission						⊜	⊜	
Electrical						⊖	⊖	
A/C						⊖	⊜	
Suspension						⊖	⊖	
Brakes						⊖	⊜	
Exhaust						⊜	⊜	
Power equip.						⊖	○	
Paint/trim/rust						⊜	⊖	
Integrity						○	⊖	
Hardware						○	⊖	
RELIABILITY VERDICT						✔	✔	

Oldsmobile 88

TROUBLE SPOTS	95	96	97	98	99	00	01	02
Engine	◒	○	○	○	⊜			
Cooling	○	◒	●	○	⊖			
Fuel	⊖	○	◒	○	○			
Ignition	⊖	⊖	○	○	⊜			
Transmission	○	○	○	○	○			
Electrical	◒	○	●	●	○			
A/C	◒	○	⊖	⊜	⊖			
Suspension	○	⊖	○	⊖	⊖			
Brakes	●	○	●	○	○			
Exhaust	⊖	⊜	⊜	⊜	⊜			
Power equip.	◒	○	○	⊜	⊖			
Paint/trim/rust	○	⊖	⊖	⊖	⊖			
Integrity	○	○	⊖	○	○			
Hardware	◒	○	○	○	○			
RELIABILITY VERDICT	✔	✔		✔	✔			

Oldsmobile Alero

TROUBLE SPOTS	95	96	97	98	99	00	01	02
Engine					○	⊖	⊖	Insufficient data
Cooling					⊖	⊜	⊜	
Fuel					⊖	⊖	⊖	
Ignition					⊖	⊜	⊖	
Transmission					⊖	⊖	⊖	
Electrical					●	○	⊖	
A/C					⊜	⊖	⊜	
Suspension					○	○	⊖	
Brakes					●	●	⊖	
Exhaust					⊜	⊜	⊜	
Power equip.					○	○	⊖	
Paint/trim/rust					⊖	⊜	⊖	
Integrity					◒	◒	○	
Hardware					◒	◒	○	
RELIABILITY VERDICT								

Oldsmobile Aurora

TROUBLE SPOTS	95	96	97	98	99	00	01	02
Engine	◒	Insufficient data	Insufficient data	Insufficient data	Insufficient data		⊜	Insufficient data
Cooling	●						⊖	
Fuel	●						⊖	
Ignition	○						⊖	
Transmission	◒						⊜	
Electrical	●						○	
A/C	●						⊜	
Suspension	◒						○	
Brakes	●						⊜	
Exhaust	⊜						⊜	
Power equip.	◒						⊖	
Paint/trim/rust	○						⊜	
Integrity	○						○	
Hardware	●						⊖	
RELIABILITY VERDICT								

Oldsmobile Bravada

TROUBLE SPOTS	95	96	97	98	99	00	01	02
Engine		Insufficient data	Insufficient data	⊖	⊖	⊜	Insufficient data	⊜
Cooling				⊖	⊖	⊜		⊜
Fuel				○	⊜	⊜		⊖
Ignition				⊖	⊜	⊖		⊜
Transmission				◒	◒	⊖		⊖
Electrical				●	◒	◒		○
A/C				○	⊖	⊜		⊜
Suspension				○	⊖	⊜		○
Brakes				⊖	⊖	⊖		⊜
Exhaust				⊜	⊖	⊜		⊜
Power equip.				◒	○	⊜		○
Paint/trim/rust				⊖	◒	⊖		⊜
Integrity				○	◒	○		○
Hardware				◒	○	○		○
RELIABILITY VERDICT						✓		

Oldsmobile Ciera, Cutlass

TROUBLE SPOTS	95	96	97	98	99	00	01	02
Engine	○	◒	○	◒	○			
Cooling	⊖	◒	◒	◒	○			
Fuel	○	◒	○	⊖	⊖			
Ignition	⊜	⊖	⊖	⊖	⊖			
Transmission	○	⊖	⊜	⊜	⊖			
Electrical	●	●	●	●	●			
A/C	○	⊖	○	◒	○			
Suspension	○	⊖	○	○	⊖			
Brakes	◒	●	●	●	●			
Exhaust	◒	⊜	⊜	⊜	⊜			
Power equip.	◒	○	⊖	○	○			
Paint/trim/rust	◒	○	⊖	⊜	⊖			
Integrity	○	○	○	◒	○			
Hardware	○	◒	○	○	○			
RELIABILITY VERDICT	✓	✓						

Oldsmobile Cutlass Supreme

TROUBLE SPOTS	95	96	97	98	99	00	01	02
Engine	○	○	⊜					
Cooling	○	○	○					
Fuel	○	◒	⊖					
Ignition	⊖	⊖	⊜					
Transmission	○	⊜	⊖					
Electrical	●	●	●					
A/C	◒	○	⊜					
Suspension	○	⊖	⊖					
Brakes	●	●	●					
Exhaust	⊖	⊜	⊜					
Power equip.	○	○	○					
Paint/trim/rust	○	○	○					
Integrity	◒	●	◒					
Hardware	◒	●	◒					
RELIABILITY VERDICT	✓	✓	✓					

Oldsmobile Intrigue

TROUBLE SPOTS	95	96	97	98	99	00	01	02
Engine				⊖	⊖	⊜	⊜	⊜
Cooling				⊖	⊖	⊜	⊜	⊜
Fuel				⊜	⊖	○	⊖	⊜
Ignition				⊜	⊖	⊜	⊜	⊜
Transmission				⊖	⊖	⊜	⊜	⊜
Electrical				◒	◒	◒	○	⊖
A/C				⊖	⊖	⊖	⊜	⊜
Suspension				○	◒	⊖	⊜	⊖
Brakes				◒	○	⊖	⊜	⊜
Exhaust				⊜	⊜	⊜	⊜	⊜
Power equip.				○	○	⊖	⊖	⊜
Paint/trim/rust				○	⊜	⊖	⊜	⊜
Integrity				○	○	○	⊖	○
Hardware				◒	○	○	⊖	○
RELIABILITY VERDICT				✓	✓	✓	(✓)	

Oldsmobile Silhouette (ext.)

TROUBLE SPOTS	95	96	97	98	99	00	01	02
Engine			○	○	○	⊜	⊜	⊜
Cooling			○	⊖	○	⊖	⊜	⊜
Fuel			○	⊖	⊖	⊖	⊖	⊜
Ignition			⊜	⊜	⊖	⊜	⊜	⊜
Transmission			⊖	⊖	○	⊖	⊜	⊜
Electrical			◒	◒	◒	◒	⊖	⊜
A/C			⊖	⊖	⊖	⊜	⊖	⊜
Suspension			○	⊖	⊖	⊖	⊖	⊜
Brakes			◒	◒	◒	○	⊜	⊜
Exhaust			⊜	⊜	⊜	⊜	⊜	⊜
Power equip.			●	●	●	◒	○	⊖
Paint/trim/rust			⊖	⊜	⊖	⊖	⊜	⊜
Integrity			●	◒	◒	◒	○	⊖
Hardware			●	●	●	●	◒	⊖
RELIABILITY VERDICT							✓	

Oldsmobile Silhouette (reg.)

TROUBLE SPOTS	95	96	97	98	99	00	01	02
Engine	◒	⊖	○	⊖	○	⊖	⊜	Insufficient data
Cooling	◒	◒	○	⊖	○	⊖	⊜	
Fuel	○	⊜	○	○	○	⊖	⊖	
Ignition	○	⊜	⊜	⊖	⊖	⊜	⊜	
Transmission	◒	○	○	⊖	◒	⊖	⊜	
Electrical	●	●	◒	●	◒	○	○	
A/C	○	⊖	⊖	⊖	⊜	⊜	⊜	
Suspension	◒	◒	○	⊖	⊖	⊖	⊜	
Brakes	●	●	◒	◒	◒	○	⊖	
Exhaust	⊖	⊜	⊜	⊜	⊜	⊜	⊜	
Power equip.	◒	◒	◒	◒	◒	○	⊖	
Paint/trim/rust	◒	◒	⊜	⊖	⊖	⊖	⊜	
Integrity	◒	○	○	○	○	○	○	
Hardware	●	◒	◒	●	●	●	○	
RELIABILITY VERDICT		✓	✓	✓			✓	

Plymouth Breeze

TROUBLE SPOTS	95	96	97	98	99	00	01	02
Engine		●	●	●	◒	⊜		
Cooling		○	○	⊜	⊜	⊜		
Fuel		○	○	⊜	⊖	⊜		
Ignition		○	⊖	⊜	⊜	⊜		
Transmission		○	○	⊖	⊖	⊖		
Electrical		◒	⊖	○	⊜	⊖		
A/C		○	○	⊖	⊖	⊖		
Suspension		●	○	○	⊖	⊖		
Brakes		◒	◒	◒	○	◒		
Exhaust		⊖	⊜	⊜	⊜	⊜		
Power equip.		○	⊖	○	⊖	○		
Paint/trim/rust		○	⊖	○	⊜	⊜		
Integrity		●	○	○	⊖	⊖		
Hardware		○	⊖	⊖	⊖	○		
RELIABILITY VERDICT					✓	✓		

Plymouth Grand Voyager V6 2WD

TROUBLE SPOTS	95	96	97	98	99	00	01	02
Engine	○	◒	○	○	⊖	⊖		
Cooling	◒	◒	◒	⊖	⊖	⊖		
Fuel	○	●	◒	⊖	⊖	⊖		
Ignition	⊖	⊖	⊜	⊜	⊜	⊜		
Transmission	●	●	○	○	◒	◒		
Electrical	◒	●	●	◒	○	○		
A/C	●	●	○	⊖	⊖	⊖		
Suspension	○	○	○	⊖	⊖	⊖		
Brakes	◒	●	◒	◒	◒	○		
Exhaust	⊜	⊜	⊜	⊜	⊜	⊜		
Power equip.	◒	●	◒	○	○	○		
Paint/trim/rust	◒	○	⊖	⊖	⊜	⊖		
Integrity	◒	◒	◒	○	○	○		
Hardware	◒	●	◒	○	○	○		
RELIABILITY VERDICT				✓	✓			

Plymouth/Chrysler Voyager V6

TROUBLE SPOTS	95	96	97	98	99	00	01	02
Engine	◒	◒	◒	○	⊖	⊖	⊜	⊜
Cooling	○	◒	○	⊖	⊜	⊜	⊜	⊜
Fuel	○	◒	○	⊖	⊖	⊜	⊜	⊜
Ignition	⊖	⊖	⊜	⊜	⊜	⊜	⊜	⊜
Transmission	●	●	◒	○	◒	◒	⊜	⊖
Electrical	◒	●	●	◒	○	⊖	○	⊜
A/C	●	●	◒	○	⊖	⊜	⊖	⊜
Suspension	○	○	○	⊖	○	⊖	⊖	⊜
Brakes	◒	●	◒	◒	○	○	⊖	⊜
Exhaust	⊜	⊜	⊜	⊜	⊜	⊜	⊜	⊜
Power equip.	○	◒	○	⊖	⊖	⊖	○	⊜
Paint/trim/rust	◒	○	⊜	⊖	⊜	⊜	⊖	⊜
Integrity	◒	◒	○	○	○	⊖	○	⊖
Hardware	◒	◒	○	○	○	○	◒	⊖
RELIABILITY VERDICT				✓		✓		

Pontiac Aztek

TROUBLE SPOTS	95	96	97	98	99	00	01	02
Engine							⊜	Insufficient data
Cooling							⊜	
Fuel							⊜	
Ignition							⊜	
Transmission							⊜	
Electrical							○	
A/C							⊜	
Suspension							⊜	
Brakes							⊜	
Exhaust							⊜	
Power equip.							⊖	
Paint/trim/rust							⊜	
Integrity							⊖	
Hardware							○	
RELIABILITY VERDICT							✓	

Pontiac Bonneville

TROUBLE SPOTS	95	96	97	98	99	00	01	02
Engine	◒	◒	◒	○	⊖	⊖	⊜	⊜
Cooling	●	◒	●	○	⊖	⊜	⊜	⊜
Fuel	○	○	○	○	○	⊖	⊜	⊜
Ignition	○	⊖	○	⊖	⊖	⊖	⊜	⊜
Transmission	○	○	○	⊖	⊖	⊖	⊜	⊜
Electrical	◒	◒	●	◒	○	○	○	⊖
A/C	◒	○	○	⊖	⊜	⊖	⊜	⊜
Suspension	○	⊖	○	⊖	⊖	◒	○	⊖
Brakes	●	○	○	○	⊜	○	⊖	⊜
Exhaust	⊜	⊜	⊜	⊜	⊜	⊜	⊜	⊜
Power equip.	●	○	⊖	⊖	○	○	⊖	⊜
Paint/trim/rust	○	⊖	⊖	⊖	⊖	○	○	⊜
Integrity	◒	○	○	○	○	◒	◒	○
Hardware	●	○	⊖	⊖	○	○	○	○
RELIABILITY VERDICT		✓		✓	✓			

Pontiac Firebird

TROUBLE SPOTS	95	96	97	98	99	00	01	02
Engine	◒	◒	○	⊜	○	⊖	Insufficient data	Insufficient data
Cooling	○	◒	○	⊜	○	⊜		
Fuel	○	◒	○	○	○	⊜		
Ignition	○	◒	○	⊖	⊖	⊜		
Transmission	⊖	⊖	⊖	○	⊖	⊖		
Electrical	●	●	●	●	◒	○		
A/C	○	○	⊖	⊜	⊖	⊖		
Suspension	⊖	○	⊖	⊖	⊖	⊜		
Brakes	●	◒	⊖	●	◒	○		
Exhaust	⊖	⊖	⊜	⊖	⊜	○		
Power equip.	●	●	●	◒	◒	○		
Paint/trim/rust	○	⊖	○	⊜	⊖	⊜		
Integrity	◒	◒	◒	◒	◒	●		
Hardware	●	○	◒	○	◒	◒		
RELIABILITY VERDICT	✓							

Pontiac Grand Am

TROUBLE SPOTS	95	96	97	98	99	00	01	02
Engine	◒	◒	◒	⊖	○	⊖	⊜	⊜
Cooling	◒	●	◒	○	⊖	⊜	⊜	⊜
Fuel	◒	◒	◒	⊖	○	○	⊖	⊖
Ignition	○	◒	◒	⊖	⊖	⊜	⊜	⊖
Transmission	○	⊖	⊖	⊖	⊜	⊜	⊜	⊜
Electrical	●	●	●	●	●	○	⊖	⊖
A/C	◒	◒	○	⊖	⊖	⊜	⊜	⊜
Suspension	○	○	○	○	○	⊖	⊖	⊜
Brakes	●	●	●	●	●	●	○	⊖
Exhaust	○	○	⊜	⊜	⊜	⊜	⊜	⊜
Power equip.	●	●	◒	○	◒	○	⊖	⊜
Paint/trim/rust	○	◒	○	⊜	○	⊜	⊖	⊜
Integrity	●	◒	◒	◒	◒	○	◒	⊖
Hardware	●	●	●	◒	◒	○	○	⊜
RELIABILITY VERDICT								

Pontiac Grand Prix

TROUBLE SPOTS	95	96	97	98	99	00	01	02
Engine	○	◒	◒	○	⊖	⊜	⊜	⊜
Cooling	○	◒	●	○	⊖	⊖	⊜	⊜
Fuel	⊖	○	○	⊖	⊖	⊖	⊖	⊜
Ignition	⊖	⊜	⊖	⊜	⊜	⊜	⊜	⊜
Transmission	○	⊖	⊖	⊖	⊖	⊖	⊖	⊜
Electrical	●	●	●	◒	○	○	⊖	⊖
A/C	⊖	⊖	⊖	⊜	⊖	⊖	⊜	⊜
Suspension	⊖	⊖	○	⊖	⊖	⊜	⊜	⊜
Brakes	●	●	○	○	○	⊖	⊜	⊜
Exhaust	⊖	⊜	⊜	⊜	⊜	⊜	⊜	⊜
Power equip.	○	◒	◒	◒	◒	⊖	⊖	⊜
Paint/trim/rust	○	○	⊜	⊜	⊜	⊖	⊜	⊖
Integrity	◒	◒	◒	○	◒	○	○	⊜
Hardware	◒	◒	◒	◒	○	⊖	⊖	⊖
RELIABILITY VERDICT	✓	✓		✓	✓	✓	✓	✓

Pontiac Sunfire

TROUBLE SPOTS	95	96	97	98	99	00	01	02
Engine	◒	○	○	⊖	⊖	⊖	⊜	⊜
Cooling	◒	◒	◒	○	⊖	⊖	⊜	⊜
Fuel	⊖	○	○	⊖	⊖	⊖	⊖	⊖
Ignition	○	○	○	⊖	○	⊜	⊜	⊜
Transmission	○	⊜	⊖	⊖	⊜	⊜	⊜	⊜
Electrical	●	●	●	◒	○	○	⊖	⊖
A/C	◒	◒	○	⊖	⊜	⊖	⊜	⊜
Suspension	○	○	○	⊖	○	⊖	⊖	⊜
Brakes	◒	◒	◒	●	◒	◒	○	⊜
Exhaust	⊜	⊖	⊖	⊜	⊜	⊜	⊜	⊜
Power equip.	⊖	⊖	○	⊖	⊖	⊖	⊖	⊜
Paint/trim/rust	◒	○	⊖	○	⊖	⊖	⊖	⊖
Integrity	◒	◒	◒	○	◒	◒	○	⊖
Hardware	◒	◒	◒	◒	○	○	⊜	○
RELIABILITY VERDICT	✔			✔	✔	✔	✔	

Pontiac TransSport, Montana (ext.)

TROUBLE SPOTS	95	96	97	98	99	00	01	02
Engine			○	○	○	⊜	⊜	⊜
Cooling			○	⊖	○	⊖	⊜	⊜
Fuel			○	⊖	⊖	⊖	⊖	⊜
Ignition			⊜	⊜	⊖	⊜	⊜	⊜
Transmission			⊖	⊖	○	⊖	⊜	⊜
Electrical			◒	◒	◒	◒	⊖	⊜
A/C			⊖	⊖	⊖	⊜	⊖	⊜
Suspension			○	⊖	⊖	⊖	⊖	⊜
Brakes			◒	◒	◒	○	⊜	⊜
Exhaust			⊜	⊜	⊜	⊜	⊜	⊜
Power equip.			●	●	●	◒	○	⊖
Paint/trim/rust			⊖	⊜	⊖	⊖	⊜	⊜
Integrity			●	◒	◒	◒	○	⊖
Hardware			●	●	●	●	◒	⊖
RELIABILITY VERDICT							✔	

Porsche Boxster

TROUBLE SPOTS	95	96	97	98	99	00	01	02
Engine			Insufficient data	Insufficient data	Insufficient data	⊜	⊖	Insufficient data
Cooling						⊜	⊜	
Fuel						⊜	⊜	
Ignition						⊜	⊖	
Transmission						⊜	⊜	
Electrical						○	⊖	
A/C						⊜	⊖	
Suspension						⊖	⊜	
Brakes						⊜	⊜	
Exhaust						⊜	⊜	
Power equip.						⊜	⊖	
Paint/trim/rust						⊜	⊜	
Integrity						⊖	○	
Hardware						⊖	⊖	
RELIABILITY VERDICT						✓	✔	

Saab 900, 9-3

TROUBLE SPOTS	95	96	97	98	99	00	01	02
Engine	○	◒	○	Insufficient data	⊜	⊜	⊜	Insufficient data
Cooling	◒	◒	⊖		⊖	⊜	⊜	
Fuel	○	◒	⊖		⊜	⊜	⊜	
Ignition	○	○	⊖		⊖	⊖	⊜	
Transmission	⊜	○	○		⊜	⊜	⊜	
Electrical	●	◒	◒		◒	⊖	⊖	
A/C	◒	◒	○		○	⊖	⊜	
Suspension	⊖	⊜	⊖		⊖	⊜	⊜	
Brakes	○	○	○		⊜	⊜	⊖	
Exhaust	◒	○	⊖		⊜	⊜	⊜	
Power equip.	◒	○	○		○	⊖	⊖	
Paint/trim/rust	⊖	○	⊜		⊖	⊜	⊜	
Integrity	○	○	⊖		◒	○	⊖	
Hardware	◒	○	⊖		●	⊖	○	
RELIABILITY VERDICT	✔		✔		✔	✓	✓	

Saab 9-5

TROUBLE SPOTS	95	96	97	98	99	00	01	02
Engine					⊖	⊜	⊖	Insufficient data
Cooling					⊖	⊜	⊜	
Fuel					⊖	⊖	⊜	
Ignition					○	⊜	⊜	
Transmission					⊜	⊜	⊜	
Electrical					●	○	⊖	
A/C					⊖	⊖	⊜	
Suspension					⊜	⊜	⊖	
Brakes					⊖	⊜	⊜	
Exhaust					⊖	⊜	⊜	
Power equip.					○	⊖	⊜	
Paint/trim/rust					⊖	⊜	⊜	
Integrity					⊜	⊖	⊜	
Hardware					⊖	○	⊜	
RELIABILITY VERDICT					✔	✓	✓	

Saturn L-Series

TROUBLE SPOTS	95	96	97	98	99	00	01	02
Engine						⊜	⊖	⊜
Cooling						○	○	⊜
Fuel						⊖	⊜	⊜
Ignition						⊖	⊖	⊜
Transmission						⊜	⊜	⊜
Electrical						◒	⊖	⊖
A/C						○	⊜	⊜
Suspension						○	⊖	⊜
Brakes						⊖	⊜	⊜
Exhaust						⊜	⊜	⊜
Power equip.						○	⊖	⊖
Paint/trim/rust						⊖	⊜	⊜
Integrity						◒	⊖	⊜
Hardware						●	⊖	⊜
RELIABILITY VERDICT								✔

Saturn SL/SW

TROUBLE SPOTS	95	96	97	98	99	00	01	02
Engine	◒	◒	○	⊖	⊖	⊖	⊜	⊜
Cooling	○	○	⊖	⊖	⊖	⊖	⊜	⊜
Fuel	○	○	◒	○	⊖	⊖	⊜	⊜
Ignition	○	○	⊖	⊖	⊜	⊜	⊜	⊜
Transmission	○	⊜	⊖	⊖	⊜	⊖	⊜	⊜
Electrical	◒	◒	●	○	○	○	⊜	⊜
A/C	⊖	⊜	⊖	⊜	⊖	⊜	⊜	⊜
Suspension	⊜	⊖	⊖	⊜	⊜	⊖	⊜	⊜
Brakes	○	○	○	⊖	○	⊖	⊜	⊜
Exhaust	⊜	⊖	⊖	○	⊖	⊖	⊜	⊜
Power equip.	⊖	○	⊖	⊖	⊖	⊖	⊜	⊜
Paint/trim/rust	⊖	⊖	⊜	⊖	⊜	⊖	⊜	⊜
Integrity	●	◒	◒	○	○	○	⊖	⊜
Hardware	○	○	○	○	○	○	⊖	⊜
RELIABILITY VERDICT	✔	✔	✔	✓	✓	✔	✓	✓

Saturn VUE

TROUBLE SPOTS	95	96	97	98	99	00	01	02
Engine								⊜
Cooling								⊜
Fuel								⊜
Ignition								⊜
Transmission								⊜
Electrical								⊖
A/C								⊜
Suspension								⊖
Brakes								⊜
Exhaust								⊖
Power equip.								⊜
Paint/trim/rust								⊜
Integrity								⊖
Hardware								⊜
RELIABILITY VERDICT								✔

Subaru Forester — TROUBLE SPOTS	95	96	97	98	99	00	01	02
Engine				○	⊖	⊜	⊜	⊜
Cooling				⊜	⊜	⊜	⊜	⊜
Fuel				⊜	⊖	○	⊖	⊜
Ignition				⊜	⊜	⊜	⊜	⊜
Transmission				⊖	⊖	⊜	⊜	⊜
Electrical				○	⊖	⊖	⊜	⊜
A/C				⊜	⊜	⊜	⊜	⊜
Suspension				⊜	⊖	⊖	⊜	⊜
Brakes				○	⊖	⊜	⊜	⊜
Exhaust				⊜	⊜	⊜	⊜	⊜
Power equip.				⊜	⊜	⊜	⊜	⊜
Paint/trim/rust				⊖	⊖	⊖	⊜	⊜
Integrity				⊖	⊖	⊖	⊖	⊜
Hardware				⊖	⊖	⊖	⊖	⊜
RELIABILITY VERDICT				✓	✓	✔	✓	✓

Subaru Impreza — TROUBLE SPOTS	95	96	97	98	99	00	01	02
Engine	○	◒	⊖	⊜	⊖	⊜		⊜
Cooling	⊖	⊖	⊜	⊜	⊜	⊜		⊜
Fuel	⊖	⊖	⊖	⊖	⊖	⊖		⊜
Ignition	⊖	⊖	⊜	⊜	⊖	⊜		⊜
Transmission	⊖	⊜	⊜	⊜	⊖	⊜		⊜
Electrical	○	⊖	⊖	⊖	⊖	⊜	Insufficient data	⊜
A/C	⊖	⊖	⊖	⊜	⊜	⊜		⊜
Suspension	○	⊖	⊖	⊖	⊜	⊜		⊜
Brakes	⊖	○	○	○	○	⊖		⊜
Exhaust	⊜	⊜	⊜	⊜	⊜	⊜		⊜
Power equip.	⊜	⊖	⊖	⊖	⊜	⊖		⊜
Paint/trim/rust	⊖	⊜	⊖	⊖	⊖	⊖		⊜
Integrity	○	⊖	⊖	⊖	⊖	○		⊖
Hardware	⊖	⊜	⊖	⊖	○	⊖		⊖
RELIABILITY VERDICT	✓	✓	✓	✓	✔	✓		✔

Subaru Legacy/Outback 4 cyl. — TROUBLE SPOTS	95	96	97	98	99	00	01	02
Engine	○	●	○	○	⊖	⊜	⊜	⊜
Cooling	⊖	⊖	⊖	⊜	⊜	⊜	⊜	⊜
Fuel	◒	⊖	⊜	⊜	⊖	⊖	⊜	⊜
Ignition	⊖	⊖	⊜	⊜	⊜	⊜	⊜	⊜
Transmission	⊖	⊜	⊜	⊖	⊖	⊜	⊜	⊜
Electrical	◒	◒	◒	○	⊖	⊖	⊜	⊜
A/C	⊖	⊖	⊜	⊖	⊜	⊜	⊜	⊜
Suspension	⊖	⊖	⊖	⊖	⊜	⊜	⊜	⊜
Brakes	○	○	○	○	⊖	⊖	⊖	⊜
Exhaust	⊜	⊜	⊜	⊜	⊜	⊜	⊜	⊜
Power equip.	⊖	⊖	⊖	⊜	⊜	⊜	⊜	⊜
Paint/trim/rust	⊖	⊖	⊜	⊖	⊜	⊜	⊜	⊜
Integrity	⊖	⊖	⊖	⊖	⊖	⊖	⊖	⊖
Hardware	○	⊖	⊖	⊖	⊖	○	⊖	⊜
RELIABILITY VERDICT	✓	✔	✓	✓	✓	✓	✓	✓

Suzuki Sidekick, Vitara/XL-7 — TROUBLE SPOTS	95	96	97	98	99	00	01	02
Engine	⊖	◒				⊖	⊜	
Cooling	○	⊖				○	⊜	
Fuel	○	○				⊖	⊜	
Ignition	⊖	⊖				⊜	⊜	
Transmission	⊜	⊖				⊖	⊜	
Electrical	◒	○				○	⊖	
A/C	◒	◒	Insufficient data	Insufficient data	Insufficient data	⊖	⊜	Insufficient data
Suspension	⊖	⊜				⊖	⊜	
Brakes	⊖	○				⊖	⊜	
Exhaust	○	⊖				⊜	⊜	
Power equip.	⊖	⊖				○	⊖	
Paint/trim/rust	⊖	○				⊖	⊜	
Integrity	●	○				◒	⊖	
Hardware	○	○				◒	⊖	
RELIABILITY VERDICT	✓	✔					✓	

Toyota 4Runner — TROUBLE SPOTS	95	96	97	98	99	00	01	02
Engine	⊖	○	⊜	⊜	⊜	⊜	⊜	⊜
Cooling	○	⊜	⊜	⊜	⊜	⊜	⊜	⊜
Fuel	⊜	⊖	⊜	⊜	⊜	⊜	⊜	⊜
Ignition	⊜	⊜	⊜	⊜	⊜	⊜	⊜	⊜
Transmission	⊜	⊜	⊜	⊜	⊜	⊜	⊜	⊜
Electrical	○	⊖	○	⊖	⊖	⊖	⊜	⊜
A/C	⊖	⊜	⊜	⊜	⊜	⊜	⊜	⊜
Suspension	○	⊖	○	⊖	⊜	⊜	⊜	⊜
Brakes	○	⊖	⊖	○	⊖	⊖	⊜	⊜
Exhaust	⊜	⊜	⊜	⊜	⊜	⊜	⊜	⊜
Power equip.	○	○	○	⊖	⊖	⊜	⊜	⊜
Paint/trim/rust	○	⊜	⊜	⊖	⊜	⊜	⊜	⊜
Integrity	○	⊜	⊜	⊖	⊖	⊜	⊖	⊖
Hardware	○	⊖	⊖	⊖	⊖	⊖	⊖	⊜
RELIABILITY VERDICT	✓	✓	✓	✓	✓	✓	✓	✓

Toyota Avalon — TROUBLE SPOTS	95	96	97	98	99	00	01	02
Engine	⊖	⊖	⊜	⊜	⊜	⊜	⊜	⊜
Cooling	⊜	⊜	⊜	⊜	⊜	⊜	⊜	⊜
Fuel	⊜	⊜	⊜	⊖	⊜	⊜	⊜	⊜
Ignition	⊜	⊜	⊜	⊜	⊜	⊜	⊜	⊜
Transmission	⊖	⊖	⊖	⊜	⊜	⊖	⊜	⊖
Electrical	○	⊖	⊖	⊖	⊖	⊖	⊖	⊜
A/C	⊖	⊖	⊜	○	⊜	⊜	⊜	⊜
Suspension	◒	○	●	◒	○	⊜	⊖	⊜
Brakes	○	⊖	⊖	⊖	⊖	⊜	⊜	⊜
Exhaust	⊜	⊜	⊜	⊜	⊜	⊜	⊜	⊜
Power equip.	◒	○	⊖	⊖	⊖	⊜	⊜	⊜
Paint/trim/rust	⊖	⊖	⊖	⊜	⊖	⊜	⊖	⊜
Integrity	◒	◒	○	○	⊖	⊖	⊖	⊖
Hardware	○	⊖	⊖	⊖	⊜	⊖	⊖	⊜
RELIABILITY VERDICT	✓	✓	✓	✓	✓	✓	✓	✓

Toyota Camry — TROUBLE SPOTS	95	96	97	98	99	00	01	02
Engine	○	○	⊖	⊜	⊜	⊜	⊜	⊜
Cooling	⊖	⊜	⊜	⊜	⊜	⊜	⊜	⊜
Fuel	⊜	⊖	⊖	⊖	⊖	⊜	⊖	⊜
Ignition	⊜	⊜	⊜	⊜	⊜	⊜	⊜	⊜
Transmission	⊖	⊜	⊜	⊜	⊜	⊜	⊜	⊜
Electrical	○	⊖	○	⊖	⊖	⊜	⊖	⊜
A/C	⊖	⊜	⊜	⊜	⊜	⊜	⊜	⊜
Suspension	○	⊖	◒	○	⊖	⊜	⊜	⊜
Brakes	○	⊖	○	⊖	⊖	⊖	⊜	⊜
Exhaust	⊖	⊜	⊜	⊜	⊜	⊜	⊜	⊜
Power equip.	○	○	⊖	⊖	⊖	⊜	⊜	⊜
Paint/trim/rust	⊖	⊖	⊖	⊜	⊖	⊜	⊜	⊖
Integrity	⊖	⊖	⊖	⊖	⊖	⊜	⊖	⊖
Hardware	⊖	⊖	⊖	⊖	⊖	⊖	⊖	⊖
RELIABILITY VERDICT	✓	✓	✓	✓	✓	✓	✓	✔

Toyota Camry Solara — TROUBLE SPOTS	95	96	97	98	99	00	01	02
Engine					⊜	⊜	⊜	⊜
Cooling					⊜	⊜	⊜	⊜
Fuel					⊖	⊜	⊖	⊜
Ignition					⊜	⊜	⊜	⊜
Transmission					⊜	⊜	⊜	⊜
Electrical					⊖	⊜	⊜	⊜
A/C					⊜	⊜	⊜	⊜
Suspension					○	⊜	⊖	⊜
Brakes					⊖	⊖	⊖	⊜
Exhaust					⊜	⊜	⊜	⊜
Power equip.					⊖	⊖	⊖	⊜
Paint/trim/rust					⊖	⊖	⊜	⊜
Integrity					○	○	⊖	⊜
Hardware					○	⊖	⊖	⊜
RELIABILITY VERDICT					✓	✓	✓	✓

Toyota Celica	95	96	97	98	99	00	01	02
Engine	○	Insufficient data	Insufficient data	Insufficient data	Insufficient data	⊖	⊜	Insufficient data
Cooling	⊖					⊜	⊜	
Fuel	⊖					⊖	⊜	
Ignition	⊜					⊜	⊜	
Transmission	⊖					⊜	⊜	
Electrical	⊖					⊖	⊖	
A/C	⊜					⊜	⊜	
Suspension	○					⊜	⊜	
Brakes	⊖					⊜	⊜	
Exhaust	⊜					⊜	⊜	
Power equip.	○					⊖	⊜	
Paint/trim/rust	⊖					⊖	⊜	
Integrity	○					⊖	⊖	
Hardware	○					⊖	⊖	
RELIABILITY VERDICT	✓					✓	✓	

Toyota Corolla	95	96	97	98	99	00	01	02
Engine	⊜	⊜	⊜	⊜	⊜	⊜	⊜	⊜
Cooling	⊜	⊜	⊜	⊜	⊜	⊜	⊜	⊜
Fuel	⊜	⊜	⊜	⊜	⊜	⊜	⊜	⊜
Ignition	⊖	⊜	⊜	⊜	⊜	⊜	⊜	⊜
Transmission	⊜	⊜	⊜	⊜	⊜	⊜	⊜	⊜
Electrical	●	○	○	⊖	⊖	⊜	⊜	⊜
A/C	⊜	⊜	⊜	⊜	⊜	⊜	⊜	⊜
Suspension	⊖	⊜	⊖	⊖	⊖	⊖	⊜	⊜
Brakes	○	○	⊖	⊖	⊖	⊖	⊜	⊜
Exhaust	⊜	⊜	⊜	⊜	⊜	⊜	⊜	⊜
Power equip.	⊖	⊖	⊖	⊖	⊜	⊜	⊜	⊜
Paint/trim/rust	⊖	⊖	⊜	⊜	⊜	⊜	⊖	⊖
Integrity	⊖	⊖	⊖	⊖	⊖	⊖	⊜	⊜
Hardware	○	⊖	○	○	⊖	⊖	⊜	⊖
RELIABILITY VERDICT	✓	✓	✓	✓	✓	✓	✓	✓

Toyota Echo	95	96	97	98	99	00	01	02
Engine						⊜	⊜	⊜
Cooling						⊜	⊜	⊜
Fuel						⊜	⊜	⊜
Ignition						⊜	⊜	⊜
Transmission						⊜	⊜	⊜
Electrical						⊜	⊜	⊜
A/C						⊜	⊜	⊜
Suspension						⊜	⊜	⊜
Brakes						○	⊜	⊜
Exhaust						⊜	⊜	⊜
Power equip.						⊜	⊜	⊜
Paint/trim/rust						⊖	⊜	⊜
Integrity						⊖	⊖	⊜
Hardware						○	⊖	⊜
RELIABILITY VERDICT						✓	✓	✓

Toyota Highlander	95	96	97	98	99	00	01	02
Engine							⊜	⊜
Cooling							⊜	⊜
Fuel							⊜	⊜
Ignition							⊜	⊜
Transmission							⊜	⊜
Electrical							⊜	⊜
A/C							⊜	⊜
Suspension							⊜	⊜
Brakes							⊖	⊜
Exhaust							⊜	⊜
Power equip.							⊜	⊜
Paint/trim/rust							⊜	⊜
Integrity							○	⊜
Hardware							⊜	⊜
RELIABILITY VERDICT							✓	✓

Toyota Land Cruiser	95	96	97	98	99	00	01	02
Engine	Insufficient data	Insufficient data	Insufficient data	Insufficient data	Insufficient data	⊜	Insufficient data	Insufficient data
Cooling						⊜		
Fuel						⊜		
Ignition						⊜		
Transmission						⊜		
Electrical						⊜		
A/C						⊜		
Suspension						⊖		
Brakes						⊜		
Exhaust						⊜		
Power equip.						⊖		
Paint/trim/rust						⊜		
Integrity						⊖		
Hardware						⊖		
RELIABILITY VERDICT						✓		

Toyota Prius	95	96	97	98	99	00	01	02
Engine							⊜	⊜
Cooling							⊜	⊜
Fuel							⊖	⊜
Ignition							⊜	⊜
Transmission							⊜	⊜
Electrical							⊖	⊜
A/C							⊜	⊜
Suspension							⊖	⊖
Brakes							⊜	⊜
Exhaust							⊜	⊜
Power equip.							⊜	⊜
Paint/trim/rust							⊜	⊜
Integrity							⊜	⊜
Hardware							⊜	⊜
RELIABILITY VERDICT							✓	✓

Toyota RAV4	95	96	97	98	99	00	01	02
Engine		⊖	⊖	⊜	⊜	⊜	⊜	⊜
Cooling		⊜	⊜	⊜	⊜	⊜	⊜	⊜
Fuel		⊖	⊖	⊖	⊜	⊜	⊖	⊜
Ignition		⊜	⊜	⊜	⊜	⊜	⊜	⊜
Transmission		⊖	⊜	⊖	⊜	⊜	⊜	⊜
Electrical		⊜	⊖	⊖	⊖	⊜	⊜	⊜
A/C		⊖	⊜	⊜	⊜	⊜	⊜	⊜
Suspension		⊜	⊜	⊜	⊖	⊜	⊜	⊜
Brakes		⊖	○	○	⊖	⊖	◒	⊜
Exhaust		⊜	⊜	⊖	⊜	⊜	⊜	⊜
Power equip.		⊜	⊖	⊖	⊖	⊖	⊜	⊜
Paint/trim/rust		⊖	⊖	⊖	⊖	⊖	⊖	⊜
Integrity		○	⊖	⊖	⊖	⊖	◒	○
Hardware		⊖	⊖	○	⊖	⊖	⊖	⊜
RELIABILITY VERDICT		✓	✓	✓	✓	✓	✔	✓

Toyota Sequoia	95	96	97	98	99	00	01	02
Engine							⊜	⊜
Cooling							⊜	⊜
Fuel							⊜	⊜
Ignition							⊜	⊜
Transmission							⊜	⊜
Electrical							⊖	⊜
A/C							⊜	⊜
Suspension							⊜	⊜
Brakes							⊖	⊜
Exhaust							⊜	⊜
Power equip.							⊖	⊜
Paint/trim/rust							⊜	⊜
Integrity							⊖	⊜
Hardware							⊖	⊜
RELIABILITY VERDICT							✓	✓

Toyota Sienna

TROUBLE SPOTS	95	96	97	98	99	00	01	02
Engine				⊜	⊜	⊜	⊜	⊜
Cooling				⊜	⊜	⊜	⊜	⊜
Fuel				⊜	⊜	⊜	⊜	⊜
Ignition				⊜	⊜	⊜	⊜	⊜
Transmission				⊜	⊜	⊜	⊜	⊜
Electrical				⊖	⊖	⊖	⊜	⊜
A/C				⊖	⊜	⊜	⊜	⊜
Suspension				⊖	⊖	⊜	⊜	⊜
Brakes				○	⊖	⊖	⊖	⊜
Exhaust				⊜	⊜	⊜	⊜	⊜
Power equip.				⊖	○	○	⊖	⊜
Paint/trim/rust				⊖	⊜	⊜	⊜	⊜
Integrity				◒	○	⊖	⊖	⊜
Hardware				●	◒	○	○	⊜
RELIABILITY VERDICT				✓	✓	✓	✓	✓

Toyota T100, Tundra 2WD

TROUBLE SPOTS	95	96	97	98	99	00	01	02
Engine	⊖	⊖	⊜	Insufficient data		⊜	⊜	⊜
Cooling	⊜	⊖	⊜			⊜	⊜	⊜
Fuel	⊜	⊜	⊖			⊖	⊜	⊜
Ignition	⊜	⊖	⊖			⊜	⊜	⊜
Transmission	⊖	⊜	⊜			⊜	⊜	⊜
Electrical	○	○	○			⊖	⊜	⊜
A/C	⊖	⊜	⊖			⊜	⊜	⊜
Suspension	⊖	⊖	⊖			⊜	⊖	⊜
Brakes	⊖	⊖	⊜			◒	⊖	⊖
Exhaust	⊖	⊖	⊜			⊜	⊜	⊜
Power equip.	⊜	⊖	⊜			⊜	⊜	⊜
Paint/trim/rust	⊖	⊖	⊜			⊜	⊖	⊜
Integrity	⊖	⊜	⊖			⊖	⊜	⊜
Hardware	⊖	○	○			⊖	⊖	⊜
RELIABILITY VERDICT	✓	✓	✓			✓	✓	✓

Toyota Tacoma 2WD

TROUBLE SPOTS	95	96	97	98	99	00	01	02
Engine	⊜	⊜	⊜	⊜	⊜	⊜	⊜	⊜
Cooling	⊜	⊜	⊖	⊜	⊜	⊜	⊜	⊜
Fuel	○	⊖	⊖	⊖	⊜	⊜	⊜	⊜
Ignition	⊜	⊜	⊜	⊜	⊜	⊜	⊜	⊜
Transmission	⊜	⊜	⊜	⊖	⊜	⊜	⊜	⊜
Electrical	⊖	○	⊖	⊖	⊖	⊜	⊜	⊜
A/C	⊜	⊜	⊖	⊜	⊜	⊜	⊜	⊜
Suspension	⊖	⊖	⊖	⊜	⊖	⊜	⊖	⊜
Brakes	⊖	○	○	○	⊜	⊖	⊜	⊜
Exhaust	⊜	⊖	⊖	⊜	⊜	⊜	⊜	⊜
Power equip.	⊜	⊜	⊜	⊜	⊜	⊜	⊖	⊜
Paint/trim/rust	⊜	⊜	⊖	⊜	⊜	⊜	○	⊖
Integrity	⊖	⊖	⊖	○	⊖	⊖	○	⊖
Hardware	⊖	⊖	⊖	○	⊜	⊜	○	⊖
RELIABILITY VERDICT	✓	✓	✓	✓	✓	✓	✔	✓

Toyota Tacoma 4WD

TROUBLE SPOTS	95	96	97	98	99	00	01	02
Engine	⊖	⊜	⊜	⊜	⊜	⊖	⊜	⊜
Cooling	⊖	⊜	⊜	⊖	⊜	⊖	⊜	⊜
Fuel	⊖	⊜	⊜	⊜	⊜	⊜	⊜	⊜
Ignition	⊖	⊜	⊜	⊜	⊜	⊜	⊜	⊜
Transmission	⊜	⊜	⊜	⊜	⊜	⊜	⊜	⊜
Electrical	◒	○	⊖	⊖	⊖	⊜	⊜	⊜
A/C	⊜	⊜	⊖	⊜	⊜	⊜	⊖	⊜
Suspension	○	⊖	⊖	⊜	⊖	⊖	⊜	⊜
Brakes	⊖	⊖	⊖	⊖	⊖	⊜	⊜	⊜
Exhaust	⊜	⊜	⊜	⊜	⊜	⊜	⊜	⊜
Power equip.	⊜	⊜	⊜	⊜	⊜	⊜	⊜	⊜
Paint/trim/rust	⊖	⊜	⊜	⊖	⊜	⊜	○	⊜
Integrity	○	⊜	⊖	⊖	⊜	⊖	○	⊖
Hardware	○	⊜	○	⊜	⊖	⊖	⊖	⊜
RELIABILITY VERDICT	✓	✓	✓	✓	✓	✓	✓	✓

Toyota Tundra 4WD

TROUBLE SPOTS	95	96	97	98	99	00	01	02
Engine						⊜	⊜	⊜
Cooling						⊜	⊜	⊜
Fuel						⊖	⊜	⊜
Ignition						⊜	⊜	⊜
Transmission						⊜	⊜	⊜
Electrical						⊖	⊜	⊜
A/C						⊜	⊜	⊜
Suspension						⊖	⊜	⊜
Brakes						◒	⊖	⊜
Exhaust						⊜	⊜	⊜
Power equip.						⊜	⊜	⊜
Paint/trim/rust						⊖	⊜	⊜
Integrity						⊖	⊖	⊜
Hardware						⊖	⊖	⊜
RELIABILITY VERDICT						✓	✓	✓

Volkswagen Golf 4 cyl.

TROUBLE SPOTS	95	96	97	98	99	00	01	02
Engine	Insufficient data	Insufficient data	Insufficient data	Insufficient data	Insufficient data	○	⊜	Insufficient data
Cooling						⊜	⊜	
Fuel						●	○	
Ignition						⊜	⊖	
Transmission						⊜	⊜	
Electrical						●	◒	
A/C						⊖	⊜	
Suspension						⊜	⊜	
Brakes						○	⊖	
Exhaust						⊜	⊜	
Power equip.						◒	○	
Paint/trim/rust						⊜	⊖	
Integrity						○	○	
Hardware						◒	○	
RELIABILITY VERDICT								

Volkswagen Jetta 4 cyl.

TROUBLE SPOTS	95	96	97	98	99	00	01	02
Engine	◒	⊖	○	⊖	⊖	⊖	⊖	⊜
Cooling	○	◒	⊜	⊜	⊜	⊜	⊜	⊜
Fuel	○	○	○	○	●	●	⊖	⊖
Ignition	○	◒	⊖	⊖	⊖	⊖	⊜	⊜
Transmission	⊖	○	○	⊖	⊖	⊖	⊖	⊜
Electrical	●	●	●	●	●	◒	○	⊖
A/C	◒	○	○	⊖	⊖	⊖	⊜	⊜
Suspension	○	⊖	⊖	⊖	⊜	⊖	⊜	⊜
Brakes	○	◒	○	⊖	⊖	⊖	⊖	⊖
Exhaust	○	○	◒	◒	⊖	⊖	⊜	⊜
Power equip.	●	◒	◒	◒	●	◒	○	⊖
Paint/trim/rust	●	●	◒	●	○	⊜	⊖	⊜
Integrity	◒	○	○	○	○	○	○	⊖
Hardware	●	◒	◒	◒	●	●	○	⊖
RELIABILITY VERDICT								

Volkswagen New Beetle

TROUBLE SPOTS	95	96	97	98	99	00	01	02
Engine				◒	⊖	⊖	⊜	⊜
Cooling				⊖	⊖	⊜	⊜	⊜
Fuel				◒	●	◒	○	⊜
Ignition				⊖	⊖	⊖	⊜	⊜
Transmission				⊜	⊖	⊜	⊖	⊜
Electrical				●	●	●	◒	○
A/C				○	○	⊜	⊜	⊜
Suspension				⊖	⊖	⊜	⊜	⊜
Brakes				○	⊖	○	⊜	⊖
Exhaust				⊜	⊖	⊜	⊜	⊜
Power equip.				●	●	◒	○	⊖
Paint/trim/rust				○	⊖	⊖	⊜	⊜
Integrity				◒	○	○	⊖	⊖
Hardware				●	●	●	○	⊖
RELIABILITY VERDICT								✔

Volkswagen Passat 4 cyl.

TROUBLE SPOTS	95	96	97	98	99	00	01	02
Engine	Insufficient data	Insufficient data	Insufficient data	○	⊖	⊖	⊜	⊜
Cooling				⊖	⊖	⊖	⊜	⊜
Fuel				○	⊖	◒	⊜	⊜
Ignition				⊖	⊖	⊜	⊖	⊜
Transmission				⊜	⊜	⊜	⊜	⊜
Electrical				●	◒	○	○	⊖
A/C				⊖	⊜	⊜	⊜	⊜
Suspension				◒	⊖	⊜	⊜	⊜
Brakes				○	⊖	⊜	⊜	⊜
Exhaust				⊜	⊜	⊖	⊜	⊜
Power equip.				●	◒	○	⊖	⊜
Paint/trim/rust				⊖	⊖	⊜	⊖	⊜
Integrity				⊖	⊖	⊖	⊖	⊖
Hardware				◒	○	○	○	⊖
RELIABILITY VERDICT					✓	✓	✓	✓

Volkswagen Passat V6

TROUBLE SPOTS	95	96	97	98	99	00	01	02
Engine	Insufficient data	Insufficient data	Insufficient data	Insufficient data	○	⊖	⊜	⊜
Cooling					○	⊖	⊜	⊜
Fuel					○	○	⊜	⊖
Ignition					⊜	⊜	⊜	⊜
Transmission					⊜	⊜	⊜	⊜
Electrical					○	○	○	⊖
A/C					⊜	⊜	⊜	⊜
Suspension					⊖	⊖	⊜	⊜
Brakes					○	⊜	⊜	⊜
Exhaust					⊜	⊜	⊜	⊜
Power equip.					○	○	⊖	⊖
Paint/trim/rust					⊜	⊜	⊜	⊖
Integrity					⊖	⊖	⊜	⊜
Hardware					○	○	○	⊖
RELIABILITY VERDICT					✓	✓	✓	✓

Volvo 850, S70

TROUBLE SPOTS	95	96	97	98	99	00	01	02
Engine	⊖	⊖	⊖	⊜	⊖	⊖		
Cooling	⊖	⊖	⊖	⊜	⊜	⊜		
Fuel	○	○	○	○	○	⊜		
Ignition	⊖	⊖	⊜	⊜	⊖	⊖		
Transmission	○	⊜	⊜	⊜	⊜	⊜		
Electrical	●	●	●	●	●	●		
A/C	●	●	◒	○	⊜	⊖		
Suspension	○	○	○	⊜	⊜	⊜		
Brakes	◒	●	◒	◒	○	⊜		
Exhaust	⊜	⊖	⊖	⊜	⊜	⊜		
Power equip.	◒	○	○	◒	○	○		
Paint/trim/rust	○	○	⊜	⊜	⊜	⊜		
Integrity	◒	○	○	○	○	⊜		
Hardware	◒	◒	○	◒	○	○		
RELIABILITY VERDICT	✓	✓	✓	✓	✓	✓		

Volvo 960, S90/V90

TROUBLE SPOTS	95	96	97	98	99	00	01	02
Engine	⊖	○	⊖	⊜				
Cooling	◒	◒	○	⊜				
Fuel	○	○	⊜	⊜				
Ignition	⊖	⊖	⊜	⊜				
Transmission	⊜	○	○	⊖				
Electrical	◒	●	●	◒				
A/C	●	●	●	●				
Suspension	⊖	○	◒	◒				
Brakes	●	●	◒	●				
Exhaust	⊜	⊖	⊜	⊜				
Power equip.	○	○	●	●				
Paint/trim/rust	○	⊜	⊜	○				
Integrity	⊜	○	○	○				
Hardware	●	●	◒	●				
RELIABILITY VERDICT	✓							

Volvo S40/V40

TROUBLE SPOTS	95	96	97	98	99	00	01	02
Engine						⊜	⊜	Insufficient data
Cooling						⊜	⊜	
Fuel						○	⊖	
Ignition						⊖	⊜	
Transmission						⊜	⊖	
Electrical						◒	○	
A/C						⊖	⊖	
Suspension						○	⊜	
Brakes						●	○	
Exhaust						⊜	⊜	
Power equip.						⊜	⊖	
Paint/trim/rust						⊖	⊖	
Integrity						○	⊖	
Hardware						○	⊖	
RELIABILITY VERDICT							✓	

Volvo S60

TROUBLE SPOTS	95	96	97	98	99	00	01	02
Engine							⊜	⊜
Cooling							⊜	⊜
Fuel							⊜	⊜
Ignition							⊜	⊜
Transmission							⊜	⊜
Electrical							○	⊖
A/C							⊜	⊜
Suspension							⊜	⊜
Brakes							⊜	⊜
Exhaust							⊜	⊜
Power equip.							◒	⊜
Paint/trim/rust							⊖	⊜
Integrity							⊜	⊜
Hardware							○	⊜
RELIABILITY VERDICT							✓	✓

Volvo S80

TROUBLE SPOTS	95	96	97	98	99	00	01	02
Engine					⊖	⊖	⊜	Insufficient data
Cooling					○	⊜	⊜	
Fuel					◒	○	⊜	
Ignition					⊖	⊖	⊜	
Transmission					⊖	⊖	⊖	
Electrical					●	◒	○	
A/C					⊖	⊜	⊜	
Suspension					◒	◒	⊖	
Brakes					○	⊖	⊜	
Exhaust					⊜	⊜	⊜	
Power equip.					◒	○	◒	
Paint/trim/rust					⊜	⊜	⊖	
Integrity					○	○	⊖	
Hardware					◒	○	○	
RELIABILITY VERDICT								

Volvo V70 Cross Country

TROUBLE SPOTS	95	96	97	98	99	00	01	02
Engine				○	○	⊜	⊜	Insufficient data
Cooling				⊖	⊜	⊜	⊜	
Fuel				○	◒	⊖	⊜	
Ignition				⊜	⊖	⊖	⊜	
Transmission				⊖	⊖	⊜	⊜	
Electrical				●	●	●	○	
A/C				○	⊜	⊜	⊜	
Suspension				○	○	○	⊖	
Brakes				●	○	○	⊜	
Exhaust				⊜	⊜	⊜	⊜	
Power equip.				◒	○	○	○	
Paint/trim/rust				⊖	⊜	⊜	⊜	
Integrity				○	○	⊖	⊖	
Hardware				◒	○	◒	○	
RELIABILITY VERDICT						✓	✓	

REFERENCE

PRODUCT RATINGS

How to use the Ratings? First, read the general buying advice for the product you're interested in. The page numbers for these reports are noted on each Ratings page. The Overall Ratings chart gives the big picture in performance. Notes on features and performance for individual models are listed under "Recommendations & notes." You can use the key numbers to move easily between the charts and the other information. CONSUMER REPORTS checked the availability for most products for this book. Some tested models may no longer be available. Models similar to the tested models, when they exist, are also listed. Such models differ in features, not essential performance, according to the manufacturers.

QUICK GUIDE

Air cleaners, room

If you have a forced-air heating/cooling system, choose a whole-house air cleaner. Otherwise, look for a room-sized cleaner that's designed to cover an area slightly larger than the one you need to treat. That way, you may be able to run it on low and still get adequate cleaning. The top three can quickly clear smoke and dust from a room; the worst is little better than nothing at all. With most room air cleaners, the cost of electricity and replacement filters can be substantial. The high-scoring Friedrich C-90A, $500, performs impressively at Low speed and has a filter that can be washed.

Excellent, Very good, Good, Fair, Poor

In performance order.

Key number	Brand & model (Similar models, in small type, comparable to tested model.)	Price	Type	Annual cost: Energy	Annual cost: Filter	Overall score (0–100: P F G VG E)	Dust: High	Dust: Low	Smoke: High	Smoke: Low	Noise: High	Noise: Low	Ease of use	Area (sq. ft.)
1	**Friedrich** C-90A	$500	EP	$56	$72		Excellent	Good	Very good	Good	Fair	Very good	Good	480
2	**Kenmore** 83202 83200 Whirlpool AP51030HO	350	F	84	220		Very good	Good	Very good	Good	Fair	Good	Good	500
3	**Whirlpool** AP45030HO	270	F	64	130		Very good	Good	Very good	Good	Fair	Very good	Good	500
4	**Bionaire** BAP-1300 Holmes HAP675RC	225	F	63	132		Very good	Fair	Very good	Fair	Poor	Good	Good	490
5	**Honeywell** Enviracare 50250	180	F	115	156		Very good	Fair	Very good	Fair	Poor	Good	Good	390
6	**Vornado** AQS35	200	F	124	43		Very good	Fair	Very good	Fair	Poor	Good	Very good	400
7	**Hunter** 30400	180	F	146	90		Good	Fair	Very good	Fair	Poor	Good	Good	400
8	**Hunter** HEPAtech 30375	150	F	106	128		Good	Fair	Very good	Fair	Poor	Very good	Good	440
9	**Hunter** 30170	160	F	57	88		Fair	Poor	Good	Fair	Good	Very good	Good	290
10	**Holmes** HAP650 GE (Wal-Mart) 106653	160	F	45	95		Good	Poor	Good	Fair	Fair	Excellent	Good	340
11	**Austin** Health Mate 400	400	F	93	30		Fair	Poor	Fair	Poor	Poor	Very good	Very good	200
12	**Holmes** HAP625 GE (Wal-Mart) 106643	120	F	25	60		Fair	Poor	Fair	Poor	Good	Very good	Good	210
13	**Honeywell** Enviracare 18150	160	F	43	100		Fair	Poor	Fair	Poor	Fair	Very good	Good	230
14	**Honeywell** Enviracare 17000 17005	110	F	54	125		Fair	Poor	Fair	Poor	Fair	Very good	Very good	200
15	**Hoover** SilentAir 4000	300	EP	7	36		Poor	Poor	Poor	Poor	Excellent	Excellent	Very good	9
16	**Sharper Image** Ionic Breeze Quadra (SI637)	350	EP	4	-		Poor	Poor	Poor	Poor	Excellent	Excellent	Good	14
17	**Honeywell** Environizer 90200	200	EP	6	-		Poor	Poor	Poor	Poor	Excellent	Excellent	Very good	2

See report, page 111. Based on tests published in Consumer Reports in October 2003.

Guide to the Ratings

Overall score is based on air-cleaning ability, noise, and ease of use. In the **type** column, **EP** denotes an electrostatic precipitator; **F** a HEPA filter. **Dust** and **smoke** scores reflect the ability to clear air of those particles at **high** and **low** speeds in a short-term, sealed-chamber test. Dust scores also indicate prowess with pet dander and larger particles, such as pollen; smoke scores also indicate prowess with other small particulates, as from cooking. For (15), (16), and (17), we used only the high setting in calculating overall score. **Noise** is based on instrument measurements and judgments at the highest and lowest speeds. **Ease of use** covers the control layout, changing the filter or cleaning collector plates, and moving the machine. **Area** is given to the nearest 10 square feet, based on AHAM guidelines. For (11), (15), (16), and (17), which do not have AHAM certification, we calculated approximate area. **Price** is approximate retail. **Annual cost** is our estimate based on operating the cleaner continuously. **Energy cost** is based on an electricity rate of about 8 cents per kilowatt-hour. **Filter cost** is based on the manufacturer's suggested retail price and recommended replacement schedule.

FIRST THINGS FIRST

Will an air cleaner address your needs?

You should be able to rely on an air cleaner to deal with: Dust, smoke particles, pollen, and pet dander.

Don't rely on an air cleaner to protect you from: Carbon monoxide, odors, viruses, and dust mites (they rarely become airborne).

Basic actions that may be more effective and less costly than using an air cleaner:

ELIMINATE CAUSES

- **Ban indoor smoking.**
- **Remove sources of pollution,** such as pressed-wood (particleboard) products. Avoid getting pets if you're allergic.
- **Get dust mites out in the laundry** with the hottest water you can. Avoid furnishings that accumulate dust.
- **Vacuum** with a low-emissions machine.

VENTILATE ROOMS

- **Open the windows** whenever weather and outdoor air quality permit.
- **Use outdoor-venting exhaust fans** in kitchen and baths to reduce moisture that can breed bacteria, insects, and dust mites.
- **Properly vent heating equipment and appliances.** Keep the equipment, chimneys, and vents in good repair.

CONTROL HARMFUL GASES

- **Test for radon** with a kit from a home center. If levels are too high, have a contractor fix the problem.
- **Use chemicals outdoors.** Try to keep solvents and pesticides outdoors. If you use them indoors, open windows and vent with a fan.
- **Use a carbon-monoxide alarm.**

Air cleaners, whole house

If you have a forced-air heating/cooling system, you can make a noticeable improvement in air quality by simply installing a filter. The 3M Filtrete Ultra 1250, $15, tops the Ratings for filters that you install yourself. Although the most expensive of its type, with an annual upkeep of $60, it's a standout for dust removal. If someone in your home smokes or has a chronic breathing problem, consider adding an electronic precipitator to your system. The four electronic models tested were 30 times more effective than conventional fiberglass furnace filters. But they cost between $600 and $700 plus installation. Three professionally installed whole-house cleaners combine excellent overall performance with a moderate price and operating cost: the Aprilaire 5000, the Trane Perfect Fit TFE2120A9FR2, and the Honeywell F50, all $600. The Trane imposes the smallest restriction on airflow.

Excellent | Very good | Good | Fair | Poor

Within groups, in performance order.

Key number	Brand & model Similar models, in small type, comparable to tested model.	Price	Type	Annual cost	Overall score 0–100 P F G VG E	Test results: Dust removal	Test results: Smoke removal	Test results: Airflow resistance
	PROFESSIONALLY INSTALLED *These can cost $200 or so to add to a heating/cooling system.*							
1	**Aprilaire** 5000	$600	EP	$48		Excellent	Excellent	Very good
2	**Trion** SE1400	700	EP	29		Excellent	Excellent	Very good
3	**Trane** Perfect Fit TFE210A9FR2	600	EP	18		Excellent	Very good	Excellent
4	**Honeywell** F50 F300	600	EP	19		Excellent	Very good	Very good
5	**Lennox** PureAir PCO-12C PCO-20C	1,100	F	303		Excellent	Fair	Very good
6	**Aprilaire** 2200 2400	350	F	45		Very good	Fair	Very good
	INSTALL-IT-YOURSELF *These replace an existing filter in the heating/cooling system.*							
7	**3M** Filtrete Ultra 1250	15	F	60		Excellent	Fair	Good
8	**Precisionaire** NaturalAire Microparticle	8	F	32		Very good	Fair	Fair
9	**3M** Filtrete 1000	12	F	48		Very good	Fair	Good
10	**3M** Filtrete 600	10	F	40		Very good	Fair	Good
11	**Purolator** PuroPleat Ultra (PPD)	7	F	28		Good	Poor	Fair
12	**American Air Filter** Dirt Demon Pleated Filter	2	F	9		Good	Poor	Good
13	**Precisionaire** NaturalAire	4	F	16		Fair	Poor	Good
14	**American Air Filter** Dirt Demon Ultra Pleat	5	F	20		Fair	Poor	Good

Within groups, in performance order.

Key number	Brand & model **Similar models,** in small type, comparable to tested model.	Price	Type	Annual cost	Overall score 0–100 (P F G VG E)	Test results: Dust removal	Smoke removal	Airflow resistance
	INSTALL-IT-YOURSELF *These replace an existing filter in the heating/cooling system.*							
15	**Precisionaire** EZ Flow	$2	F	24		●	●	⊖
16	**American Air Filter** Strata Density Premium	1	F	9		●	●	⊖
17	**Purolator** PuroPleat (Pur 40)	6	F	24		◒	●	◒
18	**American Air Filter** ElectroKlean	10	F	2		◒	●	○

See report, page 111. Based on tests published in Consumer Reports in October 2003.

Guide to the Ratings

Overall score is based mainly on the ability to remove dust and smoke particles from a test chamber equipped with ductwork to simulate one room within a house with forced-air heating and cooling. In the **type** column, **EP** denotes an electrostatic precipitator; **F** a furnace filter, which can include an electrostatic filter, fiberglass, pleated paper, or extended media. Under **test results, dust removal** and **smoke removal** scores reflect the ability to clear the air of those particles in our short-term test. Dust scores also indicate how well the machine is likely to work on pet dander and larger particles, such as pollen; smoke scores indicate prowess with other small particulates, as from cooking. **Airflow resistance** reflects how freely the model allows air to pass through it; a low score can signal a filter that may adversely affect the overall performance of the heating/cooling system. **Price** is approximate retail, not including installation. **Annual cost** is based on an electricity rate of about 8 cents per kilowatt-hour, the manufacturer's suggested retail price for filters, and the manufacturer's recommended replacement schedule. For (5), the annual cost includes operating the ultraviolet lights (not tested) built into the unit.

Blenders

You don't need to spend a bundle to get a decent blender. Most of the models we tested, even inexpensive ones, were competent at various tasks. Many have specific strengths, so choose one that suits your needs. If you make mostly fruit smoothies or icy drinks such as piña coladas, look for a model that did well in those tests. Regardless of wattage, most models had the oomph to crush ice. While all of the tested models have some shortcomings, most were judged good for convenience and were reasonably easy to use. Both the Sharp EJ-12GD, $40, and the Black & Decker ProBlend BL600, $45, were adept at all tasks and low-priced.

In performance order.

Excellent · Very good · Good · Fair · Poor

Key number	Brand & model (Similar models, in small type, comparable to the tested model.)	Price	Overall score (0–100: P F G VG E)	Test results: Convenience	Icy drinks	Smoothies	Purée	Features: Glass jar	Plastic jar	Stainless-steel jar	Removable blade	Controls	Dishwasher-safe jar
1	**Bosch** MMB 9110 UC	$300		Good	Very good	Very good	Fair		•		•	D	•
2	**Juiceman** Smoothie JMS6	125		Good	Very good	Very good	Good		•			T	
3	**Oster** in2itive 6710 6700	100		Good	Good	Very good	Very good		•		•	T	•
4	**KitchenAid** KSB3[WH]	90		Good	Very good	Good	Fair	•			•	T	•
5	**Sharp** EJ-12GD[W]	40		Good	Good	Very good	Very good	•			•	T	•
6	**Black & Decker** ProBlend BL600	45		Good	Good	Very good	Very good	•			•	P	•
7	**Oster** 6643	40		Fair	Good	Very good	Very good	•			•	P	•
8	**Hamilton Beach** Blend Master Ultra 5225[0]	35		Good	Fair	Very good	Very good	•			•	P	•
9	**KitchenAid** KSB5[SSOB]	135		Good	Very good	Good	Poor			•	•	T	•
10	**T-Fal** Magiclean 67940	45		Good	Fair	Very good	Very good		•		•	D	
11	**Proctor-Silex** 50171R12 57171	25		Good	Fair	Good	Very good		•		•	P	
12	**Oster** 6646	45		Fair	Good	Very good	Very good	•			•	P	•
13	**Oster** 6641	27		Good	Fair	Very good	Very good		•		•	P	
14	**Hamilton Beach** Turbo Twister 5615[0] D Smoothies & More 52153	35		Good	Fair	Good	Fair		•		•	P	

D *Discontinued, but similar model is available. Price is for similar model.*

See report, page 94. Based on tests published in Consumer Reports in July 2003, with updated prices and availability.

Guide to the Ratings

Overall score is based primarily on performance and convenience. We judged how well each model made icy drinks, fruit **smoothies,** vegetable **purée,** and more. For **convenience,** we judged ease of cleaning and replacing blade; clarity of controls and jar markings; pouring ease; and jar balance. **Price** is the approximate retail. Under **brand & model,** bracketed letters or numbers are the color code. A dot indicates that a model has the feature listed. Under controls, **P=push buttons, D=dial, and T=touchpad.**

HOW THEY COMPARE

Controls vary in usability and cleanability.

TOUCHPAD

Pros: Flat, smooth controls are easiest to clean. Some models have programmed settings to eliminate guesswork about time and speed.

Cons: Must often press twice–on and desired speed–to activate. On models lacking speed settings, must press up or down arrow repeatedly to reach desired speed. On programmables, small displays are hard to read.

PUSH BUTTONS

Pros: Easy to change from one speed to another with a single touch.

Cons: Hardest type of control to clean.

DIAL

Pros: Easier to clean than push buttons.

Cons: To move from low to high speed (or vice versa), must rotate dial through complete range.

SWITCH

Pros: Easier to clean than push buttons.

Cons: Limits available speeds to one or two, sometimes with a pulse option.

Camcorders

Digital camcorders offer the widest range of tape formats, the best selection of models, and the best overall performance. A digital camcorder that uses MiniDV or D8 format is the best all-around choice, especially for people who don't want to spend a lot. The **CR Best Buy** Sony DCR-TRV350 and the Canon ZR60, both $500, are two very good, inexpensive choices. Digitals that record directly onto a DVD are best-suited for those who can afford to spend more and who want their home videos on a durable, easily stored medium. For a bargain-priced DVD camcorder, try the Panasonic VDR-M30PP, $800, the least-expensive DVD recorder we tested. Analog camcorders main advantage is a low price. Picture quality is about what you'd expect from a rental video. The Sony CCD-TRV318, $300, is one of the easiest to use and has the best low-light performance of the analogs we tested

Excellent / Very good / Good / Fair / Poor

Within types, in performance order.

Key number	Brand & model	Price	Format	Overall score (0–100; P F G VG E)	Test results: Picture quality	Ease of use	Image stabilizer	Audio quality	Features: Weight (lb.)	Battery life (min.)
	DIGITAL MODELS									
1	**Canon** Elura50	$750	MiniDV		Very good	Good	Excellent	Good	1.0	60
2	**Panasonic** VDR-M30PP	800	DVD-RAM, -R		Very good	Good	Excellent	Very good	1.2	NS
3	**Panasonic** PV-DV73	700	MiniDV		Very good	Very good	Very good	Fair	1.4	NS
4	**Panasonic** PV-GS50	700	MiniDV		Very good	Very good	Good	Good	1.0	NS
5	**Sony** DCR-TRV350 **A CR BEST BUY**	500	D8		Very good	Good	Excellent	Very good	2.2	80
6	**Hitachi** DZ-MV350A	850	DVD-RAM, -R		Very good	Good	Excellent	Good	1.2	45-50
7	**Sony** DCR-PC105	1,000	MiniDV		Very good	Good	Excellent	Fair	1.2	80-90
8	**Panasonic** PV-DV203	600	MiniDV		Very good	Good	Fair	Very good	1.2	NS
9	**Sony** DCR-TRV80	1,500	MiniDV		Very good	Good	Excellent	Very good	1.8	95
10	**Canon** ZR60	500	MiniDV		Very good	Very good	Very good	Good	1.4	75
11	**Canon** ZR70MC	700	MiniDV		Very good	Very good	Very good	Good	1.4	140
12	**Hitachi** DZ-MV380A	1,000	DVD-RAM, -R		Very good	Good	Excellent	Good	1.4	45-50
13	**Panasonic** PV-DV953	1,400	MiniDV		Very good	Good	Excellent	Fair	2.0	NS
14	**Sony** DCR-TRV22	700	MiniDV		Very good	Good	Very good	Very good	1.4	90
15	**JVC** GR-DX75	600	MiniDV		Very good	Fair	Good	Fair	1.2	65
16	**Sony** DCR-TRV33	800	MiniDV		Very good	Good	Very good	Fair	1.4	90
17	**Panasonic** PV-GS70	900	MiniDV		Good	Good	Very good	Fair	1.2	NS

Within types, in performance order.

Key number	Brand & model	Price	Format	Overall score (0–100: P F G VG E)	Test results: Picture quality	Test results: Ease of use	Test results: Image stabilizer	Test results: Audio quality	Features: Weight (lb.)	Features: Battery life (min.)
	DIGITAL MODELS									
18	**Sony** DCR-TRV38	$900	MiniDV		○	○	⊖	◒	1.6	70
19	**JVC** GR-DV500	600	MiniDV		○	⊖	○	◒	1.6	70
20	**Canon** Optura 20	900	MiniDV		○	○	⊖	⊖	1.6	60
21	**JVC** GR-D70	480	MiniDV		○	○	⊖	●	1.4	70
22	**Sharp** VL-Z7U	600	MiniDV		○	◒	⊖	◒	1.2	100
23	**Samsung** SCD27	500	MiniDV		◒	○	⊖	◒	1.4	90
	ANALOG MODELS									
24	**Sony** CCD-TRV318	300	Hi8		◒	⊖	⊖	⊖	2.0	120
25	**JVC** GR-SXM250	250	SVHS/ET-C		◒	⊖	◒	●	2.4	75
26	**Canon** ES8600	280	Hi8		◒	○	◒	◒	2.0	90
27	**Samsung** SCL810	230	Hi8		◒	⊖	-	◒	2.0	90

See report, page 42. Based on tests published in Consumer Reports in November 2003, with updated prices and availability.

Guide to the Ratings

Overall score is based mainly on picture quality; ease of use, image stabilizing, and audio quality carried less weight. **Picture quality** is based on the judgments of trained panelists who viewed static images shot in good light at standard speed (SP) for tape and "fine" mode for DVDs. **Picture quality** in low light was nearly always fair or poor. **Ease of use** takes into account ergonomics, weight, how accurately the viewfinder frames scenes, and contrast in the LCD viewer. **Image stabilizer** indicates how well that circuitry worked. **Audio quality** represents accuracy using the built-in microphone, plus freedom from noise and flutter. **Weight** includes battery and tape or disk. **Battery life** is as stated by the manufacturer, using the LCD viewer. Turning off the viewer typically extends battery life by 10 to 40 minutes. "NS" indicates that the manufacturer did not provide the specification for battery life. Price is approximate retail. **Recommendations & notes** lists noteworthy features and some minor shortcomings.

Recommendations & notes

MOST CAMCORDERS HAVE: Tape counter. Backlight-compensation switch. Manual aperture control. High-speed manual shutter. Manual white balance. Simple switch for manual focus. Audio dub. Tape-position memory. Audio fade. Transitional effects. S-video signal out. Video fade. Full auto switch. Quick review. Optical zoom: 10x. LCD size: 2.5 inches. **MOST DIGITAL CAMCORDERS HAVE:** A/V input. Microphone jack. Still image digital capture.

DIGITAL MODELS

1 **CANON** Elura 50 **Very good.** Image stabilizer worked very well. Autofocus worked very well. Relatively compact. Audio practically free of flutter at slow speed. LCD size: 2 in. Lacks backlight compensation switch and manual aperture control. Canon has been among the more repair-prone brands of digital camcorders. Similar: Elura40MC.

2 **PANASONIC** VDR-M30PP **Very good.** Image stabilizer worked very well. Audio was somewhat free of background noise. Audio practically free of flutter at slow speed. Poor picture quality in low light (if used in "Auto" mode or with manual settings). How to load the tape or battery isn't obvious. Battery must be removed before connecting DC power. Uses proprietary A/V cable. Has video fade but lacks audio dub.

3 **PANASONIC** PV-DV73 **Very good.** Easy to use, overall. Audio practically free of flutter at slow speed. LCD size: 3.5 in. Poor picture quality in low light (if simply used in "Auto" mode). Battery must be removed before connecting DC power. Lacks A/V input.

4 **PANASONIC** PV-GS50 **Very good.** Easy to use, overall. Relatively compact. Audio practically free of flutter at slow speed. Uses proprietary mini jack to S-video connector. Autofocus failed to work in some situations. Poor picture quality in low light (if simply used in "Auto" mode). Battery must be removed before connecting DC power.

5 **SONY** DCR-TRV350 **A CR Best Buy Very good.** Good low-light picture quality. Image stabilizer worked very well. Has a built-in video light. Optical zoom: 20x. Discontinued, but similar DCR-TRV250[ ] is available.

6 **HITACHI** DZ-MV350A **Very good.** Relatively lighweight. LCD viewer is easy to see in bright light. Image stabilizer worked very well. You have to remove the battery before connecting a power cord. Uses proprietary A/V cable.

7 **SONY** DCR-PC105 **Very good.** Image stabilizer worked very well. Relatively compact. Audio practically free of flutter at slow speed. Uses proprietary A/V cable. Can't load tape if mounted on tripod. Lacks a high-speed manual shutter.

8 **PANASONIC** PV-DV203 **Very good.** Relatively lightweight. Good in low light if manual settings are used. But the autofocus didn't work in some situations. You have to remove the battery before connecting a power cord. Lacks a slow-speed manual shutter, A/V input and microphone jack. Similar: PV-DV103.

9 **SONY** DCR-TRV80 **Very good.** Image stabilizer worked very well. LCD size: 3.5 in. Poor performance in low light. Similar: DCR-TRV 70.

10 **CANON** ZR60 **Very good.** Easy to use. Good picture quality in low light if manual settings are used. Optical zoom: 18x. Autofocus failed to work in some situations. Lacks slow-speed manual shutter, built-in titles, custom titles, and still image digital capture. Canon has been among the more repair-prone brands of digital camcorders. Similar: ZR65MC.

11 **CANON** ZR70MC **Very good.** Easy to use and good in low light if manual settings are used. Optical zoom: 22x. But the autofocus didn't work in some situations. Lacks a slow-speed manual shutter. Canon has been among the more repair-prone brands of digital camcorders.

Recommendations & notes

12 HITACHI DZ-MV380A **Very good.** Image stabilizer worked very well. Audio practically free of flutter at slow speed, but autofocus failed to work in some situations. How to load the tape or battery isn't obvious. Battery must be removed before connecting DC power. Uses proprietary A/V cable. Lacks manual aperture control, audio dub, tape position memory, and transitional effects.

13 PANASONIC PVDV 953 **Good.** LCD viewer is easy to see in bright light. Image stabilizer worked very well. LCD size: 3.5 in. Poor performance in low light. You have to remove the battery before connecting a power cord.

14 SONY DCR-TRV22 **Good.** LCD viewer is easy to see in bright light. Similar: DCR-TRV19.

15 JVC GR-DX75U **Good.** Excellent audio accuracy. Relatively compact. Audio practically free of flutter at slow speed. Optical zoom: 16x. Somewhat hard to use, overall. Autofocus failed to work in many situations. Poor picture quality in low light. Uses proprietary A/V cable. Can't load tape if mounted on tripod. Lacks quick review, tape position memory, transitional effects, and microphone jack. JVC has been among the more repair-prone brands of digital camcorders. Similar: GR-DX95.

16 SONY DCR-TRV33 **Good overall.** Poor performance in low light. Lacks simple switch for manual focus.

17 PANASONIC PV-GS70 **Good.** Audio practically free of flutter at slow speed. Battery must be removed before connecting DC power.

18 SONY DCR-TRV38 **Good overall.** LCD viewer (3.5 in.) is easy to see in bright light. Image stabilizer worked very well. Poor performance in low light. Similar: DCR-TRV39.

19 JVC GR-DV500 **Good.** Easy to use, overall. Audio practically free of flutter at slow speed, but autofocus failed to work in many situations. Poor picture quality in low light (if simply used in "Auto" mode). Can't load tape if mounted on tripod. Can't change battery if mounted on tripod. Has video fade. Lacks quick review, tape position memory, and transitional effects. JVC has been among the more repair-prone brands of digital camcorders. Similar: GR-DV800.

20 CANON Optura 20 **Good overall.** Good performance in low light, but only if manual settings are used. Optical zoom: 16x. LCD size: 3.5 in. Lacks slow-speed manual shutter. Similar model: Optura 10.

21 JVC GR-D70 **Good.** Audio practically free of flutter at slow speed, but autofocus failed to work in many situations. Optical zoom: 16x. Poor picture quality in low light (if simply used in "Auto" mode). Audio had very noticeable background noise. Can't load tape if mounted on tripod. Lacks quick review, tape position memory, transitional effects, and microphone jack. JVC has been among the more repair-prone brands of digital camcorders. Similar: GR-D30.

22 SHARP VL-Z7U **Good.** Excellent audio accuracy, but somewhat hard to use overall. Audio practically free of flutter at slow speed. Poor picture quality in low light (if simply used in "Auto" mode). Uses proprietary A/V cable. Lacks high-speed manual shutter, quick review, tape position memory, transitional effects, and microphone jack. Similar: VL-Z3U, VL-Z5U.

23 SAMSUNG SC-D27 **Good.** Excellent audio accuracy. Autofocus worked very well. Audio practically free of flutter at slow speed. LCD size: 3.5 in. Only fair picture quality at standard speed. Poor picture quality in low light (if simply used in "Auto" mode). Can't load tape if mounted on tripod. Lacks manual white balance, simple

Recommendations & notes

switch for manual focus, transitional effects, and A/V input. Similar: SCD23.

ANALOG MODELS

24 **SONY** CCD-TRV318 **Good.** Easy to use. Good low-light picture quality. Image stabilizer worked very well. Optical zoom: 20x. Fair picture quality at standard speed, poor picture quality at low speed. Can't load tape if mounted on tripod. Lacks slow-speed manual shutter, manual white balance, quick review, audio dub, date search, tape position memory, A/V input, microphone jack, and still image digital capture. Similar model: CCD-TRV118.

25 **JVC** GR-SXM250 **Good.** Easy to use, overall. Autofocus worked very well. Optical zoom: 16x. Only fair picture quality at standard speed. Image stabilizer only slightly effective. Audio had very noticeable background noise. Relatively bulky. At slow speed, audio quality was hampered by flutter. Audio had very noticeable background noise. Lacks manual aperture control, audio dub, transitional effects, A/V input, microphone jack, and still image digital capture.

26 **CANON** ES8600 **Good.** Good picture quality in low light if manual settings are used. Optical zoom: 22x. Only fair picture quality at standard speed. Can't load tape if mounted on tripod. Lacks manual aperture control, slow-speed manual shutter, manual white balance, audio dub, custom titles, date search, tape position memory, A/V input, microphone jack, and still image digital capture.

27 **SAMSUNG** SCL810 **Fair.** Easy to use, overall. Excellent audio accuracy. Autofocus worked very well. Optical zoom: 22x. Only fair picture quality at standard speed. Lacks image stabilizer, manual aperture control, high-speed manual shutter, manual white balance, quick review, audio dub, tape position memory, transitional effects, A/V input, microphone jack, and still image digital capture.

Cameras, digital

You can expect to get high-quality prints—even 8x10 glossies—from an inexpensive digital camera. Three-megapixel cameras offer the least flexibility to manipulate images without a loss in quality. But they are typically the lightest, the most compact, and the easiest to use. The Kodak EasyShare DX4330, $280, is a 3-megapixel model with especially long battery life. If you plan on enlarging or cropping images, you'll probably want to spend a little more for a higher-resolution model. For top editing capability and a low price, consider the Olympus Camedia C-50, $480, HP Photosmart 935, $450, and the Minolta Dimage F300, $440. The Olympus and HP yield excellent images. The Minolta has a handy LCD on top to show camera status, shots remaining, battery life, and more. If you want it all—even at a price—the Nikon Coolpix 5700, $890, has excellent images and is loaded with features, including 8X optical zoom, though it is large and heavy, even for a 5-megapixel model.

Excellent ⊜ Very good ⊖ Good ○ Fair ◒ Poor ●

Within types, in performance order.

Key number	Brand and model	Price	Overall score (0–100; P F G VG E)	Test results: Print quality	Camera size	Weight (oz.)	Flash range (ft.)	Battery life (shots)	Next-shot delay (sec.)	Features: Optical zoom	Manual controls	Secure grip	Charger	AA batteries	Eyeglasses	Movie, sound
	3-MEGAPIXEL CAMERAS															
1	**Olympus** Camedia C-740 Ultra Zoom	$450		⊜	M	13	15	65	3	10X	•				•	
2	**Kodak** EasyShare DX4330	280		⊖	M	9	11	900	2	3x				•		•
3	**Canon** PowerShot A70	290		⊖	M	11	14	280	2	3X	•	•		•		•
4	**Sony** Cyber-shot DSC P8	370		⊖	C	7	11	95	2	3X			•			•
5	**Minolta** Dimage Xi	400		⊖	C	5	10	260	5	3X			•			•
6	**Sony** Cyber-shot DSC P72	310		⊖	M	9	12	260	3	3X			•	•		•
7	**Nikon** Coolpix 3100	340		⊖	C	7	10	240	3	3X		•		•		
8	**FujiFilm** Finepix F410	430		⊖	C	7	11	90	4	3X			•			•
9	**Panasonic** Lumix DMC-LC33	270		⊖	C	7	8	80	2	3X		•		•		•
10	**Pentax** Optio S	380		⊖	C	4	11	60	8	3X			•		•	•

Within types, in performance order.

Key number	Brand and model	Price	Overall score (0–100: P F G VG E)	Test results: Print quality	Camera size	Weight (oz.)	Flash range (ft.)	Battery life (shots)	Next-shot delay (sec.)	Features: Optical zoom	Manual controls	Secure grip	Charger	AA batteries	Eyeglasses	Movie, sound
	4-MEGAPIXEL CAMERAS															
11	**Nikon** Coolpix 4300	$390		⊜	M	10	12	360	3	3X	•	•	•			
12	**Konica** Digital Revio KD-400Z	450		⊜	M	8	11	100	5	3X	•		•			•
13	**Olympus** Camedia C-4000 Zoom	390		⊜	M	13	12	130	3	3X	•	•			•	
14	**Pentax** Optio 430RS	310		⊖	M	8	12	180	13	3x			•			
15	**Olympus** Stylus 400	390		⊖	C	6	12	150	4	3X			•			
16	**Kodak** EasyShare LS 443	380		⊖	M	9	11	340	3	3X			•			•
17	**Minolta** Dimage S414	390		⊖	M	16	11	55	3	4X	•	•		•		•
18	**Toshiba** PDR-4300	260		⊖	M	12	10	45	6	2.8X	•			•		
	5-MEGAPIXEL CAMERAS															
19	**Nikon** Coolpix 5700	890		⊜	L	19	13	100	3	8x	•	•	•	•	•	•
20	**Olympus** Camedia C-5050	620		⊜	L	17	18	480	3	3x	•	•	•	•	•	•
21	**Sony** Cyber-shot DSC-F717	730		⊜	L	24	15	200	2	5X	•	•	•		•	•
22	**Olympus** Camedia C-50	480		⊜	M	8	11	400	4	3x	•		•			
23	**Minolta** Dimage 7Hi	1060		⊜	L	23	11	25	2	7x	•	•	•	•	•	•
24	**HP** Photosmart 935	450		⊜	M	9	8	50	2	3X	•	•		•		•
25	**Pentax** Optio 550	540		⊖	M	8	17	120	3	5X	•		•		•	•
26	**Canon** PowerShot S50	500		⊖	M	11	16	85	3	3X	•		•			•
27	**Kyocera** Contax TVS Digital	890		⊖	M	9	10	45	7	3X	•		•		•	•
28	**Minolta** Dimage F300	440		⊖	M	7	11	260	3	3X	•			•		•
29	**Sony** CD Mavica MVC-CD500	640		⊖	L	21	16	55	2	3X	•	•	•		NA	•

See report, page 45. Based on tests published in Consumer Reports in November 2003, with updated prices and availability.

Guide to the Ratings

Overall score is based mainly on print quality, along with weight and the presence of useful features. **Print quality** is based on expert judgments, using 8x10 prints made with each camera's highest resolution and lowest image-compression settings and printed on a high-rated inkjet printer. **Camera size** denotes compact (C) models, which fit a shirt pocket; medium (M), shaped like traditional point-and-shoot cameras; and large (L) models, chunkier and bulkier. **Weight** includes battery and memory card or disc. **Flash range** is the maximum claimed range for a well-lighted subject. **Battery life** is the number of high-resolution photos taken with alkaline AAs or, if the camera cannot accept those, the rechargeables supplied; half the shots used flash, and the zoom lens was racked in and out. **Next-shot delay** is the time the camera needs to ready itself for the next photo. **Optical zoom** refers to the range of focal lengths. A 3X zoom is comparable to the 35-to-105-mm zoom lens on a film camera; 5X to 10X provides greater magnification. **Price** is approximate retail.

Recommendations & notes

3-MEGAPIXEL CAMERAS

1. **OLYMPUS** Camedia C-740 Ultra Zoom **Very good.** Has 10x zoom, electronic viewfinder, diopter adjustment, and print image matching. Amount of light emitted by flashes is adjustable.

2. **KODAK** EasyShare DX4330 **Very good.** Secure grip, simple menu system, but can't use alkaline batteries.

3. **CANON** PowerShot A70 **Very good.** Has camera direct print (with Canon printers) and adjustable flash output.

4. **SONY** Cyber-shot DSC-P8 **Very good.** Has adjustable flash level and print image matching. Can shoot and edit macro movies. Movie records in Mpeg.

5. **MINOLTA** Dimage XI **Very good.** Very compact and light. Has internal zoom and print image matching. Lacks macro focus and manual white balance.

6. **SONY** Cyber-shot DSC-P72 **Very good.** Has resizing/cropping in camera, video cutting in camera, and e-mail format. Movie records in Mpeg. Lacks manual controls.

7. **NIKON** Coolpix 3100 **Very good.** Has halo effect filter to apply after picture is taken. Lacks manual controls.

8. **FUJIFILM** FinePix F410 **Very good.** Has Super CCD and "F-Chrome" setting that sets contrast and color saturation to high. Lacks manual controls.

9. **PANASONIC** Lumix DMC-LC33 **Very good.** Has print image matching.

10. **PENTAX** Optio S **Very good.** Has 3D mode for taking 3D pictures, Slim Filter to set degree of slimness vertically or horizontally in 8 steps, and diopter adjustment.

4-MEGAPIXEL CAMERAS

11. **NIKON** Coolpix 4300 **Very good.** Has manual focus, manual controls, and best shot selector.

12. **KONICA** Digital Revio KD-400Z **Very good.** A good value. Compact size, sliding door protects lens, takes two different storage media.

Recommendations & notes

13. OLYMPUS Camedia C-4000 Zoom **Very good.** Short delay between shots. Has manual controls and focus, adjustable flash intensity, ability to make seamless panorama shots.

14. PENTAX Optio 430RS **Very good.** Compact size, diopter adjustment. Doesn't include memory card. Has built-in memory. Long delay between shots.

15. OLYMPUS Stylus 400 **Very good.** Weatherproof, has print image matching. Lacks manual controls.

16. KODAK EasyShare LS 443 **Very good.** Secure grip, simple menu system, but can't use alkaline batteries.

17. MINOLTA Dimage S414 **Very good.** Has 4x optical zoom and manual controls.

18. TOSHIBA PDR-4300 **Very good.** LCD screen is always on when shooting. Has separate switch for lens cover. Has bulb setting, IR remote controller, and manual controls.

5-MEGAPIXEL CAMERAS

19. NIKON Coolpix 5700 **Very good.** A top performer, but expensive. Has 8x optical zoom, secure grip, swing-and-flip LCD, SLR-type body, advanced menu system, and hot shoe.

20. OLYMPUS Camedia C-5050 **Very good.** A top performer. Can take three different storage media. Has tilt LCD and hot shoe.

21. SONY Cyber-shot DSC-F717 **Very good.** Unique tilt body, but heavy. Long flash range and short delay between shots. Has 5x optical zoom, up to 800 ISO setting, live histogram, hotshoe, diopter adjustment, manual focus, and electronic viewfinder. Lacks auto review.

22. OLYMPUS Camedia C-50 Zoom **Very good.** Compact size; sliding door protects lens.

23. MINOLTA Dimage 7Hi **Very good,** but expensive. Secure grip, SLR-type body, manual zoom only. Viewfinder tilts. Has PC terminal for flash, proprietary hot shoe, advanced menu system.

24. HEWLETT PACKARD Photosmart 935 **Very good.** Has direct printing with HP printers and manual controls.

25. PENTAX Optio 550 **Very good.** Has 5x optical zoom, 3D mode for taking 3D pictures, Soft Filter for producing a fuzzy effect, Multiple Exposure Mode for superimposing one picture on top of another, diopter adjustment, and print image matching.

26. CANON PowerShot S50 **Very good.** Has camera direct print (with Canon printers), and adjustable flash output.

27. KYOCERA Contax TVS Digital **Very good.** Has flash exposure compensation to allow you to modify flash output. Has diopter.

28. MINOLTA Dimage F300 **Very good.** Has flash compensation to increase or decrease the flash exposure. Has print image matching.

29. SONY CD Mavica MVC-CD500 **Very good.** Has adjustable flash level and hot shoe. Lacks viewfinder. Storage media CDR/RW.

Circular saws

If you're a serious do-it-yourselfer, look for a top-rated circular saw, which can cost $140 to $160. But you can get a fine saw for less. Among lower-priced saws, consider the Black & Decker CS1000, $40. Battery-powered saws such as the DeWalt DW939K, $260, lack the power for tough jobs but might do for occasional light work. The worm-drive DeWalt DW378GK, $155, outperformed the others in its class, but was noticeably slower than the best of the regular saws, and is primarily for contractors.

Within types, in performance order.

Excellent / Very good / Good / Fair / Poor

Key number	Brand & Model	Price	Overall Score (0–100; P F G VG E)	Test results: Cutting Speed	Power	Ease of Use	Construction	Weight (lb.)	Amps [1]
	REGULAR SAWS								
1	**Milwaukee** 6390-21	$140		Excellent	Excellent	Excellent	Excellent	11	15
2	**DeWalt** DW369CSK	140		Excellent	Excellent	Very good	Excellent	11	15
3	**DeWalt** DW364K	160		Excellent	Excellent	Very good	Excellent	12½	15
4	**Makita** 5740NB **A CR Best Buy**	90		Excellent	Good	Excellent	Very good	8½	10.5
5	**Makita** 5007NBK	130		Excellent	Excellent	Good	Excellent	11	13
6	**Craftsman** (Sears) Professional 27108	100		Very good	Excellent	Very good	Very good	11	15
7	**Bosch** 1658K	110		Very good	Very good	Good	Very good	11	13
8	**Black & Decker** CS1000	40		Good	Very good	Good	Good	11	11
9	**Black & Decker** CS1010K	50		Good	Very good	Good	Good	11	12
	BATTERY-POWERED SAWS								
10	**DeWalt** DW939K	260		Very good	Poor	Good	Good	8½	18
11	**Craftsman** (Sears) Professional 27119	200		Good	Poor	Very good	Good	10	18
12	**Makita** BSS730SHK	480		Good	Poor	Good	Very good	9½	24
13	**Bosch** 1659K	300		Good	Poor	Good	Good	9	18
	WORM-DRIVE SAWS								
14	**DeWalt** DW378GK [2]	155		Very good	Excellent	Very good	Excellent	13	15
15	**Skil** HD77	160		Fair	Excellent	Good	Very good	16	13
16	**Craftsman** (Sears) Professional 2761	140		Fair	Excellent	Good	Very good	16	13

[1] *For battery-powered saws, figure is in volts.* [2] *Hybrid design.*

See report, page 116. Based on tests published in Consumer Reports in August 2002, with updated prices and availability.

Guide to the Ratings

Overall score is based mainly on cutting speed, power, and ease of use. **Cutting speed** is how fast each saw crosscut and ripped a series of 2x12 pine and a 24-inch sheet of ¾-inch-thick hardboard; the best were up to four times as fast as the slowest. **Power,** measured with a dynamometer, indicates how well a saw can handle thick or hard wood. **Ease of use** shows how easy it was to use the cutting guide, adjust depth and bevel, and change blades, as well as our judgment of the saw's balance and handle comfort. **Construction** includes our assessment of bearings, access to motor brushes, and ruggedness of the base, housing, and adjustments. **Weight** is to the nearest half-pound with blade and, for cordless models, battery. **Price** is approximate retail.

Recommendations & notes

ALL MODELS HAVE: Blade guard that retracts when you push the saw forward. Cutting depth adjustable to at least 3½ inches. Cutting angle adjustable to 45 degrees. **MOST HAVE:** Carbide 7¼-inch blade. Blade lock to make blade changes easier. One-year warranty.

REGULAR SAWS

1 MILWAUKEE 6390-21 **Excellent.** Adjustable handle. Heavy-duty base.

2 DEWALT DW369CSK **Excellent.** Blade brake. Heavy-duty base. Earlier version of saw was subject of safety recall.

3 DEWALT DW364K **Excellent.** Blade brake. Heavy-duty base.

4 MAKITA 5740NB **A CR Best Buy Excellent.** Heavy-duty base. Safety interlock button. Attached wrench for blade change. Newest version has different front handle. An earlier version of saw was the subject of safety recall.

5 MAKITA 5007NBK **Excellent.** Heavy-duty base. Sharp bevel-angle guide can contact fingers on front handle.

6 CRAFTSMAN (Sears) Professional 27108 **Very good.** Heavy-duty base. Extra-long cord. Padded switch.

7 BOSCH 1658K **Very good.** Blade-wrench storage.

8 BLACK & DECKER CS1000 **Good.** Not supplied with carbide blade or blade lock. Short cord. Base less substantial. Blade-wrench storage. 2-yr. warranty.

9 BLACK & DECKER CS1010K **Good.** Not supplied with carbide blade. Short cord. No blade lock. Base less substantial. Blade-wrench storage. 2-yr. warranty.

BATTERY-POWERED SAWS

10 DEWALT DW939K **Good.** Safety interlock button. Blade-wrench storage.

11 CRAFTSMAN (Sears) Professional 27119 **Good.** Safety interlock button. Blade-wrench storage.

12 MAKITA BSS730SHK **Good.** Blade brake. Heavy-duty base. Safety interlock button, but it's awkward to use. Blade-wrench storage. Bevel adjustment has fasteners front and rear.

13 BOSCH 1659K **Good.** Blade brake. Safety interlock button, but it's awkward to use. Blade-wrench storage.

WORM-DRIVE SAWS

14 DEWALT DW378GK **Excellent.** Heavy-duty base. Not double-insulated. Hybrid design.

15 SKIL HD77 **Good.** Extra-long cord. Not supplied with carbide blade. Poor dust ejection. Not double-insulated.

16 CRAFTSMAN (Sears) Professional 2761 **Good.** Not supplied with carbide blade. Not double-insulated. Poor dust ejection.

Coffeemakers

Most automatic drip coffeemakers are capable of brewing good coffee, so focus on convenience features such as clear cup markings and easy-to-read displays and controls. The top-rated Cuisinart Brew Central DCC-1200, $100, has a host of handy features. For less money, consider any of the four **CR Best Buys:** the Black & Decker Smart Brew Plus DCM2500, $35, Black & Decker Smart Brew DCM2000, $25, Braun Aromaster KF 400, $20, and Mr. Coffee AR12, $20. Among thermal-carafe models, the programmable Mr. Coffee URTX83, $65, was easiest to use.

Within types, in performance order.

Key number	Brand & model	Price	Overall score (0–100; P F G VG E)	Auto on/off
	REGULAR MODELS			
1	**Cuisinart** Brew Central DCC-1200	$100		•
2	**Black & Decker** Smart Brew Plus DCM2500 **A CR Best Buy**	35		•
3	**Krups** ProAroma 12 Plus Time 453-71	100		•
4	**Black & Decker** Smart Brew DCM2000 **A CR Best Buy**	25		
5	**Braun** Aromaster KF 400 **A CR Best Buy**	20		
6	**Mr. Coffee** AR12 **A CR Best Buy**	20		
7	**Hamilton Beach** Flavor Plus 43421	40		•
8	**Proctor-Silex** Easy Morning 41331	20		
9	**Black & Decker** Spacemaker ODC325	75		•
10	**Mr. Coffee** AD10	25		
11	**Mr. Coffee** PL12	20		
12	**Mr. Coffee** PLX20	30		•
13	**Proctor-Silex** Simply Coffee 46871	20		•
14	**Proctor-Silex** Simply Coffee 46801	20		
	THERMAL-CARAFE MODELS			
15	**Mr. Coffee** Thermal Carafe URTX83	65		•
16	**Capresso** MT500 440	160		•
17	**Krups** AromaControl Therm Time 199-73	100		•
18	**Mr. Coffee** Thermal Gourmet TC80	43		
19	**Black & Decker** Thermal Select TCM300	35		

See report, page 83. Based on tests published in Consumer Reports in December 2002, with updated prices and availability.

Guide to the Ratings

Overall score is based on convenience. Tests included ease of filling, loading grounds, pouring, cleaning, and using controls. **Auto on/off** models are programmable, have a clock, and shut off after two hours. Thermal models shut off immediately. **Price** is approximate retail.

Recommendations & notes

Models listed as similar should offer performance comparable to the tested model, although features may differ. **EXCEPT AS NOTED, ALL:** Have drip-stop, "on" light, one-year warranty, clear cup markings in reservoir and/or on front-facing fill tube, or have removable reservoir with markings. Load without removing basket. Glass carafes have markings; most have flip-top lid.

REGULAR MODELS

1 **CUISINART** Brew Central DCC-1200 **Excellent, with many features and unusual design, but expensive.** 12 cups. Adjustable hotplate. Small-batch control. Water filter. Cleaning cycle. Remove lid to fill carafe. Three-year warranty.

2 **BLACK & DECKER** Smart Brew Plus DCM2500 **A CR Best Buy Very good, with good price and features.** 12 cups. Long cord; storage. But markings on side. Tested model sold only at Kmart. Similar: DCM 2575, DCM 2550.

3 **KRUPS** ProAroma 12 Plus Time 453-71 **Very good and feature-rich, but expensive.** 12 cups. Adjustable hotplate. Brew-strength/small-batch controls. Water filter. Long cord; storage. Remove lid to fill carafe. Harder to program. Similar: 453-42.

4 **BLACK & DECKER** Smart Brew DCM2000 **A CR Best Buy Inexpensive and very good, if very basic. 12 cups.** But markings on side. Tested model sold only at Kmart and Target. Similar: DCM2050, DCM2075.

5 **BRAUN** Aromaster KF 400 **A CR Best Buy Inexpensive and very good, if very basic.** 10 cups.

6 **MR. COFFEE** AR12 **A CR Best Buy Inexpensive and very good, if very basic.** 12 cups. Similar: AR13, ARX20, ARX23.

7 **HAMILTON BEACH** Flavor Plus 43421 **Very good.** 10 cups. Brew-strength control. Long cord; storage. Two-year warranty. Similar: 43424, 43425,43321

8 **PROCTOR SILEX** Easy Morning 41331 **Very good, but inconveniences.** 12 cups. Brew-strength control. But carafe harder to control when full. Two-year warranty. Similar: 41334.

9 **BLACK & DECKER** Spacemaker ODC325 **Very good if a bit expensive; mounts under cabinet.** 12 cups. Basket, reservoir pull out. Long cord; storage. But less brew than other 12-cup models. Sold only at Kmart, Target, Wal-Mart. Similar: ODC325N.

10 **MR. COFFEE** AD10 **Inexpensive and very good, if very basic.** 10 cups. Basket harder to open/close properly.

11 **MR. COFFEE** PL12 **A basic, low-cost model.** 12 cups. Basket harder to close (overflowed when not closed securely) and harder to replace on hinges. Similar: PL13.

12 **MR. COFFEE** PLX20 **Very good and reasonably priced, but inconveniences.** 12 cups. Basket harder to close (overflowed when not closed securely) and harder to replace. Display hard to read. Auto setting not obvious. Similar: PLX23.

13 **PROCTOR-SILEX** Simply Coffee 46871 **Basic model.** 12 cups. Brew-strength control. But basket won't sit upright on counter. Carafe

Recommendations & notes

harder to control when full. Six-month warranty. Similar: 46831.

14 PROCTOR-SILEX Simply Coffee 46801 **Inexpensive, but lacks conveniences.** 12 cups. Basket won't sit upright on counter. Carafe harder to control when full. Must remove basket to load. No drip-stop or "On" light. Uncoated hotplate. Markings on carafe only. Six-month warranty.

THERMAL-CARAFE MODELS

15 MR. COFFEE Thermal Carafe URTX83 **Very good, with helpful features.** 8 cups. Removable reservoir. Cleaning cycle.

16 CAPRESSO MT500 440 **Very good, but expensive; sleek silver-metal-and-black design and many features.** 10 cups. Small-batch setting. Water filter. Carafe easier to handle than other thermals. Long cord; storage. Fill tube with markings on side.

17 KRUPS AromaControl Therm Time 199-73 **Very good, but expensive; with contemporary rounded design.** 10 cups. Long cord; storage. Similar: 199-46, 197-46, 197-73, 229-45, 229-46, 229-70.

18 MR. COFFEE Thermal Gourmet TC80 **Very good, and reasonably priced for a thermal-carafe model.** 8 cups. Long cord; storage. Similar: TC81.

19 BLACK & DECKER Thermal Select TCM300 **Reasonably priced for a thermal-carafe model, but inconveniences.** 8 cups. "On" light not easily visible. Basket hard to open/close. Sold only at Target.

Cooktops

Electric smoothtops offer quick heating and easy-to-clean glass surfaces. While most electric cooktops heated quickly on their high settings and provided very low heat when turned down, most gas models didn't perform as well as the electrics on their low settings. Among electrics, the Kenmore 4270, $450, offers slightly faster heating than the Frigidaire Gallery GLEC30S8C, $500, but lacks bridge elements. Gas cooktops provide easily adjustable flame controls and choices ranging from basic to pro style. Among gas models, the Jenn-Air JGC8536AD, $850, offers excellent quick heating and two high-heat burners, while the Maytag MGC6536BD, $700, excelled at low-heat simmering. Consider the Magic Chef CGC2536AD, $350, if you're willing to trade style and features for a low price. A look at the prices for both categories reveals little correlation between price and performance.

In performance order.

Key: Excellent / Very good / Good / Fair / Poor

Key number	Product	Price	Overall score (0–100; P F G VG E)	Tests: Heating, high	Tests: Heating, low	Features: No. of elements, low	Features: Elements, medium	Features: Elements, high	Features: Bridge element	Features: Touch controls
	Similar models, in small type, comparable to tested model except that they're 36 inches wide, have an extra element or warning zone, and cost about $100 more.									
	ELECTRIC COOKTOPS									
1	**Frigidaire** Gallery GLEC30S8C[S] **A CR Best Buy** GLEC36S8C[ ]	$500		Very good	Excellent	1	2	1	•	
2	**GE** Profile JP930TC[WW] JP960TC[ ]	740		Very good	Excellent	1	2	1	•	
3	**GE** Profile JP939BH[BB]	1,200		Very good	Excellent	1	1	2		•
4	**Kenmore** (Sears) 4270[2] **A CR Best Buy** 4271[ ]	450		Excellent	Excellent	1	2	1		
5	**Kenmore** (Sears) Elite 4402[2]	600		Very good	Excellent	1	2	1	•	
6	**Jenn-Air** JEC8430AD[W]	560		Very good	Excellent	1	2	1		
7	**Thermador** CEP304Z[B]	1,300		Very good	Excellent	2		2		•
8	**Whirlpool** Gold GJC3034L[P] GJC3634L[ ]	650		Very good	Excellent	1	2	1		
9	**Bosch** NES73[2] NES93[2]	1,000		Very good	Excellent	1	2	1		•
10	**Amana** AKT3040[WW] AKT3650[ ]	550		Very good	Very good	1	2	1		

In performance order.

Excellent ⊜ Very good ⊖ Good ○ Fair ◒ Poor ●

Key number	Product	Price	Overall score (0–100; P F G VG E)	Tests: Heating, high	Tests: Heating, low	Features: No. of burners, low	Features: Burners, medium	Features: Burners, high	Style options: Stainless-steel	Style options: Glass	Style options: Enamel	Style options: Continuous grates
	Similar models, in small type, comparable to tested model except that they're 30 inches wide, have only four burners, and cost about $120 less.											
	GAS COOKTOPS											
11	**GE** Monogram ZGU375NSD[SS] ZGU375LSD [1]	$1,300		⊖	⊜		4	1	•			•
12	**Jenn-Air** JGC8536AD[S] **A CR Best Buy**	850		⊜	⊖	2	1	2	•			•
13	**Maytag** MGC6536BD[W] MGC6430BD[ ] **A CR Best Buy**	700		○	⊜	1	3	1		•		•
14	**Thermador** SGSX365Z[S]	1,500		⊖	⊖		2	3	•			•
15	**GE** Profile JGP962TEC[WW]	1,100		⊖	○	2	2	1		•		•
16	**Magic Chef** CGC2536AD[W]	350		○	⊖		4	1			•	
17	**Amana** AKS3640[SS]	600		○	⊖		4	1	•			•
18	**Kenmore** (Sears) Elite 3303[2]	750		⊖	○	1	2	1		•		
19	**Kenmore** (Sears) Elite 3321[3]	900		⊖	○	2	2	1	•			•
20	**Frigidaire** Gallery GLGC36S8C[B] GLGC30S8C[ ]	600		○	⊖	2	2	1		•		
21	**Bosch** NGT93[5]	900		⊖	◒	1	3	1	•			•

[1] *36-inch propane-only model.*

See report, page 97. *Based on tests published in Consumer Reports in September 2003, with updated prices and availability.*

Guide to the Ratings

Overall score includes high- and low-heating performance. **Heating, high** denotes how quickly the highest-powered element or burner heated 6⅓ quarts of room-temperature water to a near-boil. **Heating, low** shows how well the least-powerful element or burner melted and held chocolate without scorching it and whether the most powerful, set to low, held tomato sauce below a boil. **Price** is approximate retail. Under **Product,** brackets show a tested model's color code. Similar-model cooktops have the same highest and lowest elements or burners; other details may differ.

All 30-inch electric cooktops have: Four elements with rated powers ranging from 1,200 to between 2,200 and 2,500 watts. Expandable elements. Glass cooktop. Hot-surface indicator lights. A one-year full warranty. **Most have:** Control knobs. Limited five-year warranties on glass and elements. A 40-amp circuit requirement.

All 36-inch gas cooktops have: Control knobs. Sealed burners with lift-off base and cap for cleaning. A 120-volt connection requirement. A one-year full warranty. **Most have:** Five burners with rated power for low heat between 5,000 and 6,500 Btu/hr. and for high heat between 12,000 and 15,000 Btu/hr. A propane conversion kit.

Cookware

You don't have to pay top dollar to get even heating, comfortable handles, easy cleaning, and durability. Among nonstick sets, the Calphalon Commercial Nonstick, $500 for 10 pieces, is great for a demanding cook who's willing to pay a premium. But the two **CR Best Buys,** Simply Calphalon Nonstick, $200 for 8 pieces, and Cook's Essentials, $125 for 10 pieces, weigh less and are better choices for those on a budget. If you want an uncoated set, consider the Wolfgang Puck Bistro Collection. It has 20 pieces (including a 6-piece tool set and a nonstick frypan) and costs $150.

Within types, in performance order.

Excellent ⊜ Very good ⊖ Good ○ Fair ◒ Poor ●

Key number	Brand & Model (material)	Price	Overall score (0–100: P F G VG E)	Pieces	Test results: Even heat	Test results: Durable coating	Test results: Cleanup
	NONSTICK SETS						
1	**Calphalon** Commercial (anodized aluminum)	$500		10	Excellent	Excellent	Excellent
2	**Calphalon** Simply Calphalon **A CR Best Buy** (anodized aluminum)	200		8	Excellent	Very good	Excellent
3	**Emerilware** by All-Clad (anodized aluminum)	350		10	Excellent	Very good	Excellent
4	**Cook's Essentials A CR Best Buy** (stainless steel)	125		10	Very good	Very good	Excellent
5	**Scanpan** Titanium New Tek Classic (aluminum)	330		8	Very good	Excellent	Excellent
6	**Cuisinart** Stick Free (stainless steel)	200		7	Very good	Excellent	Excellent
7	**Meyer** Anolon Titanium (anodized aluminum)	400		10	Very good	Excellent	Excellent
8	**Meyer** Circulon Steel (stainless steel)	150		8	Good	Excellent	Very good
9	**Wearever** Soft Touch Handles (enamel on aluminum)	100		9	Good	Very good	Excellent
10	**Farberware** Millennium Satin Enamel (enamel on aluminum)	150		12	Very good	Good	Excellent
11	**Mirro** Series 500P (aluminum)	30		8	Good	Fair	Excellent
12	**Regal** Easy Clean (aluminum)	50		18	Good	Poor	Excellent
13	**T-Fal** 4U Total (enamel on aluminum)	90		8	Good	Fair	Excellent
14	**T-Fal** Encore Hard Enamel (enamel on aluminum)	80		8	Fair	Fair	Excellent

Within types, in performance order.

Key number	Brand & Model (material)	Price	Overall score (0–100; P F G VG E)	Pieces	Test results: Even heat	Test results: Durable coating	Test results: Cleanup
	UNCOATED SETS						
15	**Wolfgang Puck** Bistro Collection (stainless steel)	$150		20	⊜	⊖	○
16	**Farberware** Millennium (stainless steel, copper)	250		10	⊜	-	○
17	**Tools of the Trade** Belgique Gourmet (stainless steel, copper)	250		12	⊜	-	○
18	**Magnalite** Classic (aluminum)	115		8	⊖	-	◒
19	**Wearever** Easy Pour and Strain (stainless steel)	80		8	⊖	⊖	○
20	**Emerilware** by All-Clad (stainless steel)	150		7	⊖	-	○
21	**Calphalon** Simply Calphalon (stainless steel)	150		8	⊖	-	○
22	**Cuisinart** Multiclad (stainless steel)	200		7	○	-	○
23	**Revere** Copper Cuisine (stainless steel, copper)	60		7	⊖	-	●

See report, page 84. Based on tests published in Consumer Reports in December 2002, with updated prices and availability.

Guide to the Ratings

Overall score is based on performance and convenience. Each set includes at least these pieces: one 9.5- to 11-inch frypan with no lid, a stockpot/Dutch oven (usually 5- to 6.5-qt.) with lid, and a 2- to 3-quart saucepan with lid. Exceptions and extras are listed in Recommendations and notes. To test for **even heat,** we cooked frypan-sized pancakes at 400° F on a gas cooktop and gauged how evenly they browned. To test for **durable coating** on nonstick sets, we had a mechanical arm rub a steel-wool pad over the frypan's surface. An excellent score means the pan's coating was intact after 2,000 strokes and still released fried eggs with relative ease. **Cleanup** scores are based on the ease of removing a baked-on sauce of flour, milk, and butter from saucepans. Recommendations and notes include judgments on handle sturdiness, which indicate how well the frypans fared when we tried to bend the handle with up to 75 lb. of force and to loosen it by moving the pan up and down with 1.5 times its own weight inside. **Price** is approximate retail for the set.

Recommendations & notes

ALL COOKWARE SETS: Can be used on gas, electric coil, and electric smoothtop ranges. **EXCEPT AS NOTED, ALL:** Are dishwasher-safe and oven-safe to at least 425° F. Have a limited lifetime warranty. Have riveted handles, which are strong but can be hard to clean. Have handles that did not come loose in our tests and that stayed cool enough to hold without a potholder even while boiling water. Offer additional open stock.

NONSTICK SETS

1 **CALPHALON** Commercial (anodized aluminum) **Excels at all tasks, including simmer.** But not dishwasher-safe, and saucepan handle not well balanced. Heavy. Lifetime warranty. 8-qt. stockpot. Extras: 3-qt. chef pan, 3-qt. sauté pan & lids, 8-in. frypan.

2 **CALPHALON** Simply Calphalon **A CR Best Buy** (anodized aluminum) **Almost as good as set above, but a fraction of the price and lighter weight.** Not dishwasher-safe. Handles uncomfortable. 10-year warranty. Extras: 1-qt. saucepan & lid, 8-in. frypan.

3 **EMERILWARE** (anodized aluminum) **Well equipped, simmers very well.** But not dishwasher-safe. Heavy. Extras: 3-qt. sauté pan & lid, 3.5-qt. casserole & lid, 8-in. frypan. Made by All-Clad.

4 **COOK'S ESSENTIALS A CR Best Buy** (stainless steel) **Very good, especially simmering.** But oven-safe only to 350° F. Glass lids. Lifetime warranty. Extras: 1-qt. saucepan & lid, 12-in. sauté pan & lid, 8-in. frypan. No open stock. Available only from QVC.

5 **SCANPAN** Titanium New Tek Classic (aluminum) **Impressive overall.** But unriveted handles less comfortable and less well balanced than most. Heavy. Glass lids. Lifetime warranty. Extras: 1- qt. saucepan & lid, 8-in. frypan.

6 **CUISINART** Stick Free (stainless steel) **Very good value.** But saucepan handles got hot. Lifetime warranty. Extras: 2-qt. steamer insert, 8-in. frypan.

7 **MEYER** Anolon Titanium (anodized aluminum) **Very good.** But saucepan handles got hot. Heavy. Lifetime warranty. 8-qt stockpot. Extras: 3-qt. saucepan & lid, 5-qt. sauté pan & lid, 8-in. frypan.

8 **MEYER** Circulon Steel (stainless steel) **Commendable cooking.** But oven-safe only to 350° F. Shallow ridges slightly impede the cleaning. Has lifetime warranty. 8-qt. stockpot. Extras: 1.5-qt. saucepan & lid, 8-in. frypan.

9 **WEAREVER** Soft Touch Handles (enamel on aluminum) **Very good performance and price.** Lifetime warranty. 8-qt. stockpot. Extras: 3.5-qt. saucepan & lid, steamer, 10-in. frypan lid.

10 **FARBERWARE** Millennium Satin Enamel (enamel on aluminum) **There are better values.** Stockpot couldn't hold simmer. Lifetime warranty. 8-qt. stockpot. Extras: 3- and 1-qt. saucepans & lids, 12-in. sauté pan & lid, 8-in. frypan. Limited open stock.

11 **MIRRO** Series 500P (aluminum) **Nice overall.** Comfortable, no-rivet handles. But oven-safe only to 350° F. Glass lids. 20-yr. warranty. Extras: 1.5-qt. saucepan & lid, 8-in. frypan. Sold only at Wal-Mart.

12 **REGAL** Easy Clean (aluminum) **Lightweight, with comfortable handles.** But coating wore off quickly in tough tests. Oven-safe only to 350° F. Glass lids. 25-yr. warranty. Extras: 1.5- and 1-qt. saucepans & lids, 8-in. frypan, big frypan lid, 7-piece tool set. Open stock sold only at Wal-Mart.

13 **T-FAL** 4U Total (enamel on aluminum) **Good.** Comfortable no-rivet handles. But not oven-

Recommendations & notes

safe, and stockpot couldn't hold simmer. Lifetime warranty. Small stockpot (4.6-qt.). Extras: 11-in. frypan, 2 spatulas.

14 T-FAL Encore Hard Enamel (enamel on aluminum) **There are better sets.** Lightweight, with comfortable, no-rivet handles. But oven-safe only to 350° F. Lifetime warranty. Extras: 1-qt. saucepan & lid, 7.5-in. frypan, 3-piece tool set, recipe book.

UNCOATED SETS

15 WOLFGANG PUCK Bistro Collection (stainless steel) **Well equipped, cooks well.** 8-in. frypan is nonstick. Glass lids. Lifetime warranty. 8-qt. stockpot. Extras: 3- and 4-qt. saucepans & lids, 10-in. casserole & lid, steamer insert, 11-in. frypan & lid, 6-piece tool set. Sold through Home Shopping Network. Open stock sold through *www.wpcookware.com.*

16 FARBERWARE Millennium (stainless steel, copper) **Impressive.** Saucepan handles got hot. Lifetime warranty. 8-qt. stockpot. Extras: 12-in. sauté pan & lid, 3-qt. saucepan & lid; 4.5-qt. steamer insert.

17 TOOLS OF THE TRADE Belgique Gourmet (stainless steel, copper) **Very good performance.** Comfortable handles. Lifetime warranty. 8-qt. stockpot. Extras: 1- and 3.5-qt. saucepans & lids, 12.5-inch frypan & lid, steamer insert. Sold only at Macy's and other Federated Department Stores. Nonstick frypan available in open stock.

18 MAGNALITE Classic (aluminum) **Very good overall.** But oven-safe only to 350° F. Stockpot handles got hot. Uncomfortable, no-rivet handles. Some spouts. Heavy. 50-yr. warranty. Extras: 1-qt. saucepan & lid, meat rack. Limited open stock.

19 WEAREVER Easy Pour and Strain (stainless steel) **Good value for basic set.** But oven-safe only to 350° F, frypan handle not well balanced. Some spouts. Glass lids. Frypan is nonstick. Heavy. Lifetime warranty. Extras: 1-qt. saucepan & lid, lid for frypan.

20 EMERILWARE (stainless steel) **Very good.** Handles uncomfortable. Glass lids. Can use in broiler. Heavy. Lifetime warranty. Extras: 3-qt. casserole & lid. Made by All-Clad.

21 CALPHALON Simply Calphalon (stainless steel) **Cooks evenly, but handles uncomfortable.** Can use in broiler. Glass lids. Heavy. 10-yr. warranty. Extras: 1-qt. saucepan & lid, 8-in. frypan.

22 CUISINART Multiclad (stainless steel) **A princely sum for pauper performance.** Saucepan handles got hot. Can use in broiler. Lifetime warranty. Extras: 1.5-qt. saucepan & lid.

23 REVERE Copper Cuisine (stainless steel, copper) **Mediocre.** Stockpot couldn't hold simmer. Cleanup difficult. Glass lids. No-rivet handles. 25-year warranty. Extras: 1.5-qt. saucepan & lid. Limited open stock.

Dishwashers

Your dishes will come clean with almost all the dishwashers in our Ratings. In our latest tests, most models removed almost every trace of food. Fine performers and real values include our **CR Best Buys,** the KitchenAid KUDI01IL[BL], $550, and Maytag MDB7600A[W], $500. With our very dirty test load, the KitchenAid, with no sensor, was the more energy- and water-efficient of the two. The sensor-equipped Maytag had the most loading flexibility. While the three Bosch models that top the chart are outstanding performers, this brand has been more repair-prone than most, according to our latest survey.

Excellent · Very good · Good · Fair · Poor

In performance order.

Key number	Brand & model	Price	Washing	Energy Use	Noise	Loading	Ease of use	Cycle time (hr.:min.)	Sensor	Self-cleaning filter	Stainless-steel tub	Flatware slots
1	**Bosch** Distinctive SHU66C0[2]	$850	Excellent	Very good	Excellent	Very good	Very good	1:45	•		•	•
2	**Bosch** Distinctive SHU43C0[2]	600	Excellent	Very good	Excellent	Very good	Good	1:45	•		•	•
3	**Bosch** SHU995[2] [1]	900	Excellent	Very good	Excellent	Very good	Very good	1:45	•		•	•
4	**Viking** DFUD140	1,375	Excellent	Excellent	Very good	Good	Good	1:30			•	
5	**KitchenAid** KUDI01IL[BL] **A CR BEST BUY**	550	Excellent	Very good	Very good	Good	Very good	2:10		•	•	
6	**Frigidaire** Professional PLDB998C[C]	500	Excellent	Very good	Good	Good	Excellent	1:55	•	•	•	•
7	**KitchenAid** KUDP01DL[WH]	800	Excellent	Very good	Very good	Very good	Very good	2:10	•	•	•	•
8	**KitchenAid** Superba KUDS01FL[SS]	1,120	Excellent	Very good	Very good	Excellent	Very good	2:10	•	•		•
9	**Maytag** MDB8600AW[W]	600	Excellent	Very good	Very good	Very good	Excellent	1:50	•	•		•
10	**Maytag** MDB7600AW[W] **A CR BEST BUY**	500	Excellent	Good	Very good	Excellent	Excellent	2:00	•	•		•
11	**Miele** Novotronic G841SC Plus	850	Excellent	Very good	Very good	Good	Good	1:45		•	•	•
12	**Whirlpool** Gold GU1500XTL[Q]	570	Excellent	Good	Very good	Very good	Excellent	2:15	•	•		
13	**Whirlpool** DU943PWK[Q]	450	Excellent	Good	Good	Good	Very good	1:45	•	•		
14	**Whirlpool** Gold GU1200XTL[Q]	500	Excellent	Good	Very good	Good	Excellent	2:10	•	•		
15	**Amana** ADW862EA[W]	530	Excellent	Fair	Good	Good	Excellent	2:10	•	•		
16	**Whirlpool** DU900PWK[Q]	370	Very good	Excellent	Good	Fair	Good	1:40		•		
17	**Whirlpool** DU920PWK[B]	370	Good	Excellent	Good	Fair	Good	1:35		•		
18	**Hotpoint** HDA3700[WW]	280	Good	Excellent	Fair	Fair	Very good	1:35		•		

[1] Required custom front panel for similar Bosch SHY56A0[] is additional.

See report, page 86. Based on tests published in Consumer Reports in May 2003, with updated prices and availability.

Guide to the Ratings

Overall score stresses washing but factors in noise, energy and water use, loading, and more. **Washing** judges results with a full load of very dirty dishes, glasses, and flatware. **Energy use** is for the normal cycle. **Noise** was judged by listeners, aided by sound-level measurements. Loading reflects ability to hold extra place settings and oversized items. **Ease of use** considers controls and maintenance. Under **brand & model,** a bracketed letter or number is the color code. Similar models should perform comparably to the tested model but may differ in features. **Price** is the approximate retail. **Cycle time** is based on a normal cycle including heated dry, where that feature is available. In **key features,** a check mark indicates that a model has the feature listed. A **sensor** is intended to detect soil and adjust cycles appropriately. **Self-cleaning filter** requires no maintenance, but may make the dishwasher noisier than one with a manual-clean filter. A **stainless-steel tub** is more durable than plastic and resists stains. **Flatware slots** separate pieces for better cleaning.

Recommendations & notes

ALL DISHWASHERS: Are standard-sized, 24-inch-wide, under-the-counter models that can hold a complete 10-piece place setting with two serving bowls and one serving platter. **Most models:** Have touchpad controls and at least three cycles (light, normal, pots-and- pans). Have rinse-and-hold, heated-water, and drain/cancel control for stopping midcycle. Have a 1-year warranty on parts and labor, with 20 or more years on the door liner and tub.

1. **BOSCH** Distinctive SHU66C0[2] **Excellent.** Among the quietest models tested. But among the more repair-prone brands. More loading flexibility than most. Has an adjustable upper rack. Among the more water-efficient sensor models; uses about 7 gallons of water in the normal cycle. However, heated-dry feature can't be turned off. Hidden or partially hidden controls are available on higher-priced similar models. Similar: SH166A0[ ], SHV66A0[ ], SHY66C0[ ].

2. **BOSCH** Distinctive SHU43C0[2] **Excellent.** Among the quietest models tested. But among the more repair-prone brands. More loading flexibility than most. Has an adjustable upper rack. Among the more water-efficient sensor models; uses about 7 gallons of water in the normal cycle. However, heated-dry feature can't be turned off. Similar: SHY53A0[ ].

3. **BOSCH** SHU995[2] **Excellent.** But among the more repair-prone brands and pricey. Among the quietest and more water-efficient sensor models tested; uses about 7 gallons of water in the normal cycle. More loading flexibility than most; has an adjustable top rack. Has hidden controls, so the door must be opened to check wash progress. Has stainless-steel tub. Heated-dry feature can't be turned off. Requires a door panel, which costs extra. This model has been discontinued, but its similar model, SHY56A0[ ], is available.

4. **VIKING** DFUD140 **Excellent but expensive.** Has hidden controls. Uses less water than most, about 5.5 gallons in the normal cycle. Requires door panel, which costs extra.

5. **KITCHENAID** KUDI01IL[BL] **A CR Best Buy Excellent performance overall.** No delay start. But long cycle time. Uses about 7 gallons

Recommendations & notes

of water in the normal cycle. Hidden or partially hidden controls are available on higher-priced similar models. Similar: KUD101DL[ ], KUD101FL[ ].

6. **FRIGIDAIRE** PLDB998C[C] **Excellent performer, but among the more repair-prone brands.** Stainless-steel exterior. Uses about 9 gallons of water in the normal cycle. Similar: PLD8999C[ ].

7. **KITCHENAID** KUDP01DL[WH] **Excellent.** More loading flexibility than most. But long cycle time. Uses about 8 gallons of water in the normal cycle. Hidden controls are available on higher-priced similar models. Similar: KUDP01IL[ ], KUDP01FL[ ].

8. **KITCHENAID** Superba KUDS01FL[SS] **Excellent, but expensive.** More loading flexibility than most, with adjustable upper rack. Hidden controls. But long cycle time. Uses about 8 gallons of water in the normal cycle. Similar: KUDS01IL[ ], KUDS01DL[ ].

9. **MAYTAG** MDB8600A[W] **Excellent.** More loading flexibility than most. Has third rack at bottom, which allows loading of oversized items such as mixing bowls and platters. Center rack is adjustable. Uses about 8 gallons of water in the normal cycle. Similar: MDB9600AW[ ].

10. **MAYTAG** MDB7600A[W] **A CR Best Buy Excellent overall.** More loading flexibility than most. Has adjustable upper rack. Uses about 9 gallons of water in the normal cycle.

11. **MIELE** Novotronic G841SC Plus **Very good performer.** Holds a few more dishes than the average dishwasher. Has separate flatware rack with slots. Has an adjustable upper rack. But heated-dry option can't be turned off. No delay start. Uses about 7 gallons of water in the normal cycle.

12. **WHIRLPOOL** Gold GU1500XTL[Q] **Very good overall.** More loading flexibility than most, with adjustable rack and extra cutlery rack. But long cycle time. Uses about 10 gallons of water in the normal cycle.

13. **WHIRLPOOL** DU943PWK[Q] **Very good, at a reasonable price.** Uses about 9 gallons of water in the normal cycle. Similar: DU950PWK[ ], DU951PWK[ ], DUL200PK[ ].

14. **WHIRLPOOL** Gold GU1200XTL[Q] **Very good performance.** Much like the GU1500XTL, but fewer features. Long cycle time. Uses about 9 gallons of water in the normal cycle. Similar: DUL300XTL[ ].

15. **AMANA** ADW862EA[W] **Very good.** But long cycle time and high water use (about 12 gallons of water in the normal cycle).

16. **WHIRLPOOL** DU900PWK[Q] **Very good, basic model with excellent efficiency.** But less loading flexibility than most. Manual-control push buttons and cycle dial must be synchronized. Uses less water than most (about 5 gallons of water in the normal cycle). Similar: DU909PWK[ ], DUL100PK[ ].

17. **WHIRLPOOL** DU920PWK[B] **Very good, basic model with excellent efficiency.** Adjustable upper rack. But less loading flexibility than most. Manual-control push buttons and cycle dial must be synchronized. Used less water than most (about 5 gallons of water in the normal cycle). Door-mounted flatware basket lowers its washing performance. Similar: DU910PWK[ ], DU911PWK[ ].

18. **HOTPOINT** HDA3700G[WW] **Good performer overall.** But mechanical touchpad controls and cycle dial must be synchronized. Less loading flexibility than most. Louder than most. Uses about 7 gallons of water in the normal cycle.

Drills, cordless

Decide whether you need raw power for decks and other big jobs, easy handling for around-the-house tasks, or—like most buyers—some combination of the two. For mundane tasks and the occasional deck, consider the **CR Best Buy** 18-volt Ryobi HP1802MK2. It's nearly as capable overall as the top-rated drills, yet it weighs less and costs about half as much. Increasingly, drills with less than 14.4 volts are not worth buying. Even the highest-scoring 12-volt model we tested rated no better than a "Good" and offered less for its price. Odds are, you'll also find models in the 9.6-volt category disappointing for all but the lightest-duty tasks. Consider them only if you value minimal weight and cost over performance.

Within types, in performance order.

Excellent / Very good / Good / Fair / Poor

Key number	Brand & Model	Price	Weight (lb.)	Overall Score (0–100; P F G VG E)	Test results: Overall power	Run time	Charge time	Handling
	18-VOLT DRILLS							
1	**DeWalt** DW987K-2	$270	6.0		Excellent	Very good	Excellent	Good
2	**Craftsman** (Sears) Professional 27124	200	6.5		Very good	Very good	Excellent	Good
3	**DeWalt** DW929K-2	200	4.6		Very good	Good	Excellent	Very good
4	**Ryobi** HP1802MK2 **A CR Best Buy**	100	5.1		Very good	Good	Excellent	Good
5	**Black & Decker** FSD182K-2	110	5.2		Very good	Good	Good	Good
6	**Grizzly** G8596	70	4.2		Good	Fair	Good	Very good
	14.4-VOLT DRILLS							
7	**DeWalt** DW928K-2	180	4.3		Very good	Fair	Excellent	Very good
8	**Makita** 6228DWAE	160	3.8		Good	Fair	Excellent	Excellent
9	**Ryobi** HP1442MK2	85	4.2		Good	Fair	Excellent	Very good
10	**Black & Decker** FSD142K-2	90	4.4		Good	Fair	Good	Good
11	**Grizzly** G8595	55	3.4		Fair	Fair	Good	Very good
	12-VOLT DRILLS							
12	**DeWalt** DW927K-2	140	4.0		Very good	Fair	Excellent	Very good
13	**Makita** 6227DWE	130	3.4		Good	Fair	Excellent	Excellent
14	**Black & Decker** FSD122K	70	3.5		Fair	Fair	Good	Good
15	**Skil** 2468-02	40	3.2		Fair	Poor	Good	Very good
16	**Ryobi** HP1202MK2	70	3.4		Fair	Poor	Fair	Very good

Within types, in performance order.

Key number	Brand & Model	Price	Weight (lb.)	Overall Score (0–100; P F G VG E)	Overall power	Run time	Charge time	Handling
	9.6 VOLT AND BELOW							
17	**DeWalt** DW926K-2	$100	3.4		◒	●	⊜	⊜
18	**Black & Decker** CD9600K	60	2.9		◒	●	●	⊖

See report, page 117. Based on tests published in Consumer Reports in January 2003, with updated prices and availability.

Guide to the Ratings

Weight is to the nearest tenth of a pound for the drill and battery pack. **Overall score** is based on overall power, run time, charge time, and handling. **Overall power** denotes drilling speed and torque, or twisting force. **Run time** reflects work per battery charge, measured on a dynamometer. **Charge time** is how much time it takes to fully recharge a discharged battery. Handling includes weight, balance, and effort needed to position the head. **Price** is approximate retail. **Recommendations & notes** list noteworthy features and some minor shortcomings.

Recommendations & notes

ALL TESTED CORDLESS DRILLS HAVE: A keyless chuck. A reversible drive. **MOST HAVE:** A smart charger with 1-hour charge time. Two speed ranges: slow (0 to about 400 rpm) for driving screws, and fast (about 0 to 1,100-1,650 rpm) for drilling holes; single-speed models have a range of 0 to 600-800 rpm, which tends to compromise their driving and drilling performance. A variable clutch with at least 16 settings for limiting the tool's maximum torque. A 3⁄8-inch chuck (1⁄2-inch for 18- and 24-volt models, except as noted). A trigger lockout for safety. Bit storage. Two NiCad battery packs. A carrying case. A one-year warranty.

18-VOLT DRILLS

1. **DEWALT** DW987K-2 **Powerful and well-equipped, but heavy.** Three speed ranges.

2. **CRAFTSMAN** (Sears) Professional 27124 **Capable and well-equipped, but heavy.**

3. **DEWALT** DW929K-2 **Capable and light.** 3⁄8-inch chuck.

4. **RYOBI** HP1802MK2 **A CR Best Buy. Lots of performance for the money.** Magnetic screw holder. 2-year warranty.

5. **BLACK & DECKER** FSD182K-2 **Capable, but charging takes 3 to 6 hours.** 3⁄8-inch chuck. Quick-connect bit change. 2-year warranty.

6. **GRIZZLY** G8596 **Light, though otherwise unimpressive.** 3⁄8-inch chuck. Extra bits. Only one battery. Charging takes 3 to 5 hours.

14.4-VOLT DRILLS

7. **DEWALT** DW928K-2 **Capable overall.**

8. **MAKITA** 6228DWAE **Light and well-balanced.** No bit storage.

9. **RYOBI** HP1442MK2 **OK.** Magnetic screw holder. 2-year warranty.

10. **BLACK & DECKER** FSD142K-2 **OK, but charging takes 3 to 6 hours.** Quick-connect bit change. Level light. 1⁄2-inch chuck. 2-year warranty.

Recommendations & notes

11. GRIZZLY G8595 **There are better choices.** Only one battery. Charging takes 3 to 5 hours.

12-VOLT DRILLS

12. DEWALT DW927K-2 **Power offset by relatively short run time.**

13. MAKITA 6227DWE **Light and well-balanced, but otherwise unimpressive.** No bit storage.

14. BLACK & DECKER FSD122K **There are better choices.** Charging takes 3 to 5 hours.

15. SKIL 2468-02 **There are better choices.** Only one battery. Charging takes 3 to 5 hours. Discontinued, but similar 2467-02 is available.

16. RYOBI HP1202MK2 **There are better choices.** Charging takes 3 to 5 hours.

9.6 VOLT AND BELOW

17. DEWALT DW926K-2 **Best of an unimpressive group.** Well-balanced and well-equipped.

18. BLACK & DECKER CD9600K **There are better choices.** Only one battery. Charging takes 16 hours.

Dryers

All the full-sized dryers we tested were very good or excellent performers with ample capacity. For spacious capacity and superb drying, consider the quiet GE Profile DPSB620EC. For fine performance at a low price, look to the **CR Best Buy** Kenmore 6280 or Frigidaire Gallery GLER642A. A pricier dryer may offer fancier styling, touchpad controls, a porcelain top, a stainless-steel drum, and extras such as programmability and numerous cycles—none essential in our view. A compact washing machine and dryer is an option when space is tight, but most are pricey. A stackable full-sized washer and dryer offer more capacity and usually cost less.

Within types, in performance order.

Excellent / Very good / Good / Fair / Poor

Key number	Brand & model	Price	Overall score (0–100; P F G VG E)	Test results: Drying performance	Capacity	Noise	Features: Drying rack	Stainless-steel drum	Custom programs	Optional extended tumble
	FULL-SIZED DRYERS									
1	**GE** Profile DPSB620EC[WW]	$600		Excellent	Excellent	Excellent	●	●	●	●
2	**Kenmore** (Sears) 6280[2] **A CR Best Buy**	410		Excellent	Excellent	Very good				
3	**Kenmore** (Sears) 6490[2]	440		Excellent	Excellent	Good	●			
4	**Whirlpool** Gold GEQ9800L[W]	450		Very good	Excellent	Very good				●
5	**Kenmore** (Sears) Elite HE3 8483[2]	900		Very good	Excellent	Excellent	●			●
6	**LG** DL-E5932W	900		Very good	Excellent	Very good	●	●	●	●
7	**Maytag** Neptune MDE7500AY[W]	800		Excellent	Excellent	Good			●	●
8	**Kenmore** (Sears) Elite 6408[2]	770		Very good	Excellent	Very good	●		●	●
9	**Kenmore** (Sears) Elite HE3 8282[2]	900		Very good	Excellent	Excellent	●			●
10	**Whirlpool** Duet GEW9200L[W]	880		Very good	Excellent	Excellent	●			●
11	**Whirlpool** Gold GEW9868K[Q]	680		Very good	Excellent	Excellent	●			●
12	**Whirlpool** LEQ8000J[Q]	420		Very good	Excellent	Very good				●
13	**Whirlpool** Gold GEW9878J[Q]	560		Excellent	Excellent	Very good				●
14	**Kenmore** (Sears) Elite 6206[2]	770		Very good	Excellent	Very good	●		●	●
15	**Frigidaire** Gallery GLER642A[S] **A CR Best Buy**	350		Very good	Very good	Very good	●			●
16	**KitchenAid** KEYS850J[W]	500		Very good	Excellent	Very good	●			●

Within types, in performance order.

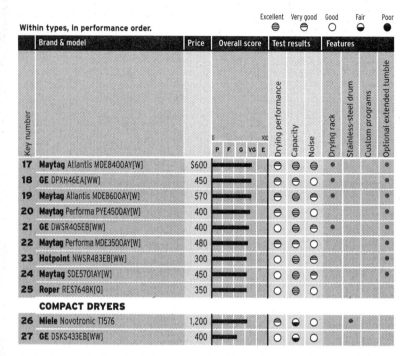

Key number	Brand & model	Price	Overall score	Test results: Drying performance	Test results: Capacity	Test results: Noise	Features: Drying rack	Features: Stainless-steel drum	Features: Custom programs	Features: Optional extended tumble
17	**Maytag** Atlantis MDE8400AY[W]	$600		Very good	Excellent	Excellent	•			•
18	**GE** DPXH46EA[WW]	450		Very good	Very good	Good	•			•
19	**Maytag** Atlantis MDE8600AY[W]	570		Very good	Excellent	Very good	•			•
20	**Maytag** Performa PYE4500AY[W]	400		Very good	Excellent	Good				•
21	**GE** DWSR405EB[WW]	400		Good	Excellent	Very good	•			•
22	**Maytag** Performa MDE3500AY[W]	480		Very good	Very good	Good				•
23	**Hotpoint** NWSR483EB[WW]	300		Good	Excellent	Very good				•
24	**Maytag** SDE5701AY[W]	450		Good	Excellent	Very good				•
25	**Roper** RES7648K[0]	350		Good	Excellent	Good				
	COMPACT DRYERS									
26	**Miele** Novotronic T1576	1,200		Very good	Fair	Good		•		
27	**GE** DSKS433EB[WW]	400		Good	Fair	Good				

Rating key: Excellent, Very good, Good, Fair, Poor. Overall score scale: 0–100 (P, F, G, VG, E).

See report, page 89. Based on tests published in Consumer Reports in August 2003, with updated prices and availability.

Guide to the Ratings

Overall score is based primarily on drying performance, capacity, and noise. Also factored in: Convenience (not shown), which considers controls, accessibility, and overall ease of use. All tested models were very good for convenience except the two tested compact dryers Miele Novotronic T1576 and GE DSKS433EB[WW], which scored lower. **Drying performance** combines tests on various-sized loads of different fabric mixed, including cotton, permanent press, and delicates. **Capacity** ranges from about 4 cubic feet for compacts to 7.5 cubic feet for the largest models; all could handle our 12-pound load. **Noise** reflects judgments by panelists. **Price** is approximate retail. Under **brand & model,** bracketed letters or numbers are color codes.

Recommendations & notes

Models judged excellent for drying were noticeably better than lower-rated units at leaving a load damp for ironing and drying delicates at low heat.

FULL-SIZED DRYERS

1 **GE** Profile DPSB620EC[WW] **Excellent overall.** Impressive on large loads. Delicates temperature lower than most, an advantage. Large door opening. Touchscreen controls. Damp dry signal to remove clothes for ironing. Gas equivalent: DPSB620GC[ ].

2 **KENMORE** (Sears) 6280[2] **A CR Best Buy Very good.** Superb drying for a good price. But warmer than most on delicates. Impressive on large loads. Fewer features than most. Similar: 6282[ ], 6481[ ]. Gas equivalent: 7280[ ], 7282[ ], 7481[ ].

3 **KENMORE** (Sears) 6490[2] **Very good overall.** Impressive on large loads. Large door opening. Similar: 6492[ ], 6493[ ]. Gas equivalent: 7490[ ] 7492[ ], 7493[ ].

4 **WHIRLPOOL** Gold GEQ9800L[W] **Very good, but warmer than most on delicates.** Impressive on large loads. Gas equivalent: GGQ9800L[ ].

5 **KENMORE** (Sears) Elite HE3 8483[2] **Very good overall.** Delicates temperature lower than most, an advantage. Damp dry signal to remove clothes for ironing. Touchscreen controls. Gas equivalent: 9483[ ].

6 **LG** DL-E5932W **Very good overall.** Delicates temperatures lower than most, an advantage. Damp dry signal to remove clothes for ironing.

7 **MAYTAG** Neptune MDE7500AY[W] **Very good.** Touch screen. Impressive on large loads. Damp dry signal to remove clothes for ironing. Similar: MDE5500AY[ ]. Gas equivalent: MDG5500AW[ ], MDG7500AW[ ].

8 **KENMORE** (Sears) Elite 6408[2] **Very good overall.** Delicates temperature lower than most, an advantage. Damp dry signal to remove clothes for ironing. Touchscreen controls. Gas equivalent: 7408[ ].

9 **KENMORE** (Sears) Elite HE3 8282[2] **A very good dryer, though pricey.** Touchpad controls. Very quiet. Pedestal available to raise dryer door to a comfortable height. Gas equivalent: 9282[ ].

10 **WHIRLPOOL** Duet GEW9200L[W] **Very good.** Much like the Kenmore (Sears) Elite HE3 8282[2]. Exceptionally quiet. Large door opening. Gas equivalent: GGW9200L[ ].

11 **WHIRLPOOL** Gold GEW9868K[Q] **Very good.** Very quiet. Impressive on large loads. Touchpad controls. Gas equivalent: GGW9868K[ ].

12 **WHIRLPOOL** LEQ8000J[Q] **Very good performance for the price.** But fewer features than most. Impressive on large loads. Similar: LEQ9858L[ ]. Gas equivalents: LGQ8000J[ ], LGQ9858L[ ].

13 **WHIRLPOOL** Gold GEW9878J[Q] **Impressive on large loads and delicates.** Discontinued, but similar GEW9878L[ ] is available. Gas equivalent: GGW9878L[ ].

14 **KENMORE** (Sears) Elite 6206[2] **Very good.** Delicate temperatures lower than most, an advantage. Large door opening. Touchpad controls. Gas equivalent: 7206[ ].

15 **FRIGIDAIRE** Gallery GLER642A[S] **A CR Best Buy A very good, no-frills machine.** Impressive on large loads. Gas equivalent: GLGR642A[ ].

16 **KITCHENAID** KEYS850J[W] **Very good.** Delicate temperatures lower than most, an

Recommendations & notes

advantage. Discontinued, but similar KEYS850L[ ] is available. Gas equivalent: KGYS850L[ ].

17 MAYTAG Atlantis MDE8400AY[W] **Very good overall.** Delicates temperature lower than most, an advantage. Large door opening. Moisture monitor. Gas equivalent: MDG8400AY[ ].

18 GE DPXH46EA[WW] **Very good.** Impressive on large loads and delicates. Gas equivalent: GE DPXH46GA[ ].

19 MAYTAG Atlantis MDE8600AY[W] **Very good.** Moisture monitor. Similar: MDE7600AY[ ]. Gas equivalents: MDG7600AW[ ], MDG8600AW[ ].

20 MAYTAG Performa PYE4500AY[W] **Very good, no-frills machine.** Drum opening smaller than most. Gas equivalent: PYG4500AY[ ].

21 GE DWSR405EB[WW] **Very good.** Not as good at drying as other sensor models. Large door opening. Gas equivalent: GE DWSR405GB[ ].

22 MAYTAG Performa MDE3500AY[W] **A very good, no-frills machine.** Moisture monitor. Gas equivalent: MDG3500AW[ ].

23 HOTPOINT NWSR483EB[WW] **A very good, spartan machine.** But no moisture sensor. Large door opening. Gas equivalent: NWSR483GB[ ].

24 MAYTAG SDE5701AY[W] **Very good, but warmer than most on delicates.** Moisture monitor. Large door opening. Gas equivalent: SDG5701.

25 ROPER RES7648K[Q] **Very good, but warmer than most on delicates.** No moisture sensor. Fewer features than most. Gas equivalent: RGS7648K[ ].

COMPACT DRYERS

26 MIELE Novotronic T1576 **Very good overall.** Delicates temperature lower than most, an advantage. Door opening smaller than most.

27 GE DSKS433EB[WW] **Good overall.** Controls on front of dryer.

Gas grills

Most grills we tested were competent overall. Spend more and you get more features, more style, better materials, and the ability to handle more cooking tasks. Superb performance makes the average-sized Jenn-Air JA460P, $600, our top pick overall. Nearly as good for less: the Weber Genesis Silver B 228[1]001, $450, and Fiesta Optima ESD45055, $200, both **CR Best Buys.** While the Fiesta lacks the Jenn-Air's porcelain-coated grates and the Weber's long-warranty burners, it provides strong performance at a low price. For large grills, the Weber Summit Gold A 526[0]001, $1,300, performs well, has a large cooking area, and lots of shelf space. But it's pricey. Among small grills, we recommend the Weber Genesis Silver A 227[1]001, **a CR Best Buy,** at $350.

Excellent ⊜ Very good ⊖ Good ○ Fair ◒ Poor ●

Within types, in performance order.

Key number	Brand & model	Price	Overall Score (0–100; P F G VG E)	Test results: Evenness	Test results: Grilling	Test results: Features and convenience	Grates: Stainless steel	Grates: Coated Cast iron	Long-warranty burners
	AVERAGE-SIZED GRILLS								
1	**Jenn-Air** JA460P	$600		Excellent	Excellent	Excellent		•	
2	**Broilmaster** P3[BL]	900 [1]		Excellent	Excellent	Very good		•	•
3	**Weber** Genesis Silver B 228[1]001 **A CR Best Buy**	450 [1]		Very good	Excellent	Very good			•
4	**TEC** Patio II PP-402-L	1,600		Excellent	Excellent	Very good	•		•
5	**Char-Broil** Professional Series 463233503	900		Very good	Excellent	Excellent	•		•
6	**Ducane** 7100 Stainless Series	1,400		Excellent	Very good	Very good	•		•
7	**Char-Broil** Commercial Series 463221503	500		Very good	Excellent	Very good		•	•
8	**Fiesta** Optima ESD45055 **A CR Best Buy**	200		Very good	Very good	Very good			
9	**Char-Broil** Big Easy 463838403	270 [1]		Very good	Excellent	Good			
10	**Ducane** 1605SHLPE	850		Very good	Very good	Very good	•		•
11	**Holland** Tradition BH421SG4	675		Excellent	Good	Good	•		•
12	**Coleman** 3300 Series DT331-BBF	470		Very good [2]	Very good	Very good		•	•
13	**Ducane** 1305SHLPE	700		Very good	Very good	Very good	•		•
14	**Char-Broil** Quickset 463728503	170 [1]		Very good	Very good	Good			
15	**Great Outdoors Grill Company** 7000W	275		Good	Very good	Very good			•
	LARGE GRILLS								
16	**Weber** Summit Gold A 526[0]001	1,300 [1]		Excellent	Very good	Excellent	•		•

Within types, in performance order.

Key number	Brand & model	Price	Overall Score (0–100; P F G VG E)	Test results: Evenness	Test results: Grilling	Test results: Features and convenience	Grates: Stainless steel	Grates: Coated Cast iron	Long-warranty burners
	SMALL GRILLS								
17	**Weber** Genesis Silver A 227[1]001 **A CR Best Buy**	$350		⊖	⊖	⊖			●
18	**Ducane** 1005SHLPE	530		⊖	⊖	⊖	●		●
19	**Americana** by Ducane AM12	250		⊖	⊖	⊖	●		
20	**Fiesta** Advantis 1000 EZA30030	125 [1]		⊖	⊖	○			
21	**Great Outdoors Grill Company** 4100W	200		◒	○	⊖			●

[1] *Price includes propane tank.* [2] *Evenness score is with the power burner off.*

See report, page 119. Based on tests published in Consumer Reports in June 2003, with updated prices and availability.

Guide to the Ratings

Under **brand & model,** brackets show a tested model's color code. **Overall score** denotes performance, features, and convenience. We tested evenness at high and low settings with temperature sensors, then combined scores. We verified results by searing 15 burgers on the high setting of the best and worst grills for 1½ minutes. Grilling is the ability to cook chicken and fish on the low setting. **Features and convenience** denotes construction and materials, accessory burners, shelves, rack space, and ease of use. **Price** is approximate retail.

Recommendations & notes

ALL GRILLS: Are on a cart. Have side shelves and hand-wheel gas fittings. Require some assembly. **ALL LARGE GRILLS HAVE:** Six burners. **MOST GRILLS HAVE:** A thermometer on the lid. Warranty from 25 years to life for castings, 3 to 5 years for burners, and 5 years for other parts. Shelf space of 200 to 550 square inches. Steel rack full of ceramic or charcoal-like briquettes, or steel triangles or plates, to distribute heat. Rotary or push-button igniter. Painted-steel cart. Plastic handles. Four wheels or casters. Spider protector on gas venturi tube to prevent webs from blocking flow. Natural-gas conversion kit or model. No propane tank ($25 to $30 extra). **MOST AVERAGE-SIZED AND SMALL GRILLS HAVE:** Dual burner controls.

AVERAGE-SIZED GRILLS

1 **JENN-AIR** JA460P **Excellent, with lots of shelf space.** Four burners. Porcelain-coated steel and aluminum lid. Electronic igniter. Side shelves can be removed for cleanup. Utensil hooks. Can be converted to natural gas. HxWxD: 50x60x25 in. Claimed output: 44,000 Btu/hr. Warranty: castings, 10 yr.; burners, 5 yr.; other parts, 5 yr.

2 **BROILMASTER** P3[BL] **Excellent.** Cooking grates can be adjusted to three different levels for more cooking flexibility. Stainless-steel cart and handle. Fold-down front shelf. Fold-up side shelf. Utensil hooks. Electronic igniter.

Recommendations & notes

Comes with natural-gas conversion kit. HxWxD: 46x54x24 in. (without front shelf up). Claimed output: 40,000 Btu/hr. Warranty: castings, life; burners, 15 yr. prorated; other parts, 5 yr.

3 WEBER Genesis Silver B 228[1]001 **A CR Best Buy Excellent.** Lots of shelf space. Porcelain-coated steel and cast-aluminum lid. Three burners. Removable thermometer on lid doubles as meat thermometer. Thermometer got hot. Stationary side shelf with pop-up section. Utensil hooks. Grill base and side shelves can be removed for cleanup. Fuel gauge. HxWxD: 43x54x24 in. with pop-up section down. Claimed output: 36,000 Btu/hr. Warranty: castings, life; burners, 10 yr.; other parts, 5 yr.

4 TEC Patio II PP-402-L **Excellent.** Infrared main burners. Stainless-steel castings, lid, and handle. Grill base can be removed for cleanup. No thermometer on lid. Only two wheels; must lift one end to move. HxWxD: 50x41x24 in. Claimed output: 37,000 Btu/hr. Warranty: castings, life; burners, 10 yr.; other parts, 10 yr.

5 CHAR-BROIL Professional Series 463233503 **Very good.** All stainless-steel construction. Lots of shelf space. Three burners. Infrared rotisserie burner with motor and spit. Grill base can be removed for cleanup. Electronic igniter. Griddle. HxWxD: 49x63x27 in. Claimed output: 55,000 Btu/hr. Warranty: castings, 99 yr.; burners, 10 yr.; other parts, 2 yr.

6 DUCANE 7100 Stainless Series **Very good.** All-stainless construction. Folding side shelf. Lots of shelf space. Electronic igniter. Flared up more than others. No thermometer on lid. HxWxD: 49x43x27 in. (with side shelf down). Claimed output: 28,000 Btu/hr. Warranty: castings, life; burners, life; other parts, 5 yr.

7 CHAR-BROIL Commercial Series 463221503 **Very good.** Stainless-steel and cast-aluminum lid. Three burners plus side burner. Griddle. Grill bottom can be removed for cleanup. Electronic igniter. No spider protector. HxWxD: 49x58x27 in. Claimed output: 45,000 Btu/hr. Warranty: castings, 99 yr.; burners, 10 yr.; other parts, 2 yr.

8 FIESTA Optima ESD45055 **A CR Best Buy Very good.** Lots of warming-rack space. Bare cast-iron grates. Auto electronic igniter (fires up with single knob turn). Utensil hooks. No thermometer on lid. Only two wheels; must lift one end to move. HxWxD: 49x65x23 in. Claimed output: 55,000 Btu/hr. Warranty: castings, life; burners, 5 yr.; other parts, 2 yr.

9 CHAR-BROIL Big Easy 463838403 **Very good.** Can use charcoal as well as gas. Side burner. Utensil hooks. Handle got hot. Only two wheels; must lift one end to move. HxWxD: 50x65x24 in. Claimed output: 40,000 Btu/hr. Warranty: castings, life; burners, 5 yr.; other parts, 1 yr.

10 DUCANE 1605SHLPE **Very good.** Lots of warming-rack space. Removable plastic side shelf doubles as a cutting board. Lit-burner indicator. Flared up more than others. Handle got hot. No thermometer on lid. HxWxD: 49x56x26 in. Claimed output: 37,000 Btu/hr. Warranty: castings, life; burners, life; other parts, 5 yr.

11 HOLLAND Tradition BH421SG4 **Very good.** Can steam and smoke as well as grill. Smoker drawer for wood chips; smoker-drawer knob got hot. Utensil hooks. Only one temperature setting; unable to turn temperature down to keep food warm. No sear marks when grilling. No warming rack. HxWxD: 49x49x26 in. Claimed output: 19,500 Btu/hr. Warranty: castings, 5 yr.; burners, life; other parts, 5 yr.

12 COLEMAN 3300 Series DT331-BBF **Very good.** Extra-hot center burner (out of three total) reduced warmup time and improved searing, but compromised evenness when on. Porcelain-coated steel and aluminum lid.

Recommendations & notes

Lots of shelf space. Deep fryer/steamer/warmer. Workbench. Electronic igniter. Utensil hooks. HxWxD: 45x48x23 in. Claimed output: 57,000 Btu/hr. Warranty: castings, life; burners, life; other parts, 5 yr.

13 DUCANE 1305SHLPE **Very good.** Removable plastic side shelf doubles as cutting board. Lit-burner indicator. Flared up more than others. Handle got hot. No thermometer on lid. HxWxD: 49x52x25 in. Claimed output: 32,000 Btu/hr. Warranty: castings, life; burners, life; other parts, 5 yr.

14 CHAR-BROIL Quickset 463728503 **Very good.** Lots of warming-rack space. Side burner. Utensil hooks. Cart judged less sturdy than others. Only two wheels; must lift one end to move. No thermometer on lid. HxWxD: 48x55x22 in. Claimed output: 43,000 Btu/hr. Warranty: castings, life; burners, 1 yr.; other parts, 1 yr.

15 GREAT OUTDOORS Grill Company 7000W **Very good.** Cast-aluminum cart. Wood handle. Utensil hooks. Handle got hot. No thermometer on lid. HxWxD: 49x59x24 in. Claimed output: 30,000 Btu/hr. Warranty: castings, 50 yr.; burners, 25-yr. prorated; other parts, 5 yr.

LARGE GRILL

16 WEBER Summit Gold A 526[0]001 **Very good.** Lots of shelf space. Stainless-steel and aluminum lid. Stainless-steel handle. Six burners. Grill base and side shelves can be removed for cleanup. Fuel gauge. Electronic igniter. Utensil hooks. Two side shelves with pop-up sections. Handle got hot. Grills sold 8/02-8/03 are subject to recall. Under certain conditions, glass cover and other parts of thermometer could break. We did not experience a problem with the thermostat when we tested this model in June 2003. HxWxD: 46x69x28 in. with pop-up sections down. Claimed output: 57,600 Btu/hr. Warranty: castings, life; burners, 10 yr.; other parts, 5 yr.

SMALL GRILLS

17 WEBER Genesis Silver A 227[1]001 **A CR Best Buy Very good.** Similar in appearance to the more expensive Weber Genesis Silver B 228[1]001, but narrower. Porcelain-coated steel and cast-aluminum lid. Utensil hooks. Removable thermometer on lid doubles as meat thermometer. Grill base and side shelves can be removed for cleanup. Fuel gauge. Thermometer got hot. HxWxD: 40x52x22 in. Claimed output: 22,000 Btu/hr. Warranty: castings, life; burners, 10 yr.; other parts, 5 yr.

18 DUCANE 1005SHLPE **Very good.** Stainless-steel cart. Lit-burner indicator. Removable side shelf doubles as a cutting board. Flared up more than others. Handle got hot. No thermometer on lid. HxWxD: 44x41x23 in. Claimed output: 25,000 Btu/hr. Warranty: castings, life; burners, life; other parts, 5 yr.

19 AMERICANA by Ducane AM12 **Very good.** Lit-burner indicator. Removable side shelf doubles as a cutting board. Flared up more than others. Handle got hot. No thermometer on lid. HxWxD: 44x41x23 in. Claimed output: 25,000 Btu/hr. Warranty: castings, 5 yr.; burners, 5 yr.; other parts, 5 yr.

20 FIESTA Advantis 1000 EZH30030 **Very good.** Utensil hooks. Wood handle. Cart judged less sturdy than others. Flared up more than others. No thermometer on lid. HxWxD: 46x57x24 in. Claimed output: 30,000 Btu/hr. Warranty: castings, life; burners, 3 yr.; other parts, 2 yr.

21 GREAT OUTDOORS GRILL COMPANY 4100W **Good.** Cast-aluminum cart. Utensil hooks. Wood handle. Handle got hot. No thermometer on lid. HxWxD: 48x56x23 in. Claimed output: 28,000 Btu/hr. Warranty: castings, 50 yr.; burners, 25-yr. prorated; other parts, 5 yr.

Home theater in a box

A home theater in a box is the easiest and usually the cheapest path to surround sound, with prices starting below $300. All these systems include a receiver and six speakers, plus wiring and instructions that make setup a relative snap. Be sure there are enough connections for your needs because some models skimp on inputs and outputs. If you're looking for a model with a DVD player, the Sony HT-1800DP, $450, holds only one disc, but its separate components offer flexibility, and its receiver has ample connections. If you don't need a DVD player, the Onkyo HT-S760B, $500, is very good. It costs more than other models without DVD players, but has more inputs and offers 6.1 support.

Excellent ⊜ Very good ⊖ Good ○ Fair ◒ Poor ●

Within types, in performance order.

Key number	Brand & model	Price	Overall score (0–100; P F G VG E)	Test results: Sound quality	Test results: Ease of use	Test results: Features	Features: No. of discs	Features: Digital-audio in (optical/coaxial)	Features: Composite-video in/out	Features: S-video in/out	Features: Component-video in/out	Features: Powered subwoofer	Features: Onscreen display	Features: Front-panel input
	MODELS WITH DVD PLAYER													
1	**Sony** HT-1800DP	$450		Very good	Very good	Very good	1	1/1	3/1	0/1	0/1	•		
2	**Pioneer** HTD-330DV	300		Very good	Good	Fair	5	0/1	0/0	0/1	0/1		•	
3	**Sony** HT-C800DP	400		Very good	Good	Good	5	0/0	1/0	0/0	0/1		•	
4	**Panasonic** SC-HT900	500		Excellent	Good	Fair	5	1/0	0/0	0/1	0/1	•	•	
5	**Panasonic** SC-MT1	400		Excellent	Good	Fair	1	0/0	0/0	0/1	0/1	•		
	MODELS WITHOUT DVD PLAYER													
6	**Pioneer** HTP-230	300		Very good	Very good	Very good	-	1/1	3/1	0/0	0/0	•		
7	**Sony** HT-DDW750	300		Very good	Very good	Very good	-	1/1	3/1	0/0	0/0	•		
8	**Onkyo** HT-S760B	500		Very good	Good	Very good	-	2/1	4/1	4/2	2/1	•		•
9	**Kenwood** HTB-306	350		Very good	Good	Fair	-	1/2	3/1	2/1	0/0			
10	**RCA** RT-2600	280		Good	Good	Good	-	2/1	4/1	2/1	0/0			•
11	**Kenwood** HTB-206	300		Very good	Good	Fair	-	1/2	3/1	0/0	0/0			

See report, page 59. Based on tests published in Consumer Reports in November 2003, with updated prices and availability.

Guide to the Ratings

Overall score is based mostly on sound quality. **Sound quality** represents the accuracy of the amplifier, front speakers, subwoofer, and center-channel speaker. **Ease of use** reflects the design of the front panel and the remote control, legibility of controls, and ease of setup. **Features** reflects the presence or absence of useful features. The inputs and outputs shown are on the receiver, if that is separate from the DVD player. On models with DVD players, the S-video and component-video outputs can be used only with a TV. **Price** is approximate retail.

Recommendations & notes

ALL TESTED MODELS HAVE: A receiver and six speakers: front left and right, center, rear-surround left and right, and subwoofer. Decoders for Dolby Digital, DTS, Dolby Pro Logic surround audio, and other digital-signal processing (DSP) modes. An FM tuner that scored very good in our tests. An AM tuner (not tested for this report) that should be good or fair, based on previous testing. Headphone jack. Mute button. Wiring and setup instructions. No phono input. **MOST TESTED MODELS:** Have bass and treble adjustment, receiver-display dimmer, at least 30 radio-station presets, sleep timer, and 1-yr. warranty. Lack on-screen display (OSD) feature, front-panel A/V inputs, loudness control, or bass-boost switch. Most with DVD player cannot play DVD-Audio and SACD discs.

MODELS WITH DVD PLAYER

1. **SONY** HT-1800DP **Very good.** Includes stand-alone single-disc DVD player. Has optical and coaxial digital-audio inputs and 2-yr. warranty. Lacks 5.1 inputs for external digital-audio decoders. Front and rear-surround speakers 6x3.75x5 in. (HWD), 1.8 lb. each; center speaker 3.75x9.25x5 in., 2.2 lb.; subwoofer 12.75x10.75x16 in., 21.6 lb.

2. **PIONEER** HTD-330DV **Very good.** Includes integrated five-disc DVD player. Has bass-boost switch and onscreen display. Coaxial digital-audio input only. Lacks 5.1 inputs for external digital-audio decoders. Front speakers 9.25x5.75x8.25 in. (HWD), 4.2 lb. each; rear-surround speakers 6.25x4.5x3.25 in., 1.7 lb. each; center speaker 4.25x12.25x3.5 in., 2.2 lb.; subwoofer 14.25x7.5x13 in., 11 lb.

3. **SONY** HT-C800DP **Very good.** Includes integrated five-disc DVD player. Has on-screen display, and bass-boost switch. 2-yr. warranty. Lacks 5.1 inputs for external digital- audio decoders. No S-video connection, sleep timer or treble adjustment. Front and rear-surround speakers 6x3.75x5 in. (HWD), 1.8 lb. each; center speaker 3.75x9.25x5 in., 2.2 lb.; subwoofer 12.75x10.75x14.25 in., 14.7 lb.

4. **PANASONIC** SC-HT900 **Very good.** Can play DVD-audio discs. Includes integrated five-disc DVD player. Has on-screen display. Optical digital-audio input only. Lacks 5.1 inputs for external digital-audio decoders. No treble adjustment. Front and rear-surround speakers 42x10x10 in. (HWD) standing (21.75x3.25x4 in. wall- mounted), 9 lb. each; center speaker 5.5x10x5.75 in. standing (3.75x9.75x4 in. wall-mounted), 3.4 lb.; subwoofer 17.75x6.25x17.75 in., 26.3 lb.

5. **PANASONIC** SC-MT1 **Very good.** Includes integrated single-disc DVD player. Can play DVD-audio discs. But lacks digital-audio input from other devices, such as digital-cable box or

Recommendations & notes

satellite receiver. Lacks 5.1 inputs for external digital-audio decoders. No treble adjustment. Front and rear-surround speakers 9x4.25x4.25 in. (HWD), 2 lb. each; center speaker 5.5x10x5.75 in., 3.4 lb.; subwoofer 17.75x6.25x17.75 in., 25.6 lb. 15 radio station presets.

MODELS WITHOUT DVD PLAYER

6. **PIONEER** HTP-230 **Very good.** Has optical and coaxial digital-audio inputs and loudness control. Has 5.1 inputs for external digital-audio decoders. Lacks component- and S-video input/output, requiring you to connect DVD player, digital-cable box, or satellite receiver directly to TV for best picture quality. No sleep timer. Front speakers 9.75x4.25x6.5 in. (HWD), 2.9 lb. each; rear-surround speakers 6x4.25x3 in., 1 lb. each; center speaker 4.25x6x3 in., 1.3 lb.; subwoofer 14.25x8.5x16 in., 17.8 lb.

7. **SONY** HT-DDW750 **Very good.** Has optical and coaxial digital-audio inputs and 2-yr. warranty. Lacks component- and S-video input/output, requiring you to connect DVD player, digital-cable box, or satellite receiver directly to TV for best picture quality. Lacks 5.1 inputs for external digital-audio decoders. Front and rear-surround speakers 6x3.75x5 in. (HWD), 1.8 lb. each; center speaker 3.75x9.25x5 in., 2.1 lb.; subwoofer 12.75x10.75x16, 21.1 lb.

8. **ONKYO** HT-S760B **Very good.** Has optical and coaxial digital-audio inputs, front-panel A/V inputs, and 2-yr. warranty. Has 5.1 inputs for external digital-audio decoders. Front speakers 16.5x7.5x9.5 in. (HWD), 11.8 lb. each; rear-surround speakers 10.5x7x5 in., 3.9 lb. each; center speaker 6.25x15.25x8 in., 7.8 lb.; subwoofer 20.25x11x15.75 in., 29.5 lb. Similar model: HT-S767C has 6-disc DVD player.

9. **KENWOOD** HTB-306 **Very good, but relatively few features for the price.** Has optical and coaxial digital-audio inputs, bass-boost switch, and loudness control. Has 5.1 inputs for external digital-audio decoders. Lacks component-video input/output, requiring you to connect HD-capable devices directly to similarly capable TV for very best picture quality. No sleep timer. Front and rear-surround speakers 7x4x5 in. (HWD), 2.1 and 1.7 lb. each respectively; center speaker 4x8x5 in., 2.2 lb.; subwoofer 13x12x17.75 in., 16.9 lb.

10. **RCA** RT-2600 **Very good.** Has optical and coaxial digital-audio inputs and front-panel A/V inputs. Has 5.1 inputs for external digital-audio decoders. Lacks component-video input/output, requiring you to connect HD-capable devices directly to similarly capable TV for very best picture quality. No receiver-display dimmer or sleep timer. Front and rear-surround speakers 7x4.75x4.5 in. (HWD), 2.9 and 2.2 lb. each respectively; center speaker 4.75x7x4.5 in., 2.9 lb.; subwoofer 14x8x13.5 in., 10.6 lb.

11. **KENWOOD** HTB-206 **Good.** Has optical and coaxial digital-audio inputs, bass-boost switch, and loudness control. Has 5.1 inputs for external digital-audio decoders. Lacks component-video input/output, requiring you to connect HD-capable devices. No sleep timer. Front speakers 7x4x5.75 in., 1.9 lb.; rear-surround speakers 7.25x4x5.75 in. (HWD), 1.5 lb. each; center speaker 4x8x5.75 in., 2 lb.; subwoofer 14.75x8x14.75 in., 13.7 lb.

Lawn mowers, push type

Push-type power mowers are fine for smaller, flatter lawns. Choose a rear-bagging model if you bag your clippings. Consider the rear-bag Yard Machines 11A-439-G, $200, **a CR Best Buy,** which was impressive at mulching and bagging. Also impressive at both those mowing tasks was the Yard Machines by MTD 11A-549G, $225. Side-bagging models often cost less. The side-bag Yard Machines 11C-084D, $180, and Poulan Pro 38618, $180, both are both **CR Best Buys.**

Within types, in performance order.

Key: Excellent ⊜ · Very good ⊖ · Good ○ · Fair ◒ · Poor ●

Key number	Brand & Model (power/swath)	Price	Overall Score	Test results: Evenness	Mulch	Bag	Side	Handling	Ease of Use
	REAR-BAG								
1	**Yard Machines** by MTD 11A-439G **A CR Best Buy** [1] 11A-436J	$200		Very good	Very good	Very good	Good	Very good	Good
2	**Yard Machines** by MTD 11A-549G [1] 11A-546U	225		Very good	Very good	Very good	Good	Good	Good
3	**Yard-Man** by MTD 11A-435D	220		Good	Good	Good	Good	Very good	Good
4	**Craftsman** (Sears) 38851	230		Good	Good	Good	Good	Very good	Good
5	**Murray** Select 204210x8 [1]	160		Good	Fair	Fair	-	Very good	Good
6	**Snapper** MR216015B	335		Good	Good	Very good	Fair	Good	Good
7	**Murray** Select 22315x8 [1]	230		Very good	Fair	Good	Fair	Fair	Good
	SIDE-BAG								
8	**Yard Machines** by MTD 11C-084D **A CR Best Buy** Bolens 11A-084C	180		Very good	Very good	Good	Good	Very good	Good
9	**Yard Machines** Gold by MTD 11A-509W [1]	250		Very good	Good	Good	Very good	Very good	Good
10	**Poulan Pro** 38618 **A CR Best Buy** [1]	180		Very good	Very good	Good	Very good	Good	Good
11	**Honda** Harmony II HRS216PDA	320		Very good	Good	Poor	Excellent	Good	Very good
12	**Yard-Man** by MTD 11B-106C [1]	200		Good	Good	Poor	Very good	Good	Good

[1] *Not sold in California, though similar models are.*

See report, page 122. *Based on tests published in Consumer Reports in May 2003, with updated prices and availability.*

Guide to the Ratings

Overall score is based mainly on cutting performance, handling, and ease of use. **Evenness** shows average cutting performance for all available modes. **Mulch** is how evenly mulched clippings are distributed over the lawn's surface. **Bag** denotes how many clippings the bag held before it filled or the chute clogged. **Side** is how evenly clippings were dispersed in the side-discharge mode. **Handling** includes ease of using the drive controls, pushing, pulling, making U-turns, and maneuvering. **Ease of use** includes ease of starting the engine, using the blade-stopping controls, shifting speeds, and adjusting cut height. **Price** is approximate retail, and includes equipment for all three mowing modes unless noted.

Recommendations & notes

MOST MODELS HAVE: A four-stroke engine with primer bulb instead of choke. An engine-kill safety system. No throttle control on handle. Stamped-steel deck. A two-year warranty.

REAR-BAGGING MODELS

1. **YARD MACHINES** by MTD 11A-439G **A CR Best Buy Well-rounded performance at a good price.** Easy to push. Cut height hard to adjust. Engine: 6 hp. Swath: 21 in. Similar: 11A-436J.

2. **YARD MACHINES** by MTD 11A-549G **Well-rounded performance, and good handling for a high-wheel model.** Easy to push. Cut height hard to adjust. Engine: 6 hp. Swath: 21 in. Similar: 11A-546U.

3. **YARD-MAN** by MTD 11A-435D **A capable, well-rounded push mower.** Side-to-side jockeying, pushing, and U-turns especially easy. Bag inconvenient to empty. Cut height hard to adjust. Uncomfortable handle. Engine: 6.5 hp. Swath: 21 in.

4. **CRAFTSMAN** (Sears) 38851 **A capable, well-rounded push mower.** Side-to-side jockeying, pushing, and U-turns especially easy. Louder than most. Engine: 6.5 hp. Swath: 21 in.

5. **MURRAY** Select 204210X8 **Good.** Side-to-side jockeying, pushing, and U-turns especially easy. Lacks side-discharge mode. Bag inconvenient to empty. Cut height hard to adjust. Uncomfortable handle. Engine: 4.5 hp. Swath: 20 in.

6. **SNAPPER** MR216015B **Good.** Mediocre vacuuming. Bag inconvenient to empty. Handle vibrates. Clippings may discharge at operator with bag off. U-turns and jockeying side to side hard. Noisier than most. Engine: 6 hp. Swath: 21 in.

7. **MURRAY** Select 22315X8 **Good.** Weak in tall grass. U-turns and jockeying side to side hard. High rear wheels. Engine: 6 hp. Swath: 22 in.

SIDE-BAGGING MODELS

8. **YARD MACHINES** by MTD 11C-084D **A CR Best Buy Well-rounded performer.** Easy to push. Bag inconvenient. Engine: 4 hp. Swath: 22 in.

9. **YARD MACHINES** Gold by MTD 11A-509W **Very good, with good handling for a high-wheel model.** Easy to push. Bag inconvenient. Handle vibrates. Engine: 6 hp. Swath: 22 in.

10. **POULAN PRO** 38618 **A CR Best Buy Very good performer at a good price.** Easy to push. Less noisy than most. High rear wheels. U-turns hard. Cut height hard to adjust. Engine: 4 hp. Swath: 22 in.

11. **HONDA** Harmony II HRS216PDA **Great for side-discharging, but pricey.** Overhead-valve engine and choke. Weak in tall grass. Bagging requires blade change. Engine: 5.5 hp. Swath: 21 in.

12. **YARD-MAN** by MTD 11B-106C **Competent performer.** Engine: 6 hp. Swath: 20 in.

Lawn mowers, self-propelled

Self-propelled power mowers are good choices for larger yards up to half an acre, or smaller, hillier terrain. Rear-bagging models generally have more bagging capacity and maneuverability than side-baggers, though they usually cost more. For fine overall mowing, consider the rear-bagging Craftsman (Sears) 37779, $500. Nearly as good for less: the rear-bagging Yard-Man by MTD 12A-978Q, $400, and Craftsman 37766, $360, both **CR Best Buys**.

Excellent ⊜ Very good ⊖ Good ○ Fair ◒ Poor ●

Within types, in performance order.

Key number	Brand & Model (power/swath)	Price	Overall Score (0–100; P F G VG E)	Evenness	Mulch	Bag	Side	Handling	Ease of Use
	REAR-BAG								
1	**Craftsman** (Sears) 37779 [1]	$500		Very good	Good	Very good	Good	Very good	Excellent
2	**John Deere** JS63C	550		Very good	Very good	Very good	Very good	Very good	Excellent
3	**John Deere** JX75 [1]	900		Very good	Good	Very good	Good	Good	Excellent
4	**Honda** Masters HR215K1HXA [1]	900		Very good	Very good	Very good	Good	Good	Excellent
5	**Honda** Harmony HRB217TDA	650		Good	Good	Good	Excellent	Very good	Excellent
6	**Troy-Bilt** Pro Cut 320 12A-998Q	530		Good	Very good	Very good	Very good	Very good	Very good
7	**Craftsman** (Sears) 37850	350		Good	Good	Excellent	Good	Very good	Very good
8	**Yard-Man** by MTD 12A-978Q **A CR Best Buy**	400		Very good	Very good	Very good	Very good	Good	Very good
9	**Toro** Super Recycler 20037	510		Very good	Very good	Very good	Very good	Good	Very good
10	**Craftsman** (Sears) 37766 **A CR Best Buy**	360		Good	Good	Good	Good	Very good	Excellent
11	**Craftsman** (Sears) 37864	340		Good	Good	Excellent	Very good	Good	Very good
12	**Yard-Man** by MTD 12AD465E	350		Very good	Good	Good	Good	Very good	Good
13	**Honda** Harmony II HRZ216TDA	555		Good	Good	Good	Good	Very good	Very good
14	**Ariens** LM21S 911514	600		Good	Good	Very good	Very good	Good	Excellent
15	**Cub Cadet** SR621 12A-977A	500		Very good	Very good	Very good	Very good	Fair	Very good
16	**Toro** Recycler 20017	360		Very good	Good	Very good	Good	Good	Very good
17	**Snapper** P2167517B1	590		Very good	Good	Very good	Good	Good	Very good
18	**Lawn-Boy** Silver Series 10324 [2]	400		Good	Very good	Good	Good	Very good	Good

Within types, in performance order.

Key number	Brand & Model (power/swath)	Price	Overall Score (0–100: P F G VG E)	Evenness	Mulch	Bag	Side	Handling	Ease of Use
	REAR-BAG								
19	**Toro** Recycler 20016	310		⊜	○	⊜	○	○	○
20	**Snapper** MRP216017B [2]	560		○	○	⊜	○	○	⊜
21	**Yard-Man** by MTD 12A-569T [2]	375		⊜	○	○	○	◒	○
22	**Murray** Select 228511x8 [2]	260		○	○	○	-	◒	○
	SIDE-BAG								
23	**Yard Machines** Gold by MTD 12A-288A [2]	$270		⊜	⊜	◒	⊜	○	○
24	**Honda** Harmony II HRS216K2SDA	370		⊜	⊜	●	⊜	○	○

See report, page 122. Based on tests published in Consumer Reports in May 2003, with updated prices and availability.

Guide to the Ratings

Overall score is based mainly on cutting performance, handling, and ease of use. **Evenness** shows average cutting performance for all available modes. **Mulch** is how evenly mulched clippings are distributed over the lawn's surface. **Bag** denotes how many clippings the bag held before it filled or the chute clogged. **Side** is how evenly clippings were dispersed in the side-discharge mode. **Handling** includes ease of using the drive controls, pushing, pulling, making U-turns, and maneuvering. **Ease of use** includes ease of starting the engine, using the blade-stopping controls, shifting speeds, and adjusting cut height. **Price** is approximate retail, and includes equipment for all three mowing modes unless noted. **Overall scores** for previously tested models may have changed because of minor changes in how we score.

Recommendations & notes

MOST MODELS HAVE: A four-stroke engine with primer bulb instead of choke. An engine-kill safety system. No throttle control on handle. Rear-wheel drive. Stamped-steel deck. A two-year warranty on mower and engine.

REAR-BAGGING MODELS

1. **CRAFTSMAN** (Sears) 37779 **Easy to use and moderately priced.** Blade-brake clutch. Throttle and choke. Engine: 5.5 hp. Swath:21 in.

2. **JOHN DEERE** JS63C **Easy to use, and a good price.** But hard to jockey side to side. Bag hard to empty. Engine: 6.5 hp. Swath: 21 in.

3. **JOHN DEERE** JX75 **Very good, with blade-brake clutch.** Easy to use, with easy bag handling. Drive starts abruptly. Throttle and choke. Aluminum deck. Engine: 6 hp. Swath: 21 in.

4. **HONDA** Masters HR215K1HXA **Easy to use, with easy bag handling, though mulching requires a blade change.** Blade-brake clutch. Throttle and choke. Aluminum deck. Engine: 5 hp. Swath: 21 in.

Recommendations & notes

5. HONDA Harmony HRB217TDA **An agile self-propelled mower** with superb side-discharging. Side-to-side jockeying and U-turns are especially easy. Engine: 6.5 hp. Swath: 21 in.

6. TROY-BILT Pro Cut 320 12A-998Q **An especially well-rounded choice.** Swivel wheels for easy U-turns, though hard to adjust cut height. Single lever cut-height adjustment for rear. Automatic choke. Hard to push and pull. Bag hard to empty. Engine: 5.5 hp. Swath: 21 in.

7. CRAFTSMAN (Sears) 37850 **A fine choice, but front-drive reduces traction.** Front wheels lifted with full bag, further reducing traction. Noisier than most. Automatic choke. Engine: 5.5 hp. Swath: 21 in.

8. YARD-MAN by MTD 12A-978Q **A CR Best Buy A fine value.** Single-lever cut-height adjustment. Automatic choke. Hard to push and pull. Bag hard to empty. Engine: 5.5 hp. Swath: 21 in. Similar: 12A-979L.

9. TORO Super Recycler 20037 **Among the less repair-prone brands.** Less noisy than most. Hard to jockey side to side. Bag inconvenient to empty. 5-year mower warranty. Engine: 6.5 hp. Swath: 21 in.

10. CRAFTSMAN (Sears) 37766 **A CR Best Buy A fine value. U-turns are especially easy.** Single-lever cut-height adjustment. Engine: 6.5 hp. Swath: 21 in.

11. CRAFTSMAN (Sears) 37864 **Inexpensive, but front-drive reduces traction.** Front wheels lifted with full bag, further reducing traction. Noisier than most. Engine: 7 hp. Swath: 21 in.

12. YARD-MAN by MTD 12AD465E **Inexpensive, but front-drive reduces traction.** Side-to-side jockeying especially easy. Bag hard to empty. Cut height hard to adjust. Engine: 6.75 hp. Swath: 21 in.

13. HONDA Harmony II HRZ216TDA **A fine, well-rounded mower.** Swivel wheels for easy U-turns. Quieter than most. Engine: 5.5 hp. Swath: 21 in.

14. ARIENS LM21S 911514 **Very good.** U-turns and jockeying side to side hard. Bag hard to empty. Tools needed to change modes. Engine: 6.5 hp. Swath: 21 in.

15. CUB CADET SR621 12A-977A **A capable though clumsy performer.** Single-lever cut-height adjustment. Hard to push, pull, U-turn, and jockey from side to side. Bag difficult to empty. Engine: 6.5 hp. Swath: 21 in. Similar: SRE621 12AE-977C

16. TORO Recycler 20017 **Very good, and among the less repair-prone brands.** Engine: 6.5 hp. Swath: 22 in.

17. SNAPPER P2167517B1 **Very good, but among the more repair-prone brands.** U-turns and jockeying side to side hard. Noisier than most. Bag inconvenient to empty. Clippings may discharge at operator with bag off. Tools needed to change modes. 3-year mower warranty. Engine: 6.5 hp. Swath: 21 in.

18. LAWN-BOY Silver Series 10324 **Very good.** Weak in tall grass. Hard to jockey side to side. Clippings may discharge at operator with bag off. Cut height hard to adjust. Two-stroke engine. Engine: 6.5 hp. Swath: 21 in.

19. TORO Recycler High Wheel 20016 **Very good.** Among the less repair-prone brands. U-turns and jockeying side to side hard. Engine: 6.5 hp. Swath: 22 in.

20. SNAPPER MRP216017B **Among the more repair-prone brands.** Mediocre vacuuming. U-turns hard. Clippings may discharge at operator with bag off. Bag inconvenient to empty. Mode changes require tools, mulching requires a blade change.

Recommendations & notes

Inconvenient shift lever. 3-year mower warranty. Engine: 6 hp. Swath: 21 in.

21. **YARD-MAN** by MTD 12A-569T **Good overall.** Push-button starter. Hard to push and pull. U-turns, jockeying side to side, and bag emptying hard. Engine: 6 hp. Swath: 21 in.

22. **MURRAY** Select 228511X8 **There are better choices among self-propelled models.** Front-drive reduces traction. Lacks side-discharge mode. Hard to push and jockey from side to side. Uncomfortable handle. Engine: 6.25 hp. Swath: 22 in.

SIDE-BAGGING MODELS

23. **YARD MACHINES** Gold by MTD 12A-288A **Hard to pull.** Bag inconvenient. Handle vibrates. Engine: 5 hp. Swath: 22 in.

24. **HONDA** Harmony II HRS216K2SDA **Capable in all modes but bagging.** Drive starts abruptly. Bagging requires blade change. Throttle and choke. Engine: 5.5 hp. Swath: 21 in.

EXTEND THE LIFE OF YOUR MACHINE

Lawn mower maintenance

Push or self-propelled gas-powered mowers. Clean beneath the deck. According to manufacturers, built-up clippings interfere with airflow and hurt performance. Especially in damp conditions and at the end of the mowing season, disconnect the spark-plug wire and remove the clippings with a plastic trowel. Sharpen the blade at least once each mowing season. A dull blade tears grass rather than cutting it, and can cause the lawn to become diseased. Remove the blade and sharpen it with a file, which costs about $10, or pay a mower shop to do it.

Once each mowing season, change the oil. Drain a four-stroke engine's crankcase and refill it with the oil recommended in the owner's manual. Check the level before each mowing and add more if needed. Two-stroke engines require no oil changes. Clean or replace the air filter when it's dirty–as often as once each mowing season in dusty conditions. Some mowers have a sponge filter you can clean and re-oil, though most now use a disposable paper filter. Replace the spark plug when the inner tip has heavy deposits–sometimes as often as once a mowing season. A new plug makes for easier starts and cleaner running. At the end of the mowing season, be sure to store the mower properly.

There are two ways to deal with gasoline remaining in the tank. With many mowers, you can drain the gasoline from the tank into an appropriate storage container and then run the engine to eliminate any gas remaining. But some manufacturers recommend filling the tank with gasoline and a gasoline stabilizer and running the engine for a few minutes so the treated gasoline gets into the fuel line and carburetor.

Electric mowers. Disconnect the cord or, on cordless models, remove the safety key, and clean beneath the deck. Keep the blade sharp, following the procedure for gas mowers. To extend the life of your mower, save the power cell. With cordless models, stop mowing and plug in the charger when the battery starts running down. Draining a battery completely shortens its life. New ones cost about $100. Manufacturers also suggest leaving the battery on "charge" whenever you're not using the mower.

Monitors

First decide if you want an LCD monitor or a CRT. If freeing up space on your desk is the priority, the LCD is the clear choice. Consider the 17-inch KDS Rad-7c, $430, and ViewSonic VA720, $500, or the 18-inch Gateway FPD 1810, $550, all of which work with both Macs and PCs. For a smaller budget, consider the $300, 15-inch Gateway FPD 1530. If display quality is important, Mac users can't do better than the 17-inch, $700 Apple Studio Display. If space isn't a concern, you can save money by purchasing a CRT monitor. Two stand-out models, both with 18-inch VIS, are the ViewSonic A90f+, which scored significantly higher than all the other CRTs, and the $200 KDS XF-9e, the least expensive 18-inch VIS CRT. For the budget-minded, look to the 16-inch VIS Gateway EV700, $150. For watching videos on a computer, both of the wide-screen displays are very good. But only the $1,000 Sony SDM-V72W accepts component signals from a DVD player.

Excellent · Very good · Good · Fair · Poor

Key number	Brand & Model	Price	Overall score (0–100: P F G VG E)	Viewable image	Test results: Display	Test results: Ease of use
	STANDARD LCD MONITORS					
1	**Apple** Studio Display	$700		17 in.	Excellent	Very good
2	**ViewSonic** VA720	500		17	Very good	Very good
3	**Sony** SDM-X52	450		15	Very good	Excellent
4	**Gateway** FPD 1730	500		17	Very good	Very good
5	**Gateway** FPD 1530	300		15	Very good	Very good
6	**Gateway** FPD 1810	550		18	Very good	Very good
7	**NEC** MultiSync LCD 1560V	330		15	Very good	Very good
8	**Samsung** SyncMaster 151V	330		15	Very good	Very good
9	**Envision** EN-5200e	275		15	Very good	Very good
10	**KDS** Rad-7c	430		17	Very good	Very good
11	**Dell** Ultra Sharp 1504FP	350		15	Very good	Excellent
12	**NEC** MultiSync LCD 1760NX	540		17	Very good	Good
	WIDE-SCREEN LCD MONITORS					
13	**Sony** SDM-V72W	1,000		17	Very good	Excellent
14	**Samsung** SyncMaster 172W	685		17	Very good	Excellent

Key number	Brand & Model	Price	Overall score (0–100: P F G VG E)	Viewable image	Test results: Display	Test results: Ease of use
	CRT MONITORS					
15	**ViewSonic** A90f+	$290		18 in.	⊖	⊖
16	**NEC** MultiSync 97F	270		18	⊖	○
17	**Samsung** SyncMaster 957MB	340		18	⊖	⊖
18	**KDS** XF-9e	200		18	⊖	⊖
19	**Dell** M782	260		16	○	⊖
20	**Envision** EN-985e	220		18	○	○
21	**Gateway** EV700	150		16	○	⊖
22	**eMachines** eView 17f	260		16	○	⊖

See report, page 144. Based on tests published in Consumer Reports in June 2003, with updated prices and availability.

Guide to the Ratings

Overall score is based primarily on display image clarity and, second, on ease of use. **Viewable image** gives a monitor's viewable image size (VIS), as measured diagonally. For CRTs only, the nominal size that's used to market models is usually one inch more than the VIS. Our viewing panelists gauged **display** quality for text and photos. **Ease of use** covers the front-panel controls, onscreen menus, tilt adjustment, and the like. **Recommendations & notes** lists noteworthy features and some minor shortcomings. **Price** is approximate retail.

Recommendations & notes

ALL MONITORS: Meet the federal government's Energy Star criteria. The LCDs consume 20 to 40 watts, depending on screen size; the 17-inch and 19-inch CRTs average 65 and 80 watts, respectively. A special "sleep" mode reduces all models' consumption to about 2 watts. Have onscreen menus. **MOST MONITORS HAVE:** A control to restore factory settings; a 3-year warranty on parts, labor, tube, or backlight; multilingual menus; detachable video cable; setup guide; no adapter for Mac. **LCDS:** Are 6½ to 9½ inches deep and weigh 8 to 16 pounds. **CRTS HAVE:** Max. resolution of 1,280x1,024 pixels (17-inch), 1,600x1,200 (19-inch). A depth an inch greater than the viewable image size. They weigh 35 to 57 pounds.

STANDARD LCD MONITORS

1 APPLE Studio Display **Excellent overall, with wide viewing angle.** But harder to tilt, and control buttons harder to use than most. No detachable video cable. Warranty only 90 days on parts, 1 yr. on labor.

2 VIEWSONIC VA720 **Very good, but harder to tilt than most.** No detachable video cable.

3 SONY SDM-X52 **Exceptionally easy to use.** Wide viewing angle. Has speakers.

4 GATEWAY FPD 1730 **Price is right for large display.** But harder to tilt than most. Warranty on parts and labor 1 yr. or less.

Recommendations & notes

5 **GATEWAY** FPD 1530 **Competitive price for very good model.** Warranty on parts and labor 1 yr. or less.

6 **GATEWAY** FPD 1810 **Very good, but pricey.** Warranty of only 1 yr. on parts and labor.

7 **NEC** MultiSync LCD 1560V **Very good,** but menu and control buttons harder to use than most.

8 **SAMSUNG** SyncMaster 151V **Very good, but harder to tilt than most.** Discontinued, but similar 152N is available.

9 **ENVISION** EN-5200e **Very good overall.**

10 **KDS** Rad-7c **Very good.** Has speakers. Warranty on parts 1 yr. or less.

11 **DELL** Ultra Sharp 1504FP **Very good, with wide viewing angle.**

12 **NEC** MultiSync LCD 1760NX **Very good,** but harder to tilt and menu harder to use than most.

WIDE-SCREEN LCD MONITORS

13 **SONY** SDM-V72W **Well-suited for HDTV broadcasts or DVD videos, but you pay extra for that.** Has speakers and composite, S-video, and component video inputs.

14 **SAMSUNG** SyncMaster 172W **Suitable for playing DVD videos, but not HDTV broadcasts.** Has digital-video input, speakers.

CRT MONITORS

15 **VIEWSONIC** A90f+ **Worth the higher price for very good performance and features.**

16 **NEC** MultiSync 97F **Very good, with easy-view flat screen.** But harder to tilt than most. Warranty on parts and labor 1 yr. or less.

17 **SAMSUNG** SyncMaster 957MB **Very good, though pricey.** Harder to tilt than most.

18 **KDS** XF-9e **A very good monitor at a good price.**

19 **DELL** M782 **Good, but harder to tilt than most.** Monitor supplied with computer.

20 **ENVISION** EN-985e **Good overall.**

21 **GATEWAY** EV700 **Very attractive price.** But control buttons harder to use than most. Curved screen. Only 1-yr. warranty on parts and labor. Monitor supplied with computer.

22 **EMACHINES** eView 17f **Good overall, but harder to tilt than most.** Only 1-yr. warranty on parts and labor. Monitor supplied with computer.

Paint, exterior

Every paint we tested will look good for at least three years. Most should last for six years. But the only paints to consider are ones that should last for a good nine years, allowing you to repaint less often. There are several models in each tested color that hold up well, and many brands that earned good marks for resisting mildew and cracking. Less common—and an important consideration—are paints that resist dirt buildup, most important if you live in an area where vehicles or factories deposit dirt.

Among white paints, the best choices for resisting dirt are the M.A. Bruder Sea Shore, California Fresh Coat Velvet, and Glidden Spred Dura semigloss. M.A. Bruder and California also resist color change, but they're sold only in the Northeast and East, respectively. The Glidden is the better value, with excellent overall performance. For a dirt-resistant blue paint, consider the Glidden Endurance semigloss, Glidden Endurance Satin, or California Fresh Coat Velvet. Keep in mind that none of the blues we tested resisted color change well. Among brown paints look first to the California Fresh Coat Velvet or Glidden Endurance (semigloss).

Within types, in performance order.

Excellent / Very good / Good / Fair / Poor

Key number	Product	Price	Overall score (0–100; P F G VG E)	Appearance: After 3 years	Appearance: After 6 years	Appearance: After 9 years	Resists: Dirt	Resists: Color change	Resists: Cracking	Resists: Mildew
	WHITE *The most common house color.*									
1	**M.A. Bruder** Sea Shore (flat)	$25		Excellent	Excellent	Excellent	•	•	•	•
2	**California** Fresh Coat Velvet (flat)	25		Excellent	Excellent	Excellent	•	•	•	•
3	**Pratt & Lambert** Accolade Eggshell (flat)	30		Excellent	Excellent	Excellent		•	•	•
4	**Sico** Supreme (flat)	C35		Excellent	Excellent	Excellent	•	•	•	•
5	**Glidden** Endurance Satin (low luster)	22		Excellent	Excellent	Excellent		•	•	•
6	**Glidden** Spred Dura Satin (low luster)	15		Excellent	Excellent	Excellent		•	•	•
7	**Glidden** Spred Dura (semigloss)	17		Excellent	Excellent	Excellent	•		•	•
8	**Glidden** Endurance (semigloss)	23		Excellent	Excellent	Very good			•	•
9	**Glidden** Endurance (flat)	19		Excellent	Very good	Very good	•		•	•
10	**Glidden** Spred Dura (flat)	15		Excellent	Very good	Good				•
11	**Sears** Best Weatherbeater (flat)	19		Excellent	Very good	Good			•	
12	**Sears** Best Weatherbeater Satin (low luster)	20		Excellent	Very good	Good			•	
13	**Sherwin-Williams** Super Paint Satin (low luster)	26		Excellent	Very good	Good			•	

Within types, in performance order.

Key number	Product	Price	Overall score (0–100: P F G VG E)	Appearance: After 3 years	Appearance: After 6 years	Appearance: After 9 years	Resists: Dirt	Resists: Color change	Resists: Cracking	Resists: Mildew
	BLUE *Typifies a range of yellows, greens, and blues, plus some grays.*									
14	**Glidden** Endurance (semigloss)	$23		⊜	⊜	⊖	•		•	•
15	**M.A. Bruder** Sea Shore (flat)	25		⊜	⊜	⊖			•	•
16	**California** Fresh Coat Velvet (flat)	25		⊜	⊜	⊖	•		•	•
17	**Glidden** Endurance Satin (low luster)	22		⊜	⊜	⊖	•		•	•
18	**Glidden** Spred Dura Satin (low luster)	15		⊜	⊜	⊖			•	•
19	**Glidden** Spred Dura (flat)	15		⊜	⊜	⊖			•	•
20	**Pratt & Lambert** Accolade Eggshell (flat)	30		⊜	⊜	⊖			•	•
21	**Glidden** Endurance (flat)	19		⊜	⊖	⊖	•		•	•
22	**Glidden** Spred Dura (semigloss)	17		⊜	⊖	⊖			•	•
23	**Sico** Supreme (flat)	C35		⊜	⊖	⊖			•	•
24	**Sherwin-Williams** Super Paint Satin (low luster)	26		⊜	⊖	○			•	
25	**Sears** Best Weatherbeater Satin (low luster)	20		⊜	⊖	○			•	
26	**Sears** Best Weatherbeater (flat)	19		⊜	⊖	◒				
	BROWN *Typifies a range of tans and other earth tones.*									
27	**California** Fresh Coat Velvet (flat)	25		⊜	⊜	⊜	•	•	•	•
28	**M.A. Bruder** Sea Shore (flat)	25		⊜	⊜	⊖	•		•	•
29	**Glidden** Endurance (flat)	19		⊜	⊜	⊖		•	•	•
30	**Glidden** Endurance (semigloss)	23		⊜	⊜	⊖	•		•	•
31	**Glidden** Endurance Satin (low luster)	22		⊜	⊜	⊖			•	•
32	**Pratt & Lambert** Accolade Eggshell (flat)	30		⊜	⊜	⊖			•	•
33	**Glidden** Spred Dura Satin (low luster)	15		⊜	⊖	⊖			•	•
34	**Glidden** Spred Dura (semigloss)	17		⊜	⊖	⊖	•		•	•
35	**Sico** Supreme (flat)	C35		⊜	⊖	⊖	•		•	•
36	**Glidden** Spred Dura (flat)	15		⊜	○	○			•	•
37	**Sherwin-Williams** Super Paint Satin (low luster)	26		⊜	⊖	○			•	
38	**Sears** Best Weatherbeater Satin (low luster)	20		⊜	⊖	○			•	
39	**Sears** Best Weatherbeater (flat)	19		⊜	⊖	◒			•	

See report, page 126. Based on tests published in Consumer Reports in August 2003. C= Canadian price. Sico (4, 23, 35) is a Canadian brand that may also be available in some U.S. stores.

Guide to the Ratings

Overall score is a weighted average of the paint's appearance scores. **Appearance** scores summarize our three-year testing cycle. One year of our tests is approximately three years of real-life exposure, so we can predict how well a paint should do after nine years. Remaining columns show specific ways, if any, in which paint held up. These standout attributes help clarify how paint actually aged. **Resists dirt** shows which paints are better than most at preventing dirt buildup. **Resists color change** shows which have the least color change. **Resists cracking** shows which provide the best protection for siding. **Resists mildew** shows which do the best job of preventing mildew growth. **Price** is approximate retail.

DOLLARS & SENSE

Measuring up

House paint is sold primarily in 1-gallon cans. A retailer or painting contractor will calculate how many gallons your home requires. Here's how to get a rough idea beforehand of what you'll need and spend:

- Each gallon of paint covers about 400 square feet. But double-check the label on the brands you're considering to be sure.
- Base calculations—and contractors' bids—on two coats, not one. Our decades of paint tests have shown that one coat does not protect as well as two. For example, a 2,300-square-foot house with an attached garage has about 3,200 square feet of wall, not counting windows and doors. That means you'll need about 16 gallons of paint to give the house two coats.
- Allow for some leeway. Figure on buying 10 percent extra for spills and other waste, and for touch-ups down the road.
- Buy everything at once. Make sure all the paint comes from the same manufacturing lot; check the numbers on the cans. Also make sure that all the paint is color-mixed at the same time. Otherwise, the color may be off slightly from one batch to another. Better still for uniformity, mix all the paint together in 5-gallon buckets.

Paint, interior

Some of the paints we tested hold their original color well and can slow the growth of mildew. Others can be scrubbed without damaging the finish. We tested most brands in three finishes: flat, low-luster, and semigloss. Fine choices for most rooms and **CR Best Buys** are the Behr Premium Plus Enamel (flat), Behr Premium Plus Satin (low-luster), and Behr Premium Plus (semigloss), all sold at Home Depot; the Valspar American Tradition (flat) and Valspar American Tradition Satin (low-luster), both sold at Lowe's; and the Dutch Boy Home (flat), Dutch Boy Home Satin (low-luster), and Dutch Boy Home (semigloss), all sold at Wal-Mart.

Within types, in performance order.

Excellent / Very good / Good / Fair / Poor

Key number	Product	Price	Overall score (0–100: P F G VG E)	Test results: Hiding	Mildew	Stains	Scrubbing: White base	Pastel base	Medium base	Appearance: Could be smoother	Tends to fade	Flatter than labeled	Glossier than labeled
	FLAT PAINTS												
1	**Behr** Premium Plus Enamel (Home Depot) **A CR Best Buy**	$20		Excellent	Excellent	Excellent	Excellent	Excellent	Excellent		•		
2	**Benjamin Moore** Regal Matte Finish	35		Excellent	Good	Excellent	Excellent	Excellent	Excellent				
3	**Valspar** American Tradition (Lowe's) **A CR Best Buy**	18		Excellent	Excellent	Very good	Excellent	Excellent	Excellent				
4	**Pratt & Lambert** Accolade	33		Very good	Fair	Excellent	Very good	Very good	Very good				
5	**Ralph Lauren** Premium Matte	23		Excellent	Fair	Very good	Very good	Very good	Excellent				
6	**Dutch Boy** Home (Wal-Mart) **A CR Best Buy**	13		Very good	Excellent	Good	Excellent	Excellent	Excellent		•		
7	**Dunn-Edwards** Decovel	23		Very good	Poor	Excellent	Very good	Very good	Excellent				
8	**Sherwin Williams** Everclean	26		Good	Excellent	Excellent	Very good	Very good	Good		•		
9	**Sico** Supreme Cashmere	C40		Good	Fair	Excellent	Good	Very good	Very good				
10	**Bob Vila** Signature Collection (Sears)	17		Excellent	Very good	Poor	Excellent	Excellent	Excellent		•		
11	**Kelly Moore** Dura-Wall	24		Good	Good	Excellent	Very good	Good	Very good	•			
12	**Glidden** Dulux Inspirations Soft Matte	23		Very good	Poor	Very good	Very good	Very good	Very good				
13	**Martha Stewart** Everyday Colors One-Coat (Kmart)	18		Very good	Good	Good	Excellent	Very good	Good		•		

Within types, in performance order.

Key number	Product	Price	Overall score (0–100; P F G VG E)	Test results: Hiding	Mildew	Stains	Scrubbing: White base	Scrubbing: Pastel base	Scrubbing: Medium base	Appearance: Could be smoother	Tends to fade	Flatter than labeled	Glossier than labeled
	FLAT PAINTS												
14	**Ace** Royal Touch	$19		E	P	VG	F	G	G				
15	**Glidden** Evermore (Home Depot)	15		VG	VG	VG	E	G	E	●			
16	**True Value** E-Z Kare	19		E	G	F	VG	F	VG				
17	**Sico** Supreme Super	C34		VG	F	E	F	F	P				
18	**Duron** Plastic Kote	24		E	P	VG	F	E	VG	●			
19	**Sears** Best Easy Living Lifetime	18		E	F	P	E	E	E				
20	**Sherwin Williams** Cashmere	30		VG	G	G	E	E	E		●		
21	**Benjamin Moore** Regal Wall Satin	18		E	F	G	VG	G	G	●			
22	**Martha Stewart** Everyday Colors (Kmart)	15		VG	G	G	E	F	VG		●		
23	**Kelly Moore** Super	19		VG	F	G	E	VG	G	●			
24	**Olympic** Premium (Lowe's)	15		VG	VG	P	G	G	G				

Within types, in performance order.

Key number	Product	Price	Overall score (0–100; P F G VG E)	Test results: Hiding	Mildew	Sticking	Scrubbing: White base	Scrubbing: Pastel base	Scrubbing: Medium base	Appearance: Could be smoother	Tends to fade	Flatter than labeled	Glossier than labeled
	LOW-LUSTER PAINTS												
25	**Behr** Premium Plus Satin (Home Depot) **A CR Best Buy**	$21		E	E	E	E	E	E	●	●		●
26	**Valspar** American Tradition Satin (Lowe's) **A CR Best Buy**	20		E	E	E	VG	E	E				
27	**Sears** Best Easy Living Lifetime Satin	20		E	G	E	E	E	E		●		

Key number	Product	Price	Overall score (0–100; P F G VG E)	Test results: Hiding	Mildew	Sticking	Scrubbing: White base	Scrubbing: Pastel base	Scrubbing: Medium base	Appearance: Could be smoother	Tends to fade	Flatter than labeled	Glossier than labeled
	LOW-LUSTER PAINTS												
28	**True Value** E-Z Kare Eggshell	$21		E	G	VG	E	E	E			●	
29	**Dutch Boy** Home Satin (Wal-Mart) **A CR Best Buy**	15		E	VG	E	E	E	VG		●		
30	**Kelly Moore** Dura-Poxy+ Eggshell	33		VG	G	E	E	E	E				
31	**MAB** Rich Lux Eggshell	25		E	P	E	E	E	E				
32	**Benjamin Moore** Regal Aquavelvet Eggshell	19		E	G	E	VG	VG	VG				●
33	**Dunn-Edwards** Decosheen Eggshell	35		VG	G	G	VG	VG	VG				●
34	**Ralph Lauren** Premium Satin	25		E	F	E	G	G	F				
35	**Martha Stewart** Everyday Colors One-Coat Satin (Kmart)	19		E	E	E	E	VG	P		●	●	
36	**Pratt & Lambert** Accolade Velvet	34		VG	G	VG	VG	VG	VG	●		●	
37	**Sherwin Williams** Everclean Satin	34		VG	E	VG	G	G	G		●	●	
38	**Ace** Royal Touch Eggshell	20		VG	P	E	E	E	VG			●	
39	**Duron** Plastic Kote Eggshell	25		VG	F	G	E	E	VG				●
40	**Glidden** Evermore Satin (Home Depot)	18		VG	G	E	VG	VG	E	●		●	
41	**Bob Vila** Signature Collection Premium Satin (Sears)	18		E	G	E	G	G	E		●	●	
42	**Glidden** Dulux Inspirations Satin Glow	23		VG	P	E	G	G	G		●		●
43	**Olympic** Premium Satin (Lowe's)	17		VG	VG	E	F	F	F				
44	**Sherwin Williams** Cashmere Low-Luster	33		VG	G	VG	F	F	P		●		●

Within types, in performance order.

Key number	Product	Price	Overall score (0–100; P F G VG E)	Test results: Hiding	Test results: Mildew	Test results: Sticking	Scrubbing: White base	Scrubbing: Pastel base	Scrubbing: Medium base	Appearance: Could be smoother	Appearance: Tends to fade	Appearance: Flatter than labeled	Appearance: Glossier than labeled
	SEMIGLOSS PAINTS												
45	**Behr** Premium Plus (Home Depot) **A CR Best Buy**	$22		⊜	⊜	⊜	⊜	⊜	⊜		•		•
46	**Dunn-Edwards** Permasheen	35		⊖	⊖	⊜	⊜	⊜	⊜				•
47	**Valspar** American Tradition (Lowe's)	21		⊜	⊜	⊜	◒	◒	◒				
48	**Sears** Best Easy Living Lifetime	22		⊜	◒	⊜	⊖	○	⊖				•
49	**Glidden** Evermore	19		⊖	⊖	⊜	⊜	⊜	○	•			•
50	**Ralph Lauren** Premium	27		⊜	◒	⊜	⊖	○	◒				•
51	**Dutch Boy** Home (Wal-Mart) **A CR Best Buy**	16		⊜	⊖	○	⊜	⊜	⊜		•		
52	**Ace** Royal Touch	24		⊜	○	⊜	⊜	⊖	○				•
53	**Kelly Moore** Dura-Poxy+	33		⊖	◒	⊜	⊜	⊜	⊜				•
54	**Bob Vila** Signature Collection (Sears)	22		⊜	⊖	◒	⊜	⊜	⊖		•		•
55	**Martha Stewart** Everyday Colors One-Coat (Kmart)	20		⊖	⊖	○	⊜	⊜	◒		•		•
56	**Martha Stewart** Everyday Colors (Kmart)	18		⊖	○	⊖	⊖	◒	◒		•		•
57	**Olympic** Premium (Lowe's)	19		⊖	⊜	●	⊖	○	○		•		•
58	**True Value** E-Z Kare	22		⊖	○	●	⊖	⊜	⊖				•
59	**Pratt & Lambert** Accolade	38		⊖	○	●	○	⊜	◒				•

See report, page 126. Based on tests published in Consumer Reports in September 2003. C=Canadian price. Sico (9, 17) is a Canadian brand that may be available in some U.S. stores.

Guide to the Ratings

We tested each paint in three versions, or tint bases, because it's the base and not the specific color that affects performance: **White** represents the lightest shades; **pastel,** light colors; **medium,** deeper tones. **Overall score** takes into account hiding, mildew resistance, scrubbing, staining or sticking, and other qualities for all three tint bases. **Hiding** is a measure of how well two coats covered a contrasting color; the higher the score, the darker a color the paint will cover. **Mildew** shows the ability to resist mildew growth. **Stains** (for flat paints only) indicates how well the paint resists staining. **Sticking** (for low-luster and semigloss paints) shows how well the paint resists the tendency to be soft and sticky; sticking is the drawback that makes vases stick to windowsills and books to shelves. **Scrubbing** shows how well the paints stood up to scrubbing with cleanser. **Appearance** highlights paints that don't go on smoothly, leaving a finish reminiscent of orange peel; whose yellows tend to fade; or that are flatter or glossier than label descriptions would have you believe. **Price** is approximate retail.

PDAs

If you're new to PDAs consider the Palm Zire, $100, an inexpensive monochrome unit with excellent battery life. If you want more than a basic organizer, the Palm m515, $300, and Tungsten T, $400, offer ample built-in memory, an expansion slot, and a color display. If you need power and room for multimedia, the Palm Zire 71, $300, and Dell Axim X5, $350, have fast processors, explandable memory, and color displays. The Zire 71 is the least expensive PDA with a built-in camera. If you need to keep the PDA with you most of the time, look for a small, thin model that fits into a pocket or purse.

Excellent · Very good · Good · Fair · Poor

	Brand & model	Price	Overall score (0–100; P F G VG E)	Test results: Ease of use	Battery life	Display	Convenience	Features: Pocket size	Memory (MB)	Expansion slot	Replaceable battery	Wireless conectivity	Display size (in.)
	PALM OS MODELS												
1	**Palm** Zire	$100		Good	Excellent	Good	Good	•	2				2.7
2	**Sony** Clié PEG-NZ90	800		Very good	Good	Good	Very good		11	MS	•	B	3.9
3	**Palm** Zire 71	300		Good	Good	Very good	Good	•	14	M			3.0
4	**Sony** Clié PEG-SJ33	300		Very good	Good	Good	Very good		15	MS			3.1
5	**Palm** m515	300		Good	Good	Good	Very good	•	16	M			3.1
6	**Palm** Tungsten T	400		Good	Good	Good	Very good	•	14	M		B	3.1
7	**Sony** Clié PEG-NX70V	600		Very good	Good	Good	Good		11	MS			3.8
8	**Sony** Clié PEG-TG50	350		Good	Good	Good	Very good	•	11	MS		B	3.0
9	**Sony** Clié PEG-SJ22	200		Very good	Good	Good	Good	•	15	MS			3.0
10	**Palm** m130	200		Good	Good	Fair	Good		8	M			2.7
	POCKET PC MODELS												
11	**Dell** Axim X5 400 MHz	350		Very good	Very good	Good	Very good		64	C, M	•		3.5
12	**Compaq** iPaq H3955	500		Very good	Good	Very good	Good		61	M			3.8
13	**HP** iPaq h1910	300		Good	Good	Good	Very good	•	47	M	•		3.5
14	**ViewSonic** Pocket PC V35	300		Very good	Good	Good	Very good	•	36	M			3.5
15	**AudioVox** Thera	600		Very good	Fair	Good	Very good		32	M		C	3.6

See report, page 147. Based on tests published in Consumer Reports in July 2003, with updated prices and availability.

Guide to the Ratings

Overall score is based primarily on ease of use, battery life, and display. **Ease of use** considers overall design, navigation among tasks, and usability of phone lists, calendar, to-do list, and memo pad. **Battery life** indicates how long fully charged batteries lasted in continuous use (with the backlight mostly turned off for monochrome models): ⊜ 20 hours or more; ⊖ 10 to 20 hours; ○ 5 to 10 hours; ⊙ fewer than 5 hours. **Display** reflects screen readability in low and normal room light and in sunlight. We scored monochrome and color displays on a different scale. **Convenience** considers battery type, expansion capability, and bundled software. **Expansion slot** describes the type of removable media or peripheral that may be added: CompactFlash (C), MultiMedia/Secure Digital Card (M), or Memory Stick (MS). **Wireless connectivity,** indicates the type of wireless connection: Bluetooth (B) or cellular phone (C). **Price** is approximate retail.

Recommendations & notes

PALM-OS MODELS

1 PALM Zire **Very good monochrome unit; while no expansion capability, among best choices in a basic organizer.** Display easy to read in bright sunlight, but no backlight for dimmer lighting. Fits easily in shirt pocket. Has expense tracker. Doesn't include backup program. Battery can't be replaced by user. 3.7 oz.

2 SONY Clié PEG-NZ90 **Very good, with exceptional color display, but too bulky for shirt pocket.** Overall hardware design better than most, and basic organizer functions easy to use. Includes built-in Bluetooth connectivity and 2-megapixel camera. Has built-in keyboard, handy jog dial, picture viewer, voice recorder, eBook reader, printed manual, and LED alarm. 10.4 oz.

3 PALM Zire 71 **Good** PDA is least expensive unit that includes a camera. Overall hardware design better than most, and screen is highly readable. Camera is VGA-quality (310-kilopixel). Fits easily in shirt pocket. Has picture viewer, expense tracker, and eBook reader. Doesn't include backup program. Battery can't be replaced by user. 5.3 oz.

4 SONY Clié PEG-SJ33 **Good choice for a model with MP3 playback, but default display font hard to read.** Overall hardware design better than most, and basic organizer functions easy to use. Has handy jog dial, picture viewer, eBook reader, printed manual, and LED alarm. Battery can't be replaced by user. 6.1 oz.

5 PALM m515 **Good; among best choices for Palm users looking to upgrade.** Basic organizer functions easy to use. Fits easily in shirt pocket. Easy to read in bright sunlight. Low-power display mode significantly lengthens battery life. Has picture viewer, expense tracker, eBook reader, printed manual, and LED and vibrating alarms. Doesn't include backup program. Battery can't be replaced by user. 5 oz.

6 PALM Tungsten T **Good; among best choices for Palm users looking to upgrade.** Overall hardware design better than most, and basic organizer functions easy to use. Fits easily in shirt pocket. Easy to read in bright sunlight. Includes built-in Bluetooth connectivity. Has picture viewer, expense tracker, voice recorder, eBook reader, and LED and vibrating alarms. Doesn't include backup program. Battery can't be replaced by user. Low-power display mode doesn't significantly lengthen battery life. 5.5 oz.

7 SONY Clié PEG-NX70V **Good; overall hardware design better than most, and basic organizer functions easy to use.** Includes

Recommendations & notes

310-kilopixel camera. Has built-in keyboard, handy jog dial, picture viewer, voice recorder, eBook reader, printed manual, and LED alarm. Battery can't be replaced by user. 7.8 oz. Similar: NX60U.

8 **SONY** Clié PEG-TG50 **Good organizer for those who prefer a built-in keyboard, but default display font hard to read.** Basic organizer functions easy to use. Fits easily in shirt pocket. Includes built-in Bluetooth connectivity. Has handy jog dial, picture viewer, voice recorder, eBook reader, printed manual, and LED alarm. Battery can't be replaced by user. 6.5 oz.

9 **SONY** Clié PEG-SJ22 **Good basic organizer, but default display font hard to read.** Overall hardware design better than most, and basic organizer functions easy to use. Fits easily in shirt pocket. Has handy jog dial, picture viewer, eBook reader, LED alarm. Battery can't be replaced by user. 4.9 oz.

10 **PALM** m130 **Good overall, but there are better choices.** Has picture viewer, eBook reader, and printed manual. Doesn't include backup program. Battery can't be replaced by user. Hard to read in bright sunlight. 5.3 oz.

POCKET PC MODELS

11 **DELL** Axim X5-400 MHz **Very good, with especially well-conceived hardware design.** A fine choice if you want to add peripherals. Basic organizer functions easy to use, and user interface better than most. Easier than most Pocket PCs to run multiple programs at once. Has picture viewer, voice recorder, eBook reader, printed manual, and LED alarm. 7.1 oz. Similar X5-300 MHz.

12 **COMPAQ** iPaq H3955 **Good, with a very good display.** Basic organizer functions easy to use, and user interface better than most. Easier than most Pocket PCs to run multiple programs at once. Has picture viewer, voice recorder, eBook reader, printed manual, and LED alarm. Battery can't be replaced by user. Too bulky for shirt pocket due to expansion sleeve. 6.4 oz.

13 **HP** iPaq h1910 **Good, and especially portable for a Pocket PC.** User interface better than most. Fits easily in shirt pocket. Has voice recorder and LED alarm. Doesn't include backup program. 4.2 oz.

14 **VIEWSONIC** Pocket PCV35 **Good basic model.** Basic organizer functions easy to use, and user interface better than most. Fits easily in shirt pocket. Has picture viewer, voice recorder, eBook reader, printed manual, and LED alarm. Battery can't be replaced by user. 4.4 oz.

15 **AUDIOVOX** Thera **Good, but there are better choices in cell phones as well as PDAs.** CDMA phone component tested good overall. Basic organizer functions easy to use, and overall hardware design and user interface better than most. Has picture viewer, voice recorder, eBook reader, and LED and vibrating alarms. Battery can't be replaced by user. 7.1 oz.

Power blowers

Among the handheld blowers most people buy, electrics rule. Besides outperforming the best gas-powered models, electric handhelds cost and weigh less while freeing you from fueling, pull-starting, and periodic tune-ups. Among the best electrics are two **CR Best Buys,** the Toro Super Blower Vac 51591, $70, and the Weed Eater 2595 Barracuda, $50. But if you can't drag an extension cord around, consider two **CR Best Buys:** the gasoline-powered Stihl BG 45, $150, which is relatively quiet, and the Weed Eater BV 1650, $100, which is a good value if loosening debris isn't a priority. A lighter model worth considering is the John Deere BH25, $190. For large properties, the Husqvarna 145BT, $350, a **CR Best Buy,** is more powerful; the Echo Pro Lite PB260L, $300, less noisy. Among wheeled units, better handling overall justifies paying more for the Little Wonder 9600-6HP, $580.

Excellent / Very good / Good / Fair / Poor

Within types, in performance order.

Key number	Brand & model	Price	Weight (lb.)	Overall score (0–100; P F G VG E)	Sweeping	Loosening debris	Vacuuming	Handling	Noise at 50 ft.	Noise at ear
	Similar models, in small type, comparable to tested model.									
	ELECTRIC HANDHELD BLOWERS									
1	**Toro** Super Blower Vac 51591 **A CR Best Buy**	$70	7		Very good	Excellent	Excellent	Excellent	Good	Good
2	**Toro** Ultra Blower Vac 51598	100	7.5		Very good	Excellent	Excellent	Excellent	Good	Good
3	**Weed Eater** 2595 Barracuda **A CR Best Buy**	50	7		Excellent	Very good	Very good	Good	Good	Good
4	**Toro** Rake and Vac 51573	65	6.5		Good	Very good	Very good	Excellent	Very good	Good
5	**Ryobi** 190r	65	7		Good	Very good	Excellent	Very good	Very good	Good
6	**Ryobi** RESV1300	80	9		Good	Very good	Good	Good	Very good	Very good
7	**Black & Decker** Leaf Hog BV2500	70	7		Fair	Good	Excellent	Excellent	Excellent	Good
8	**Toro** Power Sweep 51586	50	5		Fair	Very good	N/A	Excellent	Excellent	Very good
9	**Weed Eater** 2540 Groundskeeper	40	7		Good	Good	Good	Very good	Good	Good
10	**Black & Decker** FT1000	40	6		Fair	Good	N/A	Excellent	Excellent	Good
11	**Ryobi** 160r	45	6		Fair	Good	N/A	Very good	Excellent	Very good
12	**Craftsman** 79940	70	7		Fair	Good	Good	Excellent	Good	Good
13	**Weed Eater** 2510 Groundsweeper	30	5		Fair	Good	N/A	Very good	Very good	Good
14	**Craftsman** 79943	60	7		Fair	Fair	Very good	Excellent	Good	Good

Within types, in performance order.

Key number	Brand & model Similar models, in small type, comparable to tested model.	Price	Weight (lb.)	Overall score 0–100 (P F G VG E)	Test results: Sweeping	Loosening debris	Vacuuming	Handling	Noise at 50 ft.	Noise at ear
	GASOLINE HANDHELD BLOWERS									
15	**Stihl** BG 45 **A CR Best Buy**	$150	10		⊖	⊖	N/A	⊜	⊖	○
16	**Stihl** BG 55 [1]	195	10		⊖	⊖	⊖	⊖	○	○
17	**Echo** PB-230LN PP-231LN [2]	200	11		⊖	⊖	N/A	⊖	○	◒
18	**John Deere** BH25	190	8.5		○	⊜	N/A	⊜	○	○
19	**Weed Eater** BV 1650 **A CR Best Buy**	100	11.5		⊖	○	○	⊖	○	◒
20	**Poulan** Pro BVM200 BVM200LE [2]	130	11		○	○	⊖	⊖	◒	●
21	**Craftsman** 79712 79412 [2]	100	11		○	○	N/A	⊖	○	◒
22	**Craftsman** 79734 79434 [2]	130	11		○	○	⊖	⊖	◒	●
23	**Echo** ES-210 ES-211 [2]	200	9.5		○	○	◒	○	○	○
24	**Ryobi** RGBV3100	125	12.5		○	○	○	○	○	◒
25	**Husqvarna** 225B	180	12		○	◒	N/A	○	○	○
26	**Weed Eater** FL 1500 Featherlite	80	7.5		◒	○	N/A	○	⊖	○
27	**Ryobi** 310BVr	105	12		◒	○	⊖	◒	○	◒
	GASOLINE BACKPACK BLOWERS									
28	**Husqvarna** 145BT **A CR Best Buy**	350	22		⊜	⊜	N/A	⊜	○	●
29	**Makita** RBL500	400	24.5		⊜	⊖	N/A	⊜	○	●
30	**Poulan** Pro BP400	360	18.5		⊜	⊜	N/A	⊖	◒	●
31	**Solo** 470 D 471-KAT [2]	420	24		⊜	⊜	N/A	○	○	◒
32	**Stihl** BR340L	300	20.5		⊖	⊖	N/A	⊜	○	◒
33	**Echo** Pro Lite PB260L	300	16		⊖	⊖	N/A	⊜	⊖	◒
	GASOLINE WHEELED BLOWERS									
34	**Little Wonder** 9600-6HP	580	125.5		⊜	⊜	N/A	○	◒	◒
35	**Yard Machines** 652D	400	107.5		⊜	⊜	N/A	◒	◒	◒

[1] *Price includes optional bag ($35).* [2] *Similar models comply with California emissions rules and typically are sold in California only.* **D** *Discontinued, but similar model is available. Price is for similar model.*

See report, page 128. *Based on tests published in Consumer Reports in September 2003, with updated prices and availability.*

Guide to the Ratings

Overall score is based on sweeping and loosening performance, handling, noise, and where applicable, vacuuming. **Weight** is to the nearest half-pound in blower mode. **Sweeping** is how quickly blowers moved large leaf piles. **Loosening** is how quickly models removed embedded leaf particles from the lawn. **Vacuuming** is how quickly blowers picked up leaves and how well they mulched them. **Handling** includes ease of maneuvering while blowing and ease of controls and mode changes. **Noise** includes our measurements **at 50 feet** and at ear level. Models rated excellent or very good at 50 feet should meet typical limits of 65 decibels (dBA). For **noise at ear,** models rated fair and poor emitted 91 to 99 dBA and, we think, should be used with hearing protection. **Price** is approximate retail.

Printers

Inkjets can print color photos and graphics as well as black-and-white text pages, offering an all-around printing solution. The Canon Photo Printer, S530D, $150, a **CR Best Buy**, is a fine all-around choice combining quality, speed, and low supply costs. If you print lots of black-and-white text pages, look for a laser. Output will be faster and cheaper than with an inkjet. The Brother HL-1440, $230, and HP Laser Jet 1000, $200, provide speedy, top-quality, low-cost text. For printing, scanning, and copying at a low price, consider the compact **CR Best Buy** HP PSC 1210, $100. If you want both color and low-cost, high-speed text output, consider getting an inkjet and a laser. For about $300 total, you can buy a decent and fairly compact printer of each type.

Excellent | Very good | Good | Fair | Poor

Key number	Brand & model	Price	Overall score (0–100: P F G VG E)	Test results: Text quality	Text speed (ppm)	Text cost	Photo quality	Photo time (min.)	Photo cost	Graphics quality
	INKJET PRINTERS									
1	**Canon** Photo Printer S530D **A CR Best Buy**	$150		Excellent	8.6	3.3¢	Very good	2	0.80	Excellent
2	**HP** DeskJet 995C	385		Excellent	5.4	4.0	Very good	8	0.80	Excellent
3	**Canon** Photo Printer i850	150		Excellent	9.5	3.3	Very good	6	0.80	Good
4	**HP** DeskJet 5550	130		Excellent	4.5	6.2	Excellent	18	1.10	Excellent
5	**HP** PhotoSmart 7150	150		Excellent	4.5	6.2	Excellent	18	1.10	Excellent
6	**HP** PhotoSmart 7550	300		Excellent	4.5	6.2	Excellent	18	1.10	Excellent
7	**HP** DeskJet 3820 **A CR Best Buy**	100		Excellent	4.9	5.9	Excellent	15	0.80	Excellent
8	**HP** DeskJet 6127	250		Very good	6.9	4.0	Excellent	11	0.80	Excellent
9	**Canon** Photo Printer i470D	150		Excellent	8.2	5.2	Very good	7	0.80	Excellent
10	**Canon** Color Bubble Jet S330	60		Excellent	8	5.2	Good	3	0.80	Good
11	**Epson** Stylus Photo 825	150		Very good	2.5	5.8	Excellent	10	1.00	Excellent
12	**Epson** Stylus C62	70		Very good	8.5	4.5	Excellent	9	0.80	Excellent
13	**Epson** Stylus Photo 900	200		Very good	2.4	5.8	Excellent	11	1.00	Excellent
14	**Epson** Stylus Photo 960	350		Very good	2.6	3.2	Excellent	12	0.90	Excellent
15	**Epson** Stylus Photo 820	100		Very good	2.4	6.4	Excellent	18	1.10	Excellent
16	**Epson** Stylus C82	100		Very good	8.3	3.4	Good	10	0.80	Excellent

Key number	Brand & model	Price	Overall score (0–100: P F G VG E)	Text quality	Text speed (ppm)	Text cost	Photo quality	Photo time (min.)	Photo cost	Graphics quality
	MULTIFUNCTION INKJET PRINTER									
17	**Canon** MultiPass F30	$300		⊜	6.7	3.3	⊜	4	0.80	⊖
18	**HP** PSC 1210 all-in-one **A CR Best Buy**	100		⊜	5.5	6.2	⊖	10	0.90	⊜
19	**Dell** All-In-One Printer A940	140		⊖	8.1	9.7	⊖	8	0.90	⊖
20	**HP** PSC 2210	300		⊜	4.6	6.2	⊜	18	1.10	⊜
21	**Lexmark** X5150 All-In-One	150		⊖	8.1	9.1	⊖	8	0.90	⊖
22	**Canon** MultiPass F80	350		⊜	9.2	3.3	○	2	0.80	○
23	**Brother** MFC-5200C	250		○	6.4	3.3	⊖	5	0.80	○
	LASER PRINTER									
24	**Brother** HL-1440	230		⊜	10.9	1.8	-	-	-	⊖
25	**HP** LaserJet 1000	200		⊜	9.2	1.9	-	-	-	⊖
26	**Dell** Personal Laser Printer P1500	290		⊜	15.0	3.5	-	-	-	⊖
27	**Samsung** ML-1710	200		⊜	12.0	4.0	-	-	-	○
28	**Brother** HL-5040	300		⊜	13.3	2.0	-	-	-	○
29	**Minolta-**QMS PagePro 1250W	200		⊜	12.0	3.6	-	-	-	○

See report, page 150. Based on tests published in Consumer Reports in September 2003.

Guide to the Ratings

Overall score is based mainly on speed and text/photo quality. For multifunction models, only printing is scored. **Text quality** is for clarity and crispness of black text. **Text speed** measures pages per minutes (ppm) for a 10-page document at the default setting. **Photo quality** reflects a snapshot's appearance. **Photo time** measures, to the nearest minute, the time to print one 8x10-inch color photo at the best-quality setting. **Graphics quality** assesses illustrations, charts, and drawings. **Cost** is for one text page (for ink and plain paper) or for one 8x10-inch photo (ink and glossy 8½x11-inch paper). **Price** is the approximate retail. Under Features, water-resistant black ink (and for lasers, toner) won't run if it gets wet.

Recommendations & notes

ALL MODELS: Work with Windows XP and 2000. Can connect via USB port. **MOST MODELS:** Also work with Windows ME and 98. Support Mac OS (the manufacturer's Web site should have the latest available driver software). Use water-resistant black ink or toner. Indicate when ink supply is low. Have a 1-year parts and labor warranty. Most inkjets can print banners and lack a parallel port. Most lasers also work with Windows 95 and can connect to computers via parallel as well as USB port.

INKJET PRINTERS

1 **CANON** Photo Printer S530D **Excellent overall; a CR Best Buy.** Fast for color photos and text. Supports fast USB2 printing from compatible computer. Can print directly from memory card (using adapter) or from compatible Canon digital camera, and can transfer files to computer from memory card. Can print borderless 4x6- and 8.5x11-inch photos. Has 100-sheet and 10-envelope input.

2 **HP** DeskJet 995c **Very good overall, but expensive.** Quiet. Supports Bluetooth wireless printing on Windows 2000 or Windows XP computers and can print via infrared beam from digital cameras with HP JetSend capability. Can print from a shared Windows network. Automatic two-sided printing. USB cable included.

3 **CANON** Photo Printer i850 **Very good overall, with fast text printing.** Supports fast USB2 printing from compatible computer and has parallel port for use with older PCs. Can print from a shared Windows network. Can print borderless 4x6- and 8.5x11-inch photos.

4 **HP** DeskJet 5550 **Very good overall.** Slow for photos. Has parallel port for use with older computers. Can print from a shared Windows network. Can print borderless 4x6-inch photos. Black ink not water-resistant, and for best photo quality, photo-ink cartridge must be swapped with black before printing photos.

5 **HP** PhotoSmart 7150 **Very good overall, though slow for photos.** Can print directly from compatible HP digital cameras. Can print borderless 4x6-inch photos and has built-in tray for 4x6-inch photo paper. Black ink not water-resistant, and for best photo quality, photo-ink cartridge must be swapped with black before printing. Similar model 7350, $180, adds memory-card reader found on HP PhotoSmart 7550.

6 **HP** PhotoSmart 7550 **Very good overall, though slow for photos.** Has LCD screen for viewing and editing images. Can print directly or transfer images to computer from CompactFlash, SmartMedia, Memory Stick, MultiMedia, or Secure Digital memory card. Can print directly from compatible HP digital cameras. Can print borderless 4x6-inch photos and has built-in tray for 4x6-inch photo paper. Black ink is not water-resistant.

7 **HP** DeskJet 3820 **Very good; a CR Best Buy.** Slow for photos. Parallel port for use with older computers. Can print from a shared Windows network. Cannot print banners. Only 90-day warranty.

8 **HP** DeskJet 6127 **Very good overall.** Supports fast USB2 printing from compatible computer. Has built-in Ethernet connectivity. Similar model 6122, $200, adds parallel port but lacks built-in Ethernet.

9 **CANON** Photo Printer i470D **Very good, and fast for text.** Can print borderless 4x6-, 5x7-, and 8.5x11-inch photos. Can print directly or transfer images to computer from CompactFlash, SmartMedia, Memory Stick, Secure Digital, or MultiMedia card, and can print directly from compatible Canon cameras. Cannot print banners. Printing with output tray closed caused paper jam. Similar model Bubble Jet i450, $100, lacks memory-card reader and cannot print directly from camera.

Recommendations & notes

10 **CANON** Bubble Jet S330 **Very good.** Fast for photos and text. Only so-so quality for color photos and graphics. Supports fast USB2 printing from compatible computer. Can print from a shared Windows network. Can print borderless 4x6- and 8.5x11-inch photos.

11 **EPSON** Stylus Photo 825 **Very good overall, but slow for text.** Can print directly from memory card using adapter, and from a shared Windows network. Can print borderless 3.5x5-, 4x6-, 5x7-, 8x10-, and 8.5x11-inch photos. Noisier than most. Black ink is not water-resistant.

12 **EPSON** Stylus C62 **Very good overall and fast for text, but much slower if color added.** Parallel port for use with older computers. Noisier than most. Black ink is not water-resistant.

13 **EPSON** Stylus Photo 900 **Very good overall, but slow for text.** Parallel port for use with older computers. Can print borderless 4x6-, 5x7-, and 8x10-inch photos. Can print from a shared Windows network. Includes attachments for printing onto roll paper and printable CDs and DVDs. Black ink is not water-resistant. Printing with output tray closed caused paper jam.

14 **EPSON** Stylus Photo 960 **Very good overall, though slow for text.** Parallel port for use with older computers. Can print from a shared Windows network. Can print borderless panoramic and 3.5x5-, 4x6-, 5x7-, and 8.5x11-inch photos. Includes attachments for printing onto roll paper and printable CDs and DVDs. Black ink is not water-resistant.

15 **EPSON** Stylus Photo 820 **Good overall, but among the slowest for photos and text.** Parallel port for use with older computers. Can print from a shared Windows network. Can print borderless 3.5x5-, 4x6-, 5x7-, 8x10-, and 8.5x11-inch photos. Noisier than most. Black ink is not water-resistant.

16 **EPSON** Stylus C82 **Good overall.** Fast for text, but much slower if color added. Parallel port for use with older computers. Color ink is water-resistant on plain paper. Noisier than most. Similar model C82N, $280, adds built-in Ethernet connectivity; C82WN, $360, adds Ethernet and Wi-Fi wireless printing.

MULTIFUNCTION INKJETS

17 **CANON** MultiPass F30 **Excellent overall.** Flatbed design for scanning and copying. Fast with photos and text. Includes automatic document feeder. Noisier than most. Does not support Macs.

18 **HP** PSC 1210 all-in-one **Very good and especially compact; a CR Best Buy.** Flatbed design for scanning and copying. Can print from a shared Windows network. Can be set for only up to nine copies at a time. Black ink is not water-resistant. Cannot print banners.

19 **DELL** All-In-One Printer A940 **Very good and fast, but high per-page costs for text.** Flatbed design for scanning and copying. Has fax software and control-panel button for easy faxing via PC. Can print from a shared Windows network. Supports only Windows XP and 2000, unlike virtually identical Lexmark X5150.

20 **HP** PSC 2210 **Very good overall, but slow with photos.** Flatbed design for scanning and copying; includes built-in fax modem. Can print directly or transfer images to computer from CompactFlash, SmartMedia, Memory Stick, MultiMedia, or Secure Digital memory card. Can print from a shared Windows network. Can print borderless 4x6-inch photos. Black ink is not water-resistant, and for best photo quality, photo-ink cartridge must be swapped with black before printing photos. Similar model 2110, lacks memory-card reader and fax modem.

Recommendations & notes

21 **LEXMARK** X5150 **Very good and fast, but high per-page costs for text.** Flatbed design for scanning and copying. Has fax software and control-panel button for easy faxing via PC. Can print from a shared Windows network.

22 **CANON** MultiPass F80 **Very good; fast with photos and text.** Flatbed design for scanning and copying; includes automatic document feeder and built-in fax modem. Supports fast USB2 printing from compatible computer. Can print directly or transfer files to computer from memory card using adapter. Can print from a shared Windows network. Can print borderless 4x6- and 8.5x11-inch photos. Does not support Macs. Similar model F60, $250, lacks document feeder and fax modem.

23 **BROTHER** MFC-5200c **Very good.** Flatbed design for scanning and copying; includes automatic document feeder and built-in fax modem. Parallel port for use with older computers. Can print directly or transfer images to computer from CompactFlash, SmartMedia, or Memory Stick memory card. Can print from a shared Windows network. Black ink is not water-resistant.

LASER PRINTERS

24 **BROTHER** HL-1440 **Fast text printing and low-priced text.** Parallel port for use with older computers. Quieter than most. Stops printing when toner runs low.

25 **HP** LaserJet 1000 **Excellent printer at a good price.** Fast and low-priced text output. Does not support Macs. Lacks low-toner warning.

26 **DELL** Personal Laser Printer P1500 **Excellent overall.** Fast, but high per-page costs for text for a laser. Parallel port for use with older computers. Can print from a shared Windows network. Does not support Macs.

27 **SAMSUNG** ML-1710 **Excellent overall, and especially compact.** Fast, but high per-page costs for text for a laser. Can print from a shared Windows network. Connects via USB only. Comes with low-capacity starter toner cartridge. Lacks low-toner warning. Similar model ML-1750, $300, adds parallel port and supports faster USB2 printing.

28 **BROTHER** HL-5040 **Very good, with fast, low-cost text printing.** Supports fast USB2 printing from compatible computer. Parallel port for use with older computers. Can print from a shared Windows network. Noisier than most. Stops printing when toner runs low. Similar model HL-5050, $325, adds additional 50-sheet multipurpose tray and business-related features; HL-5070N, has built-in Ethernet connectivity. Both similar models are 0.7-inch deeper than tested model.

29 **MINOLTA-QMS** PagePro 1250W **Very good overall.** Fast, but high per-page costs for text for a laser. Can print from a shared Windows network. Parallel port for use with older computers. Does not support Macs. Comes with low-capacity starter toner cartridge.

Ranges

You can buy a competent coil-type electric range for as little as $400. Spend more and you'll get added stylishness and conveniences like a trendy glass smoothtop instead of coils, higher-power elements, a convection feature for the oven, and stainless-steel trim. The Frigidaire FEF366A[S], $600, **a CR Best Buy**, offers very good performance and outstanding value. The highly-rated GE JBP80WF[WW] and GE JBP82WF[WW] are both excellent performers. If smoothtop styling isn't a must, consider an electric-coil model, which offers the ultimate in quick cooktop heating.

You can count on impressive performance from a gas range for as little as $550. The GE JGBP35WEA[WW], $800, is a very good range from one of the more reliable brands. Spend a bit more and you typically get stainless-steel trim, higher-heat burners, and—increasingly—a convection option for oven cooking, though the time saved with this feature tends to be minimal. Pricier models (about $1,500 to $2,000) also include dual-fuel ranges, which pair a gas cooktop with an electric oven, though dual-fuel stoves delivered no clear benefits in our tests.

Within types, in performance order.

Excellent / Very good / Good / Fair / Poor

Key number	Brand And Model	Price	Overall Score (0–100: P F G VG E)	Cooktop: High	Cooktop: Low	Oven: Baking	Oven: Broiling	Oven: Capacity
	ELECTRIC SMOOTHTOP RANGES							
1	**GE** JBP80WF[WW]	$800		Very good	Excellent	Very good	Very good	Excellent
2	**GE** JBP82WF[WW]	850		Good	Excellent	Very good	Very good	Excellent
3	**Kenmore** (Sears) Elite 9901[2]	1,200		Excellent	Excellent	Very good	Very good	Very good
4	**Maytag** Accellis MER6750AA[W]	1,050		Very good	Excellent	Very good	Excellent	Good
5	**Maytag** Gemini MER6769BA[W]	1,000		Very good	Excellent	Very good	Very good	Very good
6	**Maytag** Gemini MER6872BA[W]	1,550		Very good	Excellent	Very good	Very good	Very good
7	**Kenmore** (Sears) 9582[2]	1,050		Excellent	Excellent	Very good	Good	Very good
8	**Maytag** PER5710BA[W]	565		Very good	Excellent	Excellent	Good	Very good
9	**Frigidaire** FEF366A[S] **A CR Best Buy**	600		Very good	Excellent	Very good	Very good	Very good
10	**KitchenAid** KERC500H[WH]	750		Excellent	Excellent	Very good	Very good	Good
11	**GE** Profile JS968SF[SS]	1,750		Excellent	Excellent	Very good	Very good	Good
12	**Jenn-Air** JES8850AA[W]	1,600		Very good	Very good	Good	Good	Good
13	**Whirlpool** Polara GR556LRK[P]	1,800		Very good	Excellent	Good	Good	Good

Within types, in performance order.

Key number	Brand And Model	Price	Overall Score (0–100; P F G VG E)	Cooktop: High	Cooktop: Low	Oven: Baking	Oven: Broiling	Oven: Capacity
	GAS RANGES							
14	**GE** Profile JGBP85WEB[WW]	$950		○	⊜	⊖	⊜	⊖
15	**GE** JGBP35WEA[WW]	800		○	⊜	⊖	⊜	⊖
16	**Maytag** Gemini MGR6772BD[W]	1,450		⊖	⊖	⊖	⊖	⊜
17	**Magic** Chef CGR3742CD[W]	625		○	⊜	⊜	○	⊖
18	**Maytag** MGR5880BD[W]	1,075		○	⊜	⊜	○	⊖
19	**Maytag** PGR5710BD[W]	565		○	⊜	⊜	○	⊖
20	**Jenn-Air** JGS8750AD[W]	1,500		⊖	⊖	⊖	⊜	○
21	**Kenmore** (Sears) Elite 7901[2]	1,200		○	⊜	⊖	○	○
22	**Tappan** TGF363A[W]	550		○	⊜	⊖	○	○
23	**DCS** RGSC-305	3,700		⊖	⊜	⊖	○	○
24	**Frigidaire** Gallery GLGF377A[S]	800		◒	⊜	⊖	○	○
25	**KitchenAid** KGRT607H[BS]	1,360		⊖	○	⊖	⊖	○
26	**Viking** VGSC3064B[SS]	3,890		⊖	◒	⊖	⊜	◒
	DUAL-FUEL RANGES							
27	**KitchenAid** KDRP407H[SS]	3,450		○	⊖	⊜	⊜	⊖
28	**Jenn-Air** JDS8850AA[S]	2,150		○	⊜	○	⊖	○
29	**Kenmore** (Sears) Elite 4683[3]	1,600		○	⊜	⊖	⊖	◒
30	**Jenn-Air** JDS9860AA[W]	2090		◒	⊖	⊖	⊜	○
31	**Viking** VDSC305B[SS]	3,800		⊖	⊜	○	⊖	◒
32	**Viking** VDSC3074B	4,000		⊖	⊜	○	⊖	◒
33	**GE Monogram** ZDP30N4D[SS]	3,600		○	⊖	⊖	⊖	◒

See report, page 97. Based on tests published in Consumer Reports in March 2003, with updated prices and availability.

Guide to the Ratings

Under **brand & model,** brackets show a tested model's color code. Similar models have the same high and low burners or elements, oven, and broiler; other details may differ. Overall score includes cooktop speed and simmer performance, oven capacity, baking, broiling, and self-cleaning performance. **Cooktop high** is how quickly the highest-powered burner or element heated 6⅓ quarts of room-temperature water to a near boil. **Low** shows how well the least-powerful burner or element melted and held chocolate without scorching it and whether the most powerful, set to Low, held tomato sauce below a boil. **Oven baking** is baking evenness for cakes and cookies. **Broiling** is searing performance and cooking evenness for a tray of burgers. **Capacity** is usable oven space. **Price** is approximate retail. **Recommendations & notes** list noteworthy features and some minor shortcoming.

Recommendations & notes

ALL TESTED MODELS: Are 30 inches wide. Have an oven light, anti-tip hardware, and a self-cleaning oven. **MOST HAVE:** Freestanding construction. Touchpad oven controls. Cooktop rim that holds spills. Two or three oven racks with five positions. A storage drawer. A reasonably clear oven view. Most gas ranges: Have sealed burners and cast-iron grates. Can be converted to LP gas.

ELECTRIC SMOOTHTOPS

1 **GE** JBP80WF[WW] **Excellent performance at a good price.** Has warming element and dual cooktop elements. But only small elements in rear.

2 **GE** JBP82WF[WW] **Excellent performance at a good price.** Has warming element, dual cooktop elements, and bridge element.

3 **KENMORE** (Sears) Elite 9901[2] **Excellent and nicely featured.** Has convection option, dual cooktop elements, warming drawer, warming element, and bridge element.

4 **MAYTAG** Accellis MER6750AA[W] **Feature-rich and very good,** but Maytag has been among the more repair-prone brands of electric ranges. Has microwave option to speed cooking time. Has numeric-keypad oven controls, dual cooktop elements, and "hot" light indicator for each element.

5 **MAYTAG** Gemini MER6769BA[W] **A very good model with two ovens,** but Maytag has been among the more repair-prone brands of electric ranges. Has microwave option to speed cooking time. Has numeric-keypad oven controls, dual cooktop elements, and "hot" light indicator for each element.

6 **MAYTAG** Gemini MER6872BA[W] **A very good model with two ovens,** but Maytag has been among the more repair-prone brands of electric ranges. Small upper oven can toast, bake, and broil. Lower oven mounted very low. Has convection option, dual cooktop elements, warming element, and numeric-keypad oven controls. But only small elements in rear, only one "hot" light for cooktop elements, and no storage drawer.

7 **KENMORE** (Sears) 9582[2] **Very good overall.** Has warming element, dual cooktop elements, warming drawer, and "hot" light indicator for each element. One of its three oven racks can be split. Discontinued, but may still be available.

8 **MAYTAG** PER5710BA[W] **Very good, rather basic smoothtop at a reasonable price.** Maytag has been among the more repair-prone brands of electric ranges. Similar: PER5702A[ ], PER5705BA[ ].

9 **FRIGIDAIRE** FEF366A[S] **A CR Best Buy. A good value offering very good performance.** But cooktop has no rim to contain spills.

10 **KITCHENAID** KERC500H[WH] **Very good.** Has a warming element and dual cooktop elements, but only one large element. Has "hot" indicator light for each element. Has been among the more repair-prone brands of electric ranges.

11 **GE** Profile JS968SF[SS] **Cramped controls hamper this very good smoothtop.** Slide-in model; no side panels or backsplash. Has dual cooktop elements, warming element, bridge element, "hot" light for each element, numeric-keypad oven controls, and meat probe with automatic shutoff.

12 **JENN-AIR** JES8850AA[W] **Very good, but has been among the more repair-prone brands of electric ranges.** Has numeric-keypad oven controls, convection option, dual elements, meat probe for automatic oven shutoff, "hot" light indicator for each element. But cooktop has no rim to contain spills.

Recommendations & notes

13 WHIRLPOOL Polara GR556LRK[P] **A very good smoothtop.** Has a unique feature; a refrigeration mode that allows you to set the range to keep the food cool during the day, then cook it just before you return in the evening. Has convection option, "hot" light for each element and dual cook

GAS RANGES

14 PROFILE JGBP85WEB[WW] **Very good, basic model.** Has warming drawer. Discontinued, but similar Profile JGBP86WEB[ ] and JGBP90MEB[ ] are available.

15 GE JGBP35WEA[WW] **Very good, basic model.**

16 MAYTAG Gemini MGR6772BD[W] **A very good model with two ovens,** but Maytag has been among the more repair-prone brands of gas ranges. Small upper oven can toast, bake, and broil. Lower oven mounted very low. Has numeric-keypad oven controls, and heavy, continuous grates. But no storage drawer, and large pot on rear burner blocked oven controls.

17 MAGIC CHEF CGR3742CD[W] **Very good, fairly basic range at a good price.** Has been among the more repair-prone brands of gas ranges.

18 MAYTAG MGR5880BD[W] **Has convection option, warming drawer, and numeric-keypad oven controls.** But has been among the more repair-prone brands of gas ranges. Similar: MGR5870BD[ ].

19 MAYTAG PGR5710BD[W] **Very good, fairly basic range at a good price.** But has been among the more repair-prone brands of gas ranges. Has steel grates. Similar: PGR5705BD[ ].

20 JENN-AIR JGS8750AD[W] **Very good.** Has numeric-keypad oven controls and continuous grates. Rangetop burners automatically reignite. But has been among the more repair-prone brands of gas ranges.

21 KENMORE (Sears) Elite 7901[2] **Very good and feature-filled.** Has convection option, warming drawer, warming element, and glass ceramic cooktop.

22 TAPPAN TGF363A[W] **A very good basic performer and a good value.** Roomy center workspace. Oven door and window hotter than most during self-cleaning.

23 DCS RGSC-305 **A very good pro-style range, but with only mediocre oven space.** Has convection option, heavy continuous grates, and burners that reignite if they go out. Cooktop and oven controls in front. Lacks touchpad and digital display. Only four rack positions. Large fifth burner wasn't the fastest, despite its high heat.

24 FRIGIDAIRE Gallery GLGF377A[S] **Very good overall, but fairly slow cooktop speed.** Has convection option. Similar: FGF378A[C], Gallery GLGF377C[ ].

25 KITCHENAID KGRT607H[BS] **Very good with stainless-steel touches,** but has been among the more repair-prone brands of gas ranges. Has convection option and continuous grates. Numeric keypad oven controls on front panel, but are easy to activate by mistake. Cooktop gets hot during oven and broiler use, and has no rim to contain spills. Similar: KGRT600H[].

26 VIKING VGSC3064B[SS] **Good and expensive stainless-steel stove.** Has convection option, continuous grates, and cooktop burners that auto reignite. But unsealed burners and window view not clear. Smallish oven and subpar simmering compromised performance.

DUAL-FUEL RANGES

27 KITCHENAID KDRP407H[SS] **Very good and**

Recommendations & notes

expensive dual-fuel stainless-steel range with convection option and continuous grates. Oven dial instead of touchpad controls.

28 JENN-AIR JDS8850AA[S] **A very good dual-fuel range.** Slide-in model; no side panels or backsplash. Burners reignite if they go out. Has convection option, heavy, continuous grates, meat probe with automatic oven shutoff. Door and window less hot than most during self-cleaning.

29 KENMORE (Sears) Elite 4683[3] **A very good dual-fuel model.** Has convection option, glass ceramic cooktop, warming drawer, and warming element, and continuous grates. But oven is somewhat small, cooktop has no rim to contain spills, and only four oven rack positions.

30 JENN-AIR JDS9860AA[W] **Very good.** Dual-fuel range has grill module and downdraft vent, convection option, and meat probe for auto shutoff. But fairly slow cooktop speed. Similar: JDS9860AA[P]

31 VIKING VDSC305B[SS] **Very good albeit very expensive stainless steel dual-fuel range.** Has convection option, heavy continuous grates, and burners that reignite if they go out. But has a smallish oven and unsealed burners, and is among the least effective at self-cleaning.

32 VIKING VDSC3074B **A very good dual-fuel, pro-style range.** Has convection option, heavy continuous grates, and burners that reignite if they go out. Door and window less hot than most during self-cleaning. But smallish oven, and among the least effective at self-cleaning.

33 GE MONOGRAM ZDP30N4D[SS] **Very good albeit very expensive stainless steel dual-fuel stove.** Has convection option and continuous grates. But smallish oven, unsealed burners, and only three oven-rack positions.

Receivers

You can expect very good performance at any price, but connections and features will vary. Spend around $200 and you can get a basic surround-sound (digital) model that can decode Dolby Pro Logic and Pro Logic II, along with Dolby Digital and DTS. The **CR Best Buy** Panasonic SA-HE100, $250, is a very good 5.1 receiver with ample inputs, at a great price. For $300 and up, you can get more features, such as an onscreen display and 6.1-channel decoding, which provides slightly smoother surround sound. The Yamaha RX-V440 and Onkyo TX-SR501, both $300, are very good reasonably priced choices that support three rear-surround speakers. Models priced at $500 and up typically have the most connections and features.

Excellent / Very good / Good / Fair / Poor

In performance order.

Key number	Brand & model	Price	Overall score (0–100; P F G VG E)	Test results: Amp/tuner performance	Ease of use	Features	Watts per channel: 8 ohm	6 ohm	Features: 6.1-channel decoding	Digital-audio in (optical/coaxial)	S-video in/out	Component-video in/out	Onscreen display	Front-panel input
1	**Onkyo** TX-SR701	$800		Very good	Very good	Good	130	156	•	3/1	5/3	2/1	•	•
2	**Panasonic** SA-HE100 **A CR Best Buy**	250		Very good	Very good	Very good	85	112		3/1	3/1	2/1		•
3	**Harman/Kardon** AVR325	760		Very good	Very good	Good	89	106	•	3/3	5/3	2/1	•	•
4	**Sony** STR-DE995	480		Very good	Very good	Good	131	157	•	4/1	4/2	2/1	•	•
5	**Yamaha** RX-V740	600		Very good	Very good	Very good	95	125	•	4/1	5/3	2/1	•	•
6	**Denon** AVR-2803	800		Very good	Very good	Good	91	120	•	4/2	7/3	2/1	•	
7	**Yamaha** RX-V440	300		Very good	Very good	Good	101	121	•	1/1	0/0	2/1		•
8	**Kenwood** VR-7070	500		Very good	Very good	Good	70	91	•	2/2	5/2	2/1		•
9	**Onkyo** TX-SR501	300		Very good	Good	Fair	92	111	•	2/1	4/2	2/1		•
10	**Pioneer** VSX-D912-K	400		Very good	Very good	Good	143	160	•	3/2	4/2	2/1		•
11	**Panasonic** SA-HE75	200		Very good	Very good	Good	112	125		2/1	3/1	0/0		•
12	**JVC** RX-8030VBK	400		Good	Very good	Fair	143	165	•	4/1	5/3	2/1		•
13	**Pioneer** VSX-D412-K	200		Very good	Very good	Fair	136	151		1/1	0/0	0/0		
14	**JVC** RX-6030VBK	200		Very good	Very good	Fair	95	108		1/1	2/2	2/1		
15	**Sony** STR-DE595	190		Very good	Very good	Fair	118	138		2/1	0/0	2/1		
16	**Panasonic** SA-XR45	330		Very good	Good	Fair	96	124	•	3/1	3/1	2/1	•	
17	**Kenwood** VR-705	200		Very good	Good	Poor	126	146		1/2	0/0	0/0	•	

See report, page 64. Based on tests published in Consumer Reports in November 2003, with updated prices and availability.

Guide to the Ratings

Overall score is based mainly on amplifier and AM/FM tuner performance; ease of use and features also factor in. **Amp/tuner performance** evaluates lack of noise and distortion in the amplifier, plus AM reception (which was good on all tested models) and FM reception (very good on all). **Ease of use** reflects the design of the front panel and remote control. **Features** score reflects the presence or absence of convenience features, including the number of inputs. **Watts per channel** is our measure of power when the receiver is used with 8-ohm and 6-ohm speakers; only three models (2, 5, and 7) were rated for use with 4-ohm speakers. **Price** is approximate retail. Under Features, video outputs listed include one required by TV.

Recommendations & notes

ALL TESTED MODELS: Can decode Dolby Digital, DTS, and Dolby Pro Logic and Pro Logic II surround audio. Can automatically detect which surround format requires decoding. Have a 75-ohm FM-antenna connection, output jack for powered subwoofer. Have other DSP modes besides Dolby Surround. Have test-tone function for setting sound level, remote control that can operate devices of the same brand, and display dimmer. Have an FM tuner that scored very good in our tests, and an AM tuner that scored good. Have at least 30 AM or FM station presets. Lack direct tuning of frequency on console and function to scan preset radio stations for a few seconds. **MOST TESTED MODELS:** Have 5.1 inputs for external decoder, a two-year warranty for parts and labor, sleep-timer function, universal remote control to operate devices from other manufacturers, and one or two switched AC outlets. Lack center-channel preamp output, bass-boost function, phono input, and tape monitor. Dimensions noted below are rounded up to the nearest ¼ inch.

1 ONKYO TX-SR701 **Very good, with reasonable price for a THX-certified model.** Has onscreen display (OSD) and multisource for simultaneous two-room speaker use. Bass boost. Phono input. Center-channel preamp output. 6.75x17.25x17.5 in. (HWD).

2 PANASONIC SA-HE100 **A CR Best Buy Best value among tested models.** FM tuner adjusts in full-channel increments. Radio stations can be tuned directly using remote. Troubleshooting "help" function can advise user of necessary fix. Can be used with 4-ohm speakers. Has tape monitor and phono input. Has DTS-ES (6.1) but cannot decode Dolby Digital EX surround audio. Lacks sleep timer. Warranty only 1 yr. 6.25x17x14.5 in. (HWD).

3 HARMAN/KARDON AVR-325 **Very good.** Has onscreen display (OSD) and multisource for simultaneous two-room speaker use. Can automatically calibrate sound level. Radio stations can be tuned directly using remote. Has center-channel preamp output. 6.75x17.5x16.5 in. (HWD). Similar models AVR-125 ($350) and AVR-225 permit fewer connections and have only 5.1 audio decoding.

4 SONY STR-DE995 **Very good.** Has onscreen display (OSD) and multisource for simultaneous two-room speaker use. Can program to show station call letters. Radio stations can be tuned directly using remote. Has phono input. 6.25x17x14.5 in. (HWD). Similar model STR-DE895 lacks multizone capability.

5 YAMAHA RX-V740 **Very good.** Has onscreen display (OSD) and multisource for simultaneous two-room speaker use. FM tuner adjusts in full-channel increments. Has phono input. Center-channel preamp output. Can be used

Recommendations & notes

with 4-ohm speakers. 6.75x17.25x15.5 in. (HWD). Similar model RX-V640 permits fewer connections.

6 DENON AVR-2803 **Very good.** Has onscreen display (OSD) and multisource for simultaneous two-room speaker use. FM tuner adjusts in full-channel increments. Has phono input. Center-channel preamp output. Lacks sleep timer. 6.75x18x16.25 in. (HWD).

7 YAMAHA RX-V440 **Very good.** FM tuner adjusts in full-channel increments. Can be used with 4-ohm speakers. 6.5x17.25x15.5 in. (HWD). Similar model RX-V540 permits more connections.

8 KENWOOD VR-7070 **Very good, with very low price for a THX-certified model.** Has multisource for simultaneous two-room speaker use. Has bass boost. Phono input. Center-channel preamp output. Lacks sleep timer. 6.25x17.25x15.5 in. (HWD).

9 ONKYO TX-SR501 **Very good.** 6x17.25x14.75 in. (HWD). Similar model TX-SR601 has multizone capability.

10 PIONEER VSX-D912K **Very good.** Can automatically calibrate sound level. Can program to show station call letters. Radio stations can be tuned directly using remote. Center-channel preamp output. 6.25x16.5x15.25 in. (HWD). Only 1-yr. warranty. Similar model VSX-D812K ($350) permits fewer connections; VSX-D712K has only 5.1 audio decoding.

11 PANASONIC SA-HE75 **Very good.** Troubleshooting "help" function can advise user of necessary fix. FM tuner adjusts in full-channel increments. Radio stations can be tuned directly using remote. Tape monitor. Cannot decode Dolby Digital EX or DTS-ES 6.1 surround audio. Only 1-yr. warranty. Lacks sleep timer. 6.25x17x14.25 in. (HWD).

12 JVC RX-8030VBK **Good.** Has bass boost. Phono input. Center-channel preamp output. Lacks AC outlets. 6.25x17x17.25 in. (HWD). Similar model RX-7030VBK permits fewer connections.

13 PIONEER VSX-D412-K **Good.** Can program to show station call letters. Has tape monitor. Cannot decode Dolby Digital EX or DTS-ES 6.1 surround audio. Only 1-yr. warranty. Lacks sleep timer. 6.25x16.5x16.25 in. (HWD).

14 JVC RX-6030VBK **Good.** Has bass boost. Cannot decode Dolby Digital EX or DTS-ES 6.1 surround audio. Lacks AC outlets. 5.75x18x16 in. (HWD).

15 SONY STR-DE595 **Good.** Radio stations can be tuned directly using remote. Can program to show station call letters. Cannot decode Dolby Digital EX or DTS-ES 6.1 surround audio. Lacks universal remote control, and AC outlets. 5.5x17x11.75 in. (HWD). Similar model STR-DE695 has 6.1 audio decoding.

16 PANASONIC SA-XR45 **Good.** Has onscreen display (OSD) and multisource for simultaneous two-room speaker use. FM tuner adjusts in full-channel increments. Radio stations can be tuned directly using remote. Bass and treble adjustable only via remote. Only 1-yr. warranty. Surround lacks Dolby 3 Stereo mode. Lacks AC outlets. 3x17x15 in. (HWD). Similar model SA-XR25 lacks multizone capability.

17 KENWOOD VR-705 **Good.** Has onscreen display (OSD) and bass boost. Lacks 5.1 inputs for external digital-audio decoders. Cannot decode Dolby Digital EX or DTS-ES 6.1 surround audio. Bass and treble adjustable only via remote. Lacks sleep timer and universal remote control. 5.75x17.25x12 in. (HWD). Similar model VR-707 has 6.1 audio decoding.

Refrigerators

Most refrigerators did well or very well in temperature tests; bottom-freezers and built-ins showed superior results. As a group, the bottom-freezers were noisiest. Choose the size and style, then look for the features you want, plus a brand with a good track record for reliability. Among top-freezer models, consider the Maytag MTB1956GE, $800, and the Whirlpool ET9FTTXL, $750. Among bottom-freezer models, two were super-efficient and spacious: the Amana ARB2217C, $1,250, and the 36-inch "armoire"-style Kenmore (Sears) Elite Trio 7350, $1,800. The GE GSS25JFP, $1,000, **a CR Best Buy**, is a good value that holds temperatures best among the side-by-side models. Among built-ins, the Amana ARB8057C, $1,900,is a very energy-efficient bottom-freezer model.

In performance order.

Excellent / Very good / Good / Fair / Poor

Key number	Brand & model	Price	Overall score	Test results: Energy efficiency	Temperature performance	Noise	Usable volume (cu. ft.)	Features: Meatkeeper controls	Flexible storage	Water dispenser	Stainless/SS-look avail.	Height x width (in.)
	TOP-FREEZERS *These tend to be the least expensive to run (tested models: $36-$44/yr.)*											
1	**GE** Profile Arctica PTS22LBN[WW]	$980		Excellent	Excellent	Very good	17	•	•		•	68 x 33
2	**Maytag** MTB1956GE[W]	800		Excellent	Very good	Good	14	•	•			67 x 30
3	**Maytag** MTB2156GE[W]	900		Excellent	Very good	Very good	15	•	•			67 x 33
4	**Whirlpool** ET9FTTXL[Q]	750		Excellent	Excellent	Good	15			•		67 x 30
5	**GE** GTS18KCM[WW]	650		Excellent	Very good	Good	14					67 x 30
6	**Whirlpool** Gold GR9SHKXK[Q]	830		Excellent	Very good	Good	14		•		•	66 x 30
7	**LG** LRTPC2031[W]	850		Excellent	Very good	Very good	16		•		•	69 x 30
8	**GE** GTS22KCM[WW]	750		Excellent	Very good	Good	17					68 x 33
9	**Whirlpool** ET1FTTXK[Q]	800		Excellent	Very good	Good	17		•	•		66 x 33
10	**Whirlpool** Gold GR2SHTXK[Q]	1,200		Excellent	Very good	Good	16		•	•	•	66 x 33
11	**Frigidaire** FRT18P5A[W]	500		Excellent	Very good	Very good	15	•		•	•	66 x 30
12	**GE** GTS18HBM[WW]	450		Very good	Very good	Good	13					68 x 28

In performance order.

Key number	Brand & model	Price	Overall score (0–100: P F G VG E)	Test results: Energy efficiency	Test results: Temperature performance	Test results: Noise	Test results: Usable volume (cu. ft.)	Features: Meatkeeper controls	Features: Flexible storage	Features: Water dispenser	Features: Stainless/SS-look avail.	Features: Height x width (in.)
	BOTTOM-FREEZERS *These tend to cost a bit more to run than top-freezers (tested models: $42-$46/yr.)*											
13	**Amana** ARB2217C[W]	$1,250		⊜	⊜	○	16	•	•		•	70 x 33
14	**Kenmore** (Sears) Elite Trio 7350[2]	1,800		⊜	⊜	○	18	•	•	•	•	71 x 36
15	**Maytag** Plus MBB2254GE[W]	1,000		⊜	⊜	○	16		•		•	70 x 33
16	**Amana** ARB1914C[W]	1,050		⊖	⊜	○	13		•			67 x 30
17	**Samsung** RB1855S[W]	750		⊖	⊖	○	14		•		•	70 x 33
	SIDE-BY-SIDES *More expensive to run (tested models: $49-$60/yr.).*											
18	**GE** GSS25JFP[WW] **A CR Best Buy**	1,000		⊖	⊜	⊖	17	•	•	•		70 x 36
19	**Samsung** RS2555S[W]	1,400		⊜	⊖	○	17	•	•	•	•	70 x 36
20	**Amana** ARSE66ZB[W]	1,150		⊖	⊖	○	17	•	•	•	•	71 x 36
21	**Kenmore** (Sears) 5156[2]	1,400		⊖	⊖	⊖	16	•	•	•		70 x 36
22	**Maytag** MSD2456GE[W]	1,350		⊖	⊖	○	13	•	•	•		69 x 33
23	**GE** GSS20IEM[WW]	975		○	○	○	13	•	•	•		68 x 32
24	**Maytag** Plus Wide-by Side MZD2766GE[W]	1,600		⊖	◒	○	18	•	•	•	•	71 x 36
	CABINET-DEPTH MODELS *Depth is 27-28 in. (The Amana is a bottom-freezer; others are side-by-sides.)*											
25	**Amana** ARB8057C[W]	1,900		⊖	⊜	○	14	•	•	•	•	70 x 36
26	**LG** LRSPC2031[W]	1,500		⊖	⊜	⊖	13	•	•	•	•	69 x 36
27	**Jenn-Air** JCD2389GE[W]	2,000		⊖	◒	⊖	15	•	•	•	•	71 x 36
28	**Whirlpool** Gold GC5THGXK[Q]	2,300		⊖	◒	⊖	15		•	•	•	72 x 36
	BUILT-IN BOTTOM-FREEZER MODELS *Depth is 24-25 in. Most costly to buy.*											
29	**Sub-Zero** 650/F	4,450		⊜	⊜	○	15		•		•	84 x 37
30	**GE Monogram** ZIC360NM	4,000		⊖	⊜	⊖	14		•		•	84 x 37
31	**Viking** DFBB363	4,600		⊖	⊜	○	15	•	•		•	84 x 36

[1] *Available only at Best Buy.*

See report, page 101. Based on tests published in Consumer Reports in July 2003, with updated prices and availability.

Guide to the Ratings

Overall score gives most weight to efficiency and temperature performance, then to noise; convenience was also important. **Energy efficiency** reflects consumption per EnergyGuide and usable volume. **Temperature performance** combines outcome of tests at different room temperatures, including high heat; we judge how closely and uniformly recommended settings match our ideal temperatures: Most kept main space at 37°F and freezer at 0°F with good uniformity. **Noise** gauged with compressors running. Under **Brand & model,** bracketed letter/number is color code. **Height and width** rounded up to nearest inch; depth among refrigerators in Ratings is 29 to 33 inches without handle. **Price** is approximate retail; for top-freezers, price is without icemaker, which can cost an extra $50 to $75.

Recommendations & notes

TOP-FREEZERS

1. **GE** Profile Arctica PTS22LBN[WW], **Excellent overall.** Quiet, energy efficient, with excellent temperature control. Discontinued, but a similar model, PTS22LCP[ ], is available.

2. **MAYTAG** MTB1956GE[W] **Very good performance,** with features that make it more convenient than most top-freezers.

3. **MAYTAG** MTB2156GE[W] **Very good overall,** with features that make it more convenient than most top-freezers.

4. **WHIRLPOOL** ET9FTTXL[Q] **Very good performance** from a fairly basic model.

5. **GE** GTS18KCM[WW] **Well-priced for very good performance,** with features that make it more convenient than most top-freezers. Discontinued, but a similar model, GTS18KCP [ ], is available.

6. **WHIRLPOOL** Gold GR9SHKXK[Q] **Very good overall.** Curved, smooth-surface doors.

7. **LG** LRTPC2031[W] **Very good.** Curved, textured-surface doors.

8. **GE** GTS22KCM[WW] **Well-priced for very good performance,** with features that make it more convenient than most top-freezers. But manufacturer's recommended settings left fridge and freezer too cold. Discontinued, but a similar model, GTS22KCP[ ], is available.

9. **WHIRLPOOL** ET1FTTXK[Q] **A very good performer overall.**

10. **WHIRLPOOL** Gold GR2SHTXK[Q] **Very good, with attractive features, but pricey.** Curved, smooth-surface doors. Similar: GR2SHKXK [ ].

11. **FRIGIDAIRE** FRT18P5A[W] **Very good overall and well-priced.** No pullout shelves or freezer light. Frigidaire has been among the more repair-prone brands of top-freezers with icemakers.

12. **GE** GTS18HBM[WW] **Very good performer, though a basic model.** Single control for both compartments.

BOTTOM-FREEZERS

13. **AMANA** ARB2217C[W] **Very good overall.** Bottom-freezer pulls open like a drawer.

14. **KENMORE** (Sears) Elite Trio 7350[2] **Very good model with distinctive styling.** Bottom-freezer pulls open like a drawer; refrigerator has two side-by-side doors.

15. **MAYTAG** Plus MBB2254GE[W] **Very good overall.** Bottom-freezer pulls open like a drawer.

Recommendations & notes

16. AMANA ARB1914C[W] **A very good midline offering.** Bottom-freezer pulls open like a drawer.

17. SAMSUNG RB1855S[W] **Very good but small.** Freezer has door without bins or shelves and three pullout drawers. Twin evaporators. Digital controls on front with inaccurate temperature display. Door alarm. Has hard-to-fill manual ice-making system.

SIDE-BY-SIDES

18. GE GSS25JFP[WW] **A CR Best Buy A very good model at a great price,** with excellent temperature performance. Has water filter.

19. SAMSUNG RS2555S[W] **A very good performer with dual evaporators.** Door alarm. Built-in deodorizers. Controls on door front with inaccurate temperature display. Power cool/power freeze button quickly returns fridge or freezer compartment to set temperatures. "Cool select zone" drawer.

20. AMANA ARSE66ZB[W] **A very good performer at a good price.** Beverage chiller compartment on door, quick-chill zone in freezer.

21. KENMORE (Sears) 5156[2] **A very good performer.** Has an ice-storage bin on the freezer door, dispenser locks, and a water filter. Discontinued, but a similar model, 5363[ ], is available.

22. MAYTAG MSD2456GE[W] **Very good overall,** but has been the most repair-prone side-by-side brand.

23. GE GSS20IEM[WW] **Good overall and well-priced, but not as energy-efficient as most.** Meatkeeper too warm. No spill-proof shelves or water filter. Discontinued, but a similar model, GSS20IEP[ ], is available.

24. MAYTAG Plus Wide-by-Side MZD2766GE[W] **Good overall and novel zigzag door design holds wider items than most side-by-sides.** But warm spots throughout fridge, especially butter compartment, and has been the most repair-prone side-by-side brand.

CABINET-DEPTH MODELS

25. AMANA ARB8057C[W] **A very good model.** Bottom-freezer pulls open like a drawer.

26. LG LRSPC2031[W] **Very good side-by-side model.** Controls are on front of doors. Has door alarm.

27. JENN-AIR JCD2389GE[W] **Good side-by-side performer.** Two crank-adjustable shelves. Beverage chiller on door.

28. WHIRLPOOL Gold GC5THGXK[Q] **Good side-by-side performer.** Accepts custom door panels.

BUILT-IN BOTTOM-FREEZER MODELS

29. SUB-ZERO 650/F **Very good overall and very energy-efficient.** Bottom-freezer opens like a drawer. Needs custom panels at extra cost.

30. GE MONOGRAM ZIC360NM **Very good overall and very quiet.** Bottom-freezer opens like a drawer. Needs custom panels at extra cost.

31. VIKING DFBB363 **Very good model.** Bottom-freezer opens like a drawer. Needs custom panels at extra cost.

Speakers

Most of the speakers we tested are fine performers overall. What distinguishes the best models is accuracy. Because the typical listener is unlikely to notice a difference of less than 8 points in accuracy, even models that aren't at the top of the Ratings are worth considering. Excellent, economical choices for stereo setup or for the front pair in a surround system, and **CR Best Buys,** are the Sony SS-MB35OH, $100, and the Cambridge Soundworks Model Six, $150. Both are bookshelf speakers, but on the large side. If small size is paramount, these five are among the smallest offering fine accuracy and bass handling: the Bose 201 Series V, $220; Pioneer S-DF1-K, $200; Bose 141, $100; KLH 911B, $85; and Bose Acoustimass 3 Series IV, $300.

Within types, in performance order.

Excellent / Very good / Good / Fair / Poor

Key number	Brand & model	Price	Overall score (0–100; P F G VG E)	Tests: Accuracy	Tests: Bass handling	Features: Magnetic shielding	Features: Warranty (yr.)	Features: No. of finishes
	BOOKSHELF SPEAKERS *Fairly small left and right speakers*							
1	**Cambridge Soundworks** Newton Series M80	$400		94	Very good	•	10	3
2	**Sony** SS-MB350H **A CR Best Buy**	100		92	Good	•	1	1
3	**BIC America** Venturi DV62si	200		91	Good	•	7	2
4	**Bose** 201 Series V	220		89	Very good		5	2
5	**Boston Acoustics** CR75	300		90	Fair	•	5	2
6	**Cambridge Soundworks** Model Six **A CR Best Buy**	150		89	Very good		10	1
7	**Boston Acoustics** VR-M50	700		90	Poor	•	5	2
8	**Cambridge Soundworks** Newton Series M60	300		90	Fair	•	10	3
9	**PSB** Image 2B	370		88	Excellent	•	5 [1]	2
10	**Pioneer** S-DF1-K	200		88	Very good	•	5	1
11	**Pioneer** S-DF2-K	260		88	Very good	•	5	1
12	**Boston Acoustics** CR85	400		86	Very good	•	5	1
13	**Bose** 301 Series V	330		86	Excellent		5	2
14	**Bose** 141	100		86	Good		5	1
15	**Sony** SS-X30ED	500		83	Excellent	•	1	1
16	**Polk Audio** R20	150		83	Good	•	5	1
17	**KLH** 911B	85		82	Good	•	1	1
18	**Klipsch** Synergy SB-3 Monitor	450		79	Excellent	•	5	1

Within types, in performance order.

Key number	Brand & model	Price	Overall score (0–100: P F G VG E)	Tests: Accuracy	Tests: Bass handling	Features: Magnetic shielding	Features: Warranty (yr.)	Features: No. of finishes
	FLOOR-STANDING SPEAKERS *Fairly bulky left and right speakers*							
19	**Sony** SS-MF750H	$280		91	⊜	•	1	1
20	**Cerwin Vega** E-710	300		90	⊜		5	1
21	**Polk Audio** R30	300		89	⊜	•	5	1
22	**Jensen** Champion Series C-5	180		86	⊖	•	5	1
23	**Polk Audio** R50	400		84	⊜	•	5	1
24	**Bose** 601 Series IV	600		84	⊜		5	2
25	**Bose** 701 Series II	700		82	⊖		5	1
	THREE-PIECE BOOKSHELF SETS *Two small speakers and a subwoofer*							
26	**Bose** Acoustimass 3 Series IV	300		94	⊖	•	5	2
27	**Bose** Acoustimass 5 Series III	600		94	⊖	•	5	2

[1] *Buyer must mail in completed warranty card to get 5-yr. warranty (1-yr. on subwoofer).*

Within types, in performance order.

Key number	Brand & model	Price	Overall score (0–100: P F G VG E)	Test: Accuracy	Features: Warranty (yr.)	Features: No. of finishes
	CENTER-CHANNEL SPEAKERS *One smallish speaker used near TV*					
28	**NHT** SC1	$300		92	5	1
29	**Boston Acoustics** Bravo Center	200		92	5	1
30	**Boston Acoustics** CRC	250		91	5	1
31	**B&W** VM1	200		87	5	3
32	**Acoustic Research** AR2C	450		86	5	1
33	**Polk Audio** CSi20	165		86	5	1
34	**Polk Audio** CSi30	225		84	5	1
35	**Yamaha** NS-AC40X	150		84	2	1
36	**JBL** Northridge Series N Center II	200		84	5	1
37	**Acoustic Research** AR4C	300		83	5	1

Within types, in performance order.

Key number	Brand & model	Price	Overall score (0–100; P F G VG E)	Test: Accuracy	Features: Warranty (yr.)	Features: No. of finishes
	CENTER-CHANNEL SPEAKERS *One smallish speaker used near TV*					
38	**Sony** SS-CNX70ED	$300		83	1	1
39	**Sony** SS-CN550H	100		81	1	1
40	**Jensen** Champion Series C-CS	60		80	5	1
41	**Cambridge Soundworks** CenterStage	200		79	10	1
42	**Cambridge Soundworks** Center Channel Plus	150		77	10	1
43	**Bose** VCS-10	200		73	5	2
	REAR-SURROUND SPEAKERS *Small left and right satellites*					
44	**Cambridge Soundworks** Newton Series MC100	140		91	10	2
45	**Infinity** OWS-1	275		87	5	2
46	**Bose** 161	160		84	5	2
47	**NHT** SB1	300		83	5	2
48	**JBL** Northridge Series N24 II	200		82	5	1
49	**B&W** LM1	350		81	5	5
50	**Polk Audio** RTi28	280		79	5	2
	SIX-PIECE SURROUND SETS *Five small speakers and a subwoofer*					
51	**Bose** Acoustimass 6 Series III	700		93	5	1
52	**Cambridge Soundworks** Movieworks 208	900		93	10	2
53	**Polk Audio** RM6700 with PSW303 subwoofer	1,000		91	5	3
54	**Cambridge Soundworks** Movieworks 106	400		89	10	2
55	**Cambridge Soundworks** Newton Theater MC100.2	900		89	10	2
56	**Polk Audio** RM6005 with PSW202 subwoofer	500		89	5	2
57	**Bose** Acoustimass 10 Series III	1,000		88	5	2
58	**Cambridge Soundworks** Movieworks II 5.1	650		87	10	2
59	**Atlantic Technology** System T70	1,000		86	5 [1]	1
60	**Sony** SA-VE835ED	1,000		84	1	1

[1] *Buyer must mail in completed warranty card to get 5-yr. warranty (1-yr. on subwoofer).*

See report, page 68. Based on tests published in Consumer Reports in November 2003, with updated prices and availability.

Guide to the Ratings

Overall score is based primarily on the ability to reproduce sound accurately. A score of 100 would be perfect. For bookshelf and floor-standing speakers and for three-piece bookshelf sets, **bass handling** is also factored in, reflecting the ability to play bass-heavy music loudly without buzzing or distortion. Speakers scoring poor or fair for bass handling should be avoided if you enjoy loud bass. You can expect very good or excellent bass handling from the six-piece sets, all of which have separate subwoofers. All center-channel speakers, three-piece sets, and six-piece sets have **magnetic shielding** to prevent video interference when placed near a TV. **Number of finishes** indicates the available choices. Most tested models have a black veneer finish; some are also available in other finishes, such as white, silver, oak, and cherry. **Price** is approximate retail for a pair of bookshelf, floor-standing, or rear-surround speakers; for one center-channel speaker; and for three-piece or six-piece sets.

Recommendations & notes

MOST TESTED MODELS HAVE: A five-year warranty. No included wires.

BOOKSHELF SPEAKERS

1. **CAMBRIDGE SOUNDWORKS** Newton Series M80 Excellent, with long (10-yr.) warranty. Vinyl cabinet.
2. **SONY** SS-MB350H **A CR Best Buy Excellent and well-priced,** but short (1-yr.) warranty.
3. **BIC AMERICA** Venturi DV62si **Excellent.**
4. **BOSE** 201 Series V **Excellent.** Asymmetrical; designed specifically for left or right position. Easy to wall-mount. May cause video interference near a TV.
5. **BOSTON ACOUSTICS** CR75 **Excellent overall.** But avoid if you play bass-heavy music very loud. Easy to wall-mount.
6. **CAMBRIDGE SOUNDWORKS** Model Six **A CR Best Buy Well-priced, excellent speakers** with long (10-yr.) warranty. May cause video interference near a TV.
7. **BOSTON ACOUSTICS** VR-M50 **Excellent but expensive.** Not the best choice if you play bass-heavy music very loud. Easy to wall-mount.
8. **CAMBRIDGE SOUNDWORKS** Newton Series M60 **Excellent, with long (10-yr.) warranty.** Not the best choice if you play bass-heavy music very loud. Vinyl cabinet.
9. **PSB** Image 2B **Excellent.** 5-yr. warranty only if card mailed in; otherwise 1-yr.
10. **PIONEER** S-DF1-K **Very good.**
11. **PIONEER** S-DF2-K **Very good.**
12. **BOSTON ACOUSTICS** CR85 **Very good.** Easy to wall-mount.
13. **BOSE** 301 Series V **Very good.** Easy to wall-mount. Asymmetrical; designed specifically for left or right position. May cause video interference near a TV.
14. **BOSE** 141 **Very good overall.** Small, light, and well-priced. Compact, gray vinyl cabinet. May cause video interference near a TV.
15. **SONY** SS-X30ED **Very good.** Short (1-yr.) warranty.
16. **POLK AUDIO** R20 **Very good.** Easy to wall-mount. Asymmetrical; designed specifically for left or right position.

Recommendations & notes

17. KLH 911B **Very good.** Lightweight speakers at a low price, but short (1-yr.) warranty.

18. KLIPSCH Synergy SB-3 Monitor **Good overall, with excellent bass handling.**

FLOOR-STANDING SPEAKERS

19. SONY SS-MF750H **Excellent,** but short (1-yr.) warranty.

20. CERWIN VEGA E-710 **Excellent,** though may cause video interference near a TV.

21. POLK AUDIO R30 **Excellent and well-priced.**

22. JENSEN Champion Series C-5 **Very good and well-priced.**

23. POLK AUDIO R50 **Very good.**

24. BOSE 601 Series IV **Very good.** Asymmetrical; designed specifically for left or right position. May cause video interference near a TV.

25. BOSE 701 Series II **Very good.** Has tone controls. Asymmetrical; designed specifically for left or right position. May cause video interference near a TV.

THREE-PIECE BOOKSHELF SETS

26. BOSE Acoustimass 3 Series IV **Excellent.** Vinyl cabinet. Includes speaker wires.

27. BOSE Acoustimass 5 Series III **Excellent.** Vinyl cabinet. Easy to wall-mount satellites.

CENTER-CHANNEL SPEAKERS

28. NHT SC1 **Excellent.**

29. BOSTON ACOUSTICS Bravo Center **Excellent.**

30. BOSTON ACOUSTICS CRC **Excellent.**

31. B&W VM1 **Very good.**

32. ACOUSTIC RESEARCH AR2C **Very good.** Has tone controls.

33. POLK AUDIO CSi20 **Very good.**

34. POLK AUDIO CSi30 **Very good.**

35. YAMAHA NS-AC40X **Very good,** but short (2-yr.) warranty. Has tone controls.

36. JBL Northridge Series N Center II **Very good.**

37. ACOUSTIC RESEARCH AR4C **Very good.** Easy to wall-mount.

38. SONY SS-CNX70ED **Very good,** but short (1-yr.) warranty.

39. SONY SS-CN550H **Very good, well-priced,** and more compact than most. Short (1-yr.) warranty.

40. JENSEN Champion Series C-CS **Very good and well-priced.**

41. CAMBRIDGE SOUNDWORKS CenterStage **Good.** Long (10-yr.) warranty.

42. CAMBRIDGE SOUNDWORKS Center Channel Plus **Good.** Long (10-yr.) warranty.

43. BOSE VCS-10 **Good.** But there are better choices.

REAR-SURROUND SPEAKERS

44. CAMBRIDGE SOUNDWORKS Newton Series, MC100 **Excellent and lightweight.** Long (10-yr.) warranty.

45. INFINITY OWS-1 **Very good, but larger than most.** Not stable on a horizontal surface.

46. BOSE 161 **Very good and lightweight.** Not stable on a horizontal surface.

47. NHT SB1 **Very good,** but may cause video interference near a TV.

48. JBL Northridge Series N24 II **Very good.**

Recommendations & notes

49. B&W LM1 **Very good.**

50. POLK AUDIO RTi28 **Good.**

SIX-PIECE SURROUND SYSTEMS

51. BOSE Acoustimass 6 Series III **Excellent.** Vinyl cabinets. Has tone controls.

52. CAMBRIDGE SOUNDWORKS Movieworks 208 **Excellent, with long (10-yr.) warranty.** Vinyl cabinets. Has tone controls.

53. POLK AUDIO RM6700 with PSW303 subwoofer **Excellent.** Vinyl cabinets. Has tone controls.

54. CAMBRIDGE SOUNDWORKS Movieworks 106 **Excellent and well-priced.** Long (10-yr.) warranty. Vinyl cabinets. Has tone controls.

55. CAMBRIDGE SOUNDWORKS Newton Theater MC100.2 **Excellent.** Long (10-yr.) warranty. Vinyl cabinets. Has tone controls.

56. POLK AUDIO RM6005 with PSW202 subwoofer. **Excellent and well-priced.** Vinyl cabinets. Has tone controls.

57. BOSE Acoustimass 10 Series III **Very good.** Vinyl cabinets. Has tone controls.

58. CAMBRIDGE SOUNDWORKS Movieworks II 5.1 **Very good.** Long (10-yr.) warranty. Has tone controls.

59. ATLANTIC TECHNOLOGY System T70 **Very good, but expensive.** Rear speakers differ in design from front pair.

60. SONY SA-VE835ED **Very good, but expensive.** Short (1-yr.) warranty. Metal cabinets. Has tone controls.

Stains, exterior

Opaque (solid-color) stains generally offer more years of protection and better value than semitransparent stains. Stains we test begin to differ markedly in appearance after the equivalent of three years of exposure. Latex formulations have a slight edge over oil-based stains in appearance. Overall, the best brands in any color are Sherwin-Williams Woodscapes and Olympic Premium. Among white stains, the Sherwin-Williams Woodscapes (latex) is the standout. It's the only white stain that resists cracking and color change. For green stains, the Sherwin-Williams Woodscapes (latex) is a standout; it's resistant to dirt buildup, mildew, cracking, and color change. Red stains tend to be the most resistant to dirt. The best choices are the Olympic Premium (latex) and Behr Plus 10 (alkyd). Both do a good job of resisting dirt buildup, color change, mildew, and cracking. The Behr, sold at Home Depot, is the best oil-based stain, and it cleans up with water.

Within types, in performance order.

Excellent ⊜ Very good ⊖ Good ○ Fair ◒ Poor ●

Key number	Product	Price	Overall score (0–100; P F G VG E)	Appearance: After 3 years	Appearance: After 6 years	Appearance: After 9 years	Resists: Dirt	Resists: Color change	Resists: Mildew	Resists: Cracking
	WHITE *Typifies a range of light beiges and grays.*									
1	**Sherwin-Williams** Woodscapes (latex)	$25		⊜	⊖	⊖		●		●
2	**Olympic** Premium (latex)	19		⊖	⊖	○				●
3	**Sherwin-Williams** (alkyd)	24		⊖	○	○			●	
4	**Cabot** O.V.T. 6500 (alkyd)	26		⊜	○	◒			●	
5	**Cabot** O.V.T. 0600 (latex)	23		⊖	○	◒			●	
6	**Behr** Plus 10 (Home Depot) (alkyd/water cleanup)	16		⊖	○	◒				●
7	**Olympic** WeatherScreen Water Repellent Oil (alkyd)	18		⊖	◒	●				
8	**Ace** Wood Royal House & Trim (alkyd)	18		⊖	◒	●				
	GREEN *Typifies a range of greens, yellows, and blues.*									
9	**Olympic** Premium (latex)	19		⊜	⊖	⊖	●		●	●
10	**Sherwin-Williams** Woodscapes (latex)	25		⊜	⊖	○	●	●	●	●
11	**Behr** Plus 10 (Home Depot) (alkyd/water cleanup)	16		⊖	○	○			●	●
12	**Cabot** O.V.T. 6500 (alkyd)	26		⊖	○	○	●		●	●

Within types, in performance order.

Key number	Product	Price	Overall score (0–100: P F G VG E)	Appearance: After 3 years	Appearance: After 6 years	Appearance: After 9 years	Resists: Dirt	Resists: Color change	Resists: Mildew	Resists: Cracking
	GREEN *Typifies a range of greens, yellows, and blues.*									
13	**Cabot** O.V.T. 0600 (latex)	$23		⊜	○	◒			•	•
14	**Ace** Wood Royal House & Trim (alkyd)	18		⊖	○	◒				•
15	**Sherwin-Williams** (alkyd)	24		○	◒	◒	•			
	RED *Typifies a range of browns, reds, and other earth tones.*									
16	**Olympic** Premium (latex)	19		⊜	⊖	⊖	•	•	•	•
17	**Sherwin-Williams** Woodscapes (latex)	25		⊜	⊖	⊖	•	•		•
18	**Behr** Plus 10 (Home Depot) (alkyd/water cleanup)	16		⊜	⊖	⊖	•	•	•	•
19	**Cabot** O.V.T. 6500 (alkyd)	26		⊖	○	◒	•		•	•
20	**Cabot** O.V.T. 0600 (latex)	23		⊜	○	◒	•			•
21	**Sherwin-Williams** (alkyd)	24		⊖	○	◒	•			•
22	**Olympic** WeatherScreen Water Repellent Oil (alkyd)	18		⊖	○	◒				
23	**Ace** Wood Royal House & Trim (alkyd)	18		○	●	●				

See report, page 129. Based on tests published in Consumer Reports in August 2003.

Guide to the Ratings

Overall score reflects a weighted average of the stains' appearance in three years of testing. **Appearance** scores summarize our long-term testing. One year of our tests is comparable to three years in real life, so we can say how well a stain should do after about three years, six years, and nine years. Specific attributes help you choose models that match your needs. **Resists dirt** shows which stains are better than most at preventing dirt buildup. **Resists color change** shows which change the least from the original color. **Resists mildew** shows which do the best job of preventing mildew growth. **Resists cracking** shows which provide the best protection for the siding. **Price** is the approximate retail.

Telephones, cordless

Nearly all the phones and phone-answerers we tested deliver very good or excellent voice quality. For a basic phone with excellent voice quality, consider the four CR Best Buys: the Panasonic KX-TC1484B, Uniden EXI 376 HS, GE 26938GE1, and Bell South MH9111SL. These are excellent choices for people who don't want a feature-laden phone. If you need a phone-answerer, you can find several very good models for under $100. The GE 27998GE6 $55, has excellent voice quality. For a phone with multiple handsets, consider the Panasonic KX-TG2700S, $130, or for an additional $40, the KX-TG2770S phone-answerer. In addition to supporting multiple handsets, the VTech VT20-2431, has two-line capability and can work during a power outage.

In performance order.

Excellent / Very good / Good / Fair / Poor

Key number	Brand & model	Type	Price	Overall score (0–100; P F G VG E)	Test results: Voice quality	Test results: Ease of use	Test results: Talk time (hr.)	Features: Base speakerphone	Features: Handset speakerphone	Features: Handset-to-handset talk	Features: Max. handsets supported (extra included)
1	**Panasonic** KX-TC1484B **A CR Best Buy**	900A	$30		Excellent	Very good	16				
2	**Uniden** EXI 376 HS **A CR Best Buy**	900A	30		Excellent	Very good	11				
3	**GE** 26938GE1 **A CR Best Buy**	900A	25		Excellent	Very good	11				
4	**Bell South** MH9111SL **A CR Best Buy**	900A	35		Excellent	Very good	10				
5	**Uniden** EXI 3246	2.4/900A	50		Very good	Very good	11				
6	**Panasonic** KX-TG2700S	2.4D	130		Very good	Very good	7	•	•	•	8
7	**VTech** VT5831	5.8/2.4D	160		Very good	Very good	13	•	•	•	6
8	**VTech** VT20-2431 (2-line)	2.4D	160		Very good	Very good	10	•	•	•	8
9	**Uniden** DCT 5260	2.4D	90		Very good	Very good	10		•	•	8
10	**Bell South** GH9457BK	2.4A	35		Very good	Good	8				
11	**Uniden** TRU 446-2	2.4D	100		Very good	Good	8				2 (1)

See report, page 154. Based on tests published in Consumer Reports in October 2003.

Excellent ⊜ Very good ⊖ Good ○ Fair ◒ Poor ●

In performance order.

Key number	Brand & model	Type	Price	Overall score (0–100; P F G VG E)	Test results: Phone – Voice quality	Phone – Ease of use	Phone – Talk time (hr.)	Answerer – Overall score	Answerer – Recording time (min.)	Features: Base speakerphone	Handset-to-handset talk	Max. handsets supported (extra included)	Mailboxes
	PHONE-ANSWERERS												
12	**GE** 27939GE3	2.4A	$90		⊜	○	8	⊖	16	•			1
13	**GE** 27998GE6	2.4A	55		⊜	⊖	11	○	16				1
14	**Panasonic** KX-TG2770S	2.4D	170		⊖	⊖	7	⊖	15	•	•	8	3
15	**AT&T** 5840	5.8/2.4D	180		⊖	⊖	7	⊖	31	•	•	6	3
16	**AT&T** 9357	900A	50		⊖	⊖	11	⊖	20				3
17	**RadioShack** TAD-3815	2.4D	80		⊖	⊖	8	○	13	•		8	1
18	**AT&T** 2325	2.4D	125		⊖	⊖	17	⊖	20		•	4	3
19	**VTech** VT9152	900A	30		⊖	○	5	⊖	14				1
20	**AT&T** 2255	2.4D	120		⊖	⊖	8	⊖	20			2(1)	3
21	**Uniden** TRU 5885-2	5.8D	220		⊖	○	5	○	11	•	•	2(1)	1
22	**VTech** VT2558	2.4A/900A	60		⊖	○	8	⊖	14				1
23	**Siemens** 4215	2.4D	180		⊖	⊖	10	○	18		•	4	1

Guide to the Ratings

For all: Type is as follows: 900A=900-MHz analog; 2.4A=2.4-GHz analog; 2.4D= 2.4-GHz digital spread spectrum; 5.8D=5.8-GHz digital spread spectrum; some phones use two frequency bands. **Overall score** mainly covers voice quality, ease of use, resistance to electrical damage, and privacy. **Voice quality** covers talking and listening, as judged by trained panelists. In the **Features** columns, we list the manufacturer stated maximum number of handsets that multiple-handset models can support, along with the number of extra handsets supplied with the base unit. Phones with handset-to-handset talk may cause interference to other wireless products. **Price** is the approximate retail.

For phones: Ease of use covers handset comfort, weight, talk time, setup, controls, clarity of labels. Talk time is based on continuous-use tests with fully charged batteries.

For phone answerers: Overall score for the answer includes message and greeting voice quality–judged by trained panelists; and ease of use which includes setup, controls, clarity of labels, and the ability to play new messages first and not erase unplayed. **Recording time** is based on tests using continuous speech.

Recommendations & notes

ALL TESTED PHONES HAVE: 1-yr. warranty; flash (handy with call-waiting), handset volume control, at least 10 memory-dial slots, last-number redial, low-battery indicator.
ALL TESTED ANSWERERS HAVE: Call screening, day/time stamp, remote access, selectable number of rings, repeat, and message skip.
MOST PHONES AND PHONE-ANSWERERS: Have caller ID and are wall mountable.
Models listed as similar should offer performance comparable to the tested models, although features may differ.

PHONES

1 **PANASONIC** KX-TC1484B **A CR Best Buy Very good overall.** Has any key answer.

2 **UNIDEN** EXI 376 HS **A CR Best Buy Very good overall. Includes headset.** Has auto talk. Similar: EXI 376, EXP 370.

3 **GE** 26938GE1 **A CR Best Buy Very good overall.** Similar: 26928GE1.

4 **BELL SOUTH** MH9111SL **A CR Best Buy Very good overall.** Small, lightweight handset. Has voice-mail indicator.

5 **UNIDEN** EXI 3246 **Very good overall.** Has auto talk, any key answer, voice-mail indicator. Similar: EXP 3240, EXI 3226 (2-line).

6 **PANASONIC** KX-TG2700S **Very good overall.** Has auto talk, any key answer, conferencing capable, walkie-talkielike mode, and lit keypad. KX-TG2720S (2-line).

7 **VTECH** VT5831 **Very good overall.** Can work during household AC power loss with optional battery. Has any key answer, voice-mail indicator, conferencing capable, lit keypad, adjustable sound select button, and caller ID on base also. Handset has own charging cradle that is seperate from base. Does not cause interference to other wireless devices in standby mode, but may in talk mode. High gloss keypad buttons judged difficult to read.

8 **VTECH** VT20-2431 **Very good overall.** Small, lightweight handset. Can work during household AC power loss with optional battery. Has voice-mail indicator, conferencing capable, lit keypad, data port for fax or modem. Caller ID and headset jack on base also. Can't be wall mounted.

9 **UNIDEN** DCT 5260 **Very good overall.** Small, lightweight handset. Uses two AA rechargeable batteries. Has auto talk, any key answer, voice-mail indicator, conferencing capable, lit keypad, and walkie-talkielike mode. But can't be wall mounted, phone had noticeable background noise and handset setup judged more complicated than most.

10 **BELL SOUTH** GH9457BK **Very good overall.** Small, lightweight handset. Has voice-mail indicator. We tested the 50 channel version.

11 **UNIDEN** TRU 446-2 **Very good overall.** Includes second handset with charging cradle, and shouldn't cause interference like other multiple handset capable phones. Has auto talk, any key answer, conferencing capable with call waiting deluxe, voice-mail indicator, and lit keypad. Can't be wall mounted. Similar: TRU 446, TRU 4465-2.

PHONE-ANSWERERS

12 **GE** 27939GE3 **Very good combo.** Has lit keypad, and conferencing capable. Caller ID on base also, but answerer does not play new messages first, and lacks toll saver and announce-only modes.

13 **GE** 27998GE6 **Very good phone with good answerer.** But answerer does not play new messages first, lacks toll saver and announce-only modes, messages had noticeable background noise, and greeting judged fair. Similar: 27992GE1.

14 **PANASONIC** KX-TG2770S **Very good cordless/corded combo.** Cordless handset has own charging cradle that is separate from

Recommendations & notes

base. Corded phone on base can work during household AC power loss. Has auto talk, any key answer, conferencing capable, walkie-talkie like mode, handset speakerphone, lit keypad, and caller ID on base also. Easy on answerer to accidently erase unplayed messages.

15 **AT&T** 5840 **Very good combo.** Can work during household AC power loss with optional battery. Does not cause interference to other wireless devices in standby mode, but may in talk mode. Has any key answer, conferencing capable, lit keypad, adjustable sound select button, handset speakerphone, and caller ID on base also. Answerer has audible new message alert.

16 **AT&T** 9357 **Very good combo.** Has any key answer. Answerer has audible message alert. But failed surge test. Similar: 9371.

17 **RADIO SHACK** TAD-3815 **Very good phone with good answerer.** Shouldn't cause interference like other multiple handset capable phones. Has auto talk, any key answer, conferencing capable with call waiting deluxe, and lit keypad. Answerer has audible new message alert, but messages had noticeable background noise.

18 **AT&T** 2325 **Very good combo.** Has any key answer, voice-mail indicator, conferencing capable, and handset speakerphone. Answerer has audible new message alert, but greeting judged fair.

19 **VTECH** VT9152 **Very good combo.** Has any key answer, but lacks caller ID. Answerer has audible message alert, and can record greeting using handset. Answerer lacks message counter display and setup judged more complicated than most. Similar: VT9162.

20 **AT&T** 2255 **Very good combo.** Includes second handset with charging cradle. Has auto talk, any key answer, voice-mail indicator, and conferencing capable. Answerer has audible message alert. But phone and answerer had noticeable background noise.

21 **UNIDEN** TRU 5885-2 **Very good phone with good answerer.** Includes second handset with charging cradle. Shouldn't cause interference like other multiple handset capable phones. Has auto talk, conferencing capable, handset speakerphone with call waiting deluxe, and lit keypad. Can't be wall mounted. Answerer has audible new message alert, but messages had noticeable background noise. Similar: TRU 5885.

22 **VTECH** VT2558 **Very good combo.** Has built-in TeleZapper, auto talk, and any key answer. No caller ID, can't be wall mounted. Answerer has audible new message alert, and can record greeting using handset. Answerer setup judged more complicated than most, and lacks message counter display.

23 **SIEMENS** 4215 **Very good phone with good answerer.** Small, lightweight handset. Has voice activated dialing, talking caller ID, auto talk, voice-mail indicator, handset speakerphone answerer, and multilingual menu. But failed surge test, phone and answerer had noticeable background noise, lacks headset jack. Can't be wall mounted.

Vacuum cleaners

You can get a very good vacuum cleaner for $150 to $300 or so; paying more doesn't buy better performance. Some of the priciest models are middling performers and come with relatively few features. Still, many of the least-expensive models compromise performance and convenience. Our tests also reveal that some otherwise-impressive machines don't excel in airflow through the hose, which means they have limited suction or they're more likely to lose suction as their bags or bins fill with dust. Two standout values, which are solid performers at superb prices, are the Eureka Boss Smart Vac Ultra 4870, $140 (upright), a **CR Best Buy,** and the Samsung Quiet Jet VAC-9069G, $200 (canister).

Within types, in performance order.

Excellent, Very good, Good, Fair, Poor

Key number	Brand & model	Price	Overall score (0–100: P F G VG E)	Cleaning: Carpet	Cleaning: Bare floor	Cleaning: Tools	Other results: Ease of use	Other results: Noise	Other results: Emissions	Features: Bag	Features: Brush on/off	Features: Easy on/off	Features: Manual pile adjust
	UPRIGHTS												
1	**Hoover** WindTunnel Self Propelled Ultra U6439-900	$300		Excellent	Excellent	Excellent	Good	Fair	Excellent	•	•	•	•
2	**Kenmore** (Sears) Progressive with Direct Drive 31912	330		Very good	Excellent	Very good	Very good	Good	Excellent	•	•	•	•
3	**Eureka** Boss Smart Vac Ultra 4870 **A CR Best Buy**	140		Excellent	Excellent	Good	Good	Good	Excellent	•	•		•
4	**Hoover** WindTunnel U6630-900	400		Very good	Excellent	Good	Good	Fair	Excellent		•	•	•
5	**Eureka** Ultra Whirlwind 4885	250		Very good	Excellent	Very good	Good	Good	Excellent		•	•	•
6	**Hoover** WindTunnel Bagless U5750-900	200		Excellent	Excellent	Good	Good	Fair	Excellent			•	•
7	**Dirt Devil** Platinum Force 091210	120		Excellent	Excellent	Good	Fair	Fair	Very good		•	•	•
8	**Oreck** XL21-600 [1]	700		Very good	Excellent	N/A	Very good	Good	Excellent	•		•	
9	**Panasonic** Dual Sweep MC-V7522	150		Very good	Excellent	Very good	Good	Fair	Excellent	•	•		
10	**Kenmore** (Sears) Progressive 33912	300		Very good	Excellent	Good	Good	Fair	Excellent		•	•	•
11	**Kenmore** (Sears) Progressive 34612	190		Very good	Excellent	Very good	Good	Fair	Very good	•	•	•	•
12	**Kirby** Ultimate G7D	1,300		Very good	Excellent	Very good	Good	Fair	Excellent	•		•	•
13	**Bissell** ProLite 3560-2 [1]	200		Very good	Excellent	N/A	Very good	Fair	Excellent	•		•	
14	**Dyson** DC07	400		Good	Excellent	Very good	Fair	Fair	Excellent		•		

Within types, in performance order.

Key number	Brand & model	Price	Overall score (0–100; P F G VG E)	Cleaning: Carpet	Cleaning: Bare floor	Cleaning: Tools	Other results: Ease of use	Other results: Noise	Other results: Emissions	Features: Bag	Features: Brush on/off	Features: Easy on/off	Features: Manual pile adjust
	UPRIGHTS												
15	**Panasonic** Dual Sweep Bagless MC-V7582	$180		◓	⊜	○	○	◒	◓		•		
16	**Eureka** Whirlwind Litespeed 5843	160		○	⊖	⊖	○	◒	⊜		•		•
17	**Aerus** Lux 3000	700		○	⊜	◒	○	◒	⊖	•	•	•	
18	**Dirt Devil** Featherlite Plus 085560	60		⊖	⊜	◒	⊖	●	⊖	•		•	
19	**Dirt Devil** Scorpion 088100	80		⊜	⊜	○	○	●	◒		•	•	
20	**GE** (Wal-Mart) 106585	120		○	⊖	○	○	○	⊜				•
21	**Hoover** Fold Away U5162-900	110		⊖	⊖	◒	○	◒	⊜				•
22	**Oreck** XL-2 [1]	370		○	⊜	N/A	⊖	●	⊖	•		•	
23	**Kenmore** (Sears) Progressive 32734	260		○	⊜	○	○	◒	⊜		•	•	•
24	**Eureka** Whirlwind Plus 4684	150		○	⊜	○	○	◒	⊜			•	•
25	**Sharp** Multi Floor EC-T5180A	160		○	⊜	○	○	○	●		•	•	
26	**Bosch** Turbo Jet BUH11700UC	300		○	⊜	○	◒	◒	○	•	•	•	
27	**Bissell** Powerforce 3522-1	50		○	⊜	○	○	◒	⊖	•	•		•
28	**Euro-Pro** Shark UV204	100		◒	⊜	○	○	◒	⊖	•			•
29	**Kenmore** (Sears) Quick Clean 33720	100		◒	⊖	○	⊖	◒	⊜			•	•
30	**Fantom** Twister FM740 (300SE)	160		◒	⊖	○	○	◒	⊜				
31	**Bissell** Cleanview Power Trak 3593-1	100		○	⊜	○	○	◒	◒		•		•
32	**Bissell** Cleanview Bagless 8975	80		○	⊜	○	○	●	●				•
33	**Eureka** Whirlwind Lite 4388	100		◒	◒	◒	○	◒	○			•	•
	CANISTERS												
34	**Kenmore** (Sears) Progressive 22612	380		⊖	⊜	⊖	⊖	◒	⊜	•	•	•	•
35	**Samsung** Quiet Jet VAC-9069G	200		⊖	⊜	⊖	○	⊖	⊜	•	•		
36	**GE** (Wal-Mart) 106766	150		⊖	⊜	◒	⊖	○	⊖	•	•		
37	**Miele** Plus S251	450		○	⊜	⊖	⊖	○	⊜	•	•	•	
38	**Eureka** Home Cleaning System 6984	300		⊖	⊖	○	⊖	○	⊜	•	•	•	•

Within types, in performance order.

Key number	Brand & model	Price	Overall score (0–100; P F G VG E)	Cleaning: Carpet	Cleaning: Bare floor	Cleaning: Tools	Other results: Ease of use	Other results: Noise	Other results: Emissions	Features: Bag	Features: Brush on/off	Features: Easy on/off	Features: Manual pile adjust
	CANISTERS												
39	**Aerus** Lux 7000	$750		VG	E	F	VG	G	E	•	•	•	
40	**Hoover** WindTunnel Bagless S3765-040	500		VG	E	G	G	F	G		•	•	
41	**Hoover** WindTunnel Plus S3639	300		VG	E	VG	VG	G	VG	•	•	•	
42	**Miele** Solaris Electro Plus S514	700		G	E	G	G	VG	E	•	•	•	
43	**Kenmore** (Sears) eVo 22822	380		G	E	G	G	F	E		•	•	•
44	**Oreck** Dutch Tech DTX1300C	900		F	E	VG	VG	VG	E	•	•	•	
45	**Fantom** Falcon FC251	190		VG	E	P	VG	F	VG		•		
46	**Sanyo** High Power SC-800P	200		G	E	VG	VG	F	VG	•	•	•	
47	**Hoover** PowerMax Runabout S3614	200		VG	E	G	E	F	P	•	•	•	
48	**Kenmore** (Sears) Magic Blue DX 23295	180		G	E	F	G	F	VG	•	•	•	•
49	**Rainbow** e-Series E-2	1,800		G	F	VG	VG	F	G		•		•

[1] *Comes with minicanister for cleaning with tools. Performance was fair for (13); poor for (8) and (22).*

See report, page 132. Based on tests published in Consumer Reports in November 2003, with updated prices and availability.

Guide to the Ratings

Overall score mainly reflects cleaning performance, ease of use, and emissions. Under **cleaning, carpet** denotes how much embedded talc and sand the vacuum lifted from a medium pile carpet. **Bare floor** shows how well the model vacuumed sand without dispersing it. **Tools** relates to tool use and reflects airflow with increasing amounts of dust-simulating wood "flour"; a higher score means the vac provides more airflow and maintains airflow better as dirt accumulates. **Ease of use** denotes how easy the machine is to push, pull, carry, and use beneath furniture as well as the dust bag's or bin's capacity. **Noise** denotes results using a decibel meter. **Emissions** is our measure of how much wood flour is released while vacuuming. **Features** notes whether the model has a **bag** (as opposed to being bagless), allows you to turn off the **brush** when not needed, has an **on/off switch** that is easy to access, and has manual pile-height adjustment, which can improve cleaning. **Price** is approximate retail; bag/filter prices are per unit. **Recommendations & notes** lists noteworthy features and some minor shortcomings.

Recommendations & notes

UPRIGHT VACUUMS

1. **HOOVER** WindTunnel Self Propelled Ultra U6439-900 **Excelled at cleaning, but noisy.** May not fit on some stairs. Bag: $2. Filter: $5. Similar: U6433-900, U6436-900, U6437-900.

2. **KENMORE** (Sears) Progressive with Direct Drive 31912 **Very good all around.** Bag: $4 to $5. HEPA filter: $21. Similar: 31913.

3. **EUREKA** Boss Smart Vac 4870 **A CR Best Buy Highest performance for the dollar.** Excelled at most cleaning, but hard to pull. Bag: $2.30. HEPA filter: $20.

4. **HOOVER** WindTunnel U6630-900 **Very good, but noisy, heavy, and tippy on stairs.** HEPA filter: $20. Similar: U6607-900, U6616-900, U6617-900, U6632-900, U6660-900.

5. **EUREKA** Ultra Whirlwind 4885 **A very good bagless vac, but small capacity.** HEPA filter: $20. Similar: 4880.

6. **HOOVER** WindTunnel Bagless U5750-900 **Very good.** Bagless model with excellent performance on carpets. Less prone to tipping when hose is fully extended. Small rotating brush for stairs. HEPA filter: $30 (Replace every 3 years). Similar: U5722-900, U5751-900, U5752-900, U5758-900, U5759-900.

7. **DIRT DEVIL** Platinum Force 091210 **Excelled at most cleaning, but noisy and tippy on stairs.** Bagless. Hose longer than most. Hard to push and pull. HEPA filter: $25.

8. **ORECK** XL21-600 **Very good, but no overload protection.** Filter on tested models wasn't a HEPA, despite label. Bag: $3.

9. **PANASONIC** Dual Sweep MC-V7522 **Very good overall but has a power cord shorter than most.** Also relatively noisy. Bag: $1.65. Filter: $12.

10. **KENMORE** (Sears) Progressive 33912 **Very good, full-featured machine.** Bagless. Exhaust filter: $14; chamber filter: $20. Similar: 33913.

11. **KENMORE** (Sears) Progressive 34612 **Very good, with lots of features.** Bag: $3.50. Exhaust filter: $14. Similar: 34613.

12. **KIRBY** Ultimate G7D **Very good, though ultra-expensive.** Retro design. For the money, you get a body of aluminum, instead of the more-common plastic, and better-than-average reliability. This machine also has some extra attachments, including a sprayer for shampooing carpet (not tested). Kirbys are usually sold door-to-door. Relatively heavy: 24 lbs. Bag: $3.17.

13. **BISSELL** ProLite 3560-2 **Very good, but noisy and awkward to carry.** No overload protection. Bag: $2.

14. **DYSON** DC07 **A very good bagless vac, but has confusing controls.** Hose longer than most. Noisy. Hard to push and pull. No headlamp. HEPA filter (washable): $17.50.

15. **PANASONIC** Dual Sweep MC-V7582 **Very good overall.** But relatively noisy. Filter: $25. Similar: MC-V7572.

16. **EUREKA** Whirlwind Litespeed 5843 **A good bagless vac, but noisy.** Hose longer than most. No upholstery tool. HEPA filter: $20. Similar: 5740, 5840, 5847.

17. **AERUS** Lux 3000 **Good, but pricey and noisy.** Tippy with hose extended. Unstable on stairs. Tools don't stow onboard. Bag: 12 for $18.

18. **DIRT DEVIL** Featherlite Plus 085560 **Good.** No overload protection or upholstery tool. Hose and cord shorter than most. Standard bag: $1. Microfilter bag: $3.30.

19. **DIRT DEVIL** Scorpion 088100 **Good perfor-**

Recommendations & notes

mance for the money, especially on carpet. Relatively light: 13 lbs. But noisier, with more emissions than most. Bagless. Exhaust filter: $10; HEPA filter: $25.

20. GE 106585 **A good bagless vac, but small capacity and poor furniture clearance.** HEPA filter: $16. Wal-Mart only.

21. HOOVER Fold Away U5162-900 **Good, somewhat spartan upright.** Suction for cleaning with tools not as effective as most. Unique design enables user to fold down the handle for easier storage. But we found the handle harder to grip while vacuuming. Bagless. Primary filter: $13; final filter $4. Similar: U5161-900, U5163-900, U5167-900.

22. ORECK XL-2 **Good performer, though very noisy.** Comes with minicanister for cleaning with tools; we found the performance of that machine to be poor. Bag: $2.50.

23. KENMORE (Sears) Progressive 32734 **Good bagless model, with a number of attractive features.** Exhaust filter: $14, chamber filter: $20. Similar: 32735.

24. EUREKA Whirlwind Plus 4684 **A good bagless vac, but noisy.** Tippy on stairs and with hose extended. Small capacity. Cord shorter than most. HEPA filter: $20.

25. SHARP Multi Floor EC-T5180A **Good performer, but poor on emissions.** HEPA filter: $10.

26. BOSCH Turbo Jet BUH 11700 UC **Good overall, though just so-so on emissions.** Curvy design includes front-mounted hose that we found awkward to remove. Bag: $4. Filter: $25.

27. BISSELL Powerforce 3522-1 **Good, but noisy.** Tippy with hose extended and unstable on stairs. Hard to push. Hose and power cord shorter than most. No overload protection. Bag: $3. Filter: $3.

28. EURO-PRO Shark UV204 **Good performance overall, though worse than most on carpet.** Also relatively noisy. Accessory pack, $5, includes 4 bags and 2 carbon premotor filters. HEPA filter: $13.

29. KENMORE (Sears) Quick Clean 33720 **A good bagless vac, but noisy.** Tippy on stairs and with hose extended. Hose and cord shorter than most. No upholstery tool. Tower filter: $20. Exhaust filter: $14. Similar: 33721.

30. FANTOM Twister Bagless FM740 (300SE) **Good overall, but with few amenities.** Performance on carpet worse than average. Relatively noisy. Fantom uprights ranked among the most repair-prone brands. Bagless. HEPA filter: $10.

31. BISSELL Cleanview Power Trak 3593-1 **A good bagless vac, but noisy.** Tippy with hose extended and unstable on stairs. Hard to push. No upholstery tool. HEPA filter: $10.

32. BISSELL Cleanview Bagless 8975 **There are better choices.** Upper-tank filter: $4. Premotor filter: $1.50. Postmotor filter: $3.

33. EUREKA Whirlwind Lite 4388 **There are better choices.** Bagless.

CANISTER VACUUMS

34. KENMORE (Sears) Progressive 22612 **Very good, but noisy and heavy.** Hose longer than most. Bag: $4. HEPA filter: $21. This model has been discontinued. Similar: 22613.

35. SAMSUNG Quiet Jet VAC-9069G **Very good, and quieter than most, but hard to push.** No overload protection. Bag: $2. Limited availability.

36. GE (Wal-Mart) 106766 **Very good, well-**

Recommendations & notes

priced canister, with better-than-average performance on carpet. Also relatively light: 11 lbs. On the downside, its suction for cleaning with tools was less effective than most. Available only at Wal-Mart. Bag: $1.97.

37. MIELE Plus S251 **Very good.** Less bulky and heavy than most. Cord shorter than most. Bag: $2.60.

38. EUREKA 6984 **Very good, but among the more repair-prone canister brands.** Hose longer than most. Cord shorter than most. Bag: $1.70. HEPA filter: $20.39.

39. AERUS Lux 7000 **Fine for most cleaning, but tippy on stairs.** Cord shorter than most. Bag: $2. Filter: two for $7.

40. HOOVER WindTunnel Bagless S3765-040 **A very good canister vac, with better cleaning than most on carpet.** But relatively noisy, and released dust when we emptied the bin. Dirt cup filter: $14.25. HEPA: $9.45. Similar: S3755.

41. HOOVER WindTunnel Plus S3639 **A very good, well-rounded vac.** Bag: $2.

42. MIELE Solaris Electro Plus S514 **Very good, and quieter than most, but hard to push and pull.** Cord and hose shorter than most. Filters and five-bag set: $12.

43. KENMORE (Sears) eVo 22822 **A very good bagless vac, but noisy and heavy.** Unstable on stairs. Hose longer than most. HEPA filter: $15.50.

44. ORECK DutchTech DTX1300C **Very good, but hard to push and pull.** Quieter than most. Bag: $2.80. HEPA filter: $40.

45. FANTOM Falcon FC251 **Good overall, with better-than-average cleaning on carpet.** But disconnecting the powerhead and wiring to change tools was very difficult. Vac also was relatively noisy, and released dust when bin was emptied. HEPA filter: $30.

46. SANYO High Power SC-800P **Good, but spartan for the price.** Noisy. No overload protection. Cord shorter than most. Bag: $4. Electrostatic micron filter: $9.95.

47. HOOVER PowerMAX Runabout S3614 **A good, inexpensive canister for most cleaning, but high emissions.** Noisy. No overload protection. Standard bag: $1.30. Allergen filtration bag: $2.90.

48. KENMORE (Sears) Magic Blue DX 23295 **Good overall, with lots of features.** But worse-than-average suction for cleaning with tools, and noisier than most. Bag: $1.25.

49. RAINBOW e-Series E-2 **Extremely high price not justified by performance.** Among the worst on bare floors, and relatively noisy. Unusual design utilizes water to retain dust and dirt that's been picked up; that makes the machine very heavy (32 lbs.) when filled with water. Special features include the ability to pick up wet spills (not tested), an inflator for toys and a dusting brush for plants and animals. Rainbow ranks among the more reliable brands.

Wall ovens

Based on our tests, it's hard to choose a bad wall oven; nearly all performed a variety of cooking tasks at least adequately. The best models for most, with capable cooking at a relatively low price, are the GE JTP20WF at $850 and the Frigidaire Gallery GLEB30S8C at $700. The GE lacks a convection mode, but delivers as much space and performs nearly as well as the Thermador SC301T, $1,700, for less. The Frigidaire excelled at baking, but its small capacity could be a problem if you have a large family or entertain often. If you broil lots of steak, the Thermador is a good bet.

In performance order.

Excellent · Very good · Good · Fair · Poor

Key number	Product (Similar models, in small type, comparable to tested model.)	Price	Overall score (0–100: P F G VG E)	Test results: Capacity	Bake	Broil	Features: Covered element	Meat probe	Convection cooking
1	**Thermador** SC301T[W] SC301Z[1]	$1,700		Very good	Very good	Excellent			●
2	**Kenmore** Elite 4904[2]	1,650		Good	Very good	Very good	●		●
3	**GE** Profile JT915WF[WW]	1,500		Good	Very good	Very good	●	●	●
4	**GE** JTP20WF[WW]	850		Very good	Good	Very good			
5	**Frigidaire** Gallery GLEB30S8C[S] PLEB30S8C[1]	700		Fair	Excellent	Good			●
6	**Whirlpool** Gold GBS307PD[Q]	1,220		Very good	Very good	Fair		●	●
7	**Bosch** HBL74[2] [1]	1,600		Fair	Good	Good	●	●	●

[1] *Tested model comes with stainless, typically $300 extra on others.*

See report, page 97. *Based on tests published in Consumer Reports in September 2003, with updated prices and availability.*

Guide to the Ratings

Overall score includes capacity as well as baking and broiling performance. **Capacity** is usable space; all could hold a 20-pound turkey. **Bake** shows baking evenness for cakes and cookies. **Broil** shows cooking evenness and searing for a tray of burgers. We also test the self-cleaning mode. **Price** is approximate retail. Under **Product,** brackets show a tested model's color code. Similar wall ovens have the same broiler; other details may differ. **All 30-inch electric wall ovens offer:** Timed cooking. Self-cleaning. Delay start. **Most have:** Convection. Less capacity than range ovens. Five or more rack positions. Two lights. One timer. Temperature display. A one-year full warranty. Child lockout.

Washing machines

Most of the washing machines we tested did a very good or excellent job. Paying more within a category may get you fancier styling, more settings, and a porcelain top. For very good performance at a modest price, a top-loader should fill the bill. The **CR Best Buy** Kenmore 2381 and Maytag Performa PAV2300A provide excellent washing and otherwise solid performance. If you prefer to spend more for the best performance overall and the largest capacity, get a front-loader. Two outstanding and reasonably-priced choices are the Kenmore (Sears) Elite HE3 4282[2], and the Whirlpool Duet GHW9100L[Q], both $1,100. If space is tight, the efficient and quiet Asko W6021 delivers excellent washing.

Excellent | Very good | Good | Fair | Poor

Within types, in performance order.

Key number	Brand & model	Price	Overall score (0–100: P F G VG E)	Test results: Washing performance	Energy efficiency	Water efficiency	Capacity	Gentleness	Noise	Features: Auto temp. control	Auto dispensers	Stainless-steel tub	Cycle time (min.)
	TOP-LOADING MODELS												
1	**Kenmore** (Sears) Elite Calypso 2206[2]	$1,000		Excellent	Very good	Very good	Excellent	Very good	Excellent	•	•	•	70
2	**Whirlpool** Calypso GVW9959K[Q]	1,000		Excellent	Very good	Very good	Excellent	Very good	Excellent	•	•	•	65
3	**Fisher & Paykel** GWL11	600		Very good	Very good	Good	Good	Very good	Very good			•	50
4	**GE** Profile WPRB9220C[WW]	725		Very good	Fair	Very good	Excellent	Good	Very good	•		•	50
5	**Maytag** SAV5701A[WW]	600		Very good	Good	Very good	Very good	Good	Good	•		•	50
6	**Kenmore** (Sears) 2493[2]	520		Excellent	Fair	Very good	Excellent	Good	Good	•			45
7	**Hotpoint** VWSR4150B[WW]	390		Very good	Fair	Good	Very good	Very good	Good				45
8	**Kenmore** 2381 **A CR Best Buy**	460		Very good	Good	Good	Very good	Good	Very good				40
9	**Maytag** Performa PAV2300A[WW] **A CR Best Buy**	430		Very good	Good	Good	Very good	Good	Good				50
10	**Maytag** Atlantis MAV9501E[WW]	750		Excellent	Fair	Very good	Good	Fair	Good	•		•	60
11	**Whirlpool** Gold GSW9650[W]	500		Very good	Fair	Very good	Good	Good	Good	•	•		50

Within types, in performance order.

Excellent ⊜ · Very good ⊖ · Good ○ · Fair ◒ · Poor ●

Key number	Brand & model	Price	Overall score (0–100; P F G VG E)	Washing performance	Energy efficiency	Water efficiency	Capacity	Gentleness	Noise	Auto temp. control	Auto dispensers	Stainless-steel tub	Cycle time (min.)
	FRONT-LOADING MODELS												
12	**Kenmore** (Sears) Elite HE3t 4292[2]	$1,450		Excellent	Excellent	Excellent	Excellent	Excellent	Excellent	•	•	•	70
13	**Whirlpool** Duet HT GHW9200L[W]	1,300		Excellent	Very good	Excellent	Excellent	Excellent	Excellent	•	•	•	60
14	**Kenmore** (Sears) Elite HE3 4282[2]	1,100		Excellent	Very good	Excellent	Excellent	Excellent	Excellent	•	•	•	70
15	**Whirlpool** Duet GHW9100L[Q]	1,100		Excellent	Very good	Excellent	Excellent	Excellent	Excellent	•	•	•	70
16	**LG** WM2032HW	1,000		Excellent	Very good	Excellent	Excellent	Good	Very good	•	•	•	80
17	**Kenmore** (Sears) 4304[2]	800		Excellent	Excellent	Excellent	Good	Very good	Very good	•	•	•	60
18	**Maytag** Neptune MAH6500A[WW]	1,200		Excellent	Good	Very good	Good	Good	Good	•	•	•	70
	COMPACT MODELS												
19	**Bosch** Axxis+ WFR2460UC	1,100		Good	Excellent	Excellent	Poor	Excellent	Excellent	•	•	•	60
20	**Asko** W6021	1,000		Excellent	Excellent	Excellent	Poor	Very good	Very good	•	•	•	95
21	**Bosch** Axxis WFL2060UC	930		Good	Excellent	Excellent	Poor	Excellent	Excellent	•	•	•	60
22	**Miele** Novotronic W1966	1,500		Excellent	Very good	Very good	Poor	Very good	Excellent	•	•	•	55

See report, page 106. *Based on tests published in Consumer Reports in August 2003, with updated prices and availability.*

Guide to the Ratings

Overall score is based mostly on performance, capacity, energy efficiency, and noise. Water efficiency and gentleness are also considered. **Washing performance** indicates how well each machine removed soil in the most-aggressive normal cycle. All washers of the same type used the same detergent. **Energy efficiency** is based on the electricity needed to run the washer and to heat the water for a warm wash, and the amount of water extracted in the final spin cycle (which lessens time in the dryer). **Water efficiency** reflects how much water per pound of laundry it took to do an 8-pound load and each machine's maximum load. **Capacity** measures how large a load each machine could handle effectively. Models that earned lower scores for **gentleness** are more likely to treat your clothes roughly, causing wear and tear. Panelists gauged **noise** during the fill, agitation, drain, and spin cycles. **Cycle time** is for the normal cycle, rounded to the nearest 5 minutes. **Price** is approximate retail. Under **brand & model,** bracketed letters or numbers are color codes. Ratings may differ from earlier reports because of changes to scoring.

Recommendations & notes

TOP-LOADING MODELS

1 **KENMORE** (Sears) Elite Calypso 2206[2] **An excellent, efficient washer with an especially large capacity.** Gentle on clothes. Because this is a newer model with a unique design, the Brand Repair History for top-loading Kenmores may not apply to this model. Similar model: 2408[ ].

2 **WHIRLPOOL** Calypso GVW9959K[Q] **A very good, efficient washer with an especially large capacity.** Gentle on clothes and quiet. Because this is a newer model with a unique design, the Brand Repair History for top-loading Whirlpools may not apply to this model.

3 **FISHER & PAYKEL** GWL11 **A very good washer that's gentler and more energy-efficient than most top-loaders.** Among the best at extracting water from clothes. Has selectable automatic water level. Fairly quiet.

4 **GE** Profile WPRB9220C[WW] **A very good washer with very large capacity.** Fairly quiet. Handles unbalanced loads better than most. Programmable favorites/custom keys.

5 **MAYTAG** SAV5701A[WW] **A very good washer with continuously variable water level.**

6 **KENMORE** (Sears) 2493[2] **A very good washer with very large capacity.** Similar: 2492[ ], 2490[ ].

7 **HOTPOINT** VWSR4150B[WW] **Very good.** A fine, basic performer.

8 **KENMORE** (Sears) 2381 **A CR Best Buy Very good, basic machine.** Numerous wash/spin speed combinations. But only fair at handling unbalanced loads, and fewer features than most. Discontinued, but similar 2383[ ] may still be available.

9 **MAYTAG** Performa PAV2300A[WW] **A CR Best Buy Good, strong performance for the price.** Similar: PAV2300A[ ].

10 **MAYTAG** Atlantis MAV9501E[WW] **A very good washer with selectable wash/spin speed combinations.** Has continuously variable water level. More aggressive than most in gentleness tests. Similar: MAV9750A[ ].

Recommendations & notes

11 WHIRLPOOL Gold GSW9650[W] **A good washer with continuously variable water level.** Lacks selectable spin speeds.

FRONT-LOADING MODELS

12 KENMORE (Sears)Elite HE3t 4292[2] **Excellent.** Top performance, for a price. Extremely thrifty with water and energy. Exceptionally large capacity. Very quiet. Smart controls include specialty cycle for silk and fast spin cycle to reduce drying time. Pedestal available to raise doors to a comfortable height. Similar: 4493[ ].

13 WHIRLPOOL Duet HT GHW9200L[W] **Strong performer with handy two-direction dial controls.**

14 KENMORE (Sears) Elite HE3 4282[2] **Excellent overall, with lots of features.** Exceptional capacity. Similar: 4483 [ ].

15 WHIRLPOOL Duet GHW9100L[Q] **Much like the Whirlpool Duet HT GHW9200L,** but has lower price and fewer features.

16 LG WM2032HW **An excellent washer with very large capacity.** Inner tub is angled up for easier access. Among the best at extracting water from clothes. Handles unbalanced loads better than most. Has internal water heater.

17 KENMORE (Sears) 4304[2] **A very good washer that's among the best at extracting water from clothes.** Very frugal with water and energy usage. Similar: 4314[ ], 4305[ ].

18 MAYTAG Neptune MAH6500A[WW] **A very good washer with inner tub angled up for easier access.** Has internal water heater. Remembers last cycle on Start. Maytag front-loaders have been more repair-prone than other brands. Similar: MAH5500B[ ].

COMPACT MODELS

19 BOSCH Axxis+ WFR2460UC **Very good.** Extremely thrifty with water and energy. Gentle on clothes. Can provide high temperature wash cycles using internal water heater. Requires 240 volt electrical outlet.

20 ASKO W6021 **Very good compact model; extremely thrifty with water and energy.** Has internal water heater. Requires 240-volt electrical outlet.

21 BOSCH Axxis WFL2060UC **Very good.** Extremely thrifty with water and energy. Gentle on clothes. Can provide high temperature wash cycles using internal water heater. Requires 240 volt electrical outlet.

22 MIELE Novotronic W1966 **A very good compact washer.** Among the best at extracting water from clothes. Has spin hold feature and internal water heater. Requires 240-volt electrical outlet. Similar: W1986.

Statement of Ownership, Management, and Circulation

(Required by 39 U.S.C. 3685)

1. Publication Title: Consumer Reports. 2. Publication No: 0010-7174. 3. Filing Date: September 24, 2003. 4. Issue Frequency: Monthly, except two issues in December. 5. No. of Issues Published Annually: 13. 6. Annual Subscription Price: $26.00. 7. Complete Mailing Address of Known Office of Publication: 101 Truman Avenue, Yonkers, New York 10703-1057. 8. Complete Mailing Address of Headquarters or General Business Office of Publisher: 101 Truman Avenue, Yonkers, New York 10703-1057. 9. Full Names and Complete Mailing Addresses of Publisher, Editor, and Managing Editor. Publisher: Consumers Union of United States, Inc., 101 Truman Avenue, Yonkers, New York 10703-1057. President: James A. Guest; Editor: Margot Slade; Managing Editor: Kim Kleman. 10. Owner: (If the publication is published by a nonprofit organization, its name and address must be stated.) Full Name: Consumers Union of United States, Inc., a nonprofit organization. Complete Mailing Address: 101 Truman Avenue, Yonkers, New York 10703-1057. 11. Known Bondholders, Mortgagees, and Other Security Holders Owning or Holding 1 Percent or More of Total Amount of Bonds, Mortgages, or Other Securities. If none, so state: None. 12. For Completion by Nonprofit Organizations Authorized to Mail at Special Rates: The purpose, function, and nonprofit status of this organization and the exempt status for federal income tax purposes has not changed during preceding 12 months.

15. Extent and Nature of Circulation:

	Average no. copies each issue during past 12 mo.	Actual no. copies of single issue published nearest to filing date
A. Total no. of copies (net press run)	4,383,984	4,322,948
B. Paid and/or requested circulation		
1. Sales through dealers, carriers,street vendors, counter sales (not mailed)	96,615	82,500
2. Paid or requested mail subscriptions (include advertisers' proof copies/exchange copies)	4,085,619	4,073,035
C. Total paid and/or requested circulation (sum of 15b(1) and 15b(2))	4,182,234	4,155,535
D. Free distribution by mail (samples, complimentary, and other free)	23,770	22,225
E. Free distribution outside the mail	14,657	15,006
F. Total free distribution (sum of 15d and 15e)	38,427	37,231
G. Total distribution (sum of 15c and 15f)	4,220,661	4,192,766
H. Copies not distributed		
1. Office use, leftovers, spoiled	162,479	130,182
2. Return from news agents	161,843	149,627
I. TOTAL (sum of 15g, 15h(1) and 15h(2)	4,544,983	4,472,575
J. Percent paid and/or requested circulation	99.09%	99.11%

17. I certify that the statements made by me above are correct and complete.

Louis J. Milani, Senior Director, Business Affairs & Strategic Marketing

BRAND LOCATOR

Phone numbers and Web addresses of selected manufacturers.

A		
Acura	800 382-2238	www.acura.com
Aerus (Electrolux)	800 243-9078	www.aerusonline.com
AGFA	888 988-2432	www.AGFA.com
Aiwa	800 289-2492	www.aiwa.com
Akai	888 697-2247	www.akaiusa.com
Amana	800 843-0304	www.amana.com
Apex	909 930-0132	www.apexdigitalinc.com
Apple	800 538-9696	www.apple.com
Ariens	800 678-5443	www.ariens.com
Asko	800 898-1879	www.askousa.com
AT&T	800 222-3111	www.att.com
Audi	800 367-2834	www.audiusa.com
Audiovox	800 229-1235	www.audiovox.com
B		
B&W	800 370-3740	www.bwspeakers.com
B.I.C.	888 461-4628	www.bicamerica.com
Bionaire	800 253-2764	www.bionaire.com
Bissell	800 237-7691	www.bissell.com
Black & Decker	800 544-6986	www.blackanddecker.com
BMW	800 334-4269	www.bmwusa.com
Bosch	800 944-2904	www.boschappliances.com
Bose	800 444-2673	www.bose.com
Boston Acoustics	800 246-7767	www.bostonacoustics.com
Broilmaster	800 255-0403	www.broilmaster.com
Brother	800 276-7746	www.brother.com
Buick	800 422-8425	www.buick.com
C		
Cadillac	800 333-4223	www.cadillac.com
Cambridge Soundworks	800 367-4434	www.cambridgesoundworks.com
Canon	800 652-2666	www.usa.canon.com
Carrier	800 227-7437	www.carrier.com
Casio	800 962-2746	www.casio.com
Cerwin Vega	805 584-5300	www.cerwinvega.com
Char-Broil	800 241-7548	www.charbroil.com
Chevrolet	800 950-0540	www.chevrolet.com
Chrysler	800 422-4797	www.chrysler.com
Coleman	800 356-3612	www.bbqhq.com
Compaq	800 345-1518	www.compaq.com
Craftsman	Call local Sears store	www.sears.com
Creative Labs	800 998-5227	www.creative.com
Cub Cadet	877 282-8684	www.cubcadet.com
Cuisinart	800 726-0190	www.cuisinart.com
D		
Dacor	800 793-0093	www.dacor.com
Daewoo	888 643-2396	www.daewoous.com

Dell	800 879-3355	www.dell.com
DeLonghi	800 322-3848	www.delonghiusa.com
Denon	973 396-0810	www.usa.denon.com
DeWalt	800 433-9258	www.dewalt.com
DirecTV	800 347-3288	www.direcTV.com
Dirt Devil	800 321-1134	www.dirtdevil.com
Dish Network (EchoStar)	800 333-3474	www.dishnetwork.com
Dodge	800 423-6343	www.4adodge.com
Ducane	800 382-2637	www.ducane.com
Dynamic Cooking Systems (DCS)	800 433-8466	www.dcsappliances.com
Dyson	866 693-9766	www.dyson.com
E		
Echo	800 673-1558	www.echo-usa.com
Electrolux	800 243-9078	www.electroluxusa.com
EMachines	877 566-3463	www.e4me.com
Emerson	800 898-9020	www.emersonradio.com
Envision	888 838-6388	www.envisionmonitor.com
Epson	800 463-7766	www.epson.com
Ericsson	800 374-2776	www.ericsson.com
Eureka	800 282-2886	www.eureka.com
F		
Fantom	800 668-9600	www.fantom.com
Fedders	217 342-3901	www.fedders.com
Fiesta	800 396-3838	www.fiestabbq.com
Fisher	818 998-7322	www.fisherav.com
Fisher & Paykel	888 936-7872	www.fisherpaykel.com
Ford	800 392-3673	www.fordvehicles.com
Franklin	800 266-5626	www.franklin.com
Friedrich	800 541-6645	www.friedrich.com
Frigidaire	800 374-4432	www.frigidaire.com
Fujifilm	800 800-3854	www.fujifilm.com
G		
Gateway 2000	800 846-2000	www.gateway.com
GE (appliances)	800 626-2000	www.geappliances.com
GE (electronics)	800 447-1700	www.home-electronics.net
Gibson	888 203-1389	www.frigidaire.com
GMC	800 462-8782	www.gmc.com
Goldstar	800 243-0000	www.lgeus.com
Great Outdoors Grill Company	888 869-5454	www.gogrills.com
Grizzly	570 546-9663	www.grizzly.com
H		
Haier	888 764-2437	www.haier.com
Hamilton Beach	800 851-8900	www.hambeach.com
Handspring	888 565-9393	www.handspring.com
Harman/Kardon	800 422-8027	www.harmankardon.com
Hewlett-Packard	800 752-0900	www.hp.com
Hitachi	800 448-2244	www.hitachi.com
Holland	800 880-9766	www.hollandgrill.com
Holmes	800 546-5637	www.holmesproducts.com
Homelite	800 242-4672	www.homelite.com
Honda (autos)	800 334-6632	www.honda.com
Honda (mowers)	800 426-7701	www.hondapowerequipment.com
Hoover	800 944-9200	www.hoover.com
Hotpoint	800 626-2000	www.hotpoint.com
Hughes	800 274-8995	www.hns-usa.com

Husqvarna	800 487-5962	www.husqvarna.com
Hyundai	800 826-2277	www.hyundaiusa.com
I		
IBM	800 426-7235	www.ibm.com
Infiniti	877 647-7266	www.infiniti.com
Infinity	516 674-4463	www.infinitysystems.com
Isuzu	800 726-2700	www.isuzu.com
J		
Jaguar	800 452-4827	www.usjaguar.com
JBL	516 255-4525	www.jbl.com
Jeep	800 925-5337	www.jeepunpaved.com
Jenn-Air	800 688-1100	www.jennair.com
John Deere	800 537-8233	www.deere.com
Jonsered	877 693-7729	www.usa.jonsered.com
JVC	800 252-5722	www.jvc.com
K		
KDS	800 237-9988	www.kdsusa.com
Kenmore	Call a local Sears store	www.sears.com
Kenwood	800 536-9663	www.kenwoodusa.com
Kia	800 333-4542	www.kia.com
Kirby	800 437-7170	www.kirby.com
KitchenAid	800 422-1230	www.kitchenaid.com
KLH	818 767-2843	www.klhaudio.com
Kodak	800 235-6325	www.kodak.com
Konica	800-285-6422	www.konica.com
Kyocera	800 349-4188	www.qualcomm.com
L		
Land Rover	800 346-3493	www.landrover.com
Lawn-Boy	800 526-6937	www.lawnboy.com
Lexmark	800 539-6275	www.lexmark.com
Lexus	800 872-5398	www.lexus.com
LG	800 243-0000	www.lgeus.com
Lincoln	800 521-4140	www.lincolnvehicles.com
M		
Magic Chef	800 688-1120	www.maytag.com
Magnovox	800 531-0039	www.philipsusa.com
Makita	800 462-5482	www.makita.com
Maxim	800 233-9054	www.salton-maxim.com
Maytag	800 688-9900	www.maytag.com
Mazda	800 639-1000	www.mazdausa.com
McCulloch	800 521-8559	www.mccullochpower.com
Mercedes-Benz	800 367-6372	www.mbusa.com
Mercury	800 392-3673	www.mercuryvehicles.com
Micron PC	888 719-5031	www.buympc.com
Microsoft	800 426-9400	www.microsoft.com/actimates
Microtek	310 687-5940	www.microtekusa.com
Miele	800 289-6435	www.mieleusa.com
Milwaukee	877 279-7819	www.mil-electric-tool.com
Minolta	800 808-4888	www.minoltausa.com
Mintek	866 709-9500	www.mintekdigital.com
Mitsubishi	888 648-7820	www.mitsubishicars.com
Motorola	800 331-6456	www.motorola.com
MTD	800 800-7310	www.mtdproducts.com
Murray	800 224-8940	www.murrayinc.com

N		
NEC	800 338-9549	www.necus.com
Nikon	800 645-6687	www.nikonusa.com
Nissan	800 419-7520	www.nissandriven.com
Nokia	888 665-4228	www.nokia.com
O		
Oki	800 654-3282	www.okidata.com
Oldsmobile	800 442-6537	www.oldsmobile.com
Olympus	800 622-6372	www.olympusamerica.com
Onkyo	201 785-2600	www.onkyousa.com
Optimus	Call local RadioShack	www.radioshack.com
Oreck	800 989-3535	www.oreck.com
Oster	800 597-5978	www.sunbeam.com
P		
Palm	800 881-7256	www.palm.com
Panasonic	800 211-7262	www.panasonic.com
Pentax	800 877-0155	www.pentax.com
Philips	800 531-0039	www.philipsusa.com
Pioneer	800 421-1404	www.pioneerelectronics.com
Polaroid	800 432-5355	www.polaroid.com
Polk Audio	800 377-7655	www.polkaudio.com
Pontiac	800 276-6842	www.pontiac.com
Porsche	800 767-7243	www.porsche.com
Porter-Cable	800 487-8665	www.porter-cable.com
Poulan	800 238-9333	www.poulan.com
Precor	800 477-3267	www.precor.com
Precisionaire	800 347-2220	www.precisionaire.com
Proctor-Silex	800 851-8900	www.proctorsilex.com
PSB	888 772-0000	www.psbspeakers.com
Q		
Quasar	800 211-7262	www.panasonic.com
R		
RadioShack	800 843-7422	www.radioshack.com
RCA	800 336-1900	www.rca.com
Regal	262 626-2121	www.regalware.com
Regina	228 867-8507	www.reginavac.com
Remington	616 791-7325	www.remingtonchainsaw.com
Research Products	800 545-2219	www.resprod.com
Rival	800 557-4825	www.rivalproducts.com
Roper	800 447-6737	www.roperappliances.com
Rowenta	781 396-0600	www.rowentausa.com
Royal	800 321-1134	wwww.dirtdevil.com
Ryobi	800 345-8746	www.ryobi.com
S		
Saab	800 722-2872	www.saabusa.com
Sabre by John Deere	800 537-8233	www.deere.com
Salton	800 233-9054	www.salton-maxim.com
Sampo	800 203-4429	www.sampoamericas.com
Samsung	800 726-7864	www.samsungusa.com
Sanyo	818 998-7322	www.sanyo.com
Saturn	800 522-5000	www.saturn.com
Sharp	800 237-4277	www.sharp-usa.com
Siemens	888 777-0211	www.icm.siemens.com
Simplicity (yard equipment)	262 284-8669	www.simplicitymfg.com
Simplicity (vacuum cleaners)	888 974-6759	www.simplicityvac.com

Skil	877 754 5999	www.skiltools.com
Snapper	800 762-7737	www.snapper.com
Solo	800 765-6462	www.solousa.com
Sony	800 222-7669	www.sony.com
Southwestern Bell	800 366-0937	www.southwesternbell.com
Stanley	800 788-7766	www.stanleylawnmowers.com
Stihl	800 467-8445	www.stihl.com
Subaru	800 782-2783	www.subaru.com
Sub-Zero	800 222-7820	www.subzero.com
Sunbeam	800 458-8407	www.sunbeam.com
Suzuki	877 697-8985	www.suzukiauto.com
T		
Tappan	800 537-5530	www.frigidaire.com
TEC	800 331-0097	www.tecgasgrills.com
Technics	800 211-7262	www.panasonic.com
Thermador	800 735-4328	www.thermador.com
Toastmaster	800 947-3744	www.toastmaster.com
Toro	800 348-2424	www.toro.com
Toshiba	800 631-3811	www.toshiba.com
Toyota	800 468-6968	www.toyota.com
Tripp Lite	773 869-1234	www.tripplite.com
Trion	800 338-7466	www.fedders.com
Troy-Bilt	866 840-6483	www.troybilt.com
U		
Umax	214 342-9799	www.umax.com
Uniden	800 297-1023	www.uniden.com
V		
ViewSonic	800 688-6688	www.viewsonic.com
Viking	800 467-2643	www.vikingrange.com
Visioneer	925 251-6398	www.visioneer.com
Vivitar	805 498-7008	www.vivitar.com
Volkswagen	800 444-8987	www.vw.com
Volvo	800 458-1552	www.volvocars.com
VTech	800 624-5688	www.vtech.com
W		
Walker	800 843-7422	www.radioshack.com
Waring	800 492-7464	www.waringproducts.com
Weber	800 446-1071	www.weber.com
Weed Eater	800 554-6723	www.weedeater.com
West Bend	800 367-0111	www.westbend.com
Whirlpool	800 253-1301	www.whirlpool.com
White Outdoor	800 949-4483	www.whiteoutdoor.com
White-Westinghouse	800 245-0600	www.frigidaire.com
X		
Xerox	800 832-6979	www.xerox.com
Y		
Yamaha	800 492-6242	www.yamaha.com
Yard Machines by MTD	800 800-7310	www.mtdproducts.com
Yashica	800 526-0266	www.yashica.com
Z		
Zenith	256 772-1515	www.zenith.com

PRODUCT RECALLS

Products ranging from child-safety seats to chain saws are recalled when there are safety defects. Various federal agencies, such as the Consumer Product Safety Commission (CPSC), the National Highway Traffic Safety Administration (NHTSA), the U.S. Coast Guard, and the Food and Drug Administration (FDA), monitor consumer complaints and injuries and, when there's a problem, issue a recall.

But the odds of hearing about an unsafe product are slim. Manufacturers are reluctant to issue a recall in the first place because they can be costly. And getting the word out to consumers can be haphazard. If you return the warranty card that comes with a product, you're more likely to receive notification on a recall for it.

A selection of the most far-reaching recalls appears monthly in CONSUMER REPORTS. Below is a listing of products recalled from December 2002 through November 2003, as reported in issues of CONSUMER REPORTS. For details on these products and hundreds more, go to our Web site, *www.ConsumerReports.org,* to access our free, comprehensive list of product recalls.

If you wish to report an unsafe product or get recall information, call the CPSC's hotline, 800-638-2772, or visit its Web site, *www.cpsc.gov.* Recall notices about your automobile can be obtained from a new-car dealer or by calling the NHTSA hotline at 800-424-9393 or go to *www.nhtsa.dot.gov.* Questions about food and drugs are handled by the FDA's Office of Consumer Affairs, 888-463-6332 or *www.fda.gov.*

Major product recalls in 2003

VEHICLES

'03 BMW 325i, 325Ci, 330i, and M3

'00-02 BMW X5 sport-utility vehicles

'02-03 Buick Rendezvous

'00-02 Cadillac, Chevrolet, and GMC sport-utility vehicles

'94-97 Chevrolet, GMC, and Oldsmobile minivans, pickup trucks, and sport-utility vehicles

'00 Chevrolet Suburban, Tahoe, and Silverado; GMC Yukon, Yukon XL, and Sierra

'98-02 Chrysler and Dodge cars

'97-02 Chrysler and Plymouth Prowler

'98-02 Chrysler LHS, 300M, and Concorde, and Dodge Intrepid

'01-02 Chrysler PT Cruiser

'02 Dodge Grand Caravan and Chrysler Town and Country

'02 Dodge Ram

'03 Dodge Ram 2500 and 3500 heavy-duty pickup trucks

'00-02 Ford Taurus and Mercury Sable with adjustable brake and accelerator pedals

'02-03 General Motors sport-utility vehicles

'01-02 Hyundai Santa Fe

'03 Infiniti G35

'94-95 Isuzu TF pickup trucks

'02-03 Jaguar X-Type

'01-03 Mazda models

'03 Mini Cooper

'03 Mitsubishi Outlander

'02 Nissan Altima and Xterra

'00-03 Saturn L-Series

'01-03 Subaru vehicles

'01-03 Toyota Tacoma

'01-03 Volkswagen and Audi

'00-01 Volkswagen Golf, Jetta, Cabrio, and New Beetle

CHILDREN'S PRODUCTS

Baby Trend "Trend Swing" infant swings sold at Toys 'R' Us stores

Bikepro and Oriental International Trading baby walkers

Cosco "Arriva and Turnabout" infant carrier/safety seats

First Years "2-in-1 Fold-Away Tub and Step Stool"

Fisher-Price Sparkling Symphony crib mobile

Graco SnugRide infant car seats

Home Trends Kiddy Sling Chair sold at Wal-Mart

Kolcraft toy attachments on walkers sold under Tot Rider and Carter's names

Nickelodeon "Smatter" spray foam

"Sulley and Boo" plush dolls sold at The Disney Store

"Swim Ways Deluxe Dive Buddies" weighted dive sticks

"Tiffany" and "Josephine" wooden cribs sold at Babies "R" Us stores

Wooden toy vehicles filled with candy sold at Kmart stores

HOUSEHOLD, FOOD & RECREATIONAL

Beanbag chairs sold at Wal-Mart

Black & Decker and Sears Craftsman cordless electric lawnmowers

BMX 20-inch bicycles

Brother laser printers

Campbell's Condensed Cream of Mushroom soup

Conceptual Marketing and Development Inc. (Grass Gator brand) metal blades for weed cutter attachment

Continental ContiTrac AW and General Eveready Energizer "Kidz Club" flashlights

Franzus/Travel Smart international adapter plug

Grabber AW tires

"Halo Burger" flashlights and batteries

Hamilton Beach and Proctor-Silex slow cookers

Hedstrom and NBF brand 12-, 13-, and 14-foot trampolines

Hitachi 7¼-in. circular saws

Homier Distributing Co. (HDC brand) extension cords, portable lights, and fluorescent work lights

Kawasaki KFX700 V-Force all-terrain vehicle

Kenmore Elite "TRIO" refrigerator

Kitchen Gourmet electric hot pot

Lollipop brand electric fans sold in Metropolitan New York City area

Lane "High-Leg" recliner chair

Little Red Chef food chopper sold via QVC shopping channel

Makita circular saw model number 5740NB

Maytag Gemini gas ranges

Men's Phys.Sci brand hooded sweatshirt sold at Target stores

NexL NXT Beanie motorcycle helmets

Nikon Coolpix 2000 digital camera

Panasonic rechargeable battery packs for cordless power tools

Pioneer standalone DVD recorders and DVD-R/RW drives installed in various computers

Popeil Showtime electric rotisserie

Propane-fueled camp stoves sold under Century, Hillary, and LL Bean brand names

"Pumpkin" and "Snowman" motion lamps sold at Cracker Barrel restaurants

Revel "Performa B15" subwoofer loudspeaker

Skil Warrior cordless drill battery charger

Stihl gasoline-powered chain saws

Targus ChargeSource 70-watt power adapters

Toad Lawn ball sprinkler

Trudeau brand Meat Fondue Pot

UWATEC Smart Dive scuba computer

Zenith analog projection TV sets

8-YEAR INDEX TO CONSUMER REPORTS

This index indicates when the last full report on a given subject was published in CONSUMER REPORTS. It goes back as far as 1996. Note: Beginning with Volume 61 (January 1996), CONSUMER REPORTS stopped using continuous pagination throughout each volume year. From January 1996 forward, each issue begins on page 1. **Bold type** indicates Ratings reports or brand-name discussions; *italic type* indicates corrections, followups, or Updates.

A

INDEX

B

C

D

E

F

G

H

I

J

K

L

M

N

O

P

R

S

T

V

W

Y

BUYING GUIDE INDEX

CANADA EXTRA

USING THE CANADA EXTRA

The Ratings you'll find in this 16-page section list some of the same products included in Ratings reports elsewhere in this book, but with a difference: The products listed here are those that, according to the manufacturers, are sold in Canada. You can use this section in either of two ways: Start with the main Ratings, find several products you like, and turn to this section to find whether they're sold—and for what price—in Canada. Or start here, find products sold in Canada whose price and overall score you like, and read more about them in the main report and full Ratings chart.

We've tried to make it easier to compare products in the main Ratings to products in the Canadian lists by using the same key numbers (in Ratings that use them) in both. In the Ratings of digital cameras, for example, the Canon model listed first in this section has key number 3, because it appears third in the main Ratings on page 246.

In most cases, the prices we list here are the approximate retail in Canadian dollars. We used the exchange rate that was in effect at the time of the original publication. And we include, when it's available, the manufacturer's phone number, so you can call to get information on a model you can't find in stores.

Air cleaners

Report begins on page 111; Ratings on page 235

All 6 of the professionally installed whole-house air cleaners we tested, half of the 12 install-it-yourself whole-house cleaners, and about half of the 18 room air cleaners are available.

Within types, listed in order of overall score

KEY NO.	BRAND & MODEL	PRICE	OVERALL SCORE (P F G VG E)
	Professionally installed whole-house air cleaners		
1	**Aprilaire** 5000	$1,150	
2	**Trion** SE1400	1,050	
3	**Trane** Perfect Fit TFE210A9FR2	NA	
4	**Honeywell** F50	800	
5	**Lennox** PureAir PCO-12C	1,800	
6	**Aprilaire** 2200	575	
	Install-it-yourself whole-house air cleaners		
7	**3M** Filtrete Ultra Allergen 1250	25	
9	**3M** Filtrete 1000	20	
10	**3M** Filtrete 600	15	
12	**American Air Filter** Dirt Demon Pleated Filter	6	
16	**American Air Filter** Strata Density Premium	3	
18	**American Air Filter** ElectroKlean	25	

KEY NO.	BRAND & MODEL	PRICE	OVERALL SCORE (P F G VG E)
	Room air cleaners		
1	**Friedrich** C-90A	$725	
4	**Bionaire** BAP-1300	290	
5	**Honeywell** Enviracare 50250	290	
10	**Holmes** BAP650-CN	220	
11	**Austin** Health Mate	610	
12	**Holmes** BAP625-CN	160	
13	**Honeywell** Enviracare 18159	250	
14	**Honeywell** Enviracare 17000	200	
16	**Sharper Image** Ionic Breeze Quadra (SI637)	NA	
17	**Honeywell** Environizer 90201	250	

Camcorders

Report begins on page 42; Ratings on page 241

Most of the 23 digital and 4 analog camcorders tested are available.

Within types, listed in order of overall score

Key No.	Brand & Model	Price	Overall Score (0–100: P F G VG E)
	DIGITAL MODELS		
1	**Canon** Elura50	$1,400	
2	**Panasonic** VDR-M30	1,300	
4	**Panasonic** PV-GS50S-K	1,000	
5	**Sony** DCR-TRV350	850	
6	**Hitachi** DZ-MV350A	1,300	
7	**Sony** DCRPC105	1,400	
8	**Panasonic** PV-DV203K	850	
9	**Sony** DCR-TRV80	2,300	
10	**Canon** ZR60	800	
11	**Canon** ZR70 MC	1,000	
12	**Hitachi** DZ-MV380A	1,500	
13	**Panasonic** PV-DV953	2,500	
14	**Sony** DCR-TRV22	1,100	
15	**JVC** GR-DX75U	1,200	
16	**Sony** DCR-TRV33	1,200	
17	**Panasonic** PV-GS70	1,500	
18	**Sony** DCR-TRV38	1,300	
19	**JVC** GR-DV500U	1,000	
20	**Canon** Optura20	1,300	
21	**JVC** GR-D70U	800	
22	**Sharp** VL-Z7UC	1,450	
	ANALOG MODELS		
24	**Sony** CCD-TRV318	600	
25	**JVC** GR-AXM250U	400	
27	**Samsung** SCL810	450	

Digital cameras

Report begins on page 45; Ratings on page 246

More than half of the 29 tested cameras are available.

Within types, listed in order of overall score

KEY NO.	BRAND & MODEL	PRICE	OVERALL SCORE (0–100: P F G VG E)
	3-MEGAPIXEL CAMERAS		
3	**Canon** PowerShot A70	$500	
4	**Sony** Cyber-shot DSC-P8	600	
6	**Sony** Cyber-shot DSC-P72	500	
7	**Nikon** Coolpix 3100	550	
8	**Fujifilm** FinePix F410	650	
9	**Panasonic** Lumix DMC-LC33	550	
10	**Pentax** Optio S	600	
	4-MEGAPIXEL CAMERAS		
11	**Nikon** Coolpix 4300	670	
17	**Minolta** Dimage S414	600	
18	**Toshiba** PDR-4300	NA	
	5-MEGAPIXEL CAMERAS		
21	**Sony** Cyber-shot DSC-F717	1,300	
24	**HP** PhotoSmart 935	700	
26	**Canon** PowerShot S50	800	
27	**Kyocera** Contax TVS Digital	1,800	
28	**Minolta** Dimage F300	700	
29	**Sony** CD Mavica MVC-CD500	1,000	

Dishwashers

Report begins on page 86; Ratings on page 261

Half of the 18 tested dishwashers are available, including the top-scoring Bosch models (but Bosch models have been among the more repair-prone) and KitchenAid CR Best Buy.

Listed in order of overall score

KEY NO.	BRAND & MODEL	PRICE	OVERALL SCORE (0–100: P F G VG E)
1	**Bosch** Distinctive SHU66C0[2]	$1,280	
2	**Bosch** Distinctive SHU43C0[2]	870	
4	**Viking** DFUD140	2,100	
5	**KitchenAid** KUDI01IL[BL] **A CR Best Buy**	850	
6	**Frigidaire** Professional PLDB998C[C]	775	
7	**KitchenAid** KUDP01DL[WH]	1,250	
11	**Miele** Novotronic G841SC Plus	1,450	
13	**Whirlpool** DU943PWK[2]	NA	
15	**Amana** ADW862EA[W]	790	

Drills, cordless

Report begins on page 117; Ratings on page 264

Most of the 18 tested drills are available, including the top-scoring models in the higher-voltage groups. The 18-volt Ryobi HP1802MK2 has a Canadian price low enough-$160-to earn the designation.

Within types, listed in order of overall score

KEY NO.	BRAND & MODEL	PRICE	OVERALL SCORE (0–100: P F G VG E)
	18-VOLT DRILLS		
1	**DeWalt** DW987K-2	400	
2	**Craftsman** (Sears) Professional 22044	400	
3	**DeWalt** DW929K-2	325	
4	**Ryobi** HP1802MK2 **A CR Best Buy**	160	
5	**Black & Decker** FSD182K-2	170	
	14.4-VOLT DRILLS		
7	**DeWalt** DW928K-2	225	
8	**Makita** 6228DWAE	285	
9	**Ryobi** HP1442MK2	$125	
10	**Black & Decker** FSD142K-2	140	
	12-VOLT DRILLS		
12	**DeWalt** DW927K-2	270	
13	**Makita** 6227DWE	255	
14	**Black & Decker** FSD122K	120	
15	**Skil** SK246802	85	
16	**Ryobi** HP1202MK2	95	
	9.6-VOLT DRILL		
17	**DeWalt** DW926K-2	150	
18	**Black & Decker** CD9600K	65	

Dryers

Report begins on page 89; Ratings on page 267

About half of the tested full-sized (and both of the compact) dryers are available.

Within types, listed in order of overall score

KEY NO.	BRAND & MODEL	PRICE	OVERALL SCORE (0–100: P F G VG E)
	FULL-SIZED DRYERS		
3	**Kenmore** (Sears) 6490[2]	$550	
4	**Whirlpool** Gold YGEQ9800L[W]	690	
5	**Kenmore** (Sears) Elite HE3 8283[2]	900	
6	**LG** DLE5932W	900	
7	**Maytag** Neptune MDE7500AZ[W]	970	
9	**Kenmore** (Sears) Elite HE3 8282[2]	900	
10	**Whirlpool** Duet YGEW9200L[W]	1,000	
11	**Whirlpool** Gold YGE9868K[Q]	1,000	
12	**Whirlpool** YLE8000J[Q]	590	
14	**Kenmore** (Sears) Elite 6206[2]	900	
17	**Maytag** Atlantis MDE8400AZ[W]	670	
18	**GE** DCXH46EA[WW]	730	
19	**Maytag** Atlantis MDE8600AZ[W]	670	
21	**GE** PDSR495EB[WW]	500	
23	**Hotpoint** QNSR463EB[WW]	430	
	COMPACT DRYERS		
26	**Miele** Novotronic T1576	1,600	
27	**GE** PCKS443EB[WW]	450	

PDAs

Report begins on page 147; Ratings on page 294

All of the tested Palm OS models and most of the Pocket PC models are available. Choose a Palm model for a wide variety of software, a Pocket PC model for compatibility with Windows programs.

Within types, listed in order of overall score

KEY NO.	BRAND & MODEL	PRICE	OVERALL SCORE (0–100: P F G VG E)
	PALM OS MODELS		
1	**Palm** Zire	$170	
2	**Sony** Clie´ PEG-NZ90	1,300	
3	**Palm** Zire 71	450	
4	**Sony** Clie´ PEG-SJ33	500	
5	**Palm** m515	480	
6	**Palm** Tungsten T	600	
7	**Sony** Clie´ PEG-NX70V	800	
8	**Sony** Clie´ PEG-TG50	650	
9	**Sony** Clie´ PEG-SJ22	300	
10	**Palm** m130	300	
	POCKET PC MODELS		
11	**Dell** AXIM X5400 MHz	510	
13	**HP** iPaq h1910	500	
14	**ViewSonic** Pocket PC V35	500	
15	**Audiovox** Thera	1,100	

Power blowers

Report begins on page 128; Ratings on page 297

Most of the 37 tested electric handheld, gasoline handheld, gasoline backpack, and gasoline wheeled blowers are available, but none of the Craftsman (Sears) models are sold in Canada.

Within types, listed in order of overall score

KEY NO.	BRAND & MODEL	PRICE	OVERALL SCORE (0–100; P F G VG E)
	ELECTRIC HANDHELD BLOWERS		
1	**Toro** Super Blower Vac 51591 **A CR Best Buy**	$125	
2	**Toro** Ultra Blower Vac 51598	140	
3	**Weed Eater** 2595 Barracuda **A CR Best Buy**	100	
4	**Toro** Rake and Vac 51573	105	
7	**Black & Decker** Leaf Hog BV2500-04	95	
8	**Toro** Power Sweep 51586	55	
9	**Weed Eater** 2540 Groundskeeper	80	
10	**Black & Decker** FT1000	65	
13	**Weed Eater** 2510 Groundsweeper	50	
	GASOLINE HANDHELD BLOWERS		
15	**Stihl** BG 45	290	
16	**Stihl** BG 55 [1]	250	
17	**Echo** PB-230LN	350	
18	**John Deere** BH25	290	
19	**Weed Eater** BV 1650 **A CR Best Buy**	180	
23	**Echo** ES-210	300	
25	**Husqvarna** 225B	270	
26	**Weed Eater** FL 1500 Featherlite	120	
	GASOLINE BACKPACK BLOWERS		
28	**Husqvarna** 145BT **A CR Best Buy**	430	
29	**Makita** RBL500	550	
32	**Stihl** BR 340L	650	
33	**Echo** Pro Lite PB260L	400	
	GASOLINE WHEELED BLOWER		
34	**Little Wonder** 9600-6HP	NA	

[1] *Price does not include optional vacuum kit.*

Printers

Report begins on page 150; Ratings on page 299

Most of the 29 tested inkjet, multifunction, and laser printers are available.

Within types, listed in order of overall score

KEY NO.	BRAND & MODEL	PRICE	OVERALL SCORE (0–100: P F G VG E)
	INKJET PRINTERS		
3	**Canon** Photo Printer i850	$230	
5	**HP** PhotoSmart 7150	200	
6	**HP** PhotoSmart 7550	200	
8	**HP** DeskJet 6127	400	
9	**Canon** Photo Printer i470D	310	
10	**Canon** Color Bubble Jet S330	160	
11	**Epson** Stylus Photo 825	230	
12	**Epson** Stylus C62	100	
13	**Epson** Stylus Photo 900	300	
14	**Epson** Stylus Photo 960	550	
15	**Epson** Stylus Photo 820	150	
16	**Epson** Stylus C82	150	
	MULTIFUNCTION INKJET PRINTERS		
18	**HP** PSC 1210 all-in-one **A CR Best Buy**	150	
19	**Dell** All-In-One Printer A940	200	
20	**HP** PSC 2210	450	
21	**Lexmark** X5150 All-In-One	220	
22	**Canon** MultiPass F80	750	
23	**Brother** MFC-5200C	700	
	LASER PRINTERS		
25	**HP** LaserJet 100	300	
26	**Dell** Personal Laser Printer P1500	440	
27	**Samsung** ML-1710	350	
28	**Brother** HL-5040	400	
29	**Minolta-QMS** PagePro 1250W	800	

Ranges

Report begins on page 97; Ratings on page 304

More than half of the tested electric, gas, and dual-fuel ranges are available in Canada, but none of the tested Kenmore models are available. The unique Whirlpool Polara YGR556LRK, $2,800 list, is available; that model lets you keep the food cool before and after cooking.

Within types, listed in order of overall score

KEY NO.	BRAND & MODEL	PRICE	OVERALL SCORE (0–100: P F G VG E)
	ELECTRIC SMOOTHTOP RANGES		
4	**Maytag** Accellis MER6750AA[W]	$2,270	
6	**NEW Maytag** Gemini MER6872BC[W]	2,350	
11	**GE** Profile JCS968SF[SS]	2,490	
12	**Jenn-Air** JES8850AC[W]	2,500	
13	**NEW Whirlpool** Polara YGR556LRK[P]	2,800	
	GAS RANGES		
14	**GE** Profile JGBP85WEB[WW]	1,450	
15	**GE** JGBP35WEA[WW]	1,110	
16	**Maytag** Gemini MGR6772BD[W]	2,200	
18	**Maytag** MGR5880BD[W]	1,750	
19	**Maytag** Performa PGR5710BD[W]	1,100	
20	**Jenn-Air** JGS8750AD[W]	2,350	
23	**DCS** RGSC-305	6,800	
24	**Frigidaire** Gallery GLGF377A[S]	1,100	
25	**KitchenAid** YKGRT607H[S]	2,050	
	DUAL-FUEL RANGES		
27	**KitchenAid** KDRP407H[SS]	5,000	
28	**Jenn-Air** JDS8850AC[S]	3,500	
30	**Jenn-Air** JDS9860AC[W]	3,150	
33	**GE Monogram** ZDP30N4D[SS]]	5,100	

Refrigerators

Report begins on page 101; Ratings begin on page 312

About half of the tested refrigerators are available, including all of the bottom-freezer models but only a few of the pricey cabinet-depth and built-in models.

Within types, listed in performance order

KEY NO.	BRAND & MODEL	PRICE	OVERALL SCORE (0–100: P F G VG E)
	TOP-FREEZERS		
3	**Maytag** MTB2156GE[W]	1,400	
4	**Whirlpool** ET9FTTXL[Q]	1,130	
6	**Whirlpool** Gold GR9SHKXK[Q]	1,300	
7	**LG** GR-729RN[W]	1,350	
10	**Whirlpool** Gold GR2SHTXK[Q]	1,550	
12	**GE** GTS18HBMFR[WW]	830	
	BOTTOM-FREEZERS		
13	**Amana** ARB2217C[W]	2,200	
14	**Kenmore** (Sears) Elite Trio 7350[2]	2,700	
15	**Maytag** Plus MBB2254GE[W]	1,850	
16	**Amana** ARB1914C[W]	1,750	
17	**Samsung** RB1855S[W]	1,300	
	SIDE-BY-SIDES		
19	**Samsung** RS2555S[L]	$2,400	
20	**Amana** ARSE667D[W]	3,250	
22	**Maytag** MSD2456GE[W]	2,300	
24	**Maytag** Plus MZD2766GE[W]	2,950	
	CABINET-DEPTH MODELS		
26	**LG** GR-L208NN[W]	2,025	
27	**Jenn-Air** JCD2389GE[W]	3,100	
	BUILT-IN BOTTOM-FREEZERS		
29	**Sub-Zero** 650/F	8,260	

Speakers

Report begins on page 68; Ratings on page 316

Most of the 60 tested speaker sets are available.

Within types, listed in performance order

KEY NO.	BRAND & MODEL	PRICE	OVERALL SCORE (0–100: P F G VG E)
	BOOKSHELF SPEAKERS		
1	**Cambridge Soundworks** Newton Series M80	$590	
2	**Sony** SS-MB350H **A CR Best Buy**	230	
3	**BIC** America Venturi DV62si	300	
4	**Bose** 201 Series V	350	
5	**Boston Acoustics** CR75	450	
6	**Cambridge Soundworks** Model Six **A CR Best Buy**	220	
7	**Boston Acoustics** VR-M50	1,000	
8	**Cambridge Soundworks** Newton Series M60	440	
9	**PSB** Image 2B	480	
11	**Pioneer** S-DF2-K	330	
12	**Boston Acoustics** CR85	600	
13	**Bose** 301 Series V	550	
14	**Bose** 141	200	
15	**Sony** SS-X30ED	1,000	
16	**Polk Audio** R20	150	
18	**Klipsch** Synergy SB-3	700	
	FLOOR-STANDING SPEAKERS		
19	**Sony** SS-MF750H	480	
20	**Cerwin Vega** E-710	600	
21	**Polk Audio** R30	450	
22	**Jensen** Champion Series C-5	133	
23	**Polk Audio** R50	680	
24	**Bose** 601 Series IV	1,050	
25	**Bose** 701 Series II	1,800	
	THREE-PIECE BOOKSHELF SETS		
26	**Bose** Acoustimass 3 Series IV	500	
27	**Bose** Acoustimass 5 Series III	1,200	

Within types, listed in performance order

KEY NO.	BRAND & MODEL	PRICE	OVERALL SCORE (0–100: P F G VG E)
	CENTER-CHANNEL SPEAKERS		
28	**NHT** SC1	$900	
29	**Boston Acoustics** Bravo Center	400	
30	**Boston Acoustics** CRC	300	
31	**B&W** VM1	300	
33	**Polk Audio** CSi20	215	
34	**Polk Audio** CSi30	250	
38	**Sony** SS-CNX70ED	600	
39	**Sony** SS-CN550H	150	
40	**Jensen** Champion Series C-CS	90	
41	**Cambridge Soundworks** CenterStage	440	
42	**Cambridge Soundworks** Center Channel Plus	190	
43	**Bose** VCS-10	350	
	REAR SURROUND SPEAKERS		
44	**Cambridge Soundworks** Newton Series MC100	240	
45	**Infinity** OWS-1	550	
46	**Bose** 161	300	
47	**NHT** SB1	550	
48	**JBL** Northridge Series N24 II	250	
49	**B&W** LM1	500	
50	**Polk Audio** RTi28	420	
	SIX-PIECE SURROUND SETS		
51	**Bose** Acoustimass 6 Series III	1,100	
52	**Cambridge Soundworks** Movieworks 208	1,325	
53	**Polk Audio** RM6700 with PSW303 subwoofer	1,300	
54	**Cambridge Soundworks** Movieworks 106	590	
55	**Cambridge Soundworks** Newton Theater MC100.2	1,325	
56	**Polk Audio** RM6005 with PSW202 subwoofer	800	
57	**Bose** Acoustimass 10 Series III	1,800	
58	**Cambridge Soundworks** Movieworks II 5.1	960	
59	**Atlantic Technology** System T70	NA	
60	**Sony** SA-VE835ED	1,600	

Vacuum cleaners

Report begins on page 132; Ratings on page 328

Fewer than half of the 33 tested uprights but most of the 16 canister models are available.

Within types, listed in performance order

KEY NO.	BRAND & MODEL	PRICE	OVERALL SCORE (0–100: P F G VG E)
	UPRIGHTS		
2	**Kenmore** (Sears) Progressive with Direct Drive 33900	$480	
5	**Eureka** Ultra Whirlwind 4885AT	400	
6	**Hoover** WindTunnel Bagless U5720-950	340	
8	**Oreck** XL21-600	1,000	
17	**Aerus** Lux 3000	900	
19	**Dirt Devil** Scorpion 088100CA	132	
21	**Hoover** Fold Away U5162-950	150	
22	**Oreck** XL-2	550	
23	**Kenmore** (Sears) Progressive 31910	350	
30	**Fantom** Twister FM740 300SE	230	
	CANISTERS		
34	**Kenmore** (Sears) 27115	600	
37	**Miele** Plus S251	550	
38	**Eureka** Home Cleaning System 6984A	500	
40	**Hoover** WindTunnel Electronic Bagless S3765-050	500	
41	**Hoover** WindTunnel Plus S3639-05	415	
42	**Miele** Solaris Electro Plus S514	820	
43	**Kenmore** (Sears) eVo 21960	600	
44	**Oreck** Dutch Tech DTX1300C	1,000	
45	**Fantom** Falcon FC251	280	
46	**Sanyo** High Power SC-800P	400	
48	**Kenmore** (Sears) Magic Blue DX 23150	200	
49	**Rainbow** e-Series E-2	NA	

Washing machines

Report begins on page 106; Ratings on page 335

Most of the 16 tested top-loading washers are available, and all 7 of the front-loading models and all 4 of the compact models are available.

Within types, listed in order of overall score

KEY NO.	BRAND & MODEL	PRICE	OVERALL SCORE (0–100: P F G VG E)
	TOP-LOADING MODELS		
1	**Kenmore** (Sears) Elite Calypso 2206[2]	$1,500	
2	**Whirlpool** Calypso GVW9959K[Q]	1,600	
3	**Fisher & Paykel** GWL11	1,000	
4	**GE** Profile WHSB9000B[WW]	1,100	
7	**Hotpoint** HNSR4150B[WW]	700	
8	**Kenmore** (Sears) 2383[2]	650	
9	**Maytag** Performa PAV2300A[WW] **A CR Best Buy**	600	
10	**Maytag** Atlantis MAV9501E[WW]	850	
11	**Whirlpool** Gold Ultimate Care GSW9650L[W]	790	
	FRONT-LOADING MODELS		
12	**Kenmore** (Sears) Elite HE3t 4292[2]	1,800	
13	**Whirlpool** Duet HT GHW9200L[W]	1,900	
14	**Kenmore** (Sears) Elite HE3 4282[2]	1,400	
15	**Whirlpool** Duet GHW9100L[Q]	1,500	
16	**LG** WM2032HW	1,500	
17	**Kenmore** (Sears) 4207[2]	1,050	
18	**Maytag** Neptune MAH6500A[WW]	1,550	
	COMPACT MODELS		
19	**Bosch** Axxis+ WFR2460UC	1,950	
20	**Asko** W6021	1,680	
21	**Bosch** Axxis WFL2060UC	1,550	
22	**Miele** Novotronic W1966	2,400	